INTRODUCTION TO THE STUDY OF U.S. LAW

■ ■ ■

Robert H. Klonoff
Jordan D. Schnitzer Professor of Law
Dean of the Law School, 2007–2014
Lewis & Clark Law School

AMERICAN CASEBOOK SERIES®

WEST ACADEMIC PUBLISHING

American Casebook Series is a trademark registered in the U.S. Patent and Trademark Office.

© 2016 LEG, Inc. d/b/a West Academic
 444 Cedar Street, Suite 700
 St. Paul, MN 55101
 1-877-888-1330

West, West Academic Publishing, and West Academic are trademarks of West Publishing Corporation, used under license.

Printed in the United States of America

ISBN: 978-1-62810-167-6

To my family

PREFACE

This book is designed to introduce students to the highlights of the first-year curriculum at a U.S. law school. The first chapter provides an overview of the U.S. legal system. The seven chapters that follow focus on basic foundational subjects: constitutional law, civil procedure, contracts, torts, property, criminal procedure, and criminal law, each in a separate chapter. Although the first chapter consists entirely of articles and other commentary, the other seven chapters consist mainly of edited court decisions.

All of the chapters contain notes and questions, highlighting important issues for discussion and providing citations to cases, articles, and other materials for more in-depth study. Many of the questions posed in the notes are designed to ensure that students grasp the essential legal principles of a case. Other questions invite students to assess the relative persuasiveness of various approaches for resolving a particular legal issue. The book is designed to be taught using the Socratic method, a teaching approach that is the norm at almost every U.S. law school.

I was inspired to write this book after receiving several invitations to teach U.S. law at foreign law schools. I quickly discovered that there were no textbooks that attempted to encapsulate the first-year curriculum. During my sabbatical year (2014–2015), I had a chance to test these materials in numerous countries. In many countries, law school is an undergraduate subject, so many of my students were undergraduates. At some schools, I also had graduate students (LL.M or Ph.D). In a number of instances, based on feedback from students, I ended up replacing materials that I had originally selected for this casebook.

The book is intended for several types of students:

First, it is designed for international students who are attending a U.S. law school to pursue an LL.M degree or an S.J.D. degree. Such students are at a disadvantage because they have not taken the basic first-year courses. This book gives such students the opportunity to take an intensive course on U.S. law, thus enabling them to learn the fundamental concepts before taking upper-division courses.

Second, this book is designed for international students who want to learn about U.S. law but who are not planning to attend a U.S. law school. U.S. law professors can teach the course in foreign law schools using this text, as I have done in several countries. Also, foreign professors who have been trained at a U.S. law school can teach U.S. law at their home institutions.

Third, the book is designed for an undergraduate pre-law course at a U.S. college or university. It can be taught by a law-trained undergraduate professor or by a law professor on a visiting or adjunct basis. Such a course will give undergraduates the chance to "test the waters" before deciding whether to go to law school.

Fourth, the book can be used at U.S. schools that train and certify paralegals.

All four types of students share a common desire to learn the basics of U.S. law in one course. And all four types will benefit not only from the substantive materials but also from the experience of learning multiple subject areas utilizing the Socratic method.

Because each of the seven topic areas is a separate semester or full-year course at most U.S. law schools, the materials I have selected for each subject area are necessarily condensed. The average chapter is less than 90 pages, which is less than 10 percent of the size of a standard casebook covering the same subject. Thus, I had to make difficult choices about which topics to cover and which ones to omit.

In some circumstances, I selected "landmark" cases. In other circumstances, especially where the landmark cases were difficult to understand, I opted for more modern and accessible cases. My overarching goal has been to select cases that are engaging, relatively easy to understand, and factually interesting. Not surprisingly, a number of the cases involve the intersection of law and technology. I reviewed hundreds of cases in the process of choosing those that made the final cut.

Because I wanted to keep the book under 800 pages, I had to do substantial editing of the cases. I tried, however, to retain crucial passages and to include enough of each case to allow students to understand the concepts without having to resort to secondary materials. Many of the cases involve challenging issues, and a large number contain concurring or dissenting opinions. I included excerpts from concurring and dissenting opinions when I concluded that they would provoke discussion, debate, or critical analysis. More generally, I avoided the temptation to over-edit the cases, even though that decision meant covering fewer topics. It is important for students who are unfamiliar with U.S. law to learn how to analyze court opinions, and such learning cannot occur if cases are over-edited.

I have adopted a number of conventions throughout the book. I have deleted citations contained within cases unless those citations serve a pedagogical purpose (such as allowing a student to read the cited case as background or for edification). For U.S. Supreme Court cases, I rely only on the U.S. Reporter for citation when the case has been published in that reporter. If the case is too recent for a U.S. Reporter citation, I use the Supreme Court Reporter citation. For state cases, I use both the state and regional citations when available. For material that I have edited, either in text or in the notes and questions, I use three asterisks to reflect material that I deleted. The use of ellipses (as opposed to asterisks) means that the edit was made by the court or author. Occasionally, I have modified the typeface of headings to maintain a consistent style. In numbering footnotes, I preserve the original footnote numbers, even though other footnotes have been deleted. For example, if I retain only one footnote out of three during my editing (footnote 3), that footnote will bear the number 3 even though it is the only footnote in the edited version. Also, I have corrected obvious typographical errors in the original source materials. And for the sake of simplicity, I use "he" to encompass "he or she."

I wish to thank my research assistants, who have provided superb support. Gillian Schroff and Alex Uskoski have labored with me for many months on this project and deserve special recognition for their help with research, case selection, drafting, and editing. Both started working with me shortly after completing their first year of law school, so the topics were fresh in their minds. They have done extraordinary work. Other research assistants who provided important help include Daniella Bismanovsky, Joe Callahan, Erica Hayne, Wynn Heh, Chester Hill, Dan Kubitz, Ryan Kunkel, Megan Miller-Hall, Quinton Parham, Ben Pepper, and Joy Wang. Several Lewis & Clark Law School colleagues have commented on particular chapters, including Professors Brian Blum, Michael Blumm, Henry Drummonds, William Funk, Jeffrey Jones, Laurie Mapes, James Oleske, Barbara Safriet, Juliet Stumpf, Ozan Varol, and Tung Yin.

ROBERT H. KLONOFF

March 14, 2016

ACKNOWLEDGMENTS

I wish to acknowledge the following copyright holders (listed in alphabetical order) who gave me permission to reprint excerpts from their copyrighted materials. (Apart from granting me permission to reprint excerpts in this book, the copyright holders have reserved all of their rights.)

American Bar Association, *Model Rules of Professional Conduct* (2013). Copyright © 2013 the American Bar Association. Reprinted with permission of the American Bar Association.

American Judicature Society, *Jury System Overview* (2015). Copyright © 2015 the American Judicature Society. Reprinted with permission of the American Judicature Society.

American Law Institute, *The Restatement (Second) of Contracts* (1981). Copyright © 1981 the American Law Institute. Reproduced with permission of the Institute.

American Law Institute, *The Restatement (Second) of Torts* (1965). Copyright © 1965 the American Law Institute. Reproduced with permission of the Institute.

American Law Institute, *The Restatement (Third) of Torts: Liability for Physical & Emotional Harm* (2012). Copyright © 2012 the American Law Institute. Reproduced with permission of the Institute.

Integrated Justice Information Systems Institute, *Courts 101: An Understanding of the Court System* (2012). Copyright © 2012 the Integrated Justice Information Systems Institute. Reprinted with permission of the Integrated Justice Information Systems Institute.

O'Connor, Vivienne, *Common Law and Civil Law Traditions* (2012). Copyright © 2012 the International Network to Promote the Rule of Law. Reprinted with permission of the International Network to Promote the Rule of Law.

Rakoczy, Christy, *The Arguments For and Against Tort Reform*, the Legal Finance Journal (June 24, 2013). Copyright © 2013 the Legal Finance Journal. Reprinted with permission of the Legal Finance Journal.

Rosen Weston, Cheryl, *Legal Education in the United States: Who's in Charge? Why Does it Matter?*, 24 Wis. Int'l L.J. 397 (2006). Copyright © 2006 the Wisconsin International Law Journal. Reprinted with permission of the University of Wisconsin International Law Journal.

Smith, D. Brooks, *Because Men Are Not Angels: Separation of Powers in the United States*, 47 Duq. L. Rev. 687 (2009). Copyright © 2009 the

Duquesne Law Review. Reprinted with permission of the Duquesne University Law Review.

SUMMARY OF CONTENTS

TABLE OF CONTENTS

TABLE OF CASES

The principal cases are in bold type.

INTRODUCTION TO THE STUDY OF U.S. LAW

CHAPTER 1

INTRODUCTION TO THE U.S. LEGAL SYSTEM

■ ■ ■

This chapter consists of secondary materials from scholars, judges, and other knowledgeable commentators. It addresses seven topics: the common law and civil law systems; the role of lawyers in the U.S.; the federal and state court systems; trial by jury; judicial decision-making; the U.S. Supreme Court; and U.S. legal education. These topics are the building blocks for the seven chapters that follow.

A. THE COMMON LAW SYSTEM

The U.S. legal system is classified as a "common law" system. The following excerpt addresses the differences between the common law and civil law systems.

DR. VIVIENNE O'CONNOR, COMMON LAW AND CIVIL LAW TRADITIONS
International Network to Promote the Rule of Law, 2012

II. Definitions

When we talk about civil law countries or common law countries as groups, we are referring to the fact that each group of countries shares a "distinctive heritage" or a "legal tradition." "Legal tradition" refers "to a set of deep rooted, historically conditioned attitudes about the nature of law, about the role of law in the society . . . about the proper organization and operation of a legal system, and about the way the law is or should be made, applied, studied, perfected, and taught." Legal tradition needs to be distinguished from a "legal system," which "is an operating set of legal institutions, procedures and rules." France and Germany share the same legal tradition (*i.e.*, civil law), as do Canada and Sierra Leone (*i.e.*, common law); however, France and Germany, and Canada and Sierra Leone, have variations in how their individual legal systems operate.

* * *

III. History

* * *

A.   The Civil Law Tradition

The civil law tradition is the oldest and most widely distributed legal system * * *, dating back to 450 B.C. * * *. Even though it is the older of the two systems, the civil law took exponentially longer to develop than the common law * * *.

* * *

Four hundred and fifty B.C. is designated as the beginning of the development of the civil law because this is the year of the Twelve Tablets, the first written law and rudimentary system of dispute resolution in Ancient Rome. The next significant period in the development of the civil law comes in the 6th century A.D., when the Emperor Justinian of Constantinople commissioned the Corpus Juris Civile to be written, which would codify the Roman law on family, inheritance, property, and contracts, among other areas of law. After the fall of the Roman Empire, codified Roman law was no longer in use. However, during the Enlightenment Period in Europe (11th–15th Centuries) after the so-called "Dark Ages," the Corpus Juris Civile was rediscovered. During this time the first modern European university was founded in Bologna, Italy. Students came to study the civil law from all over Europe and brought this influence back to their own countries.

As well as studying Roman law, scholars at Bologna also studied Cannon Law, developed by the church for its governance and to regulate the rights and obligations of its followers. This coupled with Roman law formed the basis of the laws applied in Europe at this time. Also influential in developing a common legal framework in Europe was commercial law that also developed in Italy and that regulated trade throughout Europe. * * *

During the Enlightenment period (11th–15th centuries), Continental European countries gradually began moving from customary norms and practices as the basis for solving disputes to formal, written laws. In most cases, national customs were integrated into the civil law sources, which partly accounts for the variations in how civil law legal systems operate in practice. "France's codification of private law, under Napoleon in 1804, was the world's first national, systematic and rational codification of law. . . . The Civil Code of Germany of 1900, advanced systematic legal thought still further." France's codes were drafted in a way so as to be accessible to ordinary citizens, an ideal replicated today in many civil law countries. Germany's, on the other hand, [was] more complex. It emphasizes legal precision and represented an ideal whereby a law could be drafted so as to cover every eventuality in a way that was rational, logical and coherent. * * *

The civil law tradition spread well beyond Europe. As European countries colonized countries in South America, Africa, the Middle East and Asia, they brought their legal systems with them.

B.   The Common Law Tradition

The development of common law has been described as a "historical accident," arising from the conquest of England by the Normans in 1066 A.D. William the Conqueror, in an effort to establish a Norman legal order in a foreign country, deputized a "corps of loyal adjudicators" (or judges) to resolve disputes at the local level and essentially make law. In more serious cases, there was a referral system to the King for adjudication. Juries were also introduced, which represented the local interests of the ordinary person to decide the case. This strategy kept the populace happy and less likely to revolt against the occupying power. Because the jury was comprised of mostly illiterate people, the proceedings were oral, the implications of which can still be seen today in the modern common law system.

In 1701, the Act of Settlement created an independent judiciary. After this, Blackstone, an eminent legal scholar, published his *Commentaries on the Laws of England*, which were carried to colonies and also influenced the development of American law.

IV. Sources of Law

A.   The Civil Law Tradition

Parliamentary legislation is the principal source of law in civil law countries. This legislation includes codes, separate statutes and ancillary legislation * * *. Within civil law countries, there is a hierarchy of laws. At the top of the hierarchy is the Constitution, followed by codes and other legislation (emanating from the executive or parliamentary branches depending upon the legal system), then executive decrees, then regulations, followed by local ordinances. Custom, as a rare source of law, sits at the bottom of the pyramid and would rarely be relied upon in court.

This reliance on codes and laws is a central characteristic of the civil law. At the heart of the civil law lies a belief in codification as a means to ensure a rational, logical, and systematic approach to law. Many civil law proponents believe that a code can address all circumstances that might need legal regulation, without the need for judicial interpretation and without the need for judges to refer to case law. Judges generally interpret codes and laws very strictly; [they do not read] existing legal provisions [expansively] to create new interpretations [or] new law * * *.

International treaties and conventions also are sources of law in civil law countries. Most civil law countries are "monist" meaning that when the country ratifies a treaty, it automatically becomes part of domestic law. This means that a judge can automatically apply it and a party in court can rely on international law in proceedings. In some countries, the judge can declare a national law or provision to be invalid if it conflicts with an international treaty or convention that the country has ratified.

Traditionally, case law did not play any role in civil law countries as a source of law. The judge would decide each case based on codes or legislation and would not look to another case for guidance even if the facts were identical. This was premised on the belief that the code contains all the information necessary to decide upon the case. It was also premised on the strong belief that the legislature makes the law, not the judges.

More recently, the role of case law has been changing. Settled lines of cases are now considered to have authority and are accepted due to the fact that they ensure consistency in the application of the law.

While case law is eschewed in many cases, "doctrine" which is the writing of prominent legal scholars, is considered an important authority in civil law countries. The origins of this may date back to the "commentators," a group of scholars in Ancient Rome based in Bologna at the new University who produced authoritative statements on the interpretation of the law. Doctrine is incredibly influential when the law is unsettled. Some areas of law will have one legal scholar who is the national authority and whose opinion is given great weight by judges.

Each code in a civil law country will likely have a set of commentaries that gives expression to the doctrine (and can sometimes summarize settled case law in a particular area of law). For example the criminal code has a set of commentaries that are drafted by the leading scholar(s) in the country on criminal law.

* * *

B.   The Common Law Tradition

The focus in the common law was originally on resolving the disputes at hand rather than creating legal principles that would be articulated in a generally applicable code. Common law developed historically on a case-by-case basis from the bottom-up (namely from judges), rather than the civil law that has always been developed top-down by the legislature.

* * *

Many common law lawyers will point with pride to the flexibility and creativity of their system. However, civil law lawyers critique what they perceive to be the unsystematic nature of the common law.

Given the central role of the judge in the common law tradition, it may come as no surprise that judicial opinions were historically the primary source of law. In contrast to the civil law tradition, where judges are tasked with applying the law only, common law judges were tasked with making the law. The development of case law, which was the authoritative source of law in the common law, led to the creation of precedents and a system called stare decisis in order to ensure certainty, fairness and consistency in the system.

Historically, laws or statutes were viewed as a secondary source of law, their role being to correct judicially-created rules. Today, legislation is far more central in common law countries. In the twentieth and twenty-first centuries, the common law underwent a crisis due to the modern trend to use the law to create new social order: the case-by-case method is not well suited to the idea of bringing about rapid and extensive social change.

Consequently, there is an increasing trend towards codification within the common law tradition, although certain distinctions should be made between a code in a common law country and a code in a civil law country. In a civil law country, the rationale for a code is to create a comprehensive legal regime and general principles on a particular area of law. In the common law, however, codification may not comprehensively address an area of law. It may not even abolish a prior law. In some cases, codes will merely incorporate prior case law, address one particular social issue or bring uniformity to an area of law.

In common law countries, a practitioner should also look for standard operating procedures (SOPs) as a source of law. SOPs are developed, with the same aim as regulations: to provide more concrete guidance to public servants and justice actors. In common law countries, SOPs may reflect both statutory law and case law, translating both into operational guidance for police, other justice actors and public servants. * * *

The final source of law in common law countries is international law, namely treaties and conventions. * * * In the common law tradition, international law is seen as a separate body of law that only begins to apply domestically when it is converted into domestic legislation by the legislature. Given the reliance on case law in the common law tradition, lawyers can invoke international treaties and case laws in court as so-called persuasive precedent but treaty provisions are not binding on the court, until they have been "domesticated" into national legislation.

V. The Court System

A. The Civil Law Tradition

Civil law countries make a theoretical and practical distinction between public law and private law—that does not hold the same importance in common law countries. What difference does this distinction make in practice? It is most evident when looking at the court structure in countries following the civil law tradition. The courts have divided according to public law cases and private law cases. Courts in civil law countries are more specialized than in the common law. There are multiple sets of courts and each has its own jurisdiction, hierarchy, judiciary and procedure. For example, in addition to ordinary courts that deal with private law matters, there may be Labor Courts, Social Security Courts, Commercial Courts, Administrative Courts and Agriculture Courts addressing public law cases.

The general rule is that private law matters are dealt with by "ordinary courts." One anomaly is that criminal law is also dealt with by ordinary courts, even though it rightly belongs in public law. Decisions of the ordinary courts can be appealed to Appellate Courts. At the head of the ordinary courts (and above Appellate Courts) sits the Court of Cassation * * *. This court decides only questions of law and the interpretation of statutes. Its purpose is to ensure uniformity in the law. It can either affirm the ruling of the Appellate Court or declare the ruling to be incorrect and refer the case back to another court of appeal for reconsideration. The latter is termed "casser" or "break," and this is where the name Court of Cassation came from.

Public law matters, namely, administrative law and constitutional law, have their own separate jurisdictions.

Traditionally, in the civil law tradition, there was no supreme administrative court that would decide upon administrative and constitutional law. Instead, like in France today, the Council of State—a government body—acts as the administrative court of last resort. * * *

The court of last resort for constitutional law, established to review whether a law is constitutional, has increasingly become the Constitutional Court. Constitutional Courts exist in [a number of] countries * * *. In other countries * * * there exists a Constitutional Council—a government body like the Council of State—to rule on the constitutionality of legislation. The reason behind the reliance on councils rather than courts is the traditional civil law view that judges cannot quash legislation as this would infringe the separation of powers doctrine (under which judges apply the law and the legislature makes, amends, or repeals the law).

* * *

B. The Common Law Tradition

Common law courts are unified, meaning that there is generally one Appeals Court and one Supreme Court in which any case may be subject to final scrutiny. The jurisdiction of inferior courts, which deal with criminal and civil matters, is limited geographically and according to the nature of the subject-matter. At the bottom of the court system may be Magistrate Courts, which originate and still exist today in the United Kingdom. * * * The exact jurisdiction of these courts will vary from country to country. There will also be variance if the country is federal, in which case the rule of law practitioner will need to determine the jurisdiction of federal (national) and state (sub-national) courts.

Of late, there has been a move towards developing specialized courts (also known as "tribunals") in common law countries such as Employment Courts, Tax Courts, Family Law Courts, and so forth. * * * In contrast to civil law countries, each of these specialized courts will not have its own Supreme Court.

VI. [Judges and Juries]

* * *

A. The Civil Law Tradition

* * *

Sitting Judge

In addition to investigating judges [who have "broad powers" to investigate cases], there are also sitting judges who hear the case in court. The sitting judge may sit alone for minor cases but, for more serious cases, will sit in a panel of judges (normally, three judges). Because of the different nature of the trial in the civil law system, the judge has a very different role to a common law judge. Rather than being an impartial referee, like a common law judge, the civil law judge is a central part of the trial. The sitting judge is the person who questions witnesses (although oral testimony is not required * * *) and experts, and calls evidence. * * *

* * *

Jury and Lay Judges

Juries are more typical in common law countries, but jury trials now exist in many civil law countries, * * * though this depends on the jurisdiction and type of case at hand. As in the common law, the role of the jury is to determine the guilt or innocence of the accused based on the facts presented. In some civil law countries, lay judges are coupled with professional judges to form a type of "mixed jury." Some systems have one professional judge and two lay judges while others have three professional judges and six lay judges, the latter forming a mini-lay jury.

* * *

B. The Common Law Tradition

* * *

Judge

The judge in the common law tradition is a much more powerful figure than in the civil law. First and foremost, * * * judges were traditionally vested with the power to make law. Today, they still have this same power but are also bound by statutes that cover many areas of the law. In interpreting statutes, judges in the common law tradition may read provisions much more expansively than judges in the civil law. This has led to novel interpretations of existing legal provisions and the broadening of the law in certain areas. * * * At trial, the judge acts like a referee with the two parties * * * taking center-stage.

* * *

The Jury

Juries have historically played a major role in the common law system. Back in the 12th century when the common law was evolving, juries were responsible for determining cases in their locality. The judge * * * is responsible for interpreting the law and instructing the jury. The role of the jury is to make a finding of fact * * *. The exact number, composition, and selection of the jury vary from country-to-country.

* * *

VII. Legal Education and Training
A.   The Civil Law Tradition

The education of law students in the civil law tradition is through an undergraduate university degree. The primary reference materials for civil law student are codes and the commentaries to these codes * * *. Case law does not play a major role in legal education. On day one, students begin at Article 1 of the code and the professor brings them through the code systematically. Rather than engaging in an interactive method of teaching, professors in the civil law lecture to a class that is usually very large.

After students complete their undergraduate education, they then make a choice as to what legal profession to pursue. Very early on, graduates must choose whether to become a government lawyer, public prosecutor, advocate, notary, judge or scholar. Lawyers do not often change careers.

If a law graduate wants to become a judge, he or she must attend a special training school for judges, pass exams and be appointed (often by a judicial council). In the alternative in some civil law countries, the judge must undertake a form of apprenticeship coupled with ongoing training. * * *

In some civil law countries, there is an office, or pool, of government lawyers to which a law graduate must apply should he or she want to take on this role. In other civil law countries, the young lawyer must apply to a particular department or agency.

To become an advocate * * *, the law graduate must undergo a period of apprenticeship in the office of an experienced lawyer. To become a notary * * *, a law graduate must also serve an apprenticeship in a notary's office and take a national exam.

The final career path—becoming an academic—is extremely challenging given the high stature of this position. Unlike in the United

States, where everyone who teaches at a law school is given the title of Professor, in many civil law countries, a professor is a person with a Ph.D who has been awarded a professorial chair. * * *

* * *

B.   The Common Law Tradition

In some common law countries * * *, a law degree is an undergraduate degree. In others, like the United States, a law degree is a graduate degree * * *.

University classes in the common law countries are usually highly interactive. Rather than professors lecturing to the class, they generally use the "Socratic method" of teaching, where the Professor asks students a series of questions and elicits responses (as well as pointing out inconsistencies in the responses or the logic of the student responses) so as to get the student to think critically.

In the common law educational system, a key learning objective is to demonstrate to students that there can be more than one answer to a particular question or that there may be no one "right" answer at all. It is important to contrast this with the civil law system where it is presumed that the codes and doctrine provide clear guidance and an answer can be easily extracted without the need for judicial interpretation or creativity * * *. The common law educational system thus rewards creative and novel interpretations of laws and cases.

In common law countries, case law rather than codes is the primary reference material for law students. Rather than refer to one set of commentaries as a civil law student would, common law students may have several textbooks that may offer differing conclusions on the same legal issue.

A common law student, at the end of his or her education, is not required to choose one particular legal career and stick to it, as a civil law student would. A common law student is more likely to switch roles during his or her career than a civil law student. For example, a practicing lawyer could become a prosecutor, then a judge, and could eventually switch to academia.

In the traditional common law, originating for the United Kingdom, a law student seeking to become a lawyer must undertake an apprenticeship. Also traditional in the common law system * * * is the division of the tasks of a lawyer into two distinct fields of practice: barristers and solicitors. To become a solicitor, a law student must undertake an apprenticeship with a senior solicitor as well as undertake professional training courses, generally organized by the Law Society of that country. In order to become a barrister, a law student must also undertake an apprenticeship (oddly enough called "deviling" in the UK system) as well as complete professional training courses.

Many common law countries [such as the United States] have departed from the traditional split between barrister and solicitor in favor of lawyers who can undertake both roles. In the United States [and certain other countries], a law graduate must complete a bar examination in order to qualify to become a lawyer. Upon passing, they are "admitted to the bar" and are then qualified to practice.

* * *

VIII.   Combining the Civil Law and Common Law? "Mixed" or "Hybrid" Systems

* * *

It has been said that today there is no pure system. * * * There has been significant borrowing between both. * * *

Witness the common law world moving toward codification—a historical trademark of the civil law tradition. * * * In the civil law world, we see the introduction of live witness testimony in court, coupled with cross-examination * * *. This stands at odds [with] the traditional judge-led trial that has been the rule in the civil law tradition. We also see in the civil law world an increasing reliance on case law to supplement the codes.

Beyond piecemeal borrowing, there are now many systems that are truly a fusion of both the civil law and the common law * * *. This can be seen also if we examine reform efforts in both developing and post-conflict countries. The trend appears to be that reformers take the best of each tradition and fuse these elements to create an overall system. * * * [O]ne system is not necessarily "better" than the other; they both have their strong points and their weak points. By fusing the best of both worlds, countries undertaking reforms arrive at stronger, more efficient systems of justice. * * *

* * *

NOTES AND QUESTIONS

1.   What are the essential features of the common law system? What are the essential features of the civil law system?

2.   How does the role of the judge differ in the two systems?

3.   How do sources of law differ in the two systems?

4.   How does the nature of legal training differ in the two systems?

5.   Despite its designation as a "common law" system, the U.S. has one of the most extensive code systems in the world. The current United States Code ("U.S.C.") contains more than 50 distinct titles, each of which contains

hundreds, if not thousands, of individual statutory laws. It is difficult to quantify the number of individual statutes. In 1982, the U.S. Justice Department oversaw an effort to count the number of federal criminal laws, which at the time spanned over 23,000 pages of statutory law. After two years, the study ended inconclusively. The researchers ultimately estimated that the U.S.C. contained approximately 3,000 distinct criminal offenses. *See* Ronald Gainer, *Report to the Attorney General on Federal Criminal Code Reform*, 1 Crim. L. Forum 99 (1989). More recent research indicates that the actual number of distinct criminal offenses may be much higher than the originally estimated 3,000. *See, e.g.*, J.S. BAKER & D.E. BENNETT, THE FEDERALIST SOCIETY FOR LAW AND PUBLIC POLICY STUDIES, MEASURING THE EXPLOSIVE GROWTH OF FEDERAL CRIME LEGISLATION (2004) (concluding that in 2004 there were more than 4,000 crimes in the U.S.C. titles). Of course, given that criminal offenses take up only a fraction of the total U.S.C., it is reasonable to assume that the U.S.C. has hundreds of thousands of statutory laws. These include laws relating to taxation, bankruptcy, the environment, antitrust regulation, securities, intellectual property, labor, immigration, and countless other subjects. There are also a number of rules governing federal trial and appellate court proceedings, including rules addressing civil procedure, criminal procedure, evidence, and appellate procedure.

In addition, each state has a large body of its own criminal and civil statutes. For example, California's statutory law consists of 29 legal code chapters, each pertaining to a distinct area of law. Similarly, New York has almost 100 chapters of state law in its publications of consolidated law. And the individual states have their own separate rules governing state court trial and appellate court proceedings.

Finally, both federal and state agencies publish and enforce regulations relating to their areas of expertise. The Code of Federal Regulations (referred to as the "C.F.R.") contains 50 titles that span over 200 volumes. They contain rules published by the numerous Executive departments and agencies of the federal government. The California Code of Regulations (referred to as the "C.C.R.") contains 28 titles that are designed to regulate over 200 administrative agencies.

6.   By the same token, with the advent of the internet, many civil law countries now publish judicial opinions on websites, and those opinions are often cited as precedent in similar cases. *See* Vincy Fon & Francesco Parisi, *Judicial Precedents in Civil Law Systems: A Dynamic Analysis*, 26 Int'l Rev. L. & Econ. 519 (2006) (describing the growing role of judicial decisions as persuasive guidance in civil law systems and comparing the use of these published decisions as a type of "soft" precedent). Given the number of statutes and regulations in the U.S., and given the increasing importance of judicial precedent in many civil law countries, is it accurate to classify current legal systems as either purely common law or purely civil law? Or is it more accurate, as Dr. O'Connor noted in the foregoing article, to characterize many systems as "hybrid"?

7. As discussed in the preceding articles, the common law legal structure was first developed in England in the Middle Ages and has since been adopted by many countries worldwide, including the United States (excluding the State of Louisiana), Canada (excluding Quebec), the United Kingdom (excluding Scotland), Australia, New Zealand, India (excluding the State of Goa), and many more. On the other hand, most countries in Europe, South America, and Africa employ a civil law structure. In total, approximately 35% of countries worldwide utilize a common law structure, while approximately 60% of countries utilize the civil law structure. The remaining approximately 5% utilize some form of hybrid system or have no defined legal structure. *See Percentage of the World Population, Civil Law and Common Law Systems*, JURIGLOBE, http://www.juriglobe.ca/eng/syst-demo/tableau-dcivil-claw.php (last visited Nov. 11, 2015).

B. THE ROLE OF THE LAWYER IN SOCIETY

As in other countries, lawyers play a crucial role in the U.S. legal system—as advocates, counselors, judges, and scholars. The following excerpt discusses various roles that lawyers play, and the methods for regulating the conduct of lawyers.

THE AMERICAN BAR ASSOCIATION'S MODEL RULES OF PROFESSIONAL CONDUCT—PREAMBLE*

© 2014 The American Bar Association

A lawyer, as a member of the legal profession, is a representative of clients, an officer of the legal system and a public citizen having special responsibility for the quality of justice.

As a representative of clients, a lawyer performs various functions. As advisor, a lawyer provides a client with an informed understanding of the client's legal rights and obligations and explains their practical implications. As advocate, a lawyer zealously asserts the client's position under the rules of the adversary system. As negotiator, a lawyer seeks a result advantageous to the client but consistent with requirements of honest dealings with others. As an evaluator, a lawyer acts by examining a client's legal affairs and reporting about them to the client or to others.

In addition to these representational functions, a lawyer may serve as a third-party neutral, a nonrepresentational role helping the parties to resolve a dispute or other matter. * * * In addition, there are Rules that apply to lawyers who are not active in the practice of law or to practicing lawyers even when they are acting in a nonprofessional capacity. For example, a lawyer who commits fraud in the conduct of a business is subject

---

* The Model Rules of Professional Conduct were adopted by the American Bar Association, a voluntary professional organization. Most states have adopted the Model Rules in whole or in part. [Ed.]

to discipline for engaging in conduct involving dishonesty, fraud, deceit or misrepresentation.

In all professional functions a lawyer should be competent, prompt and diligent. A lawyer should maintain communication with a client concerning the representation. A lawyer should keep in confidence information relating to representation of a client except so far as disclosure is required or permitted by the Rules of Professional Conduct or other law.

A lawyer's conduct should conform to the requirements of the law, both in professional service to clients and in the lawyer's business and personal affairs. A lawyer should use the law's procedures only for legitimate purposes and not to harass or intimidate others. A lawyer should demonstrate respect for the legal system and for those who serve it, including judges, other lawyers and public officials. While it is a lawyer's duty, when necessary, to challenge the rectitude of official action, it is also a lawyer's duty to uphold legal process.

As a public citizen, a lawyer should seek improvement of the law, access to the legal system, the administration of justice and the quality of service rendered by the legal profession. As a member of a learned profession, a lawyer should cultivate knowledge of the law beyond its use for clients, employ that knowledge in reform of the law and work to strengthen legal education. In addition, a lawyer should further the public's understanding of and confidence in the rule of law and the justice system because legal institutions in a constitutional democracy depend on popular participation and support to maintain their authority. A lawyer should be mindful of deficiencies in the administration of justice and of the fact that the poor, and sometimes persons who are not poor, cannot afford adequate legal assistance. Therefore, all lawyers should devote professional time and resources and use civic influence to ensure equal access to our system of justice for all those who because of economic or social barriers cannot afford or secure adequate legal counsel. A lawyer should aid the legal profession in pursuing these objectives and should help the bar regulate itself in the public interest.

Many of a lawyer's professional responsibilities are prescribed in the Rules of Professional Conduct, as well as substantive and procedural law. However, a lawyer is also guided by personal conscience and the approbation of professional peers. A lawyer should strive to attain the highest level of skill, to improve the law and the legal profession and to exemplify the legal profession's ideals of public service.

A lawyer's responsibilities as a representative of clients, an officer of the legal system and a public citizen are usually harmonious. Thus, when an opposing party is well represented, a lawyer can be a zealous advocate on behalf of a client and at the same time assume that justice is being done. So also, a lawyer can be sure that preserving client confidences ordinarily serves the public interest because people are more likely to seek legal advice, and thereby heed their legal obligations, when they know their communications will be private.

In the nature of law practice, however, conflicting responsibilities are encountered. Virtually all difficult ethical problems arise from conflict between a lawyer's responsibilities to clients, to the legal system and to the lawyer's own interest in remaining an ethical person while earning a satisfactory living. The Rules of Professional Conduct often prescribe terms for resolving such conflicts. Within the framework of these Rules, however, many difficult issues of professional discretion can arise. Such issues must be resolved through the exercise of sensitive professional and moral judgment guided by the basic principles underlying the Rules. These principles include the lawyer's obligation zealously to protect and pursue a client's legitimate interests, within the bounds of the law, while maintaining a professional, courteous and civil attitude toward all persons involved in the legal system.

The legal profession is largely self-governing. Although other professions also have been granted powers of self-government, the legal profession is unique in this respect because of the close relationship between the profession and the processes of government and law enforcement. This connection is manifested in the fact that ultimate authority over the legal profession is vested largely in the courts.

To the extent that lawyers meet the obligations of their professional calling, the occasion for government regulation is obviated. Self-regulation also helps maintain the legal profession's independence from government domination. An independent legal profession is an important force in preserving government under law, for abuse of legal authority is more readily challenged by a profession whose members are not dependent on government for the right to practice.

The legal profession's relative autonomy carries with it special responsibilities of self-government. The profession has a responsibility to assure that its regulations are conceived in the public interest and not in furtherance of parochial or self-interested concerns of the bar. Every lawyer is responsible for observance of the Rules of Professional Conduct. A lawyer should also aid in securing their observance by other lawyers. Neglect of these responsibilities compromises the independence of the profession and the public interest which it serves.

Lawyers play a vital role in the preservation of society. The fulfillment of this role requires an understanding by lawyers of their relationship to our legal system. The Rules of Professional Conduct, when properly applied, serve to define that relationship.

NOTES AND QUESTIONS

1.   Why are professional responsibility rules (such as those discussed in the above excerpt) necessary?

2.   To access the entire set of the American Bar Association's Rules of Professional Conduct, *see* Am. Bar Ass'n, *Model Rules of Professional Conduct* (2013), *available at* http://www.americanbar.org/groups/professional_responsibility/publications/model_rules_of_professional_conduct/model_rules_of_professional_conduct_table_of_contents.html.

3.   The U.S. is not the only country that has ethical rules governing a lawyer's conduct. For a discussion of lawyers' ethical obligations on a global scale, *see* JAMES MOLITERNO & PAUL PATON, GLOBAL ISSUES IN LEGAL ETHICS Ch. 1 (2d ed. 2014) (surveying the roles of lawyers and their professional rules of conduct in the United States, Japan, the European Union, and Russia).

C. DUAL FEDERAL AND STATE COURTS

The U.S. judicial system is divided into two separate legal systems: a federal judiciary and state judiciaries. The following article addresses the differences between the two court systems.

FEDERAL COURTS COMPARED TO STATE COURTS

United States Courts, 2015
http://www.uscourts.gov/about-federal-courts

<u>Why Two Court Systems?</u>

The Judicial Branch has two court systems: federal and state. While each hears certain types of cases, neither is completely independent of the other. The two systems often interact and share the goal of fairly handling legal issues.

The U.S. Constitution created a governmental structure known as federalism that calls for the sharing of powers between the national and state governments. The Constitution gives certain powers to the federal government and reserves the rest for the states.

The federal court system deals with legal issues expressly or implicitly granted to it by the U.S. Constitution. The state court systems deal with their respective state constitutions and the legal issues that the U.S. Constitution did not give to the federal government or explicitly deny to the states.

For example, because the Constitution gives Congress sole authority to make uniform laws concerning bankruptcies, a state court would lack jurisdiction. Likewise, since the Constitution does not give the federal government authority in most family law matters, a federal court would lack jurisdiction in a divorce case.

Comparing State & Federal Courts

* * *

The U.S. Constitution is the supreme law of the land in the United States. It creates a federal system of government in which power is shared between the federal government and the state governments. Due to federalism, both the federal government and each of the state governments have their own court systems. * * *

1.   Court Structure

The Federal Court System	The State Court System
Article III of the Constitution invests the judicial power of the United States in the federal court system. Article III, Section 1 specifically creates the U.S. Supreme Court and gives Congress the authority to create the lower federal courts.	The Constitution and laws of each state establish the state courts. A court of last resort, often known as a Supreme Court, is usually the highest court. Some states also have an intermediate Court of Appeals. Below these appeals courts are the state trial courts. Some are referred to as Circuit or District Courts.
Congress has used this power to establish the 13 U.S. Courts of Appeals, the 94 U.S. District Courts, the U.S. Court of Claims, and the U.S. Court of International Trade. U.S. Bankruptcy Courts handle bankruptcy cases. Magistrate Judges handle some District Court matters.	States also usually have courts that handle specific legal matters, *e.g.*, probate court (wills and estates); juvenile court; family court; etc.
Parties dissatisfied with a decision of a U.S. District Court, the U.S. Court of Claims, and/or the U.S. Court of International Trade may appeal to a U.S. Court of Appeals.	Parties dissatisfied with the decision of the trial court may take their case to the intermediate Court of Appeals.

A party may ask the U.S. Supreme Court to review a decision of the U.S. Court of Appeals, but the Supreme Court usually is under no obligation to do so. The U.S. Supreme Court is the final arbiter of federal constitutional questions.	Parties have the option to ask the highest state court to hear the case.
	Only certain [state court] cases are eligible for review by the U.S. Supreme Court.

2.   Selection of Judges

The Federal Court System	The State Court System
The Constitution states that federal judges are to be nominated by the President and confirmed by the Senate. They hold office during good behavior, typically for life. Through Congressional impeachment proceedings, federal judges may be removed from office for misbehavior.	State court judges are selected in a variety of ways, including • election, • appointment for a given number of years, • appointment for life, and • combinations of these methods, *e.g.*, appointment followed by election.

3.   Types of Cases Heard

The Federal Court System	The State Court System
• Cases that deal with the constitutionality of a law; • Cases involving the laws and treaties of the U.S.; • Cases involving ambassadors and public ministers; • Admiralty law; • Bankruptcy; and • Habeas corpus issues.	• Most criminal cases, probate (involving wills and estates) • Most contract cases, tort cases (personal injuries), family law (marriages, divorces, adoptions), etc.

	State courts are the final arbiters of state laws and constitutions. Their interpretations of federal law or the U.S. Constitution may be appealed to the U.S. Supreme Court. The Supreme Court may choose to hear or not to hear such cases.

4. Article I Courts

Congress has created several Article I or legislative courts that do not have full judicial power. Judicial power is the authority to be the final decider in all questions of constitutional law and all questions of federal law, and to hear claims at the core of habeas corpus issues.

Article I courts are U.S. Court of Veterans' Appeals, the U.S. Court of Military Appeals, and the U.S. Tax Court.

5. Cases in Federal and State Courts

Find out what types of cases are heard in federal courts and state courts. How are they different? How are they similar?

State Courts	Federal Courts	State or Federal Courts
• Crimes under state legislation. • State constitutional issues and cases involving state laws or regulations. • Family law issues. • Real property issues. • Most private contract disputes (except those resolved under bankruptcy law).	• Crimes under statutes enacted by Congress. • Most cases involving federal laws or regulations (for example: tax, Social Security, broadcasting, civil rights). • Matters involving interstate and international commerce, including airline	• Certain civil rights claims. • "Class action" cases. • Environmental regulations. • Certain disputes involving federal law.

• Most issues involving the regulation of trades and professions. • Most professional malpractice issues. • Most issues involving the internal governance of business associations such as partnerships and corporations. • Most personal injury lawsuits. • Most workers' injury claims. • Probate and inheritance matters. • Most traffic violations and registration of motor vehicles.	and railroad regulation. • Cases involving securities and commodities regulation, including takeover of publicly held corporations. • Admiralty cases. • International trade law matters. • Patent, copyright, and other intellectual property issues. • Cases involving rights under treaties, foreign states, and foreign nationals. • State law disputes when "diversity of citizenship" exists. • Bankruptcy matters. • Disputes between states. • Habeas corpus actions. • Traffic violations and other misdemeanors occurring on certain federal property.	

THE FEDERAL COURT SYSTEM OF THE UNITED STATES

Administrative Office of the U.S. Courts, 2010

* * *

The Structure of the Federal Courts

With certain notable exceptions, the federal courts have jurisdiction to hear a broad variety of cases. The same federal judges handle both civil and criminal cases, public law and private law disputes, cases involving individuals and cases involving corporations and government entities, appeals from administrative agency decisions, and law and equity matters. There are no separate constitutional courts, because all federal courts and judges may decide issues regarding the constitutionality of federal laws and other governmental actions that arise in the cases they hear.

Trial Courts

The United States district courts are the principal trial courts in the federal court system. The district courts have jurisdiction to hear nearly all categories of federal cases. There are 94 federal judicial districts, including one or more in each state, the District of Columbia, Puerto Rico, and the overseas territories.

Each federal judicial district includes a United States bankruptcy court operating as a unit of the district court. The bankruptcy court has nationwide jurisdiction over almost all matters involving insolvency cases, except criminal issues. Once a case is filed in a bankruptcy court, related matters pending in other federal and state courts can be removed to the bankruptcy court. The bankruptcy courts are administratively managed by the bankruptcy judges.

Two special trial courts within the federal judicial branch have nationwide jurisdiction over certain types of cases. The Court of International Trade addresses cases involving international trade and customs issues. The United States Court of Federal Claims has jurisdiction over disputes involving federal contracts, the taking of private property by the federal government, and a variety of other monetary claims against the United States.

Trial court proceedings are conducted by a single judge, sitting alone or with a jury of citizens as finders of fact. * * *

Appellate Courts

The 94 judicial districts are organized into 12 regional circuits, each of which has a United States court of appeals. A court of appeals hears appeals from the district courts located within its circuit, as well as appeals from certain federal administrative agencies. In addition, the Court of Appeals for the Federal Circuit has nationwide jurisdiction to hear appeals in specialized cases, such as those involving patent laws and cases decided by the Court of International Trade and the Court of Federal Claims.

There is a right of appeal in every federal case in which a district court enters a final judgment. The courts of appeals typically sit in panels of three judges. They are not courts of cassation, and they may review a case only if one or more parties files a timely appeal from the decision of a lower court or administrative agency. When an appeal is filed, a court of appeals reviews the decision and record of proceedings in the lower court or administrative agency. The court of appeals does not hear additional evidence, and generally must accept the factual findings of the trial judge. If additional fact-finding is necessary, the court of appeals may remand the case to the trial court or administrative agency. Remand is unnecessary in most cases, however, and the court of appeals either affirms or reverses the lower court or agency decision in a written order or written opinion.

In cases of unusual importance, a court of appeals may sit "en banc"— that is, with all the appellate judges in the circuit present—to review the decisions of a three-judge panel. The full court may affirm or reverse the panel decision.

The United States Supreme Court

The United States Supreme Court is the highest court in the federal judiciary. It consists of the Chief Justice of the United States and eight associate justices. The court always sits en banc, with all nine justices hearing and deciding all cases together. The jurisdiction of the Supreme Court is almost completely discretionary, and, to be exercised, requires the agreement of at least four justices to hear a case. (In a small number of special cases, such as boundary disputes between the states, the Supreme Court acts either as the court of first instance or exercises mandatory appellate review). As a general rule, the Court only agrees to decide cases where there is a split of opinion among the courts of appeals or where there is an important constitutional question or issue of federal law that needs to be clarified.

* * *

COURTS 101: AN UNDERSTANDING OF THE COURT SYSTEM
Integrated Justice Information Systems Institute, 2012

* * *

State Court System

The organizational structure of a state court is determined by individual state constitutions—none are exactly the same—but the following levels of courts * * * exist in the majority of states.

Courts of Limited Jurisdiction

Courts of limited jurisdiction generally comprise the first tier of the judicial systems in the states. The reference to limited jurisdiction indicates that state legislatures limited the scope of these courts when they were created. These courts usually hear "less serious" or minor cases, including, but not limited to: small claims (*e.g.* landlord/tenant actions, debt matters, non-injury accident claims, etc.) where, typically, self-represented litigants bring claims of a "limited," up to a pre-set, monetary value; traffic cases; city ordinance violations; and, specialized cases, such as juvenile or family matters.

Courts of limited jurisdiction also tend to be where the first appearance, charging, and bail setting for criminal cases happens in an arrest or criminal matter.

Courts of General Jurisdiction

Courts of general jurisdiction represent the second tier of the judicial systems in the states, and are considered the "trial courts" in the state systems. They serve a similar function to district courts in the federal system. Although caseloads vary from state to state, general jurisdiction courts typically handle: felony cases, both criminal and civil; higher-level misdemeanor cases; special case types, such as probate, mental health, and juvenile cases; family and domestic violence; and, appeals from limited jurisdiction courts. Courts of general jurisdiction are where most jury trials occur. It should also be noted that some states combine the jurisdiction of the limited and general jurisdiction court into a single general jurisdiction court with different divisions for minor versus major matters, or specialize by case type.

Appellate Courts

Appellate courts are commonly considered review courts only and not courts where citizens initiate cases. All states have an appellate level of court; some have a multi-tiered level. Most appellate matters are cases where one of the parties is not happy with the decision from the trial court and petitions the appeals court in their state to get a review of the matter. Some states have "Intermediate Appellate Courts" (see below), which handle specific appeals to which an appeal is almost guaranteed. Appeals to the "Court of Last Resort" in those states are generally discretionary. There are states, however, which do not have an intermediate appellate court and, in this case, all appeals generally go directly to the single Appellate level "Court of Last Resort."

State court systems generally follow this structure of limited/high volume courts—trial/general jurisdiction courts—appellate/review courts; however, there are three common variations * * * that are important to integrated justice: specialty courts, juvenile courts, and intermediate appellate courts, which have many anomalies at the state level.

Specialty Courts

There are many types of limited or general jurisdiction courts—*specialty courts*—that have been established to deal with a specific type of case or a specific problem. These courts are established as stand-alone separate courts, a separate division of a larger court, or just a separate docket (calendar) of a larger court. Specialty courts may be part of the Judicial Branch or the Executive Branch, depending on the state constitution. While specialty courts may occur at the limited jurisdiction level, they are more common at the trial level. Some examples include: specific courts assigned to deal with issues such as complex litigation (business courts), tax issues (tax courts), environmental issues (water or environmental courts), or drug offenses (drug courts), and, most recently, gun courts to fast track weapons-specific offenses.

Juvenile Courts

Juvenile courts are special courts or departments of a trial court that deal with underage defendants charged with delinquency—committing offenses that would be criminal matters if committed by an adult, [and] status offenses (violations that occur because of their age[, such as] underage drinking, truancy, [and] runaways)—or minors who are involved in abuse and neglect matters. The normal age of these defendants is under 18, with some states allowing juveniles usually over age 14 to also be charged as adults. The juvenile court does not have jurisdiction in these cases in which minors are charged as adults. The procedure in juvenile court is not adversarial (although the minor is entitled to legal representation by a lawyer), and is seen more as a mediation and consultative environment. There is often the involvement of advocates, social services, and probation officers in the process to achieve positive results and to save the minor from involvement in further crimes; however, serious crimes and repeated offenses can result in sentencing juvenile offenders to a juvenile correctional or detention facility, and later transfer to state prison upon reaching adulthood with limited maximum sentences. Where abuse, neglect, and family support (care and safety of the child) are at issue, the juvenile court may work with foster care agencies and the child may be treated as a ward of the court.

Intermediate Appellate Courts

Many, but not all, states have *intermediate appellate courts*, which are located between the trial courts of general jurisdiction and the highest court in the state. Any party, except in a case where a defendant in a criminal trial has been found not guilty, who is not satisfied with the judgment of a state trial court may appeal the matter to an appropriate intermediate appellate court. Such appeals are usually a matter of right (meaning the court must hear them); however, these courts address only alleged procedural mistakes and errors of law made by the trial court. They do not generally review the judgment of the lower court (guilt/innocence) and do not review the facts of the case, which have been established during the trial, nor do they accept additional evidence. Instead, these courts look to see that the process and procedures [were correct] (*e.g.*, jury instructions were correctly provided; evidence was properly admitted; parties were given their rights in court; discovery during the trial process, etc.). These courts usually sit in panels of two or three judges. Moreover, appellate decisions are normally to uphold the verdict/decision of the lower court, to reverse the decision of the lower court, or to return the case for re-hearing.

* * *

NOTES AND QUESTIONS

1.   There is a common saying in the U.S.: "Don't make a federal case out of it." The assumption underlying that saying is that federal cases are typically important, while state cases are usually less consequential. *See* JAMES CLAPP ET AL., LAWTALK: THE UNKNOWN STORIES BEHIND FAMILIAR LEGAL EXPRESSIONS 160–65 (2011) (describing how that phrase originated in New York in the 1940s after the federal judicial system had grown in importance in the 1930s). As discussed above, however, state courts have exclusive or primary jurisdiction over matters such as marriage, divorce, child custody, most types of street crime (*e.g.*, most murders, rapes, and robberies), landlord-tenant disputes, most estate matters, most matters involving real property, most personal injury matters, and most matters relating to professional conduct (such as that of doctors and lawyers). Is it correct to assume that, in general, federal cases are more "important" than state cases?

2.   As the preceding pages demonstrate, it is not uncommon for state and federal courts to have jurisdiction over the same subject matter or issues in dispute. For example, in what is known as federal "diversity jurisdiction" under 28 U.S.C. § 1332 (a topic that will be discussed in greater detail in Chapter 3), federal courts have jurisdiction over state law claims when the adverse parties are citizens of different states and the lawsuit involves an amount in controversy in excess of $75,000. In addition to basic "diversity jurisdiction," there are several situations in which a federal court and a state court may have overlapping jurisdiction based on separate legal grounds, including: a state murder charge and a federal civil rights prosecution (where, for example, the murder involved racial animus); environmental enforcement at both the federal and state level; a violation of both federal and state employment laws, etc. And in various circumstances, alleged violations of the U.S. Constitution or federal statutes can be asserted in either federal or state court. For example, one of the lawsuits comprising the famous school desegregation litigation (*Brown v. Board of Education*, 347 U.S. 483 (1954)) was originally brought in the Delaware state court system, even though it raised claims based on the Fourteenth Amendment to the U.S. Constitution (equal protection). *See Gebhart v. Belton*, 33 Del.Ch. 144, 91 A.2d 137 (1952). *Brown v. Board of Education* will be discussed in greater detail in Chapter 2.

3.   Federal judges are nominated by the President of the United States, confirmed by the U.S. Senate, and typically hold their positions for life or until they resign (as long as "good behavior" is maintained). The power of federal judges (including U.S. Supreme Court Justices) is granted by Article III of the U.S. Constitution, and Congress controls the number of judges and justices that are appointed. Since 1869, the number of Supreme Court justices has remained at nine. As of 2014, Congress had authorized 179 federal court of appeals judgeships and 677 federal district court judgeships. For detailed information on the federal appointment process, *see* http://www.uscourts.gov/judges-judgeships. Although state judges in some states are appointed by the Governor and are granted life tenure, the majority of states have some sort of election scheme whereby judges are elected (by voters residing in the particular jurisdiction) and lose their positions if not re-elected. Terms vary depending on the state. Examples include Minnesota (6-year election terms); Kentucky (8-year election terms); and Pennsylvania (10-year election terms).

4.   What are the advantages and disadvantages of a system in which judges are appointed? What are the advantages and disadvantages of a system in which judges are elected? *See, e.g., Republican Party of Minn. v. White*, 536 U.S. 765, 788–89 (2002) (O'Connor, J., concurring) (criticizing state election policies and noting: "[I]f judges are subject to regular elections they are likely to feel that they have at least some personal stake in the outcome of every publicized case. Elected judges cannot help being aware that if the public is not satisfied with the outcome of a particular case, it could hurt their reelection prospects."); Mark Cady & Jess Phelps, *Preserving the Delicate Balance Between Judicial Accountability and Independence: Merit Selection in the Post-White World*, 17 Cornell J.L. & Pub. Pol'y 343 (2008) (arguing for a middle ground in selecting state court judges, with an initial appointment and a subsequent option for a retention election, and asserting that such a middle ground is preferable because it maintains a meaningful balance between judicial accountability and independence); Peter Olszweski, Sr., *Who's Judging Whom? Why Popular Elections Are Preferable to Merit Selection Systems*, 109 Penn St. L. Rev. 1 (2004) (supporting the judicial election system and arguing that popular elections for judges are the most democratic, representative, and efficient method of judicial selection because they give citizens a direct role in choosing the judges who represent them); Mark Behrens & Cary Silverman, *The Case for Adopting Appointive Judicial Selection Systems for State Court Judges*, 11 Cornell J.L. & Pub. Pol'y 273 (2002) (condemning judicial elections and advocating for states to adopt systems of judicial appointment). In recent years, the U.S. Supreme Court has twice sided with litigants who have raised concerns about ethical conflicts arising out of judicial elections. *See Williams-Yulee v. Fla. Bar*, 575 U.S. ___, 135 S. Ct. 1656 (2015) (holding that a state regulation that prohibited judicial candidates from personally soliciting to support a campaign fund did not violate the First Amendment's right to free speech); *Caperton v. A.T. Massey Coal Co., Inc.*, 556 U.S. 868 (2009) (requiring a state judge to recuse himself from participation in a case involving a party

that had donated $3 million to his election campaign because the situation posed a high risk of actual bias).

D. TRIAL BY JURY

One of the seminal features of American law (in both criminal and civil cases) is the right to a jury trial. The following articles discuss the U.S. jury system.

HISTORY OF JURY DUTY

U.S. District Court, Western District of Missouri, 2015
http://www.mow.uscourts.gov/district/jury/jury_history.html#grand_jury

History of the Jury

By the time the United States Constitution and the Bill of Rights were drafted and ratified, the institution of trial by jury was almost universally revered, so revered that its history had been traced back to Magna Carta. The jury began in the form of a grand or presentment jury with the role of inquest and was started by Frankish conquerors to discover the King's rights. Henry II regularized this type of proceeding to establish royal control over the machinery of justice, first in civil trials and then in criminal trials. Trial by petit jury was not employed at least until the reign of Henry III, in which the jury was first essentially a body of witnesses, called for their knowledge of the case; not until the reign of Henry VI did it become the trier of evidence. It was during the Seventeenth Century that the jury emerged as a safeguard for the criminally accused. Thus, in the Eighteenth Century, Blackstone could commemorate the institution as part of a "strong and two-fold barrier . . . between the liberties of the people and the prerogative of the crown" because "the truth of every accusation . . . [must] be confirmed by the unanimous suffrage of twelve of his equals and neighbors indifferently chosen and superior to all suspicion." The right was guaranteed in the constitutions of the original 13 States, was guaranteed in the body of the Constitution and in the Sixth Amendment, and the constitution of every State entering the Union thereafter in one form or another protected the right to jury trial in criminal cases. "Those who emigrated to this country from England brought with them this great privilege 'as their birthright and inheritance, as a part of that admirable common law which had fenced around and interposed barriers on every side against the approaches of arbitrary power.' "

* * * "The framers of the constitutions strove to create an independent judiciary but insisted upon further protection against arbitrary action. * * * [T]he jury trial provisions . . . reflect a fundamental decision about the exercise of official power—a reluctance to entrust plenary powers over the life and liberty of the citizen to one judge or to a group of judges. * * * "

History of the Grand Jury

A Grand Jury derives its name from the fact that it usually has a greater number of jurors than a trial (petit) jury. One of the earliest concepts of Grand Juries dates back to early Greece where the Athenians used an accusatory body. In early Briton, the Saxons also used something similar to a Grand Jury System. During the years 978 to 1016, one of the Dooms (laws) stated that for each 100 men, 12 were to be named to act as an accusing body. They were cautioned "not to accuse an innocent man or spare a guilty one."

The Grand Jury can also be traced to the time of the Norman conquest of England in 1066. There is evidence that the courts of that time summoned a body of sworn neighbors to present crimes that had come to their knowledge. Since the members of that accusing jury were selected from small jurisdictions, it was natural that they could present accusations based on their personal knowledge.

Historians agree that the Assize [court session or assembly] of Clarendon in 1166 provided the ground work for our present Grand Jury system. During the reign of Henry II (1154–1189), to regain for the crown the powers usurped by Thomas Becket, Chancellor of England, 12 "good and lawful men" in each village were assembled to reveal the names of those suspected of crimes. It was during this same period that juries were divided into two types, civil and criminal, with the development of each influencing the other.

The oath taken by these jurors provided that they would carry out their duties faithfully, that they would aggrieve no one through enmity nor deference to anyone through love, and that they would conceal those things that they had heard.

By the year 1290, these accusing juries were given the authority to inquire into the maintenance of bridges and highways, defects of jails, and whether the Sheriff had kept in jail anyone who should have been brought before the justices. "Le Grand Inquest" evolved during the reign of Edward III (1368), when the "accusatory jury" was increased in number from 12 to 23, with a majority vote necessary to indict anyone accused of crime.

In America, the Massachusetts Bay Colony impaneled the first Grand Jury in 1635 to consider cases of murder, robbery and wife beating. As early as 1700, the value of the Grand Jury was recognized as opposing the Royalists. These colonial Grand Juries expressed their independence by refusing to indict leaders of the Stamp Act (1765), and refusing to bring libel charges against the editors of the Boston Gazette (1765). A union with other colonies to oppose British taxes was supported by the Philadelphia Grand Jury in 1770.

By the end of the Colonial Period, the Grand Jury had become an indispensable adjunct of Government: "they proposed new laws, protested against abuses in government, and wielded the tremendous authority in their power to determine who should and who should not face trial."

JURY SYSTEM OVERVIEW
American Judicature Society, 2015
(formerly available online; AJS dissolved in 2015)

* * *

Right to a Jury Trial

The right to a jury trial is governed by three different sets of rules that apply to three different types of cases: civil cases in federal court[;] [c]ivil cases in state court; and [c]riminal cases (whether in federal court or state court).

Civil cases in federal court

In civil cases in federal court, the right to a jury trial is governed by the Seventh Amendment:

> In Suits at Common Law, where the value in controversy shall exceed twenty dollars, the right of trial by jury shall be preserved, and no fact tried to a jury, shall be otherwise reexamined in any Court of the United States, than according to the rules of the Common Law.

It is clear that the Amendment does not provide for jury trials in all federal civil cases because as of the time of the Amendment's adoption in 1791 there were several kinds of cases that were not "Suits at Common Law," like suits in equity or admiralty; those suits were not entitled to jury trials in 1791, and still are not. But subsequently many kinds of suits have come into being that did not exist at all in 1791, and the law/equity distinction was abolished in 1938. In this drastically changed legal landscape, it is sometimes difficult to decide what jury trial rights "shall be preserved" under the Seventh Amendment. One rule of thumb is that if the suit seeks money damages—the traditional remedy under the common law—there is almost surely a right to a jury trial, while if the suit seeks only equitable relief—like an injunction—there almost surely is no right to a jury trial. * * *

* * *

Civil cases in state court

In civil cases in state court, the right to a jury trial is governed by the state's constitution and statutes. The Supreme Court has repeatedly held that the Seventh Amendment right to a jury trial applies only to federal courts, not to state courts. As a practical matter, though, most states make jury trials widely available for many kinds of civil cases above the level of small claims court.

Criminal cases

The governing law for criminal cases in both federal and state courts is the Sixth Amendment, which provides in part:

In all criminal prosecutions, the accused shall enjoy the right to a speedy and public trial, by an impartial jury of the State and district wherein the crime shall have been committed. . . .

While this provision originally only applied to federal criminal prosecutions, in 1968 the Supreme Court decided that a right to trial by jury in most criminal cases is so fundamental that it constitutes an element of due process that the state is obligated to provide by the Fourteenth Amendment's Due Process Clause. However, the Court later decided that a right to jury trial is constitutionally required only for "serious" offenses. An offense is always "serious" if the potential punishment for the crime is greater than six months' imprisonment, although sometimes additional statutory and regulatory penalties may make a crime "serious" even if the potential imprisonment is less than six months. Of course, states are free to provide the right to a jury trial even in cases where it is not constitutionally required. And a criminal defendant is always free to waive the right to a trial by jury.

* * *

Jury Powers

The traditional description of the jury's role gives it two powers: (1) to decide the facts, and (2) to apply the law to the facts. * * *

Power to decide facts

The facts the jury has the power to determine are the nitty-gritty details of the event that is the subject of the litigation. These facts pertain to what are sometimes called the "journalist's questions:" who, what, when, where, why, and how? The jurors listen to the evidence of each party concerning a disputed fact. Then the jurors, through deliberations, determine which version of a disputed fact they find more convincing. Often, this task requires the jurors to evaluate the credibility of witnesses.

Jurors have a great deal of freedom in determining the facts. No judicial officer is present during the deliberations to impose any particular approach upon the jurors. Jurors are not required to explain the verdict, so what went on in the jury room is usually shrouded in mystery. And even if jurors are willing to talk about the deliberations afterward, the rules of most jurisdictions establish that testimony about what went on in the jury room is usually inadmissible to cast doubt on the verdict.

Nonetheless, this freedom to determine the facts is supposed to be exercised rationally by the jurors, not emotionally or arbitrarily. Thus, for example, it is impermissible to award damages to a plaintiff who has not proven the case just because the jurors feel sorry for the plaintiff. Similarly, it is impermissible for a jury to decide a case by flipping a coin, or by employing a "quotient verdict" (one arrived at by each juror writing down a damages amount, adding all the figures, and dividing by the number of jurors to get an average).

Due to the secrecy of the deliberations, it is often impossible to determine whether a verdict was arrived at rationally. But there are procedural mechanisms designed to assure, to the extent possible, that jurors use rational processes to reach rational results.

Several mechanisms available to trial judges are designed to remove from jury consideration factual issues on which the evidence is entirely one-sided, thereby avoiding irrational findings by the jury. Primary among these mechanisms are summary judgments and directed verdicts (although the Constitution forbids their use against defendants in criminal cases). Further, trial judges also have mechanisms to deal with irrational jury verdicts after-the-fact, including judgments notwithstanding the verdict, grants of new trials, and additur (ordering a new trial unless the losing party agrees to an increase in the amount of damages awarded by the jury) and remittitur (ordering a new trial unless the winning party agrees to a decrease in the amount of damages awarded by the jury).

Not only do trial judges have some power to prevent irrational jury results, so do appellate judges. Appellate courts have the power to overturn a verdict that is contrary to the great weight of the evidence (although this power does not exist as to an acquittal in a criminal case, since the Double Jeopardy Clause prevents retrial of an acquitted defendant, no matter how irrational the acquittal may have been).

Power to apply the law to the facts

The traditional statement that the jury is to take the law given by the judge and apply it to the facts misleadingly suggests that juries have no role in determining what the law is. In fact, juries determine what the law is in every case to a limited extent. This is true because even the clearest instructions on the law still require juries to make some judgments about what the instructions mean (although the more completely a legal term is defined in the instructions, the less room there is for juror interpretation of the law). For example, words describing the burden of persuasion ("by a preponderance of the evidence" in most civil cases; "beyond a reasonable doubt" in all criminal cases) inevitably require jurors to interpret what those phrases mean in the context of the facts of the case, no matter how carefully the phrases are explained. And some important legal questions are explicitly structured so as to provide for juror interpretation of what the law is. A primary example is negligence, which is defined in terms of how a "reasonable person" would have behaved, and the jurors are responsible for determining the behavior of a "reasonable person." * * *

One mechanism for attempting to limit jury interpretation of law is the "special verdict" form. A special verdict form asks the jurors to answer specific questions about the case, as contrasted with a "general verdict" form that simply asks the jurors to report which party won. Presumably, a jury will engage in more legal interpretation when a general verdict form is used. * * *

NOTES AND QUESTIONS

1.   In the U.S., the right to a jury trial is available in most criminal cases and some civil cases. *See, e.g., Tull v. United States*, 481 U.S. 412 (1987) (noting that a civil plaintiff has a Seventh Amendment right to a jury trial where the claim constitutes an action "at law" as opposed to an action "in equity"); *Duncan v. Louisiana*, 391 U.S. 145 (1968) (set forth in Chapter 7) (holding that the Sixth Amendment affords criminal defendants an absolute right to a jury trial in cases where a conviction could result in more than six months in jail or more than a $500 fine). Despite this right, however, parties may choose to waive the right to a jury and opt for the case to be decided by a judge (known as a "bench trial"). Why might a party prefer a bench trial over a jury trial? *See, e.g.*, Andrew Leipold, *Why Are Judges So Acquittal Prone?*, 83 Wash. U. L.Q. 151 (2005) (analyzing criminal acquittal rates in bench trials and finding that, statistically, federal judges acquit defendants far more frequently than juries across all categories of cases). The topic of jury trials will be discussed in greater detail in Chapter 3 and Chapter 7.

2.   In addition to the Sixth Amendment right to a jury trial, in criminal cases, the Constitution provides (in the Fifth Amendment) that "[n]o person shall be held to answer for a capital, or otherwise infamous crime, unless on a presentment or indictment of a grand jury * * *." A grand jury indictment is not a criminal conviction, but is merely a determination that sufficient evidence exists to warrant taking the defendant to trial. Evidentiary standards and the burden of proof are less rigorous in a grand jury proceeding than in a criminal trial. *See, e.g., Lawn v. United States*, 355 U.S. 339 (1958) (stating the general rule that a grand jury can rely on any and all evidence in determining whether to return an indictment, even if the evidence was illegally obtained or would be otherwise inadmissible at the defendant's trial). Unlike the Sixth Amendment right to a jury trial in criminal cases, which applies to the states, the U.S. Constitution does not guarantee the right to a grand jury in state criminal courts, and thus states are under no obligation to convene a grand jury before charging an individual with a crime. *See Hurtado v. California*, 110 U.S. 516 (1884) (holding that the Due Process clause of the Fourteenth Amendment does not require a grand jury indictment in a state prosecution). Nonetheless, many states have adopted provisions in their own state constitutions (or other laws) that grant a defendant a right to a grand jury indictment before a criminal trial may commence. *E.g.*, New York (granting a defendant a state constitutional right to a grand jury under N.Y. Const. art. I, § 6); Mississippi (granting a defendant a state constitutional right to a grand jury under Miss. Const. § 27). Other states have adopted alternative

preliminary hearing procedures where a judge or prosecutor determines whether there is probable cause to charge a suspect with a crime. *E.g.*, California (providing a statutory right under Cal. Penal Code § 872 to have a preliminary hearing before a judge to determine probable cause). Preliminary probable cause hearings may also be conducted in federal criminal court prior to a grand jury indictment. *See* Fed. R. Crim. P. 5.1 (stating that a defendant charged with a felony in federal court has a right to a preliminary hearing unless the defendant has already been indicted or waives (gives up) the right to the hearing). Even if a judge deems that there is probable cause to charge the defendant after a Federal Rule 5.1 hearing, however, a defendant charged with a felony in federal court always retains the right under the Fifth Amendment to a grand jury indictment before criminal proceedings may be commenced against him.

3.   Trial and appellate judges have authority to overturn a jury verdict in certain limited situations (although the Fifth Amendment's Double Jeopardy Clause prohibits a court from reversing a jury verdict in a criminal case if the jury finds the defendant not guilty). For example, in criminal cases, judges have the power to grant a "judgment of acquittal," whereby a judge can set aside a guilty verdict if the judge finds the evidence insufficient to sustain a conviction. *See* Fed. R. Crim. P. 29. Similarly, in a civil trial, a judge has the authority to set aside a jury verdict and grant "judgment as a matter of law" if "a reasonable jury would not have a legally sufficient evidentiary basis to find for the party on [an] issue." *See* Fed. R. Civ. P. 50. Understandably, courts are generally reluctant overturn a jury's verdict. Some scholars, however, have argued that judicial discretion to overturn jury verdicts actually reinforces and protects the right to a jury trial in some circumstances. *See, e.g.*, Cassandra Burke Robertson, *Judging Jury Verdicts*, 83 Tul. L. Rev. 157 (2008) (urging more extensive verdict review powers to ensure that parties are afforded the right to a second (additional) jury trial where there was manifest error in the first jury's verdict).

4.   It is important to recognize the difference between a trial court and an appellate court. At the trial level, the jury (or in some cases the judge) determines the facts of the case; the judge determines the law that will apply; and the trier of fact then applies the law to the facts. The judge can then reject the jury's verdict in certain circumstances. After a trial, the parties in the case may have an opportunity to appeal the outcome of the trial based on potential legal errors that may have occurred during the trial process. To this end, an appellate court does not generally consider new facts or evidence, but instead usually bases its legal assessment on the facts that were presented in the trial court. An appellate court's job is to rule on legal issues and to assess whether the trial court made any legal errors during the trial process. There are no juries during the appellate process. An appellate court is usually comprised of a panel of judges (three or more) who must decide the merits of the case by a majority vote. An appellate court reviews the legal issues of a case and then renders a written decision discussing the legal rulings (or decides the case summarily without a written opinion). If the appellate court rules that there were indeed legal errors made during the trial, the appellate court may reverse

the trial court's decision and send the case back to the trial court for a new trial based on the new legal ruling (or to modify the judgment without another trial). The vast majority of cases included in this casebook are decisions authored and published by appellate courts. The next section will discuss this process of judicial review and judicial decision-making.

E. JUDICIAL REVIEW AND JUDICIAL DECISIONS

Although many legal disputes involve a simple application of the law to the facts, many cases involve disputes over the meaning or constitutionality of the law in question. To that end, trial and appellate courts often engage in a process of decision-making known as "judicial review." Judicial review is the process by which a court reviews law or legislation to determine its meaning or constitutionality. Judicial review lies at the heart of the American legal system. The following article discusses the concept of judicial review as well as the process by which judges interpret the law and render decisions.

THE COURT AND CONSTITUTIONAL INTERPRETATION
Supreme Court of the United States, 2015
http://www.supremecourt.gov/about/constitutional.aspx

* * *

"EQUAL JUSTICE UNDER LAW"—These words, written above the main entrance to the Supreme Court Building, express the ultimate responsibility of the Supreme Court of the United States. The Court is the highest tribunal in the Nation for all cases and controversies arising under the Constitution or the laws of the United States. As the final arbiter of the law, the Court is charged with ensuring the American people the promise of equal justice under law and, thereby, also functions as guardian and interpreter of the Constitution.

The Supreme Court is "distinctly American in concept and function," as Chief Justice Charles Evans Hughes observed. Few other courts in the world have the same authority of constitutional interpretation and none have exercised it for as long or with as much influence. A century and a half ago, the French political observer Alexis de Tocqueville noted the unique position of the Supreme Court in the history of nations and of jurisprudence. "The representative system of government has been adopted in several states of Europe," he remarked, "but I am unaware that any nation of the globe has hitherto organized a judicial power in the same manner as the Americans. . . . A more imposing judicial power was never constituted by any people."

The unique position of the Supreme Court stems, in large part, from the deep commitment of the American people to the Rule of Law and to constitutional government. The United States has demonstrated an unprecedented determination to preserve and protect its written Constitution, thereby providing the American "experiment in democracy" with the oldest written Constitution still in force.

The Constitution of the United States is a carefully balanced document. It is designed to provide for a national government sufficiently strong and flexible to meet the needs of the republic, yet sufficiently limited and just to protect the guaranteed rights of citizens; it permits a balance between society's need for order and the individual's right to freedom. To assure these ends, the Framers of the Constitution created three independent and coequal branches of government. That this Constitution has provided continuous democratic government through the periodic stresses of more than two centuries illustrates the genius of the American system of government.

The complex role of the Supreme Court in this system derives from its authority to invalidate legislation or executive actions which, in the Court's considered judgment, conflict with the Constitution. This power of "judicial review" has given the Court a crucial responsibility in assuring individual rights, as well as in maintaining a "living Constitution" whose broad provisions are continually applied to complicated new situations.

While the function of judicial review is not explicitly provided in the Constitution, it had been anticipated before the adoption of that document. Prior to 1789, state courts had already overturned legislative acts which conflicted with state constitutions. Moreover, many of the Founding Fathers expected the Supreme Court to assume this role in regard to the Constitution; Alexander Hamilton and James Madison, for example, had underlined the importance of judicial review in the Federalist Papers, which urged adoption of the Constitution.

Hamilton had written that through the practice of judicial review the Court ensured that the will of the whole people, as expressed in their Constitution, would be supreme over the will of a legislature, whose statutes might express only the temporary will of part of the people. And Madison had written that constitutional interpretation must be left to the reasoned judgment of independent judges, rather than to the tumult and conflict of the political process. If every constitutional question were to be decided by public political bargaining, Madison argued, the Constitution would be reduced to a battleground of competing factions, political passion and partisan spirit.

Despite this background the Court's power of judicial review was not confirmed until 1803, when it was invoked by Chief Justice Marshall in *Marbury v. Madison*[, 5 U.S. (1 Cranch) 137 (1803)]. In this decision, the Chief Justice asserted that the Supreme Court's responsibility to overturn unconstitutional legislation was a necessary consequence of its sworn duty to uphold the Constitution. That oath could not be fulfilled any other way.

"It is emphatically the province of the judicial department to say what the law is," he declared.

In retrospect, it is evident that constitutional interpretation and application were made necessary by the very nature of the Constitution. The Founding Fathers had wisely worded that document in rather general terms leaving it open to future elaboration to meet changing conditions. As Chief Justice Marshall noted in *McCulloch v. Maryland*[, 17 U.S. 316 (1819)], a constitution that attempted to detail every aspect of its own application "would partake of the prolixity of a legal code, and could scarcely be embraced by the human mind. . . . Its nature, therefore, requires that only its great outlines should be marked, its important objects designated, and the minor ingredients which compose those objects be deduced from the nature of the objects themselves."

The Constitution limits the Court to dealing with "Cases" and "Controversies." John Jay, the first Chief Justice, clarified this restraint early in the Court's history by declining to advise President George Washington on the constitutional implications of a proposed foreign policy decision. The Court does not give advisory opinions; rather, its function is limited only to deciding specific cases.

The Justices must exercise considerable discretion in deciding which cases to hear, since more than 10,000 civil and criminal cases are filed in the Supreme Court each year from the various state and federal courts. The Supreme Court also has "original jurisdiction" in a very small number of cases arising out of disputes between States or between a State and the Federal Government.

When the Supreme Court rules on a constitutional issue, that judgment is virtually final; its decisions can be altered only by the rarely used procedure of constitutional amendment or by a new ruling of the Court. However, when the Court interprets a statute, new legislative action can be taken.

Chief Justice Marshall expressed the challenge which the Supreme Court faces in maintaining free government by noting: "We must never forget that it is a constitution we are expounding . . . intended to endure for ages to come, and consequently, to be adapted to the various crises of human affairs."

NOTES AND QUESTIONS

1.   As noted in the above excerpt, judicial review is a concept that was articulated in the landmark decision of *Marbury v. Madison*, 5 U.S. (1 Cranch) 137 (1803). The topic will be discussed in more detail in Chapter 2. The concept of judicial review illustrates two important features of the U.S. system of government: "separation of powers" and "checks and balances."

"Separation of powers" means that the essential functions of government are divided among the three co-equal branches: Legislative, Executive, and Judicial. That phrase, however, is nowhere mentioned in the Constitution. As one U.S. appellate judge has explained:

> While the notion of "separation of powers" was a driving force behind the Constitution, it is notable that the words themselves are not found in the text of our Constitution. That is because our federal government is structured around the concept; our Constitution as a whole manifests this principle by giving shape to that government. Article I vests in Congress specific powers, such as the ability to write and enact laws, raise taxes, and declare war; yet it also requires that Congress engage in the affairs of the other branches—Congress creates lower federal courts and has the power to impeach the President and offers a check on Congress in the form of presidential presentment before a bill can become law.[1] Likewise, Article II gives the President the power to conduct war, make treaties, and pardon.[2] * * * [T]he Constitution gives the executive a role in the other departments by giving the President the power to appoint judges[3] and the authority to execute enacted laws[4] while, concurrently, Article II also makes the executive accountable to the other branches by requiring confirmation of the President's candidates for officers, judges, and ambassadors of the United States[5] and establishing the impeachment process for judges and the President.[6] Finally, Article III maintains a similar structure: it confers all the judicial power in the Supreme Court,[7] but it gives Congress the authority to create lower courts[8] and make exceptions to the jurisdiction of the federal courts.[9] Each branch, therefore, has a defined role, and yet each branch must coexist, often interdependently, with the others and find balance.

D. Brooks Smith, *Because Men Are Not Angels: Separation of Powers in the United States*, 47 Duq. L. Rev. 687, 691 (2009).

Separation of powers is also related to a second, albeit similar, concept of U.S. law—"checks and balances." That phrase connotes the fact that each branch of government has some degree of control over the other branches. For example, the President may veto legislation passed by Congress (thereby requiring a 2/3 vote of both houses to override the veto); the Supreme Court (and lower federal courts) may review and invalidate legislation passed by

---

[1] U.S. CONST. art. I, §§ 1, 7–8.
[2] U.S. CONST. art. II, § 2.
[3] U.S. CONST. art. II, § 2, cl. 2.
[4] U.S. CONST. art. II, § 3.
[5] U.S. CONST. art. II, § 2.
[6] U.S. CONST. art. II, § 4.
[7] U.S. CONST. art III, § 2.
[8] U.S. CONST. art. I, § 8.
[9] U.S. CONST. art. III, § 2.

Congress; and Congress may remove the President and members of the Judiciary from office based on certain kinds of misconduct. Together, "separation of powers" and "checks and balances" prevent the usurpation of power by a single branch, ensuring that the United States will preserve its democratic form of government.

2.   It is sometimes argued that judicial review undermines the principles of democracy because an unelected judicial body has the power to determine how the law will be applied. Some scholars have argued that such a task is better left to the legislature, which is democratically elected by a majority vote of the citizens. *See, e.g.*, RICHARD BELLAMY, POLITICAL CONSTITUTIONALISM: A REPUBLICAN DEFENCE OF THE CONSTITUTIONALITY OF DEMOCRACY 5 (2007) (raising concern that judicial review gives judges the power to overrule elected officials and negates the notion of democratic representation); Jeremy Waldron, *The Core of the Case Against Judicial Review*, 115 Yale L.J. 1346 (2006) (expressing concern about giving unelected judges controlling authority on matters that concern the will of the majority). Other scholars, however, argue that judicial review is necessary because the federal judiciary is largely insulated from politics, allowing it to interpret the law in an objective fashion. *See, e.g.*, COREY BRETTSCHNEIDER, DEMOCRATIC RIGHTS AND THE SUBSTANCE OF SELF-GOVERNMENT 152 (2007) (reasoning that judicial review can, in some instances, support democracy by advancing core democratic principles, such as the minority's right to participate in the political process); ALEXANDER BICKEL, THE LEAST DANGEROUS BRANCH: THE SUPREME COURT AT THE BAR OF POLITICS 24–26 (1962) (arguing that having the acts of government reviewed by the judiciary is beneficial because the political insulation of federal judges allows them to enforce long-term constitutional values even when those values conflict with short-term political goals). Which perspective on judicial review is most persuasive?

3.   The U.S. system of judicial review is unlike that in any other country. *See, e.g.*, Mark Tushnet, Marbury v. Madison *Around the World*, 71 Tenn. L. Rev. 251 (2004) (comparing judicial review in the U.S. with that in other nations, and concluding that the U.S. system is unique because of the judiciary's broad authority to interpret the law and thereby bind the Executive and Legislative Branches of government). Should the U.S. style of judicial review be adopted by other nations? Why or why not?

F. THE U.S. SUPREME COURT

REMARKS BY CHIEF JUSTICE WILLIAM H. REHNQUIST

Lecture at the Faculty of Law of the University of Guanajuato, Mexico
Thursday, September 27, 2001
http://www.supremecourt.gov/publicinfo/speeches/viewspeech/sp_09–27–01

* * *

The Supreme Court of the United States has been in existence for more than 200 years. Because it has the power of judicial review—that is, the authority to declare an act of Congress or of the Executive unconstitutional and void—it is bound on occasion to antagonize these other branches. Fifty years ago, during the Korean War, President Truman seized the country's steel mills from their private owners in order to avoid a strike. The Supreme Court ordered him to return them to their owners, and he did so.

Some 25 years ago, President Nixon refused to turn over to a court in which a criminal case was pending tapes of his conversations which bore on the case. The Supreme Court told him that he must turn them over. He did so, and resigned from office as a result.

Several years ago, the Court told President Clinton that he was answerable in a private lawsuit even though he was President. He answered.

How has a court so engaged in controversy not only survived, but maintained its authority for more than two centuries? There are a number of reasons, but first and foremost is the fact that it is genuinely independent of both the Executive and the Legislative Branches. We are far from infallible—but our mistakes are our own, and not imposed on us by Congress or the President.

There are nine Justices on the Supreme Court of the United States. Justices are appointed by the President, with the approval of a majority of the Senate. * * * [I]n the United States all federal judges appointed under Article III of our Constitution are appointed for life.

My first experience with the Supreme Court was not as a lawyer or as a Justice, but as a law clerk. In December 1951, I had just been graduated from Stanford Law School in Palo Alto, California. I did not start out to be a lawyer—prior to law school, I had studied political science and government with the idea of being a college professor.

In those days, when people did not easily travel across the country for a job interview, the great majority of Supreme Court law clerks were graduates of law schools in the Eastern half of the United States. Justice William Douglas had roots in the West, so he made an effort to select clerks from the West. The chance of getting a clerkship with one of the other Justices seemed remote to me.

But as luck would have it, Justice Jackson came to Stanford to dedicate the new Stanford Law School building in the summer of 1951 and one of my professors arranged for an interview. Justice Jackson was pleasant and rather informal. After a few questions about my background and legal education, he asked whether my last name was Swedish. When I said it was, Justice Jackson told several anecdotes about Swedish clients he had represented while practicing law in New York. It was an enjoyable conversation, but when the interview was over, I was sure that I was not going to get the job. To my surprise, in November I received a letter offering me a clerkship beginning the following February.

Twenty years later, in 1972, I was appointed to the Supreme Court by President Nixon as an Associate Justice. In 1986, I was chosen by President Reagan to be Chief Justice and I will remain in that position until I retire. * * *

Because I am the Chief Justice, people are often surprised to hear what a small staff I have in my chambers, or office. In addition to my three law clerks, I have two secretaries and one aide. The law clerks have usually been out of law school for just a year or two when they come to the Court and most have first served as law clerks to lower federal court judges. The law clerks serve for only one year. Most of the Justices have four law clerks, but [some] have [only] three because that is the number [they] prefer. One of the most distinguished of the Court's past Justices, Louis D. Brandeis, was asked why he thought that people respected the Court. His reply was short and pithy: "Because we do our own work."

Today, the work of the Court consists essentially of three different functions. First, we select which cases we will decide. Second, we actually decide those cases, which consists of studying the papers filed, hearing the oral arguments of the lawyers and voting which way the case will come out. Third, we prepare written opinions supporting and explaining the result reached by the majority, and there are often separate concurring or dissenting opinions by those Justices who do not agree with the reasoning of the majority opinion.

The authority to decide for itself which cases it will hear is essential to a court of last resort such as ours. We have not always had it. For about the first hundred years of our Court's existence, from 1789 until 1891, it served as an appeals court for the federal trial courts. If a party to a suit in a lower court was dissatisfied, he had a right to a direct appeal to the Supreme Court. As the size and population of the United States increased, so did the number of federal trial courts, and as Congress conferred wider jurisdiction on those federal trial courts, the number of cases filed in the Supreme Court became too numerous for the Court to handle efficiently.

Although Congress created the intermediate courts of appeals—called circuit courts—in 1891, it was not until 1925 that Congress passed the Certiorari Act, which gave the Supreme Court discretion as to which cases to hear. Chief Justice William Howard Taft was the person mainly responsible for the passage of that statute.

Taft was an interesting fellow in his own right. * * * He is the only person ever to serve as both President of the United States and Chief Justice. * * * When he was appointed Chief Justice, the Court had fallen nearly five years behind in its docket. He resolved this caseload congestion in the Court by convincing Congress to give the Court discretion as to which cases to hear. Some members of Congress were doubtful—why shouldn't every litigant have a right to get a decision on his case from the Supreme Court? Taft responded that in each case, there had already been one trial and one appeal. "Two courts are enough for justice," he said. To obtain still a third hearing in the Supreme Court, there should be some question involved more important than just who wins this lawsuit.

Under the Certiorari Act, a party dissatisfied with a decision in either a state court of last resort or a federal appeals court may file a petition for a writ of certiorari with the Supreme Court and the Court decides whether or not to grant the petition and hear the case. Rather than serving as an appellate court that simply attempts to correct errors in cases involving no generally important principle of law, the Court instead tries to pick those cases involving unsettled questions of federal constitutional or statutory law of general interest. When the Court renders a decision, it is binding on and must be followed by the lower courts not only in that case, but in any case that presents the same question.

When I joined the Court in 1972, about 4,000 petitions for certiorari were filed each year with the Court, and we selected about 150 cases to hear on the merits. Today, about 7,000 petitions are filed each year and we hear about 80. Now, if you do the math, you will see that 7,000 petitions per year means an average of about 135 petitions each week. In order to manage this volume, we rely on our law clerks to summarize the petitions.

Although our Court otherwise operates by majority rule, in order to grant a petition for certiorari—and decide to accept a case for decision—it only takes four, rather than five, votes. During the time the Court is sitting, from the first Monday in October through sometime in June, the nine members of the Court meet in conference each week to vote on the petitions and decide which cases to accept. These conferences take place in a conference room in the Supreme Court building. Only the nine Justices are present. The conferences are not open to the public or any Court staff.

Shortly before each conference, I send out a list of the petitions to be decided during that conference that I want to discuss. Each of the other Justices may ask to have additional cases put on the "discuss list." If at any particular conference there are 100 petitions to be decided, there may be anywhere from 15 to 30 that are on the discuss list. The petitions for certiorari that are not discussed are denied without any recorded vote.

Whether or not to grant certiorari is a rather subjective decision, made up in part of intuition and in part of legal judgment. One important factor is whether the case being considered has been decided differently from a very similar case decided by another lower court. Another factor that makes a difference is whether the lower court decision seems to have incorrectly applied a Supreme Court decision that the Justices believe should have directed the outcome of the case.

Now when a case is filed with the Supreme Court, the Court's job is to pick from the several thousand cases it is asked to review each year those cases involving unsettled questions of federal constitutional or statutory law of general interest.

After the Court performs its first function of picking which cases to decide, it must move on to hear and decide them. Several weeks before oral argument is scheduled, the parties must file briefs that conform with specific Court rules. The rules direct what information must be included in a brief, describe the size of paper and type of print, and limit the number of pages. Even the colors of the covers of the briefs are specified: the petitioner's brief must have a blue cover and the respondent's must have a red cover. The Court also often receives briefs from amici curiae—or friends of the Court—in particular cases, and these must have a green cover. This color-coding comes in very handy when you have a stack of eight or ten briefs in a particular case and can locate the brief you want by its color without having to read the covers of each.

Each Justice of course prepares for argument in his own way. Some of my colleagues get memos from their law clerks summarizing and analyzing the arguments made by each side. I do not do this because it does not suit my working style. When I begin to prepare for a case that will be orally argued, I first read the opinion of the lower court that is to be reviewed. I find this a good starting point because it has been produced by another court which, like ours, is sworn to uphold the Constitution and laws and has presumably done its best to decide the case fairly. Then I read the petitioner's brief and then the respondent's brief.

One of my law clerks will have done the same thing so that we can discuss the case. And when we are both ready, that is what we do. * * * We discuss our reactions to certain arguments and if I think the briefs do not cover a particular point adequately, I may ask the clerk to write a memorandum on that point. Then I go back and read the main Supreme Court opinions relied upon by one side or the other in their briefs.

The oral arguments are the only publicly visible part of the Supreme Court's decision process. It is the time set aside for all nine Justices to gather to hear the advocates for both sides argue the case and to ask our own questions. We hear arguments in the courtroom of the Supreme Court building fourteen weeks out of each year; two weeks each in the months of October through April. During the weeks of oral argument, the Court sits on the bench from ten o'clock in the morning until noon on Monday, Tuesday and Wednesday. On each day, it hears two cases, allotting a half hour to the lawyers representing each side in each case. Oral arguments are open to the public and if you were to visit Washington during an oral argument week, you could come to the Court in the morning and stand in line to see an argument or part of one.

Once a case has been argued, we must decide which way it will come out. For cases argued on Mondays, we meet in conference on Wednesday afternoon. For cases argued on Tuesdays and Wednesdays, we meet in conference on Friday. At the appointed time the nine members of the Court meet in the conference room. We all shake hands with one another when we come in and we have whatever materials we want with us. As I said before, there is no one in the room except the nine of us. If our conference is interrupted by a knock on the door indicating that there is a message for one of the Justices, the most junior Justice answers the door and delivers it. * * *

The Chief Justice begins the discussion of the cases that have been argued by reviewing the facts and the decision of the lower court, outlining what he understands is the applicable case law and indicating either that he votes to affirm the decision of the lower court or to reverse it. The discussion then proceeds to the most senior Associate Justice, on down to the most junior Justice. The time taken to discuss any particular case obviously depends upon its complexity. By the time the most junior Justice has finished his discussion, it will usually be evident that a majority of the Court has agreed upon a basis for either affirming or reversing the decision under discussion, and I announce how I am recording the vote so that others may disagree with my count if they believe I am mistaken.

Once we have decided which way a case will come out, we must address the third function of the Court: the preparation of written opinions supporting and explaining the result reached by the majority. And, as I said earlier, there are often separate concurring or dissenting opinions by those Justices who do not agree with the reasoning of the majority opinion.

In every case in which the Chief Justice votes with the majority, he decides who will write the opinion of the Court. If the Chief Justice is not in the majority, the most senior Justice in the majority assigns the case. The assignment of cases is, as you would expect, very important to each member of the Court. The signed opinions are to a very large extent the only visible record of a Justice's work on the Court. As an Associate Justice I eagerly awaited the assignments, and I think my law clerks awaited them more eagerly than I did. If I was assigned 17 or 18 opinions a year, each of my clerks—who serve for only a year—might have an opportunity to work on five or six opinions.

When I assign a case to myself, I sit down with the clerk who is responsible for the case and go over my notes and recollections from conference with him. This usually provides an adequate basis for discussion between me and the clerk of the views expressed by the majority at conference, and of the way in which an opinion supporting the result reached by the majority can be drafted. After this discussion, I ask the clerk to prepare a first draft of a Court opinion and to have it for me in ten days or two weeks. That first draft is really a rough draft that I may very well substantially rewrite.

I go through the draft with a view to shortening it, simplifying it, and clarifying it. I have a rule of thumb that I picked up from a lawyer I worked with before I came on the Court: If a sentence takes up more than six lines of type on an ordinary page, it is probably too long. The rule is simple, but I apply it to every draft I review.

After I have revised the draft, I return it to the law clerk, who refines it further. We print the finished product so that we may circulate it to the other chambers. And then we wait to see what the reaction of the other Justices will be, especially those who voted with the majority at conference.

If a Justice agrees with the draft and has no criticisms or suggestions, he will send a letter saying that he would like to join in the opinion. If a Justice agrees with the general import of the draft but wishes changes to be made in it before joining, a letter to that effect will be sent. The Justice who is writing the opinion will, if possible, accommodate the suggested changes.

The senior Justice among those who disagree with the result reached by the majority at conference usually assigns the preparation of the dissenting opinion in the case, if there is to be one. The draft dissent will be circulated in due course.

The decision-making process has now been completed. A case in which certiorari was granted somewhere from six months to a year ago has been briefed, orally argued and now finally decided by the Supreme Court of the United States.

* * *

NOTES AND QUESTIONS

1.   As the above remarks indicate, each year as many as 10,000 losing parties (in both civil and criminal cases) seek review by the U.S. Supreme Court. The Court, however, hears only a small fraction of that number. The Judiciary Act of 1925 granted the Court discretionary review in the vast majority of cases, and the Supreme Court Selections Act of 1988 all but eliminated mandatory appellate jurisdiction in the Supreme Court. If the Supreme Court does decide to review a case, the process is called granting "a petition for writ of certiorari" ("certiorari" is Latin for "to be more informed"). Although there is no formal rule that so provides, unless there is some basis for mandatory jurisdiction (see below), Supreme Court review occurs only if four Justices vote to grant certiorari. That principle (which Chief Justice Rehnquist describes above) has become known as the "rule of four." *See, e.g.,* Ira Robbins, *Justice by the Numbers: The Supreme Court and the Rule of Four—Or Is It Five?*, 36 Suffolk U. L. Rev. 1 (2002). What is the logic of having discretionary review? Should Supreme Court review be mandatory in significant categories of cases, such as death penalty cases, or cases in which a lower court has declared a law unconstitutional?

2.   Chief Justice Rehnquist noted that in 1972, the Court heard about 150 cases per year. By 2001 (the year he gave his remarks), that number had

fallen to 80 cases per year. During the ten years that John G. Roberts, Jr. has served as Chief Justice, that number has continued to fall. For example, in the 2014 term, the Court decided only 66 cases (after full briefing and oral argument), and for the 2013 term, the number was only 68. Erwin Chemerinsky, *Chemerinsky: 10 lessons from Chief Justice Roberts' first 10 years*, ABA JOURNAL (Sept. 30, 2015), *available at* http://www.abajournal.com/ news/article/chemerinsky_10_lessons_from_chief_justice_roberts_first_10_ years. Commentators have speculated as to why the Court hears so few cases, and why that number has decreased significantly in recent years. *See, e.g.,* Ryan Owens & David Simon, *Explaining the Supreme Court's Shrinking Docket*, 53 Wm. & Mary L. Rev. 1219 (2012) (concluding that the decrease in caseload stems from an ideologically fractured court and changes that have eliminated most grounds for mandatory jurisdiction).

3. As Chief Justice Rehnquist's remarks reveal, the Supreme Court considers several factors when deciding whether to grant review, including: (1) whether there is a split in authority (a conflict) on an important federal issue among the federal appellate courts or state supreme courts, or (2) whether there is an important federal issue that should be addressed by the Court even in the absence of a lower court conflict. A more detailed description of the certiorari process can be found in Rule 10 of the published Supreme Court Rules, available online at http://www.supremecourt.gov/ctrules/2013Rulesof theCourt.pdf.

4. As noted, the Supreme Court's appellate jurisdiction is almost entirely discretionary. The Court, however, also has "original jurisdiction" over certain types of cases, meaning that in those cases the Supreme Court serves as a type of trial court. Under Article III, Section 2 of the Constitution, the Supreme Court has original jurisdiction "[i]n all cases affecting Ambassadors, other public ministers and Consuls and those in which a State shall be a party." Additionally, 28 U.S.C. § 1251 prescribes some additional situations in which the Supreme Court's original jurisdiction may be invoked. In those situations, the Supreme Court is a court of both first *and* last resort. *See generally* ROBERT KLONOFF & GREGORY CASTANIAS, FEDERAL APPELLATE PRACTICE AND PROCEDURE IN A NUTSHELL 401–04 (2008) (discussing Supreme Court's original jurisdiction).

5. Once the Supreme Court grants review in a case, the parties to the case file written briefs and present oral arguments. In many Supreme Court cases, *amicus curiae* ("friend of the Court") briefs are filed as well. Both briefing and oral arguments are important, but most experts agree that briefs play a greater role in the outcome than oral argument. *See, e.g.,* Ruth Bader Ginsburg, *Remarks on Appellate Advocacy*, 50 S.C. L. Rev. 567, 567–68 (1999) (observations of a sitting Supreme Court justice, who notes that briefing is far more important in the Court's decision-making process, and stating, "Oral argument is fleeting—here today, it may be forgotten tomorrow"); Terry Rombeck, *Justice Takes Time for Q & A*, LAWRENCE J.—WORLD, Oct. 30, 2002, at 5B, *available at* http://www2.ljworld.com/news/2002/oct/30/justice_ takes_time/ (interviewing Justice Clarence Thomas regarding oral argument,

and quoting the Justice as stating: "I don't see a need for all those questions . . . I think justices, 99 percent of the time, have their minds made up when they go to the bench"); Nancy Winkelman, *Just a Brief Writer?*, 29 Litig. 50, 52 (2003) (noting that "judges overwhelmingly agree that cases are decided primarily on the basis of the briefs"). For a detailed look at the role of oral arguments and briefing in the Court's decision-making process, *see* ISAAC UNAH, THE SUPREME COURT IN AMERICAN POLITICS 118 (2010).

6.   As Chief Justice Rehnquist noted, every Justice on the U.S. Supreme Court has at least three law clerks to assist in research, opinion writing, and other tasks. Most clerks have completed a clerkship with a lower court judge and may also have had a brief period in private practice. Clerking on the Supreme Court is perhaps the most prestigious job that a recent U.S. law school graduate can hold. The role of law clerks in the work of the Court should not be underestimated. For example, as Chief Justice Rehnquist's remarks illustrate, law clerks frequently write the first drafts of opinions. Also, law clerks play a major role in evaluating the petitions for certiorari that are filed in the Court. A recent study has shown that law clerks play a major role in influencing the cases that the Court chooses to review. *See* Ryan Black & Christina Boyd, *The Role of Law Clerks in the U.S. Supreme Court's Agenda-Setting Process*, 40 Am. Pol. Research 147 (2012) (detailed study demonstrating impact of law clerks on the certiorari process). Should a recent law school graduate have such a large role in the Court's review process?

7.   The U.S. Constitution is written in extremely broad terms. A major debate among the Justices and among constitutional law scholars concerns how the document should be interpreted in resolving cases before the Court. Several competing approaches have been proposed.

Some justices and scholars have embraced interpreting the Constitution based upon the "original intent" of the framers who drafted the document. That approach often involves a complex historical analysis of the personal and public writings of the framers around the time that the Constitution was drafted (1787). This theory has its supporters and its critics. *See, e.g.*, Jamal Greene, *The Case for Original Intent*, 80 Geo. Wash. L. Rev. 1683, 1705 (2012) (arguing that scholars need to consider the framers' intent in constitutional analysis because it is a "time-honored form of ethical argument" that allows for a more comprehensive view of constitutional interpretation); Robert Bennett, *Originalist Theories of Constitutional Interpretation*, 73 Cornell L. Rev. 355 (1988) (asserting that the original intent argument is subject to major analytical problems, including (1) a historical problem in compiling all relevant historical documents to decipher comprehensive intent, (2) a "summing" problem whereby it is difficult to formulate one coherent intent because each of the founders may have had a distinct subjective intent, and (3) a malleability problem whereby a finding of general intent can be manipulated in many different ways).

Another approach is to interpret the Constitution by its "plain meaning" or "original text," which does not look solely at the intent of the framers, but rather at the meaning of constitutional terms as they were understood at the time they were drafted. Once again, that approach requires an historical analysis of societal language and understandings at the time the Constitution was drafted. That theory also has its supporters and critics. *See, e.g.*, ROBERT BORK, THE TEMPTING OF AMERICA: THE POLITICAL SEDUCTION OF THE LAW (1990) (warning of the dangers of interpreting law based on politics rather than text, and stating that the textualist approach is the only approach sufficient to protect the democratic legitimacy of the judiciary because it does not consider political influence); Antonin Scalia, *Address Before the Attorney General's Conference on Economic Liberties in Washington, D.C.—June 14, 1986, in* ORIGINAL MEANING JURISPRUDENCE: A SOURCEBOOK 103 (1987) (future Supreme Court Justice argues that the appropriate constitutional inquiry is "the most plausible meaning of the words of the Constitution to the society that adopted it—regardless of what the Framers might secretly have intended"). *But see, e.g.*, Michael Dorf, *Foreword: The Limits of Socratic Deliberation*, 112 Harv. L. Rev. 4, 4 (1998) (noting that "[b]ecause textualism as practiced by its proponents on the Court is backward-looking, it is particularly ill-suited to the problems of a rapidly changing world to which the Court must constantly apply statutory and constitutional text"); Robert Post, *Theories of Constitutional Interpretation* (Yale Faculty Scholarship Series, Paper 209, 1990), *available at* http://digitalcommons.law.yale.edu/fss_papers/209/ (criticizing the plain meaning approach, and stating: "[I]f for any reason that meaning has become questionable, it is no help at all to instruct a judge to follow the 'plain meaning' of the constitutional text. A meaning that has ceased to be plain cannot be made so by sheer force of will").

Finally, some scholars follow a "pragmatic" approach to interpretation. That approach maintains that the Constitution is a living document that is meant to evolve over time based on changing norms, technology, and other circumstances. Thus, the pragmatist does not view the original meaning or intent of the document to be the sole (or even primary) principle guiding interpretation. Once again, that approach has both supporters and detractors. *See, e.g.*, STEPHEN BREYER, ACTIVE LIBERTY: INTERPRETING OUR DEMOCRATIC CONSTITUTION 18 (2005) (promoting the pragmatic constitutional interpretive approach and the concept of a "living constitution," and stating that the Constitution is "a continuing instrument of government" to apply to new subject matter); Richard Posner, *Foreword: A Political Court*, 119 Harv. L. Rev. 31 (2005) (stating that pragmatism is preferable because it allows judges to focus on the practical consequences of their decisions and often creates more socially desirable outcomes); Daniel Farber, *Legal Pragmatism and the Constitution*, 72 Minn. L. Rev. 1331, 1378 (1988) (supporting a pragmatic approach to constitutional interpretation and concluding that "[t]he pragmatist's answers may be less elegant, but in the end I believe they are more satisfying than those that any grand theory could provide"). *But see, e.g.*, ANTONIN SCALIA, A MATTER OF INTERPRETATION: FEDERAL COURTS AND THE LAW (Amy Gutmann ed. 1997) (criticizing the pragmatic approach to constitutional interpretation because it undermines the principles of democracy and allows judges to wrongfully place themselves in the role of the legislature); Jeffrey Rosen, *Overcoming Posner*, 105 Yale L.J. 581, 601 (1995) (criticizing the pragmatic approach and stating: "In addition to being hard to reconcile with democracy, it requires a degree of empirical rigor and prophetic ability that is virtually impossible for run-of-the-mill * * * judges to achieve").

In analyzing U.S. Supreme Court cases interpreting the Constitution (including many of the cases in this textbook), it is useful to reflect upon which interpretative approach the Court is using to decide the dispute. Sometimes more than one approach may be involved.

RUTH BADER GINSBURG, THE ROLE OF DISSENTING OPINIONS

The 20th Annual Leo and Berry Eizenstat Memorial Lecture
October 21, 2007
http://www.supremecourt.gov/publicinfo/speeches/viewspeech/sp_10–21–07
Associate Justice
Supreme Court of the United States

* * *

Artworks in my chambers display in Hebrew letters the command from Deuteronomy: *Zedek, zedek tirdof*—"Justice, justice shalt thou pursue." These postings serve as ever-present reminders of what judges must do "that they may thrive." In the Supreme Court of the United States, with difficult cases on which reasonable minds may divide, sometimes intensely, one's sense of Justice may demand a departure from the majority's view, expressed in a dissenting opinion. This audience, I thought, might find of interest some reflections on the role dissents play in the U.S. judicial system.

Our Chief Justice, in his confirmation hearings, expressed admiration for the nation's fourth Chief Justice, John Marshall, in my view, shared by many, the greatest Chief Justice in U.S. history. Our current Chief admired, particularly, Chief Justice Marshall's unparalleled ability to achieve consensus among his colleagues. During his tenure, the Court spoke with one voice most of the time.

In Chief Justice Roberts's first year at the helm, which was also Justice O'Connor's last term on our bench, it appeared that the Chief's hope for greater unanimity might be realized. In the 2005–2006 Term, 45% of the cases we took up for review were decided unanimously, with but one opinion for the Court, and 55% were unanimous in the bottom line judgment. This past term, however, revealed that predictions of more consensus decision-making were off the mark. We spoke with one voice in only 25% of the cases presented, and were unanimous in the bottom line judgment less than 40% of the time. Fully one-third of the cases we took up—the highest share in at least a decade—were decided by a bare majority of five.

Typically, when Court decisions are announced from the bench, only the majority opinion is summarized. Separate opinions, concurring or dissenting, are noted, but not described. A dissent presented orally therefore garners immediate attention. It signals that, in the dissenters' view, the Court's opinion is not just wrong, but importantly and grievously misguided. Last term, a record seven dissents were summarized from the bench, six of them in cases the Court decided by 5–4 votes.

I described from the bench two dissenting opinions. The first deplored the Court's approval of a federal ban on so-called "partial-birth abortion." Departing from decades of precedent, the Court placed its imprimatur on an anti-abortion measure that lacked an exception safeguarding a woman's health. Next, I objected to the Court's decision making it virtually impossible for victims of pay discrimination to mount a successful Title VII challenge. (Commenting on these orally announced dissents, Linda Greenhouse, the New York Times' star Supreme Court reporter, wrote that last term will be remembered as the one in which I "found [my] voice, and used it." That appraisal surprised my husband, my children, my chambers staff, and even my colleagues at the Court. All of them have heard me use my voice, sometimes to stirring effect. But it is true, as Linda Greenhouse knew, that only six times before, in thirteen terms on the Court, and never twice in the same term, did I find it appropriate to underscore a dissent by reading a summary of it aloud in the Courtroom.)

Our practice of revealing dissents, it bears emphasis, is hardly universal. In the civil law tradition that holds sway in Europe, and in countries once controlled by a continental power, courts issue a collective judgment, written in an impersonal style. The author of the judgment is neither named nor otherwise identifiable. Disagreement, if it exists, is not disclosed. That pattern prevails without exception in French tribunals, and it is also followed by the European Court of Justice, the High Court of the European Union, seated in Luxembourg.

The British common law tradition lies at the opposite pole. In appeals in that tradition, there was conventionally no "opinion for the court" disposing of a case under review. Instead, the judges hearing the matter composed their own individual opinions which, taken together, revealed the court's disposition. Changes in British practice and in some European tribunals have brought these divergent systems closer together. The European Court of Human Rights, for example, seated in Strasbourg, publishes signed dissenting opinions. But, by and large, the historical traditions hold.

Our system occupies a middle ground between the continental and the British patterns. In the earliest days of our national existence, the U.S. Supreme Court, like the House of Lords, Britain's highest tribunal, issued *seriatim* opinions. Each Justice spoke for himself whenever more than a memorandum judgment issued. But John Marshall, who served as Chief Justice from 1801 until 1835, thought that practice ill-advised. In its place, he established the practice of announcing judgments in a single opinion for the Court, which he generally wrote himself. Opinions that speak for the Court remain the custom today. But unlike courts in civil law systems, and in line with the British tradition, each member of the Court has the prerogative to speak out separately.

What is right for one system and society may not be right for another. The civil law-style judgment is suited to a system in which judges train for and embark on career service soon after university graduation. Promotions in such systems generally depend upon the recommendation of longer-tenured, higher-ranking judges. Common law judges, in contrast, are recruited at middle age from the senior ranks of the practicing bar or of law faculties.

In civilian systems, the nameless, stylized judgment, and the disallowance of dissent, are thought to foster the public's perception of the law as dependably stable and secure. Our tradition, on the other hand, safeguards the independence of the individual judge and prizes the transparency of the process of wielding judicial power.

No doubt, as Chief Justice Roberts suggested, the U.S. Supreme Court may attract greater deference, and provide clearer guidance, when it speaks with one voice. And I agree that a Justice, contemplating publication of a separate writing, should ask himself: Is this dissent or concurrence really necessary? Consider the extra weight carried by the Court's unanimous opinion in *Brown v. Board of Education* [set forth in Chapter 2]. In that case, all nine Justices signed on to one opinion making it clear that the Constitution does not tolerate legally enforced segregation in our Nation's schools. With similar heft, in a follow-up case, *Cooper v. Aaron*, all nine Justices jointly authored a statement for the Court powerfully reaffirming—in the face of official resistance in Little Rock, Arkansas—that desegregation in public schools is indeed the law of the land.

On the utility of dissenting opinions, I will mention first their in-house impact. My experience teaches that there is nothing better than an impressive dissent to improve an opinion for the Court. A well-reasoned dissent will lead the author of the majority opinion to refine and clarify her initial circulation. An illustration: I wrote for the Court in the Virginia Military Institute case [set forth in Chapter 2], which held that VMI's denial of admission to women violated the Equal Protection Clause. The published opinion was ever so much better than my first draft, thanks to Justice Scalia's attention-grabbing dissent.

Sometimes a dissent is written, then buried by its author. An entire volume is devoted to the unpublished separate opinions of Justice Brandeis. He would suppress his dissent if the majority made ameliorating alterations or, even if he gained no accommodations, if he thought the Court's opinion was of limited application and unlikely to cause real harm in future cases.

On rare occasions, a dissent will be so persuasive that it attracts the votes necessary to become the opinion of the Court. I had the heady experience once of writing a dissent for myself and just one other Justice that became the opinion of the Court from which only two of my colleagues, in the end, dissented.

Are there lasting rifts sparked by sharply worded dissents? Justice Scalia spoke to that question nicely. He said: "I doubt whether any two [J]ustices have dissented from one another's opinions any more regularly, or any more sharply, than did my former colleague Justice William Brennan and I. I always considered him, however, one of my best friends on the Court, and I think that feeling was reciprocated." The same might be said about my close friendship with Justice Scalia.

Describing the external impact of dissenting opinions, Chief Justice Hughes famously said: "A dissent in a Court of last resort is an appeal . . . to the intelligence of a future day, when a later decision may possibly correct the error into which the dissenting judge believes the court to have been betrayed."

A classic example is Justice Benjamin Curtis's dissent from the Court's now notorious 1856 decision in *Dred Scott v. Sanford*. The Court held, 7–2, in *Dred Scott* that people of African descent whose ancestors were brought here as slaves could never become American citizens. Justice Curtis disagreed in an opinion remarkable for its time. At the founding of our Nation, he wrote, Blacks were "citizens of at least five States, and so in every sense part of the people of the United States," thus "among those for whom and whose posterity the Constitution was ordained and established."

Dissents of this order, Justice Scalia rightly commented, "augment rather than diminish the prestige of the Court." He explained: "When history demonstrates that one of the Court's decisions has been a truly horrendous mistake, it is comforting . . . to look back and realize that at least some of the [J]ustices saw the danger clearly and gave voice, often eloquent voice, to their concern."

Though Justice Scalia would not agree with me in this further example, I would place Justice Breyer's dissent in [the October 2006] term's school integration cases in the same category. In those cases, the Court invalidated student assignment plans adopted in Seattle, Washington and Louisville, Kentucky. The plans were designed by the cities' authorities to counter resegregation in the local public schools. The question was whether local communities had leeway to use race-conscious criteria for the purpose of bringing about the kind of racially integrated education *Brown v. Board of Education* anticipated. The Court held, 5–4, that the Constitution proscribed Louisville's and Seattle's efforts.

Justice Breyer's exhaustive dissent concluded: "[T]he very school districts that once spurned integration now strive for it. The long history of their efforts reveals the complexities and difficulties they have faced. . . . [T]hey have asked us not to take from their hands the instruments they have used to rid their schools of racial segregation, instruments . . . they believe are needed to overcome the problems of cities divided by race and poverty. . . . The last half-century has witnessed great strides towards racial equality, but we have not yet realized the promise of *Brown*. To invalidate the plans under review is to threaten [*Brown*'s promise]. . . . This is a decision . . . the Court and the Nation will come to regret."

One of the two dissenting opinions I read from the bench in the 2006–2007 term serves as my last illustration of an appeal "to the intelligence of a future day." Seven years ago, the Court held Nebraska's ban on so-called "partial-birth" abortion unconstitutional, in part because it contained no exception safeguarding the health of the woman. Three years later, in a deliberate effort to undo the Court's ruling, Congress passed a federal ban on the same procedure, also without a health exception. The federal ban was promptly challenged and found unconstitutional in the lower courts. A Supreme Court, which no longer included Justice O'Connor, held, 5–4, that the federal ban survived review for constitutionality.

I recalled, in my dissent, that the Court had repeatedly reaffirmed the State's unconditional obligation, when regulating abortion, to safeguard the woman's health. Not only did the Court, last term, refuse to take seriously once solid precedent demanding a health exception, but the majority also, and alarmingly in my judgment, resurrected "ancient notions about women's place in the family and under the Constitution." Both the federal ban, and the majority's approval of it, I observed, were endeavors "to chip away at a [constitutional] right declared again and again by th[e] Court," and, until the Court's *volte-face*, "with increasing comprehension of its centrality to women's lives." "A decision" of the character the Court rendered, I said in conclusion, "should not have staying power."

I turn now to another genre of dissent, one aiming to attract immediate public attention and to propel legislative change. My example is the second dissent I read from the bench last term. The case involved a woman, Lilly Ledbetter, who worked as an area manager at a Goodyear tire plant in Alabama—in 1997, the only woman in Goodyear to hold such a post. Her starting salary (in 1979) was in line with the salaries of men performing similar work. But over time, her pay slipped. By the end of 1997, there was a *15 to 40 percent* disparity between Ledbetter's pay and the salaries of her fifteen male counterparts. A federal jury found it "more likely than not that [Goodyear] paid [Ledbetter] a[n] unequal salary because of her sex." The Supreme Court nullified that verdict, holding that Ledbetter filed her claim too late.

It was incumbent on Ledbetter, the Court said, to file charges of discrimination each time Goodyear failed to increase her salary commensurate with the salaries of her male peers. Any annual pay decision not contested promptly (within 180 days), the Court ruled, became grandfathered, beyond the province of Title VII (our principal law outlawing employment discrimination) ever to repair.

The Court's ruling, I observed for the dissenters, ignored real-world employment practices that Title VII was meant to govern: "Sue early on," the majority counseled, when it is uncertain whether discrimination accounts for the pay disparity you are beginning to experience, and when you may not know that men are receiving more for the same work. (Of course, you will likely lose such a less-than-fully baked case.) If you sue only when the pay disparity becomes steady and large enough to enable you to mount a winnable case, you will be cut off at the court's threshold for suing too late. That situation, I urged, could not be what Congress intended when, in Title VII, it outlawed discrimination based on race, color, religion, sex, or national origin in our Nation's workplaces.

Several members of Congress responded within days after the Court's decision issued. A corrective measure passed the House on July 31, 2007. Senator Kennedy introduced a parallel bill, with 21 co-sponsors. The response was just what I contemplated when I wrote: "The ball is in Congress's court. . . . to correct [the Supreme] Court's parsimonious reading of Title VII." * * **

Another type of dissent that may sound an alarm and propel change in the law is one at the intermediate appellate court level. When a judge on a mid-level court writes separately, he or she may persuade other courts at that level, thus creating a conflict among appellate courts in different regions of the country, one that the Supreme Court eventually may resolve. An impressive dissent, even in the absence of a division among intermediate courts, may alert the Supreme Court that an issue is difficult, important, and worthy of the Justices' attention.

* * * I will continue to give voice to my dissent if, in my judgment, the Court veers in the wrong direction when important matters are at stake. I *stress* important matters because I try to follow Justice Brandeis's counsel. He cautioned that "in most matters it is more important that the applicable rule of law be settled than that it be settled right." One might put in that category an ambiguous provision of a complex statutory regime—the [tax code], for example. Justices take comfort in such cases from the knowledge that Congress can amend the provision if it believes the Court has gone astray.

On when to acquiesce in the majority's view, and when to take an independent stand, Judge Jerome Frank wrote of the model Brandeis set:

> Brandeis was a great institutional man. He realized that . . . random dissents . . . weaken the institutional impact of the Court

---

* The measure was later enacted as the Lilly Ledbetter Fair Pay Act of 2009, Pub. L. 111–2, the first bill signed into law by President Obama. [Ed.]

and handicap it in the doing of its fundamental job. Dissents . . . need to be saved for major matters if the Court is not to appear indecisive and quarrelsome. . . . To have discarded some of [his separate] opinions is a supreme example of [Brandeis's] sacrifice to [the] strength and consistency of the Court. And he had his reward: his shots [were] all the harder because he chose his ground.

In the years I am privileged to serve on the Court I hope I will be granted similar wisdom in choosing my ground.

NOTES AND QUESTIONS

1.   Dissenting opinions, by their very nature, demonstrate to the public that the court is in disagreement about a particular issue. Is it important to publish different interpretations of the law? Or do dissenting opinions cause too much confusion and contribute to a lack of respect for the law?

2.   Over the past two centuries, several important dissenting opinions later formed the bases for majority opinions in landmark cases. For example, Justice Harlan's dissent in *Plessy v. Ferguson*, 163 U.S. 537 (1896), a case upholding "separate but equal" facilities used to separate blacks and whites, represents one of the most important dissents in U.S. history. His dissent was undoubtedly influential in the seminal case of *Brown v. Board of Education*, 347 U.S. 483 (1954), when the Supreme Court rejected the "separate but equal" doctrine and ruled that racial segregation in schools was unconstitutional. Justice Blackmun's dissenting opinion in *Bowers v. Hardwick*, 478 U.S. 186 (1986), a case that upheld criminal prohibitions on consensual homosexual sex, is another example of a highly influential dissenting opinion. His dissent was a key factor in the decision by the Supreme Court to overrule *Bowers* 17 years later in *Lawrence v. Texas*, 539 U.S. 558 (2003) (holding that it was unconstitutional to criminalize consensual homosexual sex). (The subject of gay rights is also discussed in Chapter 2.) For a discussion of the history of dissenting opinions, *see* Edward McGlynn Gaffney, Jr., *The Importance of Dissent and the Imperative of Judicial Civility*, 28 Val. U.L. Rev. 583 (1994) (analyzing the role of dissenting opinions over the past two centuries and concluding that such opinions play a crucial part in the development of appellate precedent).

3.   Dissenting opinions have long been important in the United States, but in recent years they have become increasingly important in other parts of the world. For example, as Katalin Kelemen notes in her article, *Dissenting Opinions in Constitutional Courts*, 14 German L.J. 1345 (2013), published dissenting opinions are becoming more common throughout European legal systems.

4.   In addition to dissenting opinions, there are times when an appellate judge will write a concurring opinion. One major reason for a concurring opinion is to discuss issues or points not addressed by the majority. Because of

the importance of both concurring and dissenting opinions, the excerpts in the following chapters include many such opinions.

G. LEGAL EDUCATION IN THE UNITED STATES

A career as a lawyer or legal scholar in the United States almost always involves formal legal education in a law school. The following article discusses the current law school experience in the United States.

LEGAL EDUCATION IN THE UNITED STATES: WHO'S IN CHARGE? WHY DOES IT MATTER?

Cheryl Rosen Weston
24 Wis. Int'l L.J. 397 (2006)

I. Regulators and Stakeholders in U.S. Legal Education

* * *

Just as the regulation of lawyers has increased, so has regulation of legal education. Yet the forces which shape legal education are complex and include the government, voluntary institutions, professional organizations, the market, and even the media.

The role of the federal government in legal education in the United States is indirect. There is nothing equivalent to a Ministry of Education as found in other countries. The United States Department of Education does not approve law schools. Rather, it is required to maintain a list of agencies deemed suitable for accrediting higher education institutions, law schools among them. The list is divided into two segments: regional accrediting authorities, which focus on general standards for college and universities, and specialist accrediting bodies, which focus on distinct subject-matter programs.

The accreditation process is non-governmental and voluntary, but it has an important effect on law students. In the broadest sense, it serves as a status symbol that enhances the value of the degree offered. In relation to the power of the federal government, it is an essential prerequisite for attaining federal financial support. In the United States, students are individually responsible for a significant proportion of the costs of their education. The federal government provides approximately 70 percent of all financial aid to post-secondary students in the United States, * * * amounting [as of 2006] to more than $67 billion per year. Eighty percent of U.S. law students use educational loans as their primary source of financial aid. Law schools receive federal funds in a variety of other ways including research grants and payment for contracted services. Thus, the power of the federal government in legal education is largely the power of the purse. Financial aid, although principally in the form of loans requiring repayment, makes legal education widely available to those academically qualified. The ensuing debt impacts career choices because salary needs are influenced by loan repayment demands. The requirement that students attend accredited law schools to qualify for financial aid significantly influences their choice of law school.

The role of state governments is similarly indirect, but more powerful. It is illegal to practice law in the United States without a license and licensure is the exclusive province of state government. State authorities, located within the judicial branch, are responsible for determining admission to the bar and continuing eligibility to practice law. Typically, states require proof of competence, character, and fitness as the prerequisites of licensure. Competence is described as having a suitable educational credential, plus obtaining a passing grade on a bar examination. Thus the determination of what constitutes a "suitable educational credential" is a required precondition of entry into the profession under state law. Of the fifty-six jurisdictions that admit lawyers to practice, twenty will not permit an applicant to sit for the bar examination without having first graduated from an ABA [American Bar Association]-approved law school. Of the remaining, eleven other jurisdictions permit non-ABA-approved school graduates to take the exam only if they have been licensed in another state and have practiced there from periods ranging from three to ten years; twenty jurisdictions have varying provisions permitting graduates of foreign law schools to take the bar exam; and seven states permit taking the exam conditioned upon law office study, or an office/law school combination of studies. A handful of jurisdictions have unique requirements, such as a certain number of credits obtained at an ABA-approved school, a degree from a provisionally ABA-approved school, or additional years of law study. Unless one has completed his or her legal studies outside of the United States, or wishes to take the bar after being licensed and having practiced for a number of years in a different state, few states will license an individual who has graduated from a non-ABA-approved law school. In effect, state governments influence legal education by heavily favoring ABA-accredited schools in the licensing process.

U.S. law schools are subject to myriad regulations that, though unrelated to schools' educational mission, potentially impact the educational process. For example, laws concerning employment, including working conditions and prohibitions against discrimination; laws affecting student admissions, such as disability accommodations; and the management of student records may be addressed on the federal, state, and/or local level. Law schools located within larger colleges or universities must comply with institution-wide hierarchical policies addressing such diverse issues as course approvals and faculty tenure. Consequently, the indirect nature of federal and state control of legal education is supplemented by numerous legal requirements of a diverse nature which must be satisfied on an ongoing basis.

Neither public nor private law schools are immune from financial distress. Alumni and employers of school graduates see themselves as stakeholders in the institution, and they are identified by the administration as potential donors. In addition, a strong pool of student applicants is critical to financial viability. The need to court these funding sources, as well as to attract dollars from grant-bestowing entities, places pressure on law schools to effectively market themselves to multiple constituencies and distinguish themselves from peers. In recent years the publication of U.S. News and World Report's annual ranking of law schools has undisputedly impacted individual schools' ability to attract students, much to the consternation of administration and faculty critical of the accuracy of the rankings yet willing to manipulate data and take actions to improve their institutions' rank. It is increasingly common for law schools to identify themselves as special in a variety of ways, including overall quality, distinct areas of specialization, flexible class scheduling, emphasis on the use of technology, and/or regional or global focus. Individual schools see themselves as participants in a competitive market and seek to distinguish themselves in order to gain advantage.

Three voluntary organizations are of particular importance to the structure of legal education: the National Conference of Bar Examiners, the American Association of Law Schools, and above all, the American Bar Association.

The National Conference of Bar Examiners (NCBE) was created in 1931 as a non-profit corporation that works in conjunction with others to develop, maintain, and apply reasonable and uniform standards of education and character for eligibility for admission to practice law. The NCBE develops the Multistate Bar Examination (MBE) (a multiple choice exam on substantive areas of law) and the Multistate Professional Responsibility Examination (MPRE) (a multiple choice exam on [the] law of lawyer conduct) as well as the less-widely used Multistate Performance Test (MPE) (comprised of three ninety-minute questions attempting to determine lawyering skills) and the Multistate Essay Examination (MEE) (comprised of six thirty-minute essay questions within ten pre-announced areas of substantive law). In addition, the NCBE conducts character examinations, publishes statistical information, performs research, and assists bar admission authorities in general matters.

The American Association of Law Schools (AALS) is a non-profit association of * * * [more than 150] law schools. The purpose of the association is "the improvement of the legal profession through legal education." It serves as the learned society for law teachers and is legal education's principal representative to the federal government and to other national higher education organizations and learned societies. Membership consists of law schools; individual faculty and administrative staff are involved in the AALS's governance activities and participate in [numerous] sections of subject-matter interest.

The AALS is known for its annual meeting, a national gathering of law faculty that offers workshops and scholarly presentations, its faculty recruitment conference, and an applicant registry service. It further plays an important role in participating in ABA-accreditation site visits to member schools, reviewing conditions of key concern to faculty.

Chief among influential voluntary organizations is the American Bar Association. The ABA is a membership organization claiming membership of over 400,000 of the United States' [more than 1 million] lawyers. The ABA seeks "to be the national representative of the legal profession, serving the public and the profession by promoting justice, professional excellence and respect for the law." While the ABA's membership consists of a minority of the profession, it has no substantial competitors.

In the context of legal education, the primacy of influence of the ABA results from its position as the sole accreditor of law schools recognized by the United States government. The organization first published standards for law schools in the late 1920s. A decade later, twenty states required bar applicants to be graduates of ABA-approved schools. The accreditation process is accomplished by way of a determination of whether the school has satisfied the ABA's Standards for Approval of Law Schools. The process has two primary components, self-study and site visits.

The self-study process commences more than a year in advance of the year of the site visit. The process contemplates consultation with all constituencies of the school, including the faculty, administration, students, and alumni as well as the bench and bar. The resulting document identifies the components of the law school's educational program and its goals; it also analyzes the school's strengths, weaknesses, and educational output, such as bar examination performance and placement data in relation to its goals.

* * *

Site visit teams for schools seeking provisional approval—those determined to be operating in substantial compliance with the accreditation standards with a reliable plan for attaining full compliance within three years—are visited annually by teams of five to seven members.

Fully approved schools are normally visited by seven-member teams. Teams consist of a lawyer, judge, or public member; a university administrator; and members of faculty or staff at other law schools. The visit, typically lasting three days, consists of numerous classroom visits; time spent examining clinical programs, including field placements; and evaluation of the library, physical facilities, technological capabilities, and student and administrative services. The visit encompasses extensive conversations with the dean; meetings with individual faculty, professional staff, and student leaders; and open meetings with students. Also expected is a records review including a sample of examinations, student-written work, faculty scholarship, admission files, and financial records. The culmination of the visit results in a site evaluation report tendered to the ABA Accrediting Committee, which is composed of legal educators, judges, practicing lawyers, bar examiners and public non-lawyer members. The committee finds full compliance and continues accreditation, specifically identifies non-compliance, or seeks additional information. The entire process occurs every seven years. * * *

* * * When the ABA site visit is to an AALS member school, one member of the ABA site evaluation team is an AALS member responsible for both participating in the ABA review and writing a separate report to the AALS membership review committee for compliance with its membership requirements. * * *

The final major influence on the American law school is the institutional faculty. Embedded in U.S. higher education is the value of faculty governance. Within the constraints of budget, accreditation, and rules of the parent institution, faculty members are responsible for the fundamental decisions concerning curriculum and program, hires, employment security, and job duties. * * *

* * *

II. The Resulting Shape of Legal Education

A. Law School Offerings

* * *

The first year of instruction is largely standardized and consists of courses in contracts, torts, property, criminal law, and civil procedure. Students are exposed to a substantial amount of doctrine and focus on mastering basic legal reasoning and analysis. In the 1870s, Professor Christopher Langdell of Harvard Law School promoted the practice of learning law through the analysis of appellate court opinions, commonly referred to as the case method. Case books evolved into compilations of "Cases and Materials," supplementing the selected opinions with notes and problems. Classes consist of varying degrees of lecture and calling upon students to explicate the reasoning and holding of the opinions, statutes, and rules under consideration. Within these courses, the focus varies. Emphasizing national or local law, looking for rules or identifying policy considerations, examining the impacts of other disciplines, or focusing on the problem method and cultivating practitioner's skills are some of the distinct approaches that distinguish schools or the predilections of individual law teachers.

The second- and third-year curriculum offerings are far more diverse. Trends indicate an explosive growth in the number of course offerings. A recent study found that between 1994 and 1997, eighty-three responding law schools added 1,574 new courses and seminars, with a mean of nineteen and a median of fifteen new courses added. Upper-level courses include large sections of courses addressing subjects of core contemporary legal knowledge such as evidence, administrative law, constitutional law, taxation, trusts and estates, labor law, and business associations. Numerous seminars, often reflecting individual faculty members' areas of interest, are common. A significant number of additional courses focus on skills training, whether through focus on legal writing, simulation courses [such] as negotiations, trial advocacy, alternative dispute resolution, or various field and clinical placements.

A review of the history of law school offerings must be seen, not as the transition from the vocational training of the apprenticeship model to the ivory tower, but rather as an attempt to strike a balance between skills-based training and the theoretical study of law as science. * * *

* * *

B.   Law School Teachers

The continuing debate over what law schools should teach is accompanied by the question of who shall teach it. The creation of the academic law school gave rise to the profession of law professor. Early law schools were staffed by practitioners and judges. The transition to the academic law school brought recognition that the talents of one distinguished within the profession do not necessarily translate into skill as a teacher. * * *

* * *

Academic affiliation gave rise to the role of law teacher as scholar. It became expected that as academics, law professors would contribute to the body of legal knowledge, chiefly through scholarly publications. The view of law as a science further generated interest in empirical research and exploration of the "law and" disciplines. Law professors as social thinkers advanced schools of thought, such as legal realism and critical legal studies. Law professors also became activists both as technicians, drafting legislation and model laws, and as policy consultants on a national and international level. These roles are accepted within our society as a natural extension of professorial duties. They are clearly distinct, however, from teaching, and call for different talents.

As clinical programs and skills-oriented courses became more integrated into the curriculum, the lack of talented practitioners on staff became a real deficiency. Law schools have attempted to fill the gap by hiring clinicians—full-time instructors with practice experience who combine classroom instruction with supervision of students in practice settings, or specialize in teaching legal writing—and adjuncts—local practitioners and judges with specialization or skills expertise who wish to teach on a part-time basis. * * *

* * *

NOTES AND QUESTIONS

1.   For many years, law school has remained a three-year graduate program (commencing after a student completes an undergraduate degree, which typically involves a four-year program). In recent years, however, some scholars have proposed limiting law school to two years. For example, in a 2013 New York Times opinion article entitled, *Make Law Schools Earn a Third Year*, Professor Samuel Estreicher and Dean Daniel Rodriguez proposed changes that would make students eligible to take the bar exam after two years of law school, with a third year being optional. The article argues that a two-year program would cut educational costs for students and would thus provide more financial flexibility for students to work in less lucrative public interest fields. The Estreicher/Rodriguez proposal is available at http://www.nytimes.com/2013/01/18/opinion/practicing-law-should-not-mean-living-in-bankruptcy.html. President Barack Obama has also voiced his support for two-year law school programs. Speaking at New York's Binghamton University in 2013, the President opined that law schools should eliminate the required third year of education. As he stated, students would "be better off clerking or practicing in a firm [in their third year] even if they weren't getting paid that much * * *." *See* Phillip Rucker, *Obama Emphasizes Focus on Middle Class in Biden's Home Town of Scranton*, WASH. POST, August 23, 2014, *available at* https://www.washingtonpost.com/politics/obama-at-binghamton-university-comments-on-law-schools-tuition-congress/2013/08/23/b2b804e8-0c1b-11e3-8974-f97ab3b3c677_story.html. Some scholars, however, have criticized the two-year proposal. *See, e.g.*, Erwin Chemerinsky & Carrie Menkel-Meadow, *Don't Skimp on Legal Training*, N.Y. TIMES, Apr. 14, 2014, *available at* http://www.nytimes.com/2014/04/15/opinion/dont-skimp-on-legal-training.html (arguing that law schools need to expand (rather than reduce) their curriculum to keep up with modern legal issues). What benefits would two-year programs have over the traditional three-year model? What are the costs of a two-year approach? Which approach is preferable?

2.   Some law schools offer a curriculum that is heavily focused on legal doctrine. Numerous scholars have supported a law school model that focuses more on practical skills and less on pure legal doctrine. *See, e.g.*, James Moliterno, *The Future of Legal Education Reform*, 40 Pepp. L. Rev. 423 (2013) (arguing that in addition to basic legal doctrine, law schools need to focus more on practical skills necessary to be an effective lawyer); Susan Sturm & Lani Guinier, *The Law School Matrix: Reforming Legal Education in a Culture of Competition and Conformity,* 60 Vand. L. Rev. 515, 516 (2007) (stating that the current law school curriculum "over-emphasizes adjudication and discounts many of the important global, transactional, and facilitative dimensions of legal practice," and arguing that law schools need to focus more on offering

practical skills necessary for effective advocacy). In recent years, many law schools have increased significantly their offerings in practical skills. What should the balance be between traditional law school courses and courses offering practical training or experience?

CHAPTER 2

CONSTITUTIONAL LAW

■ ■ ■

Constitutional law covers many topics. These include, among others: judicial, legislative, and executive powers; federalism; due process; equal protection; freedom of speech; freedom of religion; and privacy. Many constitutional law casebooks exceed 1,000 pages. Although this chapter cannot cover all of the major topics, it does highlight several important and controversial issues.

Two issues that arise frequently throughout this chapter involve (1) the determination of the proper level of scrutiny, and (2) the determination whether a particular guarantee of the Bill of Rights applies to the states or only to the federal government. These issues are discussed below.

Level of Scrutiny: When dealing with laws affecting "fundamental rights" and "suspect classifications" (*e.g.*, the right to vote, race, national origin, or sex), an issue arises as to the appropriate standard of scrutiny. For example, laws involving classifications based on ethnicity or race are subject to the "most rigid scrutiny," commonly referred to as strict scrutiny. *Loving v. Virginia*, 388 U.S. 1, 11 (1967). Similarly, where fundamental rights are involved, such as the right to marriage and procreation, *Skinner v. Okla. ex rel. Williamson*, 316 U.S. 535, 541 (1942), and the right to vote, *Harper v. Va. Bd. of Elections*, 383 U.S. 663, 670 (1966), classifications "must be closely scrutinized and carefully confined." *Id.* The Supreme Court has explained that "strict scrutiny means that the [law] is not entitled to the usual presumption of validity, that the [government] rather than the complainants must carry a 'heavy burden of justification,' that the [government] must demonstrate that [the law] has been structured with 'precision,' and is 'tailored' narrowly to serve legitimate objectives and that it has selected the 'less drastic means' for effectuating its objectives." *San Antonio Indep. Sch. Dist. v. Rodriguez*, 411 U.S. 1, 16–17 (1973). In short, to withstand strict scrutiny, laws must be "narrowly tailored measures that further compelling governmental interests." *Adarand Constructors, Inc. v. Pena*, 515 U.S. 200, 227 (1995).

Some classifications, such as those based on gender, are also subject to heightened scrutiny, but not to the same degree as strict scrutiny. Under such intermediate scrutiny, "a statutory classification must be substantially related to an important governmental objective." *Clark v.*

Jeter, 486 U.S. 456, 461 (1988) (striking down classification that burdened illegitimate children).

Laws that do not involve a suspect classification or a fundamental right are subject to the lowest standard of review—rational basis review. Under rational basis review, a law need only be "rationally related to a legitimate governmental purpose." *Id.* Most statutes are subject to rational basis review, including statutes involving classifications based on mental disability, *City of Cleburne v. Cleburne Living Ctr.*, 473 U.S. 432 (1985), age, *Mass. Bd. of Ret. v. Murgia*, 427 U.S. 307 (1976), and wealth, *Rodriguez, supra.*

Applicability of the Bill of Rights to the States: Because the Bill of Rights (the first ten amendments to the Constitution) initially applied only to the federal government, *Barron v. Baltimore*, 32 U.S. (7 Pet.) 243 (1833), the question arises whether those rights also apply to the states. The Supreme Court has held—as a result of the Fourteenth Amendment command that "[n]o State" shall "deprive any person of life, liberty, or property, without due process of law * * *," U.S. CONST. amend. XIV, § 1— that some provisions of the Bill of Rights apply to the states. For example, addressing the right to counsel, the Court has held that "a provision of the Bill of Rights which is 'fundamental and essential to a fair trial' is made obligatory upon the States by the Fourteenth Amendment." *Gideon v. Wainwright*, 372 U.S. 335, 342 (1963). Through a process of "selective incorporation," the Supreme Court has held in various opinions that most, but not all, provisions of the Bill of Rights apply to the states. *See McDonald v. City of Chicago*, 561 U.S. 742, 763 (2010). Most recently, the Court has indicated that the relevant inquiry is "whether a particular Bill of Rights guarantee is fundamental to *our* scheme of ordered liberty and system of justice." *Id.* at 764 (emphasis in original). Currently, the only provisions in the Bill of Rights that have *not* been made applicable to the states are the Third Amendment (forbidding "quartering" of soldiers in private homes without owner consent), the Fifth Amendment grand jury indictment requirement, the Sixth Amendment right to a *unanimous* jury verdict in criminal cases (although the basic Sixth Amendment jury trial right is applicable to the states), the Seventh Amendment right to a jury trial in civil cases, and the Eighth Amendment prohibition on excessive fines. *See id.* at 765 n.13.

———————

This chapter begins with an examination of one of the core constitutional guarantees: the right to freedom of speech.

A. FREEDOM OF SPEECH

The First Amendment to the U.S. Constitution states in part that "Congress shall make no law * * * abridging the freedom of speech."

Despite that seemingly unambiguous mandate, it is not always clear—especially given modern technology—what constitutes "speech." Moreover, it should be obvious that not all speech is protected. For example, one could not reasonably contend that a robber has a First Amendment right to say to a robbery victim, "your money or your life," and be free of any legal consequences for the expression used to facilitate a crime. But many situations are not as clear. This section explores a variety of issues that can arise in the context of free speech claims.

1. SYMBOLIC SPEECH

TEXAS V. JOHNSON
Supreme Court of the United States, 1989
491 U.S. 397

JUSTICE BRENNAN delivered the opinion of the Court.

After publicly burning an American flag as a means of political protest, Gregory Lee Johnson was convicted of desecrating a flag in violation of Texas law. This case presents the question whether his conviction is consistent with the First Amendment. We hold that it is not.

I

While the Republican National Convention was taking place in Dallas in 1984, respondent Johnson participated in a political demonstration dubbed the "Republican War Chest Tour." As explained in literature distributed by the demonstrators and in speeches made by them, the purpose of this event was to protest the policies of the Reagan administration and of certain Dallas-based corporations. The demonstrators marched through the Dallas streets, chanting political slogans and stopping at several corporate locations to stage "die-ins" intended to dramatize the consequences of nuclear war. On several occasions they spray-painted the walls of buildings and overturned potted plants, but Johnson himself took no part in such activities. He did, however, accept an American flag handed to him by a fellow protestor who had taken it from a flagpole outside one of the targeted buildings.

The demonstration ended in front of Dallas City Hall, where Johnson unfurled the American flag, doused it with kerosene, and set it on fire. While the flag burned, the protestors chanted: "America, the red, white, and blue, we spit on you." After the demonstrators dispersed, a witness to the flag burning collected the flag's remains and buried them in his backyard. No one was physically injured or threatened with injury, though several witnesses testified that they had been seriously offended by the flag burning.

Of the approximately 100 demonstrators, Johnson alone was charged with a crime. The only criminal offense with which he was charged was the desecration of a venerated object in violation of [the Texas Penal Code. Johnson was convicted at trial but his conviction was reversed by the Texas Court of Criminal Appeals. The U.S. Supreme Court granted the State's petition for a writ of certiorari.]

* * *

II

Johnson was convicted of flag desecration for burning the flag rather than for uttering insulting words. This fact somewhat complicates our consideration of his conviction under the First Amendment. We must first determine whether Johnson's burning of the flag constituted expressive conduct, permitting him to invoke the First Amendment in challenging his conviction. If his conduct was expressive, we next decide whether the State's regulation is related to the suppression of free expression. If the State's regulation is not related to expression, then the less stringent standard we announced in *United States v. O'Brien*[, 391 U.S. 367 (1968)] for regulations of noncommunicative conduct controls. If it is, then we are outside of *O'Brien*'s test, and we must ask whether this interest justifies Johnson's conviction under a more demanding standard. A third possibility is that the State's asserted interest is simply not implicated on these facts, and in that event the interest drops out of the picture.

The First Amendment literally forbids the abridgment only of "speech," but we have long recognized that its protection does not end at the spoken or written word. While we have rejected "the view that an apparently limitless variety of conduct can be labeled 'speech' whenever the person engaging in the conduct intends thereby to express an idea," we have acknowledged that conduct may be "sufficiently imbued with elements of communication to fall within the scope of the First and Fourteenth Amendments."

In deciding whether particular conduct possesses sufficient communicative elements to bring the First Amendment into play, we have asked whether "[a]n intent to convey a particularized message was present, and [whether] the likelihood was great that the message would be understood by those who viewed it." Hence, we have recognized the expressive nature of students' wearing of black armbands to protest American military involvement in Vietnam; of a sit-in by blacks in a "whites only" area to protest segregation; of the wearing of American military uniforms in a dramatic presentation criticizing American involvement in Vietnam; and of picketing about a wide variety of causes.

Especially pertinent to this case are our decisions recognizing the communicative nature of conduct relating to flags. Attaching a peace sign to the flag; refusing to salute the flag; and displaying a red flag, we have held, all may find shelter under the First Amendment. That we have had little difficulty identifying an expressive element in conduct relating to flags should not be surprising. The very purpose of a national flag is to serve as a symbol of our country; it is, one might say, "the one visible manifestation of two hundred years of nationhood." * * *

* * *

We have not automatically concluded, however, that any action taken with respect to our flag is expressive. * * *

The State of Texas conceded * * * in this case that Johnson's conduct was expressive conduct, and this concession seems to us [a] prudent [one] * * *. Johnson burned an American flag as part—indeed, as the culmination—of a political demonstration that coincided with the convening of the Republican Party and its renomination of Ronald Reagan for President. The expressive, overtly political nature of this conduct was both intentional and overwhelmingly apparent. At his trial, Johnson explained his reasons for burning the flag as follows: "The American Flag was burned as Ronald Reagan was being renominated as President. And a more powerful statement of symbolic speech, whether you agree with it or not, couldn't have been made at that time. It's quite a [juxtaposition]. We had new patriotism and no patriotism." In these circumstances, Johnson's burning of the flag was conduct "sufficiently imbued with elements of communication" to implicate the First Amendment.

III

The government generally has a freer hand in restricting expressive conduct than it has in restricting the written or spoken word. It may not, however, proscribe particular conduct *because* it has expressive elements. " * * * A law *directed at* the communicative nature of conduct must, like a law directed at speech itself, be justified by the substantial showing of need that the First Amendment requires." * * *

Thus, although we have recognized that where " 'speech' and 'nonspeech' elements are combined in the same course of conduct, a sufficiently important governmental interest in regulating the nonspeech element can justify incidental limitations on First Amendment freedoms," we have limited the applicability of *O'Brien*'s relatively lenient standard to those cases in which "the governmental interest is unrelated to the suppression of free expression." * * *

In order to decide whether *O'Brien*'s test applies here, therefore, we must decide whether Texas has asserted an interest in support of Johnson's conviction that is unrelated to the suppression of expression. * * * The State offers two separate interests to justify this conviction: preventing breaches of the peace and preserving the flag as a symbol of nationhood and national unity. We hold that the first interest is not implicated on this record and that the second is related to the suppression of expression.

A

Texas claims that its interest in preventing breaches of the peace justifies Johnson's conviction for flag desecration. However, no disturbance of the peace actually occurred or threatened to occur because of Johnson's burning of the flag. Although the State stresses the disruptive behavior of the protestors during their march toward City Hall, it admits that "no actual breach of the peace occurred at the time of the flag burning or in response to the flag burning." The State's emphasis on the protestors' disorderly actions prior to arriving at City Hall is not only somewhat surprising given that no charges were brought on the basis of this conduct, but it also fails to show that a disturbance of the peace was a likely reaction to *Johnson's* conduct. The only evidence offered by the State at trial to show the reaction to Johnson's actions was the testimony of several persons who had been seriously offended by the flag burning.

The State's position, therefore, amounts to a claim that an audience that takes serious offense at particular expression is necessarily likely to disturb the peace and that the expression may be prohibited on this basis. Our precedents do not countenance such a presumption. On the contrary, they recognize that a principal "function of free speech under our system of government is to invite dispute. * * * "

Thus, we have not permitted the government to assume that every expression of a provocative idea will incite a riot, but have instead required careful consideration of the actual circumstances surrounding such expression, asking whether the expression "is directed to inciting or producing imminent lawless action and is likely to incite or produce such action." * * *

Nor does Johnson's expressive conduct fall within that small class of "fighting words" that are "likely to provoke the average person to retaliation, and thereby cause a breach of the peace." No reasonable onlooker would have regarded Johnson's generalized expression of dissatisfaction with the policies of the Federal Government as a direct personal insult or an invitation to exchange fisticuffs.

We thus conclude that the State's interest in maintaining order is not implicated on these facts. * * *

* * *

IV

It remains to consider whether the State's interest in preserving the flag as a symbol of nationhood and national unity justifies Johnson's conviction.

* * * Johnson was not * * * prosecuted for the expression of just any idea; he was prosecuted for his expression of dissatisfaction with the

policies of this country, expression situated at the core of our First Amendment values.

Moreover, Johnson was prosecuted because he knew that his politically charged expression would cause "serious offense." If he had burned the flag as a means of disposing of it because it was dirty or torn, he would not have been convicted of flag desecration under this Texas law: federal law designates burning as the preferred means of disposing of a flag "when it is in such condition that it is no longer a fitting emblem for display," and Texas has no quarrel with this means of disposal. The Texas law is thus not aimed at protecting the physical integrity of the flag in all circumstances, but is designed instead to protect it only against impairments that would cause serious offense to others. * * *

Whether Johnson's treatment of the flag violated Texas law thus depended on the likely communicative impact of his expressive conduct. * * *

* * * Johnson's political expression was restricted because of the content of the message he conveyed. We must therefore subject the State's asserted interest in preserving the special symbolic character of the flag to "the most exacting scrutiny."

Texas argues that its interest in preserving the flag as a symbol of nationhood and national unity survives this close analysis. * * * According to Texas, if one physically treats the flag in a way that would tend to cast doubt on either the idea that nationhood and national unity are the flag's referents or that national unity actually exists, the message conveyed thereby is a harmful one and therefore may be prohibited.

If there is a bedrock principle underlying the First Amendment, it is that the government may not prohibit the expression of an idea simply because society finds the idea itself offensive or disagreeable.

We have not recognized an exception to this principle even where our flag has been involved. * * *

* * *

* * * [N]othing in our precedents suggests that a State may foster its own view of the flag by prohibiting expressive conduct relating to it. To bring its argument outside our precedents, Texas attempts to convince us that even if its interest in preserving the flag's symbolic role does not allow it to prohibit words or some expressive conduct critical of the flag, it does permit it to forbid the outright destruction of the flag. The State's argument cannot depend here on the distinction between written or spoken words and nonverbal conduct. That distinction, we have shown, is of no moment where the nonverbal conduct is expressive, as it is here, and where the regulation of that conduct is related to expression, as it is here.

Texas's focus on the precise nature of Johnson's expression, moreover, misses the point of our prior decisions * * *. If we were to hold that a State may forbid flag burning wherever it is likely to endanger the flag's symbolic role, but allow it wherever burning a flag promotes that role—as where, for example, a person ceremoniously burns a dirty flag—we would be saying that * * * the flag itself may be used as a symbol * * * only in one direction. We would be permitting a State to "prescribe what shall be orthodox" by saying that one may burn the flag to convey one's attitude toward it and its referents only if one does not endanger the flag's representation of nationhood and national unity.

We never before have held that the Government may ensure that a symbol be used to express only one view of that symbol or its referents. * * *

* * * To conclude that the government may permit designated symbols to be used to communicate only a limited set of messages would be to enter territory having no discernible or defensible boundaries. Could the government, on this theory, prohibit the burning of state flags? Of copies of the Presidential seal? Of the Constitution? In evaluating these choices under the First Amendment, how would we decide which symbols were sufficiently special to warrant this unique status? To do so, we would be forced to consult our own political preferences, and impose them on the citizenry, in the very way that the First Amendment forbids us to do.

There is, moreover, no indication—either in the text of the Constitution or in our cases interpreting it—that a separate juridical category exists for the American flag alone. * * *

It is not the State's ends, but its means, to which we object. It cannot be gainsaid that there is a special place reserved for the flag in this Nation, and thus we do not doubt that the government has a legitimate interest in making efforts to "preserv[e] the national flag as an unalloyed symbol of our country." * * * Congress has, for example, enacted precatory regulations describing the proper treatment of the flag, and we cast no doubt on the legitimacy of its interest in making such recommendations. To say that the government has an interest in encouraging proper treatment of the flag, however, is not to say that it may criminally punish a person for burning a flag as a means of political protest. * * *

We are fortified in today's conclusion by our conviction that forbidding criminal punishment for conduct such as Johnson's will not endanger the special role played by our flag or the feelings it inspires. * * * Indeed, Texas's argument that the burning of an American flag " 'is an act having a high likelihood to cause a breach of the peace,' " and its statute's implicit assumption that physical mistreatment of the flag will lead to "serious offense," tend to confirm that the flag's special role is not in danger; if it were, no one would riot or take offense because a flag had been burned.

We are tempted to say, in fact, that the flag's deservedly cherished place in our community will be strengthened, not weakened, by our holding today. Our decision is a reaffirmation of the principles of freedom and inclusiveness that the flag best reflects, and of the conviction that our toleration of criticism such as Johnson's is a sign and source of our strength. * * *

The way to preserve the flag's special role is not to punish those who feel differently about these matters. It is to persuade them that they are wrong. * * * We can imagine no more appropriate response to burning a flag than waving one's own, no better way to counter a flag burner's message than by saluting the flag that burns, no surer means of preserving the dignity even of the flag that burned than by—as one witness here did— according its remains a respectful burial. We do not consecrate the flag by punishing its desecration, for in doing so we dilute the freedom that this cherished emblem represents.

V

Johnson was convicted for engaging in expressive conduct. The State's interest in preventing breaches of the peace does not support his conviction * * *. Nor does the State's interest in preserving the flag as a symbol of nationhood and national unity * * *. The judgment of the Texas Court of Criminal Appeals is therefore

Affirmed.

[Concurring opinion by JUSTICE KENNEDY is omitted.]

CHIEF JUSTICE REHNQUIST, with whom JUSTICE WHITE and JUSTICE O'CONNOR join, dissenting.

* * * For more than 200 years, the American flag has occupied a unique position as the symbol of our Nation, a uniqueness that justifies a governmental prohibition against flag burning in the way respondent Johnson did here.

At the time of the American Revolution, the flag served to unify the Thirteen Colonies at home, while obtaining recognition of national sovereignty abroad. * * *

* * *

One immediate result of the flag's adoption was that American vessels harassing British shipping sailed under an authorized national flag. Without such a flag, the British could treat captured seamen as pirates and hang them summarily; with a national flag, such seamen were treated as prisoners of war.

During the War of 1812, British naval forces sailed up Chesapeake Bay and marched overland to sack and burn the city of Washington. They then sailed up the Patapsco River to invest the city of Baltimore, but to do so it was first necessary to reduce Fort McHenry in Baltimore Harbor. Francis Scott Key, a Washington lawyer, had been granted permission by the British to board one of their warships to negotiate the release of an American who had been taken prisoner. That night, waiting anxiously on the British ship, Key watched the British fleet firing on Fort McHenry. Finally, at daybreak, he saw the fort's American flag still flying; the British attack had failed. Intensely moved, he began to scribble on the back of an envelope the poem [describing what he saw] that became our national anthem ["The Star-Spangled Banner"].

* * *

The American flag played a central role in our Nation's most tragic conflict, when the North fought against the South. The lowering of the American flag at Fort Sumter was viewed as the start of the war. The Southern States, to formalize their separation from the Union, adopted the "Stars and Bars" of the Confederacy. The Union troops marched to the sound of "Yes We'll Rally Round The Flag Boys, We'll Rally Once Again." President Abraham Lincoln refused proposals to remove from the American flag the stars representing the rebel States, because he considered the conflict not a war between two nations but an attack by 11 States against the National Government. By war's end, the American flag again flew over "an indestructible union, composed of indestructible states." * * *

* * *

In the First and Second World Wars, thousands of our countrymen died on foreign soil fighting for the American cause. At Iwo Jima in the Second World War, United States Marines fought hand to hand against thousands of Japanese. By the time the Marines reached the top of Mount Suribachi, they raised a piece of pipe upright and from one end fluttered a flag. That ascent had cost nearly 6,000 American lives. The Iwo Jima Memorial in Arlington National Cemetery memorializes that event. President Franklin Roosevelt authorized the use of the flag on labels, packages, cartons, and containers intended for export as lend-lease aid, in order to inform people in other countries of the United States' assistance.

During the Korean war, the successful amphibious landing of American troops at Inchon was marked by the raising of an American flag within an hour of the event. Impetus for the enactment of the Federal Flag Desecration Statute in 1967 came from the impact of flag burnings in the United States on troop morale in Vietnam. * * *

The flag symbolizes the Nation in peace as well as in war. It signifies our national presence on battleships, airplanes, military installations, and public buildings from the United States Capitol to the thousands of county courthouses and city halls throughout the country. Two flags are prominently placed in our courtroom. Countless flags are placed by the graves of loved ones each year on what * * * is now called Memorial Day. The flag is traditionally placed on the casket of deceased members of the Armed Forces, and it is later given to the deceased's family. Congress has provided that the flag be flown at half-staff upon the death of the President, Vice President, and other government officials "as a mark of respect to their memory." The flag identifies United States merchant ships, and "[t]he laws of the Union protect our commerce wherever the flag of the country may float."

No other American symbol has been as universally honored as the flag. In 1931, Congress declared ["The Star-Spangled Banner"] to be our national anthem. In 1949, Congress declared June 14th to be Flag Day. In 1987, John Philip Sousa's "The Stars and Stripes Forever" was designated as the national march. Congress has also established "The Pledge of Allegiance to the Flag" and the manner of its deliverance. The flag has appeared as the principal symbol on approximately 33 United States postal stamps and in the design of at least 43 more, more times than any other symbol.

Both Congress and the States have enacted numerous laws regulating misuse of the American flag. Until 1967, Congress left the regulation of misuse of the flag up to the States. Now, however, 18 U.S.C. § 700(a) provides that:

> Whoever knowingly casts contempt upon any flag of the United States by publicly mutilating, defacing, defiling, burning, or trampling upon it shall be fined not more than $1,000 or imprisoned for not more than one year, or both.

Congress has also prescribed, *inter alia*, detailed rules for the design of the flag, the time and occasion of flag's display, the position and manner of its display, respect for the flag, and conduct during hoisting, lowering, and passing of the flag. With the exception of Alaska and Wyoming, all of the States now have statutes prohibiting the burning of the flag. Most of the state statutes are patterned after the Uniform Flag Act of 1917, which * * * provides: "No person shall publicly mutilate, deface, defile, defy, trample upon, or by word or act cast contempt upon any such flag, standard, color, ensign or shield." Most were passed by the States at about the time of World War I.

The American flag, then, throughout more than 200 years of our history, has come to be the visible symbol embodying our Nation. * * *

* * *

Here * * * the public burning of the American flag by Johnson was no essential part of any exposition of ideas, and at the same time it had a tendency to incite a breach of the peace. Johnson was free to make any verbal denunciation of the flag that he wished; indeed, he was free to burn the flag in private. He could publicly burn other symbols of the Government or effigies of political leaders. He did lead a march through the streets of Dallas, and conducted a rally in front of the Dallas City Hall. He engaged in a "die-in" to protest nuclear weapons. He shouted out various slogans during the march, including: "Reagan, Mondale which will it be? Either one means World War III"; "Ronald Reagan, killer of the hour, Perfect example of U.S. power"; and "red, white and blue, we spit on you, you stand for plunder, you will go under." For none of these acts was he arrested or prosecuted; it was only when he proceeded to burn publicly an American flag stolen from its rightful owner that he violated the Texas statute.

* * * Johnson's public burning of the flag in this case * * * convey[ed] Johnson's bitter dislike of his country. But his act * * * conveyed nothing that could not have been conveyed and was not conveyed just as forcefully in a dozen different ways. * * *

The result of the Texas statute is obviously to deny one in Johnson's frame of mind one of many means of "symbolic speech." Far from being a case of "one picture being worth a thousand words," flag burning is the equivalent of an inarticulate grunt or roar that, it seems fair to say, is most likely to be indulged in not to express any particular idea, but to antagonize others. * * * The Texas statute deprived Johnson of only one rather inarticulate symbolic form of protest—a form of protest that was profoundly offensive to many—and left him with a full panoply of other symbols and every conceivable form of verbal expression to express his deep disapproval of national policy. * * *

* * *

* * * The Court decides that the American flag is just another symbol, about which not only must opinions pro and con be tolerated, but for which the most minimal public respect may not be enjoined. The government may conscript men into the Armed Forces where they must fight and perhaps die for the flag, but the government may not prohibit the public burning of the banner under which they fight. I would uphold the Texas statute as applied in this case.

JUSTICE STEVENS, dissenting.

* * *

A country's flag is a symbol of more than "nationhood and national unity." It also signifies the ideas that characterize the society that has chosen that emblem as well as the special history that has animated the growth and power of those ideas. * * *

So it is with the American flag. It is more than a proud symbol of the courage, the determination, and the gifts of nature that transformed 13 fledgling Colonies into a world power. It is a symbol of freedom, of equal opportunity, of religious tolerance, and of good will for other peoples who share our aspirations. The symbol carries its message to dissidents both at home and abroad who may have no interest at all in our national unity or survival.

The value of the flag as a symbol cannot be measured. * * * Conceivably that value will be enhanced by the Court's [decision] * * *. But I am unpersuaded. The creation of a federal right to post bulletin boards and graffiti on the Washington Monument might enlarge the market for free expression, but at a cost I would not pay. Similarly, * * * sanctioning the public desecration of the flag will tarnish its value—both for those who cherish the ideas for which it waves and for those who desire to don the robes of martyrdom by burning it. That tarnish is not justified by the trivial burden on free expression occasioned by requiring that an available, alternative mode of expression—including uttering words critical of the flag—be employed.

* * *

* * * Respondent was prosecuted because of the method he chose to express his dissatisfaction with [the government's] policies. Had he chosen to spray-paint—or perhaps convey with a motion picture projector—his message of dissatisfaction on the facade of the Lincoln Memorial, there would be no question about the power of the Government to prohibit his means of expression. The prohibition would be supported by the legitimate interest in preserving the quality of an important national asset. Though the asset at stake in this case is intangible, given its unique value, the same interest supports a prohibition on the desecration of the American flag.

The ideas of liberty and equality have been an irresistible force in motivating [our leaders and soldiers]. * * * If those ideas are worth fighting for—and our history demonstrates that they are—it cannot be true that the flag that uniquely symbolizes their power is not itself worthy of protection from unnecessary desecration.

I respectfully dissent.

NOTES AND QUESTIONS

1. What arguments did the State of Texas advance for outlawing flag desecration? How did the Supreme Court respond to each argument?

2. Why did the Supreme Court believe that its decision striking down Johnson's conviction on First Amendment grounds would strengthen, not weaken, the flag's special place in the U.S.? Was that portion of the opinion persuasive?

3. Justice Stevens, who dissented, is normally passionate about protecting the First Amendment. For example, he dissented in *Morse v. Frederick* (set forth *infra*). Why did he disagree with the majority's pro-First Amendment holding in *Johnson*? Is his reasoning persuasive? Chief Justice Rehnquist, joined by two other Justices, also dissented. Why did he disagree with the majority? Is his opinion persuasive?

4. In *Snyder v. Phelps*, 562 U.S. 443 (2011), the father of a slain military service member brought suit against the Westboro Baptist Church for protesting at his son's funeral with signs such as "Thank God for Dead Soldiers." The Supreme Court held that this speech was protected: "Given that Westboro's speech was at a public place on a matter of public concern, that speech is entitled to 'special protection' under the First Amendment. Such speech cannot be restricted simply because it is upsetting or arouses contempt." *Id.* at 458. Should this type of speech be protected under the First Amendment? Is the Westboro Baptist Church's speech distinguishable from Johnson's speech? If so, which one is more deserving of First Amendment protection?

5. For further discussion of *Johnson* and flag desecration, *see, e.g.*, D. Wes Sullenger, *Burning the Flag: A Conservative Defense of Radical Speech and Why It Matters Now*, 43 Brandeis L.J. 597 (2005) (discussing the flag as an American symbol and arguing that the Supreme Court chose to permit flag burning only because holding otherwise would have required overturning a substantial body of First Amendment jurisprudence); Norman Dorsen, *Flag Desecration in Courts, Congress, and Country*, 17 T.M. Cooley L. Rev. 417 (2000) (discussing the history of flag-desecration laws in the United States, both before and after *Johnson*, and suggesting that the flag debate and proposals for a constitutional amendment banning flag burning have continued because of the powerful force that patriotism plays in the discussion); Robert Justin Goldstein, *The Great 1989–1990 Flag Flap: An Historical, Political, and Legal Analysis*, 45 U. Miami L. Rev. 19 (1990) (examining the history of flag desecration in the United States and arguing that such desecration is a form of peaceful protest that should have full First Amendment protection).

2. TECHNOLOGY

BROWN V. ENTERTAINMENT MERCHANTS ASS'N

Supreme Court of the United States, 2011
564 U.S. ___, 131 S. Ct. 2729

JUSTICE SCALIA delivered the opinion of the Court.

We consider whether a California law imposing restrictions on violent video games comports with the First Amendment.

I

[The California Civil Code] prohibits the sale or rental of "violent video games" to minors, and requires their packaging to be labeled "18." The Act covers games "in which the range of options available to a player includes killing, maiming, dismembering, or sexually assaulting an image of a human being, if those acts are depicted" in a manner that "[a] reasonable person, considering the game as a whole, would find appeals to a deviant or morbid interest of minors," that is "patently offensive to prevailing standards in the community as to what is suitable for minors," and that "causes the game, as a whole, to lack serious literary, artistic, political, or scientific value for minors." Violation of the [statute] is punishable by a civil fine of up to $1,000.

Respondents, representing the video-game and software industries, brought a preenforcement challenge to the [statute] in the United States District Court for the Northern District of California. That court concluded that the Act violated the First Amendment and permanently enjoined its enforcement. [The Court of Appeals affirmed, and the Supreme Court granted certiorari.]

II

California correctly acknowledges that video games qualify for First Amendment protection. The Free Speech Clause exists principally to protect discourse on public matters, but we have long recognized that it is difficult to distinguish politics from entertainment, and dangerous to try. "Everyone is familiar with instances of propaganda through fiction. What is one man's amusement, teaches another's doctrine." Like the protected books, plays, and movies that preceded them, video games communicate ideas—and even social messages—through many familiar literary devices (such as characters, dialogue, plot, and music) and through features distinctive to the medium (such as the player's interaction with the virtual world). That suffices to confer First Amendment protection. Under our Constitution, "esthetic and moral judgments about art and literature . . . are for the individual to make, not for the Government to decree, even with the mandate or approval of a majority." And whatever the challenges of applying the Constitution to ever-advancing technology, "the basic principles of freedom of speech and the press, like the First Amendment's command, do not vary" when a new and different medium for communication appears.

The most basic of those principles is this: "[A]s a general matter, . . . government has no power to restrict expression because of its message, its ideas, its subject matter, or its content." There are of course exceptions. * * * These limited areas—such as obscenity, incitement, and fighting words—represent "well-defined and narrowly limited classes of speech, the prevention and punishment of which have never been thought to raise any Constitutional problem."

Last Term, in *United States v. Stevens*, 559 U.S. 460 (2010), we held that new categories of unprotected speech may not be added to the list by a legislature that concludes certain speech is too harmful to be tolerated. *Stevens* concerned a federal statute purporting to criminalize the creation, sale, or possession of certain depictions of animal cruelty. The statute covered depictions "in which a living animal is intentionally maimed, mutilated, tortured, wounded, or killed" if that harm to the animal was illegal where the "the creation, sale, or possession t[ook] place." A saving clause largely borrowed from our obscenity jurisprudence, exempted depictions with "serious religious, political, scientific, educational, journalistic, historical, or artistic value." We held that statute to be an impermissible content-based restriction on speech. There was no American tradition of forbidding the *depiction of* animal cruelty—though States have long had laws against *committing* it.

The Government argued in *Stevens* that lack of a historical warrant did not matter; that it could create new categories of unprotected speech by applying a "simple balancing test" that weighs the value of a particular category of speech against its social costs and then punishes that category of speech if it fails the test. We emphatically rejected that "startling and dangerous" proposition. * * * [W]ithout persuasive evidence that a novel restriction on content is part of a long (if heretofore unrecognized) tradition of proscription, a legislature may not revise the "judgment [of] the American people," embodied in the First Amendment, "that the benefits of its restrictions on the Government outweigh the costs."

That holding controls this case. As in *Stevens*, California has tried to make violent-speech regulation look like obscenity regulation by appending a saving clause required for the latter. That does not suffice. Our cases have been clear that the obscenity exception to the First Amendment does not cover whatever a legislature finds shocking, but only depictions of "sexual conduct."

* * *

Because speech about violence is not obscene, it is of no consequence that California's statute mimics the New York statute regulating obscenity-for-minors that we upheld in *Ginsberg v. New York*, 390 U.S. 629 (1968). That case approved a prohibition on the sale to minors of *sexual* material that would be obscene from the perspective of a child. We held that the legislature could "adjus[t] the definition of obscenity 'to social realities by permitting the appeal of this type of material to be assessed in terms of the sexual interests . . . ' of . . . minors." And because "obscenity is not protected expression," the New York statute could be sustained so long as the legislature's judgment that the proscribed materials were harmful to children "was not irrational."

The California [statute] is something else entirely. It does not adjust the boundaries of an existing category of unprotected speech to ensure that a definition designed for adults is not uncritically applied to children. California does not argue that it is empowered to prohibit selling offensively violent works *to adults*—and it is wise not to, since that is but a hair's breadth from the argument rejected in *Stevens*. Instead, it wishes to create a wholly new category of content-based regulation that is permissible only for speech directed at children.

That is unprecedented and mistaken. "[M]inors are entitled to a significant measure of First Amendment protection, and only in relatively narrow and well-defined circumstances may government bar public dissemination of protected materials to them." * * *

California's argument would fare better if there were a longstanding tradition in this country of specially restricting children's access to depictions of violence, but there is none. Certainly the *books* we give children to read—or read to them when they are younger—contain no shortage of gore. Grimm's Fairy Tales, for example, are grim indeed. As her just deserts for trying to poison Snow White, the wicked queen is made to dance in red hot slippers "till she fell dead on the floor, a sad example of envy and jealousy." Cinderella's evil stepsisters have their eyes pecked out by doves. And Hansel and Gretel (children!) kill their captor by baking her in an oven.

High-school reading lists are full of similar fare. Homer's Odysseus blinds Polyphemus the Cyclops by grinding out his eye with a heated stake. In the Inferno, Dante and Virgil watch corrupt politicians struggle to stay submerged beneath a lake of boiling pitch, lest they be skewered by devils above the surface. And Golding's Lord of the Flies recounts how a schoolboy called Piggy is savagely murdered *by other children* while marooned on an island.

This is not to say that minors' consumption of violent entertainment has never encountered resistance. In the 1800's, dime novels depicting crime and "penny dreadfuls" (named for their price and content) were blamed in some quarters for juvenile delinquency. * * * For a time, our Court did permit broad censorship of movies because of their capacity to be "used for evil," but we eventually reversed course. Radio dramas were next, and then came comic books. Many in the late 1940's and early 1950's blamed comic books for fostering a "preoccupation with violence and horror" among the young, leading to a rising juvenile crime rate. But efforts to convince Congress to restrict comic books failed. And, of course, after comic books came television and music lyrics.

California claims that video games present special problems because they are "interactive," in that the player participates in the violent action on screen and determines its outcome. The latter feature is nothing new: Since at least the publication of The Adventures of You: Sugarcane Island in 1969, young readers of choose-your-own-adventure stories have been able to make decisions that determine the plot by following instructions about which page to turn to. As for the argument that video games enable participation in the violent action, that seems to us more a matter of degree than of kind. * * * [A]ll literature is interactive. * * *

Justice ALITO has done considerable independent research to identify video games in which "the violence is astounding." * * * Justice ALITO recounts all these disgusting video games in order to disgust us—but disgust is not a valid basis for restricting expression. * * *

III

Because the Act imposes a restriction on the content of protected speech, it is invalid unless California can demonstrate that it passes strict scrutiny—that is, unless it is justified by a compelling government interest and is narrowly drawn to serve that interest. The State must specifically identify an "actual problem" in need of solving, and the curtailment of free speech must be actually necessary to the solution. That is a demanding standard. * * *

California cannot meet that standard. At the outset, it acknowledges that it cannot show a direct causal link between violent video games and harm to minors. Rather, * * * the State claims that it need not produce such proof because the legislature can make a predictive judgment that such a link exists, based on competing psychological studies. But * * * California * * * bears the risk of uncertainty, [and] ambiguous proof will not suffice.

The State's evidence is not compelling. California relies primarily on the research of Dr. Craig Anderson and a few other research psychologists whose studies purport to show a connection between exposure to violent video games and harmful effects on children. These studies have been rejected by every court to consider them, and with good reason: They do not prove that violent video games *cause* minors to *act* aggressively (which would at least be a beginning). Instead, "[n]early all of the research is based on correlation, not evidence of causation, and most of the studies suffer from significant, admitted flaws in methodology." They show at best some correlation between exposure to violent entertainment and minuscule real-world effects, such as children's feeling more aggressive or making louder noises in the few minutes after playing a violent game than after playing a nonviolent game.

Even taking for granted Dr. Anderson's conclusions that violent video games produce some effect on children's feelings of aggression, those effects are both small and indistinguishable from effects produced by other media. In his testimony in a similar lawsuit, Dr. Anderson admitted that the "effect sizes" of children's exposure to violent video games are "about the same" as that produced by their exposure to violence on television. And he admits that the *same* effects have been found when children watch cartoons starring Bugs Bunny or the Road Runner, or when they play video games like Sonic the Hedgehog that are rated "E" (appropriate for all ages), or even when they "vie[w] a picture of a gun."

Of course, California has (wisely) declined to restrict Saturday morning cartoons, the sale of games rated for young children, or the distribution of pictures of guns. The consequence is that its regulation is wildly underinclusive when judged against its asserted justification, which in our view is alone enough to defeat it. Underinclusiveness raises serious doubts about whether the government is in fact pursuing the interest it invokes, rather than disfavoring a particular speaker or viewpoint. Here, California has singled out the purveyors of video games for disfavored treatment—at least when compared to booksellers, cartoonists, and movie producers—and has given no persuasive reason why.

The Act is also seriously underinclusive in another respect—and a respect that renders irrelevant the contentions of the concurrence and the dissents that video games are qualitatively different from other portrayals of violence. The California Legislature is perfectly willing to leave this dangerous, mind-altering material in the hands of children so long as one parent (or even an aunt or uncle) says it's OK. And there are not even any requirements as to how this parental or avuncular relationship is to be verified; apparently the child's or putative parent's, aunt's, or uncle's say-so suffices. That is not how one addresses a serious social problem.

California claims that the Act is justified in aid of parental authority: By requiring that the purchase of violent video games can be made only by adults, the Act ensures that parents can decide what games are appropriate. At the outset, we note our doubts that punishing third parties for conveying protected speech to children *just in case* their parents disapprove of that speech is a proper governmental means of aiding parental authority. Accepting that position would largely vitiate the rule that "only in relatively narrow and well-defined circumstances may government bar public dissemination of protected materials to [minors]."

But leaving that aside, California cannot show that the Act's restrictions meet a substantial need of parents who wish to restrict their children's access to violent video games but cannot do so. The video-game industry has in place a voluntary rating system designed to inform consumers about the content of games. The system, implemented by the Entertainment Software Rating Board (ESRB), assigns age-specific ratings to each video game submitted: EC (Early Childhood); E (Everyone); E10+ (Everyone 10 and older); T (Teens); M (17 and older); and AO (Adults Only—18 and older). The Video Software Dealers Association encourages retailers to prominently display information about the ESRB system in their stores; to refrain from renting or selling adults-only games to minors; and to rent or sell "M" rated games to minors only with parental consent. In 2009, the Federal Trade Commission (FTC) found that, as a result of this system, "the video game industry outpaces the movie and music industries" in "(1) restricting target-marketing of mature-rated products to children; (2) clearly and prominently disclosing rating information; and (3) restricting children's access to mature-rated products at retail." This system does much to ensure that minors cannot purchase seriously violent games on their own, and that parents who care about the matter can readily evaluate the games their children bring home. Filling the remaining modest gap in concerned-parents' control can hardly be a compelling state interest.

And finally, the Act's purported aid to parental authority is vastly overinclusive. Not all of the children who are forbidden to purchase violent video games on their own have parents who *care* whether they purchase violent video games. While some of the legislation's effect may indeed be in support of what some parents of the restricted children actually want, its entire effect is only in support of what the State thinks parents *ought* to want. This is not the narrow tailoring to "assisting parents" that restriction of First Amendment rights requires.

* * *

California's effort to regulate violent video games is the latest episode in a long series of failed attempts to censor violent entertainment for minors. While we have pointed out above that some of the evidence brought forward to support the harmfulness of video games is unpersuasive, we do not mean to demean or disparage the concerns that underlie the attempt to regulate them—concerns that may and doubtless do prompt a good deal of parental oversight. We have no business passing judgment on the view of the California Legislature that violent video games (or, for that matter, any other forms of speech) corrupt the young or harm their moral development. Our task is only to say whether or not such works constitute a "well-defined and narrowly limited class of speech, the prevention and punishment of which have never been thought to raise any Constitutional problem," (the answer plainly is no); and if not, whether the regulation of such works is justified by that high degree of necessity we have described as a compelling state interest (it is not). Even where the protection of children is the object, the constitutional limits on governmental action apply.

California's legislation straddles the fence between (1) addressing a serious social problem and (2) helping concerned parents control their children. Both ends are legitimate, but when they affect First Amendment rights they must be pursued by means that are neither seriously underinclusive nor seriously overinclusive. * * * California's [l]egislation * * * cannot survive strict scrutiny.

We affirm the judgment below.

* * *

JUSTICE ALITO, with whom THE CHIEF JUSTICE joins, concurring in the judgment.

* * * Although the California statute is well intentioned, its terms are not framed with the precision that the Constitution demands, and I therefore agree with the Court that this particular law cannot be sustained.

I disagree, however, with the approach taken in the Court's opinion. In considering the application of unchanging constitutional principles to new and rapidly evolving technology, this Court should proceed with caution. We should make every effort to understand the new technology. * * * We should not jump to the conclusion that new technology is fundamentally the same as some older thing with which we are familiar. And we should not hastily dismiss the judgment of legislators, who may be in a better position than we are to assess the implications of new technology. The opinion of the Court exhibits none of this caution.

In the view of the Court, all those concerned about the effects of violent video games—federal and state legislators, educators, social scientists, and parents—are unduly fearful, for violent video games really present no serious problem. * * *

The Court is sure of this; I am not. * * *

I

Respondents in this case, representing the video-game industry, ask us to strike down the California law on two grounds: The broad ground adopted by the Court and the narrower ground that the law's definition of "violent video game" is impermissibly vague. Because I agree with the latter argument, I see no need to reach the broader First Amendment issues addressed by the Court.

[Justice Alito concluded that "the California law does not define 'violent video games' with the 'narrow specificity' that the Constitution demands."]

II

* * * I will now briefly elaborate on my reasons for questioning the wisdom of the Court's approach. * * *

A

The Court is wrong in saying that the holding in *United States v. Stevens*, 559 U.S. 460 (2010), "controls this case." First, the statute in *Stevens* differed sharply from the statute at issue here. *Stevens* struck down a law that broadly prohibited *any person* from creating, selling, or possessing depictions of animal cruelty for commercial gain. The California law involved here, by contrast, is limited to the sale or rental of violent video games *to minors*. * * *

Second, *Stevens* does not support the proposition that a law like the one at issue must satisfy strict scrutiny. The portion of *Stevens* on which the Court relies rejected the Government's contention that depictions of animal cruelty were categorically outside the range of *any* First Amendment protection. Going well beyond *Stevens*, the Court now holds that any law that attempts to prevent minors from purchasing violent video games must satisfy strict scrutiny. * * *

Third, *Stevens* expressly left open the possibility that a more narrowly drawn statute targeting depictions of animal cruelty might be compatible with the First Amendment. In this case, the Court's sweeping opinion will likely be read by many, both inside and outside the video-game industry, as suggesting that no regulation of minors' access to violent video games is allowed—at least without supporting evidence that may not be realistically obtainable given the nature of the phenomenon in question.

B

* * * I certainly agree with the Court that the government has no "free-floating power to restrict the ideas to which children may be exposed," but the California law does not exercise such a power. If parents want their child to have a violent video game, the California law does not interfere with that parental prerogative. * * *

* * *

C

Finally, the Court is far too quick to dismiss the possibility that the experience of playing video games (and the effects on minors of playing violent video games) may be very different from anything that we have seen before. * * *

Today's most advanced video games create realistic alternative worlds in which millions of players immerse themselves for hours on end. These games feature visual imagery and sounds that are strikingly realistic, and in the near future video-game graphics may be virtually indistinguishable from actual video footage. Many of the games already on the market can produce high definition images, and it is predicted that it will not be long before video-game images will be seen in three dimensions. It is also forecast that video games will soon provide sensory feedback. By wearing a special vest or other device, a player will be able to experience physical sensations supposedly felt by a character on the screen.* * *

Persons who play video games also have an unprecedented ability to participate in the events that take place in the virtual worlds that these games create. Players can create their own video-game characters and can use photos to produce characters that closely resemble actual people. A person playing a sophisticated game can make a multitude of choices and can thereby alter the course of the action in the game. In addition, the means by which players control the action in video games now bear a closer relationship to the means by which people control action in the real world. While the action in older games was often directed with buttons or a joystick, players dictate the action in newer games by engaging in the same motions that they desire a character in the game to perform. For example, a player who wants a video-game character to swing a baseball bat—either to hit a ball or smash a skull—could bring that about by simulating the motion of actually swinging a bat.

These present-day and emerging characteristics of video games must be considered together with characteristics of the violent games that have already been marketed.

In some of these games, the violence is astounding. Victims by the dozens are killed with every imaginable implement, including machine guns, shotguns, clubs, hammers, axes, swords, and chainsaws. Victims are dismembered, decapitated, disemboweled, set on fire, and chopped into little pieces. They cry out in agony and beg for mercy. Blood gushes, splatters, and pools. Severed body parts and gobs of human remains are graphically shown. In some games, points are awarded based, not only on the number of victims killed, but on the killing technique employed.

It also appears that there is no antisocial theme too base for some in the video-game industry to exploit. There are games in which a player can take on the identity and reenact the killings carried out by the perpetrators of the murders at Columbine High School and Virginia Tech. The objective of one game is to rape a mother and her daughters; in another, the goal is to rape Native American women. There is a game in which players engage in "ethnic cleansing" and can choose to gun down African-Americans, Latinos, or Jews. In still another game, players attempt to fire a rifle shot into the head of President Kennedy as his motorcade passes by the Texas School Book Depository.

* * *

When all of the characteristics of video games are taken into account, there is certainly a reasonable basis for thinking that the experience of playing a video game may be quite different from the experience of reading a book, listening to a radio broadcast, or viewing a movie. And if this is so, then for at least some minors, the effects of playing violent video games may also be quite different. The Court acts prematurely in dismissing this possibility out of hand.

* * *

For all these reasons, I would hold only that the particular law at issue here fails to provide the clear notice that the Constitution requires. I would not squelch legislative efforts to deal with what is perceived by some to be a significant and developing social problem. * * *

JUSTICE THOMAS, dissenting.

The Court's decision today does not comport with the original public understanding of the First Amendment. * * * The practices and beliefs of the founding generation establish that "the freedom of speech," as originally understood, does not include a right to speak to minors (or a right of minors to access speech) without going through the minors' parents or guardians. I would hold that the law at issue is not facially unconstitutional under the First Amendment * * *.

* * *

JUSTICE BREYER, dissenting.

* * * I would uphold the statute as constitutional on its face and would consequently reject the industries' facial challenge.

* * *

II

In my view, California's statute provides "fair notice of what is prohibited," and consequently it is not impermissibly vague. * * *

* * *

III

Video games combine physical action with expression. Were physical activity to predominate in a game, government could appropriately intervene, say by requiring parents to accompany children when playing a game involving actual target practice, or restricting the sale of toys presenting physical dangers to children. But because video games also embody important expressive and artistic elements, I agree with the Court that the First Amendment significantly limits the State's power to regulate. And I would determine whether the State has exceeded those limits by applying a strict standard of review.

* * *

A

California's law imposes no more than a modest restriction on expression. The statute prevents no one from playing a video game, it prevents no adult from buying a video game, and it prevents no child or adolescent from obtaining a game provided a parent is willing to help. All it prevents is a child or adolescent from buying, without a parent's assistance, a gruesomely violent video game of a kind that the industry *itself* tells us it wants to keep out of the hands of those under the age of 17.

Nor is the statute, if upheld, likely to create a precedent that would adversely affect other media, say films, or videos, or books. A typical video game involves a significant amount of physical activity. And pushing buttons that achieve an interactive, virtual form of target practice (using images of human beings as targets), while containing an expressive component, is not just like watching a typical movie.

B

* * *

* * * [T]here is considerable evidence that California's statute significantly furthers [a] compelling interest. That is, in part, because video games are excellent teaching tools. Learning a practical task often means developing habits, becoming accustomed to performing the task, and receiving positive reinforcement when performing that task well. Video games can help develop habits, accustom the player to performance of the task, and reward the player for performing that task well. Why else would the Armed Forces incorporate video games into its training?

When the military uses video games to help soldiers train for missions, it is using this medium for a beneficial purpose. But California argues that when the teaching features of video games are put to less desirable ends, harm can ensue. In particular, extremely violent games can harm children by rewarding them for being violently aggressive in play, and thereby often teaching them to be violently aggressive in life. And video games can cause more harm in this respect than can typically passive media, such as books or films or television programs.

There are many scientific studies that support California's views. Social scientists, for example, have found *causal* evidence that playing these games results in harm. Longitudinal studies, which measure changes over time, have found that increased exposure to violent video games causes an increase in aggression over the same period.

Experimental studies in laboratories have found that subjects randomly assigned to play a violent video game subsequently displayed more characteristics of aggression than those who played nonviolent games.

Surveys of 8th and 9th grade students have found a correlation between playing violent video games and aggression.

Cutting-edge neuroscience has shown that "virtual violence in video game playing results in those neural patterns that are considered characteristic for aggressive cognition and behavior."

And "meta-analyses," *i.e.*, studies of all the studies, have concluded that exposure to violent video games "was positively associated with aggressive behavior, aggressive cognition, and aggressive affect," and that "playing violent video games is a *causal* risk factor for long-term harmful outcomes."

Some of these studies take care to explain in a commonsense way why video games are potentially more harmful than, say, films or books or television. In essence, they say that the closer a child's behavior comes, not to watching, but to *acting* out horrific violence, the greater the potential psychological harm.

Experts debate the conclusions of all these studies. Like many, perhaps most, studies of human behavior, each study has its critics, and some of those critics have produced studies of their own in which they reach different conclusions. * * * But associations of public health professionals who do possess that expertise have reviewed many of these studies and found a significant risk that violent video games, when compared with more passive media, are particularly likely to cause children harm.

* * *

C

I can find no "less restrictive" alternative to California's law that would be "at least as effective." The majority points to a voluntary alternative: The industry tries to prevent those under 17 from buying extremely violent games by labeling those games with an "M" (Mature) and encouraging retailers to restrict their sales to those 17 and older. But this voluntary system has serious enforcement gaps. When California enacted its law, a Federal Trade Commission (FTC) study had found that nearly 70% of unaccompanied 13- to 16-year-olds were able to buy M-rated video games. Subsequently the voluntary program has become more effective. But as of the FTC's most recent update to Congress, 20% of those under 17 are still able to buy M-rated video games * * *.

* * *

IV

The upshot is that California's statute, as applied to its heartland of applications (*i.e.*, buyers under 17; extremely violent, realistic video games), imposes a restriction on speech that is modest at most. That restriction is justified by a compelling interest (supplementing parents' efforts to prevent their children from purchasing potentially harmful violent, interactive material). And there is no equally effective, less restrictive alternative. * * *

* * *

* * * Education * * * is about choices. Sometimes, children need to learn by making choices for themselves. Other times, choices are made for children—by their parents, by their teachers, and by the people acting democratically through their governments. In my view, the First Amendment does not disable government from helping parents make such a choice here—a choice not to have their children buy extremely violent, interactive video games, which they more than reasonably fear pose only the risk of harm to those children.

For these reasons, I respectfully dissent.

NOTES AND QUESTIONS

1.   What is the basis for the respondents' argument in *Brown* that California's restrictions on violent video games violated the First Amendment?

2.   Given that the State of California agreed that video games are entitled to First Amendment protection, what was its argument for why the

California statute did not violate the First Amendment? Was the State of California wise to concede that the First Amendment applied to video games?

3.   How did the Court rule? How does the approach of Justice Alito in his concurring opinion (joined by the Chief Justice) differ from that of the majority? Why does Justice Thomas dissent? Why does Justice Breyer dissent? (Note that Justice Thomas, a conservative, is on the opposite end of the political spectrum from Justice Breyer, a liberal.) Which of the four opinions is most persuasive?

4.   For scholarly discussion of *Brown* and the treatment of video games under the First Amendment, *see* Jessica Fisher, Brown v. Entertainment Merchants Association*: "Modern Warfare" on First Amendment Protection of Violent Video Games*, 8 J. Bus. & Tech. L. 525 (2013) (arguing that speech in video games cannot be analyzed like speech in other forms of media and that the Supreme Court in *Brown* should have deferred to the legislature); William Lee, *Books, Video Games, and Foul-Mouthed Hollywood Glitteratae: The Supreme Court and the Technology-Neutral Interpretation of the First Amendment*, 14 Colum. Sci. & Tech. L. Rev. 295 (2013) (arguing that *Brown* correctly focused on the regulation of violent content in general, rather than on the unique qualities of video games).

5.   In addition to the video game context, the intersection of the First Amendment and technology also arises in the context of social media. For example, in *People v. Marquan M.*, 24 N.Y.3d 1, 19 N.E.3d 1 (2014), a high school student posted offensive information about other students on Facebook. The student who did the posting was prosecuted under a local law that addressed "cyberbullying." The defendant student challenged the law, arguing that it violated the First Amendment's Free Speech Clause because it was overly broad and included protected expression. New York's highest court recognized that the government has a compelling interest in preventing online bullying and that the online forum presents unique challenges:

> There is undoubtedly general consensus that defendant's Facebook communications were repulsive and harmful to the subjects of his rants, and potentially created a risk of physical or emotional injury based on the private nature of the comments. He identified specific adolescents with photographs, described their purported sexual practices and posted the information on a website accessible world-wide. Unlike traditional bullying, which usually takes place by a face-to-face encounter, defendant used the advantages of the internet to attack his victims from a safe distance, 24 hours a day, while cloaked in anonymity.

Id. at 12. Nonetheless, the court held that the law was unconstitutional because it also applied to non-bullying behavior and to online communications involving adults.

In *Elonis v. United States*, 575 U.S. ___, 135 S. Ct. 2001 (2015), the U.S. Supreme Court reversed a criminal prosecution for posting death threats on Facebook because of an erroneous jury instruction. Given its disposition of the case, it did not address any First Amendment issues. Such issues are certain to arise, however, in future cases involving criminal prosecutions for postings on social media websites.

3. OFFENSIVE SPEECH

HUSTLER MAGAZINE, INC. V. FALWELL
Supreme Court of the United States, 1988
485 U.S. 46

CHIEF JUSTICE REHNQUIST delivered the opinion of the Court.

Petitioner Hustler Magazine, Inc., is a magazine of nationwide circulation. Respondent Jerry Falwell, a nationally known minister who has been active as a commentator on politics and public affairs, sued petitioner and its publisher, petitioner Larry Flynt, to recover damages for invasion of privacy, libel, and intentional infliction of emotional distress. The District Court directed a verdict against respondent on the privacy claim, and submitted the other two claims to a jury. The jury found for petitioners on the defamation claim, but found for respondent on the claim for intentional infliction of emotional distress and awarded damages. We now consider whether this award is consistent with the First and Fourteenth Amendments of the United States Constitution.

The inside front cover of the November 1983 issue of Hustler Magazine featured a "parody" of an advertisement for Campari Liqueur that contained the name and picture of respondent and was entitled "Jerry Falwell talks about his first time." This parody was modeled after actual Campari ads that included interviews with various celebrities about their "first times." Although it was apparent by the end of each interview that this meant the first time they sampled Campari, the ads clearly played on the sexual double entendre of the general subject of "first times." Copying the form and layout of these Campari ads, Hustler's editors chose respondent as the featured celebrity and drafted an alleged "interview" with him in which he states that his "first time" was during a drunken incestuous rendezvous with his mother in an outhouse. The Hustler parody portrays respondent and his mother as drunk and immoral, and suggests that respondent is a hypocrite who preaches only when he is drunk. In small print at the bottom of the page, the ad contains the disclaimer, "ad parody—not to be taken seriously." The magazine's table of contents also lists the ad as "Fiction; Ad and Personality Parody."

Soon after the November issue of Hustler became available to the public, respondent brought this diversity action in the United States District Court for the Western District of Virginia against Hustler Magazine, Inc., Larry C. Flynt, and Flynt Distributing Co., Inc. Respondent stated in his complaint that publication of the ad parody in Hustler entitled him to recover damages for libel, invasion of privacy, and intentional infliction of emotional distress. The case proceeded to trial. At the close of the evidence, the District Court granted a directed verdict for petitioners on the invasion of privacy claim. The jury then found against respondent on the libel claim, specifically finding that the ad parody could not "reasonably be understood as describing actual facts about [respondent] or actual events in which [he] participated." The jury ruled for respondent on the intentional infliction of emotional distress claim, however, and stated that he should be awarded $100,000 in compensatory damages, as well as $50,000 each in punitive damages from petitioners. * * *

On appeal, the United States Court of Appeals for the Fourth Circuit affirmed the judgment against petitioners. * * * Given the importance of the constitutional issues involved, we granted certiorari.

This case presents us with a novel question involving First Amendment limitations upon a State's authority to protect its citizens from the intentional infliction of emotional distress. We must decide whether a public figure may recover damages for emotional harm caused by the publication of an ad parody offensive to him, and doubtless gross and repugnant in the eyes of most. Respondent would have us find that a State's interest in protecting public figures from emotional distress is sufficient to deny First Amendment protection to speech that is patently offensive and is intended to inflict emotional injury, even when that speech could not reasonably have been interpreted as stating actual facts about the public figure involved. This we decline to do.

At the heart of the First Amendment is the recognition of the fundamental importance of the free flow of ideas and opinions on matters of public interest and concern. * * *

The sort of robust political debate encouraged by the First Amendment is bound to produce speech that is critical of those who hold public office or those public figures who are "intimately involved in the resolution of important public questions or, by reason of their fame, shape events in areas of concern to society at large." * * *

Of course, this does not mean that *any* speech about a public figure is immune from sanction in the form of damages. Since *New York Times Co. v. Sullivan,* [376 U.S. 254 (1964)], we have consistently ruled that a public figure may hold a speaker liable for the damage to reputation caused by publication of a defamatory falsehood, but only if the statement was made "with knowledge that it was false or with reckless disregard of whether it was false or not." * * *

Respondent argues, however, that a different standard should apply in this case because here the State seeks to prevent not reputational damage, but the severe emotional distress suffered by the person who is the subject of an offensive publication. In respondent's view, and in the view of the Court of Appeals, so long as the utterance was intended to inflict emotional distress, was outrageous, and did in fact inflict serious emotional distress, it is of no constitutional import whether the statement was a fact or an opinion, or whether it was true or false. * * *

Generally speaking[,] the law does not regard the intent to inflict emotional distress as one which should receive much solicitude, and it is quite understandable that most if not all jurisdictions have chosen to make it civilly culpable where the conduct in question is sufficiently "outrageous." But in the world of debate about public affairs, many things done with motives that are less than admirable are protected by the First Amendment. In *Garrison v. Louisiana*, 379 U.S. 64 (1964), we held that even when a speaker or writer is motivated by hatred or ill will his expression was protected by the First Amendment[.] * * *

Thus while such a bad motive may be deemed controlling for purposes of tort liability in other areas of the law, we think the First Amendment prohibits such a result in the area of public debate about public figures.

Were we to hold otherwise, there can be little doubt that political cartoonists and satirists would be subjected to damages awards without any showing that their work falsely defamed its subject. Webster's defines a caricature as "the deliberately distorted picturing or imitating of a person, literary style, etc. by exaggerating features or mannerisms for satirical effect." The appeal of the political cartoon or caricature is often based on exploitation of unfortunate physical traits or politically embarrassing events—an exploitation often calculated to injure the feelings of the subject of the portrayal. The art of the cartoonist is often not reasoned or evenhanded, but slashing and one-sided. * * *

* * *

* * * [F]rom the early cartoon portraying George Washington as an ass down to the present day, graphic depictions and satirical cartoons have played a prominent role in public and political debate. Nast's castigation of the Tweed Ring, Walt McDougall's characterization of presidential candidate James G. Blaine's banquet with the millionaires at Delmonico's as "The Royal Feast of Belshazzar," and numerous other efforts have undoubtedly had an effect on the course and outcome of contemporaneous debate. Lincoln's tall, gangling posture, Teddy Roosevelt's glasses and teeth, and Franklin D. Roosevelt's jutting jaw and cigarette holder have been memorialized by political cartoons with an effect that could not have been obtained by the photographer or the portrait artist. From the viewpoint of history it is clear that our political discourse would have been considerably poorer without them.

Respondent contends, however, that the caricature in question here was so "outrageous" as to distinguish it from more traditional political cartoons. * * * "Outrageousness" in the area of political and social discourse has an inherent subjectiveness about it which would allow a jury to impose liability on the basis of the jurors' tastes or views, or perhaps on the basis of their dislike of a particular expression. An "outrageousness" standard thus runs afoul of our longstanding refusal to allow damages to be awarded because the speech in question may have an adverse emotional impact on the audience. * * *

* * *

We conclude that public figures and public officials may not recover for the tort of intentional infliction of emotional distress by reason of publications such as the one here at issue without showing in addition that the publication contains a false statement of fact which was made with "actual malice," *i.e.*, with knowledge that the statement was false or with reckless disregard as to whether or not it was true. This is not merely a "blind application" of the *New York Times* standard, it reflects our considered judgment that such a standard is necessary to give adequate "breathing space" to the freedoms protected by the First Amendment.

Here it is clear that respondent Falwell is a "public figure" for purposes of First Amendment law. * * * [F]or reasons heretofore stated [his intentional infliction of emotional distress] claim cannot, consistently with the First Amendment, form a basis for the award of damages when the conduct in question is the publication of a caricature such as the ad parody involved here. The judgment of the Court of Appeals is accordingly

Reversed.

[Concurring opinion by JUSTICE WHITE is omitted.]

NOTES AND QUESTIONS

1.   Why did Hustler Magazine create a fictitious advertisement portraying Jerry Falwell in a negative light? Did Hustler intend for its readers to take the ad seriously?

2.   Both the district court and the court of appeals agreed that it was appropriate to award damages to Jerry Falwell for intentional infliction of emotional distress. Why did the Supreme Court unanimously disagree with the lower courts?

3.   The Supreme Court treated Jerry Falwell as a public figure. Why did it do so? Was that treatment important to the Supreme Court's holding in the case?

4.   Was the Supreme Court correct in shielding Hustler Magazine from liability for intentionally injurious speech? Is it surprising that the Court's decision was unanimous—gaining the votes of both liberals and conservatives?

5.   For additional reading on *Falwell* and related concepts, *see, e.g.*, Sandra Davidson Scott, *From Satirical to Satyrical: When Is A Joke Actionable?*, 13 Hastings Comm. & Ent. L.J. 141 (1991) (arguing that statements can be damaging, and should be actionable, even if they cannot

reasonably be interpreted as true); Robert Post, *The Constitutional Concept of Public Discourse: Outrageous Opinion, Democratic Deliberation, and* Hustler Magazine v. Falwell, 103 Harv. L. Rev. 601 (1990) (discussing *Falwell* and concluding that the boundaries of public discourse are in constant flux based on the competing influences of community values, the practical purpose of speech as an instrumentality, and the traditional public discourse purpose of freedom of interaction).

6. For a realistic portrayal of the Supreme Court oral argument in *Falwell, see* the movie THE PEOPLE VS. LARRY FLYNT (Columbia Pictures Corp. 1996).

4. SCHOOLS

MORSE V. FREDERICK
Supreme Court of the United States, 2007
551 U.S. 393

CHIEF JUSTICE ROBERTS delivered the opinion of the Court.

At a school-sanctioned and school-supervised event, a high school principal saw some of her students unfurl a large banner conveying a message she reasonably regarded as promoting illegal drug use. Consistent with established school policy prohibiting such messages at school events, the principal directed the students to take down the banner. One student— among those who had brought the banner to the event—refused to do so. The principal confiscated the banner and later suspended the student. The Ninth Circuit held that the principal's actions violated the First Amendment, and that the student could sue the principal for damages.

Our cases make clear that students do not "shed their constitutional rights to freedom of speech or expression at the schoolhouse gate." At the same time, we have held that "the constitutional rights of students in public school are not automatically coextensive with the rights of adults in other settings," and that the rights of students "must be 'applied in light of the special characteristics of the school environment.'" Consistent with these principles, we * * * conclude that the school officials in this case did not violate the First Amendment by confiscating the pro-drug banner and suspending the student responsible for it.

I

On January 24, 2002, the Olympic Torch Relay passed through Juneau, Alaska, on its way to the winter games in Salt Lake City, Utah. The torchbearers were to proceed along a street in front of Juneau-Douglas High School (JDHS) while school was in session. Petitioner Deborah Morse, the school principal, decided to permit staff and students to participate in the Torch Relay as an approved social event or class trip. Students were allowed to leave class to observe the relay from either side of the street. Teachers and administrative officials monitored the students' actions.

Respondent Joseph Frederick, a JDHS senior, was late to school that day. When he arrived, he joined his friends (all but one of whom were JDHS students) across the street from the school to watch the event. Not all the students waited patiently. Some became rambunctious, throwing plastic cola bottles and snowballs and scuffling with their classmates. As the torchbearers and camera crews passed by, Frederick and his friends unfurled a 14-foot banner bearing the phrase: "BONG HiTS 4 JESUS." The large banner was easily readable by the students on the other side of the street.

Principal Morse immediately crossed the street and demanded that the banner be taken down. Everyone but Frederick complied. Morse confiscated the banner and told Frederick to report to her office, where she suspended him for 10 days. Morse later explained that she told Frederick to take the banner down because she thought it encouraged illegal drug use, in violation of established school policy. Juneau School Board Policy No. 5520 states: "The Board specifically prohibits any assembly or public expression that . . . advocates the use of substances that are illegal to minors. . . ." In addition, Juneau School Board Policy No. 5850 subjects "[p]upils who participate in approved social events and class trips" to the same student conduct rules that apply during the regular school program.

Frederick administratively appealed his suspension, but the Juneau School District Superintendent upheld it, limiting it to time served (eight days). In a memorandum setting forth his reasons, the superintendent determined that Frederick had displayed his banner "in the midst of his fellow students, during school hours, at a school-sanctioned activity." He further explained that Frederick "was not disciplined because the principal of the school 'disagreed' with his message, but because his speech appeared to advocate the use of illegal drugs."

The superintendent continued:

> The common-sense understanding of the phrase 'bong hits' is that it is a reference to a means of smoking marijuana. Given [Frederick's] inability or unwillingness to express any other credible meaning for the phrase, I can only agree with the principal and countless others who saw the banner as advocating the use of illegal drugs. * * *

* * * [T]he superintendent concluded that the principal's actions were permissible because Frederick's banner was "speech or action that intrudes upon the work of the schools." The Juneau School District Board of Education upheld the suspension.

Frederick then filed suit under 42 U.S.C. § 1983, alleging that the school board and Morse had violated his First Amendment rights. He sought declaratory and injunctive relief, unspecified compensatory damages, punitive damages, and attorney's fees. The District Court granted summary judgment for the school board and Morse * * *. The court found that Morse reasonably interpreted the banner as promoting illegal drug use * * * [and thus] " * * * had the authority, if not the obligation, to stop such messages at a school-sanctioned activity."

The Ninth Circuit reversed. [It] * * * found a violation of Frederick's First Amendment rights because the school punished Frederick without demonstrating that his speech gave rise to a "risk of substantial disruption." * * *

We granted certiorari. * * *

II

At the outset, we reject Frederick's argument that this is not a school speech case—as has every other authority to address the question. The event occurred during normal school hours. It was sanctioned by Principal Morse "as an approved social event or class trip," and the school district's rules expressly provide that pupils in "approved social events and class trips are subject to district rules for student conduct." Teachers and administrators were interspersed among the students and charged with supervising them. The high school band and cheerleaders performed. Frederick, standing among other JDHS students across the street from the school, directed his banner toward the school, making it plainly visible to most students. Under these circumstances, * * * Frederick cannot "stand in the midst of his fellow students, during school hours, at a school-sanctioned activity and claim he is not at school." * * *

III

The message on Frederick's banner is cryptic. It is no doubt offensive to some, perhaps amusing to others. To still others, it probably means nothing at all. Frederick himself claimed "that the words were just nonsense meant to attract television cameras." But Principal Morse thought the banner would be interpreted by those viewing it as promoting illegal drug use, and that interpretation is plainly a reasonable one.

As Morse later explained in a declaration, when she saw the sign, she thought that "the reference to a 'bong hit' would be widely understood by high school students and others as referring to smoking marijuana." She further believed that "display of the banner would be construed by students, District personnel, parents and others witnessing the display of the banner, as advocating or promoting illegal drug use"—in violation of school policy. * * *

We agree with Morse. At least two interpretations of the words on the banner demonstrate that the sign advocated the use of illegal drugs. First, the phrase could be interpreted as an imperative: "[Take] bong hits . . ."—

a message equivalent, as Morse explained in her declaration, to "smoke marijuana" or "use an illegal drug." Alternatively, the phrase could be viewed as celebrating drug use—"bong hits [are a good thing]," or "[we take] bong hits"—and we discern no meaningful distinction between celebrating illegal drug use in the midst of fellow students and outright advocacy or promotion.

The pro-drug interpretation of the banner gains further plausibility given the paucity of alternative meanings the banner might bear. The best Frederick can come up with is that the banner is "meaningless and funny." The dissent similarly refers to the sign's message as "curious," "ambiguous," "nonsense," "ridiculous," "obscure," "silly," "quixotic," and "stupid." Gibberish is surely a possible interpretation of the words on the banner, but it is not the only one, and dismissing the banner as meaningless ignores its undeniable reference to illegal drugs.

The dissent mentions Frederick's "credible and uncontradicted explanation for the message—he just wanted to get on television." But that is a description of Frederick's *motive* for displaying the banner; it is not an interpretation of what the banner says. The *way* Frederick was going to fulfill his ambition of appearing on television was by unfurling a pro-drug banner at a school event, in the presence of teachers and fellow students.

Elsewhere in its opinion, the dissent emphasizes the importance of political speech * * *. But not even Frederick argues that the banner conveys any sort of political or religious message. Contrary to the dissent's suggestion, this is plainly not a case about political debate over the criminalization of drug use or possession.

IV

The question thus becomes whether a principal may, consistent with the First Amendment, restrict student speech at a school event, when that speech is reasonably viewed as promoting illegal drug use. We hold that she may.

In *Tinker* [*v. Des Moines Independent Community School Dist.*, 393 U.S. 503 (1969)], this Court made clear that "First Amendment rights, applied in light of the special characteristics of the school environment, are available to teachers and students." *Tinker* involved a group of high school students who decided to wear black armbands to protest the Vietnam War. School officials learned of the plan and then adopted a policy prohibiting students from wearing armbands. When several students nonetheless wore armbands to school, they were suspended. The students sued, claiming that their First Amendment rights had been violated, and this Court agreed.

Tinker held that student expression may not be suppressed unless school officials reasonably conclude that it will "materially and substantially disrupt the work and discipline of the school." The essential facts of *Tinker* are quite stark * * *. The students sought to engage in political speech, using the armbands to express their "disapproval of the Vietnam hostilities and their advocacy of a truce, to make their views known, and, by their example, to influence others to adopt them." Political speech, of course, is "at the core of what the First Amendment is designed to protect." The only interest the Court discerned underlying the school's actions was the "mere desire to avoid the discomfort and unpleasantness that always accompany an unpopular viewpoint," or "an urgent wish to avoid the controversy which might result from the expression." That interest was not enough to justify banning "a silent, passive expression of opinion, unaccompanied by any disorder or disturbance."

This Court's next student speech case was [*Bethel School Dist. No. 403 v.*] *Fraser*, 478 U.S. 675 [(1986)]. Matthew Fraser was suspended for delivering a speech before a high school assembly in which he employed what this Court called "an elaborate, graphic, and explicit sexual metaphor." Analyzing the case under *Tinker*, the District Court and Court of Appeals found no disruption, and therefore no basis for disciplining Fraser. This Court reversed, holding that the "School District acted entirely within its permissible authority in imposing sanctions upon Fraser in response to his offensively lewd and indecent speech."

* * *

We * * * distill from *Fraser* two basic principles. First, *Fraser's* holding demonstrates that "the constitutional rights of students in public school are not automatically coextensive with the rights of adults in other settings." Had Fraser delivered the same speech in a public forum outside the school context, it would have been protected. In school, however, Fraser's First Amendment rights were circumscribed * * *. Second, *Fraser* established that the mode of analysis set forth in *Tinker* is not absolute. Whatever approach *Fraser* employed, it certainly did not conduct the "substantial disruption" analysis prescribed by *Tinker*.

Our most recent student speech case, *Hazelwood School Dist. v. Kuhlmeier*, 484 U.S. 260 (1988), concerned "expressive activities that students, parents, and members of the public might reasonably perceive to bear the imprimatur of the school." Staff members of a high school newspaper sued their school when it chose not to publish two of their articles. * * * This Court [held] that "educators do not offend the First Amendment by exercising editorial control over the style and content of student speech in school-sponsored expressive activities so long as their actions are reasonably related to legitimate pedagogical concerns."

Kuhlmeier does not control this case because no one would reasonably believe that Frederick's banner bore the school's imprimatur. The case is nevertheless instructive because * * * *Kuhlmeier* acknowledged that schools may regulate some speech "even though the government could not censor similar speech outside the school." And, like *Fraser*, it confirms that the rule of *Tinker* is not the only basis for restricting student speech.

Drawing on the principles applied in our student speech cases, we have held in the Fourth Amendment context that "while children assuredly do not 'shed their constitutional rights . . . at the schoolhouse gate,' . . . the nature of those rights is what is appropriate for children in school." In particular, "the school setting requires some easing of the restrictions to which searches by public authorities are ordinarily subject."

Even more to the point, these cases also recognize that deterring drug use by schoolchildren is an "important—indeed, perhaps compelling" interest. Drug abuse can cause severe and permanent damage to the health and well-being of young people[.]

* * *

The problem remains serious today. About half of American 12th graders have used an illicit drug, as have more than a third of 10th graders and about one-fifth of 8th graders. Nearly one in four 12th graders has used an illicit drug in the past month. Some 25% of high schoolers say that they have been offered, sold, or given an illegal drug on school property within the past year.

Congress has declared that part of a school's job is educating students about the dangers of illegal drug use. It has provided billions of dollars to support state and local drug-prevention programs, and required that schools receiving federal funds * * * certify that their drug-prevention programs "convey a clear and consistent message that . . . the illegal use of drugs [is] wrong and harmful."

Thousands of school boards throughout the country—including JDHS—have adopted policies aimed at effectuating this message. Those school boards know that peer pressure is perhaps "the single most important factor leading schoolchildren to take drugs," and that students are more likely to use drugs when the norms in school appear to tolerate such behavior. Student speech celebrating illegal drug use at a school event, in the presence of school administrators and teachers, thus poses a particular challenge for school officials working to protect those entrusted to their care from the dangers of drug abuse.

The "special characteristics of the school environment," and the governmental interest in stopping student drug abuse—reflected in the policies of Congress and myriad school boards, including JDHS—allow schools to restrict student expression that they reasonably regard as promoting illegal drug use. * * *

Petitioners urge us to adopt the broader rule that Frederick's speech is proscribable because it is plainly "offensive" as that term is used in *Fraser*. We think this stretches *Fraser* too far; that case should not be read to encompass any speech that could fit under some definition of "offensive." After all, much political and religious speech might be perceived as offensive to some. The concern here is not that Frederick's speech was offensive, but that it was reasonably viewed as promoting illegal drug use.

* * *

School principals have a difficult job, and a vitally important one. When Frederick suddenly and unexpectedly unfurled his banner, Morse had to decide to act—or not act—on the spot. It was reasonable for her to conclude that the banner promoted illegal drug use—in violation of established school policy—and that failing to act would send a powerful message to the students in her charge, including Frederick, about how serious the school was about the dangers of illegal drug use. The First Amendment does not require schools to tolerate at school events student expression that contributes to those dangers.

The judgment of the United States Court of Appeals for the Ninth Circuit is reversed, and the case is remanded for further proceedings consistent with this opinion.

It is so ordered.

[Concurring opinion by JUSTICE THOMAS is omitted.]

[Concurring opinion by JUSTICE ALITO, joined by JUSTICE KENNEDY, is omitted.]

[Concurring and dissenting opinion by JUSTICE BREYER is omitted.]

JUSTICE STEVENS, with whom JUSTICE SOUTER and JUSTICE GINSBURG join, dissenting.

A significant fact barely mentioned by the Court sheds a revelatory light on the motives of both the students and the principal of Juneau-Douglas High School (JDHS). On January 24, 2002, the Olympic Torch Relay gave those Alaska residents a rare chance to appear on national television. As Joseph Frederick repeatedly explained, he did not address the curious message—"BONG HiTS 4 JESUS"—to his fellow students. He just wanted to get the camera crews' attention. Moreover, concern about a nationwide evaluation of the conduct of the JDHS student body would have justified the principal's decision to remove an attention-grabbing 14-foot banner, even if it had merely proclaimed "Glaciers Melt!"

* * * I would hold * * * that the school's interest in protecting its students from exposure to speech "reasonably regarded as promoting illegal drug use" cannot justify disciplining Frederick for his attempt to make an ambiguous statement to a television audience simply because it contained an oblique reference to drugs. The First Amendment demands more, indeed, much more.

The Court holds otherwise only after laboring to establish two uncontroversial propositions: first, that the constitutional rights of students in school settings are not coextensive with the rights of adults, and second, that deterring drug use by schoolchildren is a valid and terribly important interest. As to the first, I take the Court's point that the message on Frederick's banner is not *necessarily* protected speech, even though it unquestionably would have been had the banner been unfurled elsewhere. As to the second, I am willing to assume that the Court is correct that the pressing need to deter drug use supports JDHS' rule prohibiting willful conduct that expressly "advocates the use of substances that are illegal to minors." But it is a gross non sequitur to draw from these two unremarkable propositions the remarkable conclusion that the school may suppress student speech that was never meant to persuade anyone to do anything.

In my judgment, the First Amendment protects student speech if the message itself neither violates a permissible rule nor expressly advocates conduct that is illegal and harmful to students. This nonsense banner does neither, and the Court does serious violence to the First Amendment in upholding—indeed, lauding—a school's decision to punish Frederick for expressing a view with which it disagreed.

I

In December 1965, we were engaged in a controversial war, a war that "divided this country as few other issues ever have." Having learned that some students planned to wear black armbands as a symbol of opposition to the country's involvement in Vietnam, officials of the Des Moines public school district adopted a policy calling for the suspension of any student who refused to remove the armband. * * * Because the school officials had insufficient reason to believe that those disturbances would "materially and substantially interfere with the requirements of appropriate discipline in the operation of the school," we found [in *Tinker*] the justification for the rule to lack any foundation and therefore held that the censorship violated the First Amendment.

* * *

[Under *Tinker*] censorship based on the content of speech, particularly censorship that depends on the viewpoint of the speaker, is subject to the most rigorous burden of justification.

* * *

Yet today the Court fashions a test that trivializes [*Tinker.*] The Court's test invites stark viewpoint discrimination. In this case, for example, the principal has unabashedly acknowledged that she disciplined Frederick because she disagreed with the pro-drug viewpoint she ascribed to the message on the banner, a viewpoint, incidentally, that Frederick has disavowed. * * *

It is also perfectly clear that "promoting illegal drug use," comes nowhere close to proscribable "incitement to imminent lawless action." Encouraging drug use might well increase the likelihood that a listener will try an illegal drug, but that hardly justifies censorship.

* * *

No one seriously maintains that drug advocacy (much less Frederick's ridiculous sign) comes within the vanishingly small category of speech that can be prohibited because of its feared consequences.

II

The Court rejects outright these twin foundations of *Tinker* because, in its view, the unusual importance of protecting children from the scourge of drugs supports a ban on all speech in the school environment that promotes drug use. Whether or not such a rule is sensible as a matter of policy, carving out pro-drug speech for uniquely harsh treatment finds no support in our case law and is inimical to the values protected by the First Amendment.

* * * Given that the relationship between schools and students "is custodial and tutelary, permitting a degree of supervision and control that could not be exercised over free adults," it might well be appropriate to tolerate some targeted viewpoint discrimination in this unique setting. And while conventional speech may be restricted only when likely to "incit[e] . . . imminent lawless action," it is possible that our rigid imminence requirement ought to be relaxed at schools.

But it is one thing to restrict speech that *advocates* drug use. It is another thing entirely to prohibit an obscure message with a drug theme that a third party subjectively—and not very reasonably—thinks is tantamount to express advocacy. * * *

* * *

There is absolutely no evidence that Frederick's banner's reference to drug paraphernalia "willful[ly]" infringed on anyone's rights or interfered with any of the school's educational programs. * * * JDHS must [therefore] show that Frederick's supposed advocacy stands a meaningful chance of making otherwise-abstemious students try marijuana.

But instead of demanding that the school make such a showing, the Court punts. * * * On occasion, the Court suggests it is deferring to the principal's "reasonable" judgment that Frederick's sign qualified as drug advocacy. At other times, the Court seems to say that *it* thinks the banner's message constitutes express advocacy. Either way, its approach is indefensible.

To the extent the Court defers to the principal's ostensibly reasonable judgment, it abdicates its constitutional responsibility. The beliefs of third parties, reasonable or otherwise, have never dictated which messages amount to proscribable advocacy. * * *

* * *

To the extent the Court independently finds that "BONG HiTS 4 JESUS" *objectively* amounts to the advocacy of illegal drug use—in other words, that it can *most* reasonably be interpreted as such—that conclusion practically refutes itself. This is a nonsense message, not advocacy. The Court's feeble effort to divine its hidden meaning is strong evidence of that. Frederick's credible and uncontradicted explanation for the message—he just wanted to get on television—is also relevant because a speaker who does not intend to persuade his audience can hardly be said to be advocating anything. But most importantly, it takes real imagination to read a "cryptic" message (the Court's characterization, not mine) with a slanting drug reference as an incitement to drug use. Admittedly, some high school students (including those who use drugs) are dumb. Most students, however, do not shed their brains at the schoolhouse gate, and most students know dumb advocacy when they see it. The notion that the message on this banner would actually persuade either the average student or even the dumbest one to change his or her behavior is most implausible. That the Court believes such a silly message can be proscribed as advocacy underscores the novelty of its position, and suggests that the principle it articulates has no stopping point.

* * *

Among other things, the Court's ham-handed, categorical approach is deaf to the constitutional imperative to permit unfettered debate, even among high school students, about the wisdom of the war on drugs or of legalizing marijuana for medicinal use. * * *

Consider, too, that the school district's rule draws no distinction between alcohol and marijuana, but applies evenhandedly to all "substances that are illegal to minors." Given the tragic consequences of teenage alcohol consumption—drinking causes far more fatal accidents than the misuse of marijuana—the school district's interest in deterring teenage alcohol use is at least comparable to its interest in preventing marijuana use. Under the Court's reasoning, must the First Amendment give way whenever a school seeks to punish a student for any speech mentioning beer, or indeed anything else that might be deemed risky to teenagers? While I find it hard to believe the Court would support punishing Frederick for flying a "WINE SiPS 4 JESUS" banner—which could quite reasonably be construed either as a protected religious message or as a pro-alcohol message—the breathtaking sweep of its opinion suggests it would.

III

Although this case began with a silly, nonsensical banner, it ends with the Court inventing out of whole cloth a special First Amendment rule permitting the censorship of any student speech that mentions drugs, at least so long as someone could perceive that speech to contain a latent pro-drug message. * * *

* * *

I respectfully dissent.

NOTES AND QUESTIONS

1.   In *Morse*, did the fact that the students engaged in speech during a school-sanctioned event make the Court more sympathetic or less sympathetic to their First Amendment claims?

2.   In the majority's view, what message did "BONG HiTS 4 JESUS" convey?

3.   In rejecting Frederick's First Amendment argument, how did the Court distinguish its prior decision in *Tinker*?

4.   On what grounds did Justice Stevens, in his dissent, disagree with the majority? How did Justice Stevens interpret BONG HiTS 4 JESUS?

5.   For interesting articles on *Morse, see, e.g.*, Kenneth Starr, *From Fraser to Frederick: Bong Hits and the Decline of Civic Culture*, 42 U.C. Davis L. Rev. 661 (2009) (article by attorney who argued in the Supreme Court on behalf of the principal; author discusses the progression of case law on student speech in schools from *Tinker* to *Morse*); Stephen Kanter, *Bong Hits 4 Jesus as a Cautionary Tale of Two Cities*, 12 Lewis & Clark L. Rev. 61 (2008) (analyzing the *Morse* decision and criticizing the Court's curtailment of student free speech rights through an unnecessarily broad holding that does not account for the unique facts of the case); Richard Garnett, *Can There Really Be "Free Speech" in Public Schools?*, 12 Lewis & Clark L. Rev. 45 (2008) (arguing that the applicability of the First Amendment depends on the nature of the institution, and questioning whether the right to free speech is compatible with public schools because those schools are designed to instill uniform, socially desirable values and behaviors rather than to promote diversity of thought and expression).

B. RELIGIOUS CLAUSES

In addition to protecting freedom of speech, the First Amendment also states that "Congress shall make no law respecting an establishment of religion, or prohibiting the free exercise thereof." The first clause, known as the Establishment Clause, prohibits the government from adopting an official religion or endorsing a particular religion. The second clause, known as the Free Exercise Clause, prohibits the government from limiting an individual's ability to practice his religion. The following sections focus on those two clauses.

1.   THE FREE EXERCISE CLAUSE

EMPLOYMENT DIVISION, DEPARTMENT OF HUMAN RESOURCES OF OREGON V. SMITH

Supreme Court of the United States, 1990
494 U.S. 872

JUSTICE SCALIA delivered the opinion of the Court.

This case requires us to decide whether the Free Exercise Clause of the First Amendment permits the State of Oregon to include religiously inspired peyote use within the reach of its general criminal prohibition on use of that drug, and thus permits the State to deny unemployment benefits to persons dismissed from their jobs because of such religiously inspired use.

I

Oregon law prohibits the knowing or intentional possession of a "controlled substance" unless the substance has been prescribed by a medical practitioner. The law defines "controlled substance" as a drug classified in Schedules I through V of the Federal Controlled Substances Act, as modified by the State Board of Pharmacy. Persons who violate this provision by possessing a controlled substance listed on Schedule I are "guilty of a Class B felony." As compiled by the State Board of Pharmacy under its statutory authority, Schedule I contains the drug peyote, a hallucinogen derived from the plant *Lophophora williamsii Lemaire.**

Respondents Alfred Smith and Galen Black (hereinafter respondents) were fired from their jobs with a private drug rehabilitation organization because they ingested peyote for sacramental purposes at a ceremony of the Native American Church, of which both are members. [They were not criminally prosecuted for using the drug. Rather, they were denied certain government benefits. In particular,] [w]hen respondents applied to petitioner Employment Division (hereinafter petitioner) for unemployment compensation, they were determined to be ineligible for benefits because they had been discharged for work-related "misconduct." [The Oregon Court of Appeals reversed, finding a First Amendment violation. The Oregon Supreme Court agreed that respondents were entitled to payment of unemployment benefits. The U.S. Supreme Court granted certiorari and remanded because the Oregon Supreme Court did not address whether religious use of peyote was in fact a crime. The Oregon Supreme Court

---

*   Although the federal act classified peyote as a "controlled substance," there was an exception under federal law (but not under Oregon law) for the use of peyote in religious ceremonies of the Native American Church. [Ed.]

confirmed that such use was a crime but held that the state violated the First Amendment by denying unemployment benefits to respondents.]

We again granted certiorari.

II

* * *

A

The Free Exercise Clause of the First Amendment, which has been made applicable to the States by incorporation into the Fourteenth Amendment, provides that "Congress shall make no law respecting an establishment of religion, or *prohibiting the free exercise thereof. . . .*" The free exercise of religion means, first and foremost, the right to believe and profess whatever religious doctrine one desires. Thus, the First Amendment obviously excludes all "governmental regulation of religious *beliefs* as such." The government may not compel affirmation of religious belief, punish the expression of religious doctrines it believes to be false, or lend its power to one or the other side in controversies over religious authority or dogma.

But the "exercise of religion" often involves not only belief and profession but the performance of (or abstention from) physical acts: assembling with others for a worship service, participating in sacramental use of bread and wine, proselytizing, abstaining from certain foods or certain modes of transportation. It would be true, we think (though no case of ours has involved the point), that a State would be "prohibiting the free exercise [of religion]" if it sought to ban such acts or abstentions only when they are engaged in for religious reasons, or only because of the religious belief that they display. It would doubtless be unconstitutional, for example, to ban the casting of "statues that are to be used for worship purposes," or to prohibit bowing down before a golden calf.

Respondents in the present case, however, seek to carry the meaning of "prohibiting the free exercise [of religion]" one large step further. They contend that their religious motivation for using peyote places them beyond the reach of a criminal law that is not specifically directed at their religious practice, and that is concededly constitutional as applied to those who use the drug for other reasons. * * *

* * * We have never held that an individual's religious beliefs excuse him from compliance with an otherwise valid law prohibiting conduct that the State is free to regulate. On the contrary, the record of more than a century of our free exercise jurisprudence contradicts that proposition. * * *

[This Court's] decisions have consistently held that the right of free exercise does not relieve an individual of the obligation to comply with a "valid and neutral law of general applicability on the ground that the law proscribes (or prescribes) conduct that his religion prescribes (or proscribes)." In *Prince v. Massachusetts*, 321 U.S. 158 (1944), we held that a mother could be prosecuted under the child labor laws for using her children to dispense literature in the streets, her religious motivation notwithstanding. We found no constitutional infirmity in "excluding [these children] from doing there what no other children may do." In *Gillette v. United States*, 401 U.S. 437 (1971), we sustained the military Selective Service System against the claim that it violated free exercise by conscripting persons who opposed a particular war on religious grounds.

Our most recent decision [on the subject] was *United States v. Lee*, 455 U.S. 252 (1982). There, an Amish employer, on behalf of himself and his employees, sought exemption from collection and payment of Social Security taxes on the ground that the Amish faith prohibited participation in governmental support programs. We rejected the claim that an exemption was constitutionally required. There would be no way, we observed, to distinguish the Amish believer's objection to Social Security taxes from the religious objections that others might have to the collection or use of other taxes. * * *

The only decisions in which we have held that the First Amendment bars application of a neutral, generally applicable law to religiously motivated action have involved not the Free Exercise Clause alone, but the Free Exercise Clause in conjunction with other constitutional protections, such as freedom of speech and of the press.

The present case does not present such a hybrid situation, but a free exercise claim unconnected with any communicative activity or parental right. Respondents urge us to hold, quite simply, that when otherwise prohibitable conduct is accompanied by religious convictions, not only the convictions but the conduct itself must be free from governmental regulation. We have never held that, and decline to do so now. * * *

B

Respondents argue that even though exemption from generally applicable criminal laws need not automatically be extended to religiously motivated actors, at least the claim for a religious exemption must be evaluated under the balancing test set forth in *Sherbert v. Verner*, 374 U.S. 398 (1963). Under the *Sherbert* test, governmental actions that substantially burden a religious practice must be justified by a compelling governmental interest. Applying that test we have, on three occasions, invalidated state unemployment compensation rules that conditioned the availability of benefits upon an applicant's willingness to work under conditions forbidden by his religion. We have never invalidated any governmental action on the basis of the *Sherbert* test except the denial of unemployment compensation. Although we have sometimes purported to apply the *Sherbert* test in contexts other than that, we have always found the test satisfied. In recent years we have abstained from applying the

Sherbert test (outside the unemployment compensation field) at all. [The Court discussed several prior cases.]

Even if we were inclined to breathe into *Sherbert* some life beyond the unemployment compensation field, we would not apply it to require exemptions from a generally applicable criminal law. * * *

* * * Although, * * * we have sometimes used the *Sherbert* test to analyze free exercise challenges [to across-the-board criminal prohibitions], we have never applied the test to invalidate one. We conclude today that the sounder approach, and the approach in accord with the vast majority of our precedents, is to hold the test inapplicable to such challenges. The government's ability to enforce generally applicable prohibitions of socially harmful conduct, like its ability to carry out other aspects of public policy, "cannot depend on measuring the effects of a governmental action on a religious objector's spiritual development." * * *

The "compelling government interest" requirement seems benign, because it is familiar from other fields. But using it as the standard that must be met before the government may accord different treatment on the basis of race, or before the government may regulate the content of speech, is not remotely comparable to using it for the purpose asserted here. What it produces in those other fields—equality of treatment and an unrestricted flow of contending speech—are constitutional norms; what it would produce here—a private right to ignore generally applicable laws—is a constitutional anomaly.

Nor is it possible to limit the impact of respondents' proposal by requiring a "compelling state interest" only when the conduct prohibited is "central" to the individual's religion. It is no more appropriate for judges to determine the "centrality" of religious beliefs before applying a "compelling interest" test in the free exercise field, than it would be for them to determine the "importance" of ideas before applying the "compelling interest" test in the free speech field. What principle of law or logic can be brought to bear to contradict a believer's assertion that a particular act is "central" to his personal faith? * * *

If the "compelling interest" test is to be applied at all, then, it must be applied across the board, to all actions thought to be religiously commanded. Moreover, if "compelling interest" really means what it says (and watering it down here would subvert its rigor in the other fields where it is applied), many laws will not meet the test. Any society adopting such a system would be courting anarchy, but that danger increases in direct proportion to the society's diversity of religious beliefs, and its determination to coerce or suppress none of them. Precisely because "we are a cosmopolitan nation made up of people of almost every conceivable religious preference," and precisely because we value and protect that religious divergence, we cannot afford the luxury of deeming *presumptively invalid*, as applied to the religious objector, every regulation of conduct that does not protect an interest of the highest order. The rule respondents favor would open the prospect of constitutionally required religious exemptions from civic obligations of almost every conceivable kind—ranging from compulsory military service, to the payment of taxes, to health and safety regulation such as manslaughter and child neglect laws, compulsory vaccination laws, drug laws, and traffic laws, to social welfare legislation such as minimum wage laws, child labor laws, animal cruelty laws, environmental protection laws, and laws providing for equality of opportunity for the races. The First Amendment's protection of religious liberty does not require this.

Values that are protected against government interference through enshrinement in the Bill of Rights are not thereby banished from the political process. * * * It is * * * not surprising that a number of States have made an exception to their drug laws for sacramental peyote use. But to say that a nondiscriminatory religious-practice exemption is permitted, or even that it is desirable, is not to say that it is constitutionally required * * *.

Because respondents' ingestion of peyote was prohibited under Oregon law, and because that prohibition is constitutional, Oregon may, consistent with the Free Exercise Clause, deny respondents unemployment compensation when their dismissal results from use of the drug. The decision of the Oregon Supreme Court is accordingly reversed.

It is so ordered.

JUSTICE O'CONNOR, with whom JUSTICE BRENNAN, JUSTICE MARSHALL, and JUSTICE BLACKMUN join as to Parts I and II, concurring in the judgment.

Although I agree with the result the Court reaches in this case, I cannot join its opinion. In my view, today's holding dramatically departs from well-settled First Amendment jurisprudence, appears unnecessary to resolve the question presented, and is incompatible with our Nation's fundamental commitment to individual religious liberty.

* * *

II

* * * [T]he Court holds that where the law is a generally applicable criminal prohibition, our usual free exercise jurisprudence does not * * * apply. To reach this sweeping result, however, the Court must not only give a strained reading of the First Amendment but must also disregard our [prior decisions] * * *.

A

* * *

The Court * * * interprets the [Free Exercise] Clause to permit the government to prohibit, without justification, conduct mandated by an individual's religious beliefs, so long as that prohibition is generally applicable. But a law that prohibits certain conduct—conduct that happens to be an act of worship for someone—manifestly does prohibit that person's free exercise of his religion. A person who is barred from engaging in religiously motivated conduct is barred from freely exercising his religion. Moreover, that person is barred from freely exercising his religion regardless of whether the law prohibits the conduct only when engaged in for religious reasons, only by members of that religion, or by all persons. It is difficult to deny that a law that prohibits religiously motivated conduct, even if the law is generally applicable, does not at least implicate First Amendment concerns.

The Court responds that generally applicable laws are "one large step" removed from laws aimed at specific religious practices. The First Amendment, however, does not distinguish between laws that are generally applicable and laws that target particular religious practices. Indeed, few States would be so naive as to enact a law directly prohibiting or burdening a religious practice as such. Our free exercise cases have all concerned generally applicable laws that had the effect of significantly burdening a religious practice. If the First Amendment is to have any vitality, it ought not be construed to cover only the extreme and hypothetical situation in which a State directly targets a religious practice. * * *

To say that a person's right to free exercise has been burdened, of course, does not mean that he has an absolute right to engage in the conduct. Under our established First Amendment jurisprudence, we have recognized that the freedom to act, unlike the freedom to believe, cannot be absolute. Instead, we have respected both the First Amendment's express textual mandate and the governmental interest in regulation of conduct by requiring the government to justify any substantial burden on religiously motivated conduct by a compelling state interest and by means narrowly tailored to achieve that interest. * * *

* * *

That we [based the decisions on "hybrid" grounds, not just on Free Exercise, or that we] rejected the free exercise claims * * * hardly calls into question the applicability of First Amendment doctrine in the first place. * * *

B

Respondents, of course, do not contend that their conduct is automatically immune from all governmental regulation simply because it is motivated by their sincere religious beliefs. The Court's rejection of that argument might therefore be regarded as merely harmless dictum. Rather, respondents invoke our traditional compelling interest test to argue that the Free Exercise Clause requires the State to grant them a limited exemption from its general criminal prohibition against the possession of peyote. The Court today, however, denies them even the opportunity to make that argument * * *.

In my view, however, the essence of a free exercise claim is relief from a burden imposed by government on religious practices or beliefs, whether the burden is imposed directly through laws that prohibit or compel specific religious practices, or indirectly through laws that, in effect, make abandonment of one's own religion or conformity to the religious beliefs of others the price of an equal place in the civil community. * * *

A State that makes criminal an individual's religiously motivated conduct burdens that individual's free exercise of religion in the severest manner possible, for it "results in the choice to the individual of either abandoning his religious principle or facing criminal prosecution." I would have thought it beyond argument that such laws implicate free exercise concerns.

Indeed, we have never distinguished between cases in which a State conditions receipt of a benefit on conduct prohibited by religious beliefs and cases in which a State affirmatively prohibits such conduct. * * *

Legislatures, of course, have always been "left free to reach actions which were in violation of social duties or subversive of good order." Yet because of the close relationship between conduct and religious belief, "[i]n every case the power to regulate must be so exercised as not, in attaining a permissible end, unduly to infringe the protected freedom." Once it has been shown that a government regulation or criminal prohibition burdens the free exercise of religion, we have consistently asked the government to demonstrate that unbending application of its regulation to the religious objector "is essential to accomplish an overriding governmental interest," or represents "the least restrictive means of achieving some compelling state interest." To me, the sounder approach * * * is to apply this test in each case to determine whether the burden on the specific plaintiffs before us is constitutionally significant and whether the particular criminal interest asserted by the State before us is compelling. Even if, as an empirical matter, a government's criminal laws might usually serve a compelling interest in health, safety, or public order, the First Amendment at least requires a case-by-case determination of the question, sensitive to the facts of each particular claim. Given the range of conduct that a State might legitimately make criminal, we cannot assume, merely because a law carries criminal sanctions and is generally applicable, that the First Amendment *never* requires the State to grant a limited exemption for religiously motivated conduct.

* * *

* * * [T]he Court today suggests that the disfavoring of minority religions is an "unavoidable consequence" under our system of government and that accommodation of such religions must be left to the political process. In my view, however, the First Amendment was enacted precisely to protect the rights of those whose religious practices are not shared by the majority and may be viewed with hostility. * * *

III

The Court's holding today not only misreads settled First Amendment precedent; it appears to be unnecessary to this case. I would reach the same result applying our established free exercise jurisprudence.

A

There is no dispute that Oregon's criminal prohibition of peyote places a severe burden on the ability of respondents to freely exercise their religion. Peyote is a sacrament of the Native American Church and is regarded as vital to respondents' ability to practice their religion. * * *

There is also no dispute that Oregon has a significant interest in enforcing laws that control the possession and use of controlled substances by its citizens. * * *

B

Thus, the critical question in this case is whether exempting respondents from the State's general criminal prohibition "will unduly interfere with fulfillment of the governmental interest." Although the question is close, I would conclude that uniform application of Oregon's criminal prohibition is "essential to accomplish" its overriding interest in preventing the physical harm caused by the use of a Schedule I controlled substance. Oregon's criminal prohibition represents that State's judgment that the possession and use of controlled substances, even by only one person, is inherently harmful and dangerous. Because the health effects caused by the use of controlled substances exist regardless of the motivation of the user, the use of such substances, even for religious purposes, violates the very purpose of the laws that prohibit them. Moreover, in view of the societal interest in preventing trafficking in controlled substances, uniform application of the criminal prohibition at issue is essential to the effectiveness of Oregon's stated interest in preventing any possession of peyote.

For these reasons, I believe that * * * the Free Exercise Clause does not require the State to accommodate respondents' religiously motivated conduct. * * *

* * *

JUSTICE BLACKMUN, with whom JUSTICE BRENNAN and JUSTICE MARSHALL join, dissenting.

* * *

* * * I agree with Justice O'CONNOR's analysis of the applicable free exercise doctrine, and I join parts I and II of her opinion. * * * I * * * disagree, however, with her specific [conclusion].

I

In weighing the clear interest of respondents Smith and Black (hereinafter respondents) in the free exercise of their religion against Oregon's asserted interest in enforcing its drug laws, it is important to articulate in precise terms the state interest involved. It is not the State's broad interest in fighting the critical "war on drugs" that must be weighed against respondents' claim, but the State's narrow interest in refusing to make an exception for the religious, ceremonial use of peyote. Failure to reduce the competing interests to the same plane of generality tends to distort the weighing process in the State's favor.

The State's interest in enforcing its prohibition, in order to be sufficiently compelling to outweigh a free exercise claim, cannot be merely abstract or symbolic. The State cannot plausibly assert that unbending application of a criminal prohibition is essential to fulfill any compelling interest, if it does not, in fact, attempt to enforce that prohibition. In this case, the State actually has not evinced any concrete interest in enforcing its drug laws against religious users of peyote. Oregon has never sought to prosecute respondents, and does not claim that it has made significant enforcement efforts against other religious users of peyote. The State's asserted interest thus amounts only to the symbolic preservation of an unenforced prohibition. But a government interest in "symbolism, even symbolism for so worthy a cause as the abolition of unlawful drugs," cannot suffice to abrogate the constitutional rights of individuals.

* * *

The State proclaims an interest in protecting the health and safety of its citizens from the dangers of unlawful drugs. It offers, however, no evidence that the religious use of peyote has ever harmed anyone. * * *

The fact that peyote is classified as a Schedule I controlled substance does not, by itself, show that any and all uses of peyote, in any circumstance, are inherently harmful and dangerous. * * *

The carefully circumscribed ritual context in which respondents used peyote is far removed from the irresponsible and unrestricted recreational use of unlawful drugs. The Native American Church's internal restrictions on, and supervision of, its members' use of peyote substantially obviate the State's health and safety concerns.

* * * Not only does the church's doctrine forbid nonreligious use of peyote; it also generally advocates self-reliance, familial responsibility, and abstinence from alcohol. There is considerable evidence that the spiritual and social support provided by the church has been effective in combating the tragic effects of alcoholism on the Native American population. * * * Far from promoting the lawless and irresponsible use of drugs, Native American Church members' spiritual code exemplifies values that Oregon's drug laws are presumably intended to foster.

The State also seeks to support its refusal to make an exception for religious use of peyote by invoking its interest in abolishing drug trafficking. There is, however, practically no illegal traffic in peyote. * * *

Finally, the State argues that granting an exception for religious peyote use would erode its interest in the uniform, fair, and certain enforcement of its drug laws. The State fears that, if it grants an exemption for religious peyote use, a flood of other claims to religious exemptions will follow. * * *

The State's apprehension of a flood of other religious claims is purely speculative. Almost half the States, and the Federal Government, have maintained an exemption for religious peyote use for many years, and apparently have not found themselves overwhelmed by claims to other religious exemptions. Allowing an exemption for religious peyote use would not necessarily oblige the State to grant a similar exemption to other religious groups. The unusual circumstances that make the religious use of peyote compatible with the State's interests in health and safety and in preventing drug trafficking would not apply to other religious claims. Some religions, for example, might not restrict drug use to a limited ceremonial context, as does the Native American Church. Some religious claims involve drugs such as marijuana and heroin, in which there is significant illegal traffic, with its attendant greed and violence, so that it would be difficult to grant a religious exemption without seriously compromising law enforcement efforts. That the State might grant an exemption for religious peyote use, but deny other religious claims arising in different circumstances, would not violate the Establishment Clause. * * *

II

Finally, * * * I do not think * * * that the courts must turn a blind eye to the severe impact of a State's restrictions on the adherents of a minority religion.

Respondents believe, and their sincerity has *never* been at issue, that the peyote plant embodies their deity, and eating it is an act of worship and communion. Without peyote, they could not enact the essential ritual of their religion.

* * *

* * * [T]his Court must scrupulously apply its free exercise analysis to the religious claims of Native Americans, however unorthodox they may be. * * *

III

For these reasons, I conclude that * * * [t]he State of Oregon cannot, consistently with the Free Exercise Clause, deny respondents unemployment benefits.

I dissent.

NOTES AND QUESTIONS

1.   Why did Smith and Black argue that their rights under the Free Exercise Clause were violated? How did the Supreme Court rule and why?

2.   Justice O'Connor, writing for herself and (in part) for three other Justices, concurred in the judgment but disagreed with the majority. What was the basis of her disagreement?

3.   Justice Blackmun, joined by two other Justices, agreed with much of Justice O'Connor's analysis but nonetheless dissented. Why did Justice Blackmun dissent?

4.   Which opinion—the majority, Justice O'Connor's concurrence, or Justice Blackmun's dissent—is the most persuasive?

5.   In 1978, Congress passed the American Indian Religious Freedom Act (AIRFA), 42 U.S.C. § 1996 (2012), which stated generally the policy of the U.S. to permit American Indians to engage in freedom of worship through "ceremonial and traditional rites." Notwithstanding that statute, the Court in *Smith* held that Native Americans could be denied unemployment benefits based on the religious use of peyote. In response to *Smith*, Congress passed the American Indian Religious Freedom Act Amendments of 1994, 42 U.S.C. § 1996a(b)(1) (2012), which make it lawful for Indians to use, possess, or transport peyote "for bona fide traditional ceremonial purposes."

6.   The Free Exercise Clause has generated significant litigation. For example, in *Wisconsin v. Yoder*, 406 U.S. 205 (1972), Amish parents were criminally prosecuted for failing to send their children to school after eighth grade (in violation of a state requirement that children attend school through the tenth grade). Members of the Amish Church defended their conduct on religious grounds—they refrain from various elements of modern life, including not only advanced education but also the use of electricity and automobiles. The Supreme Court held that the religious interests of the Amish

outweighed any interest that the state had in requiring the students to go to school for two more years. In *Church of the Lukumi Babalu Aye, Inc. v. Hialeah*, 508 U.S. 520 (1993), a church practicing Santeria, a religion involving animal sacrifice, challenged a city ordinance that prohibited the killing of animals as part of a ritual (unless the primary purpose of the ritual was for food consumption). Based on *Smith*, the Supreme Court applied strict scrutiny—because the ordinance was not neutral or generally applicable. The Court concluded that the ordinance violated the Free Exercise Clause because, although the city might have had a compelling interest in preventing animal cruelty, the ordinance was not narrowly tailored to that goal. In *Watchtower Bible & Tract Society of New York v. Village of Stratton*, 536 U.S. 150 (2002), a case involving a Jehovah's Witnesses organization (which distributes religious reading material door-to-door), the Supreme Court held that a city ordinance requiring a permit for door-to-door advocacy was unconstitutional under the Free Speech and Free Exercise provisions of the First Amendment because the city did not have a sufficient interest to justify such a limitation on religious activity.

7.   In *Hosanna-Tabor Evangelical Lutheran Church and School v. E.E.O.C.*, 565 U.S. ___, 132 S. Ct. 694 (2012), the Court addressed—in the context of a religious organization—an alleged violation of a federal law protecting people with disabilities. The plaintiff in the case was a teacher at a Church-run school who brought a claim for wrongful discharge after she was terminated. Prior to her termination, the teacher had been diagnosed with narcolepsy (a neurological condition that causes sleepiness even during the daytime) and took a medical leave from the school. When the teacher returned, she was told to leave the premises and was later advised that she was going to be fired. In response, the teacher informed the Church that she planned to take legal action. Subsequently, the Church terminated her employment. The teacher alleged that the Church had discriminated against her based on her disability and thus violated the Americans with Disabilities Act (ADA). The Church argued that, under the Free Exercise Clause of the First Amendment (and under the Establishment Clause, discussed *infra*), the government could not interfere with a religious organization's hiring decisions. The Church's argument was based on what is known as the "ministerial exception," under which courts may not interfere with a religious organization's selection of its religious leaders. The teacher, however, argued that she was not a minister and should be protected by the anti-discrimination laws. The Supreme Court held that, under the Free Exercise Clause (and the Establishment Clause), the ministerial exception applied: "The exception * * * ensures that the authority to select and control who will minister to the faithful—a matter 'strictly ecclesiastical'—is the [C]hurch's alone." *Id.* at 709.

8.   For additional discussion of the Free Exercise Clause, *see, e.g.*, Richard Schragger & Micah Schwartzman, *Against Religious Institutionalism*, 99 Va. L. Rev. 917 (2013) (criticizing *Hosanna-Tabor* and similar decisions for focusing on the free exercise rights of institutions and arguing that the right to freedom of religion belongs to individuals); Ronald Krotoszynski, Jr., *If Judges Were Angels: Religious Equality, Free Exercise, and the*

(Underappreciated) Merits of Smith, 102 Nw. U. L. Rev. 1189 (2008) (proposing an approach to the Free Exercise Clause that would put the burden of disproving discriminatory treatment on the government, rather than putting the burden on the religionist to prove discrimination, when the government applies a neutral law in a way that burdens religious conduct); Michael McConnell, *The Origins and Historical Understanding of Free Exercise of Religion*, 103 Harv. L. Rev. 1409 (1990) (discussing the historical development of the Free Exercise Clause and concluding that it should be read to mandate widespread religious exemptions to all laws to better support religious pluralism).

2. THE ESTABLISHMENT CLAUSE

TOWN OF GREECE, NEW YORK V. GALLOWAY

Supreme Court of the United States, 2014
572 U.S. ___, 134 S. Ct. 1811

JUSTICE KENNEDY delivered the opinion of the Court, except as to Part II-B.*

The Court must decide whether the town of Greece, New York, imposes an impermissible establishment of religion by opening its monthly board meetings with a prayer. * * *

I

Greece, a town with a population of 94,000, is in upstate New York. For some years, it began its monthly town board meetings with a moment of silence. In 1999, the newly elected town supervisor, John Auberger, decided to replicate the prayer practice he had found meaningful while serving in the county legislature. Following the roll call and recitation of the Pledge of Allegiance, Auberger would invite a local clergyman to the front of the room to deliver an invocation. After the prayer, Auberger would thank the minister for serving as the board's "chaplain for the month" and present him with a commemorative plaque. The prayer was intended to place town board members in a solemn and deliberative frame of mind, invoke divine guidance in town affairs, and follow a tradition practiced by Congress and dozens of state legislatures.

The town followed an informal method for selecting prayer givers, all of whom were unpaid volunteers. A town employee would call the congregations listed in a local directory until she found a minister available for that month's meeting. The town eventually compiled a list of willing "board chaplains" who had accepted invitations and agreed to return in the future. The town at no point excluded or denied an opportunity to a would-be prayer giver. Its leaders maintained that a minister or layperson of any

---

* In Part II–B, Justice Kennedy offered additional rationales for the outcome, but that section (omitted here) was not supported by a majority of the Court. [Ed.]

persuasion, including an atheist, could give the invocation. But nearly all of the congregations in town were Christian; and from 1999 to 2007, all of the participating ministers were too.

Greece neither reviewed the prayers in advance of the meetings nor provided guidance as to their tone or content, in the belief that exercising any degree of control over the prayers would infringe both the free exercise and speech rights of the ministers. The town instead left the guest clergy free to compose their own devotions. The resulting prayers often sounded both civic and religious themes. Typical were invocations that asked the divinity to abide at the meeting and bestow blessings on the community:

> Lord we ask you to send your spirit of servanthood upon all of us gathered here this evening to do your work for the benefit of all in our community. We ask you to bless our elected and appointed officials so they may deliberate with wisdom and act with courage. Bless the members of our community who come here to speak before the board so they may state their cause with honesty and humility. . . . Lord we ask you to bless us all, that everything we do here tonight will move you to welcome us one day into your kingdom as good and faithful servants. We ask this in the name of our brother Jesus. Amen.

Some of the ministers spoke in a distinctly Christian idiom; and a minority invoked religious holidays, scripture, or doctrine, as in the following prayer:

> Lord, God of all creation, we give you thanks and praise for your presence and action in the world. We look with anticipation to the celebration of Holy Week and Easter. It is in the solemn events of next week that we find the very heart and center of our Christian faith. We acknowledge the saving sacrifice of Jesus Christ on the cross. We draw strength, vitality, and confidence from his resurrection at Easter. . . . We pray for peace in the world, an end to terrorism, violence, conflict, and war. We pray for stability, democracy, and good government in those countries in which our armed forces are now serving, especially in Iraq and Afghanistan. . . . Praise and glory be yours, O Lord, now and forever more. Amen.

Respondents Susan Galloway and Linda Stephens attended town board meetings to speak about issues of local concern, and they objected that the prayers violated their religious or philosophical views. At one meeting, Galloway admonished board members that she found the prayers "offensive," "intolerable," and an affront to a "diverse community." After respondents complained that Christian themes pervaded the prayers, to the exclusion of citizens who did not share those beliefs, the town invited a Jewish layman and the chairman of the local Baha'i temple to deliver prayers. A Wiccan priestess who had read press reports about the prayer controversy requested, and was granted, an opportunity to give the invocation.

Galloway and Stephens brought suit in the United States District Court for the Western District of New York. They alleged that the town violated the First Amendment's Establishment Clause by preferring Christians over other prayer givers and by sponsoring sectarian prayers, such as those given "in Jesus's name." They did not seek an end to the prayer practice, but rather requested an injunction that would limit the town to "inclusive and ecumenical" prayers that referred only to a "generic God" and would not associate the government with any one faith or belief.

The District Court * * * upheld the prayer practice as consistent with the First Amendment. It found no impermissible preference for Christianity, noting that the town had opened the prayer program to all creeds and excluded none. * * *

* * *

The Court of Appeals for the Second Circuit reversed. It held that some aspects of the prayer program, viewed in their totality by a reasonable observer, conveyed the message that Greece was endorsing Christianity. * * *

* * * [T]he Court now reverses the judgment of the Court of Appeals.

II

In *Marsh v. Chambers*, [463 U.S. 783 (1983),] the Court found no First Amendment violation in the Nebraska Legislature's practice of opening its sessions with a prayer delivered by a chaplain paid from state funds. The decision concluded that legislative prayer, while religious in nature [was] compatible with the Establishment Clause. As practiced by Congress since the framing of the Constitution, legislative prayer lends gravity to public business, reminds lawmakers to transcend petty differences in pursuit of a higher purpose, and expresses a common aspiration to a just and peaceful society. * * *

Marsh is sometimes described as "carving out an exception" to the Court's Establishment Clause jurisprudence, because it sustained legislative prayer without subjecting the practice to "any of the formal 'tests' that have traditionally structured" this inquiry. The Court in *Marsh* found those tests unnecessary because history supported the conclusion that legislative invocations are compatible with the Establishment Clause. The First Congress made it an early item of business to appoint and pay official chaplains, and both the House and Senate have maintained the office virtually uninterrupted since that time. When *Marsh* was decided, in 1983, legislative prayer had persisted in the Nebraska Legislature for more than a century, and the majority of the other States also had the same, consistent practice. Although no information has been cited by the parties to indicate how many local legislative bodies open their meetings with prayer, this practice too has historical precedent. * * *

Yet *Marsh* must not be understood as permitting a practice that would amount to a constitutional violation if not for its historical foundation. The case teaches instead that the Establishment Clause must be interpreted "by reference to historical practices and understandings." That the First Congress provided for the appointment of chaplains only days after approving language for the First Amendment demonstrates that the Framers considered legislative prayer a benign acknowledgment of religion's role in society. In the 1850's, the judiciary committees in both the House and Senate reevaluated the practice of official chaplaincies after receiving petitions to abolish the office. The committees concluded that the office posed no threat of an establishment because lawmakers were not compelled to attend the daily prayer; no faith was excluded by law, nor any favored; and the cost of the chaplain's salary imposed a vanishingly small burden on taxpayers. *Marsh* stands for the proposition that it is not necessary to define the precise boundary of the Establishment Clause where history shows that the specific practice is permitted. * * *

The Court's inquiry, then, must be to determine whether the prayer practice in the town of Greece fits within the tradition long followed in Congress and the state legislatures. * * *

A

Respondents maintain that [under the Establishment Clause] prayer must be nonsectarian, or not identifiable with any one religion; and they fault the town for permitting guest chaplains to deliver prayers that "use overtly Christian terms" or "invoke specifics of Christian theology." A prayer is fitting for the public sphere, in their view, only if it contains the " 'most general, nonsectarian reference to God,' " and eschews mention of doctrines associated with any one faith. * * *

An insistence on nonsectarian or ecumenical prayer as a single, fixed standard is not consistent with the tradition of legislative prayer outlined in the Court's cases. The Court found the prayers in *Marsh* consistent with the First Amendment not because they espoused only a generic theism but because our history and tradition have shown that prayer in this limited context could "coexis[t] with the principles of disestablishment and religious freedom." The Congress that drafted the First Amendment would have been accustomed to invocations containing explicitly religious themes of the sort respondents find objectionable. * * *

The contention that legislative prayer must be generic or nonsectarian derives from dictum in *Allegheny v. ACLU*, 492 U.S. 573 (1989), that was disputed when written and has been repudiated by later cases. There the Court held that a crèche placed on the steps of a county courthouse to celebrate the Christmas season violated the Establishment Clause because it had "the effect of endorsing a patently Christian message." Four dissenting Justices disputed that endorsement could be the proper test, as it likely would condemn a host of traditional practices that recognize the role religion plays in our society, among them legislative prayer and the "forthrightly religious" Thanksgiving proclamations issued by nearly every President since Washington. The Court sought to counter this criticism by recasting *Marsh* to permit only prayer that contained no overtly Christian references:

> However history may affect the constitutionality of nonsectarian references to religion by the government, history cannot legitimate practices that demonstrate the government's allegiance to a particular sect or creed. . . . The legislative prayers involved in *Marsh* did not violate this principle because the particular chaplain had "removed all references to Christ." [Quoting *Marsh*.]

This proposition is irreconcilable with the facts of *Marsh* and with its holding and reasoning. *Marsh* nowhere suggested that the constitutionality of legislative prayer turns on the neutrality of its content. The opinion noted that Nebraska's chaplain, the Rev. Robert E. Palmer, modulated the "explicitly Christian" nature of his prayer and "removed all references to Christ" after a Jewish lawmaker complained. With this footnote, the Court did no more than observe the practical demands placed on a minister who holds a permanent, appointed position in a legislature and chooses to write his or her prayers to appeal to more members, or at least to give less offense to those who object. *Marsh* did not suggest that Nebraska's prayer practice would have failed had the chaplain not acceded to the legislator's request. Nor did the Court imply the rule that prayer violates the Establishment Clause any time it is given in the name of a figure deified by only one faith or creed. * * *

To hold that invocations must be nonsectarian would force the legislatures that sponsor prayers and the courts that are asked to decide these cases to act as supervisors and censors of religious speech, a rule that would involve government in religious matters to a far greater degree than is the case under the town's current practice of neither editing or approving prayers in advance nor criticizing their content after the fact. Our Government is prohibited from prescribing prayers to be recited in our public institutions in order to promote a preferred system of belief or code of moral behavior. It would be but a few steps removed from that prohibition for legislatures to require chaplains to redact the religious content from their message in order to make it acceptable for the public sphere. Government may not mandate a civic religion that stifles any but the most generic reference to the sacred any more than it may prescribe a religious orthodoxy.

Respondents argue, in effect, that legislative prayer may be addressed only to a generic God. The law and the Court could not draw this line for each specific prayer or seek to require ministers to set aside their nuanced and deeply personal beliefs for vague and artificial ones. There is doubt, in any event, that consensus might be reached as to what qualifies as generic or nonsectarian. Honorifics like "Lord of Lords" or "King of Kings" might strike a Christian audience as ecumenical, yet these titles may have no place in the vocabulary of other faith traditions. * * * Because it is unlikely that prayer will be inclusive beyond dispute, it would be unwise to adopt what respondents think is the next-best option: permitting those religious words, and only those words, that are acceptable to the majority, even if they will exclude some. The First Amendment is not a majority rule, and government may not seek to define permissible categories of religious speech. Once it invites prayer into the public sphere, government must permit a prayer giver to address his or her own God or gods as conscience dictates, unfettered by what an administrator or judge considers to be nonsectarian.

In rejecting the suggestion that legislative prayer must be nonsectarian, the Court does not imply that no constraints remain on its content. The relevant constraint derives from its place at the opening of legislative sessions, where it is meant to lend gravity to the occasion and reflect values long part of the Nation's heritage. Prayer that is solemn and respectful in tone, that invites lawmakers to reflect upon shared ideals and common ends before they embark on the fractious business of governing, serves that legitimate function. If the course and practice over time shows that the invocations denigrate nonbelievers or religious minorities, threaten damnation, or preach conversion, many present may consider the prayer to fall short of the desire to elevate the purpose of the occasion and to unite lawmakers in their common effort. That circumstance would present a different case than the one presently before the Court.

The tradition reflected in *Marsh* permits chaplains to ask their own God for blessings of peace, justice, and freedom that find appreciation among people of all faiths. That a prayer is given in the name of Jesus, Allah, or Jehovah, or that it makes passing reference to religious doctrines, does not remove it from that tradition. * * *

It is thus possible to discern in the prayers offered to Congress a commonality of theme and tone. While these prayers vary in their degree of religiosity, they often seek peace for the Nation, wisdom for its lawmakers, and justice for its people, values that count as universal and that are embodied not only in religious traditions, but in our founding documents and laws. * * *

* * *

From the earliest days of the Nation, these invocations have been addressed to assemblies comprising many different creeds. These ceremonial prayers strive for the idea that people of many faiths may be united in a community of tolerance and devotion. Even those who disagree as to religious doctrine may find common ground in the desire to show respect for the divine in all aspects of their lives and being. Our tradition assumes that adult citizens, firm in their own beliefs, can tolerate and perhaps appreciate a ceremonial prayer delivered by a person of a different faith.

The prayers delivered in the town of Greece do not fall outside the tradition this Court has recognized. A number of the prayers did invoke the name of Jesus, the Heavenly Father, or the Holy Spirit, but they also invoked universal themes, as by celebrating the changing of the seasons or calling for a "spirit of cooperation" among town leaders. Among numerous examples of such prayer in the record is the invocation given by the Rev. Richard Barbour at the September 2006 board meeting:

> Gracious God, you have richly blessed our nation and this community. Help us to remember your generosity and give thanks for your goodness. Bless the elected leaders of the Greece Town Board as they conduct the business of our town this evening. Give them wisdom, courage, discernment and a single-minded desire to serve the common good. We ask your blessing on all public servants, and especially on our police force, firefighters, and emergency medical personnel. . . . Respectful of every religious tradition, I offer this prayer in the name of God's only son Jesus Christ, the Lord, Amen.

Respondents point to other invocations that disparaged those who did not accept the town's prayer practice. One guest minister characterized objectors as a "minority" who are "ignorant of the history of our country," while another lamented that other towns did not have "God-fearing" leaders. Although these two remarks strayed from the rationale set out in *Marsh*, they do not despoil a practice that on the whole reflects and embraces our tradition. * * * *Marsh* * * * requires an inquiry into the prayer opportunity as a whole, rather than into the contents of a single prayer.

Finally, the Court disagrees with the view taken by the Court of Appeals that the town of Greece contravened the Establishment Clause by inviting a predominantly Christian set of ministers to lead the prayer. The town made reasonable efforts to identify all of the congregations located within its borders and represented that it would welcome a prayer by any minister or layman who wished to give one. That nearly all of the congregations in town turned out to be Christian does not reflect an aversion or bias on the part of town leaders against minority faiths. So long as the town maintains a policy of nondiscrimination, the Constitution does not require it to search beyond its borders for non-Christian prayer givers in an effort to achieve religious balancing. The quest to promote "a 'diversity' of religious views" would require the town "to make wholly inappropriate judgments about the number of religions [it] should sponsor and the relative frequency with which it should sponsor each," a form of government entanglement with religion that is far more troublesome than the current approach.

* * *

The town of Greece does not violate the First Amendment by opening its meetings with prayer that comports with our tradition and does not coerce participation by nonadherents. The judgment of the U.S. Court of Appeals for the Second Circuit is reversed.

* * *

[Concurring opinion by JUSTICE ALITO, joined by JUSTICE SCALIA, is omitted.]

[Concurring opinion by JUSTICE THOMAS, joined in part by JUSTICE SCALIA, is omitted.]

[Dissenting opinion by JUSTICE BREYER is omitted.]

JUSTICE KAGAN, with whom JUSTICE GINSBURG, JUSTICE BREYER, and JUSTICE SOTOMAYOR join, dissenting.

* * *

I respectfully dissent * * *.

I

To begin to see what has gone wrong in the Town of Greece, consider several hypothetical scenarios * * *. [Justice Kagan hypothesized prayers taking place in a courtroom before the commencement of a trial; in a polling place on election day; and during a naturalization ceremony to become a citizen.]

I would hold that the government officials responsible for the above practices—that is, for prayer repeatedly invoking a single religion's beliefs in these settings—crossed a constitutional line. I have every confidence the Court would agree. * * * Why?

The reason, of course, has nothing to do with Christianity as such. This opinion is full of Christian prayers, because those were the only invocations offered in the Town of Greece. But if my hypotheticals involved the prayer of some other religion, the outcome would be exactly the same. [Justice Kagan gave examples of Jewish and Muslim prayers.] * * *

* * *

By authorizing and overseeing prayers associated with a single religion—to the exclusion of all others—the government officials in my hypothetical cases (whether federal, state, or local does not matter) have * * * embarked on a course of religious favoritism anathema to the First Amendment.

And making matters still worse: They have done so in a place where individuals come to interact with, and participate in, the institutions and processes of their government. A person goes to court, to the polls, to a naturalization ceremony—and a government official or his hand-picked minister asks her, as the first order of official business, to stand and pray with others in a way conflicting with her own religious beliefs. Perhaps she feels sufficient pressure to go along—to rise, bow her head, and join in whatever others are saying * * *. Or perhaps she is made of stronger mettle, and she opts not to participate in what she does not believe— indeed, what would, for her, be something like blasphemy. She then must make known her dissent * * *. And so a civic function of some kind brings religious differences to the fore * * *.

That is not the country we are, because that is not what our Constitution permits. * * *

II

* * * *Marsh* upheld (I think correctly) the Nebraska Legislature's practice of opening each day with a chaplain's prayer as "a tolerable acknowledgment of beliefs widely held among the people of this country." And so I agree with the majority that the issue here is "whether the prayer practice in the Town of Greece fits within the tradition long followed in Congress and the state legislatures."

Where I depart from the majority is in my reply to that question. The town hall here is a kind of hybrid. Greece's Board indeed has legislative functions, as Congress and state assemblies do—and that means some opening prayers are allowed there. But much as in my hypotheticals, the Board's meetings are also occasions for ordinary citizens to engage with and petition their government, often on highly individualized matters. That feature calls for Board members to exercise special care to ensure that the prayers * * * respect each and every member of the community as an equal citizen. But the Board, and the clergy members it selected, made no such effort. * * *

A

Start by comparing two pictures, drawn precisely from reality. The first is of Nebraska's (unicameral) Legislature, as this Court and the state senators themselves described it. The second is of town council meetings in Greece * * *.

It is morning in Nebraska, and senators are beginning to gather in the State's legislative chamber * * *. The chaplain rises to give the daily invocation. That prayer * * * is "directed only at the legislative membership, not at the public at large." Any members of the public who happen to be in attendance—not very many at this early hour—watch only from the upstairs visitors' gallery.

The longtime chaplain says something like the following * * *: "*O God*, who has given all persons talents and varying capacities, Thou dost only require of us that we utilize Thy gifts to a maximum. In this Legislature to which Thou has entrusted special abilities and opportunities, may each recognize his stewardship for the people of the State." The chaplain is a Presbyterian minister, and "some of his earlier prayers" explicitly invoked Christian beliefs, but he "removed all references to Christ" after a single legislator complained. The chaplain also previously invited other clergy members to give the invocation, including local rabbis.

Now change the channel: It is evening in Greece, New York, and the Supervisor of the Town Board calls its monthly public meeting to order. Those meetings (so says the Board itself) are "the most important part of Town government." They serve assorted functions, almost all actively involving members of the public. The Board may swear in new Town employees and hand out awards for civic accomplishments; it always provides an opportunity (called a Public Forum) for citizens to address local issues and ask for improved services or new policies * * *.

The Town Supervisor, Town Clerk, Chief of Police, and four Board members sit at the front of the meeting room on a raised dais. But the setting is intimate: There are likely to be only 10 or so citizens in attendance. A few may be children or teenagers, present to receive an award or fulfill a high school civics requirement.

As the first order of business, the Town Supervisor introduces a local Christian clergy member—denominated the chaplain of the month—to lead the assembled persons in prayer. The pastor steps up to a lectern (emblazoned with the Town's seal) at the front of the dais, and with his back to the Town officials, he faces the citizens present. He asks them all to stand and to "pray as we begin this evening's town meeting." And he says:

> The beauties of spring . . . are an expressive symbol of the new life of the risen Christ. The Holy Spirit was sent to the apostles at Pentecost so that they would be courageous witnesses of the Good News to different regions of the Mediterranean world and beyond. The Holy Spirit continues to be the inspiration and the source of strength and virtue, which we all need in the world of today. And so . . . [w]e pray this evening for the guidance of the Holy Spirit as the Greece Town Board meets.

After the pastor concludes, Town officials behind him make the sign of the cross, as do some members of the audience, and everyone says "Amen." The Supervisor then announces the start of the Public Forum, and a citizen stands up to complain about the Town's contract with a cable company.

B

Let's count the ways in which these pictures diverge. First, the governmental proceedings at which the prayers occur differ significantly in nature and purpose. The Nebraska Legislature's floor sessions—like those of the U.S. Congress and other state assemblies—are of, by, and for elected lawmakers. Members of the public take no part in those proceedings; any few who attend are spectators only, watching from a high-up visitors' gallery. * * * Greece's town meetings, by contrast, revolve around ordinary members of the community. * * *

Second (and following from what I just said), the prayers in these two settings have different audiences. In the Nebraska Legislature, the chaplain spoke to, and only to, the elected representatives. * * *

The very opposite is true in Greece: * * * [T]he prayers there are directed squarely at the citizens. * * *

And third, the prayers themselves differ in their content and character. *Marsh* * * * stated * * * that the chaplain had removed all explicitly Christian references at a senator's request. * * *

But no one can fairly read the prayers from Greece's Town meetings as anything other than explicitly Christian—constantly and exclusively so. From the time Greece established its prayer practice in 1999 until litigation loomed nine years later, all of its monthly chaplains were Christian clergy. And after a brief spell surrounding the filing of this suit (when a Jewish layman, a Wiccan priestess, and a Baha'i minister appeared at meetings), the Town resumed its practice of inviting only clergy from neighboring Protestant and Catholic churches. About two-thirds of the prayers given over this decade or so invoked "Jesus," "Christ," "Your Son," or "the Holy Spirit"; in the 18 months before the record closed, 85% included those references. Many prayers contained elaborations of Christian doctrine or recitations of scripture. And the prayers usually close with phrases like "in the name of Jesus Christ" or "in the name of Your son."

Still more, the prayers betray no understanding that the American community is today, as it long has been, a rich mosaic of religious faiths. The monthly chaplains appear almost always to assume that everyone in the room is Christian * * *. The Town itself has never urged its chaplains to reach out to members of other faiths, or even to recall that they might be present. * * *

C

Those three differences, taken together, remove this case from the protective ambit of *Marsh* and the history on which it relied. * * *

* * *

Everything about [the Greece] situation, I think, infringes the First Amendment. * * *

None of this means that Greece's town hall must be religion-or prayer-free. * * * What the circumstances here demand is the recognition that we are a pluralistic people too. When citizens of all faiths come to speak to each other and their elected representatives in a legislative session, the government must take especial care to ensure that the prayers they hear will seek to include, rather than serve to divide. * * *

And contrary to the majority's * * * view, that is not difficult to do. If the Town Board had let its chaplains know that they should speak in nonsectarian terms, common to diverse religious groups, then no one would have valid grounds for complaint. Priests and ministers, rabbis and imams give such invocations all the time; there is no great mystery to the project. * * * Or if the Board preferred, it might have invited clergy of many faiths to serve as chaplains, * * *. When one month a clergy member refers to Jesus, and the next to Allah or Jehovah * * *, the government does not identify itself with one religion or align itself with that faith's citizens, and the effect of even sectarian prayer is transformed. * * *

But Greece could not do what it did: infuse a participatory government body with one (and only one) faith * * *.

III

How, then, does the majority go so far astray, allowing the Town of Greece to turn its assemblies for citizens into a forum for Christian prayer? * * * [T]he error reflects two kinds of blindness. First, the majority misapprehends the facts of this case * * *. And second, the majority misjudges the essential meaning of the religious worship in Greece's town hall, along with its capacity to exclude and divide.

* * * When the majority analyzes the "setting" and "audience" for prayer, it focuses almost exclusively on Congress and the Nebraska Legislature; it does not stop to analyze how far those factors differ in Greece's meetings. The majority thus gives short shrift to the gap—more like, the chasm—between a legislative floor session involving only elected officials and a town hall revolving around ordinary citizens. And similarly the majority neglects to consider how the prayers in Greece are mostly addressed to members of the public, rather than (as in the forums it discusses) to the lawmakers. * * *

And of course—as the majority sidesteps as well—to pray in the name of Jesus Christ. In addressing the sectarian content of these prayers, the majority again changes the subject, preferring to explain what happens in *other* government bodies. * * * But that case is not this one * * * because in Greece only Christian clergy members speak, and then mostly in the voice of their own religion * * *.

And the month in, month out sectarianism the Board chose for its meetings belies the majority's refrain that the prayers in Greece were "ceremonial" in nature. Ceremonial references to the divine surely abound: The majority is right that "the Pledge of Allegiance, inaugural prayer, or the recitation of 'God save the United States and this honorable Court'" each fits the bill. But prayers evoking "the saving sacrifice of Jesus Christ on the cross," "the plan of redemption that is fulfilled in Jesus Christ," "the life and death, resurrection and ascension of the Savior Jesus Christ," the workings of the Holy Spirit, the events of Pentecost, and the belief that God "has raised up the Lord Jesus" and "will raise us, in our turn, and put us by His side"? No. These are statements of profound belief and deep meaning, subscribed to by many, denied by some. * * *

* * * [T]he not-so-implicit message of the majority's opinion—"What's the big deal, anyway?"—is mistaken. The content of Greece's prayers *is* a big deal, to Christians and non-Christians alike. * * *

IV

* * *

* * * When the citizens of this country approach their government, they do so only as Americans, not as members of one faith or another. I * * * respectfully dissent from the Court's decision.

NOTES AND QUESTIONS

1. What is the purpose of the Establishment Clause?

2. What facts were critical to the majority's holding that the town of Greece did not violate the Establishment Clause? Did the dissent disagree with the majority on factual grounds, legal grounds, or both? Which decision is more persuasive?

3. *Town of Greece* arose in the context of monthly town board meetings. Establishment Clause issues arise in several other contexts. This note discusses three such contexts.

  a. **Public Funding of Religious Schools:** In *Lemon v. Kurtzman*, 403 U.S. 602 (1971), the Supreme Court addressed the claim that providing state aid to religious schools violated the Establishment Clause. Two states, Rhode Island and Pennsylvania, had statutes under which the state provided financial assistance to religious schools for secular activities. The Court used a three-part test, now known as the *"Lemon"* test, to analyze whether the statutes violated the Establishment Clause: (1) Did the statute have a secular legal purpose? (2) Was the primary effect of the statute to advance religion? (3) Did the statute lead to excessive entanglement between government and religion? Ultimately, the Court relied on the third question, holding that "the cumulative impact of the entire relationship arising under the statutes in each State involves excessive entanglement between government and religion" because the state would have to consistently monitor the schools to ensure that the funds were not used for religious purposes. *Id.* at 614. For additional discussion of public funding of religious schools, *see, e.g.*, *Bd. of Educ. of Westside Cmty. Schs. v. Mergens*, 496 U.S. 226 (1990) (religious group's use of school property after school hours did not violate the Establishment Clause); *Everson v. Bd. of Educ. of Ewing Twp.*, 330 U.S. 1 (1947) (upholding the use of city buses to transport students to Catholic school).

b. Religious Activity in Schools: In *Engel v. Vitale*, 370 U.S. 421 (1962), the Court addressed the question of whether the use of an official prayer in schools violated the Establishment Clause. In that case, the Board of Education directed schools to begin each day with student recitation of the prayer in the presence of a teacher. The prayer stated: "Almighty God, we acknowledge our dependence upon Thee, and we beg Thy blessings upon us, our parents, our teachers, and our Country." *Id.* at 422. The Court held that this practice violated the Establishment Clause: "[P]etitioners argue[] the State's use of the * * * prayer in its public school system breaches the constitutional wall of separation between Church and State. We agree with that contention since we think that the [the Establishment Clause] must at least mean that in this country it is no part of the business of government to compose official prayers for any group of the American people to recite as a part of a religious program carried on by government." *Id.* at 425. For additional discussion of religion in public schools, *see, e.g.*, *Santa Fe Indep. Sch. Dist. v. Doe*, 530 U.S. 290 (2000) (student-led prayer before school football games violated the Establishment Clause); *Lee v. Weisman*, 505 U.S. 577 (1992) (clergy-led prayers at a middle school graduation ceremony violated the Establishment Clause); *Sch. Dist. of Abington Twp. v. Schempp*, 374 U.S. 203 (1963) (school-sponsored Bible readings violated the Establishment Clause).

c. Use of Religious Symbols in Government Spaces: In *County of Allegheny v. American Civil Liberties Union Greater Pittsburgh Chapter*, 492 U.S. 573 (1989), the Supreme Court applied the *"Lemon"* test to determine whether the erection of a crèche (a representation of the birth of Jesus described in the Christian Bible) in a county courthouse violated the Establishment Clause. The Court concluded: "[B]y permitting the display of the crèche in this particular physical setting, the county sends an unmistakable message that it supports and promotes the Christian praise to God that is the crèche's religious message." *Id.* at 600. The Court further explained that, "by prohibiting government endorsement of religion, the Establishment Clause prohibits precisely what occurred here: the government's lending its support to the communication of a religious organization's religious message." *Id.* at 601. In the same case, however, the Court held that the erection at a City-County building of a Menorah, a Jewish religious symbol associated with the Jewish holiday of Chanukah, and a Christmas tree, associated with the Christian holiday of Christmas, did not violate the Establishment Clause. The Court reasoned that the Christmas tree was not necessarily a religious symbol, there was no alternative secular symbol to recognize Chanukah, and the display included a sign explaining that "during the holiday season the city salutes liberty." *Id.* at 619. For other cases discussing government use of religious symbols, *see, e.g.,* *Van Orden v. Perry,* 545 U.S. 677 (2005) (Ten Commandments monument on the grounds of the Texas State Capitol did not violate the Establishment Clause); *Lynch v. Donnelly,* 465 U.S. 668 (1984) (Christmas display that included a nativity scene, Santa, and reindeers was not an endorsement of religion and thus did not violate the Establishment Clause); *Stone v. Graham,* 449 U.S. 39 (1980) (requirement that the Ten Commandments be displayed in public classrooms violated the Establishment Clause).

4.   For further reading on the Establishment Clause, *see, e.g.,* Steven Gey, *Reconciling the Supreme Court's Four Establishment Clauses,* 8 U. Pa. J. Const. L. 725 (2006) (identifying inconsistencies in the Supreme Court's Establishment Clause jurisprudence and suggesting that these inconsistencies arise because there is ongoing conflict as to the role of religion in government and whether the government is, or should be, secular); John Jeffries, Jr. & James Ryan, *A Political History of the Establishment Clause,* 100 Mich. L. Rev. 279 (2001) (evaluating Establishment Clause cases as if they were political contests among interest groups and arguing that that approach helps to account for the results in the cases and to explain the instability of the doctrine as a product of changing political forces).

C. EQUAL PROTECTION (AND RELATED ISSUES)

In response to the American Civil War (1861–1865) and the racial tensions over slavery that were at the heart of the war, Congress passed the so-called Civil War Amendments—the Thirteenth, Fourteenth, and Fifteenth Amendments to the Constitution. One clause of the Fourteenth Amendment, known as the Equal Protection Clause, states that "No state shall * * * deny to any person within its jurisdiction the equal protection of the laws." The Supreme Court has also found that there is an implicit guarantee of equal protection within the Fifth Amendment Due Process Clause. The equal protection guarantee has been applied in many contexts to prevent discrimination against minority groups. The following cases explore some of the parameters of equal protection (and the related concept of due process).

1.   RACE/SCHOOL DESEGREGATION

BROWN V. BOARD OF EDUCATION
Supreme Court of the United States, 1954
347 U.S. 483

CHIEF JUSTICE WARREN delivered the opinion of the Court.

These cases come to us from the States of Kansas, South Carolina, Virginia, and Delaware. They are premised on different facts and different local conditions, but a common legal question justifies their consideration together in this consolidated opinion.

In each of the cases, minors of the Negro race, through their legal representatives, seek the aid of the courts in obtaining admission to the public schools of their community on a nonsegregated basis. In each instance, they have been denied admission to schools attended by white children under laws requiring or permitting segregation according to race. This segregation was alleged to deprive the plaintiffs of the equal protection of the laws under the Fourteenth Amendment. In each of the cases other than the Delaware case, a three-judge federal district court denied relief to the plaintiffs on the so-called "separate but equal" doctrine announced by this Court in *Plessy v. Ferguson*, 163 U.S. 537 (1896). Under that doctrine, equality of treatment is accorded when the races are provided substantially equal facilities, even though these facilities be separate. In the Delaware case, the Supreme Court of Delaware adhered to that doctrine, but ordered that the plaintiffs be admitted to the white schools because of their superiority to the Negro schools.

The plaintiffs contend that segregated public schools are not "equal" and cannot be made "equal," and that hence they are deprived of the equal protection of the laws. Because of the obvious importance of the question presented, the Court took jurisdiction. * * *

* * * The most avid proponents of the post-War Amendments [Thirteenth, Fourteenth, and Fifteenth] undoubtedly intended them to remove all legal distinctions among "all persons born or naturalized in the United States." Their opponents, just as certainly, were antagonistic to both the letter and the spirit of the Amendments and wished them to have the most limited effect. What others in Congress and the state legislatures had in mind cannot be determined with any degree of certainty.

An additional reason for the inconclusive nature of the [Fourteenth] Amendment's history, with respect to segregated schools, is the status of public education at that time. In the South, the movement toward free common schools, supported by general taxation, had not yet taken hold.

Education of white children was largely in the hands of private groups. Education of Negroes was almost nonexistent, and practically all of the race were illiterate. In fact, any education of Negroes was forbidden by law in some states. Today, in contrast, many Negroes have achieved outstanding success in the arts and sciences as well as in the business and professional world. It is true that public school education at the time of the Amendment had advanced further in the North, but the effect of the Amendment on Northern States was generally ignored in the congressional debates. Even in the North, the conditions of public education did not approximate those existing today. The curriculum was usually rudimentary; ungraded schools were common in rural areas; the school term was but three months a year in many states; and compulsory school attendance was virtually unknown. As a consequence, it is not surprising that there should be so little in the history of the Fourteenth Amendment relating to its intended effect on public education.

In the first cases in this Court construing the Fourteenth Amendment, decided shortly after its adoption, the Court interpreted it as proscribing all state-imposed discriminations against the Negro race. The doctrine of "separate but equal" did not make its appearance in this court until 1896 in the case of *Plessy v. Ferguson*, involving not education but transportation. American courts have since labored with the doctrine for over half a century. In this Court, there have been six cases involving the "separate but equal" doctrine in the field of public education. * * * In none of these cases was it necessary to re-examine the doctrine to grant relief to the Negro plaintiff. * * *

In the instant cases, that question is directly presented. Here, * * * there are findings below that the Negro and white schools involved have been equalized, or are being equalized, with respect to buildings, curricula, qualifications and salaries of teachers, and other "tangible" factors. Our decision, therefore, cannot turn on merely a comparison of these tangible factors in the Negro and white schools involved in each of the cases. We must look instead to the effect of segregation itself on public education.

In approaching this problem, we cannot turn the clock back to 1868 when the Amendment was adopted, or even to 1896 when *Plessy v. Ferguson* was written. We must consider public education in the light of its full development and its present place in American life throughout the Nation. Only in this way can it be determined if segregation in public schools deprives these plaintiffs of the equal protection of the laws.

Today, education is perhaps the most important function of state and local governments. Compulsory school attendance laws and the great expenditures for education both demonstrate our recognition of the importance of education to our democratic society. It is required in the performance of our most basic public responsibilities, even service in the armed forces. It is the very foundation of good citizenship. Today it is a principal instrument in awakening the child to cultural values, in preparing him for later professional training, and in helping him to adjust normally to his environment. In these days, it is doubtful that any child may reasonably be expected to succeed in life if he is denied the opportunity of an education. Such an opportunity, where the state has undertaken to provide it, is a right which must be made available to all on equal terms.

We come then to the question presented: Does segregation of children in public schools solely on the basis of race, even though the physical facilities and other "tangible" factors may be equal, deprive the children of the minority group of equal educational opportunities? We believe that it does.

In *Sweatt v. Painter*, 339 U.S. 629 (1950), in finding that a segregated law school for Negroes could not provide them equal educational opportunities, this Court relied in large part on "those qualities which are incapable of objective measurement but which make for greatness in a law school." In *McLaurin v. Oklahoma State Regents*, 339 U.S. 637 (1950), the Court, in requiring that a Negro admitted to a white graduate school be treated like all other students, again resorted to intangible considerations: ". . . his ability to study, to engage in discussions and exchange views with other students, and, in general, to learn his profession." Such considerations apply with added force to children in grade and high schools. To separate them from others of similar age and qualifications solely because of their race generates a feeling of inferiority as to their status in the community that may affect their hearts and minds in a way unlikely ever to be undone. The effect of this separation on their educational opportunities was well stated by a finding in the Kansas case by a court which nevertheless felt compelled to rule against the Negro plaintiffs:

> Segregation of white and colored children in public schools has a detrimental effect upon the colored children. The impact is greater when it has the sanction of the law; for the policy of separating the races is usually interpreted as denoting the inferiority of the Negro group. A sense of inferiority affects the motivation of a child to learn. Segregation with the sanction of law, therefore, has a tendency to (retard) the educational and mental development of Negro children and to deprive them of some of the benefits they would receive in a racial[ly] integrated school system.

Whatever may have been the extent of psychological knowledge at the time of *Plessy v. Ferguson*, this finding is amply supported by modern authority.[11] Any language in *Plessy v. Ferguson* contrary to this finding is rejected.

We conclude that in the field of public education the doctrine of "separate but equal" has no place. Separate educational facilities are

---

[11] [The Court cited several articles on the psychological effects of segregation.]

inherently unequal. Therefore, we hold that the plaintiffs and others similarly situated for whom the actions have been brought are, by reason of the segregation complained of, deprived of the equal protection of the laws guaranteed by the Fourteenth Amendment. This disposition makes unnecessary any discussion whether such segregation also violates the Due Process Clause of the Fourteenth Amendment.

Because these are class actions, because of the wide applicability of this decision, and because of the great variety of local conditions, the formulation of decrees in these cases presents problems of considerable complexity. * * * We have now announced that such segregation is a denial of the equal protection of the laws. In order that we may have the full assistance of the parties in formulating decrees, the cases will be restored to the docket, and the parties are requested to present further argument on [the issues that should be covered in the Court's decrees]. The Attorney General of the United States is again invited to participate. The Attorneys General of the states requiring or permitting segregation in public education will also be permitted to appear as amici curiae * * *.

It is so ordered.

Cases ordered restored to docket for further argument on question of appropriate decrees.

NOTES AND QUESTIONS

1.   What was the relief sought by plaintiffs in *Brown*? What was the legal basis for their claim? Why would plaintiffs choose to sue as a class action through "legal representatives" and unnamed class members?

2.   What did the Court in *Brown* hold? Why did the Court reject its previous approach in *Plessy v. Ferguson*?

3.   If it is assumed that the separate black and white schools at issue in *Brown* were "equal" in terms of building facilities, curricula, faculty, and other "tangible factors," was the Court correct in ruling for the plaintiffs? Why or why not?

4.   Dr. Kenneth Clark was one of various social scientists who testified in the district court in *Brown* about the effect of segregation on children. In the 1940s, Drs. Kenneth and Mamie Clark conducted a series of experiments known as the "doll tests" to study how segregation affected African American children. The test consisted of providing four different dolls, identical apart from their color, to African American children between the ages of three and seven. The children were asked to describe the race of the dolls and to choose the doll that they preferred. A majority of the children preferred the white dolls. The Clarks' research was cited by the *Brown* Court in footnote 11 of its opinion.

5.   In a subsequent opinion, *Brown v. Board of Education of Topeka, Kansas* (*Brown II*), 349 U.S. 294 (1955), the Court addressed the

implementation of *Brown*. The Court recognized that individual school districts might encounter difficulties "in making the transition to school systems operated in accordance with" *Brown*, and stated that once the school districts begin, "the courts may find that additional time is necessary to carry out the ruling in an effective manner." *Id.* at 300. The Court instructed the school districts to implement *Brown* "with all deliberate speed." *Id.*

Indeed, implementation proved to be protracted and controversial. Following *Brown* and *Brown II*, there was significant public outcry about the Court's decisions, particularly in the South. One of the most publicized acts of defiance occurred in Little Rock, Arkansas, where the governor ordered National Guard troops to prevent African American students from attending an all-white high school. In response, President Eisenhower sent a thousand paratroopers to Little Rock and federalized the National Guard to facilitate integration. The school board requested relief from a federal district judge that would have allowed the board to postpone desegregation. The district court granted the request, but the court of appeals reversed. In *Cooper v. Aaron*, 358 U.S. 1 (1958), the Supreme Court affirmed the court of appeals' decision, denying the school board's requested relief, and reaffirming the state's obligation to follow the law as announced by the U.S. Supreme Court. The opinion was signed by all nine Justices. *See* David Strauss, *Little Rock and the Legacy of* Brown, 52 St. Louis U. L.J. 1065 (2008) (describing the aftermath of *Brown*, the events at Little Rock, and *Cooper v. Aaron*). As other school districts continued to delay the integration of their schools, the Supreme Court repeatedly demanded that its earlier rulings be followed. *See, e.g., Alexander v. Holmes Cnty. Bd. of Educ.*, 396 U.S. 19 (1969) (holding that desegregation must be implemented "at once"); *Swann v. Charlotte-Mecklenburg Bd. of Educ.*, 402 U.S. 1 (1971) (approving busing to achieve racial desegregation in schools); *Keyes v. Sch. Dist. No. 1*, 413 U.S. 189 (1973) (same).

6.   Many judges and scholars consider *Brown* to be one of the Supreme Court's most important decisions of all time. *See, e.g.*, BERNARD SCHWARTZ, A HISTORY OF THE SUPREME COURT 286 (1993) (noting that "*Brown* was the watershed constitutional case of this century" and quoting Justice Stanley Reed, who stated that "if [*Brown*] was not the most important decision in the history of the Court, it was very close"); J. HARVIE WILKINSON III, FROM BROWN TO BAKKE: THE SUPREME COURT AND SCHOOL INTEGRATION: 1954–1978 6 (1979) ("*Brown* may be the most important political, social, and legal event in America's twentieth-century history."). The fact that the decision was unanimous is especially noteworthy. *See, e.g.*, Randall Shepard, *The Changing Nature of Judicial Leadership*, 42 Ind. L. Rev. 767 (2009) (describing Chief Justice Earl Warren's efforts to produce a unanimous opinion in *Brown*); John David Fassett et al., *Supreme Court Law Clerks' Recollections of* Brown v. Board of Education, 78 St. John's L. Rev. 515 (2004) (recollections of law clerks who served at the time of *Brown* about the process of reaching a unanimous decision).

7.   For additional discussion of *Brown* and its aftermath, *see, e.g.*, MARTHA MINOW, IN BROWN'S WAKE: LEGACIES OF AMERICA'S EDUCATIONAL

LANDMARK (2010) (concluding that, while American schools remain largely segregated by race, *Brown* was a landmark decision, and urging that there be a recommitment to *Brown*'s vision); Jack Weinstein, Brown v. Board of Education *After Fifty Years*, 26 Cardozo L. Rev. 289 (2004) (authored by a federal judge who was part of the team of lawyers in *Brown*, who noted that there is more work to be done to reach *Brown*'s goal of desegregation and educational equality); Michael Klarman, Brown, *Racial Change, and the Civil Rights Movement*, 80 Va. L. Rev. 7 (1994) (questioning the traditional understanding of *Brown* as a turning point in U.S. race relations and suggesting that *Brown*, far from advancing the cause of civil rights, actually led to more racial tension in the South, contributing to the violent suppression of African Americans seen during the Civil Rights Movement of the 1960s).

8.   A related topic, affirmative action, is discussed at the end of this chapter.

2. GAY RIGHTS

OBERGEFELL V. HODGES
Supreme Court of the United States, 2015
576 U.S. ___, 135 S. Ct. 2584

JUSTICE KENNEDY delivered the opinion of the Court.

The Constitution promises liberty to all within its reach, a liberty that includes certain specific rights that allow persons, within a lawful realm, to define and express their identity. The petitioners in these cases seek to find that liberty by marrying someone of the same sex and having their marriages deemed lawful on the same terms and conditions as marriages between persons of the opposite sex.

I

These cases come from Michigan, Kentucky, Ohio, and Tennessee, States that define marriage as a union between one man and one woman. The petitioners are 14 same-sex couples and two men whose same-sex partners are deceased. The respondents are state officials responsible for enforcing the laws in question. The petitioners claim the respondents violate the Fourteenth Amendment by denying them the right to marry or to have their marriages, lawfully performed in another State, given full recognition.

Petitioners filed these suits in United States District Courts in their home States. Each District Court ruled in their favor. * * * The respondents appealed the decisions * * *. [The U.S. Court of Appeals for the Sixth Circuit] consolidated the cases and reversed the judgments of the District Courts. [It] held that a State has no constitutional obligation to license same-sex marriages or to recognize same-sex marriages performed out of State.

The petitioners sought certiorari. This Court granted review [on the questions of] whether the Fourteenth Amendment requires a State to license a marriage between two people of the same sex * * * [and] whether the Fourteenth Amendment requires a State to recognize a same-sex marriage licensed and performed in a State which does grant that right.

II

Before addressing the principles and precedents that govern these cases, it is appropriate to note the history of the subject now before the Court.

A

From their beginning to their most recent page, the annals of human history reveal the transcendent importance of marriage. The lifelong union of a man and a woman always has promised nobility and dignity to all persons, without regard to their station in life. * * *

The centrality of marriage to the human condition makes it unsurprising that the institution has existed for millennia and across civilizations. Since the dawn of history, marriage has transformed strangers into relatives, binding families and societies together. [The Court quoted Confucius and Cicero on the importance of marriage.] * * * It is fair and necessary to say these [quotes] were based on the understanding that marriage is a union between two persons of the opposite sex.

That history is the beginning of these cases. The [state officials] say it should be the end as well. To them, it would demean a timeless institution if the concept and lawful status of marriage were extended to two persons of the same sex. * * *

The petitioners acknowledge this history but contend that these cases cannot end there. * * * Far from seeking to devalue marriage, the petitioners seek it for themselves because of their respect—and need—for its privileges and responsibilities. And their immutable nature dictates that same-sex marriage is their only real path to this profound commitment.

Recounting the circumstances of three of these cases illustrates the urgency of the petitioners' cause from their perspective. Petitioner James Obergefell, a plaintiff in the Ohio case, met John Arthur over two decades ago. They fell in love and started a life together, establishing a lasting, committed relation. In 2011, however, Arthur was diagnosed with amyotrophic lateral sclerosis, or ALS. This debilitating disease is progressive, with no known cure. Two years ago, Obergefell and Arthur decided to commit to one another, resolving to marry before Arthur died. To fulfill their mutual promise, they traveled from Ohio to Maryland, where same-sex marriage was legal. It was difficult for Arthur to move, and so the couple were wed inside a medical transport plane as it remained on the tarmac in Baltimore. Three months later, Arthur died. Ohio law does not permit Obergefell to be listed as the surviving spouse on Arthur's death certificate. By statute, they must remain strangers even in death * * *. He brought suit to be shown as the surviving spouse on Arthur's death certificate.

April DeBoer and Jayne Rowse are co-plaintiffs in the case from Michigan. They celebrated a commitment ceremony to honor their permanent relation in 2007. They both work as nurses, DeBoer in a neonatal unit and Rowse in an emergency unit. In 2009, DeBoer and Rowse fostered and then adopted a baby boy. Later that same year, they welcomed another son into their family. The new baby, born prematurely and abandoned by his biological mother, required around-the-clock care. The next year, a baby girl with special needs joined their family. Michigan, however, permits only opposite-sex married couples or single individuals to adopt, so each child can have only one woman as his or her legal parent. If an emergency were to arise, schools and hospitals may treat the three children as if they had only one parent. And, were tragedy to befall either DeBoer or Rowse, the other would have no legal rights over the children she had not been permitted to adopt. This couple seeks relief from the continuing uncertainty their unmarried status creates in their lives.

Army Reserve Sergeant First Class Ijpe DeKoe and his partner Thomas Kostura, co-plaintiffs in the Tennessee case, fell in love. In 2011, DeKoe received orders to deploy to Afghanistan. Before leaving, he and Kostura married in New York. A week later, DeKoe began his deployment, which lasted for almost a year. When he returned, the two settled in Tennessee, where DeKoe works full-time for the Army Reserve. Their lawful marriage is stripped from them whenever they reside in Tennessee, returning and disappearing as they travel across state lines. DeKoe, who served this Nation to preserve the freedom the Constitution protects, must endure a substantial burden.

The cases now before the Court involve other petitioners as well, each with their own experiences. Their stories reveal that they seek not to denigrate marriage but rather to live their lives, or honor their spouses' memory, joined by its bond.

B

* * * The history of marriage is one of both continuity and change. That institution—even as confined to opposite-sex relations—has evolved over time.

For example, marriage was once viewed as an arrangement by the couple's parents based on political, religious, and financial concerns; but by the time of the Nation's founding it was understood to be a voluntary contract between a man and a woman. As the role and status of women changed, the institution further evolved. Under the centuries-old doctrine of coverture, a married man and woman were treated by the State as a single, male-dominated legal entity. As women gained legal, political, and property rights, and as society began to understand that women have their own equal dignity, the law of coverture was abandoned. These and other developments in the institution of marriage over the past centuries * * * worked deep transformations in its structure, affecting aspects of marriage long viewed by many as essential.

These new insights have strengthened, not weakened, the institution of marriage. Indeed, changed understandings of marriage are characteristic of a Nation where new dimensions of freedom become apparent to new generations, often through perspectives that begin in pleas or protests and then are considered in the political sphere and the judicial process.

This dynamic can be seen in the Nation's experiences with the rights of gays and lesbians. Until the mid-20th century, same-sex intimacy long had been condemned as immoral by the state itself in most Western nations, a belief often embodied in the criminal law. * * * A truthful declaration by same-sex couples of what was in their hearts had to remain unspoken. Even when a greater awareness of the humanity and integrity of homosexual persons came in the period after World War II, the argument that gays and lesbians had a just claim to dignity was in conflict with both law and widespread social conventions. Same-sex intimacy remained a crime in many States. Gays and lesbians were prohibited from most government employment, barred from military service, excluded under immigration laws, targeted by police, and burdened in their rights to associate.

For much of the 20th century, moreover, homosexuality was treated as an illness. When the American Psychiatric Association published the first Diagnostic and Statistical Manual of Mental Disorders in 1952, homosexuality was classified as a mental disorder, a position adhered to until 1973. Only in more recent years have psychiatrists and others recognized that sexual orientation is both a normal expression of human sexuality and immutable.

In the late 20th century, following substantial cultural and political developments, same-sex couples began to lead more open and public lives and to establish families. * * * As a result, questions about the rights of gays and lesbians soon reached the courts * * *.

This Court first gave detailed consideration to the legal status of homosexuals in *Bowers v. Hardwick*, 478 U.S. 186 (1986). There it upheld the constitutionality of a Georgia law deemed to criminalize certain homosexual acts. Ten years later, in *Romer v. Evans*, 517 U.S. 620 (1996), the Court invalidated an amendment to Colorado's Constitution that sought to foreclose any branch or political subdivision of the State from protecting persons against discrimination based on sexual orientation.

Then, in 2003, the Court overruled *Bowers*, holding that laws making same-sex intimacy a crime "demea[n] the lives of homosexual persons." *Lawrence v. Texas*, 539 U.S. 558, 575 (2003).

Against this background, the legal question of same-sex marriage arose. In 1993, the Hawaii Supreme Court held Hawaii's law restricting marriage to opposite-sex couples constituted a classification on the basis of sex and was therefore subject to strict scrutiny under the Hawaii Constitution. * * * So too in 1996, Congress passed the Defense of Marriage Act (DOMA), 110 Stat. 2419, defining marriage for all federal-law purposes as "only a legal union between one man and one woman as husband and wife." 1 U.S.C. § 7.

* * * In 2003, the Supreme Judicial Court of Massachusetts held the State's Constitution guaranteed same-sex couples the right to marry. After that ruling, some additional States granted marriage rights to same-sex couples, either through judicial or legislative processes. * * * [I]n *United States v. Windsor*, 133 S. Ct. 2675 (2013), this Court invalidated DOMA to the extent it barred the Federal Government from treating same-sex marriages as valid even when they were lawful in the State where they were licensed. * * *

Numerous cases about same-sex marriage have reached the United States Courts of Appeals in recent years. * * * [Most have struck down bans on same-sex marriage.] There also have been many thoughtful District Court decisions addressing same-sex marriage—and most of them, too, have concluded same-sex couples must be allowed to marry. In addition the highest courts of many States have contributed to this ongoing dialogue in decisions interpreting their own State Constitutions. * * *

After years of litigation, legislation, referenda, and the discussions that attended these public acts, the States are now divided on the issue of same-sex marriage. * * *

III

Under the Due Process Clause of the Fourteenth Amendment, no State shall "deprive any person of life, liberty, or property, without due process of law." The fundamental liberties protected by this Clause include most of the rights enumerated in the Bill of Rights. In addition these liberties extend to certain personal choices central to individual dignity and autonomy, including intimate choices that define personal identity and beliefs.

The identification and protection of fundamental rights is an enduring part of the judicial duty to interpret the Constitution. * * *

The nature of injustice is that we may not always see it in our own times. The generations that wrote and ratified the Bill of Rights and the Fourteenth Amendment did not presume to know the extent of freedom in all of its dimensions, and so they entrusted to future generations a charter protecting the right of all persons to enjoy liberty as we learn its meaning. When new insight reveals discord between the Constitution's central protections and a received legal stricture, a claim to liberty must be addressed.

Applying these established tenets, the Court has long held the right to marry is protected by the Constitution. In *Loving v. Virginia*, 388 U.S. 1, 12 (1967) which invalidated bans on interracial unions, a unanimous Court held marriage is "one of the vital personal rights essential to the orderly pursuit of happiness by free men." The Court reaffirmed that holding in *Zablocki v. Redhail*, 434 U.S. 374, 384 (1978), which held the right to marry was burdened by a law prohibiting fathers who were behind on child support from marrying. The Court again applied this principle in *Turner v. Safley*, 482 U.S. 78, 95 (1987), which held the right to marry was abridged by regulations limiting the privilege of prison inmates to marry. Over time and in other contexts, the Court has reiterated that the right to marry is fundamental under the Due Process Clause.

* * *

* * * The four principles and traditions to be discussed demonstrate that the reasons marriage is fundamental under the Constitution apply with equal force to same-sex couples.

A first premise of the Court's relevant precedents is that the right to personal choice regarding marriage is inherent in the concept of individual autonomy. This abiding connection between marriage and liberty is why *Loving* invalidated interracial marriage bans under the Due Process Clause. * * *

Choices about marriage shape an individual's destiny. * * *

* * *

A second principle in this Court's jurisprudence is that the right to marry is fundamental because it supports a two-person union unlike any other in its importance to the committed individuals. * * *

* * * The right to marry * * * dignifies couples who "wish to define themselves by their commitment to each other." Marriage responds to the universal fear that a lonely person might call out only to find no one there. It offers the hope of companionship and understanding and assurance that while both still live there will be someone to care for the other.

As this Court held in *Lawrence*, same-sex couples have the same right as opposite-sex couples to enjoy intimate association. * * *

A third basis for protecting the right to marry is that it safeguards children and families and thus draws meaning from related rights of childrearing, procreation, and education. * * * By giving recognition and legal structure to their parents' relationship, marriage allows children "to understand the integrity and closeness of their own family and its concord with other families in their community and in their daily lives." Marriage also affords the permanency and stability important to children's best interests.

As all parties agree, many same-sex couples provide loving and nurturing homes to their children, whether biological or adopted. And hundreds of thousands of children are presently being raised by such couples. Most States have allowed gays and lesbians to adopt, either as individuals or as couples, and many adopted and foster children have same-sex parents. This provides powerful confirmation from the law itself that gays and lesbians can create loving, supportive families.

Excluding same-sex couples from marriage thus conflicts with a central premise of the right to marry. Without the recognition, stability, and predictability marriage offers, their children suffer the stigma of knowing their families are somehow lesser. They also suffer the significant material costs of being raised by unmarried parents, relegated through no fault of their own to a more difficult and uncertain family life. The marriage laws at issue here thus harm and humiliate the children of same-sex couples.

That is not to say the right to marry is less meaningful for those who do not or cannot have children. An ability, desire, or promise to procreate is not and has not been a prerequisite for a valid marriage in any State. * * * The constitutional marriage right has many aspects, of which childbearing is only one.

Fourth and finally, this Court's cases and the Nation's traditions make clear that marriage is a keystone of our social order.

* * *

For that reason, just as a couple vows to support each other, so does society pledge to support the couple, offering symbolic recognition and material benefits to protect and nourish the union. Indeed, while the States are in general free to vary the benefits they confer on all married couples, they have throughout our history made marriage the basis for an expanding list of governmental rights, benefits, and responsibilities. These aspects of marital status include: taxation; inheritance and property rights; rules of intestate succession; spousal privilege in the law of evidence; hospital access; medical decision-making authority; adoption rights; the rights and benefits of survivors; birth and death certificates; professional ethics rules; campaign finance restrictions; workers' compensation benefits; health insurance; and child custody, support, and visitation rules. Valid marriage under state law is also a significant status for over a thousand provisions of federal law. The States have contributed to the fundamental character of the marriage right by placing that institution at the center of so many facets of the legal and social order.

There is no difference between same-and opposite-sex couples with respect to this principle. Yet by virtue of their exclusion from that institution, same-sex couples are denied the constellation of benefits that the States have linked to marriage. * * * Same-sex couples are consigned to an instability many opposite-sex couples would deem intolerable in their own lives. As the State itself makes marriage all the more precious by the significance it attaches to it, exclusion from that status has the effect of teaching that gays and lesbians are unequal in important respects. It demeans gays and lesbians for the State to lock them out of a central institution of the Nation's society. * * *

The limitation of marriage to opposite-sex couples may long have seemed natural and just, but its inconsistency with the central meaning of the fundamental right to marry is now manifest. With that knowledge must come the recognition that laws excluding same-sex couples from the marriage right impose stigma and injury of the kind prohibited by our basic charter.

* * *

The right of same-sex couples to marry that is part of the liberty promised by the Fourteenth Amendment is derived, too, from that Amendment's guarantee of the equal protection of the laws. * * **

* * * [The Court explained that both *Loving* and *Zablocki* were based on the Due Process Clause and the Equal Protection Clause.] * * *

Indeed, in interpreting the Equal Protection Clause, the Court has recognized that new insights and societal understandings can reveal unjustified inequality within our most fundamental institutions that once passed unnoticed and unchallenged. [The Court described, by way of example, "invidious sex-based classifications in marriage" favoring the husband that existed into the mid-20th Century, until the Supreme Court invalidated them on equal protection grounds.] Like *Loving* and *Zablocki*, these precedents show the Equal Protection Clause can help to identify and correct inequalities in the institution of marriage, vindicating precepts of liberty and equality under the Constitution.

* * *

* * * [T]he challenged laws burden the liberty of same-sex couples, and it must be further acknowledged that they abridge central precepts of equality. Here the marriage laws enforced by the respondents are in essence unequal: same-sex couples are denied all the benefits afforded to opposite-sex couples and are barred from exercising a fundamental right.

---

* The pertinent language provides: "No State shall * * * deny any person within its jurisdiction the equal protection of the laws." [Ed.]

* * * The imposition of this disability on gays and lesbians serves to disrespect and subordinate them. * * *

These considerations lead to the conclusion that the right to marry is a fundamental right inherent in the liberty of the person, and under the Due Process and Equal Protection Clauses of the Fourteenth Amendment couples of the same-sex may not be deprived of that right and that liberty. The Court now holds that same-sex couples may exercise the fundamental right to marry. * * *

IV

There may be an initial inclination in these cases to proceed with caution—to await further legislation, litigation, and debate. * * *

Yet there has been far more deliberation than this argument acknowledges. There have been referenda, legislative debates, and grassroots campaigns, as well as countless studies, papers, books, and other popular and scholarly writings. There has been extensive litigation in state and federal courts. * * * [M]any of the central institutions in American life—state and local governments, the military, large and small businesses, labor unions, religious organizations, law enforcement, civic groups, professional organizations, and universities—have devoted substantial attention to the question. * * *

Of course, the Constitution contemplates that democracy is the appropriate process for change, so long as that process does not abridge fundamental rights. * * * But * * * "[t]he freedom secured by the Constitution consists, in one of its essential dimensions, of the right of the individual not to be injured by the unlawful exercise of governmental power." Thus, when the rights of persons are violated, "the Constitution requires redress by the courts," notwithstanding the more general value of democratic decision-making. This holds true even when protecting individual rights affects issues of the utmost importance and sensitivity.

The dynamic of our constitutional system is that individuals need not await legislative action before asserting a fundamental right. The Nation's courts are open to injured individuals who come to them to vindicate their own direct, personal stake in our basic charter. * * * This is why "fundamental rights may not be submitted to a vote * * *."

* * *

* * * Were the Court to uphold the challenged laws as constitutional, it would teach the Nation that these laws are in accord with our society's most basic compact. Were the Court to stay its hand to allow slower, case-by-case determination of the required availability of specific public benefits to same-sex couples, it still would deny gays and lesbians many rights and responsibilities intertwined with marriage.

The respondents also argue allowing same-sex couples to wed will harm marriage as an institution by leading to fewer opposite-sex marriages. This may occur, the respondents contend, because licensing same-sex marriage severs the connection between natural procreation and marriage. That argument, however, rests on a counterintuitive view of opposite-sex couple's decision-making processes regarding marriage and parenthood. Decisions about whether to marry and raise children are based on many personal, romantic, and practical considerations; and it is unrealistic to conclude that an opposite-sex couple would choose not to marry simply because same-sex couples may do so. * * *

Finally, it must be emphasized that religions, and those who adhere to religious doctrines, may continue to advocate with utmost, sincere conviction that, by divine precepts, same-sex marriage should not be condoned. The First Amendment ensures that religious organizations and persons are given proper protection as they seek to teach the principles that are so fulfilling and so central to their lives and faiths, and to their own deep aspirations to continue the family structure they have long revered. The same is true of those who oppose same-sex marriage for other reasons. In turn, those who believe allowing same-sex marriage is proper or indeed essential, whether as a matter of religious conviction or secular belief, may engage those who disagree with their view in an open and searching debate. The Constitution, however, does not permit the State to bar same-sex couples from marriage on the same terms as accorded to couples of the opposite sex.

V

These cases also present the question whether the Constitution requires States to recognize same-sex marriages validly performed out of State. As made clear by the case of Obergefell and Arthur, and by that of DeKoe and Kostura, the recognition bans inflict substantial and continuing harm on same-sex couples.

Being married in one State but having that valid marriage denied in another is one of "the most perplexing and distressing complication[s]" in the law of domestic relations. * * *

* * * [I]f States are required by the Constitution to issue marriage licenses to same-sex couples, the justifications for refusing to recognize those marriages performed elsewhere are undermined. The Court, in this decision, holds same-sex couples may exercise the fundamental right to marry in all States. It follows that the Court also must hold—and it now does hold—that there is no lawful basis for a State to refuse to recognize a lawful same-sex marriage performed in another State on the ground of its same-sex character.

* * *

No union is more profound than marriage, for it embodies the highest ideals of love, fidelity, devotion, sacrifice, and family. In forming a marital union, two people become something greater than once they were. As some of the petitioners in these cases demonstrate, marriage embodies a love that may endure even past death. It would misunderstand these men and women to say they disrespect the idea of marriage. Their plea is that they do respect it, respect it so deeply that they seek to find its fulfillment for themselves. Their hope is not to be condemned to live in loneliness, excluded from one of civilization's oldest institutions. They ask for equal dignity in the eyes of the law. The Constitution grants them that right.

The judgment of the Court of Appeals for the Sixth Circuit is reversed.

It is so ordered.

CHIEF JUSTICE ROBERTS, with whom JUSTICE SCALIA and JUSTICE THOMAS join, dissenting.

Petitioners make strong arguments rooted in social policy and considerations of fairness. They contend that same-sex couples should be allowed to affirm their love and commitment through marriage, just like opposite-sex couples. That position has undeniable appeal; over the past six years, voters and legislators in eleven States and the District of Columbia have revised their laws to allow marriage between two people of the same sex.

But this Court is not a legislature. Whether same-sex marriage is a good idea should be of no concern to us. Under the Constitution, judges have power to say what the law is, not what it should be. * * *

Although the policy arguments for extending marriage to same-sex couples may be compelling, the legal arguments for requiring such an extension are not. The fundamental right to marry does not include a right to make a State change its definition of marriage. And a State's decision to maintain the meaning of marriage that has persisted in every culture throughout human history can hardly be called irrational. In short, our Constitution does not enact any one theory of marriage. The people of a State are free to expand marriage to include same-sex couples, or to retain the historic definition.

Today, however, the Court takes the extraordinary step of ordering every State to license and recognize same-sex marriage. Many people will rejoice at this decision, and I begrudge none their celebration. But for those who believe in a government of laws, not of men, the majority's approach is deeply disheartening. Supporters of same-sex marriage have achieved considerable success persuading their fellow citizens—through the democratic process—to adopt their view. That ends today. Five lawyers have closed the debate and enacted their own vision of marriage as a matter of constitutional law. Stealing this issue from the people will for many cast a cloud over same-sex marriage, making a dramatic social change that much more difficult to accept.

The majority's decision is an act of will, not legal judgment. The right it announces has no basis in the Constitution or this Court's precedent. * * * [T]he Court invalidates the marriage laws of more than half the States and orders the transformation of a social institution that has formed the basis of human society for millennia * * *. Just who do we think we are?

It can be tempting for judges to confuse our own preferences with the requirements of the law. But as this Court has been reminded throughout our history, the Constitution "is made for people of fundamentally differing views." Accordingly, "courts are not concerned with the wisdom or policy of legislation." The majority today neglects that restrained conception of the judicial role. It seizes for itself a question the Constitution leaves to the people, at a time when the people are engaged in a vibrant debate on that question. And it answers that question based not on neutral principles of constitutional law, but on its own "understanding of what freedom is and must become." I have no choice but to dissent.

Understand well what this dissent is about: It is not about whether, in my judgment, the institution of marriage should be changed to include same-sex couples. It is instead about whether, in our democratic republic, that decision should rest with the people acting through their elected representatives, or with five lawyers who happen to hold commissions authorizing them to resolve legal disputes according to law. The Constitution leaves no doubt about the answer.

I

* * * There is no serious dispute that, under our precedents, the Constitution protects a right to marry and requires States to apply their marriage laws equally. The real question in these cases is what constitutes "marriage," or—more precisely—*who decides* what constitutes "marriage"?

The majority largely ignores these questions * * *.

A

As the majority acknowledges, marriage "has existed for millennia and across civilizations." For all those millennia, across all those civilizations, "marriage" referred to only one relationship: the union of a man and a woman. * * *

* * *

This singular understanding of marriage has prevailed in the United States throughout our history. * * *

The Constitution itself says nothing about marriage, and the Framers thereby entrusted the States with "[t]he whole subject of the domestic relations of husband and wife." * * * There is no dispute that every State at the founding—and every State throughout our history until a dozen years ago—defined marriage in the traditional, biologically rooted way. The four States in these cases are typical. Their laws, before and after statehood, have treated marriage as the union of a man and a woman. The meaning of "marriage" went without saying.

* * *

B

Shortly after this Court struck down racial restrictions on marriage in *Loving*, a gay couple in Minnesota sought a marriage license. They argued that the Constitution required States to allow marriage between people of the same sex for the same reasons that it requires States to allow marriage between people of different races. The Minnesota Supreme Court rejected their analogy to *Loving*, and this Court summarily dismissed an appeal [in 1972].

In the decades after [1972], greater numbers of gays and lesbians began living openly, and many expressed a desire to have their relationships recognized as marriages. Over time, more people came to see marriage in a way that could be extended to such couples. Until recently, this new view of marriage remained a minority position. * * *

Over the last few years, public opinion on marriage has shifted rapidly. In 2009, the legislatures of Vermont, New Hampshire, and the District of Columbia became the first in the Nation to enact laws that revised the definition of marriage to include same-sex couples, while also providing accommodations for religious believers. In 2011, the New York Legislature enacted a similar law. In 2012, voters in Maine did the same, reversing the result of a referendum just three years earlier in which they had upheld the traditional definition of marriage.

In all, voters and legislators in eleven States and the District of Columbia have changed their definitions of marriage to include same-sex couples. The highest courts of five States have decreed that same result under their own Constitutions. The remainder of the States retain the traditional definition of marriage.

Petitioners [argue] that the Due Process and Equal Protection Clauses of the Fourteenth Amendment compel their States to license and recognize marriages between same-sex couples. [The Court of Appeals] concluded that petitioners had not made "the case for constitutionalizing the definition of marriage * * *." I would affirm.

II

Petitioners first contend that the marriage laws of their States violate the Due Process Clause. * * *

The majority purports to identify four "principles and traditions" in this Court's due process precedents that support a fundamental right for same-sex couples to marry. * * * Stripped of its shiny rhetorical gloss, the majority's argument is that the Due Process Clause gives same-sex couples a fundamental right to marry because it will be good for them and for society. If I were a legislator, I would certainly consider that view as a matter of social policy. But as a judge, I find the majority's position indefensible as a matter of constitutional law.

A

Petitioners' "fundamental right" claim falls into the most sensitive category of constitutional adjudication. Petitioners do not contend that their States' marriage laws violate an *enumerated* constitutional right, such as the freedom of speech protected by the First Amendment. * * * They argue instead that the laws violate a right *implied* by the Fourteenth Amendment's requirement that "liberty" may not be deprived without "due process of law."

This Court has interpreted the Due Process Clause to include a "substantive" component that protects certain liberty interests against state deprivation "no matter what process is provided." The theory is that some liberties are "so rooted in the traditions and conscience of our people as to be ranked as fundamental," and therefore cannot be deprived without compelling justification.

Allowing unelected federal judges to select which unenumerated rights rank as "fundamental"—and to strike down state laws on the basis of that determination—raises obvious concerns about the judicial role. Our precedents have accordingly insisted that judges "exercise the utmost care" in identifying implied fundamental rights, "lest the liberty protected by the Due Process Clause be subtly transformed into the policy preferences of the Members of this Court."

* * *

Proper reliance on history and tradition of course requires looking beyond the individual law being challenged, so that every restriction on liberty does not supply its own constitutional justification. * * * Expanding a right suddenly and dramatically is likely to require tearing it up from its roots. * * * The only way to ensure restraint in this delicate enterprise is "continual insistence upon respect for the teachings of history, solid recognition of the basic values that underlie our society, and wise appreciation of the great roles [of] the doctrines of federalism and separation of powers."

B

* * *

1

The majority's driving themes are that marriage is desirable and petitioners desire it. * * * As a matter of constitutional law, however, the sincerity of petitioners' wishes is not relevant.

When the majority turns to the law, it relies primarily on precedents discussing the fundamental "right to marry." These cases do not hold, of course, that anyone who wants to get married has a constitutional right to do so. They instead require a State to justify barriers to marriage as that institution has always been understood. In *Loving*, the Court held that racial restrictions on the right to marry lacked a compelling justification. In *Zablocki*, restrictions based on child support debts did not suffice. In *Turner*, restrictions based on status as a prisoner were deemed impermissible.

None of the laws at issue in those cases purported to change the core definition of marriage as the union of a man and a woman. * * *

In short, the "right to marry" cases stand for the important but limited proposition that particular restrictions on access to marriage *as traditionally defined* violate due process. These precedents say nothing at all about a right to make a State change its definition of marriage, which is the right petitioners actually seek here. * * *

2

The majority suggests that "there are other, more instructive precedents" informing the right to marry. * * *

* * *

Neither *Lawrence* nor any other precedent [involving the right to privacy] supports the right that petitioners assert here. Unlike criminal laws banning contraceptives and sodomy [which have been struck down on right to privacy grounds], the marriage laws at issue here involve no government intrusion. They create no crime and impose no punishment. Same-sex couples remain free to live together, to engage in intimate conduct, and to raise their families as they see fit. No one is "condemned to live in loneliness" by the laws challenged in these cases—no one. At the same time, the laws in no way interfere with the "right to be let alone."

* * *

In sum, the privacy cases provide no support for the majority's position, because petitioners do not seek privacy. Quite the opposite, they seek public recognition of their relationships, along with corresponding government benefits. * * * Thus, although the right to privacy recognized by our precedents certainly plays a role in protecting the intimate conduct of same-sex couples, it provides no affirmative right to redefine marriage and no basis for striking down the laws at issue here.

3

* * *

* * * The truth is that today's decision rests on nothing more than the majority's own conviction that same-sex couples should be allowed to marry because they want to, and that "it would disparage their choices and diminish their personhood to deny them this right." Whatever force that belief may have as a matter of moral philosophy, it has no * * * basis in the Constitution * * *.

* * *

One immediate question invited by the majority's position is whether States may retain the definition of marriage as a union of two people. Although the majority randomly inserts the adjective "two" in various places, it offers no reason at all why the two-person element of the core definition of marriage may be preserved while the man-woman element may not. Indeed, from the standpoint of history and tradition, a leap from opposite-sex marriage to same-sex marriage is much greater than one from a two-person union to plural unions, which have deep roots in some cultures around the world. If the majority is willing to take the big leap, it is hard to see how it can say no to the shorter one.

It is striking how much of the majority's reasoning would apply with equal force to the claim of a fundamental right to plural marriage. If "[t]here is dignity in the bond between two men or two women who seek to marry and in their autonomy to make such profound choices," why would there be any less dignity in the bond between three people who, in exercising their autonomy, seek to make the profound choice to marry? If a same-sex couple has the constitutional right to marry because their children would otherwise "suffer the stigma of knowing their families are somehow lesser," why wouldn't the same reasoning apply to a family of three or more persons raising children? If not having the opportunity to marry "serves to disrespect and subordinate" gay and lesbian couples, why wouldn't the same "imposition of this disability" serve to disrespect and subordinate people who find fulfillment in polyamorous relationships?

I do not mean to equate marriage between same-sex couples with plural marriages in all respects. There may well be relevant differences that compel different legal analysis. But if there are, petitioners have not pointed to any. * * *

4

* * *

The majority's understanding of due process lays out a tantalizing vision of the future for Members of this Court: If an unvarying social institution enduring over all of recorded history cannot inhibit judicial policymaking, what can? But this approach is dangerous for the rule of law. The purpose of insisting that implied fundamental rights have roots in the history and tradition of our people is to ensure that when unelected judges strike down democratically enacted laws, they do so based on something more than their own beliefs. * * *

III

* * *

[T]he marriage laws at issue here do not violate the Equal Protection Clause, because distinguishing between opposite-sex and same-sex couples is rationally related to the States' "legitimate state interest" in "preserving the traditional institution of marriage."

It is important to note with precision which laws petitioners have challenged. Although they discuss some of the ancillary legal benefits that accompany marriage, such as hospital visitation rights and recognition of spousal status on official documents, petitioners' lawsuits target the laws defining marriage generally rather than those allocating benefits specifically. The equal protection analysis might be different, in my view, if we were confronted with a more focused challenge to the denial of certain tangible benefits. Of course, those more selective claims will not arise now that the Court has taken the drastic step of requiring every State to license and recognize marriages between same-sex couples.

IV

The legitimacy of this Court ultimately rests "upon the respect accorded to its judgments." That respect flows from the perception—and reality—that we exercise humility and restraint in deciding cases according to the Constitution and law. The role of the Court envisioned by the majority today, however, is anything but humble or restrained. * * *

* * *

When decisions are reached through democratic means, some people will inevitably be disappointed with the results. But those whose views do not prevail at least know that they have had their say, and accordingly are—in the tradition of our political culture—reconciled to the result of a fair and honest debate. In addition, they can gear up to raise the issue later, hoping to persuade enough on the winning side to think again. * * *

But today the Court puts a stop to all that. By deciding this question under the Constitution, the Court removes it from the realm of democratic decision. There will be consequences to shutting down the political process on an issue of such profound public significance. Closing debate tends to close minds. People denied a voice are less likely to accept the ruling of a court on an issue that does not seem to be the sort of thing courts usually decide. * * * Indeed, however heartened the proponents of same-sex marriage might be on this day, it is worth acknowledging what they have lost, and lost forever: the opportunity to win the true acceptance that comes from persuading their fellow citizens of the justice of their cause. And they lose this just when the winds of change were freshening at their backs.

* * * Today's decision * * * creates serious questions about religious liberty. Many good and decent people oppose same-sex marriage as a tenet of faith, and their freedom to exercise religion is—unlike the right imagined by the majority—actually spelled out in the [First Amendment].

Respect for sincere religious conviction has led voters and legislators in every State that has adopted same-sex marriage democratically to include accommodations for religious practice. The majority's decision imposing same-sex marriage cannot, of course, create any such accommodations. * * *

Hard questions arise when people of faith exercise religion in ways that may be seen to conflict with the new right to same-sex marriage—when, for example, a religious college provides married student housing only to opposite-sex married couples, or a religious adoption agency declines to place children with same-sex married couples. * * * There is little doubt that these and similar questions will soon be before this Court. Unfortunately, people of faith can take no comfort in the treatment they receive from the majority today.

Perhaps the most discouraging aspect of today's decision is the extent to which the majority feels compelled to sully those on the other side of the debate. * * * It is one thing for the majority to conclude that the Constitution protects a right to same-sex marriage; it is something else to portray everyone who does not share the majority's "better informed understanding" as bigoted.

* * *

If you are among the many Americans—of whatever sexual orientation—who favor expanding same-sex marriage, by all means celebrate today's decision. Celebrate the achievement of a desired goal. Celebrate the opportunity for a new expression of commitment to a partner. Celebrate the availability of new benefits. But do not celebrate the Constitution. It had nothing to do with it.

I respectfully dissent.

JUSTICE SCALIA, with whom JUSTICE THOMAS joins, dissenting.

* * *

The substance of today's decree is not of immense personal importance to me. The law can recognize as marriage whatever sexual attachments and living arrangements it wishes, and can accord them favorable civil consequences, from tax treatment to rights of inheritance. Those civil consequences—and the public approval that conferring the name of marriage evidences—can perhaps have adverse social effects, but no more adverse than the effects of many other controversial laws. So it is not of special importance to me what the law says about marriage. It is of overwhelming importance, however, who it is that rules me. Today's decree says that my Ruler, and the Ruler of 320 million Americans coast-to-coast, is a majority of the nine lawyers on the Supreme Court. * * *

I

Until the courts put a stop to it, public debate over same-sex marriage displayed American democracy at its best. Individuals on both sides of the issue passionately, but respectfully, attempted to persuade their fellow citizens to accept their views. * * * That is exactly how our system of government is supposed to work.

* * *

But the Court ends this debate, in an opinion lacking even a thin veneer of law. Buried beneath the mummeries and straining-to-be-memorable passages of the opinion is a candid and startling assertion: No matter *what* it was the People ratified, the Fourteenth Amendment protects those rights that the Judiciary, in its "reasoned judgment," thinks the Fourteenth Amendment ought to protect. * * *

* * *

This is a naked judicial claim to legislative—indeed, *super-legislative*—power; a claim fundamentally at odds with our system of government. * * *

Judges are selected precisely for their skill as lawyers; whether they reflect the policy views of a particular constituency is not (or should not be) relevant. * * * [T]o allow the policy question of same-sex marriage to be considered and resolved by a select, patrician, highly unrepresentative panel of nine is to violate a principle even more fundamental than no taxation without representation: no social transformation without representation.

II

But what really astounds is the hubris reflected in today's judicial Putsch. The five Justices who compose today's majority are entirely comfortable concluding that every State violated the Constitution for all of the 135 years between the Fourteenth Amendment's ratification and Massachusetts' permitting of same-sex marriages in 2003. * * *

The opinion is couched in a style that is as pretentious as its content is egotistic. It is one thing for separate concurring or dissenting opinions to contain extravagances, even silly extravagances, of thought and expression; it is something else for the official opinion of the Court to do so. * * * The stuff contained in today's opinion has to diminish this Court's reputation for clear thinking and sober analysis.

* * *

[Dissenting opinions by JUSTICE THOMAS and JUSTICE ALITO are omitted.]

NOTES AND QUESTIONS

1. What is the rationale of the majority in striking down bans on same-sex marriage? Why does Chief Justice Roberts disagree with the majority? Why does Justice Scalia disagree with the majority? Which opinion is most persuasive and why?

2. For additional discussion of same-sex marriage in the United States, see, e.g., Katie Eyer, Brown, Not Loving: Obergefell and the Unfinished Business of Formal Equality, 125 Yale L.J. Forum 1 (2015) (discussing Obergefell before the Court had issued its opinion and arguing that, even if the right to marriage was extended to same-sex couples, the lack of formal equality under the law for homosexuals in general would remain problematic and allow for discrimination in areas such as housing and employment); Casey Faucon, Polygamy After Windsor: What's Religion Got to Do with It?, 9 Harv. L. & Pol'y Rev. 471 (2015) (discussing the state of polygamy under the law after Windsor and Obergefell and suggesting that the same equal protection and substantive due process analysis could aid polygamists as they seek recognition and protection under the law); Daniel Conkle, Evolving Values, Animus, and Same-Sex Marriage, 89 Ind. L.J. 27 (2014) (exploring the right to same-sex marriage under the Fourteenth Amendment pre-Obergefell and arguing that such a right exists as a result of changing national values).

3. GENDER DISCRIMINATION

As the Supreme Court has recognized, "throughout much of the 19th century the position of women in our society was, in many respects, comparable to that of blacks under the pre-Civil War slave codes." Frontiero v. Richardson, 411 U.S. 677, 685 (1973). In fact, "[n]either slaves nor women could hold office, serve on juries, or bring suit in their own names, and married women traditionally were denied the legal capacity to hold or convey property or to serve as legal guardians of their own children." Id. Women were not even permitted to vote in the U.S. until the passage of the Nineteenth Amendment in 1919. Over the course of the twentieth century, the role of women in American society changed drastically, with many women entering the workforce and abandoning traditional gender roles. As women struggled for equality, advocates challenged various forms of gender discrimination. The following case is one example.

UNITED STATES V. VIRGINIA

Supreme Court of the United States, 1996
518 U.S. 515

JUSTICE GINSBURG delivered the opinion of the Court.

Virginia's public institutions of higher learning include an incomparable military college, Virginia Military Institute (VMI). The United States maintains that the Constitution's equal protection guarantee precludes Virginia from reserving exclusively to men the unique educational opportunities VMI affords. We agree.

I

Founded in 1839, VMI is today the sole single-sex school among Virginia's 15 public institutions of higher learning. VMI's distinctive mission is to produce "citizen-soldiers," men prepared for leadership in civilian life and in military service. VMI pursues this mission through pervasive training of a kind not available anywhere else in Virginia. Assigning prime place to character development, VMI uses an "adversative method" modeled on English public schools and once characteristic of military instruction. VMI constantly endeavors to instill physical and mental discipline in its cadets and impart to them a strong moral code. The school's graduates leave VMI with heightened comprehension of their capacity to deal with duress and stress, and a large sense of accomplishment for completing the hazardous course.

VMI has notably succeeded in its mission to produce leaders; among its alumni are military generals, Members of Congress, and business executives. The school's alumni overwhelmingly perceive that their VMI training helped them to realize their personal goals. VMI's endowment reflects the loyalty of its graduates; VMI has the largest per-student endowment of all public undergraduate institutions in the Nation.

Neither the goal of producing citizen-soldiers nor VMI's implementing methodology is inherently unsuitable to women. And the school's impressive record in producing leaders has made admission desirable to some women. Nevertheless, Virginia has elected to preserve exclusively for men the advantages and opportunities a VMI education affords.

II

A

From its establishment in 1839 as one of the Nation's first state military colleges, VMI has remained financially supported by Virginia and "subject to the control of the [Virginia] General Assembly." * * *

VMI today enrolls about 1,300 men as cadets. Its academic offerings in the liberal arts, sciences, and engineering are also available at other public colleges and universities in Virginia. But VMI's mission is special. It is the mission of the school

> to produce educated and honorable men, prepared for the varied work of civil life, imbued with love of learning, confident in the functions and attitudes of leadership, possessing a high sense of public service, advocates of the American democracy and free enterprise system, and ready as citizen-soldiers to defend their country in time of national peril.

In contrast to the federal service academies, institutions maintained "to prepare cadets for career service in the armed forces," VMI's program "is directed at preparation for both military and civilian life"; "[o]nly about 15% of VMI cadets enter career military service."

VMI produces its "citizen-soldiers" through "an adversative, or doubting, model of education" which features "[p]hysical rigor, mental stress, absolute equality of treatment, absence of privacy, minute regulation of behavior, and indoctrination in desirable values." As one Commandant of Cadets described it, the adversative method " 'dissects the young student,' " and makes him aware of his " 'limits and capabilities,' " so that he knows " 'how far he can go with his anger, . . . how much he can take under stress, . . . [and] exactly what he can do when he is physically exhausted.' "

VMI cadets live in spartan barracks where surveillance is constant and privacy nonexistent; they wear uniforms, eat together in the mess hall, and regularly participate in drills. Entering students are incessantly exposed to the rat line, "an extreme form of the adversative model," comparable in intensity to Marine Corps boot camp. Tormenting and punishing, the rat line bonds new cadets to their fellow sufferers and, when they have completed the 7-month experience, to their former tormentors.

VMI's "adversative model" is further characterized by a hierarchical "class system" of privileges and responsibilities, a "dyke system" for assigning a senior class mentor to each entering class "rat," and a stringently enforced "honor code," which prescribes that a cadet " 'does not lie, cheat, steal, nor tolerate those who do.' "

VMI attracts some applicants because of its reputation as an extraordinarily challenging military school, and "because its alumni are exceptionally close to the school." "[W]omen have no opportunity anywhere to gain the benefits of [the system of education at VMI]."

B

In 1990, prompted by a complaint filed with the Attorney General by a female high-school student seeking admission to VMI, the United States sued the Commonwealth of Virginia and VMI, alleging that VMI's exclusively male admission policy violated the Equal Protection Clause of the Fourteenth Amendment. Trial of the action consumed six days and involved an array of expert witnesses on each side.

* * *

The District Court ruled in favor of VMI * * * and rejected the equal protection challenge pressed by the United States.

* * *

The Court of Appeals for the Fourth Circuit disagreed and vacated the District Court's judgment. * * *

* * *

C

In response to the Fourth Circuit's ruling, Virginia proposed a parallel program for women: Virginia Women's Institute for Leadership (VWIL). The 4-year, state-sponsored undergraduate program would be located at Mary Baldwin College, a private liberal arts school for women, and would be open, initially, to about 25 to 30 students. Although VWIL would share VMI's mission—to produce "citizen-soldiers"—the VWIL program would differ, as does Mary Baldwin College, from VMI in academic offerings, methods of education, and financial resources.

The average combined SAT score of entrants at Mary Baldwin is about 100 points lower than the score for VMI freshmen. Mary Baldwin's faculty holds "significantly fewer Ph.D.'s than the faculty at VMI," and receives significantly lower salaries. While VMI offers degrees in liberal arts, the sciences, and engineering, Mary Baldwin, at the time of trial, offered only bachelor of arts degrees. * * *

Experts in educating women at the college level composed the Task Force charged with designing the VWIL program; Task Force members were drawn from Mary Baldwin's own faculty and staff. Training its attention on methods of instruction appropriate for "most women," the Task Force determined that a military model would be "wholly inappropriate" for VWIL.

VWIL students would participate in ROTC programs and a newly established, "largely ceremonial" Virginia Corps of Cadets, but the VWIL House would not have a military format, and VWIL would not require its students to eat meals together or to wear uniforms during the schoolday. In lieu of VMI's adversative method, the VWIL Task Force favored "a cooperative method which reinforces self-esteem." In addition to the standard bachelor of arts program offered at Mary Baldwin, VWIL students would take courses in leadership, complete an off-campus leadership externship, participate in community service projects, and assist in arranging a speaker series.

Virginia represented that it will provide equal financial support for in-state VWIL students and VMI cadets, and the VMI Foundation agreed to supply a $5.4625 million endowment for the VWIL program. Mary Baldwin's own endowment is about $19 million; VMI's is $131 million. Mary Baldwin will add $35 million to its endowment based on future commitments; VMI will add $220 million. The VMI Alumni Association has developed a network of employers interested in hiring VMI graduates. The Association has agreed to open its network to VWIL graduates, but those graduates will not have the advantage afforded by a VMI degree.

D

Virginia returned to the District Court seeking approval of its proposed remedial plan, and the court decided the plan met the requirements of the Equal Protection Clause. * * *

A divided Court of Appeals affirmed the District Court's judgment. * * *

* * *

III

[This case] present[s] two ultimate issues. First, does Virginia's exclusion of women from the educational opportunities provided by VMI—extraordinary opportunities for military training and civilian leadership development—deny to women "capable of all of the individual activities required of VMI cadets," the equal protection of the laws guaranteed by the Fourteenth Amendment? Second, if VMI's "unique" situation—as Virginia's sole single-sex public institution of higher education—offends the Constitution's equal protection principle, what is the remedial requirement?

IV

* * * Parties who seek to defend gender-based government action must demonstrate an "exceedingly persuasive justification" for that action.

Today's skeptical scrutiny of official action denying rights or opportunities based on sex responds to volumes of history. * * * "[O]ur Nation has had a long and unfortunate history of sex discrimination." * * *

In 1971, for the first time in our Nation's history, this Court ruled in favor of a woman who complained that her State had denied her the equal protection of its laws. *Reed v. Reed*, 404 U.S. 71 [(1971)]. Since *Reed*, the Court has repeatedly recognized that neither federal nor state government acts compatibly with the equal protection principle when a law or official policy denies to women, simply because they are women, * * * equal opportunity to aspire, achieve, participate in and contribute to society based on their individual talents and capacities.

Without equating gender classifications, for all purposes, to classifications based on race or national origin, the Court, in post-*Reed* decisions, has carefully inspected official action that closes a door or denies opportunity to women (or to men). To summarize the Court's current directions for cases of official classification based on gender: Focusing on the differential treatment for denial of opportunity for which relief is sought, the reviewing court must determine whether the proffered justification is "exceedingly persuasive." The burden of justification is demanding and it rests entirely on the State. The State must show "at least that the [challenged] classification serves 'important governmental objectives and that the discriminatory means employed' are 'substantially related to the achievement of those objectives.' " The justification must be genuine, not hypothesized or invented *post hoc* in response to litigation. And it must not rely on overbroad generalizations about the different talents, capacities, or preferences of males and females.

The heightened review standard our precedent establishes does not make sex a proscribed classification. Supposed "inherent differences" are no longer accepted as a ground for race or national origin classifications. Physical differences between men and women, however, are enduring: "[T]he two sexes are not fungible; a community made up exclusively of one [sex] is different from a community composed of both."

Inherent differences between men and women, we have come to appreciate, remain cause for celebration, but not for denigration of the members of either sex or for artificial constraints on an individual's opportunity. Sex classifications may be used to compensate women "for particular economic disabilities [they have] suffered," to "promot[e] equal employment opportunity," to advance full development of the talent and capacities of our Nation's people. But such classifications may not be used, as they once were, to create or perpetuate the legal, social, and economic inferiority of women.

Measuring the record in this case against the review standard just described, we conclude that Virginia has shown no "exceedingly persuasive justification" for excluding all women from the citizen-soldier training afforded by VMI. We therefore affirm the Fourth Circuit's initial judgment, which held that Virginia had violated the Fourteenth Amendment's Equal Protection Clause. Because the remedy proffered by Virginia—the Mary Baldwin VWIL program—does not cure the constitutional violation, *i.e.*, it does not provide equal opportunity, we reverse the Fourth Circuit's final judgment in this case.

V

* * *

A

Single-sex education affords pedagogical benefits to at least some students, Virginia emphasizes, and that reality is uncontested in this litigation. Similarly, it is not disputed that diversity among public educational institutions can serve the public good. * * *

* * *

* * * [W]e find no persuasive evidence in this record that VMI's male-only admission policy "is in furtherance of a state policy of 'diversity.' " * * * A purpose genuinely to advance an array of educational options * * * is not served by VMI's historic and constant plan—a plan to "affor[d] a unique educational benefit only to males." However "liberally" this plan serves the Commonwealth's sons, it makes no provision whatever for her daughters. That is not *equal* protection.

B

Virginia next argues that VMI's adversative method of training provides educational benefits that cannot be made available, unmodified, to women. Alterations to accommodate women would necessarily be "radical," so "drastic," Virginia asserts, as to transform, indeed "destroy," VMI's program. * * *

The District Court forecast from expert witness testimony, and the Court of Appeals accepted, that coeducation would materially affect "at least these three aspects of VMI's program—physical training, the absence of privacy, and the adversative approach." And it is uncontested that women's admission would require accommodations, primarily in arranging housing assignments and physical training programs for female cadets. It is also undisputed, however, that "the VMI methodology could be used to educate women." The District Court even allowed that some women may prefer it to the methodology a women's college might pursue. * * * The parties, furthermore, agree that "*some* women can meet the physical standards [VMI] now impose[s] on men." In sum, as the Court of Appeals stated, "neither the goal of producing citizen soldiers," VMI's *raison d'être*, "nor VMI's implementing methodology is inherently unsuitable to women."

* * *

It may be assumed, for purposes of this decision, that most women would not choose VMI's adversative method. * * * Education, to be sure, is not a "one size fits all" business. The issue, however, is not whether "women—or men—should be forced to attend VMI"; rather, the question is whether the Commonwealth can constitutionally deny to women who have the will and capacity, the training and attendant opportunities that VMI uniquely affords.

The notion that admission of women would downgrade VMI's stature, destroy the adversative system and, with it, even the school, is a judgment hardly proved, a prediction hardly different from other "self-fulfilling prophec[ies]," once routinely used to deny rights or opportunities. * * *

* * *

Surely [the school's] goal [of "producing citizen soldiers"] is great enough to accommodate women, who today count as citizens in our American democracy equal in stature to men. Just as surely, the Commonwealth's great goal is not substantially advanced by women's categorical exclusion, in total disregard of their individual merit, from the Commonwealth's premier "citizen-soldier" corps. * * *

VI

In the second phase of the litigation, Virginia presented its remedial plan—maintain VMI as a male-only college and create VWIL as a separate program for women. * * *

A

A remedial decree, this Court has said, must closely fit the constitutional violation; it must be shaped to place persons unconstitutionally denied an opportunity or advantage in "the position they would have occupied in the absence of [discrimination]." The constitutional violation in this suit is the categorical exclusion of women from an extraordinary educational opportunity afforded men. A proper remedy for an unconstitutional exclusion * * * aims to "eliminate [so far as possible] the discriminatory effects of the past" and to "bar like discrimination in the future."

Virginia chose not to eliminate, but to leave untouched, VMI's exclusionary policy. For women only, however, Virginia proposed a separate program, different in kind from VMI and unequal in tangible and intangible facilities. * * *

* * *

B
* * *

Virginia, * * * while maintaining VMI for men only, has failed to provide any "comparable single-gender women's institution." Instead, the Commonwealth has created a VWIL program fairly appraised as a "pale shadow" of VMI in terms of the range of curricular choices and faculty stature, funding, prestige, alumni support, and influence.

* * *

VII

* * *

VMI * * * offers an educational opportunity no other Virginia institution provides, and the school's "prestige"—associated with its success in developing "citizen-soldiers"—is unequaled. Virginia has closed this facility to its daughters and, instead, has devised for them a "parallel program," with a faculty less impressively credentialed and less well paid, more limited course offerings, fewer opportunities for military training and for scientific specialization. VMI, beyond question, "possesses to a far greater degree" than the VWIL program "those qualities which are incapable of objective measurement but which make for greatness in a . . . school," including "position and influence of the alumni, standing in the community, traditions, and prestige." Women seeking and fit for a VMI-quality education cannot be offered anything less, under the Commonwealth's obligation to afford them genuinely equal protection.

* * * There is no reason to believe that the admission of women capable of all the activities required of VMI cadets would destroy the Institute rather than enhance its capacity to serve the "more perfect Union."

For the reasons stated, the initial judgment of the Court of Appeals is affirmed, the final judgment of the Court of Appeals is reversed, and the case is remanded for further proceedings consistent with this opinion.

JUSTICE THOMAS took no part in the consideration or decision of these cases.

[Concurring opinion by JUSTICE REHNQUIST is omitted.]

JUSTICE SCALIA, dissenting.

Today the Court shuts down an institution that has served the people of the Commonwealth of Virginia with pride and distinction for over a century and a half. To achieve that desired result, it rejects * * * the factual findings of two courts below, sweeps aside the precedents of this Court, and ignores the history of our people. * * *

Much of the Court's opinion is devoted to deprecating the closed-mindedness of our forebears with regard to women's education, and even with regard to the treatment of women in areas that have nothing to do with education. Closed-minded they were—as every age is, including our own, with regard to matters it cannot guess, because it simply does not consider them debatable. The virtue of a democratic system with a First Amendment is that it readily enables the people, over time, to be persuaded that what they took for granted is not so, and to change their laws accordingly. That system is destroyed if the smug assurances of each age are removed from the democratic process and written into the Constitution.

So to counterbalance the Court's criticism of our ancestors, let me say a word in their praise: They left us free to change. The same cannot be said of this most illiberal Court, which has embarked on a course of inscribing one after another of the current preferences of the society (and in some cases only the counter-majoritarian preferences of the society's law-trained elite) into our Basic Law. Today it enshrines the notion that no substantial educational value is to be served by an all-men's military academy—so that the decision by the people of Virginia to maintain such an institution denies equal protection to women who cannot attend that institution but can attend others. Since it is entirely clear that the Constitution of the United States—the old one—takes no sides in this educational debate, I dissent.

* * *

NOTES AND QUESTIONS

1.   On what ground did the Court find that VMI's all-male admissions policy violated the Equal Protection Clause? Why did the Court hold that the VWIL did not adequately remedy the problem? Are Justice Scalia's criticisms valid?

2.   Justice Ginsburg, who authored *United States v. Virginia*, played a major role as a U.S. Supreme Court advocate in gender discrimination cases before becoming a judge on the D.C. Circuit (and later a Justice on the Supreme Court). She represented parties alleging discrimination in a variety of cases. *See, e.g., Duren v. Missouri*, 439 U.S. 357 (1979) (holding that the jury proceedings in the defendant's criminal trial were flawed because women received an automatic exemption from jury service upon request); *Weinberger v. Wiesenfeld*, 420 U.S. 636 (1975) (holding that a provision of the Social Security Act providing different survivors' benefits based on gender was unconstitutional); *see also* Ruth Bader Ginsburg, *Sex Equality and the Constitution*, 52 Tul. L. Rev. 451 (1978) (surveying the development of women's rights in the United States).

3.   For examples from the vast literature on gender discrimination, *see, e.g.*, Linda Wharton, *State Equal Rights Amendments Revisited: Evaluating Their Effectiveness in Advancing Protection Against Sex Discrimination*, 36 Rutgers L.J. 1201 (2005) (arguing that various state constitutional amendments granting equal rights to women have been an important tool for advancing gender equality); Deborah Brake, *Sex as a Suspect Class: An Argument for Applying Strict Scrutiny to Gender Discrimination*, 6 Seton Hall Const. L.J. 953 (1996) (arguing that applying strict scrutiny to sex discrimination (as for race discrimination) would support equal opportunity for women and would recognize that sex discrimination is inherently invidious).

D. THE RIGHT TO PRIVACY

In addition to the rights that are enumerated in the Constitution, the Supreme Court has held that some rights are implied through the Bill of

Rights. One such right is the right to privacy. The following case discusses that right in the context of abortion.

ROE V. WADE

Supreme Court of the United States, 1973
410 U.S. 113

JUSTICE BLACKMUN delivered the opinion of the Court.

This Texas federal appeal and its Georgia companion present constitutional challenges to state criminal abortion legislation. * * *

We forthwith acknowledge our awareness of the sensitive and emotional nature of the abortion controversy, of the vigorous opposing views, even among physicians, and of the deep and seemingly absolute convictions that the subject inspires. * * *

* * *

Our task, of course, is to resolve the issue by constitutional measurement, free of emotion and of predilection. * * *

I

The Texas statutes that concern us here are [various articles] of the State's Penal Code. These make it a crime to "procure an abortion," as therein defined, or to attempt one, except with respect to "an abortion procured or attempted by medical advice for the purpose of saving the life of the mother." Similar statutes are in existence in a majority of the States.

Texas first enacted a criminal abortion statute in 1854. This was soon modified into language that has remained substantially unchanged to the present time. The final article in each of these compilations provided the same exception, as docs thc [current statute], for an abortion by "medical advice for the purpose of saving the life of the mother."

II

Jane Roe, a single woman who was residing in Dallas County, Texas, instituted this federal action in March 1970 against the District Attorney of the county. She sought a declaratory judgment that the Texas criminal abortion statutes were unconstitutional on their face, and an injunction restraining the defendant from enforcing the statutes.

Roe alleged that she was unmarried and pregnant; that she wished to terminate her pregnancy by an abortion "performed by a competent, licensed physician, under safe, clinical conditions"; that she was unable to get a "legal" abortion in Texas because her life did not appear to be threatened by the continuation of her pregnancy; and that she could not afford to travel to another jurisdiction in order to secure a legal abortion under safe conditions. She claimed that the Texas statutes were unconstitutionally vague and that they abridged her right of personal privacy * * *. [She] purported to sue "on behalf of herself and all other women" similarly situated.

[The Court's discussion of the complex procedural history of the case is omitted.]

III

* * *

IV

We are * * * confronted with issues of justiciability, standing, and abstention. [Has] Roe * * * established that "personal stake in the outcome of the controversy" that insures that "the dispute sought to be adjudicated will be presented in an adversary context and in a form historically viewed as capable of judicial resolution?" * * *

* * * Despite the use of the pseudonym, no suggestion is made that Roe is a fictitious person. For purposes of her case, we accept as true, and as established, her existence; her pregnant state, as of the inception of her suit in March 1970 and as late as May 21 of that year when she filed an alias affidavit with the District Court; and her inability to obtain a legal abortion in Texas.

Viewing Roe's case as of the time of its filing and thereafter until as late as May, there can be little dispute that it then presented a case or controversy and that, wholly apart from the class aspects, she, as a pregnant single woman thwarted by the Texas criminal abortion laws, had standing to challenge those statutes. * * *

The appellee notes, however, that * * * Roe's case must now be moot because she and all other members of her class are no longer subject to any 1970 pregnancy.

The usual rule in federal cases is that an actual controversy must exist at stages of appellate or certiorari review, and not simply at the date the action is initiated.

But when, as here, pregnancy is a significant fact in the litigation, the normal 266-day human gestation period is so short that the pregnancy will come to term before the usual appellate process is complete. If that termination makes a case moot, pregnancy litigation seldom will survive much beyond the trial stage, and appellate review will be effectively denied. Our law should not be that rigid. * * *

We, therefore [hold] that Jane Roe had standing to undertake this litigation, that she presented a justiciable controversy, and that the termination of her 1970 pregnancy has not rendered her case moot.

* * *

[The Court found that three other plaintiffs did not present a case or controversy: a husband and wife, where the wife was not pregnant; and a physician who was subject to two pending criminal prosecutions under the Texas statutes and could challenge the constitutionality of the statutes in those pending cases.]

V

The principal thrust of [Roe's] attack on the Texas statutes is that they improperly invade a right, said to be possessed by the pregnant woman, to choose to terminate her pregnancy. Appellant would discover this right in the concept of personal "liberty" embodied in the Fourteenth Amendment's Due Process Clause; or in personal marital, familial, and sexual privacy said to be protected by the Bill of Rights or its penumbras, or among those rights reserved to the people by the Ninth Amendment. Before addressing this claim, we feel it desirable briefly to survey, in several aspects, the history of abortion, for such insight as that history may afford us, and then to examine the state purposes and interests behind the criminal abortion laws.

VI

* * * [T]he restrictive criminal abortion laws in effect in a majority of States today are of relatively recent vintage. Those laws, generally proscribing abortion or its attempt at any time during pregnancy except when necessary to preserve the pregnant woman's life, * * * derive from statutory changes effected, for the most part, in the latter half of the 19th century.

1. *Ancient attitudes.* These are not capable of precise determination. We are told that at the time of the Persian Empire * * * abortions were severely punished. We are also told, however, that abortion was practiced in Greek times as well as in the Roman Era, and that "it was resorted to without scruple." * * * Greek and Roman law afforded little protection to the unborn. If abortion was prosecuted in some places, it seems to have been based on a concept of a violation of the father's right to his offspring. Ancient religion did not bar abortion.

2. *The Hippocratic Oath.* What then of the famous Oath that has stood so long as the ethical guide of the medical profession and that bears the name of the great Greek (460(?)–377(?) B.C.), who has been described as the Father of Medicine * * *? The Oath varies somewhat according to the particular translation, but in any translation the content is clear: "I will give no deadly medicine to anyone if asked, nor suggest any such counsel; and in like manner I will not give to a woman a pessary to produce abortion," or "I will neither give a deadly drug to anybody if asked for it, nor will I make a suggestion to this effect. Similarly, I will not give to a woman an abortive remedy."

Although the Oath is not mentioned in any of the principal briefs * * *, it represents the apex of the development of strict ethical concepts in medicine, and its influence endures to this day. Why did not the authority of Hippocrates dissuade abortion practice in his time and that of Rome? [One prominent theory is that] [t]he Oath was not uncontested even in Hippocrates's day * * *. Most Greek thinkers * * * commended abortion, at least prior to viability. * * *

* * *

3.   *The common law.* It is undisputed that at common law, abortion performed before "quickening"—the first recognizable movement of the fetus in utero, appearing usually from the 16th to the 18th week of pregnancy—was not an indictable offense. The absence of a common-law crime for pre-quickening abortion appears to have developed from a confluence of earlier philosophical, theological, and civil and canon law concepts of when life begins. These disciplines variously approached the question in terms of the point at which the embryo or fetus became "formed" or recognizably human, or in terms of when a "person" came into being, that is, infused with a "soul" or "animated." A loose consensus evolved in early English law that these events occurred at some point between conception and live birth. * * * Although Christian theology and the canon law came to fix the point of animation at 40 days for a male and 80 days for a female, a view that persisted until the 19th century, there was otherwise little agreement about the precise time of formation or animation. There was agreement, however, that prior to this point the fetus was to be regarded as part of the mother, and its destruction, therefore, was not homicide. * * *

Whether abortion of a quick fetus was a felony at common law, or even a lesser crime, is still disputed. [The Court described conflicting viewpoints among common law scholars.]

4.   *The English statutory law.* England's first criminal abortion statute came in 1803. It made abortion of a quick fetus a capital crime, but it provided lesser penalties for the felony of abortion before quickening * * *. This contrast * * * disappeared, however, together with the death penalty, in 1837, and did not reappear in the Offenses Against the Person Act of 1861 that formed the core of English anti-abortion law until the liberalizing reforms of 1967. * * *

* * *

[In 1967,] Parliament enacted a new abortion law. * * * The [law] permits a licensed physician to perform an abortion where two other licensed physicians agree (a) "that the continuance of the pregnancy would involve risk to the life of the pregnant woman, or of injury to the physical or mental health of the pregnant woman or any existing children of her family, greater than if the pregnancy were terminated," or (b) "that there is a substantial risk that if the child were born it would suffer from such physical or mental abnormalities as to be seriously handicapped." * * * It also permits a physician, without the concurrence of others, to terminate a pregnancy where he is of the good-faith opinion that the abortion "is immediately necessary to save the life or to prevent grave permanent injury to the physical or mental health of the pregnant woman."

5. *The American law.* In this country, the law in effect in all but a few States until mid-19th century was the pre-existing English common law. * * * It was not until after the War Between the States [which ended in 1865] that legislation began generally to replace the common law. Most of these initial statutes dealt severely with abortion after quickening but were lenient with it before quickening. * * *

Gradually, in the middle and late 19th century the quickening distinction disappeared from the statutory law of most States and the degree of the offense and the penalties were increased. By the end of the 1950's a large majority of the jurisdictions banned abortion, however and whenever performed, unless done to save or preserve the life of the mother. * * * In the past several years, however, a trend toward liberalization of abortion statutes has resulted in adoption, by about one-third of the States, of less stringent laws * * *.

It is thus apparent that at common law, at the time of the adoption of our Constitution, and throughout the major portion of the 19th century * * * a woman enjoyed a substantially broader right to terminate a pregnancy than she does in most States today. * * *

6. *The position of the American Medical Association.* The anti-abortion mood prevalent in this country in the late 19th century was shared by the medical profession. Indeed, the attitude of the profession may have played a significant role in the enactment of stringent criminal abortion legislation during that period.

An AMA Committee on Criminal Abortion was appointed in May 1857. * * * [Its] report observed that the Committee had been appointed to investigate criminal abortion "with a view to its general suppression." It deplored abortion and its frequency * * *.

* * *

The Committee * * * offered, and the Association adopted, resolutions protesting "against such unwarrantable destruction of human life," calling upon state legislatures to revise their abortion laws, and requesting the cooperation of state medical societies "in pressing the subject."

In 1871 a long and vivid report was submitted by the Committee on Criminal Abortion. * * * It proffered resolutions, adopted by the Association, recommending, among other things, that it "be unlawful and unprofessional for any physician to induce abortion or premature labor, without the concurrent opinion of at least one respectable consulting physician, and then always with a view to the safety of the child—if that be possible," and calling "the attention of the clergy of all denominations to the perverted views of morality entertained by a large class of females— aye, and men also, on this important question."

Except for periodic condemnation of the criminal abortionist, no further formal AMA action took place until 1967. In that year, the Committee on Human Reproduction urged the adoption of a stated policy of opposition to induced abortion, except when there is "documented medical evidence" of a threat to the health or life of the mother, or that the child "may be born with incapacitating physical deformity or mental deficiency," or that a pregnancy "resulting from legally established statutory or forcible rape or incest may constitute a threat to the mental or physical health of the patient," two other physicians "chosen because of their recognized professional competency have examined the patient and have concurred in writing," and the procedure "is performed in a hospital accredited by the Joint Commission on Accreditation of Hospitals." * * *

In 1970, after the introduction of a variety of proposed resolutions, and of a report from its Board of Trustees, a * * * committee noted "polarization of the medical profession on this controversial issue" * * *. On June 25, 1970, the House of Delegates adopted preambles and most of the resolutions proposed by the * * * committee. The preambles emphasized "the best interests of the patient," "sound clinical judgment," and "informed patient consent," in contrast to "mere acquiescence to the patient's demand." The resolutions asserted that abortion is a medical procedure that should be performed by a licensed physician in an accredited hospital only after consultation with two other physicians and in conformity with state law, and that no party to the procedure should be required to violate personally held moral principles. * * *

7. *The position of the American Public Health Association.* In October 1970, the Executive Board of the APHA adopted Standards for Abortion Services. These were five in number:

a.   Rapid and simple abortion referral * * *.

b.   Counseling [that would] simplify and expedite the provision of abortion services * * *.

c.   Psychiatric consultation * * * should be sought for definite indications and not on a routine basis.

d.   A wide range of individuals from appropriately trained, sympathetic volunteers to highly skilled physicians may qualify as abortion counselors.

e.   Contraception and/or sterilization should be discussed with each abortion patient. * * *

Among factors pertinent to life and health risks associated with abortion were * * *:

a.   the skill of the physician,

b.   the environment in which the abortion is performed, and above all

c.   the duration of pregnancy, as determined by uterine size and confirmed by menstrual history.

* * * [I]t was recommended that abortions in the second trimester and early abortions in the presence of existing medical complications be performed in hospitals as inpatient procedures. For pregnancies in the first trimester, abortion in the hospital with or without overnight stay "is probably the safest practice." * * * It was said that * * * abortions should be performed by physicians or osteopaths who are licensed to practice and who have "adequate training."

8.   The position of the American Bar Association. At its meeting in February 1972 the ABA House of Delegates approved [a model statute providing that abortions could be performed only by a physician in a hospital, or by a female upon herself based on a physician's advice, within twenty weeks after the commencement of the pregnancy, or more than twenty weeks if the physician believed that there was a risk to the life of the mother, the child would be born with a grave defect, or if the pregnancy resulted from rape, incest, or illicit intercourse with a minor. Any person who performed or procured an abortion outside of those constraints would be guilty of a felony and subject to a fine.]

VII

Three reasons have been advanced to explain historically the enactment of criminal abortion laws in the 19th century and to justify their continued existence.

It has been argued occasionally that these laws were the product of a Victorian social concern to discourage illicit sexual conduct. Texas, however, does not advance this justification in the present case * * *.

A second reason is concerned with abortion as a medical procedure. When most criminal abortion laws were first enacted, the procedure was a hazardous one for the woman. * * * [P]erhaps until as late as the development of antibiotics in the 1940's, standard modern techniques * * * were not nearly so safe as they are today. Thus, it has been argued that a State's real concern in enacting a criminal abortion law was to protect the pregnant woman * * *.

Modern medical techniques have altered this situation. * * * Mortality rates for women undergoing early abortions, where the procedure is legal, appear to be as low as or lower than the rates for normal childbirth. * * * Of course, * * * [t]he State has a legitimate interest in seeing to it that abortion, like any other medical procedure, is performed under circumstances that insure maximum safety for the patient. This interest obviously extends at least to the performing physician and his staff, to the facilities involved, to the availability of after-care, and to adequate provision for any complication or emergency that might arise. The prevalence of high mortality rates at illegal "abortion mills" strengthens * * * the State's interest in regulating the conditions under which abortions are performed. Moreover, the risk to the woman increases as her pregnancy continues. * * *

The third reason is the State's interest * * * in protecting prenatal life. Some of the argument for this justification rests on the theory that a new human life is present from the moment of conception. The State's interest and general obligation to protect life then extends, it is argued, to prenatal life. Only when the life of the pregnant mother herself is at stake, balanced against the life she carries within her, should the interest of the embryo or fetus not prevail. Logically, of course, a legitimate state interest in this area need not stand or fall on acceptance of the belief that life begins at conception or at some other point prior to life birth. In assessing the State's interest, recognition may be given to the less rigid claim that as long as at least potential life is involved, the State may assert interests beyond the protection of the pregnant woman alone.

* * *

It is with these interests, and the weight to be attached to them, that this case is concerned.

VIII

The Constitution does not explicitly mention any right of privacy. In a line of decisions, however, * * * the Court has recognized that a right of personal privacy, or a guarantee of certain areas or zones of privacy, does exist under the Constitution. In varying contexts, the Court or individual Justices have, indeed, found at least the roots of that right in the First Amendment; in the Fourth and Fifth Amendments; in the penumbras of the Bill of Rights; in the Ninth Amendment; or in the concept of liberty guaranteed by the first section of the Fourteenth Amendment. These decisions make it clear that only personal rights that can be deemed "fundamental" or "implicit in the concept of ordered liberty" are included in this guarantee of personal privacy. They also make it clear that the right has some extension to activities relating to marriage; procreation; contraception; family relationships; and child rearing and education.

This right of privacy, whether it be founded in the Fourteenth Amendment's concept of personal liberty and restrictions upon state action, as we feel it is, or, as the [lower court] determined, in the Ninth Amendment's reservation of rights to the people, is broad enough to encompass a woman's decision whether or not to terminate her pregnancy.

The detriment that the State would impose upon the pregnant woman by denying this choice altogether is apparent. Specific and direct harm medically diagnosable even in early pregnancy may be involved. Maternity, or additional offspring, may force upon the woman a distressful life and future. Psychological harm may be imminent. Mental and physical health may be taxed by child care. There is also the distress, for all concerned, associated with the unwanted child, and there is the problem of bringing a child into a family already unable, psychologically and otherwise, to care for it. In other cases, as in this one, the additional difficulties and continuing stigma of unwed motherhood may be involved. All these are factors the woman and her responsible physician necessarily will consider in consultation.

On the basis of elements such as these, appellant and some amici argue that the woman's right is absolute and that she is entitled to terminate her pregnancy at whatever time, in whatever way, and for whatever reason she alone chooses. With this we do not agree. * * * As noted above, a State may properly assert important interests in safeguarding health, in maintaining medical standards, and in protecting potential life. At some point in pregnancy, these respective interests become sufficiently compelling to sustain regulation of the factors that govern the abortion decision. * * *

* * *

Where certain "fundamental rights" are involved, the Court has held that regulation limiting these rights may be justified only by a "compelling state interest."

* * *

IX

* * * Appellant * * * claims an absolute right that bars any state imposition of criminal penalties in the area. Appellee argues that the State's determination to recognize and protect prenatal life from and after conception constitutes a compelling state interest. As noted above, we do not agree fully with either formulation.

A. The appellee and certain amici argue that the fetus is a "person" within the language and meaning of the Fourteenth Amendment. In support of this, they outline at length and in detail the well-known facts of fetal development. If this suggestion of personhood is established, the appellant's case, of course, collapses, for the fetus's right to life would then be guaranteed specifically by the Amendment. * * * On the other hand, the appellee conceded * * * that no case could be cited that holds that a fetus is a person within the meaning of the Fourteenth Amendment.

The Constitution does not define "person" in so many words. Section 1 of the Fourteenth Amendment contains three references to "person." The first, in defining "citizens," speaks of "persons born or naturalized in the United States." The word also appears both in the Due Process Clause and in the Equal Protection Clause. "Person" is used in other places in the Constitution: [the Court cited numerous provisions]. But in nearly all these instances, the use of the word is such that it has application only postnatally. None indicates, with any assurance, that it has any possible prenatal application.

All this, together with our observation, that throughout the major portion of the 19th century prevailing legal abortion practices were far freer than they are today, persuades us that the word "person," as used in the Fourteenth Amendment, does not include the unborn. * * *

This conclusion, however, does not of itself fully answer the contentions raised by Texas, and we pass on to other considerations.

B.   The pregnant woman cannot be isolated in her privacy. She carries an embryo and, later, a fetus, if one accepts the medical definitions of the developing young in the human uterus. The situation therefore is inherently different from marital intimacy, or bedroom possession of obscene material, or marriage, or procreation * * *. [I]t is reasonable and appropriate for a State to decide that at some point in time another interest, that of health of the mother or that of potential human life, becomes significantly involved. * * *

Texas urges that, apart from the Fourteenth Amendment, life begins at conception and is present throughout pregnancy, and that, therefore, the State has a compelling interest in protecting that life from and after conception. We need not resolve the difficult question of when life begins. When those trained in the respective disciplines of medicine, philosophy, and theology are unable to arrive at any consensus, the judiciary * * * is not in a position to speculate as to the answer.

* * *

In areas other than criminal abortion, the law has been reluctant to endorse any theory that life * * * begins before live birth or to accord legal rights to the unborn except in narrowly defined situations and except when the rights are contingent upon [live] birth. For example, the traditional rule of tort law denied recovery for prenatal injuries even though the child was born alive. That rule has been changed in almost every jurisdiction. In most States, recovery is said to be permitted only if the fetus was viable, or at least quick, when the injuries were sustained, though few courts have squarely so held. * * * [S]ome States permit the parents of a stillborn child to maintain an action for wrongful death because of prenatal injuries. Such an action, however, would appear to be one to vindicate the parents' interest and is thus consistent with the view that the fetus, at most, represents only the potentiality of life. Similarly, unborn children have been recognized as acquiring rights or interests by way of inheritance or other devolution of property, and have been represented by guardians ad litem. Perfection of the interests involved, again, has generally been contingent upon live birth. In short, the unborn have never been recognized in the law as persons in the whole sense.

X

In view of all this, we do not agree that, by adopting one theory of life, Texas may override the rights of the pregnant woman that are at stake. We repeat, however, that the State does have an important and legitimate interest in preserving and protecting the health of the pregnant woman * * * [and] in protecting the potentiality of human life. These interests are separate and distinct. Each grows in substantiality as the woman approaches term and, at a point during pregnancy, each becomes "compelling."

With respect to the State's important and legitimate interest in the health of the mother, the "compelling" point, in the light of present medical knowledge, is at approximately the end of the first trimester. This is so because of the now-established medical fact, that until the end of the first trimester mortality in abortion may be less than mortality in normal childbirth. It follows that, from and after this point, a State may regulate the abortion procedure to the extent that the regulation reasonably relates to the preservation and protection of maternal health. Examples of permissible state regulation in this area are requirements as to the qualifications of the person who is to perform the abortion; as to the licensure of that person; as to the facility in which the procedure is to be performed, that is, whether it must be a hospital or may be a clinic or some other place of less-than-hospital status; as to the licensing of the facility; and the like.

This means, on the other hand, that, for the period of pregnancy prior to this "compelling" point, the attending physician, in consultation with his patient, is free to determine, without regulation by the State, that, in his medical judgment, the patient's pregnancy should be terminated. If that decision is reached, the judgment may be effectuated by an abortion free of interference by the State.

With respect to the State's important and legitimate interest in potential life, the "compelling" point is at viability. This is so because the fetus then presumably has the capability of meaningful life outside the mother's womb. State regulation protective of fetal life after viability thus has both logical and biological justifications. If the State is interested in protecting fetal life after viability, it may go so far as to proscribe abortion during that period, except when it is necessary to preserve the life or health of the mother.

Measured against these standards, * * * the Texas Penal Code, in restricting legal abortions to those "procured or attempted by medical advice for the purpose of saving the life of the mother," sweeps too broadly. The statute makes no distinction between abortions performed early in pregnancy and those performed later, and it limits to a single reason, "saving" the mother's life, the legal justification for the procedure. The statute, therefore, cannot survive the constitutional attack made upon it here.

* * *

XI

To summarize and to repeat:

1.   A state criminal abortion statute of the current Texas type, that excepts from criminality only a *life-saving* procedure on behalf of the mother, without regard to pregnancy stage and without recognition of the other interests involved, is violative of the Due Process Clause of the Fourteenth Amendment.

> (a) For the stage prior to approximately the end of the first trimester, the abortion decision and its effectuation must be left to the medical judgment of the pregnant woman's attending physician.

> (b) For the stage subsequent to approximately the end of the first trimester, the State, in promoting its interest in the health of the mother, may, if it chooses, regulate the abortion procedure in ways that are reasonably related to maternal health.

> (c) For the stage subsequent to viability, the State in promoting its interest in the potentiality of human life may, if it chooses, regulate, and even proscribe, abortion except where it is necessary, in appropriate medical judgment, for the preservation of the life or health of the mother.

2.   The State may define the term "physician" * * * to mean only a physician currently licensed by the State, and may proscribe any abortion by a person who is not a physician as so defined.

* * *

[Concurring opinions by CHIEF JUSTICE BURGER, JUSTICE STEWART, and JUSTICE DOUGLAS are omitted.]

[Dissenting opinion by JUSTICE WHITE, joined by JUSTICE REHNQUIST, is omitted.]

JUSTICE REHNQUIST, dissenting.

The Court's opinion brings to the decision * * * both extensive historical fact and a wealth of legal scholarship. * * * I find myself nonetheless in fundamental disagreement with those parts of it that invalidate the Texas statute in question, and therefore dissent.

I

* * *

[Justice Rehnquist initially stated that the Court should not have decided the case because it was not clear what trimester of pregnancy the plaintiff was in when she filed her complaint. If she was in her third trimester, the state might have properly prohibited her abortion even under the majority opinion.]

II

Even if there were a plaintiff in this case capable of litigating the issue which the Court decides, I would reach a conclusion opposite to that reached by the Court. I have difficulty in concluding, as the Court does, that the right of "privacy" is involved in this case. Texas, by the statute here challenged, bars the performance of a medical abortion by a licensed physician on a plaintiff such as Roe. A transaction resulting in an operation such as this is not "private" in the ordinary usage of that word. Nor is the "privacy" that the Court finds here even a distant relative of the freedom from searches and seizures protected by the Fourth Amendment to the Constitution, which the Court has referred to as embodying a right to privacy.

If the Court means by the term "privacy" no more than that the claim of a person to be free from unwanted state regulation of consensual transactions may be a form of "liberty" protected by the Fourteenth Amendment, there is no doubt that similar claims have been upheld in our earlier decisions * * *. [L]iberty is not guaranteed absolutely against deprivation, only against deprivation without due process of law. The test traditionally applied in the area of social and economic legislation is whether or not a law such as that challenged has a rational relation to a valid state objective. * * * If the Texas statute were to prohibit an abortion even where the mother's life is in jeopardy, I have little doubt that such a statute would lack a rational relation to a valid state objective * * *. But the Court's sweeping invalidation of any restrictions on abortion during the first trimester is impossible to justify under that standard, and the conscious weighing of competing factors [in] the Court's opinion * * * is far more appropriate to a legislative judgment than to a judicial one.

* * *

The fact that a majority of the States * * * have had restrictions on abortions for at least a century is a strong indication * * * that the asserted right to an abortion is not "so rooted in the traditions and conscience of our people as to be ranked as fundamental." Even today, when society's views on abortion are changing, the very existence of the debate is evidence that the "right" to an abortion is not so universally accepted as the appellant would have us believe.

* * * By the time of the adoption of the Fourteenth Amendment in 1868, there were at least 36 laws enacted by state or territorial legislatures limiting abortion. While many States have amended or updated their laws, 21 of the laws on the books in 1868 remain in effect today. Indeed, the Texas statute struck down today was * * * first enacted in 1857 and "has remained substantially unchanged to the present time."

* * * The only conclusion possible from this history is that the drafters did not intend to have the Fourteenth Amendment withdraw from the States the power to legislate with respect to this matter.

III

* * * [Still another concern is that t]he Texas statute is struck down *in toto*, even though the Court apparently concedes that at later periods of pregnancy Texas might impose these selfsame statutory limitations on abortion. My understanding of past practice is that a statute found to be invalid as applied to a particular plaintiff, but not unconstitutional as a whole, is not simply "struck down" but is, instead, declared unconstitutional as applied to the fact situation before the Court.

For all of the foregoing reasons, I respectfully dissent.

NOTES AND QUESTIONS

1.   What did the majority hold in *Roe v. Wade*? Which provisions of the Constitution did it rely upon in reaching its decision? What was the basis for Justice Rehnquist's dissent? Which opinion is more persuasive?

2.   The Court in *Roe v. Wade* initially addressed the constitutional requirements of "standing" and "mootness," which are derived from Article III's limitation of judicial power to "cases" or "controversies." Standing has three requirements:

> First, the plaintiff must have suffered an "injury in fact"—an invasion of a legally protected interest which is (a) concrete and particularized, and (b) "actual or imminent, not 'conjectural' or 'hypothetical.'" Second, there must be a causal connection between the injury and the conduct complained of—the injury has to be "fairly . . . trace[able] to the challenged action of the defendant, and not . . . th[e] result [of] the independent action of some third party not before the court." Third, it must be "likely," as opposed to merely "speculative," that the injury will be "redressed by a favorable decision."

Lujan v. Defenders of Wildlife, 504 U.S. 555, 560–61 (1992). This doctrine ensures that the plaintiff has a sufficient stake in the outcome of the proceeding, and thus will argue aggressively. Mootness is a related doctrine that restricts the class of judicially reviewable cases to those that present "live" controversies. A case might become moot, for example, because a plaintiff has relocated and is no longer exposed to the alleged wrongful conduct (such as when a prisoner who complains about poor prison conditions is transferred to a different facility). Standing thus examines the factual circumstances at the time of filing of the action, whereas mootness examines post-filing developments.

In some circumstances, however, claims that appear moot might still be subject to judicial review. For example, when a defendant voluntarily stops engaging in challenged conduct, the case might not be moot because of a concern that the defendant might " 'return to his old ways.' " *Friends of the Earth, Inc., v. Laidlaw Envtl. Servs. (TOC), Inc.*, 528 U.S. 167, 189 (2000). There is also a class of issues that are "capable of repetition, yet evading review" because they remain "live" issues only for a limited time. For example, in *Gerstein v. Pugh*, 420 U.S. 103 (1975), which involved allegedly unconstitutional detentions pending trial, the Court noted:

> Pretrial detention is by nature temporary, and it is most unlikely that any given individual could have his constitutional claim decided on appeal before he is either released or convicted. The individual could nonetheless suffer repeated deprivations, and it is certain that other persons similarly situated will be detained under the allegedly unconstitutional procedures. The claim, in short, is one that is distinctly "capable of repetition, yet evading review."

Id. at 110 n.11. How did the plaintiff in *Roe* satisfy the standing requirements? With respect to mootness, given the fact that pregnancy, like pretrial detention, is temporary in nature, was it appropriate for the Court to hear Roe's claim under the mootness doctrine?

One additional Article III concept should be noted: the doctrine of ripeness. That doctrine examines whether the facts and circumstances have become sufficiently clear and definite to justify judicial review. Ripeness issues frequently arise, for example, in the context of challenges to actions by administrative agencies. In that context, the aim of the doctrine is "to prevent the courts, through avoidance of premature adjudication, from entangling themselves in abstract disagreements over administrative policies, and also to protect the agencies from judicial interference until an administrative decision has been formalized and its effects felt in a concrete way by the challenging parties." *Abbott Labs. v. Gardner*, 387 U.S. 136, 148–49 (1967).

3.   Despite the 7–2 vote in *Roe v. Wade*, the changing composition of the Court has raised the specter that the case might be overruled. During President Reagan's administration in the 1980s, three conservative Justices—O'Connor, Scalia, and Kennedy—joined the Court, and many assumed that the new conservative majority would overturn *Roe*. In *Webster v. Reproductive Health Services*, 492 U.S. 490 (1989), the Supreme Court declined to overrule *Roe*, but the Court did uphold a state law that imposed significant restrictions on the use of state funds for abortion services. The state statute that the Court upheld specifically prohibited the use of public employees and facilities for elective abortions and the use of public funds to encourage or counsel women on the option of choosing to have an abortion. The Court dealt a more severe blow to *Roe* in *Planned Parenthood of Southeastern Pennsylvania v. Casey*, 505

U.S. 833 (1992). Although the Supreme Court again declined to overrule *Roe*, it abolished *Roe*'s strict scrutiny test in favor of an "undue burden" standard, which would permit restrictions on abortion as long as they do not make it significantly more difficult for a woman to obtain an abortion. Applying that standard, the Court upheld requirements that a woman receive counseling informing her of the details and risks of the abortion procedure and the gestational age and stage of development of the fetus, wait 24 hours after the counseling before having an abortion, and receive parental consent if she is a minor. The Court also upheld the requirement that the medical facility file a report for each abortion performed detailing the physician, the facility, the referring physician, the woman's age, and several other pieces of information. The Court, however, rejected a requirement that a woman tell her husband before she obtained an abortion. Then, in *Gonzalez v. Carhart*, 550 U.S. 124 (2007), the Supreme Court upheld the Partial-Birth Abortion Ban Act of 2003, a law that completely banned one type of late-term abortive procedure—the intact dilation and evacuation procedure—in which a fetus is aborted during the second trimester of pregnancy by removing the entire fetal body, intact except for its skull, from the uterus. In 2015, the Supreme Court granted certiorari in *Whole Woman's Health v. Cole*, 136 S. Ct. 499 (2015), which involves a challenge to Texas laws requiring abortion clinics to maintain the same facilities as a surgical center and requiring physicians performing abortions to have admitting privileges at a hospital within 30 miles from where the abortion is being performed. The decision in that case was pending when this text went to press.

4.   For additional reading on *Roe v. Wade*, *see* FAYE GINSBURG, CONTESTED LIVES (1998) (discussing the abortion debate in the United States, including the shift in the 1990s towards more violent forms of anti-abortion protest); Richard Myers, *Re-Reading* Roe v. Wade, 71 Wash. & Lee L. Rev. 1025 (2014) (analyzing the *Roe* opinion and arguing that its weaknesses justify overruling it); Dahlia Lithwick, *Foreword:* Roe v. Wade *at Forty*, 74 Ohio St. L.J. 5 (2013) (reflecting on the *Roe* holding and noting that the litigation strategies and the medical understanding have changed, but that other factors, such as the percentage of Americans identifying as pro-choice and pro-life, have remained fairly constant); Paul Benjamin Linton, *The Legal Status of Abortion in the States If* Roe v. Wade *Is Overruled*, 23 Issues L. & Med. 3 (2007) (analyzing state abortion laws and suggesting that very little would change if *Roe* were to be overruled because most state statutory schemes permit abortion); Linda Wharton et al., *Preserving the Core of* Roe: *Reflections on* Planned Parenthood v. Casey, 18 Yale J.L. & Feminism 317 (2006) (discussing the viability of the *Roe* decision after *Casey* and suggesting that the undue burden standard be clarified to better align with *Roe*); Sarah Weddington, *Reflections on the Twenty-Fifth Anniversary of* Roe v. Wade, 62 Alb. L. Rev. 811 (1999) (an analysis of *Roe* and its aftermath from the perspective of the attorney who argued the case in the Supreme Court on behalf of Roe); Sylvia Law, *Abortion Compromise—Inevitable and Impossible*, 1992 U. Ill. L. Rev. 921 (1992) (examining the pro-life and pro-choice viewpoints and concluding that the fundamental premises of the two viewpoints are irreconcilable).

5.   Abortion is controversial not just in the U.S. but also in many other parts of the world. *See, e.g.*, ANDRZEJ KULCZUCKI, THE ABORTION DEBATE IN THE WORLD ARENA (1999) (describing the development of abortion policies in Kenya, Mexico, and Poland and analyzing the roles of cultural history, women's movements, the Catholic Church, and international influences on that development); Jill Replogle, *Abortion Debate Heats Up in Latin America*, LANCET, July 28, 2007 (describing changes in abortion policies in Latin America and the polarization of the debate between pro-choice and anti-abortion activists).

6.   Another controversial privacy issue is the "right to die" through physician-assisted suicide. The case of *Cruzan v. Director, Missouri Department of Health*, 497 U.S. 261 (1990), concerned a young woman who had entered into a vegetative state following a car accident. After determining that there was no chance that their daughter would regain cognitive functioning, the woman's parents sought to discontinue the artificial methods that were keeping their daughter alive. The hospital employees, however, declined to discontinue care because there was no clear directive by the daughter that she opposed life-preserving treatment. The parents brought a claim in Missouri state court, and the court agreed that the hospital should discontinue treatment. On appeal, the Missouri Supreme Court reversed, finding that there was insufficient evidence that the woman would have wanted to end her life under the circumstances. The U.S. Supreme Court granted certiorari and affirmed, holding that it was proper for Missouri to require clear evidence of the individual's desire to discontinue treatment before permitting the termination of her life. The Court explained that, while a competent individual had a privacy interest in deciding whether to receive or decline treatment:

> An incompetent person is not able to make an informed and voluntary choice to exercise a hypothetical right to refuse treatment * * *. Such a "right" must be exercised * * * by some sort of surrogate. Here, Missouri has * * * recognized that under certain circumstances a surrogate may act for the patient in electing to have hydration and nutrition withdrawn in such a way as to cause death, but it has established a procedural safeguard to assure that the action of the surrogate conforms as best it may to the wishes expressed by the patient while competent. * * *
>
> * * *
>
> The choice between life and death is a deeply personal decision of obvious and overwhelming finality. We believe Missouri may legitimately seek to safeguard the personal element of this choice through the imposition of heightened evidentiary requirements.

Id. at 280–81.

Following *Cruzan*, the Supreme Court again addressed physician-assisted suicide in *Washington v. Glucksberg*, 521 U.S. 702 (1997), and *Vacco v. Quill*, 521 U.S. 793 (1997). In *Glucksberg*, the Court upheld a Washington state ban on assisted suicide, holding:

The history of the law's treatment of assisted suicide in this country
has been and continues to be one of the rejection of nearly all efforts
to permit it. That being the case, * * * [we] conclude that the asserted
"right" to assistance in committing suicide is not a fundamental
liberty interest protected by the Due Process Clause. The
Constitution also requires, however, that Washington's assisted-
suicide ban be rationally related to legitimate government interests.
This requirement is unquestionably met here.

Glucksberg, 521 U.S. at 728. Similarly, in *Vacco* the Court upheld, against an
equal protection challenge, a New York statute making it a crime to aid
another in committing suicide (even though a patient may refuse lifesaving
treatment). As the Court reasoned:

[W]e [reject the argument] that the distinction between refusing
lifesaving medical treatment and assisted suicide is "arbitrary" and
"irrational." * * * Logic and contemporary practice support New
York's judgment that the two acts are different, and New York may
therefore, consistent with the Constitution, treat them differently. By
permitting everyone to refuse unwanted medical treatment while
prohibiting anyone from assisting a suicide, New York law follows a
longstanding and rational distinction.

Vacco, 521 U.S. at 807–08.

For additional discussion of the "right to die," *see, e.g.*, Lois Shepherd, *The
End of End-of-Life Law*, 92 N.C. L. Rev. 1693 (2014) (suggesting that end-of-
life laws should be eliminated and that end-of-life medical decisions should be
treated like any other important medical decision); Browne Lewis, *A Graceful
Exit: Redefining Terminal to Expand the Availability of Physician-Facilitated
Suicide*, 91 Or. L. Rev. 457 (2012) (discussing current physician-assisted
suicide laws, proposing that the laws be expanded to include any individual
with an irreversible and incurable disease, and recommending that physician-
assisted suicide statutes be enacted in more states to allow for greater access
to death with dignity).

E. SEPARATION OF POWERS AND JUDICIAL REVIEW

The following case addresses "separation of powers" and "judicial
review" in the context of a dispute that ultimately led to the resignation of
a U.S. president. The dispute arose following the criminal indictment of
suspects in a burglary at the Democratic National Committee
headquarters at the Watergate Hotel in Washington, D.C. (The series of
events later came to be known as the "Watergate scandal.") The burglary
occurred several months prior to the 1972 presidential election, in which
President Richard Nixon was reelected. President Nixon was not one of the
indicted defendants, but the burglars were linked to the President's
reelection campaign. After a congressional hearing revealed that the

President had installed a tape-recording device in the Oval Office, the special prosecutor in charge of the criminal investigation obtained a subpoena ordering the President to turn over certain tapes and documents that were potentially relevant to the Watergate scandal. The President turned over only edited transcripts of some of the requested materials, and moved to quash (rescind) the subpoena. The district court denied that motion and ordered the President to turn over all of the materials for review by the court. The President appealed, and the Supreme Court granted expedited review.

UNITED STATES V. NIXON

Supreme Court of the United States, 1974
418 U.S. 683

CHIEF JUSTICE BURGER delivered the opinion of the Court.

This litigation presents for review the denial of a motion, filed in the District Court on behalf of the President of the United States, * * * to quash a third-party subpoena *duces tecum* issued by the United States District Court for the District of Columbia, pursuant to Fed. R. Crim. P. 17(c) [governing subpoenas for the production of evidence in federal criminal cases]. The subpoena directed the President to produce certain tape recordings and documents relating to his conversations with aides and advisers. The court rejected the President's [various arguments]. The President appealed to the Court of Appeals. We granted [review] before judgment because of the public importance of the issues presented and the need for their prompt resolution.

On March 1, 1974, a grand jury * * * returned an indictment charging seven named individuals with various offenses, including conspiracy to defraud the United States and to obstruct justice. Although he was not designated as such in the indictment, the grand jury named the President, among others, as an unindicted coconspirator. On April 18, 1974, upon motion of the Special Prosecutor, a subpoena *duces tecum* was issued pursuant to Rule 17(c) to the President by the * * * District Court and made returnable on May 2, 1974. This subpoena required the production, in advance of the September 9 trial date, of certain tapes, memoranda, papers, transcripts or other writings relating to certain precisely identified meetings between the President and others. The Special Prosecutor was able to fix the time, place, and persons present at these discussions because the White House daily logs and appointment records had been delivered to him. On April 30, the President publicly released edited transcripts of 43 conversations; portions of 20 conversations subject to subpoena in the present case were included. On May 1, 1974, the President's counsel filed * * * a motion to quash the subpoena * * *. This motion was accompanied by a formal claim of privilege. * * *

On May 20, 1974, the District Court denied the motion to quash * * *. It further ordered "the President or any subordinate officer, official, or employee with custody or control of the documents or objects subpoenaed," to deliver to the District Court, on or before May 31, 1974, the originals of all subpoenaed items, as well as an index and analysis of those items, together with tape copies of those portions of the subpoenaed recordings for which transcripts had been released to the public by the President on April 30. * * *

* * *

[This Court subsequently granted expedited review.]

I

* * *

II

JUSTICIABILITY

In the District Court, the President's counsel argued that the court lacked jurisdiction to issue the subpoena because the matter was an intra-branch dispute between a subordinate and superior officer of the Executive Branch and hence not subject to judicial resolution. That argument has been renewed in this Court with emphasis on the contention that the dispute does not present a "case" or "controversy" which can be adjudicated in the federal courts. The President's counsel argues that the federal courts should not intrude into areas committed to the other branches of Government. He views the present dispute as essentially a "jurisdictional" dispute within the Executive Branch which he analogizes to a dispute between two congressional committees. Since the Executive Branch has exclusive authority and absolute discretion to decide whether to prosecute a case, it is contended that a President's decision is final in determining what evidence is to be used in a given criminal case. Although his counsel concedes that the President has delegated certain specific powers to [a] Special Prosecutor [appointed specifically to investigate the Watergate scandal], he has not "waived nor delegated to the Special Prosecutor the President's duty to claim privilege as to all materials . . . which fall within the President's inherent authority to refuse to disclose to any executive officer." The Special Prosecutor's demand for the items therefore presents, in the view of the President's counsel, a political question under *Baker v. Carr*, 369 U.S. 186 (1962), since it involves a "textually demonstrable" grant of power under Art. II.

The mere assertion of a claim of an "intra-branch dispute," without more, has never operated to defeat federal jurisdiction; justiciability does not depend on such a surface inquiry. * * *

Our starting point is the nature of the proceeding for which the evidence is sought—here a pending criminal prosecution. It is a judicial proceeding in a federal court alleging violation of federal laws and is brought in the name of the United States as sovereign. Under the authority of Art. II, § 2, Congress has vested in the Attorney General [by statute] the power to conduct the criminal litigation of the United States Government. It has also vested in him the power to appoint subordinate officers to assist him in the discharge of his duties. Acting pursuant to those statutes, the Attorney General has delegated the authority to represent the United States in these particular matters to a Special Prosecutor with unique authority and tenure. The regulation gives the Special Prosecutor explicit power to contest the invocation of executive privilege in the process of seeking evidence deemed relevant to the performance of these specially delegated duties.

* * *

Here, * * * it is theoretically possible for the Attorney General to amend or revoke the regulation defining the Special Prosecutor's authority. But he has not done so. So long as this regulation remains in force the Executive Branch is bound by it, and indeed the United States as the sovereign composed of the three branches is bound to respect and to enforce it. Moreover, the delegation of authority to the Special Prosecutor in this case is not an ordinary delegation by the Attorney General to a subordinate officer: with the authorization of the President, the Acting Attorney General provided in the regulation that the Special Prosecutor was not to be removed without the "consensus" of eight designated leaders of Congress.

The demands of and the resistance to the subpoena present an obvious controversy in the ordinary sense, but that alone is not sufficient to meet constitutional standards. In the constitutional sense, controversy means more than disagreement and conflict; rather it means the kind of controversy courts traditionally resolve. Here at issue is the production or nonproduction of specified evidence deemed by the Special Prosecutor to be relevant and admissible in a pending criminal case. It is sought by one official of the Executive Branch within the scope of his express authority; it is resisted by the Chief Executive on the ground of his duty to preserve the confidentiality of the communications of the President. Whatever the correct answer on the merits, these issues are "of a type which are traditionally [within the scope of the judiciary]." * * *

* * * [T]he fact that both parties are officers of the Executive Branch cannot be viewed as a barrier to [judicial review]. It would be inconsistent with the applicable law and regulation, and the unique facts of this case to conclude other than that * * * a justiciable controversy is presented for decision.

III

* * *

* * * We * * * conclude that the Special Prosecutor has made a sufficient showing to justify a subpoena for production before trial. The subpoenaed materials are not available from any other source, and their examination and processing should not await trial in the circumstances shown.

IV

THE CLAIM OF PRIVILEGE

A

* * * [W]e turn to the claim that the subpoena should be quashed because it demands "confidential conversations between a President and his close advisors that it would be inconsistent with the public interest to produce." The first contention is a broad claim that the separation of powers doctrine precludes judicial review of a President's claim of privilege. The second contention is that if he does not prevail on the claim of absolute privilege, the court should hold as a matter of constitutional law that the privilege prevails over the subpoena *duces tecum*.

In the performance of assigned constitutional duties each branch of the Government must initially interpret the Constitution, and the interpretation of its powers by any branch is due great respect from the others. The President's counsel * * * reads the Constitution as providing an absolute privilege of confidentiality for all Presidential communications. Many decisions of this Court, however, have unequivocally reaffirmed the holding of *Marbury v. Madison*, 1 Cranch, 137, 2 L. Ed. 60 (1803), that "[i]t is emphatically the province and duty of the judicial department to say what the law is."

No holding of the Court has defined the scope of judicial power specifically relating to the enforcement of a subpoena for confidential Presidential communications for use in a criminal prosecution, but other exercises of power by the Executive Branch and the Legislative Branch have been found invalid as in conflict with the Constitution. * * *

Our system of government "requires that federal courts on occasion interpret the Constitution in a manner at variance with the construction given the document by another branch." * * * [I]n *Baker v. Carr*, the Court stated:

> [D]eciding whether a matter has in any measure been committed by the Constitution to another branch of government, or whether the action of that branch exceeds whatever authority has been committed, is itself a delicate exercise in constitutional

interpretation, and is a responsibility of this Court as ultimate interpreter of the Constitution.

Notwithstanding the deference each branch must accord the others, the "judicial Power of the United States" vested in the federal courts by Art. III, § 1, of the Constitution can no more be shared with the Executive Branch than the Chief Executive, for example, can share with the Judiciary the veto power, or the Congress share with the Judiciary the power to override a Presidential veto. Any other conclusion would be contrary to the basic concept of separation of powers and the checks and balances that flow from the scheme of a tripartite government. * * *

B

In support of his claim of absolute privilege, the President's counsel urges two grounds * * *. The first ground is the valid need for protection of communications between high Government officials and those who advise and assist them in the performance of their manifold duties; the importance of this confidentiality is too plain to require further discussion. Human experience teaches that those who expect public dissemination of their remarks may well temper candor with a concern for appearances and for their own interests to the detriment of the decision-making process. Whatever the nature of the privilege of confidentiality of Presidential communications in the exercise of Art. II powers, the privilege can be said to derive from the supremacy of each branch within its own assigned area of constitutional duties. Certain powers and privileges flow from the nature of enumerated powers; the protection of the confidentiality of Presidential communications has similar constitutional underpinnings.

The second ground asserted by the President's counsel in support of the claim of absolute privilege rests on the doctrine of separation of powers. Here it is argued that the independence of the Executive Branch within its own sphere, insulates a President from a judicial subpoena in an ongoing criminal prosecution, and thereby protects confidential Presidential communications.

However, neither the doctrine of separation of powers, nor the need for confidentiality of high-level communications, without more, can sustain an absolute, unqualified Presidential privilege of immunity from judicial process under all circumstances. The President's need for complete candor and objectivity from advisers calls for great deference from the courts. However, when the privilege depends solely on the broad, undifferentiated claim of public interest in the confidentiality of such conversations, a confrontation with other values arises. Absent a claim of need to protect military, diplomatic, or sensitive national security secrets, we find it difficult to accept the argument that even the very important interest in confidentiality of Presidential communications is significantly diminished by production of such material for *in camera* [private judicial] inspection with all the protection that a district court will be obliged to provide.

The impediment that an absolute, unqualified privilege would place in the way of the primary constitutional duty of the Judicial Branch to do justice in criminal prosecutions would plainly conflict with the function of the courts under Art. III. In designing the structure of our Government and dividing and allocating the sovereign power among three co-equal branches, the Framers of the Constitution sought to provide a comprehensive system, but the separate powers were not intended to operate with absolute independence.

* * *

To read the Art. II powers of the President as providing an absolute privilege as against a subpoena essential to enforcement of criminal statutes on no more than a generalized claim of the public interest in confidentiality of nonmilitary and nondiplomatic discussions would upset the constitutional balance of "a workable government" and gravely impair the role of the courts under Art. III.

C

Since we conclude that the legitimate needs of the judicial process may outweigh Presidential privilege, it is necessary to resolve those competing interests in a manner that preserves the essential functions of each branch. The right and indeed the duty to resolve that question does not free the Judiciary from according high respect to the representations made on behalf of the President.

The expectation of a President to the confidentiality of his conversations and correspondence, like the claim of confidentiality of judicial deliberations, for example, has all the values to which we accord deference for the privacy of all citizens and, added to those values, is the necessity for protection of the public interest in candid, objective, and even blunt or harsh opinions in Presidential decision-making. A President and those who assist him must be free to explore alternatives in the process of shaping policies and making decisions and to do so in a way many would be unwilling to express except privately. These are the considerations justifying a presumptive privilege for Presidential communications. The privilege is fundamental to the operation of Government and inextricably rooted in the separation of powers under the Constitution.

But this presumptive privilege must be considered in light of our historic commitment to the rule of law. This is nowhere more profoundly manifest than in our view that "the twofold aim (of criminal justice) is that guilt shall not escape or innocence suffer." We have elected to employ an adversary system of criminal justice in which the parties contest all issues before a court of law. The need to develop all relevant facts in the adversary system is both fundamental and comprehensive. * * * To ensure that justice is done, it is imperative to the function of courts that compulsory process be available for the production of evidence needed either by the prosecution or by the defense.

* * *

* * * [E]xceptions to the demand for every man's evidence are not lightly created nor expansively construed, for they are in derogation of the search for truth.

In this case the President challenges a subpoena served on him as a third party requiring the production of materials for use in a criminal prosecution; he does so on the claim that he has a privilege against disclosure of confidential communications. He does not place his claim of privilege on the ground they are military or diplomatic secrets. As to these areas of Art. II duties the courts have traditionally shown the utmost deference to Presidential responsibilities. * * *

* * *

No case of the Court, however, has extended this high degree of deference to a President's generalized interest in confidentiality. Nowhere in the Constitution * * * is there any explicit reference to a privilege of confidentiality, yet to the extent this interest relates to the effective discharge of a President's powers, it is constitutionally based.

The right to the production of all evidence at a criminal trial similarly has constitutional dimensions. The Sixth Amendment explicitly confers upon every defendant in a criminal trial the right "to be confronted with the witnesses against him" and "to have compulsory process for obtaining witnesses in his favor." Moreover, the Fifth Amendment also guarantees that no person shall be deprived of liberty without due process of law. It is the manifest duty of the courts to vindicate those guarantees, and to accomplish that it is essential that all relevant and admissible evidence be produced.

In this case we must weigh the importance of the general privilege of confidentiality of Presidential communications in performance of the President's responsibilities against the inroads of such a privilege on the fair administration of criminal justice. The interest in preserving confidentiality is weighty indeed and entitled to great respect. However, we cannot conclude that advisers will be moved to temper the candor of their remarks by the infrequent occasions of disclosure because of the possibility that such conversations will be called for in the context of a criminal prosecution.

On the other hand, the allowance of the privilege to withhold evidence that is demonstrably relevant in a criminal trial would cut deeply into the guarantee of due process of law and gravely impair the basic function of the courts. * * * Without access to specific facts a criminal prosecution may be totally frustrated. The President's broad interest in confidentiality of communications will not be vitiated by disclosure of a limited number of conversations preliminarily shown to have some bearing on the pending criminal cases.

We conclude that when the ground for asserting privilege as to subpoenaed materials sought for use in a criminal trial is based only on the generalized interest in confidentiality, it cannot prevail over the fundamental demands of due process of law in the fair administration of criminal justice. * * *

D

* * * Accordingly, we affirm the order of the District Court that subpoenaed materials be transmitted to that court. We now turn to the important question of the District Court's responsibilities in conducting the in camera examination of Presidential materials or communications delivered under the compulsion of the subpoena *duces tecum.*

E

* * * It is elementary that *in camera* inspection of evidence is always a procedure calling for scrupulous protection against any release or publication of material not found by the court, at that stage, probably admissible in evidence and relevant to the issues of the trial for which it is sought. That being true of an ordinary situation, it is obvious that the District Court has a very heavy responsibility to see to it that Presidential conversations, which are either not relevant or not admissible, are accorded that high degree of respect due the President of the United States. * * *

* * * We have no doubt that the District Judge will at all times accord to Presidential records [a] high degree of deference * * * and will discharge his responsibility to see to it that until released to the Special Prosecutor no in camera material is revealed to anyone. This burden applies with even greater force to excised material; once the decision is made to excise, the material is restored to its privileged status and should be returned under seal to its lawful custodian.

* * *

Affirmed.

NOTES AND QUESTIONS

1.   At the time of *Nixon*, four members of the Supreme Court (including Chief Justice Burger) were Nixon appointees. One Justice, Justice Rehnquist, recused himself because he had served in the Nixon administration as Assistant Attorney General. With respect to the remaining three Justices, is it surprising that they would vote against the President who appointed them? The *Nixon* decision ultimately had grave consequences for President Nixon, because one of the tapes revealed that he personally approved plans to cover up the facts involving the break-in. The Supreme Court decided *Nixon* on July

24, 1974, and Nixon resigned from office approximately two weeks later, on August 8, 1974. *See, e.g.*, Carroll Kilpatrick, *Nixon Resigns*, WASH. POST, Aug. 9, 1974, at A01, *available at* http://www.washingtonpost.com/wp-srv/national/longterm/watergate/articles/080974-3.htm.

2. What was the Court's rationale for rejecting the President's argument that he, not the courts, decides questions of executive privilege? What was the Court's rationale for rejecting, on the merits, the President's argument that the tapes were protected by executive privilege?

3. In *Nixon*, the Supreme Court had to interpret the Constitution to determine the degree of confidentiality accorded to presidential communications. Thus, *Nixon* is an important application of the principle announced in *Marbury v. Madison* that it is the duty of the Supreme Court to say what the law is. *See* Chapter 1. Is the Court's decision in *Nixon* consistent with the holding in *Marbury*?

4. Federal courts can only hear issues that are "justiciable." Among other things, to be justiciable the issue must not raise a political question. In *Baker v. Carr*, 369 U.S. 186 (1962), cited in *Nixon*, voters in Tennessee sought a declaratory judgment that the state apportionment statute (which established voting districts) violated the Equal Protection Clause, as well as injunctive relief from that violation. The argument was that, because of population migration from rural to urban areas with no change in district lines, the votes of urban voters were diluted. The state claimed that the issue was a nonjusticiable political question. The Court rejected that argument, holding that the issue was justiciable.

For additional discussion of justiciability and the political question doctrine, *see, e.g.*, Rachel Barkow, *More Supreme Than Court? The Fall of the Political Question Doctrine and the Rise of Judicial Supremacy*, 102 Colum. L. Rev. 237 (2002) (exploring the decline of the political question doctrine); Robert Pushaw, Jr., *Judicial Review and the Political Question Doctrine: Reviving the Federalist "Rebuttable Presumption" Analysis*, 80 N.C. L. Rev. 1165 (2002) (arguing that the *Baker* political question test gives judges too much discretion to hear political cases).

5. For additional discussion of *Nixon*, *see, e.g.*, Eric Lane et al., *Too Big a Canon in the President's Arsenal: Another Look at* United States v. Nixon, 17 Geo. Mason L. Rev. 737 (2010) (arguing that the *Nixon* decision's presumption of secrecy for presidential communications is inconsistent with the structure of the Constitution when used to thwart a congressional inquiry); Philip Allen Lacovara, United States v. Nixon: *The Prelude*, 83 Minn. L. Rev. 1061 (1999) (describing the legal process leading up to *Nixon* after it became known that there was a tape recorder in the Oval Office); K.A. McNeely-Johnson, United States v. Nixon, *Twenty Years After: The Good, the Bad and the Ugly—An Exploration of Executive Privilege*, 14 N. Ill. U. L. Rev. 251 (1993) (suggesting that the judiciary should control the use of executive privilege by increasing in camera inspection, putting the burden on the President to show privilege, and

extending such procedures to traditionally unreviewable fields such an national security).

6.   A landmark case regarding separation of powers is *Youngstown Sheet & Tube Co. v. Sawyer*, 343 U.S. 579 (1952), often referred to as the "Steel Seizure Case." In *Youngstown*, the Supreme Court addressed a challenge to President Truman's seizure of the nation's steel industry during labor disputes between steelworkers and steel industry management. The Korean War had increased the demand for steel, and the President authorized the Secretary of Commerce to take possession of the steel mills to avoid a strike and keep them running to support the military. The Supreme Court declared the President's actions unconstitutional. It explained that the President's powers must be rooted in an act of Congress or an explicit delegation of power in the Constitution. It held that the President did not have the power to seize private property as Commander-in-Chief of the military, nor the authority "implied from the aggregate of his powers under the Constitution." *Id.* at 587.

The most frequently cited language in *Youngstown* appeared in a concurring opinion by Justice Jackson, which set forth a three-part test to determine the reach of executive power:

> (1) When the President acts pursuant to an express or implied authorization of Congress, his authority is at its maximum, for it includes all [authority] that he possesses in his own right plus all that Congress can delegate. * * *

> (2) When the President acts in the absence of either a congressional grant or denial of authority, he can only rely upon his own independent powers, but there is a zone * * * in which he and Congress may have concurrent authority, or in which its distribution is uncertain. * * *

> (3) When the President takes measures incompatible with the expressed or implied will of Congress, his power is at its lowest ebb, for then he can rely only upon his own constitutional powers minus any constitutional powers of Congress over the matter. * * *

Id. at 635–36 (Jackson, J., concurring).

F. COMMERCE CLAUSE AND FEDERALISM

The Commerce Clause appears in Article I, Section 8, Clause 3 of the Constitution. It grants Congress the power "[t]o regulate Commerce with foreign Nations, and among the several States, and with the Indian Tribes." The Supreme Court's interpretation of that language has played a major role in determining the balance of power between the federal government and the states. The Commerce Clause has often been interpreted broadly, allowing the federal government to regulate a wide range of matters, from interstate navigation, *Gibbons v. Ogden*, 22 U.S. 1 (1824), to labor standards, *United States v. Darby Lumber Co.*, 312 U.S. 100 (1941), to agricultural production for personal use, *Wickard v. Filburn*,

317 U.S. 111 (1942). Indeed, it has provided authority for much of the federal legislation promulgated since the late nineteenth century. *See Gonzales v. Raich*, 545 U.S. 1, 16 & n.27 (2005) (noting that industrialization in the late 1800s gave rise to "a new era of federal regulation under the commerce power").

Between 1933 and 1939, President Franklin Roosevelt advanced a policy called the New Deal, designed to stimulate the economy in the face of the Great Depression (which began in 1929). Some of his New Deal legislation, enacted by Congress, was invalidated by the Supreme Court as beyond federal authority under the Commerce Clause. *See, e.g., Carter v. Carter Coal Co.*, 298 U.S. 238 (1936) (invalidating legislation regulating the coal industry); *Schechter Poultry Corp. v. United States*, 295 U.S. 495 (1935) (invalidating statute authorizing the President to establish codes of fair competition for particular industries). Frustrated with the Supreme Court's repeated interference with his policies, President Roosevelt threatened to pursue legislation to increase the number of justices on the Supreme Court and presumably fill the new spots with justices who would support his policies. That step was avoided when the Supreme Court upheld Roosevelt's policies in *West Coast Hotel Co. v. Parrish*, 300 U.S. 379 (1937). Subsequently, no exercise of Congress's Commerce Clause power was overturned as unconstitutional for a period of nearly 60 years, from the New Deal era to 1995 (in the case below).

The principle of federalism is intertwined with Commerce Clause considerations. As explained by the Founding Fathers in the Federalist Papers, under the system of federalism:

> The States will retain, under the proposed Constitution, a very extensive portion of active sovereignty. * * * The powers delegated by the proposed Constitution to the federal government, are few and defined. Those which are to remain in the State governments are numerous and indefinite. The former will be exercised principally on external objects, as war, peace, negotiation, and foreign commerce; with which last the power of taxation will, for the most part, be connected. The powers reserved to the several States will extend to all the objects which, in the ordinary course of affairs, concern the lives, liberties, and properties of the people, and the internal order, improvement, and prosperity of the State.

Federalist 45 (James Madison). Thus, "[a]lthough the Constitution grants broad powers to Congress, our federalism requires that Congress treat the States in a manner consistent with their status as residuary sovereigns and joint participants in the governance of the Nation." *Alden v. Maine*, 527 U.S. 706, 748 (1999). Although the balance of power between the states and the federal government has shifted over time, the states, as sovereigns, maintain almost complete control over some aspects of governance, such as "street crime, running public schools, and zoning property for development." *Nat'l Fed. of Indep. Bus. v. Sebelius*, 567 U.S. ___, 132 S. Ct. 2566, 2578 (2012). In other areas, like commerce and economic concerns, the states and the federal government have overlapping powers: "[T]he grant of power to Congress by the Commerce Clause did not wholly withdraw from the states the authority to regulate the commerce with respect to matters of local concern, on which Congress has not spoken." *Parker v. Brown*, 317 U.S. 341, 360 (1943).

The following case involves the intersection of the Commerce Clause and federalism.

UNITED STATES V. LOPEZ

Supreme Court of the United States, 1995
514 U.S. 549

CHIEF JUSTICE REHNQUIST delivered the opinion of the Court.

In the Gun-Free School Zones Act of 1990, Congress made it a federal offense "for any individual knowingly to possess a firearm at a place that the individual knows, or has reasonable cause to believe, is a school zone." 18 U.S.C. § 922(q)(1)(A) (1988 ed., Supp. V). The Act neither regulates a commercial activity nor contains a requirement that the possession be connected in any way to interstate commerce. We hold that the Act exceeds the authority of Congress "[t]o regulate Commerce . . . among the several States. . . ." U.S. CONST. art. I, § 8, cl. 3.

On March 10, 1992, respondent, who was then a 12th-grade student, arrived at Edison High School in San Antonio, Texas, carrying a concealed .38-caliber handgun and five bullets. Acting upon an anonymous tip, school authorities confronted respondent, who admitted that he was carrying the weapon. He was arrested and charged under Texas law with firearm possession on school premises. The next day, the state charges were dismissed after federal agents charged respondent * * * with violating the Gun-Free School Zones Act of 1990.[1]

A federal grand jury indicted respondent on one count of knowing possession of a firearm at a school zone, in violation of § 922(q). Respondent moved to dismiss his federal indictment on the ground that § 922(q) "is unconstitutional as it is beyond the power of Congress to legislate control over our public schools." [The district court upheld the constitutionality of § 922(g), but the Fifth Circuit reversed.] * * *

[W]e * * * affirm.

We start with first principles. The Constitution creates a Federal Government of enumerated powers. * * * "Just as the separation and

---

[1]   The term "school zone" is defined as "in, or on the grounds of, a public, parochial or private school" or "within a distance of 1,000 feet from the grounds of a public, parochial or private school." 18 U.S.C. § 921(a)(25).

independence of the coordinate branches of the Federal Government serve to prevent the accumulation of excessive power in any one branch, a healthy balance of power between the States and the Federal Government will reduce the risk of tyranny and abuse from either front."

The Constitution delegates to Congress the power "[t]o regulate Commerce with foreign Nations, and among the several States, and with the Indian Tribes." Art. I, § 8, cl. 3. The Court, through Chief Justice Marshall, first defined the nature of Congress's commerce power in *Gibbons v. Ogden*, 9 Wheat. 1, 189–90, 6 L. Ed. 23 (1824):

> Commerce, undoubtedly, is traffic, but it is something more: it is intercourse. It describes the commercial intercourse between nations, and parts of nations, in all its branches, and is regulated by prescribing rules for carrying on that intercourse.

The commerce power "is the power to regulate; that is, to prescribe the rule by which commerce is to be governed. This power, like all others vested in Congress, is complete in itself, may be exercised to its utmost extent, and acknowledges no limitations, other than are prescribed in the Constitution." [But] * * * limitations on the commerce power are inherent in the very language of the Commerce Clause.

* * *

For nearly a century [after *Gibbons*], the Court's Commerce Clause decisions dealt but rarely with the extent of Congress's power, and almost entirely with the Commerce Clause as a limit on state legislation that discriminated against interstate commerce. * * *

[The Court reviewed decades of its Commerce Clause jurisprudence beginning in the mid-1800s, noting the great expansion of Congress's authority under the Commerce Clause starting in 1937.]

In part, this [expansion] was a recognition of the great changes that had occurred in the way business was carried on in this country. Enterprises that had once been local or at most regional in nature had become national in scope. But the doctrinal change also reflected a view that earlier Commerce Clause cases artificially had constrained the authority of Congress to regulate interstate commerce.

But even these modern-era precedents which have expanded congressional power under the Commerce Clause confirm that this power is subject to outer limits. * * *

* * *

Consistent with this structure, we have identified three broad categories of activity that Congress may regulate under its commerce power. First, Congress may regulate the use of the channels of interstate commerce. Second, Congress is empowered to regulate and protect the instrumentalities of interstate commerce, or persons or things in interstate commerce, even though the threat may come only from intrastate activities. Finally, Congress's commerce authority includes the power to regulate * * * those activities that substantially affect interstate commerce.

* * *

We now turn to consider the power of Congress, in the light of this framework, to enact § 922(q). The first two categories of authority may be quickly disposed of: § 922(q) is not a regulation of the use of the channels of interstate commerce * * *; nor can § 922(q) be justified as a regulation by which Congress has sought to protect an instrumentality of interstate commerce or a thing in interstate commerce. Thus, if § 922(q) is to be sustained, it must be under the third category * * *.

* * * [W]e have upheld a wide variety of congressional [a]cts regulating intrastate economic activity where we have concluded that the activity substantially affected interstate commerce. Examples include the regulation of intrastate coal mining; extortionate credit transactions; restaurants utilizing substantial interstate supplies; inns and hotels catering to interstate guests; and production and consumption of homegrown wheat. These examples are by no means exhaustive, but the pattern is clear. * * *

* * *

Section 922(q) is a criminal statute that by its terms has nothing to do with "commerce" or any sort of economic enterprise, however broadly one might define those terms.[3] Section 922(q) is not an essential part of a larger regulation of economic activity, in which the regulatory scheme could be undercut unless the intrastate activity were regulated. It cannot, therefore, be sustained [as an activity that] * * * substantially affects interstate commerce.

[Moreover], § 922(q) * * * has no express jurisdictional element which might limit its reach to a discrete set of firearm possessions that additionally have an explicit connection with or effect on interstate commerce.

Although as part of our independent evaluation of constitutionality under the Commerce Clause we of course consider legislative findings, and indeed even congressional committee findings, regarding effect on interstate commerce, the Government concedes that "[n]either the statute nor its legislative history contain[s] express congressional findings regarding the effects upon interstate commerce of gun possession in a school zone." We agree with the Government that Congress normally is not

---

[3] Under our federal system, the " 'States possess primary authority for defining and enforcing the criminal law.' " When Congress criminalizes conduct already denounced as criminal by the States, it effects a " 'change in the sensitive relation between federal and state criminal jurisdiction.' " * * *

required to make formal findings as to the substantial burdens that an activity has on interstate commerce. But to the extent that congressional findings would enable us to evaluate the legislative judgment that the activity in question substantially affected interstate commerce, * * * they are lacking here.

* * *

The Government's essential contention * * * is that we may determine here that § 922(q) is valid because possession of a firearm in a local school zone does indeed substantially affect interstate commerce. The Government argues that possession of a firearm in a school zone may result in violent crime and that violent crime can be expected to affect the functioning of the national economy in two ways. First, the costs of violent crime are substantial, and * * * are spread throughout the population. Second, violent crime reduces the willingness of individuals to travel to areas within the country that are perceived to be unsafe. The Government also argues that the presence of guns in schools poses a substantial threat to the educational process by threatening the learning environment. A handicapped educational process, in turn, will result in a less productive citizenry. That, in turn, would have an adverse effect on the Nation's economic well-being. As a result, the Government argues that Congress could rationally have concluded that § 922(q) substantially affects interstate commerce.

We pause to consider the implications of the Government's arguments. The Government admits, under its "costs of crime" reasoning, that Congress could regulate not only all violent crime, but all activities that might lead to violent crime, regardless of how tenuously they relate to interstate commerce. Similarly, under the Government's "national productivity" reasoning, Congress could regulate any activity that it found was related to the economic productivity of individual citizens: family law (including marriage, divorce, and child custody), for example. Under the theories that the Government presents in support of § 922(q), it is difficult to perceive any limitation on federal power, even in areas such as criminal law enforcement or education where States historically have been sovereign. Thus, if we were to accept the Government's arguments, we are hard pressed to posit any activity by an individual that Congress is without power to regulate.

* * *

For instance, * * * Congress could determine that a school's curriculum has a "significant" effect on the extent of classroom learning. As a result, Congress could mandate a federal curriculum for local elementary and secondary schools * * *.

* * *

* * * The possession of a gun in a local school zone is in no sense an economic activity that might, through repetition elsewhere, substantially affect any sort of interstate commerce. Respondent was a local student at a local school; there is no indication that he had recently moved in interstate commerce, and there is no requirement that his possession of the firearm have any concrete tie to interstate commerce.

To uphold the Government's contentions here, we would have to pile inference upon inference in a manner that would * * * convert congressional authority under the Commerce Clause to a general police power of the sort retained by the States. Admittedly, some of our prior cases have taken long steps down that road, giving great deference to congressional action. * * * [B]ut we decline here to proceed any further.

For the foregoing reasons the judgment of the Court of Appeals is

Affirmed.

[Concurring opinion by JUSTICE KENNEDY, joined by JUSTICE O'CONNOR, is omitted.]

[Concurring opinion by JUSTICE THOMAS is omitted.]

[Dissenting opinions by JUSTICE STEVENS and JUSTICE SOUTER are omitted.]

JUSTICE BREYER, with whom JUSTICE STEVENS, JUSTICE SOUTER, and JUSTICE GINSBURG join, dissenting.

The issue in this case is whether the Commerce Clause authorizes Congress to enact a statute that makes it a crime to possess a gun in, or near, a school. In my view, the statute falls well within the scope of the commerce power * * *.

I

In reaching this conclusion, I apply three basic principles of Commerce Clause interpretation. First, the power to "regulate Commerce . . . among the several States," U.S. CONST. art. I, § 8, cl. 3, encompasses the power to regulate local activities insofar as they significantly affect interstate commerce. * * * Second, in determining whether a local activity will likely have a significant effect upon interstate commerce, a court must consider, not the effect of an individual act (a single instance of gun possession), but rather the cumulative effect of all similar instances (*i.e.*, the effect of all guns possessed in or near schools). * * *

Third, * * * [c]ourts must give Congress a degree of leeway in determining the existence of a significant factual connection between the regulated activity and interstate commerce—both because the Constitution delegates the commerce power directly to Congress and because the determination requires an empirical judgment of a kind that a legislature is more likely than a court to make with accuracy. The traditional words "rational basis" capture this leeway. * * *

* * *

II

[W]e must ask * * *: Could Congress rationally have found that "violent crime in school zones," through its effect on the "quality of education," significantly (or substantially) affects "interstate" or "foreign commerce"? 18 U.S.C. §§ 922(q)(1)(F), (G). As long as one views the commerce connection, not as a "technical legal conception," but as "a practical one," the answer to this question must be yes. * * *

For one thing, reports, hearings, and other readily available literature make clear that the problem of guns in and around schools is widespread and extremely serious. These materials report, for example, that four percent of American high school students (and six percent of inner-city high school students) carry a gun to school at least occasionally; that 12 percent of urban high school students have had guns fired at them; that 20 percent of those students have been threatened with guns; and that, in any 6-month period, several hundred thousand schoolchildren are victims of violent crimes in or near their schools. And, they report that this widespread violence in schools throughout the Nation significantly interferes with the quality of education in those schools. Based on reports such as these, * * * Congress could * * * have found a substantial educational problem—teachers unable to teach, students unable to learn—and concluded that guns near schools contribute substantially to the size and scope of that problem.

Having found that guns in schools significantly undermine the quality of education in our Nation's classrooms, Congress could also have found, given the effect of education upon interstate and foreign commerce, that gun-related violence in and around schools is a commercial, as well as a human, problem. Education * * * has long been inextricably intertwined with the Nation's economy. When this Nation began, most workers received their education in the workplace, typically * * * as apprentices. As late as the 1920s, many workers still received general education directly from their employers * * *. As public school enrollment grew in the early 20th century, the need for industry to teach basic educational skills diminished. But, the direct economic link between basic education and industrial productivity remained. * * *

In recent years the link between secondary education and business has strengthened * * *. Scholars * * * report that technological changes and innovations in management techniques have altered the nature of the workplace so that more jobs now demand greater educational skills. * * *

Increasing global competition also has made primary and secondary education economically more important. The portion of the American economy attributable to international trade nearly tripled between 1950 and 1980, and more than 70 percent of American-made goods now compete with imports. Yet, lagging worker productivity has contributed to negative trade balances and to real hourly compensation that has fallen below wages in ten other industrialized nations. At least some significant part of this serious productivity problem is attributable to students who emerge from classrooms without the reading or mathematical skills necessary to compete with their European or Asian counterparts. * * *

Finally, there is evidence that, today more than ever, many firms base their location decisions upon the presence, or absence, of a workforce with a basic education. * * *

The economic links I have just sketched seem fairly obvious. * * * [G]uns in the hands of six percent of inner-city high school students and gun-related violence throughout a city's schools must threaten the trade and commerce that those schools support. The only question, then, is whether the latter threat is * * * "substantial." The evidence of (1) the *extent* of the gun-related violence problem, (2) the *extent* of the resulting negative effect on classroom learning, and (3) the *extent* of the consequent negative commercial effects, when taken together, indicate a threat to trade and commerce that is "substantial." At the very least, Congress could rationally have concluded that the links are "substantial."

Specifically, Congress could have found that gun-related violence near the classroom poses a serious economic threat (1) to consequently inadequately educated workers who must endure low-paying jobs, and (2) to communities and businesses that might (in today's "information society") otherwise gain, from a well-educated work force, an important commercial advantage. * * * To hold this statute constitutional is not to "obliterate" the "distinction between what is national and what is local" * * *. In sum, a holding that the particular statute before us falls within the commerce power would * * * simply * * * apply preexisting law to changing economic circumstances. * * *

* * *

NOTES AND QUESTIONS

1.   Why did the majority find that § 922(g) exceeds Congress's authority under the Commerce Clause? Why did the four dissenting Justices disagree? Which opinion is more persuasive?

2.   *Lopez* has generated extensive commentary, both favorable and unfavorable. *See, e.g.*, Richard Epstein, *Constitutional Faith and the Commerce Clause*, 71 Notre Dame L. Rev. 167 (1996) (arguing that *Lopez* did not go far enough in narrowing the application of the Commerce Clause and proposing a return to the pre-1937 understanding of the Commerce Clause); Robert Wax, United States v. Lopez: *The Continued Ambiguity of Commerce Clause*

Jurisprudence, 69 Temp. L. Rev. 275 (1996) (arguing that *Lopez* was flawed because it misapplied precedent and failed to announce a clear test to guide lower courts); Steven Calabresi, *"A Government of Limited and Enumerated Powers": In Defense of* United States v. Lopez, 94 Mich. L. Rev. 752 (1995) (arguing that *Lopez* restores important federalism considerations to Commerce Clause jurisprudence).

3.   In *United States v. Morrison*, 529 U.S. 598 (2000), the Supreme Court relied on *Lopez* to invalidate the civil remedy provision of the Violence Against Women Act. The provision allowed victims of gender-based crimes of violence to pursue compensatory and punitive damages claims and claims for equitable relief against the perpetrators of those crimes. The Court found that, as in *Lopez*, Congress had failed to establish a true interstate nexus for the law: "We * * * reject the argument that Congress may regulate noneconomic, violent criminal conduct based solely on that conduct's aggregate effect on interstate commerce."

4.   The Court continued to apply this narrower construction of the Commerce Clause in *National Federation of Independent Business v. Sebelius*, 567 U.S. ___, 132 S. Ct. 2566 (2012). *Sebelius* concerned the constitutionality of the Affordable Care Act, commonly known as "Obamacare." The Act included an "individual mandate" that required individuals to obtain health insurance. The Court held that such a mandate was not authorized under the Commerce Clause because it compelled action rather than regulating existing commercial activity. As the Court noted: "[c]onstruing the Commerce Clause to permit Congress to regulate individuals precisely *because* they are doing nothing would open a new and potentially vast domain to congressional authority." *Id.* at 2587. The Court ultimately upheld the mandate under the Taxing and Spending Clause. The case is discussed further at the end of the chapter.

Even after *Lopez*, *Morrison*, and *Sebelius*, Congress continues to have broad powers under the Commerce Clause. For example, in *Gonzales v. Raich*, 545 U.S. 1 (2005), the Supreme Court held that, under the Commerce Clause, Congress could regulate the manufacture, distribution, and possession of medical marijuana—even if those acts were committed intrastate—because such activities would affect the larger national market for marijuana.

5.   For other scholarly discussions of the Commerce Clause, *see, e.g.,* Grant Nelson, *A Commerce Clause Standard for the New Millennium: "Yes" to Broad Congressional Control over Commercial Transactions; "No" to Federal Legislation on Social and Cultural Issues*, 55 Ark. L. Rev. 1213 (2003) (arguing that Congress needs ample power to regulate commercial transactions that have effects in multiple states, but that such power should not generally extend to cultural and social issues that have only an attenuated connection to commerce); Richard Epstein, *The Proper Scope of the Commerce Power*, 73 Va. L. Rev. 1387 (1987) (arguing in favor of a narrow construction of the Commerce Clause).

6.   A concept that arises from the Commerce Clause is the "dormant Commerce Clause," which stands for the principle that states may not pass

laws that unduly burden interstate commerce. *See, e.g., City of Philadelphia v. New Jersey*, 437 U.S. 617 (1978) (invalidating a New Jersey law restricting the importation of out-of-state waste); *Dean Milk Co. v. City of Madison*, 340 U.S. 349 (1951) (invalidating a Madison, Wisconsin ordinance requiring that all milk sold in the city be pasteurized locally).

7.   For other scholarly discussions of federalism, *see, e.g.*, Larry Kramer, *Understanding Federalism*, 47 Vand. L. Rev. 1485 (1994) (discussing the appropriate role of federalism in the U.S.); Herbert Wechsler, *The Political Safeguards of Federalism: The Role of the States in the Composition and Selection of the National Government*, 54 Colum. L. Rev. 543 (1954) (arguing that Congress, not the courts, plays the primary role in ensuring that the federal government does not usurp state authority).

G. ADDITIONAL TOPICS OF INTEREST

In addition to the topics covered in detail in this chapter, the following topics are frequently addressed in an introductory constitutional law course.

a.   Affirmative Action: In 1965, President Johnson issued an executive order requiring government contractors to "take affirmative action" to hire minority employees. Exec. Order No. 11,246, 3 C.F.R. 339 (1964–1965). Subsequently, some universities adopted affirmative action programs to admit a greater number of diverse students. Although designed to eliminate the consequences of segregation, affirmative action programs have been challenged as violating the Equal Protection Clause of the Fourteenth Amendment by discriminating against Caucasian people.

In *Regents of the University of California v. Bakke*, 438 U.S. 265 (1978), Bakke, a Caucasian man, challenged his denial of admission to the medical school of the University of California at Davis. The school had a general admissions process for all students and a parallel process for minority applicants, with 16 of the 100 admissions spots reserved for minority applicants. Minority students were considered under both processes, while non-minority students could only be admitted through the general process. Bakke twice applied to the medical school and was rejected, despite the fact that special applicants with lower grades and test scores were admitted. Bakke alleged that that system discriminated against him based on his race because his application was not given the same consideration as those of minority students.

Six of the nine Justices on the Supreme Court wrote opinions in *Bakke*. Four Justices concluded that the university's use of a "racial quota" was unconstitutional, and four Justices concluded that the consideration of race in admissions was permissible. Justice Powell wrote a separate opinion that was endorsed in part by one group of four Justices and endorsed in other parts by the other group of four. As a result, Justice Powell's opinion became the controlling opinion of the Court. In his opinion, Justice Powell concluded that U.C. Davis's admissions program was "a line drawn on the basis of race and ethnic status." *Id.* at 289. He noted that "[i]f petitioner's purpose is to assure within its student body some specified percentage of a particular group merely because of its race or ethnic origin, such a preferential purpose must be rejected * * * as facially invalid." *Id.* at 307. According to Justice Powell, however, race can be a legitimate factor in admissions as long as the applicants are evaluated based on all of their individual traits, not just race.

Subsequently, the Court addressed affirmative action in two decisions involving the University of Michigan, *Grutter v. Bollinger*, 539 U.S. 306 (2003), and *Gratz v. Bollinger*, 539 U.S. 244 (2003). *Grutter* concerned the University of Michigan Law School's admissions procedures: "The hallmark of that policy is its focus on academic ability coupled with a flexible assessment of applicants' talents, experiences, and potential to contribute to the learning of those around them." *Grutter*, 539 U.S. at 315. Within that analysis, the law school also considers racial and ethnic diversity, with the goal of "enrolling a 'critical mass' of [underrepresented] minority students * * *." *Id.* at 316. As in *Bakke*, a white applicant denied admission claimed that the policy was discriminatory. The Court, however, rejected that argument, reasoning that "[t]he Law School's interest is not simply to assure within its student body some specified percentage of a particular group merely because of its race or ethnic origin. * * * Rather, the Law School's concept of critical mass is defined by reference to the educational benefits that diversity is designed to produce." *Id.* at 329–30. Because diversity was only one factor in the admissions policy, the policy was not unconstitutional. By contrast, *Gratz* involved the University of Michigan's undergraduate admissions policy, under which applicants were awarded points based on various factors, and a point total of 100 was needed to guarantee admission. The policy at issue automatically gave 20 points to every minority student, solely because of race. The Court held that such a standard was unconstitutional because the "automatic distribution of 20 points has the effect of making 'the factor of race . . . decisive' for virtually every minimally qualified underrepresented minority applicant." *Gratz*, 539 U.S. at 272.

In *Fisher v. University of Texas*, 570 U.S. ___, 133 S. Ct. 2411 (2013), the Court addressed whether the University of Texas's consideration of race in its admissions policy was constitutional. In response to *Grutter* and *Gratz*, the university adopted a policy designed to obtain a "critical mass" of minority students, but did not give race a specific numerical weight in the admissions process. The U.S. Court of Appeals for the Fifth Circuit upheld the program by giving deference to the university's policy decisions. The Supreme Court, however, held that in granting that deference, the Fifth Circuit had failed to apply the strict scrutiny required for affirmative action programs. The Court explained: "[S]trict scrutiny * * * require[s] a court to examine with care, and not defer to, a university's 'serious, good faith consideration of workable race-neutral alternatives.'" *Id.* at 2420. Two Justices (Scalia and Thomas) wrote concurring opinions arguing that the Fourteenth Amendment prohibited any discrimination based on race. In dissent, Justice Ginsburg argued that the university policy fell directly within the holding of *Grutter* and *Bakke* and thus the Fifth Circuit had properly upheld the policy.

On remand, the Fifth Circuit again found in favor of the university. In 2015, the plaintiff in *Fisher* again sought—and the Supreme Court again granted—review. 135 S. Ct. 2888 (U.S. June 29, 2015) (14–981). The decision was pending when this text went to press.

For additional reading on affirmative action, *see, e.g.*, Matthew Gaertner & Melissa Hart, *From Access to Success: Affirmative Action Outcomes in a Class-Based System*, 86 U. Colo. L. Rev. 431 (2015) (citing data from Colorado universities that students admitted through affirmative action tend to lag behind academically, and arguing that the best solution is to implement programs to support affirmative action students, rather than eliminating affirmative action); Girardeau Spann, *Good Faith Discrimination*, 23 Wm. & Mary Bill Rts. J. 585 (2015) (noting that current Supreme Court affirmative action jurisprudence seems "artificial, internally inconsistent, and even conceptually incoherent" and proposing a good faith standard for evaluating race-based discrimination); Anita Bernstein, *Diversity May Be Justified*, 64 Hastings L.J. 201 (2012) (offering justifications for affirmative action).

b.   Taxation: Before the ratification of the Constitution, the federal government had only limited power because it did not have a direct source of funding. As a result, it could not establish an effective military or fully enforce federal laws. To resolve this problem, Article I, Section 8, Clause 1 of the Constitution grants Congress "Power To lay and collect Taxes, Duties, Imposts and Excises, to pay the Debts and provide for the common Defence and general Welfare of the United States." The Taxing and Spending Clause, as this provision is commonly called, has been generally understood to allow Congress to enact taxes as necessary to fund governmental activities.

In one pathbreaking case, the Taxing and Spending Clause was the basis for the Supreme Court to uphold a major program of the Obama Administration. In *National Federation of Independent Business v. Sebelius*, 567 U.S. ___, 132 S. Ct. 2566 (2012), the Court addressed a challenge to the Affordable Care Act, or "Obamacare," a program designed to expand medical insurance coverage through federal intervention. A major legal challenge involved two elements of the Act: the individual mandate, which would require individuals to obtain health insurance or pay a penalty, and an expansion of Medicaid, an income-based federal insurance program that would require states to accept the expansion or lose their Medicaid funding. The Supreme Court held that the Medicaid expansion was unconstitutional because it effectively coerced the states to accept the expansion. The Court upheld the individual mandate, however, relying on the Taxing and Spending Clause. In its 5–4 decision, the Court explained that the penalty for not having insurance could be construed as a tax, and that such a tax was permitted by the Taxing and Spending Clause.

c.   **Habeas Corpus and the War on Terrorism:** The writ of habeas corpus comes from the English common law tradition. The phrase "habeas corpus" translates roughly to "you shall have the body." It was initially used in the 14th century to bring prisoners from private courts into royal courts of law when the prisoner was potentially entitled to release under the monarch's law. Today, a writ of habeas corpus is a remedy for unlawful imprisonment. The right to habeas corpus is codified in the U.S. Constitution as Article I, Section 9, Clause 2. An example of a criminal case involving a petition for a writ of habeas corpus is *Gideon v. Wainwright*, 372 U.S. 335 (1963) (set forth in Chapter 7), where a criminal defendant had been forced to go to trial without the appointment of counsel.

Habeas corpus issues have arisen as a result of the terrorist attacks against the United States on September 11, 2001. For instance, in *Hamdi v. Rumsfeld*, 542 U.S. 507 (2004), a U.S. citizen challenged his detention as an enemy combatant. The government alleged that Hamdi joined the Taliban (a fundamentalist Islamic group that has operated in Afghanistan and Pakistan) following the September 11th attacks. Hamdi was detained in Afghanistan as an enemy combatant and eventually transferred to the U.S. Naval Base in Guantanamo Bay, Cuba. When authorities learned that Hamdi was an American citizen, he was transferred to Norfolk, Virginia. Because the government was holding Hamdi as an enemy combatant, it argued that Hamdi could be detained in the U.S. indefinitely without any formal charges or proceedings. Hamdi's father challenged his son's detention by petitioning for a writ of habeas corpus. In response, the government argued that the Supreme Court should not interfere in the sensitive realm of national security involved in the case. The Supreme Court rejected the government's position, holding that, under the Due Process Clause, U.S. citizens held in the U.S. as enemy combatants must at least be given an opportunity to contest their detention before a neutral decision maker. *See also Hamdan v. Rumsfeld*, 548 U.S. 557 (2006) (holding that the military commissions under which Guantanamo Bay, Cuba detainees were to be tried violated the Uniform Code of Military Justice and the Geneva Conventions); *Boumediene v. Bush*, 553 U.S. 723 (2008) (holding that enemy combatants detained at Guantanamo Bay were entitled to challenge their detention through habeas corpus proceedings in U.S. district court).

d.   **Freedom of Speech: Campaign Finance:** The right to contribute money to political campaigns is a controversial issue in U.S. law.

In *Citizens United v. Federal Election Commission*, 558 U.S. 310 (2010), the Supreme Court (in a 5–4 decision) invalidated—on First Amendment grounds—a federal regulation that prohibited certain types of campaign spending by corporations, unions, and other associations. Although such associations are not permitted to donate directly to individual campaigns, they are entitled (after *Citizens United*) to spend unlimited funds on political ads and broadcasts. The case has generated significant criticism. *See, e.g.*, Mark Alexander, Citizens United *and Equality Forgotten*, 35 N.Y.U. Rev. L & Soc. Change 499 (2011) (arguing that *Citizens United* is a threat to republican government because it allows wealthy people to exert disproportionate control over politics); Richard Briffault, *On Dejudicializing American Campaign Finance Law*, 27 Ga. St. U. L. Rev. 887 (2011) (arguing, in response to *Citizens United*, that the Supreme Court should not control campaign finance law because it has so far failed to adopt a consistent and practical approach). *But see, e.g.*, James Bopp, Jr. & Kaylan Lytle Phillips, *The Limits of* Citizens United v. Federal Election Commission*: Analytical and Practical Reasons Why the Sky is Not Falling*, 46 U.S.F. L. Rev. 281 (2011) (responding to criticism that *Citizens United* encourages corruption and gives unwarranted rights to corporations by arguing that the primary focus of the case was the protection of First Amendment rights); Joel Gora, *The First Amendment . . . United*, 27 Ga. St. U. L. Rev. 935 (2010) (arguing that the *Citizens United* holding was required under the First Amendment and that it will result in increased political speech and a more informed electorate).

Subsequent to *Citizens United*, the Supreme Court held in *McCutcheon v. Federal Election Commission*, 572 U.S. ___, 134 S. Ct. 1434 (2014), that limits (during a two-year period) on the total amount that individuals could contribute to multiple candidates ($48,600 for federal candidates and $74,600 for other political committees, for a total contribution limit of $123,200) were unconstitutional because they restricted political speech. Even after *McCutcheon*, there are limits on contributions: for example, an individual cannot give more than $2,700 per election to a single candidate, or more than $5,000 per year to a political action committee. *See* Federal Elections Commission, *Contributions*, February 2015, *available at* http://www.fec.gov/pages/brochures/contrib.shtml#Contribution.

e.   **Gun Rights:** The Second Amendment to the Constitution states: "A well regulated Militia, being necessary to the security of a free State, the right of the people to keep and bear Arms, shall not be infringed." In *District of Columbia v. Heller*, 554 U.S. 570 (2008), the Supreme Court addressed the Second Amendment in the context of a District of Columbia law that effectively prohibited the possession of handguns. The plaintiff sued the District, seeking to enjoin enforcement of the ban on handguns within an individual's home. The district court dismissed the complaint, but the U.S. Court of Appeals for the District of Columbia Circuit reversed, holding that the Second Amendment protects an individual's right to possess firearms. The Supreme Court affirmed the D.C. Circuit. It analyzed the text and historical context of the Second Amendment and held that a prohibition on the possession of handguns violated the Second Amendment. The Court explained:

> The handgun ban amounts to a prohibition of an entire class of "arms" that is overwhelmingly chosen by American society for [a] lawful purpose. The prohibition extends, moreover, to the home, where the need for defense of self, family, and property is most acute. Under any of the standards of scrutiny that we have applied to enumerated constitutional rights, banning from the home "the most preferred firearm in the nation to 'keep' and use for protection of one's home and family," would fail constitutional muster.

Id. at 628–29. The Court did recognize, however, that there may be exceptions, such as carrying firearms in certain places (*e.g.*, schools and government buildings); possession of firearms by felons or the mentally ill; and possession of certain particularly dangerous weapons. In dissent, Justice Breyer noted that gun use, and particularly handgun use, is a significant problem in the U.S.:

> From 1993 to 1997, there were 180,533 firearm-related deaths in the United States, an average of over 36,000 per year. * * * Handguns are involved in a majority of firearm deaths and injuries in the United States. From 1993 to 1997, 81% of firearm-homicide victims were killed by handgun. * * * Handguns also appear to be a very popular weapon among criminals. In a 1997 survey of inmates who were armed during the crime for which they were incarcerated, 83.2% of state inmates and 86.7% of federal inmates said that they were armed with a handgun.

Id. at 696–98.

Two years after *Heller*, the Supreme Court decided *McDonald v. City of Chicago*, 561 U.S. 742 (2010). *McDonald* concerned Illinois handgun bans similar to those in *Heller*. The city of Chicago had instituted an ordinance prohibiting the possession of firearms without a registration certificate and prohibiting the registration of most handguns, effectively banning the possession of handguns. Two Chicago residents sued, claiming that they wanted to keep handguns in their homes for self-defense, but could not do so under the ordinance. Because the District of Columbia is governed by the federal government and is not a state, the Second Amendment applies directly to D.C. It was an open question, however, whether the Second Amendment applied to the states. In *McDonald*, the Court extended the *Heller* holding to the states by holding that the Second Amendment applies to the states.

CHAPTER 3

CIVIL PROCEDURE

■ ■ ■

Civil procedure focuses on the procedural rules for civil actions (such as private actions for money damages). Criminal procedure, by contrast, focuses on the procedural rules governing criminal prosecutions—actions by federal or state authorities for violation of criminal laws. (Criminal procedure is the focus of Chapter 7.)

All U.S. courts (both federal and state) have written rules governing such matters as what type of document a plaintiff must file to start a civil lawsuit, how the defendant is notified of a plaintiff's claim, how much time the parties are allowed to complete various tasks, and how the parties go about asking each other for documents and other information that relates to the litigation. Civil procedure addresses those issues. It also addresses issues such as where a lawsuit may be brought and what law should apply to the case. The focus of this chapter is on civil procedure in federal courts, but many similar issues arise in state courts.

A. DUE PROCESS RIGHT TO FAIR PROCEDURES

The Fifth Amendment to the U.S. Constitution states in relevant part: "No person shall be deprived of life, liberty, or property, without due process of law." This provision is known as the "Due Process Clause." The following case, *Goldberg v. Kelly*, discusses procedural due process rights in the context of the termination of public assistance benefits. It is a landmark decision because it addresses the contours of the right to be heard. As one scholar has noted: "*Goldberg* details the key features of procedural systems—notice, exchange of information between disputants in writing or oral hearings, and decision-making by a third party who is constrained in some respects." Judith Resnik, *The Story of* Goldberg*: Why this Case is Our Shorthand*, in CIVIL PROCEDURE STORIES 473, 476 (Kevin Clermont ed., 2d ed. 2008). The case "stands as a central statement that just outcomes depend on adequate process and offers a framework for what constitutes fair process." *Id.* at 476.

GOLDBERG V. KELLY
Supreme Court of the United States, 1970
397 U.S. 254

JUSTICE BRENNAN delivered the opinion of the Court.

The question for decision is whether a State that terminates public assistance payments to a particular recipient without affording him the opportunity for an evidentiary hearing prior to termination denies the recipient procedural due process in violation of the Due Process Clause of the Fourteenth Amendment.

This action was brought in the District Court for the Southern District of New York by residents of New York City receiving financial aid under the federally assisted program of Aid to Families with Dependent Children (AFDC) or under New York State's general Home Relief program.[1] Their complaint alleged that the New York State and New York City officials administering these programs terminated, or were about to terminate, such aid without prior notice and hearing, thereby denying them due process of law. At the time the suits were filed there was no requirement of prior notice or hearing of any kind before termination of financial aid. However, the State and city adopted procedures for notice and hearing after the suits were brought, and the plaintiffs, appellees here, then challenged the constitutional adequacy of those procedures.

The State Commissioner of Social Services amended the State Department of Social Services' Official Regulations to require that local social services officials proposing to discontinue or suspend a recipient's financial aid do so according to a procedure that conforms to either subdivision (a) or subdivision (b) of § 351.26 of the regulations as amended. The City of New York elected to promulgate a local procedure according to subdivision (b). That subdivision, so far as here pertinent, provides that the local procedure must include the giving of notice to the recipient of the reasons for a proposed discontinuance or suspension at least seven days prior to its effective date, with notice also that upon request the recipient may have the proposal reviewed by a local welfare official holding a position superior to that of the supervisor who approved the proposed discontinuance or suspension, and, further, that the recipient may submit, for purposes of the review, a written statement to demonstrate why his grant should not be discontinued or suspended. The decision by the reviewing official whether to discontinue or suspend aid must be made expeditiously, with written notice of the decision to the recipient. The section further expressly provides that "[a]ssistance shall not be discontinued or suspended prior to the date such notice of decision is sent

---

[1] AFDC * * * assists any person unable to support himself or to secure support from other sources.

to the recipient and his representative, if any, or prior to the proposed effective date of discontinuance or suspension, whichever occurs later."

Pursuant to subdivision (b), the New York City Department of Social Services promulgated Procedure No. 68–18. A caseworker who has doubts about the recipient's continued eligibility must first discuss them with the recipient. If the caseworker concludes that the recipient is no longer eligible, he recommends termination of aid to a unit supervisor. If the latter concurs, he sends the recipient a letter stating the reasons for proposing to terminate aid and notifying him that within seven days he may request that a higher official review the record, and may support the request with a written statement prepared personally or with the aid of an attorney or other person. If the reviewing official affirms the determination of ineligibility, aid is stopped immediately and the recipient is informed by letter of the reasons for the action. Appellees' challenge to this procedure emphasizes the absence of any provisions for the personal appearance of the recipient before the reviewing official, for oral presentation of evidence, and for confrontation and cross-examination of adverse witnesses. However, the letter does inform the recipient that he may request a post-termination "fair hearing." This is a proceeding before an independent state hearing officer at which the recipient may appear personally, offer oral evidence, confront and cross-examine the witnesses against him, and have a record made of the hearing. If the recipient prevails at the "fair hearing" he is paid all funds erroneously withheld. A recipient whose aid is not restored by a "fair hearing" decision may have judicial review. The recipient is so notified.

I

The constitutional issue to be decided, therefore, is the narrow one whether the Due Process Clause requires that the recipient be afforded an evidentiary hearing before the termination of benefits. The District Court held that only a pre-termination evidentiary hearing would satisfy the constitutional command, and rejected the argument of the state and city officials that the combination of the post-termination "fair hearing" with the informal pre-termination review disposed of all due process claims. * * * Although state officials were party defendants in the action, only the Commissioner of Social Services of the City of New York appealed. [The case was appealed directly from a three-judge district court panel to the Supreme Court.] We affirm.

Appellant does not contend that procedural due process is not applicable to the termination of welfare benefits. Such benefits are a matter of statutory entitlement for persons qualified to receive them.[8]

---

[8]   It may be realistic today to regard welfare entitlements as more like "property" than a "gratuity." Much of the existing wealth in this country takes the form of rights that do not fall within traditional common-law concepts of property. It has been aptly noted that

Their termination involves state action that adjudicates important rights. The constitutional challenge cannot be answered by an argument that public assistance benefits are "a 'privilege' and not a 'right.'" Relevant constitutional restraints apply as much to the withdrawal of public assistance benefits as to disqualification for unemployment compensation; or to denial of a tax exemption; or to discharge from public employment. The extent to which procedural due process must be afforded the recipient is influenced by the extent to which he may be "condemned to suffer grievous loss," and depends upon whether the recipient's interest in avoiding that loss outweighs the governmental interest in summary adjudication. Accordingly, * * * "consideration of what procedures due process may require under any given set of circumstances must begin with a determination of the precise nature of the government function involved as well as of the private interest that has been affected by governmental action."

It is true, of course, that some governmental benefits may be administratively terminated without affording the recipient a pre-termination evidentiary hearing. But we agree with the District Court that when welfare is discontinued, only a pre-termination evidentiary hearing provides the recipient with procedural due process. For qualified recipients, welfare provides the means to obtain essential food, clothing, housing, and medical care. Thus the crucial factor in this context—a factor not present in the case of the blacklisted government contractor, the discharged government employee, the taxpayer denied a tax exemption, or virtually anyone else whose governmental entitlements are ended—is that termination of aid pending resolution of a controversy over eligibility may deprive an eligible recipient of the very means by which to live while he waits. Since he lacks independent resources, his situation becomes immediately desperate. His need to concentrate upon finding the means for daily subsistence, in turn, adversely affects his ability to seek redress from the welfare bureaucracy.

Moreover, important governmental interests are promoted by affording recipients a pre-termination evidentiary hearing. From its founding the Nation's basic commitment has been to foster the dignity and well-being of all persons within its borders. We have come to recognize that

---

[s]ociety today is built around entitlement. The automobile dealer has his franchise, the doctor and lawyer their professional licenses, the worker his union membership, contract, and pension rights, the executive his contract and stock options; all are devices to aid security and independence. Many of the most important of these entitlements now flow from government: subsidies to farmers and businessmen; routes for airlines and channels for television stations; long term contracts for defense, space, and education; social security pensions for individuals. Such sources of security, whether private or public, are no longer regarded as luxuries or gratuities; to the recipients they are essentials, fully deserved, and in no sense a form of charity. It is only the poor whose entitlements, although recognized by public policy, have not been effectively enforced.

Charles Reich, *Individual Rights and Social Welfare: The Emerging Legal Issues*, 74 Yale L.J. 1245, 1255 (1965). *See also* Charles Reich, *The New Property*, 73 Yale L.J. 733 (1964).

forces not within the control of the poor contribute to their poverty. This perception, against the background of our traditions, has significantly influenced the development of the contemporary public assistance system. Welfare, by meeting the basic demands of subsistence, can help bring within the reach of the poor the same opportunities that are available to others to participate meaningfully in the life of the community. At the same time, welfare guards against the societal malaise that may flow from a widespread sense of unjustified frustration and insecurity. Public assistance, then, is not mere charity, but a means to "promote the general Welfare, and secure the Blessings of Liberty to ourselves and our Posterity." The same governmental interests that counsel the provision of welfare, counsel as well its uninterrupted provision to those eligible to receive it; pre-termination evidentiary hearings are indispensable to that end.

Appellant does not challenge the force of these considerations but argues that they are outweighed by countervailing governmental interests in conserving fiscal and administrative resources. These interests, the argument goes, justify the delay of any evidentiary hearing until after discontinuance of the grants. Summary adjudication protects the public fisc by stopping payments promptly upon discovery of reason to believe that a recipient is no longer eligible. Since most terminations are accepted without challenge, summary adjudication also conserves both the fisc and administrative time and energy by reducing the number of evidentiary hearings actually held.

We agree with the District Court, however, that these governmental interests are not overriding in the welfare context. The requirement of a prior hearing doubtless involves some greater expense, and the benefits paid to ineligible recipients pending decision at the hearing probably cannot be recouped, since these recipients are likely to be judgment-proof. But the State is not without weapons to minimize these increased costs. Much of the drain on fiscal and administrative resources can be reduced by developing procedures for prompt pre-termination hearings and by skillful use of personnel and facilities. * * * Thus, the interest of the eligible recipient in uninterrupted receipt of public assistance, coupled with the State's interest that his payments not be erroneously terminated, clearly outweighs the State's competing concern to prevent any increase in its fiscal and administrative burdens. As the District Court correctly concluded, "[t]he stakes are simply too high for the welfare recipient, and the possibility for honest error or irritable misjudgment too great, to allow termination of aid without giving the recipient a chance, if he so desires, to be fully informed of the case against him so that he may contest its basis and produce evidence in rebuttal."

II

We also agree with the District Court, however, that the pre-termination hearing need not take the form of a judicial or quasi-judicial trial. We bear in mind that the statutory "fair hearing" will provide the recipient with a full administrative review.[14] Accordingly, the pre-termination hearing has one function only: to produce an initial determination of the validity of the welfare department's grounds for discontinuance of payments in order to protect a recipient against an erroneous termination of his benefits. Thus, a complete record and a comprehensive opinion, which would serve primarily to facilitate judicial review and to guide future decisions, need not be provided at the pre-termination stage. We recognize, too, that both welfare authorities and recipients have an interest in relatively speedy resolution of questions of eligibility, that they are used to dealing with one another informally, and that some welfare departments have very burdensome caseloads. These considerations justify the limitation of the pre-termination hearing to minimum procedural safeguards, adapted to the particular characteristics of welfare recipients, and to the limited nature of the controversies to be resolved. We wish to add that we * * * recognize the importance of not imposing upon the States or the Federal Government in this developing field of law any procedural requirements beyond those demanded by rudimentary due process.

"The fundamental requisite of due process of law is the opportunity to be heard." The hearing must be "at a meaningful time and in a meaningful manner." In the present context these principles require that a recipient have timely and adequate notice detailing the reasons for a proposed termination, and an effective opportunity to defend by confronting any adverse witnesses and by presenting his own arguments and evidence orally. These rights are important in cases such as those before us, where recipients have challenged proposed terminations as resting on incorrect or misleading factual premises or on misapplication of rules or policies to the facts of particular cases.[15]

We are not prepared to say that the seven-day notice currently provided by New York City is constitutionally insufficient *per se*, although there may be cases where fairness would require that a longer time be given. Nor do we see any constitutional deficiency in the content or form of the notice. New York employs both a letter and a personal conference with a caseworker to inform a recipient of the precise questions raised about his continued eligibility. Evidently the recipient is told the legal and factual

---

[14] Due process does not, of course, require two hearings. If, for example, a State simply wishes to continue benefits until after a "fair" hearing there will be no need for a preliminary hearing.

[15] This case presents no question requiring our determination whether due process requires only an opportunity for written submission, or an opportunity both for written submission and oral argument, where there are no factual issues in dispute or where the application of the rule of law is not intertwined with factual issues.

bases for the Department's doubts. This combination is probably the most effective method of communicating with recipients.

The city's procedures presently do not permit recipients to appear personally with or without counsel before the official who finally determines continued eligibility. Thus a recipient is not permitted to present evidence to that official orally, or to confront or cross-examine adverse witnesses. These omissions are fatal to the constitutional adequacy of the procedures.

The opportunity to be heard must be tailored to the capacities and circumstances of those who are to be heard. It is not enough that a welfare recipient may present his position to the decision-maker in writing or second-hand through his caseworker. Written submissions are an unrealistic option for most recipients, who lack the educational attainment necessary to write effectively and who cannot obtain professional assistance. Moreover, written submissions do not afford the flexibility of oral presentations; they do not permit the recipient to mold his argument to the issues the decision maker appears to regard as important. Particularly where credibility and veracity are at issue, as they must be in many termination proceedings, written submissions are a wholly unsatisfactory basis for decision. The second-hand presentation to the decision-maker by the caseworker has its own deficiencies; since the caseworker usually gathers the facts upon which the charge of ineligibility rests, the presentation of the recipient's side of the controversy cannot safely be left to him. Therefore a recipient must be allowed to state his position orally. Informal procedures will suffice; in this context due process does not require a particular order of proof or mode of offering evidence.

In almost every setting where important decisions turn on questions of fact, due process requires an opportunity to confront and cross-examine adverse witnesses. What we said in *Greene v. McElroy*, 360 U.S. 474 (1959), is particularly pertinent here:

> * * * [W]here governmental action seriously injures an individual, and the reasonableness of the action depends on fact findings, the evidence used to prove the Government's case must be disclosed to the individual so that he has an opportunity to show that it is untrue. While this is important in the case of documentary evidence, it is even more important where the evidence consists of the testimony of individuals whose memory might be faulty or who, in fact, might be perjurers or persons motivated by malice, vindictiveness, intolerance, prejudice, or jealousy. * * *

Welfare recipients must therefore be given an opportunity to confront and cross-examine the witnesses relied on by the department.

"The right to be heard would be, in many cases, of little avail if it did not comprehend the right to be heard by counsel." We do not say that counsel must be provided at the pre-termination hearing, but only that the recipient must be allowed to retain an attorney if he so desires. Counsel can help delineate the issues, present the factual contentions in an orderly manner, conduct cross-examination, and generally safeguard the interests of the recipient. We do not anticipate that this assistance will unduly prolong or otherwise encumber the hearing. * * *

Finally, the decision-maker's conclusion as to a recipient's eligibility must rest solely on the legal rules and evidence adduced at the hearing. To demonstrate compliance with this elementary requirement, the decision maker should state the reasons for his determination and indicate the evidence he relied on, though his statement need not amount to a full opinion or even formal findings of fact and conclusions of law. And, of course, an impartial decision maker is essential. We agree with the District Court that prior involvement in some aspects of a case will not necessarily bar a welfare official from acting as a decision maker. He should not, however, have participated in making the determination under review.

Affirmed.

[Dissenting opinion by JUSTICE BLACK is omitted.]

NOTES AND QUESTIONS

1.   What was the issue in *Goldberg*? What did the majority hold?

2.   In his dissent, Justice Black disagreed with the majority's conclusion that the Fourteenth Amendment required a hearing before a welfare benefit could be revoked. Instead, Justice Black opined that the government should be allowed to revoke such benefits without a prior hearing, unless Congress decided otherwise. Justice Black predicted that many people would abuse the welfare system if they could continue to receive payments to which they were not entitled pending a hearing. Similarly, in the companion case to *Goldberg*, Chief Justice Burger dissented from the majority opinion because he thought that it was inappropriate for the Court to constitutionalize this emerging area of the law prior to the development of administrative regulations. *Wheeler v. Montgomery*, 397 U.S. 280 (1970) (Burger, C.J., dissenting). Justice Stewart also dissented in *Wheeler*, stating: "Although the question is for me a close one, I do not believe that the procedures that New York * * * now follow[s] in terminating welfare payments are violative of the United States Constitution." *Id.* at 285 (Stewart, J., dissenting). Which position is more persuasive: that of the majority or that of the various dissents?

3.   Why did the Court in *Goldberg* deem it critical that the hearing be held prior to termination of welfare benefits? What countervailing arguments did the state officials make?

4.   How does the hearing envisioned by the majority differ from a judicial proceeding in court? How is it similar?

5.   One important element of the right to be heard in court cases is the right to a jury trial. Although the right to a jury trial exists in both criminal and civil matters, different constitutional provisions are involved. The right in criminal cases stems from the Sixth Amendment ("In all criminal prosecutions, the accused shall enjoy the right * * * to have the Assistance of Counsel for his defence"). The right in civil cases stems from the Seventh Amendment ("In Suits at common law, where the value in controversy shall exceed twenty dollars, the right of trial by jury shall be preserved."). The contours of the Seventh Amendment right to jury trial are narrower than those of its Sixth Amendment counterpart. For example, the Seventh Amendment right is inapplicable to state trials, *see City of Monterey v. Del Monte Dunes at Monterey, Ltd.*, 526 U.S. 687, 719 (1999) ("It is settled law that the Seventh Amendment does not apply in the[ ] context [of suits brought in state court]."), and the right only applies to "suits at law" (as opposed to "suits in equity"). In assessing whether the right being asserted is "at law" or "in equity," courts must determine whether the claim is more similar to those tried (in 18th Century England) in courts of law or in courts of equity. That analysis is sometimes complex. *See, e.g., Feltner v. Columbia Pictures Television, Inc.*, 523 U.S. 340 (1998) (holding that the Copyright Act provided a right to jury trial under the Seventh Amendment because the lawsuit sought "monetary relief," which is generally considered a legal remedy in a "suit at law"); *Tull v. United States*, 481 U.S. 412 (1987) (analyzing the Seventh Amendment right to a jury trial in a civil penalties lawsuit brought by the federal government under the Clean Water Act, and finding that the petitioner was entitled to a jury trial to determine his liability under the Act because the suit was analogous to an action in debt under the common law).

6.   In addition to the right to a hearing, an important element of due process is notice. In *Mullane v. Central Hanover Bank & Trust Co.*, 339 U.S. 306 (1950), the U.S. Supreme Court addressed the issue of notice. In that case, Central Hanover Bank and Trust Company was the trustee for a common trust fund and sought to settle the account. Kenneth Mullane was appointed as a special guardian to represent the interests of the beneficiaries of the trust. The whereabouts of some of the beneficiaries were unknown, but in many circumstances the mailing addresses of beneficiaries were available. Central Hanover issued notice of the proceedings through a local newspaper publication. Mullane argued that the notice was insufficient under the Due Process Clause of the Fourteenth Amendment. The Supreme Court agreed. It articulated the principle that notice must be "reasonably calculated, under all the circumstances, to apprise interested parties of the pendency of the action and afford them an opportunity to present their objections. * * * [P]rocess which is a mere gesture is not due process." *Id.* at 314. For beneficiaries whose whereabouts were known, publication notice was insufficient: "[W]e find no tenable ground for dispensing with a serious effort to inform them personally of the accounting, at least by ordinary mail to the record addresses." *Id.* at 318. As for beneficiaries whose whereabouts were unknown, however, the Court held that the published notice was sufficient: "[I]n the case of persons missing or unknown, employment of an indirect and even a probably futile means of

notification is all that the situation permits and creates no constitutional bar
to a final decree foreclosing their rights." *Id.* at 317.

Given modern technology—and a decrease in newspaper readership—
what type of notice would suffice for unknown beneficiaries such as those in
Mullane? For the known beneficiaries, would email or website notice suffice in
lieu of notice by mail?

7.   *Mullane*'s "reasonable under the circumstances" test for notice has
been applied in various contexts. For example, in *Dusenbery v. United States*,
534 U.S. 161 (2002), a federal inmate had property and money seized and
disposed of through civil forfeiture (a practice permitted under various
criminal statutes that allows the government to seize all proceeds and goods
traceable to criminal activity). The inmate challenged this forfeiture, claiming
that he received insufficient notice. Under the relevant statute in *Dusenbery*,
the government was required to send written notice to interested parties and
publish notice in the newspaper for at least three successive weeks. The
government did so. The inmate, however, argued that the government should
have been required to provide "actual notice," meaning that the government
should have ensured that the notice actually reached the inmate. The Supreme
Court rejected this argument, holding that the Due Process Clause did not
require "actual notice" and that "the use of the mail addressed to petitioner at
the penitentiary was clearly acceptable * * * [because it] was 'reasonably
calculated, under the circumstances, to apprise [petitioner] of the pendency of
the action.' " *Id.* at 172–73.

In *Jones v. Flowers*, 547 U.S. 220 (2006), the State of Arkansas mailed
notice to an individual that his property was to be sold at a tax sale. The mailed
notice, however, was returned, meaning that it was not received by the
property owner. Arkansas did nothing more to notify the property owner and
instead proceeded with the sale. The property owner sued, claiming that his
due process rights had been violated because he had not received notice of the
sale. Applying *Mullane*, the Supreme Court agreed: "We do not think that a
person who actually desired to inform a real property owner of an impending
tax sale of a house he owns would do nothing when a certified letter sent to the
owner is returned unclaimed." *Id.* at 229.

8.   In *Goldberg*, the district court decision was reviewed by the Supreme
Court without prior review by a circuit court of appeals. That situation is
extremely rare. *See generally* GREGORY CASTANIAS & ROBERT KLONOFF,
FEDERAL APPELLATE PRACTICE AND PROCEDURE IN A NUTSHELL 362–67 (2008).

9.   *Goldberg* has been applied in many contexts. The outcome in each
case has turned on the precise circumstances. *See, e.g., Goss v. Lopez*, 419 U.S.
565 (1975) (holding that public school students are entitled to notice and a
hearing before they can be suspended from school); *Arnett v. Kennedy*, 416 U.S.
134 (1974) (holding that a government employee was not entitled to a hearing
prior to removal; a post-termination hearing satisfied due process); *Board of
Regents of State Colleges v. Roth*, 408 U.S. 564 (1972) (holding that a non-
tenured university professor was not entitled to a hearing prior to nonrenewal;

the professor could not show a "liberty" or "property" interest in continued employment); *Fuentes v. Shevin*, 407 U.S. 67 (1972) (holding that Florida and Pennsylvania statutes allowing allegedly stolen goods to be repossessed and returned to the claimed owner before a hearing violated due process); *Morrissey v. Brewer*, 408 U.S. 471 (1972) (holding that parolees have a due process right to two-step process: to a preliminary hearing shortly after their arrest to determine if there is probable cause that their parole was violated, and then, soon after the defendant is placed in custody, to a more elaborate revocation hearing prior to revocation of parole).

10.   For further discussion of procedural due process under *Goldberg* and it progeny, *see, e.g.*, Rebecca Hollander-Blumoff, *The Psychology of Procedural Justice in the Federal Courts*, 63 Hastings L.J. 127 (2011) (arguing that courts and lawmakers should devote more attention to the litigants' perceptions of justice because positive perceptions give legitimacy to legal authority); Sylvia Law, *Some Reflections on* Goldberg v. Kelly *at Twenty Years*, 56 Brook. L. Rev. 805 (1990) (describing *Goldberg* from the perspective of a lawyer who represented the welfare recipients in the case and arguing that the case did not go far enough in protecting the rights of poor individuals to be heard).

B. PERSONAL JURISDICTION

The following cases discuss the concept of "personal jurisdiction." Personal jurisdiction is a court's ability to exercise power over a party that has been sued. It can be established through "general jurisdiction" or "specific jurisdiction." Specific jurisdiction exists when a person has minimum contacts with the forum state (the place where a claim is brought) that are directly related to the subject matter of the claim. General jurisdiction is satisfied when a person has such strong connections with the forum state that the court has authority over any claim, regardless of whether the contacts are related to the claim. Personal jurisdiction is automatically established if the defendant is a citizen of the forum state. Personal jurisdiction can be waived by a defendant (for instance, by voluntarily submitting to the jurisdiction of the court). As the *Walden v. Fiore* case below illustrates, the issues are sometimes complicated.

1. SPECIFIC JURISDICTION

WALDEN V. FIORE
Supreme Court of the United States, 2014
571 U.S. ___, 134 S. Ct. 1115

JUSTICE THOMAS delivered the opinion for a unanimous Court.

This case asks us to decide whether a court in Nevada may exercise personal jurisdiction over a defendant on the basis that he knew his allegedly tortious conduct in Georgia would delay the return of funds to plaintiffs with connections to Nevada. Because the defendant had no other contacts with Nevada, and because a plaintiff's contacts with the forum State cannot be "decisive in determining whether the defendant's due process rights are violated," we hold that the court in Nevada may not exercise personal jurisdiction under these circumstances.

I

Petitioner Anthony Walden serves as a police officer for the city of Covington, Georgia. In August 2006, petitioner was working at the Atlanta Hartsfield-Jackson Airport as a deputized agent of the Drug Enforcement Administration (DEA). As part of a task force, petitioner conducted investigative stops and other law enforcement functions in support of the DEA's airport drug interdiction program.

On August 8, 2006, Transportation Security Administration agents searched respondents Gina Fiore and Keith Gipson and their carry-on bags at the San Juan airport in Puerto Rico. They found almost $97,000 in cash. Fiore explained to DEA agents in San Juan that she and Gipson had been gambling at a casino known as the El San Juan, and that they had residences in both California and Nevada (though they provided only California identification). After respondents were cleared for departure, a law enforcement official at the San Juan airport notified petitioner's task force in Atlanta that respondents had boarded a plane for Atlanta, where they planned to catch a connecting flight to Las Vegas, Nevada.

When respondents arrived in Atlanta, petitioner and another DEA agent approached them at the departure gate for their flight to Las Vegas. In response to petitioner's questioning, Fiore explained that she and Gipson were professional gamblers. Respondents maintained that the cash they were carrying was their gambling " 'bank' " and winnings. After using a drug-sniffing dog to perform a sniff test, petitioner seized the cash. Petitioner advised respondents that their funds would be returned if they later proved a legitimate source for the cash. Respondents then boarded their plane.

After respondents departed, petitioner moved the cash to a secure location and the matter was forwarded to DEA headquarters. The next day, petitioner received a phone call from respondents' attorney in Nevada seeking return of the funds. On two occasions over the next month, petitioner also received documentation from the attorney regarding the legitimacy of the funds.

At some point after petitioner seized the cash, he helped draft an affidavit to show probable cause for forfeiture of the funds and forwarded that affidavit to a United States Attorney's Office in Georgia. According to respondents, the affidavit was false and misleading because petitioner misrepresented the encounter at the airport and omitted exculpatory information regarding the lack of drug evidence and the legitimate source of the funds. In the end, no forfeiture complaint was filed, and the DEA returned the funds to respondents in March 2007.

Respondents filed suit against petitioner in the United States District Court for the District of Nevada, seeking money damages * * *. Respondents alleged that petitioner violated their Fourth Amendment rights by (1) seizing the cash without probable cause; (2) keeping the money after concluding it did not come from drug-related activity; (3) drafting and forwarding a probable cause affidavit to support a forfeiture action while knowing the affidavit contained false statements; (4) willfully seeking forfeiture while withholding exculpatory information; and (5) withholding that exculpatory information from the United States Attorney's Office.

The District Court granted petitioner's motion to dismiss [the complaint for lack of personal jurisdiction]. Relying on this Court's decision in *Calder v. Jones*, 465 U.S. 783 (1984), the court determined that petitioner's search of respondents and his seizure of the cash in Georgia did not establish a basis to exercise personal jurisdiction in Nevada. The court concluded that even if petitioner caused harm to respondents in Nevada while knowing they lived in Nevada, that fact alone did not confer jurisdiction. * * *

On appeal, a divided panel of the United States Court of Appeals for the Ninth Circuit reversed. * * * [It] found the District Court's exercise of personal jurisdiction to be proper. * * *

We granted certiorari * * * [and now] * * * reverse.

II

* * *

The Due Process Clause of the Fourteenth Amendment constrains a State's authority to bind a nonresident defendant to a judgment of its courts. Although a nonresident's physical presence within the territorial jurisdiction of the court is not required, the nonresident generally must have "certain minimum contacts . . . such that the maintenance of the suit does not offend 'traditional notions of fair play and substantial justice.' " *Int'l Shoe Co. v. Washington*, 326 U.S. 310, 316 (1945).

This case addresses the "minimum contacts" necessary to create specific jurisdiction. The inquiry whether a forum State may assert specific jurisdiction over a nonresident defendant "focuses on 'the relationship among the defendant, the forum, and the litigation.' " For a State to exercise jurisdiction consistent with due process, the defendant's suit-related conduct must create a substantial connection with the forum State. Two related aspects of this necessary relationship are relevant in this case.

First, the relationship must arise out of contacts that the "defendant *himself*" creates with the forum State. Due process limits on the State's adjudicative authority principally protect the liberty of the nonresident defendant—not the convenience of plaintiffs or third parties. We have consistently rejected attempts to satisfy the defendant-focused "minimum contacts" inquiry by demonstrating contacts between the plaintiff (or third parties) and the forum State. We have thus rejected a plaintiff's argument that a Florida court could exercise personal jurisdiction over a trustee in Delaware based solely on the contacts of the trust's settlor, who was domiciled in Florida and had executed powers of appointment there. *Hanson v. Denckla*, 357 U.S. 235 (1958). We have likewise held that Oklahoma courts could not exercise personal jurisdiction over an automobile distributor that supplies New York, New Jersey, and Connecticut dealers based only on an automobile purchaser's act of driving it on Oklahoma highways. *World-Wide Volkswagen Corp. v. Woodson*, 444 U.S. 286 (1980). Put simply, however significant the plaintiff's contacts with the forum may be, those contacts cannot be "decisive in determining whether the defendant's due process rights are violated."

Second, our "minimum contacts" analysis looks to the defendant's contacts with the forum State itself, not the defendant's contacts with persons who reside there. Accordingly, we have upheld the assertion of jurisdiction over defendants who have purposefully "reach[ed] out beyond" their State and into another by, for example, entering a contractual relationship that "envisioned continuing and wide-reaching contacts" in the forum State, or by circulating magazines to "deliberately exploi[t]" a market in the forum State. And although physical presence in the forum is not a prerequisite to jurisdiction, physical entry into the State—either by the defendant in person or through an agent, goods, mail, or some other means—is certainly a relevant contact.

But the plaintiff cannot be the only link between the defendant and the forum. Rather, it is the defendant's conduct that must form the necessary connection with the forum State that is the basis for its jurisdiction over him. To be sure, a defendant's contacts with the forum State may be intertwined with his transactions or interactions with the plaintiff or other parties. But a defendant's relationship with a plaintiff or third party, standing alone, is an insufficient basis for jurisdiction. Due process requires that a defendant be haled into court in a forum State based on his own affiliation with the State, not based on the "random, fortuitous, or attenuated" contacts he makes by interacting with other persons affiliated with the State.

These same principles apply when intentional torts are involved. In that context, it is likewise insufficient to rely on a defendant's "random, fortuitous, or attenuated contacts" or on the "unilateral activity" of a plaintiff. A forum State's exercise of jurisdiction over an out-of-state intentional tortfeasor must be based on intentional conduct by the defendant that creates the necessary contacts with the forum.

Calder v. Jones illustrates the application of these principles. In *Calder*, a California actress brought a libel suit in California state court against a reporter and an editor, both of whom worked for the National Enquirer at its headquarters in Florida. The plaintiff's libel claims were based on an article written and edited by the defendants in Florida for publication in the National Enquirer, a national weekly newspaper with a California circulation of roughly 600,000.

We held that California's assertion of jurisdiction over the defendants was consistent with due process. Although we recognized that the defendants' activities "focus[ed]" on the plaintiff, our jurisdictional inquiry "focuse[d] on 'the relationship among the defendant, the forum, and the litigation.'" Specifically, we examined the various contacts the defendants had created with California (and not just with the plaintiff) by writing the allegedly libelous story.

We found those forum contacts to be ample: The defendants relied on phone calls to "California sources" for the information in their article; they wrote the story about the plaintiff's activities in California; they caused reputational injury in California by writing an allegedly libelous article that was widely circulated in the State; and the "brunt" of that injury was suffered by the plaintiff in that State. "In sum, California [wa]s the focal point both of the story and of the harm suffered." Jurisdiction over the defendants was "therefore proper in California based on the 'effects' of their Florida conduct in California."

The crux of *Calder* was that the reputation-based "effects" of the alleged libel connected the defendants to California, not just to the plaintiff. The strength of that connection was largely a function of the nature of the libel tort. However scandalous a newspaper article might be, it can lead to a loss of reputation only if communicated to (and read and understood by) third persons. Accordingly, the reputational injury caused by the defendants' story would not have occurred but for the fact that the defendants wrote an article for publication in California that was read by a large number of California citizens. Indeed, because publication to third persons is a necessary element of libel, the defendants' intentional tort actually occurred *in* California. In this way, the "effects" caused by the defendants' article—*i.e.*, the injury to the plaintiff's reputation in the estimation of the California public—connected the defendants' conduct to *California*, not just to a plaintiff who lived there. That connection, combined with the various facts that gave the article a California focus, sufficed to authorize the California court's exercise of jurisdiction.

III

Applying the foregoing principles, we conclude that petitioner lacks the "minimal contacts" with Nevada that are a prerequisite to the exercise of jurisdiction over him. It is undisputed that no part of petitioner's course of conduct occurred in Nevada. Petitioner approached, questioned, and searched respondents, and seized the cash at issue, in the Atlanta airport. It is alleged that petitioner later helped draft a "false probable cause affidavit" in Georgia and forwarded that affidavit to a United States Attorney's Office in Georgia to support a potential action for forfeiture of the seized funds. Petitioner never traveled to, conducted activities within, contacted anyone in, or sent anything or anyone to Nevada. In short, when viewed through the proper lens—whether the *defendant's* actions connect him to the *forum*—petitioner formed no jurisdictionally relevant contacts with Nevada.

* * *

Relying on *Calder*, respondents emphasize that they suffered the "injury" caused by petitioner's allegedly tortious conduct (*i.e.*, the delayed return of their gambling funds) while they were residing in the forum. This emphasis is likewise misplaced. As previously noted, *Calder* made clear that mere injury to a forum resident is not a sufficient connection to the forum. Regardless of where a plaintiff lives or works, an injury is jurisdictionally relevant only insofar as it shows that the defendant has formed a contact with the forum State. The proper question is not where the plaintiff experienced a particular injury or effect but whether the defendant's conduct connects him to the forum in a meaningful way.

Respondents' claimed injury does not evince a connection between petitioner and Nevada. Even if we consider the continuation of the seizure in Georgia to be a distinct injury, it is not the sort of effect that is tethered to Nevada in any meaningful way. Respondents (and only respondents) lacked access to their funds in Nevada not because anything independently occurred there, but because Nevada is where respondents chose to be at a time when they desired to use the funds seized by petitioner. Respondents would have experienced this same lack of access in California, Mississippi, or wherever else they might have traveled and found themselves wanting more money than they had. Unlike the broad publication of the forum-focused story in *Calder*, the effects of petitioner's conduct on respondents are not connected to the forum State in a way that makes those effects a proper basis for jurisdiction.

* * * [O]ther possible contacts with Nevada [are] unavailing. Respondents' Nevada attorney contacted petitioner in Georgia, but that is precisely the sort of "unilateral activity" of a third party that "cannot satisfy the requirement of contact with the forum State." Respondents allege that some of the cash seized in Georgia "originated" in Nevada, but that attenuated connection was not created by petitioner, and the cash was in Georgia, not Nevada, when petitioner seized it. Finally, the funds were eventually returned to respondents in Nevada, but petitioner had nothing to do with that return (indeed, it seems likely that it was respondents' unilateral decision to have their funds sent to Nevada).

* * *

* * * In this case, * * * those principles [are] clear: Petitioner's relevant conduct occurred entirely in Georgia, and the mere fact that his conduct affected plaintiffs with connections to the forum State does not suffice to authorize jurisdiction. We therefore reverse the judgment of the Court of Appeals.

It is so ordered.

2. GENERAL JURISDICTION

DAIMLER AG v. BAUMAN

Supreme Court of the United States, 2014
571 U.S. ___, 134 S. Ct. 746

JUSTICE GINSBURG delivered the opinion of the Court.

* * *

In *Goodyear Dunlop Tires Operations, S.A. v. Brown*, 564 U.S. ___, 131 S. Ct. 2846 (2011), we addressed the distinction between general or all-purpose jurisdiction, and specific or conduct-linked jurisdiction. As to the former, we held that a court may assert jurisdiction over a foreign corporation "to hear any and all claims against [it]" only when the corporation's affiliations with the State in which suit is brought are so constant and pervasive "as to render [it] essentially at home in the forum State." Instructed by *Goodyear*, we conclude Daimler [AG, a German public stock company] is not "at home" in California, and cannot be sued there for injuries plaintiffs attribute[d] to conduct in Argentina.

I

In 2004, plaintiffs (respondents here) filed suit in the United States District Court for the Northern District of California, alleging that MB [Mercedes–Benz] Argentina [a subsidiary of Daimler AG] collaborated with Argentinian state security forces to kidnap, detain, torture, and kill plaintiffs and their relatives during the military dictatorship in place there from 1976 through 1983, a period known as Argentina's "Dirty War." Based on those allegations, plaintiffs asserted claims under [two federal statutes permitting suits for various violations of international law], as well as claims for wrongful death and intentional infliction of emotional distress under the laws of California and Argentina. The incidents recounted in the complaint center on MB Argentina's plant in Gonzalez Catan, Argentina; no part of MB Argentina's alleged collaboration with Argentinian authorities took place in California or anywhere else in the United States.

Plaintiffs' operative complaint names only one corporate defendant: Daimler, the petitioner here. Plaintiffs seek to hold Daimler vicariously liable for MB Argentina's alleged malfeasance. Daimler is a German

Aktiengesellschaft (public stock company) that manufactures Mercedes–Benz vehicles in Germany and has its headquarters in Stuttgart. At times relevant to this case, MB Argentina was a subsidiary wholly owned by Daimler's predecessor in interest.

Daimler moved to dismiss the action for want of personal jurisdiction. Opposing the motion, plaintiffs submitted declarations and exhibits purporting to demonstrate the presence of Daimler itself in California. Alternatively, plaintiffs maintained that jurisdiction over Daimler could be founded on the California contacts of MBUSA, a distinct corporate entity that, according to plaintiffs, should be treated as Daimler's agent for jurisdictional purposes.

MBUSA, an indirect subsidiary of Daimler, is a Delaware limited liability corporation. MBUSA serves as Daimler's exclusive importer and distributor in the United States, purchasing Mercedes–Benz automobiles from Daimler in Germany, then importing those vehicles, and ultimately distributing them to independent dealerships located throughout the Nation. Although MBUSA's principal place of business is in New Jersey, MBUSA has multiple California-based facilities, including a regional office in Costa Mesa, a Vehicle Preparation Center in Carson, and a Classic Center in Irvine. According to the record developed below, MBUSA is the largest supplier of luxury vehicles to the California market. In particular, over 10% of all sales of new vehicles in the United States take place in California, and MBUSA's California sales account for 2.4% of Daimler's worldwide sales.

The relationship between Daimler and MBUSA is delineated in a General Distributor Agreement, which sets forth requirements for MBUSA's distribution of Mercedes–Benz vehicles in the United States. That agreement established MBUSA as an "independent contracto[r]" that "buy[s] and sell[s] [vehicles] . . . as an independent business for [its] own account." The agreement "does not make [MBUSA] . . . a general or special agent, partner, joint venturer or employee of DAIMLERCHRYSLER or any DaimlerChrysler Group Company"; MBUSA "ha[s] no authority to make binding obligations for or act on behalf of DAIMLERCHRYSLER or any DaimlerChrysler Group Company."

* * * [T]he District Court granted Daimler's motion to dismiss. Daimler's own affiliations with California, the court first determined, were insufficient to support the exercise of all-purpose jurisdiction over the corporation. Next, the court declined to attribute MBUSA's California contacts to Daimler on an agency theory, concluding that plaintiffs failed to demonstrate that MBUSA acted as Daimler's agent.

The Ninth Circuit [initially] affirmed the District Court's judgment [but on rehearing reversed itself]. * * *

We granted certiorari * * *.

II

* * *

III

* * *

"The canonical opinion in this area remains *International Shoe [Co. v. Washington]*, 326 U.S. 310 (1945), in which we held that a State may authorize its courts to exercise personal jurisdiction over an out-of-state defendant if the defendant has 'certain minimum contacts' with [the State] such that the maintenance of the suit does not offend 'traditional notions of fair play and substantial justice.'" * * *

International Shoe's conception of "fair play and substantial justice" presaged the development of two categories of personal jurisdiction. The first category is represented by *International Shoe* itself, a case in which the in-state activities of the corporate defendant "ha[d] not only been continuous and systematic, but also g[a]ve rise to the liabilities sued on." * * * Adjudicatory authority of this order, in which the suit "aris[es] out of or relate[s] to the defendant's contacts with the forum," is today called "specific jurisdiction."

International Shoe distinguished between, on the one hand, exercises of specific jurisdiction, as just described, and on the other, situations where a foreign corporation's "continuous corporate operations within a state [are] so substantial and of such a nature as to justify suit against it on causes of action arising from dealings entirely distinct from those activities." As we have since explained, "[a] court may assert general jurisdiction over foreign (sister-state or foreign-country) corporations to hear any and all claims against them when their affiliations with the State are so 'continuous and systematic' as to render them essentially at home in the forum State."

Since *International Shoe*, "specific jurisdiction has become the centerpiece of modern jurisdiction theory, while general jurisdiction [has played] a reduced role." * * *

Our post-*International Shoe* opinions on general jurisdiction * * * are few. "[The Court's] 1952 decision in *Perkins v. Benguet Consolidated Mining Co.*, 342 U.S. 437 (1952), remains the textbook case of general jurisdiction appropriately exercised over a foreign corporation that has not consented to suit in the forum." The defendant in *Perkins*, Benguet, was a company incorporated under the laws of the Philippines, where it operated gold and silver mines. Benguet ceased its mining operations during the Japanese occupation of the Philippines in World War II; its president moved to Ohio, where he kept an office, maintained the company's files, and oversaw the company's activities. The plaintiff, an Ohio resident, sued Benguet on a claim that neither arose in Ohio nor related to the corporation's activities in that State. We held that the Ohio courts could exercise general jurisdiction over Benguet without offending due process. That was so, we later noted, because "Ohio was the corporation's principal, if temporary, place of business."

The next case on point, *Helicopteros* [*Nacionales de Colombia, S.A. v. Hall*], 466 U.S. 408 (1984), arose from a helicopter crash in Peru. Four U.S. citizens perished in that accident; their survivors and representatives brought suit in Texas state court against the helicopter's owner and operator, a Colombian corporation. That company's contacts with Texas were confined to "sending its chief executive officer to Houston for a contract-negotiation session; accepting into its New York bank account checks drawn on a Houston bank; purchasing helicopters, equipment, and training services from [a Texas-based helicopter company] for substantial sums; and sending personnel to [Texas] for training." Notably, those contacts bore no apparent relationship to the accident that gave rise to the suit. We held that the company's Texas connections did not resemble the "continuous and systematic general business contacts . . . found to exist in *Perkins*." "[M]ere purchases, even if occurring at regular intervals," we clarified, "are not enough to warrant a State's assertion of *in personam* jurisdiction over a nonresident corporation in a cause of action not related to those purchase transactions."

Most recently, in *Goodyear*, we answered the question: "Are foreign subsidiaries of a United States parent corporation amenable to suit in state court on claims unrelated to any activity of the subsidiaries in the forum State?" That case arose from a bus accident outside Paris that killed two boys from North Carolina. The boys' parents brought a wrongful-death suit in North Carolina state court alleging that the bus's tire was defectively manufactured. The complaint named as defendants not only The Goodyear Tire and Rubber Company (Goodyear), an Ohio corporation, but also Goodyear's Turkish, French, and Luxembourgian subsidiaries. Those foreign subsidiaries, which manufactured tires for sale in Europe and Asia, lacked any affiliation with North Carolina. A small percentage of tires manufactured by the foreign subsidiaries were distributed in North Carolina, however, and on that ground, the North Carolina Court of Appeals held the subsidiaries amenable to the general jurisdiction of North Carolina courts.

We reversed, observing that the North Carolina court's analysis "elided the essential difference between case-specific and all-purpose (general) jurisdiction." Although the placement of a product into the stream of commerce "may bolster an affiliation germane to *specific* jurisdiction," we explained, such contacts "do not warrant a determination that, based on those ties, the forum has *general* jurisdiction over a defendant." As *International Shoe* itself teaches, a corporation's "continuous activity of some sorts within a state is not enough to support the demand that the corporation be amenable to suits unrelated to that activity." Because Goodyear's foreign subsidiaries were "in no sense at home in North Carolina," we held, those subsidiaries could not be required to submit to the general jurisdiction of that State's courts.

* * *

IV

* * *

With this background, we turn directly to the question whether Daimler's affiliations with California are sufficient to subject it to the general (all-purpose) personal jurisdiction of that State's courts. In the proceedings below, the parties agreed on, or failed to contest, certain points we now take as given. Plaintiffs have never attempted to fit this case into the *specific* jurisdiction category. Nor did plaintiffs challenge on appeal the District Court's holding that Daimler's own contacts with California were, by themselves, too sporadic to justify the exercise of general jurisdiction. * * *

Daimler * * * failed to object below to plaintiffs' assertion that the California courts could exercise all-purpose jurisdiction over MBUSA. We will assume then, for purposes of this decision only, that MBUSA qualifies as at home in California.

A

In sustaining the exercise of general jurisdiction over Daimler, the Ninth Circuit relied on an agency theory, determining that MBUSA acted as Daimler's agent for jurisdictional purposes and then attributing MBUSA's California contacts to Daimler. * * *

This Court has not yet addressed whether a foreign corporation may be subjected to a court's general jurisdiction based on the contacts of its in-state subsidiary. * * * But we need not pass judgment on invocation of an agency theory in the context of general jurisdiction, for in no event can the appeals court's analysis be sustained.

The Ninth Circuit's agency finding rested primarily on its observation that MBUSA's services were "important" to Daimler, as gauged by Daimler's hypothetical readiness to perform those services itself if MBUSA did not exist. * * * The Ninth Circuit's agency theory thus appears to subject foreign corporations to general jurisdiction whenever they have an in-state subsidiary or affiliate, an outcome that would sweep beyond even the "sprawling view of general jurisdiction" we rejected in *Goodyear*.

B

Even if we were to assume that MBUSA is at home in California, and further to assume MBUSA's contacts are imputable to Daimler, there would still be no basis to subject Daimler to general jurisdiction in

California, for Daimler's slim contacts with the State hardly render it at home there.

Goodyear made clear that only a limited set of affiliations with a forum will render a defendant amenable to all-purpose jurisdiction there. "For an individual, the paradigm forum for the exercise of general jurisdiction is the individual's domicile; for a corporation, it is an equivalent place, one in which the corporation is fairly regarded as at home." With respect to a corporation, the place of incorporation and principal place of business are "paradig[m] . . . bases for general jurisdiction." Those affiliations have the virtue of being unique—that is, each ordinarily indicates only one place— as well as easily ascertainable. These bases afford plaintiffs recourse to at least one clear and certain forum in which a corporate defendant may be sued on any and all claims.

* * * Plaintiffs would have us look beyond the exemplar bases *Goodyear* identified, and approve the exercise of general jurisdiction in every State in which a corporation "engages in a substantial, continuous, and systematic course of business." That formulation, we hold, is unacceptably grasping.

As noted, the words "continuous and systematic" were used in *International Shoe* to describe instances in which the exercise of *specific* jurisdiction would be appropriate. Turning to all-purpose jurisdiction, in contrast, *International Shoe* speaks of "instances in which the continuous corporate operations within a state [are] so substantial and of such a nature as to justify suit . . . *on causes of action arising from dealings entirely distinct from those activities.*" Accordingly, the inquiry under *Goodyear* is not whether a foreign corporation's in-forum contacts can be said to be in some sense "continuous and systematic," it is whether that corporation's "affiliations with the State are so 'continuous and systematic' as to render [it] essentially at home in the forum State."[19]

Here, neither Daimler nor MBUSA is incorporated in California, nor does either entity have its principal place of business there. If Daimler's California activities sufficed to allow adjudication of this Argentina-rooted case in California, the same global reach would presumably be available in every other State in which MBUSA's sales are sizable. Such exorbitant exercises of all-purpose jurisdiction would scarcely permit out-of-state defendants "to structure their primary conduct with some minimum assurance as to where that conduct will and will not render them liable to suit."

---

[19] We do not foreclose the possibility that in an exceptional case a corporation's operations in a forum other than its formal place of incorporation or principal place of business may be so substantial and of such a nature as to render the corporation at home in that State. But this case presents no occasion to explore that question, because Daimler's activities in California plainly do not approach that level. * * *

It was therefore error for the Ninth Circuit to conclude that Daimler, even with MBUSA's contacts attributed to it, was at home in California, and hence subject to suit there on claims by foreign plaintiffs having nothing to do with anything that occurred or had its principal impact in California.

C

* * *

For the reasons stated, the judgment of the United States Court of Appeals for the Ninth Circuit is

Reversed.

JUSTICE SOTOMAYOR, concurring in the judgment.

* * *

I

I begin with the point on which the majority and I agree: The Ninth Circuit's decision should be reversed.

Our personal jurisdiction precedents call for a two-part analysis. The contacts prong asks whether the defendant has sufficient contacts with the forum State to support personal jurisdiction; the reasonableness prong asks whether the exercise of jurisdiction would be unreasonable under the circumstances. * * * I would decide this case under the reasonableness prong without foreclosing future consideration of whether that prong should be limited to the specific jurisdiction context.

We identified the factors that bear on reasonableness in *Asahi Metal Industry Co. v. Superior Court of California, Solano County*, 480 U.S. 102 (1987): "the burden on the defendant, the interests of the forum State," "the plaintiff's interest in obtaining relief" in the forum State, and the interests of other sovereigns in resolving the dispute. We held in *Asahi* that it would be "unreasonable and unfair" for a California court to exercise jurisdiction over a claim between a Taiwanese plaintiff and a Japanese defendant that arose out of a transaction in Taiwan, particularly where the Taiwanese plaintiff had not shown that it would be more convenient to litigate in California than in Taiwan or Japan.

The same considerations resolve this case. It involves Argentine plaintiffs suing a German defendant for conduct that took place in Argentina. Like the plaintiffs in *Asahi*, respondents have failed to show that it would be more convenient to litigate in California than in Germany, a sovereign with a far greater interest in resolving the dispute. *Asahi* thus makes clear that it would be unreasonable for a court in California to subject Daimler to its jurisdiction.

II

* * *

[Justice Sotomayor expressed concern that the Court decided the case on a ground that was neither briefed nor argued by the parties in the lower courts.]

III

While the majority's decisional process is problematic enough, I fear that process leads it to an even more troubling result.

A

Until today, our precedents had established a straightforward test for general jurisdiction: Does the defendant have "continuous corporate operations within a state" that are "so substantial and of such a nature as to justify suit against it on causes of action arising from dealings entirely distinct from those activities"? * * *

* * *

Had the majority applied our settled approach, it would have had little trouble concluding that Daimler's California contacts rise to the requisite level, given the majority's assumption that MBUSA's contacts may be attributed to Daimler and given Daimler's concession that those contacts render MBUSA "at home" in California. * * *

Under this standard, Daimler's concession that MBUSA is subject to general jurisdiction in California (a concession the Court accepts) should be dispositive. For if MBUSA's California contacts are so substantial and the resulting benefits to MBUSA so significant as to make MBUSA "at home" in California, the same must be true of Daimler when MBUSA's contacts and benefits are viewed as its own. * * *

B

The majority today concludes otherwise. Referring to the "continuous and systematic" contacts inquiry that has been taught to generations of first-year law students as "unacceptably grasping," the majority announces the new rule that in order for a foreign defendant to be subject to general jurisdiction, it must not only possess continuous and systematic contacts with a forum State, but those contacts must also surpass some unspecified level when viewed in comparison to the company's "nationwide and worldwide" activities.

* * *

C

* * *

* * * [T]he rule that [the Court] adopts will produce deep injustice in at least four respects.

First, the majority's approach unduly curtails the States' sovereign authority to adjudicate disputes against corporate defendants who have engaged in continuous and substantial business operations within their boundaries. The majority does not dispute that a State can exercise general jurisdiction where a corporate defendant has its corporate headquarters, and hence its principal place of business within the State. Yet it never explains why the State should lose that power when, as is increasingly common, a corporation "divide[s] [its] command and coordinating functions among officers who work at several different locations." * * * Put simply, the majority's rule defines the Due Process Clause so narrowly and arbitrarily as to contravene the States' sovereign prerogative to subject to judgment defendants who have manifested an unqualified "intention to benefit from and thus an intention to submit to the[ir] laws."

Second, the proportionality approach will treat small businesses unfairly in comparison to national and multinational conglomerates. Whereas a larger company will often be immunized from general jurisdiction in a State on account of its extensive contacts outside the forum, a small business will not be. * * *

Third, the majority's approach creates the incongruous result that an individual defendant whose only contact with a forum State is a one-time visit will be subject to general jurisdiction if served with process during that visit, but a large corporation that owns property, employs workers, and does billions of dollars' worth of business in the State will not be, simply because the corporation has similar contacts elsewhere (though the visiting individual surely does as well).

Finally, it should be obvious that the ultimate effect of the majority's approach will be to shift the risk of loss from multinational corporations to the individuals harmed by their actions. * * * I cannot agree with the majority's conclusion that the Due Process Clause requires these results.

The Court * * * adopts a new rule of constitutional law that is unmoored from decades of precedent. Because I would reverse the Ninth Circuit's decision on the narrower ground that the exercise of jurisdiction over Daimler would be unreasonable in any event, I respectfully concur in the judgment only.

NOTES AND QUESTIONS

1.   What are the policy reasons for requiring personal jurisdiction? Are those reasons sound?

2. What is the difference between specific jurisdiction and general jurisdiction?

3. It is well established that "the requirement of personal jurisdiction may be intentionally waived" by the defendant. *Ins. Corp. of Ireland v. Compagnie de Guinee*, 456 U.S. 694, 704 (1982). Why is the defendant permitted to submit voluntarily to the jurisdiction of the court?

4. How did the Supreme Court rule in *Walden*? What were the crucial facts that led to its decision? How did the Court distinguish *Calder v. Jones*? Is that distinction persuasive?

5. What was the issue in *Daimler AG*? How did the majority resolve the case? Justice Sotomayor concurred in the result only. On what ground would she have reversed the court of appeals? What was the basis for her disagreement with the majority? Which approach is more persuasive: the majority's or Justice Sotomayor's?

6. The issue of personal jurisdiction has become increasingly complicated with advances in technology. Should communication over the internet be sufficient to establish minimum contacts with a state? In *Rio Properties, Inc. v. Rio International Interlink*, 284 F.3d 1007 (9th Cir. 2002), a Nevada casino sued a foreign business in Nevada for trademark infringement based on the use of a website domain name previously registered by the plaintiff. The Ninth Circuit held that the court had personal jurisdiction over the foreign business because the business had both advertised for its website in Nevada and knowingly injured the casino there. As the court explained: "All told, [defendant's] actions in Nevada, including its radio and print advertisements, demonstrate an insistent marketing campaign directed toward Nevada. Therefore, we have no problem finding that * * * the purposeful availment requirement for the exercise of personal jurisdiction is satisfied." *Id.* at 1020–21.

By contrast, in *Cybersell, Inc. v. Cybersell, Inc.*, 130 F.3d 414 (9th Cir. 1997), the Ninth Circuit held that there was no jurisdiction based on internet contacts. An Arizona corporation, Cybersell, Inc., claimed that a Florida corporation by the same name had infringed its federally registered name. The Arizona corporation argued that, because the Florida website was accessible to internet users in Arizona, the Florida corporation should be subject to suit in Arizona. The Ninth Circuit, however, held that "it would not comport with 'traditional notions of fair play and substantial justice' for Arizona to exercise personal jurisdiction over an allegedly infringing Florida web site advertiser who has no contacts with Arizona other than maintaining a home page that is accessible to Arizonans, and everyone else, over the internet." *Id.* at 415. Can *Rio Properties* and *Cybersell, Inc.* be reconciled? If so, on what ground?

For further discussion of personal jurisdiction and modern technology, *see* C. Douglas Floyd & Shima Baradaran-Robison, *Toward a Unified Test of Personal Jurisdiction in an Era of Widely Diffused Wrongs: The Relevance of Purpose and Effects*, 81 Ind. L.J. 601 (2006) (noting that, for purposes of personal jurisdiction, the internet is not significantly different from other forms of communication, and proposing a test that focuses on whether a defendant could reasonably anticipate the risk of suit in the forum state).

C. SUBJECT MATTER JURISDICTION

Subject matter jurisdiction pertains to a court's power to hear a case involving the subject matter at issue. Under the U.S. Constitution (Art. III, § 2), federal courts have limited jurisdiction, and thus the plaintiff must establish either "federal question" jurisdiction or "diversity" jurisdiction. A federal question exists when a claim arises under federal law. Diversity jurisdiction exists when the parties are "diverse" (*i.e.*, they reside in different states or one is not a U.S. citizen) and the amount in controversy exceeds $75,000. This section examines both types of subject matter jurisdiction. It should be noted that if a claim is within a federal court's subject matter jurisdiction, the court may also adjudicate all other claims that "are so related to claims in the action within such original jurisdiction that they form part of the same case or controversy * * *." 28 U.S.C. § 1367(a). Thus, for example, if a claim raises a question under a federal statute, a court can also adjudicate state-law claims that are factually intertwined with the federal claim. Unlike personal jurisdiction, subject matter jurisdiction cannot be waived by the parties, because it is limited by the Constitution and by statute.

1. FEDERAL QUESTION JURISDICTION

As authorized by Art. III, § 2 of the U.S. Constitution, Congress established in 28 U.S.C. § 1331 that federal "district courts shall have original jurisdiction of all civil actions arising under the Constitution, laws, or treaties of the United States." Thus, federal questions include issues involving the U.S. Constitution, federal statutes, federal regulations, executive orders, or U.S. treaties.

The Supreme Court has construed federal question jurisdiction narrowly. "[A] suit arises under the Constitution and laws of the United States only when the plaintiff's statement of his own cause of action shows that it is based upon those laws or that Constitution." *Beneficial Nat'l Bank v. Anderson*, 539 U.S. 1, 6 (2003). If the action is based on state law, the possibility that the defendant might invoke federal law as a defense or on a counterclaim (where the defendant seeks relief from plaintiff as part of defendant's answer) does not create federal question jurisdiction. *See, e.g., Holmes Grp., Inc. v. Vornado Air Circulation Sys., Inc.*, 535 U.S. 826, 831 (2002) ("[A] counterclaim * * * cannot serve as the basis for 'arising under' jurisdiction"). On the other hand, even if a complaint purports to be based solely on state law, if federal law completely bars or preempts state law, then a federal question exists. For example, the Employee Retirement Income Security Act of 1974 ("ERISA"), 29 U.S.C. § 1132(a) *et seq.*, establishes a uniform law governing employee benefit plans. Section 502(a) of ERISA provides for a comprehensive enforcement scheme, and thus "any state-law cause of action that duplicates, supplements, or supplants the ERISA civil enforcement remedy * * * [is] pre-empted." *Aetna Health Inc. v. Davila*, 542 U.S. 200, 209 (2004). Moreover, under the "artful-pleading" doctrine, a plaintiff cannot avoid federal jurisdiction by characterizing what is in fact a federal claim as a state-law claim. *Federated Dept. Stores, Inc. v. Moitie*, 452 U.S. 394, 397 n.2 (1981). And a federal question exists "where the vindication of a right under state law necessarily turn[s] on some construction of federal law." *Franchise Tax Bd. v. Constr. Laborers Vacation Trust*, 463 U.S. 1, 8–9 (1983).

2. DIVERSITY JURISDICTION AND CHOICE OF LAW

Diversity jurisdiction allows parties to bring state-law claims in federal court, rather than state court, if (1) the parties are diverse—*i.e.*, no plaintiff is a citizen of the same state as any defendant (or the case involves U.S. citizens on one side and foreign parties on the other), and (2) the amount in controversy is greater than $75,000. 28 U.S.C. § 1332(a). Diversity jurisdiction was created to ensure that out-of-state parties have access to a neutral forum—a federal court—that will not favor in-state residents. If a plaintiff brings a case in state court that satisfies the requirements of diversity, the defendant has 30 days after receiving the complaint to "remove" the case to federal court. 28 U.S.C. § 1446(b). This section addresses various diversity jurisdiction issues. The first featured case addresses the issue of how a corporation's citizenship is determined. The second featured case addresses some of the complications that arise when a federal district court must decide what law governs (federal or state law) when the court is exercising diversity jurisdiction.

i. Diversity Jurisdiction Principles

HERTZ CORP. v. FRIEND
Supreme Court of the United States, 2010
559 U.S. 77

JUSTICE BREYER delivered the opinion of the Court.

The federal diversity jurisdiction statute provides that "a corporation shall be deemed to be a citizen of any State by which it has been incorporated *and of the State where it has its principal place of business*." 28 U.S.C. § 1332(c)(1) (emphasis added [by the Court]). We seek here to resolve different interpretations that the Circuits have given this phrase. In doing so, we place primary weight upon the need for judicial administration of a jurisdictional statute to remain as simple as possible. And we conclude that the phrase "principal place of business" refers to the place where the corporation's high level officers direct, control, and coordinate the corporation's activities. Lower federal courts have often metaphorically called that place the corporation's "nerve center." We believe that the "nerve center" will typically be found at a corporation's headquarters.

I

In September 2007, respondents Melinda Friend and John Nhieu, two California citizens, sued petitioner, the Hertz Corporation, in a California state court. They sought damages for what they claimed were violations of California's wage and hour laws. And they requested relief on behalf of a potential class composed of California citizens who had allegedly suffered similar harms.

Hertz filed a notice seeking removal to a federal court. 28 U.S.C. §§ 1332(d)(2), 1453. Hertz claimed that the plaintiffs and the defendant were citizens of different States. §§ 1332(a)(1), (c)(1). Hence, the federal court possessed diversity-of-citizenship jurisdiction. Friend and Nhieu, however, claimed that the Hertz Corporation was a California citizen, like themselves, and that, hence, diversity jurisdiction was lacking.

To support its position, Hertz submitted a declaration by an employee relations manager that sought to show that Hertz's "principal place of business" was in New Jersey, not in California. The declaration stated, among other things, that Hertz operated facilities in 44 States; and that California—which had about 12% of the Nation's population—accounted for 273 of Hertz's 1,606 car rental locations; about 2,300 of its 11,230 full-time employees; about $811 million of its $4.371 billion in annual revenue; and about 3.8 million of its approximately 21 million annual transactions, *i.e.*, rentals. The declaration also stated that the "leadership of Hertz and its domestic subsidiaries" is located at Hertz's "corporate headquarters" in Park Ridge, New Jersey; that its "core executive and administrative functions . . . are carried out" there and "to a lesser extent" in Oklahoma City, Oklahoma; and that its "major administrative operations . . . are found" at those two locations.

The District Court of the Northern District of California accepted Hertz's statement of the facts as undisputed. But it concluded that, given those facts, Hertz was a citizen of California. * * *

Hertz appealed the District Court's remand order. 28 U.S.C. § 1453(c). The Ninth Circuit affirmed in a brief memorandum opinion. * * * [W]e granted the writ [of certiorari].

II

[The Court rejected respondents' argument that it lacked jurisdiction to decide the issue.]

III

[The Court discussed the history of the "principal place of business" language in § 1332(c)(1), going back to Congress's authorization of diversity jurisdiction in 1789. The Court then described how, in 1958, Congress determined that a corporation should "be deemed a citizen of any State by which it has been incorporated and of the State where it has its principal place of business."]

IV

The phrase "principal place of business" has proved more difficult to apply than its originators likely expected. * * *

After Congress's [1958 legislation], courts were * * * uncertain as to where to look to determine a corporation's "principal place of business" for diversity purposes. If a corporation's headquarters and executive offices were in the same State in which it did most of its business, the test seemed straightforward. The "principal place of business" was located in that State.

But suppose those corporate headquarters, including executive offices, are in one State, while the corporation's plants or other centers of business activity are located in other States? In 1959 a distinguished federal district judge [gave the following answer]:

> Where a corporation is engaged in far-flung and varied activities which are carried on in different states, its principal place of business is the nerve center from which it radiates out to its constituent parts and from which its officers direct, control and coordinate all activities without regard to locale, in the furtherance of the corporate objective. The test * * * is that place where the corporation has an "office from which its business was directed and controlled"—the place where "all of its business was under the supreme direction and control of its officers."

Numerous Circuits have since followed this rule, applying the "nerve center" test for corporations with "far-flung" business activities.

[The] analysis, however, did not go far enough. For it did not answer what courts should do when the operations of the corporation are not "far-flung" but rather limited to only a few States. When faced with this question, various courts have focused more heavily on where a corporation's actual business activities are located.

Perhaps because corporations come in many different forms, involve many different kinds of business activities, and locate offices and plants for different reasons in different ways in different regions, a general "business activities" approach has proved unusually difficult to apply. Courts must decide which factors are more important than others: for example, plant location, sales or servicing centers; transactions, payrolls, or revenue generation.

The number of factors grew as courts explicitly combined aspects of the "nerve center" and "business activity" tests to look to a corporation's "total activities," sometimes to try to determine what treatises have described as the corporation's "center of gravity." * * * Not surprisingly, different circuits (and sometimes different courts within a single circuit) have applied these highly general multifactor tests in different ways.

This complexity may reflect an unmediated judicial effort to apply the statutory phrase "principal place of business" in light of the general purpose of diversity jurisdiction, *i.e.*, an effort to find the State where a corporation is least likely to suffer out-of-state prejudice when it is sued in a local court. But, if so, that task seems doomed to failure. After all, the relevant purposive concern—prejudice against an out-of-state party—will often depend upon factors that courts cannot easily measure, for example, a corporation's image, its history, and its advertising, while the factors that courts can more easily measure, for example, its office or plant location, its sales, its employment, or the nature of the goods or services it supplies, will sometimes bear no more than a distant relation to the likelihood of prejudice. At the same time, this approach is at war with administrative simplicity. And it has failed to achieve a nationally uniform interpretation of federal law, an unfortunate consequence in a federal legal system.

V

A

In an effort to find a single, more uniform interpretation of the statutory phrase, we have reviewed the Courts of Appeals' divergent and increasingly complex interpretations. * * * We conclude that "principal place of business" is best read as referring to the place where a corporation's officers direct, control, and coordinate the corporation's activities. It is the place that Courts of Appeals have called the corporation's "nerve center." And in practice it should normally be the place where the corporation maintains its headquarters—provided that the headquarters is the actual center of direction, control, and coordination, *i.e.*, the "nerve center," and not simply an office where the corporation holds its board meetings (for example, attended by directors and officers who have traveled there for the occasion).

Three sets of considerations, taken together, convince us that this approach, while imperfect, is superior to other possibilities. First, the statute's language supports the approach. The statute's text deems a corporation a citizen of the "State where it has its principal place of business." 28 U.S.C. § 1332(c)(1). The word "place" is in the singular, not the plural. The word "principal" requires us to pick out the "main, prominent" or "leading" place. 12 Oxford English Dictionary 495 (2d ed. 1989) (def.(A)(I)(2)). And the fact that the word "place" follows the words "State where" means that the "place" is a place *within* a State. It is not the State itself.

A corporation's "nerve center," usually its main headquarters, is a single place. The public often (though not always) considers it the corporation's main place of business. And it is a place within a State. By contrast, the application of a more general business activities test has led some courts, as in the present case, to look, not at a particular place within a State, but incorrectly at the State itself, measuring the total amount of business activities that the corporation conducts there and determining whether they are "significantly larger" than in the next-ranking State.

This approach invites greater litigation and can lead to strange results * * *. Namely, if a "corporation may be deemed a citizen of California on th[e] basis" of "activities [that] roughly reflect California's larger population . . . nearly every national retailer—no matter how far flung its operations—will be deemed a citizen of California for diversity purposes." But why award or decline diversity jurisdiction on the basis of a State's population, whether measured directly, indirectly (say proportionately), or with modifications?

Second, administrative simplicity is a major virtue in a jurisdictional statute. Complex jurisdictional tests complicate a case, eating up time and money as the parties litigate, not the merits of their claims, but which court is the right court to decide those claims. Complex tests produce appeals and reversals, encourage gamesmanship, and, again, diminish the likelihood that results and settlements will reflect a claim's legal and factual merits. Judicial resources too are at stake. Courts have an independent obligation to determine whether subject-matter jurisdiction exists, even when no party challenges it. So courts benefit from straightforward rules under which they can readily assure themselves of their power to hear a case.

Simple jurisdictional rules also promote greater predictability. Predictability is valuable to corporations making business and investment decisions. Predictability also benefits plaintiffs deciding whether to file suit in a state or federal court.

A "nerve center" approach, which ordinarily equates that "center" with a corporation's headquarters, is simple to apply *comparatively speaking*. The metaphor of a corporate "brain," while not precise, suggests a single location. By contrast, a corporation's general business activities more often lack a single principal place where they take place. That is to say, the corporation may have several plants, many sales locations, and employees located in many different places. If so, it will not be as easy to determine which of these different business locales is the "principal" or most important "place."

Third, [the Court discusses the statute's legislative history, concluding that a "nerve center" test is consistent with such history but a "general business activities test" is not.]

B

We recognize that there may be no perfect test that satisfies all administrative and purposive criteria. We recognize as well that, under the "nerve center" test we adopt today, there will be hard cases. For example, in this era of telecommuting, some corporations may divide their command and coordinating functions among officers who work at several different locations, perhaps communicating over the internet. That said, our test nonetheless points courts in a single direction, towards the center of overall direction, control, and coordination. Courts do not have to try to weigh corporate functions, assets, or revenues different in kind, one from the other. Our approach provides a sensible test that is relatively easier to apply, not a test that will, in all instances, automatically generate a result.

We also recognize that the use of a "nerve center" test may in some cases produce results that seem to cut against the basic rationale for 28 U.S.C. § 1332. For example, if the bulk of a company's business activities visible to the public take place in New Jersey, while its top officers direct those activities just across the river in New York, the "principal place of business" is New York. One could argue that members of the public in New Jersey would be *less* likely to be prejudiced against the corporation than persons in New York—yet the corporation will still be entitled to remove a New Jersey state case to federal court. And note too that the same corporation would be unable to remove a New York state case to federal court, despite the New York public's presumed prejudice against the corporation.

We understand that such seeming anomalies will arise. However, in view of the necessity of having a clearer rule, we must accept them. Accepting occasionally counterintuitive results is the price the legal system must pay to avoid overly complex jurisdictional administration while producing the benefits that accompany a more uniform legal system.

The burden of persuasion for establishing diversity jurisdiction, of course, remains on the party asserting it. When challenged on allegations of jurisdictional facts, the parties must support their allegations by competent proof. * * * [I]f the record reveals attempts at manipulation—for example, that the alleged "nerve center" is nothing more than a mail drop box, a bare office with a computer, or the location of an annual executive retreat—the courts should instead take as the "nerve center" the place of actual direction, control, and coordination, in the absence of such manipulation.

VI

Petitioner's unchallenged declaration suggests that Hertz's center of direction, control, and coordination, its "nerve center," and its corporate headquarters are one and the same, and they are located in New Jersey, not in California. Because respondents should have a fair opportunity to litigate their case in light of our holding, however, we vacate the Ninth Circuit's judgment and remand the case for further proceedings consistent with this opinion.

It is so ordered.

NOTES AND QUESTIONS

1. In filing a lawsuit, the plaintiff makes the initial decision whether a case is brought in state or federal court. The defendant, however, can attempt to change that decision when certain requirements are met. If the case is initially brought in state court and the defendant believes that there is a basis for federal jurisdiction, the defendant can "remove," or transfer, the case to federal court. The plaintiff can then challenge the removal by filing a "motion to remand" the case to state court. That motion is decided by the federal court.

2. Diversity jurisdiction was established because of fears of local bias against out-of-state parties. One court has explained this justification as follows:

> The primary purpose of the diversity statute is to avoid prejudice against "outsiders." [Parties] who have minimal contact with the public in a particular state are not likely to be recognized as "locals." The Congress that provided for diversity jurisdiction was concerned that a local jury sitting in state court might exhibit bias in favor of a "local" party who was suing an out-of-state party. Because federal courts draw from a wider jury pool, removal to federal court, so the theory goes, provides a more neutral forum. In contrast, parties who have a great deal of contact with the public in a particular state are not likely to be considered outsiders and, therefore, are not likely to be victims of discrimination by "local" jurors sitting in state court.

Ho v. Ikon Office Solutions, Inc., 143 F. Supp. 2d 1163, 1164 (N.D. Cal. 2001). In addition, the Supreme Court has observed that "federal judges appointed for life are more likely to enforce the constitutional rights of unpopular minorities than elected state judges" because they do not have to worry about pleasing their constituents. *England v. La. State Bd. of Med. Exam'rs*, 375 U.S. 411, 427 (1964).

3. When a defendant removes a case from state court to federal court, myriad requirements must be met. As noted in the introduction, there must be "complete diversity," and the jurisdictional amount must be satisfied. Also, a defendant has only a limited (30-day) period to remove. In addition, the removal must be to the federal court in the district where the state court is located. 28 U.S.C. § 1441(a). Some additional requirements are: (1) all properly joined and served defendants must join in or consent to the removal (28 U.S.C. § 1446(b)(2)(A)); (2) the case cannot be removed if any defendant is a citizen of the state where the action was brought (28 U.S.C. § 1441(b)(2)); and (3) if the grounds for removal emerge later in the litigation (and not when the case was filed), removal is not permitted more than one year after the case was commenced (unless the plaintiff deliberately withheld information that would

have allowed an earlier removal) (28 U.S.C. §§ 1446(c)(1) & (c)(3)(B)). For a concise survey of issues that can arise in the diversity context, *see* MARY KAY KANE, CIVIL PROCEDURE IN A NUTSHELL 13–39 (7th ed. 2013).

4.   Some commentators have questioned whether the concerns underlying diversity jurisdiction are still relevant today. *See, e.g.,* Larry Kramer, *Diversity Jurisdiction*, 1990 BYU L. Rev. 97 (1990) (arguing that diversity jurisdiction should be all but eliminated, in part because diversity suits have overloaded the federal court system, but suggesting exceptions to the general elimination of diversity jurisdiction, including suits involving aliens and complex multistate litigation); Elmo Hunter, *Federal Diversity Jurisdiction: The Unnecessary Precaution*, 46 UMKC L. Rev. 347, 349 (1978) (noting that "[w]hatever prejudice as may have existed in 1789 today is acknowledged to be minimal or nonexistent" because most Americans travel between states during their lifetimes and state courts generally adjudicate cases objectively); Felix Frankfurter, *Distribution of Judicial Power Between United States and State Courts*, 13 Cornell L. Q. 499 (1928) (asserting that a decline in state patriotism and a rise in national unity has eliminated the bias rationale underlying diversity jurisdiction). Other commentators believe that the historical purposes for diversity jurisdiction are still valid today. *See, e.g.,* F. Andrew Hessick, *Cases, Controversies, and Diversity*, 109 Nw. U. L. Rev. 57 (2014) (arguing that diversity jurisdiction is still necessary because of state court bias).

5.   Why did it matter in *Hertz* where Hertz's principal place of business was located? What did Hertz argue was its principal place of business? What was plaintiffs' argument?

6.   What did the Supreme Court hold in *Hertz*? What test did the Supreme Court adopt for determining a corporation's principal place of business?

7.   For further reading on *Hertz*, its background, and its implications, *see, e.g.,* Case Note, *Corporate Citizenship*, 124 Harv. L. Rev. 309 (2010) (characterizing *Hertz* as a rule-based holding and noting that the use of clear rules, rather than flexible standards, results in additional clarity but sacrifices fairness because rules do not allow for the consideration of individual circumstances); Michael Chaplin, *Resolving the Principal Place of Business Conundrum: Adopting a Single Test for Federal Diversity Jurisdiction*, 30 Rev. Litig. 75 (2010) (examining the consequences of *Hertz* and concluding that, although the new test generally clarifies the jurisdiction issue, the approach will be difficult to apply when corporations divide their important management functions between multiple locations in different states).

ii.   Choice of Law

An important question that arises in cases based on diversity jurisdiction is whether, on various issues, state law should apply (because the case involves state-law claims) or whether federal law should apply (because the case is in federal court). This section addresses the choice-of-law issues that can arise under diversity jurisdiction. The featured case, *Walker v. Armco Steel Corp.*, discusses several landmark Supreme Court cases, including *Erie Railroad Co. v. Tompkins.*

WALKER V. ARMCO STEEL CORP.

Supreme Court of the United States, 1980
446 U.S. 740

JUSTICE MARSHALL delivered the opinion of the Court.

This case presents the issue whether in a diversity action the federal court should follow state law or, alternatively, Rule 3 of the Federal Rules of Civil Procedure in determining when an action is commenced for the purpose of tolling [suspending the running of] the state statute of limitations.

I

According to the allegations of the complaint, petitioner, a carpenter, was injured on August 22, 1975, in Oklahoma City, Okla., while pounding a Sheffield nail into a cement wall. Respondent was the manufacturer of the nail. Petitioner claimed that the nail contained a defect which caused its head to shatter and strike him in the right eye, resulting in permanent injuries. The defect was allegedly caused by respondent's negligence in manufacture and design.

Petitioner is a resident of Oklahoma, and respondent is a foreign corporation having its principal place of business in a State other than Oklahoma. Since there was diversity of citizenship, petitioner brought suit in the United States District Court for the Western District of Oklahoma. The complaint was filed on August 19, 1977. Although summons was issued that same day, service of process was not made on respondent's authorized service agent until December 1, 1977. On January 5, 1978, respondent filed a motion to dismiss the complaint on the ground that the action was barred by the applicable Oklahoma statute of limitations. Although the complaint had been filed within the 2-year statute of limitations, state law does not deem the action "commenced" for purposes of the statute of limitations until service of the summons on the defendant, Okla. Stat., Tit. 12, § 97 (1971). If the complaint is filed within the limitations period, however, the action is deemed to have commenced from that date of filing if the plaintiff serves the defendant within 60 days, even though that service may occur outside the limitations period. *Id.* In this case, service was not effectuated until long after this 60-day period had expired. Petitioner in his reply brief to the motion to dismiss admitted that his case would be foreclosed in state court, but he argued that Rule 3 of the Federal Rules of Civil Procedure governs the manner in which an action is commenced in federal court for all purposes, including the tolling of the state statute of limitations.

The District Court dismissed the complaint as barred by the Oklahoma statute of limitations. The court concluded that Tit. 12, § 97 was "an integral part of the Oklahoma statute of limitations," and therefore, under *Ragan v. Merchants Transfer & Warehouse Co.*, 337 U.S. 530 (1949), state law applied. The court rejected the argument that *Ragan* had been implicitly overruled in *Hanna v. Plumer*, 380 U.S. 460 (1965).

The United States Court of Appeals for the Tenth Circuit affirmed. That court concluded that Tit. 12, § 97 was in "direct conflict" with Rule 3. However, the Oklahoma statute was "indistinguishable" from the statute involved in *Ragan*, and the court felt itself "constrained" to follow *Ragan*.

We granted certiorari * * *. We now affirm.

II

The question whether state or federal law should apply on various issues arising in an action based on state law which has been brought in federal court under diversity of citizenship jurisdiction has troubled this Court for many years. In the landmark decision of *Erie Railroad Co. v. Tompkins*, 304 U.S. 64 (1938), we overturned the rule expressed in *Swift v. Tyson*, 16 Pet. 1, 10 L. Ed. 865 (1842), that federal courts exercising diversity jurisdiction need not, in matters of "general jurisprudence," apply the nonstatutory law of the State. The Court noted that "[d]iversity of citizenship jurisdiction was conferred in order to prevent apprehended discrimination in state courts against those not citizens of the State," *Erie R.R. Co. v. Tompkins, supra*. The doctrine of *Swift v. Tyson* had led to the undesirable results of discrimination in favor of noncitizens, prevention of uniformity in the administration of state law, and forum shopping. In response, we established the rule that "[e]xcept in matters governed by the Federal Constitution or by Acts of Congress, the law to be applied in any [diversity] case is the law of the State."

In *Guaranty Trust Co. v. York*, 326 U.S. 99 (1945), we addressed ourselves to "the narrow question whether, when no recovery could be had in a State court because the action is barred by the statute of limitations, a federal court in equity can take cognizance of the suit because there is diversity of citizenship between the parties." The Court held that the *Erie* doctrine applied to suits in equity as well as to actions at law. In construing *Erie* we noted that "[i]n essence, the intent of that decision was to insure that, in all cases where a federal court is exercising jurisdiction solely because of the diversity of citizenship of the parties, the outcome of the litigation in the federal court should be substantially the same, so far as legal rules determine the outcome of a litigation, as it would be if tried in a State court." We concluded that the state statute of limitations should be applied. "Plainly enough, a statute that would completely bar recovery in a suit if brought in a State court bears on a State-created right vitally and not merely formally or negligibly. As to consequences that so intimately affect recovery or non-recovery a federal court in a diversity case should follow State law."

The decision in *York* led logically to our holding in *Ragan v. Merchants Transfer & Warehouse Co.* In *Ragan*, the plaintiff had filed his complaint in federal court on September 4, 1945, pursuant to Rule 3 of the Federal Rules of Civil Procedure. The accident from which the claim arose had occurred on October 1, 1943. Service was made on the defendant on December 28, 1945. The applicable statute of limitations supplied by Kansas law was two years. Kansas had an additional statute which provided: "An action shall be deemed commenced within the meaning of [the statute of limitations], as to each defendant, at the date of the summons which is served on him. . . . An attempt to commence an action shall be deemed equivalent to the commencement thereof within the meaning of this article when the party faithfully, properly and diligently endeavors to procure a service; but such attempt must be followed by the first publication or service of the summons within sixty days." Kan. Gen. Stat. § 60–308 (1935). The defendant moved for summary judgment on the ground that the Kansas statute of limitations barred the action since service had not been made within either the 2-year period or the 60-day period. It was conceded that had the case been brought in Kansas state court it would have been barred. Nonetheless, the District Court held that the statute had been tolled by the filing of the complaint. The Court of Appeals reversed because "the requirement of service of summons within the statutory period was an integral part of that state's statute of limitations."

We affirmed, relying on *Erie* and *York*. "We cannot give [the cause of action] longer life in the federal court than it would have had in the state court without adding something to the cause of action. We may not do that consistently with *Erie Railroad Co. v. Tompkins*." We rejected the argument that Rule 3 of the Federal Rules of Civil Procedure governed the manner in which an action was commenced in federal court for purposes of tolling the state statute of limitations. Instead, we held that the service of summons statute controlled because it was an integral part of the state statute of limitations, and under *York* that statute of limitations was part of the state-law cause of action.

Ragan was not our last pronouncement in this difficult area, however. In 1965 we decided *Hanna v. Plumer*, holding that in a civil action where federal jurisdiction was based upon diversity of citizenship, Rule 4(d)(1) of the Federal Rules of Civil Procedure, rather than state law, governed the manner in which process was served. Massachusetts law required in-hand service on an executor or administrator of an estate, whereas Rule 4 permits service by leaving copies of the summons and complaint at the defendant's home with some person "of suitable age and discretion." The Court noted that in the absence of a conflicting state procedure, the Federal

Rule would plainly control. We stated that the "outcome-determination" test of *Erie* and *York* had to be read with reference to the "twin aims" of *Erie*: "discouragement of forum-shopping and avoidance of inequitable administration of the laws." We determined that the choice between the state in-hand service rule and the Federal Rule "would be of scant, if any, relevance to the choice of a forum," for the plaintiff "was not presented with a situation where application of the state rule would wholly bar recovery; rather, adherence to the state rule would have resulted only in altering the way in which process was served." This factor served to distinguish that case from *York* and *Ragan*.

The Court in *Hanna*, however, pointed out "a more fundamental flaw" in the defendant's argument in that case. The Court concluded that the *Erie* doctrine was simply not the appropriate test of the validity and applicability of one of the Federal Rules of Civil Procedure:

> The *Erie* rule has never been invoked to void a Federal Rule. It is true that there have been cases where this Court had held applicable a state rule in the face of an argument that the situation was governed by one of the Federal Rules. But the holding of each such case was not that *Erie* commanded displacement of a Federal Rule by an inconsistent state rule, but rather that the scope of the Federal Rule was not as broad as the losing party urged, and therefore, there being no Federal Rule which covered the point in dispute, *Erie* commanded the enforcement of state law.

The Court cited *Ragan* as one of the examples of this proposition. The Court explained that where the Federal Rule was clearly applicable, as in *Hanna*, the test was whether the Rule was within the scope of the Rules Enabling Act, 28 U.S.C. § 2072, and if so, within a constitutional grant of power such as the Necessary and Proper Clause of Art. I.

III

The present case is indistinguishable from *Ragan*. The statutes in both cases require service of process to toll the statute of limitations, and in fact the predecessor to the Oklahoma statute in this case was derived from the predecessor to the Kansas statute in *Ragan*. Here, as in *Ragan*, the complaint was filed in federal court under diversity jurisdiction within the 2-year statute of limitations, but service of process did not occur until after the 2-year period and the 60-day service period had run. In both cases the suit would concededly have been barred in the applicable state court, and in both instances the state service statute was held to be an integral part of the statute of limitations by the lower court more familiar than we with state law. Accordingly, as the Court of Appeals held below, the instant action is barred by the statute of limitations unless *Ragan* is no longer good law.

Petitioner argues that the analysis and holding of *Ragan* did not survive our decision in *Hanna*. Petitioner's position is that Tit. 12, § 97 is in direct conflict with the Federal Rule. Under *Hanna*, petitioner contends, the appropriate question is whether Rule 3 is within the scope of the Rules Enabling Act and, if so, within the constitutional power of Congress. In petitioner's view, the Federal Rule is to be applied unless it violates one of those two restrictions. This argument ignores both the force of *stare decisis* and the specific limitations that we carefully placed on the *Hanna* analysis.

* * *

This Court in *Hanna* distinguished *Ragan* rather than overruled it, and for good reason. Application of the *Hanna* analysis is premised on a "direct collision" between the Federal Rule and the state law. In *Hanna* itself the "clash" between Rule 4(d)(1) and the state in-hand service requirement was "unavoidable."

The first question must therefore be whether the scope of the Federal Rule in fact is sufficiently broad to control the issue before the Court. It is only if that question is answered affirmatively that the *Hanna* analysis applies.[9]

As has already been noted, we recognized in *Hanna* that the present case is an instance where "the scope of the Federal Rule [is] not as broad as the losing party urge[s], and therefore, there being no Federal Rule which cover[s] the point in dispute, *Erie* command[s] the enforcement of state law." Rule 3 simply states that "[a] civil action is commenced by filing a complaint with the court." There is no indication that the Rule was intended to toll a state statute of limitations, much less that it purported to displace state tolling rules for purposes of state statutes of limitations. In our view, in diversity actions Rule 3 governs the date from which various timing requirements of the Federal Rules begin to run, but does not affect state statutes of limitations.

In contrast to Rule 3, the Oklahoma statute is a statement of a substantive decision by that State that actual service on, and accordingly actual notice by, the defendant is an integral part of the several policies served by the statute of limitations. The statute of limitations establishes a deadline after which the defendant may legitimately have peace of mind; it also recognizes that after a certain period of time it is unfair to require the defendant to attempt to piece together his defense to an old claim. A requirement of actual service promotes both of those functions of the statute. It is these policy aspects which make the service requirement an "integral" part of the statute of limitations both in this case and in *Ragan*. As such, the service rule must be considered part and parcel of the statute

---

[9]   This is not to suggest that the Federal Rules of Civil Procedure are to be narrowly construed in order to avoid a "direct collision" with state law. The Federal Rules should be given their plain meaning. If a direct collision with state law arises from that plain meaning, then the analysis developed in *Hanna v. Plumer* applies.

of limitations. Rule 3 does not replace such policy determinations found in state law. Rule 3 and Tit. 12, § 97 can exist side by side, therefore, each controlling its own intended sphere of coverage without conflict.

Since there is no direct conflict between the Federal Rule and the state law, the *Hanna* analysis does not apply. Instead, the policies behind *Erie* and *Ragan* control the issue whether, in the absence of a federal rule directly on point, state service requirements which are an integral part of the state statute of limitations should control in an action based on state law which is filed in federal court under diversity jurisdiction. The reasons for the application of such a state service requirement in a diversity action in the absence of a conflicting federal rule are well explained in *Erie* and *Ragan*, and need not be repeated here. It is sufficient to note that although in this case failure to apply the state service law might not create any problem of forum shopping,[15] the result would be an "inequitable administration" of the law. There is simply no reason why, in the absence of a controlling federal rule, an action based on state law which concededly would be barred in the state courts by the state statute of limitations should proceed through litigation to judgment in federal court solely because of the fortuity that there is diversity of citizenship between the litigants. The policies underlying diversity jurisdiction do not support such a distinction between state and federal plaintiffs, and *Erie* and its progeny do not permit it.

The judgment of the Court of Appeals is

Affirmed.

NOTES AND QUESTIONS

1.   When a federal court hears a case as a result of diversity jurisdiction, how does the court determine what law applies to questions going to substance? How does the court determine what law applies to questions of procedure? What law did the Supreme Court apply in *Walker*? Why did the decision of which law to apply matter in the case?

2.   As in *Walker*, choice of law will often determine whether plaintiffs can bring a claim at all. For example, in *Shady Grove Orthopedic Associates, P.A. v. Allstate Insurance Co.*, 559 U.S. 393 (2010), a medical provider brought a class action against an insurance company in New York federal court based on diversity. Plaintiff alleged that the insurance company routinely refused to pay interest on its overdue payments. The district court dismissed the case for lack of jurisdiction based on a provision of New York state law prohibiting class actions seeking only penalties. Despite Federal Rule of Civil Procedure 23, which allows for class actions (*i.e.*, representative suits on behalf of a group of similarly situated people), the district court concluded that the New York state

---

[15]   There is no indication that when petitioner filed his suit in federal court he had any reason to believe that he would be unable to comply with the service requirements of Oklahoma law or that he chose to sue in federal court in an attempt to avoid those service requirements.

provision applied in federal court. Thus, the case, which sought only tax penalties, could not proceed. On appeal, the Second Circuit affirmed, holding that the New York provision applied because it did not conflict with Rule 23. The Supreme Court reversed, holding that the two laws *did* conflict because both addressed whether a claim could be brought as a class action. Because the laws were in conflict, the Supreme Court held that the New York statute did not apply in federal court and remanded the case for further proceedings.

3.   For further reading on diversity jurisdiction and choice of law, *see, e.g.*, Kevin Clermont, *The Repressible Myth of* Shady Grove, 86 Notre Dame L. Rev. 987 (2011) (analyzing the development of the *Erie* doctrine and concluding that *Shady Grove* added little, but clarified the doctrine); Adam Steinman, *What Is the* Erie *Doctrine? (and What Does It Mean for the Contemporary Politics of Judicial Federalism?)*, 84 Notre Dame L. Rev. 245 (2008) (arguing that state summary judgment, class certification, and pleading rules should apply in federal court because those rules directly impact a litigant's ability to bring a substantive claim and because differences between state and federal court promote forum shopping).

D. VENUE

"Venue," a concept that is distinct from jurisdiction, focuses on the proper place for a lawsuit to be heard. As with other parts of this chapter, this section focuses on venue in federal district court. Venue issues also arise in state court, however. Depending on the case, the proper venue may be where the litigants live, where the events underlying the claim took place, where witnesses and evidence are located, or perhaps even some other location agreed to by the litigants. The general venue statute is 28 U.S.C. § 1391, but other statutes address venue in particular circumstances. Like personal jurisdiction, but unlike subject matter jurisdiction, venue can be waived. In many instances, venue may exist in more than one federal district court. Thus, it is often the case that a party will seek to transfer a case from one proper venue to another under 28 U.S.C. § 1404 "[f]or the convenience of parties and witnesses, in the interest of justice * * *." When a district court does not have proper venue, it still has authority to transfer a case (as an alternative to dismissal) under 28 U.S.C. § 1406.

The following case from the U.S. Court of Appeals for the Fifth Circuit discusses venue under 28 U.S.C. § 1391 and a request to transfer under 28 U.S.C. § 1404. The district court denied the request to transfer, an order that is not normally appealable. Thus, the Fifth Circuit addressed "mandamus," which, among other things, allows appellate court review of non-final orders in extraordinary circumstances.

IN RE VOLKSWAGEN OF AMERICA, INC.
United States Court of Appeals, Fifth Circuit En Banc, 2008
545 F.3d 304

JOLLY, CIRCUIT JUDGE.

The overarching question before the *en banc* Court is whether a writ of mandamus should issue directing the transfer of this case from the Marshall Division of the Eastern District of Texas * * * to the Dallas Division of the Northern District of Texas * * *. We grant the petition and direct the district court to transfer this case to the Dallas Division.

I.

A.

On the morning of May 21, 2005, a Volkswagen Golf automobile traveling on a freeway in Dallas, Texas, was struck from behind and propelled rear-first into a flat-bed trailer parked on the shoulder of the freeway. Ruth Singleton was driving the Volkswagen Golf. Richard Singleton was a passenger. And Mariana Singleton, Richard and Ruth Singleton's seven-year-old granddaughter, was also a passenger. Richard Singleton was seriously injured in the accident. Mariana Singleton was also seriously injured in the accident, and she later died as a result of her injuries.

Richard Singleton, Ruth Singleton, and Amy Singleton (Mariana's mother) filed suit against Volkswagen AG and Volkswagen of America, Inc., in the Marshall Division of the Eastern District of Texas, alleging that design defects in the Volkswagen Golf caused Richard's injuries and Mariana's death.

In response to the Singletons' suit, Volkswagen filed a third-party complaint against the driver of the automobile that struck the Singletons, alleging that the Singletons had the ability to sue him but did not and that his negligence was the only proximate cause of the damages.

B.

Pursuant to 28 U.S.C. § 1404(a),[1] Volkswagen moved to transfer venue to the Dallas Division. Volkswagen asserted that a transfer was warranted as the Volkswagen Golf was purchased in Dallas County, Texas; the accident occurred on a freeway in Dallas, Texas; Dallas residents witnessed the accident; Dallas police and paramedics responded and took action; a Dallas doctor performed the autopsy; the third-party defendant lives in Dallas County, Texas; none of the plaintiffs live in the Marshall Division; no known party or non-party witness lives in the Marshall Division; no known source of proof is located in the Marshall Division; and none of the

---

[1] Section 1404(a) provides: "For the convenience of parties and witnesses, in the interest of justice, a district court may transfer any civil action to any other district or division where it might have been brought."

facts giving rise to this suit occurred in the Marshall Division. These facts are undisputed.

The district court denied Volkswagen's transfer motion [and later denied reconsideration]. * * *

C.

Volkswagen then petitioned this Court for a writ of mandamus [a writ ordering the lower court to correct a clear violation of law]. * * * [A] divided panel of this Court denied the petition and declined to issue a writ. The panel majority held that the district court did not clearly abuse its discretion in denying Volkswagen's transfer motion. * * *

Volkswagen then filed a petition for rehearing. * * * [A] panel granted Volkswagen's petition and issued a writ directing the district court to transfer this case to the Dallas Division.

The Singletons then filed a petition for rehearing *en banc*, which the Court * * * [now rules on].

II.

In this opinion, we will first address whether mandamus is an appropriate means to test a district court's ruling on a venue transfer motion. * * *

III.

* * *

Although the Supreme Court has never decided mandamus in the context of § 1404(a), the Supreme Court holds that mandamus is an appropriate remedy for "exceptional circumstances amounting to a judicial usurpation of power or a clear abuse of discretion." Thus, the specific standard that we apply here is that mandamus will be granted upon a determination that there has been a clear abuse of discretion.

* * *

IV.

Because the writ is an extraordinary remedy, the Supreme Court has established three requirements that must be met before a writ may issue: (1) "the party seeking issuance of the writ [must] have no other adequate means to attain the relief he desires * * * "; (2) "the petitioner must [show] that [his] right to issuance of the writ is clear and indisputable"; and (3) " * * * the issuing court, in the exercise of its discretion, [must be] satisfied that the writ is appropriate under the circumstances." *Cheney v. U.S. Dist. Ct.*, 542 U.S. 367 (2004). * * *

* * * We shall first address the second requirement because it captures the essence of the disputed issue presented in this petition.

A.

The second requirement is that the petitioner must have a clear and indisputable right to issuance of the writ. If the district court clearly abused its discretion * * * in denying Volkswagen's transfer motion, then Volkswagen's right to issuance of the writ is necessarily clear and indisputable.

* * *

* * * We therefore turn to examine the district court's exercise of its discretion in denying Volkswagen's transfer motion.

1.

The preliminary question under § 1404(a) is whether a civil action "might have been brought" in the destination venue. Volkswagen seeks to transfer this case to the Dallas Division of the Northern District of Texas. All agree that this civil action originally could have been filed in the Dallas Division.

2.

Beyond this preliminary and undisputed question, the parties sharply disagree. * * *

(a)

When no special, restrictive venue statute applies, the general venue statute, 28 U.S.C. § 1391, controls a plaintiff's choice of venue. Under § 1391(a)(1), a diversity action may be brought in "a judicial district where any defendant resides, if all defendants reside in the same State." Under § 1391(c), when a suit is filed in a multi-district state, like Texas, a corporation is "deemed to reside in any district in that State within which its contacts would be sufficient to subject it to personal jurisdiction if that district were a separate State." Because large corporations, like Volkswagen, often have sufficient contacts to satisfy the requirement of § 1391(c) for most, if not all, federal venues, the general venue statute "has the effect of nearly eliminating venue restrictions in suits against corporations."

Congress, however, has tempered the effects of this general venue statute by enacting the venue transfer statute, 28 U.S.C. § 1404. The underlying premise of § 1404(a) is that courts should prevent plaintiffs from abusing their privilege under § 1391 by subjecting defendants to venues that are inconvenient * * *. Thus, while a plaintiff has the privilege of filing his claims in any judicial division appropriate under the general venue statute, § 1404(a) tempers the effects of the exercise of this privilege.

(b)

With this understanding of the competing statutory interests, we turn to the legal precedents. We first turn to *Gulf Oil Corp. v. Gilbert*, 330 U.S.

501 (1947), because of its historic and precedential importance to § 1404(a), even today.

In 1947, in *Gilbert*, the Supreme Court firmly established in the federal courts the common-law doctrine of *forum non conveniens*. The essence of the *forum non conveniens* doctrine is that a court may decline jurisdiction and may actually dismiss a case, even when the case is properly before the court, if the case more conveniently could be tried in another forum.

Shortly after the *Gilbert* decision, in 1948, the venue transfer statute became effective. The essential difference between the *forum non conveniens* doctrine and § 1404(a) is that under § 1404(a) a court does not have authority to dismiss the case; the remedy under the statute is simply a transfer of the case within the federal system to another federal venue more convenient to the parties, the witnesses, and the trial of the case. Thus, * * * "Congress, by the term 'for the convenience of parties and witnesses, in the interest of justice,' intended to permit courts to grant transfers upon a lesser showing of inconvenience."[8]

That § 1404(a) venue transfers may be granted "upon a lesser showing of inconvenience" than *forum non conveniens* dismissals * * * impl[ies] that the burden that a moving party must meet to justify a venue transfer is less demanding than that a moving party must meet to warrant a *forum non conveniens* dismissal. And we have recognized as much, noting that the "heavy *burden* traditionally imposed upon defendants by the *forum non conveniens* doctrine—dismissal permitted only in favor of a substantially more convenient alternative—was dropped in the § 1404(a) context. In order to obtain a new federal [venue], the statute requires only that the transfer be '[f]or the convenience of the parties, in the interest of justice.'" Thus, the district court, [which required] Volkswagen to show that the § 1404(a) factors must substantially outweigh the plaintiffs' choice of venue, erred by applying the stricter *forum non conveniens* dismissal standard and thus giving inordinate weight to the plaintiffs' choice of venue.

As to the appropriate standard, * * * "he who seeks the transfer must show good cause." * * * When viewed in the context of § 1404(a), to show good cause means that a moving party, in order to support its claim for a transfer, must satisfy the statutory requirements and clearly demonstrate that a transfer is "[f]or the convenience of parties and witnesses, in the interest of justice." * * * When the movant demonstrates that the transferee venue is clearly more convenient, * * * it has shown good cause and the district court should therefore grant the transfer.

---

[8]   The district courts are permitted to grant transfers upon a lesser showing of inconvenience under § 1404(a) because § 1404(a) venue transfers do not have the serious consequences of *forum non conveniens* dismissals.

3.

We thus turn to examine the showing that Volkswagen made under § 1404(a) * * *.

* * * [W]e have adopted the private and public interest factors first enunciated in *Gilbert*, a *forum non conveniens* case, as appropriate for the determination of whether a § 1404(a) venue transfer is for the convenience of parties and witnesses and in the interest of justice.

The private interest factors are: "(1) the relative ease of access to sources of proof; (2) the availability of compulsory process to secure the attendance of witnesses; (3) the cost of attendance for willing witnesses; and (4) all other practical problems that make trial of a case easy, expeditious and inexpensive." The public interest factors are: "(1) the administrative difficulties flowing from court congestion; (2) the local interest in having localized interests decided at home; (3) the familiarity of the forum with the law that will govern the case; and (4) the avoidance of unnecessary problems of conflict of laws [or in] the application of foreign law."

* * * [T]he *Gilbert* factors * * * are not necessarily exhaustive or exclusive. Moreover, we have noted that "none . . . can be said to be of dispositive weight."

(a)

Before the district court, Volkswagen asserted that a transfer was warranted because: (1) the relative ease of access to sources of proof favors transfer as all of the documents and physical evidence relating to the accident are located in the Dallas Division, as is the collision site; (2) the availability of compulsory process favors transfer as the Marshall Division does not have absolute subpoena power over the non-party witnesses; (3) the cost of attendance for willing witnesses factor favors transfer as the Dallas Division is more convenient for all relevant witnesses; and (4) the local interest in having localized interests decided at home favors transfer as the Volkswagen Golf was purchased in Dallas County, Texas; the accident occurred on a freeway in Dallas, Texas; Dallas residents witnessed the accident; Dallas police and paramedics responded and took action; a Dallas doctor performed the autopsy; the third-party defendant lives in Dallas County, Texas; none of the plaintiffs live in the Marshall Division; no known party or non-party witness lives in the Marshall Division; no known source of proof is located in the Marshall Division; and none of the facts giving rise to this suit occurred in the Marshall Division.

(b)

Applying the *Gilbert* factors, however, the district court concluded that: (1) the relative ease of access to sources of proof is neutral because of advances in copying technology and information storage; (2) the availability of compulsory process is neutral because, despite its lack of absolute subpoena power, the district court could deny any motion to quash and ultimately compel the attendance of third-party witnesses found in Texas; (3) the cost of attendance for willing witnesses is neutral because Volkswagen did not designate "key" witnesses and because, given the proximity of Dallas to the Marshall Division, the cost of having witnesses attend a trial in Marshall would be minimal; and (4) the local interest in having localized interests decided at home factor is neutral because, although the accident occurred in Dallas, Texas, the citizens of Marshall, Texas, "would be interested to know whether there are defective products offered for sale in close proximity to the Marshall Division." Based on this analysis, the district court concluded that Volkswagen "has not satisfied its burden of showing that the balance of convenience and justice weighs in favor of transfer."

(c)

We consider first the private interest factor concerning the relative ease of access to sources of proof. Here, the district court's approach reads the sources of proof requirement out of the § 1404(a) analysis * * *. That access to some sources of proof presents a lesser inconvenience now than it might have absent recent developments does not render this factor superfluous. All of the documents and physical evidence relating to the accident are located in the Dallas Division, as is the collision site. Thus, the district court erred in applying this factor * * *.

The second private interest factor is the availability of compulsory process to secure the attendance of witnesses. * * * [T]he non-party witnesses located in the city where the collision occurred "are outside the Eastern District's subpoena power for deposition under Fed. R. Civ. P. 45(c)(3)(A)(ii)," and any "trial subpoenas for these witnesses to travel more than 100 miles would be subject to motions to quash under Fed. R. Civ. P. 45(c)(3)." Moreover, a proper venue that does enjoy *absolute* subpoena power for both depositions and trial—the Dallas Division—is available. * * * [T]hat a district court can deny any motions to quash does not address concerns regarding the convenience of parties and witnesses. Thus, the district court erred in applying this factor * * *.

The third private interest factor is the cost of attendance for willing witnesses. Volkswagen has submitted a list of potential witnesses that included the third-party defendant, accident witnesses, accident investigators, treating medical personnel, and the medical examiner—all of whom reside in Dallas County or in the Dallas area. Volkswagen also has submitted two affidavits, one from an accident witness and the other from the accident investigator, that stated that traveling to the Marshall Division would be inconvenient. Volkswagen also asserts that the testimony of these witnesses, including an accident witness and an accident investigator, is critical to determining causation and liability in this case.

In [prior case law,] we set a 100-mile threshold as follows: "When the distance between an existing venue for trial of a matter and a proposed venue under § 1404(a) is more than 100 miles, the factor of inconvenience to witnesses increases in direct relationship to the additional distance to be traveled." We said, further, that it is an "obvious conclusion" that it is more convenient for witnesses to testify at home and that "[a]dditional distance means additional travel time; additional travel time increases the probability for meal and lodging expenses; and additional travel time with overnight stays increases the time which these fact witnesses must be away from their regular employment." The district court disregarded our precedent relating to the 100-mile rule. As to the witnesses * * *, it is apparent that it would be more convenient for them if this case is tried in the Dallas Division, as the Marshall Division is 155 miles from Dallas. Witnesses not only suffer monetary costs, but also the personal costs associated with being away from work, family, and community. Moreover, the plaintiffs, Richard Singleton and Ruth Singleton, also currently reside in the Dallas Division (Amy Singleton resides in Kansas). The Singletons have not argued that a trial in the Dallas Division would be inconvenient to them; they actually have conceded that the Dallas Division would be a convenient venue. The district court erred in applying this factor * * *.

The only contested public interest factor is the local interest in having localized interests decided at home. Here, * * * again, this factor weighs heavily in favor of transfer: the accident occurred in the Dallas Division, the witnesses to the accident live and are employed in the Dallas Division, Dallas police and paramedics responded and took action, the Volkswagen Golf was purchased in Dallas County, the wreckage and all other evidence are located in Dallas County, two of the three plaintiffs live in the Dallas Division (the third lives in Kansas), not one of the plaintiffs has ever lived in the Marshall Division, and the third-party defendant lives in the Dallas Division. In short, there is no relevant factual connection to the Marshall Division.

Furthermore, the district court's provided rationale—that the citizens of Marshall have an interest in this product liability case because the product is available in Marshall, and that for this reason jury duty would be no burden—stretches logic in a manner that eviscerates the public interest that this factor attempts to capture. The district court's provided rationale could apply virtually to any judicial district or division in the United States * * *. In contrast [to the residents of the Marshall Division], the residents of the Dallas Division have extensive connections with the events that gave rise to this suit. Thus, the district court erred in applying this factor * * *.

4.

* * * The remaining question as to [the] second [mandamus] requirement is whether the errors we have noted warrant mandamus relief * * *. The errors of the district court * * * were extraordinary errors. Indeed, "[t]he only connection between this case and the Eastern District of Texas is plaintiffs' choice to file there."

In the light of the above, we hold that the district court's errors resulted in a patently erroneous result. * * * [T]he second requirement * * * for granting a petition for a writ of mandamus is therefore satisfied.

B.

We now return to the first and the third [mandamus] requirements * * *.

The first requirement * * * is certainly satisfied here. * * * [A] petitioner "would not have an adequate remedy for an improper failure to transfer the case by way of an appeal from an adverse final judgment because [the petitioner] would not be able to show that it would have won the case had it been tried in a convenient [venue]." * * * And the harm inconvenience to witnesses, parties and other—will already have been done * * *.

As to the third requirement for granting * * * mandamus, we must assure ourselves that [mandamus relief] is appropriate in this case. We have addressed most of the reasons outlined above. * * * Further, writs of mandamus are supervisory in nature and are particularly appropriate when the issues also have an importance beyond the immediate case. Because venue transfer decisions are rarely reviewed, the district courts have developed their own tests, and they have applied these tests with too little regard for consistency of outcomes. Thus, * * * the issues presented and decided above have an importance beyond this case. * * *

We therefore conclude that all three of the *Cheney* requirements * * * are met in this case.

V.

Thus, * * * we grant Volkswagen's petition for a writ of mandamus. The Clerk of this Court shall * * * direct[ ] the district court to transfer this case to the United States District Court for the Northern District of Texas, Dallas Division.

KING, CIRCUIT JUDGE, with whom DAVIS, WIENER, BENAVIDES, STEWART, DENNIS, and PRADO, CIRCUIT JUDGES, join, dissenting:

* * *

Before getting into the majority's analysis and its flaws, it is important to describe the case actually presented to the district court. The majority notes briefly that this is a products liability case, but its entire opinion proceeds as if this were simply a case in which the victims of a Dallas traffic accident were suing the driver of the offending car. That is not this case. The Singletons' Volkswagen Golf was indeed hit on its left rear panel by Colin Little, spun around, and slid rear-first into a flat-bed trailer parked by the side of the road. Emergency personnel found an unconscious Richard Singleton in his fully reclined passenger seat with Mariana Singleton (who was seated directly behind him) trapped underneath. Mariana later died from the head trauma she received from the seat, and Richard was left paraplegic. The Singletons sued Volkswagen, alleging that the seat adjustment mechanism of Richard's seat was defectively designed, resulting in a collapse of the seat during the accident. Thus, the case before the district court is first and foremost a products liability, design defect case that will depend heavily on expert testimony from both the plaintiffs and Volkswagen. No claim is made by Volkswagen that any of its experts is Dallas-based, and whether this case is tried in Marshall or Dallas will make little, if any, difference—Volkswagen will be able to get its experts (from Germany or elsewhere) to trial regardless. The Dallas connections with the original accident become relevant if there is a finding of a design defect and the court turns to the third party action by Volkswagen against Colin Little, raising issues of causation and damages. Pretrial discovery and the trial itself will have to address those issues, but they are not the only, or even the primary, focus of this case. Finally, Little, the other party to the accident, has explicitly stated that the Eastern District is not an inconvenient forum for him.

The majority has correctly identified the three requirements for the issuance of a writ [of mandamus] * * *. Where we differ is in the application of *Cheney*'s three requirements. In particular, * * * the majority fundamentally misconstrues [the] second requirement * * *.

* * * [T]he majority states that Volkswagen's right is clear and indisputable if the district court clearly abused its discretion. * * * Because Volkswagen concedes that the district court considered all the proper § 1404(a) transfer factors and no improper ones, the majority must reweigh these factors in order to find [a clear abuse of discretion]. The majority's findings * * * do not bear close inspection.

The district court first allegedly erred because it assigned too much weight to the plaintiffs' choice of venue by applying the *forum non conveniens* dismissal standard. * * * For the majority, the district court's use of the word "substantially" indicates that it was requiring Volkswagen to make the showing necessary to obtain a *forum non conveniens* dismissal. But that is simply not the case. * * * [T]he district court drew upon several formulations common to the venue transfer context to describe the unremarkable notion that the party seeking transfer bears some heightened burden in demonstrating that a transfer is warranted. It did not apply the *forum non conveniens* dismissal standard.

Additionally under the plaintiff's choice analysis, the majority distorts the relationship between §§ 1391 and 1404. Congress has afforded plaintiffs a broad venue privilege in § 1391(a) and (c). And although aspersions are often cast on plaintiffs' "forum shopping," frequently by defendants also "forum shopping," we have explicitly stated that a plaintiff's motive for choosing a forum "is ordinarily of no moment * * *." Section 1404(a) does temper plaintiffs' broad statutory right in venue selection, but how Congress went about doing so is telling. Congress did not restrict the range of permissible venues available to plaintiffs * * *. Rather, § 1404(a) vests a district court with the authority to transfer a case in its discretion. Section 1404(a), therefore, is * * * a discretionary tool * * *. The majority's review of the plaintiffs' choice, then, is both misleading as to the facts and wrong on the law.

* * * [T]he majority * * * [also] fails to take account of the realities that surround a transfer decision and the realities in this particular case. Generally speaking, venue transfer motions are filed very early in the case. * * * At this early stage, assessing what best serves the "convenience of parties and witnesses" and "interests of justice" is hardly an exact science * * *. But the district court can draw on its experience with the day-to-day reality of litigation issues—an area in which appellate courts lack expertise. * * *

* * * The majority would have us believe that since this case involves only a Dallas traffic accident, Dallas is the only convenient location for the Singletons' suit. But, while the convenience inquiry may begin with listing this case's Dallas connections, it does not end there. First for the Dallas documents: * * * the district court considered the reality that the Northern and Eastern Districts have required ECF (electronic case filing) for a long time and that all the courtrooms are electronic. This means that the documents will be converted to electronic form, and whether they are displayed on monitors in Dallas or Marshall makes no difference to their availability. Secondly, the court's subpoena power runs throughout the state, and an experienced district court can properly discount the likelihood of an avalanche of motions to quash. * * * Thirdly, the Dallas witnesses will not likely be inconvenienced because (as Volkswagen recognizes) discovery will be, in all likelihood, conducted in Dallas. Additionally, witnesses necessary to establish damages for Mariana's wrongful death—her teachers, neighbors, and friends—all reside in the Eastern District (where the Singletons resided at the time of the accident). And the majority's "100-mile rule" is no proxy for considering the realistic costs and inconvenience for witnesses that will attend the trial, particularly in a state as expansive as Texas. As for the two non-party fact witnesses who submitted identical affidavits asserting inconvenience, if the case goes to trial and if they end up testifying (two very big "ifs," the district court was no doubt aware), the court could reasonably conclude that traveling 150 miles, or two hours on a four-lane interstate (I-20), each way is only minimally inconvenient. And

finally, with regard to the local interests factor, * * * [a] Dallas traffic accident may have triggered the events that revealed a possibly defective product, but that does not change the nature of this suit. Drivers in the Eastern District could be connected to the actual issues in this case as they may be interested to learn of a possibly defective product that they may be driving or that is on their roads. Thus, the majority's "careful review" under the § 1404(a) transfer factors is both erroneous * * * and misleading * * *.

Having identified [various] "errors" in the district court's § 1404(a) analysis, the majority moves on to declare the sum of these errors as a "clear abuse" justifying the writ * * *.

The majority moves on to *Cheney*'s remaining requirements. [Regarding the] first requirement, * * * [w]e are told * * * that direct appeal is effectively unavailable to address a possible error in a § 1404(a) transfer decision. That is flat wrong. Direct appeal is available to review a transfer decision [after an adverse final judgment] * * *. That such an appeal may have limited success due to the [difficulty in showing that the location of the trial affected the outcome] does not mean—here or anywhere else that I know of—that direct appeal is "unavailable." But it is telling that a refusal to transfer from Marshall to Dallas is unlikely, in the majority's view, to affect Volkswagen's substantial rights: if Volkswagen's substantial rights will not likely be affected, how can this case satisfy the * * * stringent requirements for mandamus?

The third *Cheney* requirement * * * is, for the majority, easily met. Because "[t]he district court clearly abused its discretion," "Volkswagen has no other adequate remedy," and "district courts . . . have applied [venue transfer tests] with too little regard for consistency of outcomes," the majority convinces itself that mandamus is appropriate and issues the writ.

* * * As the majority opinion seems to recognize, but then ignores, the Supreme Court has been explicit on repeated occasions that mandamus must not devolve into "interlocutory review of nonappealable orders on the mere ground that they may be erroneous."

* * *

In order to enable the majority to correct the district court's "errors" in applying § 1404(a), the majority misapplies the "clear abuse of discretion" standard provided by the Supreme Court by divorcing the standard from the context that gave it meaning. * * *

* * * There is no claim here that the district court did not have the judicial power to deny the transfer motion. The claim is that it erred in the judgment that it made when it exercised the power that it concededly has. That is not the basis for a writ.

* * *

Cheney describes mandamus as a " 'drastic and extraordinary' remedy 'reserved for really extraordinary causes.' " To say the least, this is anything but a "really extraordinary cause." Volkswagen seeks no more than to transfer this case 150 miles from the Eastern District of Texas to the Northern District of Texas. * * * [This situation] does not justify an extraordinary writ.

* * *

NOTES AND QUESTIONS

1.   In *In re Volkswagen*, the Singletons had a clear strategic reason for filing in the Marshall Division rather than in Dallas. *See* Saurabh Vishnubhakat, *Reconceiving the Patent Rocket Docket: An Empirical Study of Infringement Litigation 1985–2010*, 11 J. Marshall Rev. Intell. Prop. L. 58, 65 (2011) (explaining, based on empirical research involving patent litigation, that the Marshall Division had a reputation for being plaintiff-friendly and "return[ed] verdicts in favor of plaintiffs in seventy-eight percent of the patent cases that [went] to trial" during the period studied in the article); Elizabeth Offen-Brown, *Forum Shopping and Venue Transfer in Patent Cases*, 25 Berkeley Tech. L.J. 61 (2010) (also noting that the Marshall Division is known for being plaintiff-friendly in patent cases). Although *In re Volkswagen* was not a patent case, the plaintiffs' attorneys no doubt concluded that they too could benefit from a plaintiff-friendly judicial division.

2.   How does the venue transfer statute, 28 U.S.C. § 1404, work in conjunction with the general venue statute, 28 U.S.C. § 1391?

3.   What is forum non conveniens? What are the differences between transfer of venue under § 1404 and forum non conveniens?

4.   What are the so-called *Gilbert* factors? How did the Fifth Circuit en banc majority resolve the transfer issues under those factors?

5.   What is a writ of mandamus? Why did Volkswagen need to seek a writ of mandamus to challenge the district court's denial of Volkswagen's transfer motion?

6.   What are the three requirements for securing mandamus relief? The appellate court first applied the second requirement for securing mandamus. How did the court analyze that issue? The court then applied the first requirement. How did the court analyze that issue? Finally, the court applied the third requirement. How did the court analyze that issue?

7.   On what grounds did the dissenting judges disagree with the majority's analysis? Which view is more persuasive?

8.   For additional readings on venue, transfer of venue, and forum non conveniens, *see, e.g.,* Simona Grossi, *Forum Non Conveniens as a Jurisdictional Doctrine*, 75 U. Pitt. L. Rev. 1 (2013) (arguing that, because the consequence of forum non conveniens is a dismissal, the doctrine should apply only in exceptional circumstances); Debra Lyn Bassett, *The Forum Game*, 84

N.C. L. Rev. 333 (2006) (analyzing the strategy involved in choosing a forum and arguing that "forum-shopping" is not necessarily unfair, but instead incorporates many valid elements of litigation strategy, such as choosing between federal and state court and choosing a court based on convenience).

E. THRESHOLD PLEADINGS

A civil lawsuit begins when the plaintiff files a "complaint." The complaint includes the plaintiff's claim against the defendant, an explanation of the court's jurisdiction over the claim, and a statement of the plaintiff's desired relief. The defendant may respond with an "answer," which addresses the plaintiff's claims. (In many cases, as in the *Iqbal* case set out below, a defendant may file a motion, such as a motion to dismiss the case, in lieu of—or prior to—filing an answer.)

The *Iqbal* case discusses the level of factual detail that must be included in a complaint. At the time of pleading, a plaintiff may not have access to all of the evidence it needs because it cannot obtain defendants' evidence until later in the litigation through "discovery." Thus, it may be difficult for some plaintiffs to set forth a high level of factual detail.

Iqbal involved a suit for damages against a number of federal officials for alleged misconduct. Special considerations come into play when a suit involves a government official who is being sued for conduct occurring as part of the person's governmental duties. As one commentator has explained: "[J]udges and prosecutors are absolutely immune from suit for any violations of constitutional rights they commit as part of their official duties." Alexander Volokh, *Supreme Court Clarifies Standards for Qualified Immunity in Civil Rights Cases—Or Does It?*, REASON FOUND., Apr. 5, 2013, *available at* http://reason.org/news/show/privatization-qualified-immunity. Executive officials are subject to "qualified immunity" and thus "are only subject to suit if they violate a 'clearly established right.'" *Id.* Actions against federal officials for violations of various constitutional rights were authorized by the U.S. Supreme Court in *Bivens v. Six Unknown Agents of the Federal Bureau of Narcotics*, 403 U.S. 388 (1971). Actions against state officials are authorized by a federal statute (enacted in 1871), 42 U.S.C. § 1983.

ASHCROFT V. IQBAL

Supreme Court of the United States, 2009
556 U.S. 662

JUSTICE KENNEDY delivered the opinion of the Court.

Respondent Javaid Iqbal is a citizen of Pakistan and a Muslim. In the wake of the September 11, 2001, terrorist attacks he was arrested in the United States on criminal charges and detained by federal officials. Respondent claims he was deprived of various constitutional protections while in federal custody. To redress the alleged deprivations, respondent filed a complaint against numerous federal officials, including John Ashcroft, the former Attorney General of the United States, and Robert Mueller, the Director of the Federal Bureau of Investigation (FBI). Ashcroft and Mueller are the petitioners in the case now before us. As to these two petitioners, the complaint alleges that they adopted an unconstitutional policy that subjected respondent to harsh conditions of confinement on account of his race, religion, or national origin.

* * *

* * * This case [raises the following] question: Did respondent, as the plaintiff in the District Court, plead factual matter that, if taken as true, states a claim that petitioners deprived him of his clearly established constitutional rights. We hold respondent's pleadings are insufficient.

I

Following the 2001 attacks, the FBI and other entities within the Department of Justice began an investigation of vast reach to identify the assailants and prevent them from attacking anew. The FBI dedicated more than 4,000 special agents and 3,000 support personnel to the endeavor. By September 18 "the FBI had received more than 96,000 tips or potential leads from the public."

In the ensuing months the FBI questioned more than 1,000 people with suspected links to the attacks in particular or to terrorism in general. Of those individuals, some 762 were held on immigration charges; and a 184-member subset of that group was deemed to be "of 'high interest'" to the investigation. The high-interest detainees were held under restrictive conditions designed to prevent them from communicating with the general prison population or the outside world.

Respondent was one of the detainees. According to his complaint, in November 2001 agents of the FBI and Immigration and Naturalization Service arrested him on charges of fraud in relation to identification documents and conspiracy to defraud the United States. Pending trial for those crimes, respondent was housed at the Metropolitan Detention Center (MDC) in Brooklyn, New York. Respondent was designated a person "of high interest" to the September 11 investigation and in January 2002 was placed in a section of the MDC known as the Administrative Maximum Special Housing Unit (ADMAX SHU). As the facility's name indicates, the ADMAX SHU incorporates the maximum security conditions allowable under Federal Bureau of Prison regulations. ADMAX SHU detainees were kept in lockdown 23 hours a day, spending the remaining hour outside their cells in handcuffs and leg irons accompanied by a four-officer escort.

* * * The defendants range from the correctional officers who had day-to-day contact with respondent during the term of his confinement, to the wardens of the MDC facility, all the way to petitioners—officials who were at the highest level of the federal law enforcement hierarchy.

* * *

The allegations against petitioners [Ashcroft and Mueller] are the only ones relevant here. The complaint contends that petitioners designated respondent a person of high interest on account of his race, religion, or national origin, in contravention of the First and Fifth Amendments to the Constitution. The complaint alleges that "the [FBI], under the direction of Defendant Mueller, arrested and detained thousands of Arab Muslim men . . . as part of its investigation of the events of September 11." It further alleges that "[t]he policy of holding post-September-11th detainees in highly restrictive conditions of confinement until they were 'cleared' by the FBI was approved by Defendants Ashcroft and Mueller in discussions in the weeks after September 11, 2001." Lastly, the complaint posits that petitioners "each knew of, condoned, and willfully and maliciously agreed to subject" respondent to harsh conditions of confinement "as a matter of policy, solely on account of [his] religion, race, and/or national origin and for no legitimate penological interest." The pleading names Ashcroft as the "principal architect" of the policy, and identifies Mueller as "instrumental in [its] adoption, promulgation, and implementation."

Petitioners moved to dismiss the complaint for failure to state sufficient allegations to show their own involvement in clearly established unconstitutional conduct. The District Court denied their motion. * * * [The U.S. Court of Appeals for the Second Circuit affirmed.]

* * *

* * * We granted certiorari and now reverse.

II

[The Court held that the district court's order was appealable under an exception to the general rule that only final judgments are appealable.]

III

* * * Here * * * we begin by taking note of the elements a plaintiff must plead to state a claim of unconstitutional discrimination against officials entitled to assert the defense of qualified immunity.

In *Bivens* [*v. Six Unknown Agents of the Federal Bureau of Narcotics*, 403 U.S. 388 (1971)]—proceeding on the theory that a right suggests a remedy—this Court "recognized for the first time an implied private action for damages against federal officers alleged to have violated a citizen's constitutional rights." * * *

In the limited settings where *Bivens* does apply, the implied cause of action is the "federal analog to suits brought against state officials under * * * 42 U.S.C. § 1983." Based on the rules our precedents establish, respondent correctly concedes that Government officials may not be held liable for the unconstitutional conduct of their subordinates * * *. [A] plaintiff must plead that each Government-official defendant, through the official's own individual actions, has violated the Constitution.

The factors necessary to establish a *Bivens* violation will vary with the constitutional provision at issue. Where the claim is invidious discrimination in contravention of the First and Fifth Amendments, our decisions make clear that the plaintiff must plead and prove that the defendant acted with discriminatory purpose. * * * [P]urposeful discrimination requires more than "intent as volition or intent as awareness of consequences." It instead involves a decision-maker's undertaking a course of action " 'because of,' not merely 'in spite of,' [the action's] adverse effects upon an identifiable group." It follows that, to state a claim based on a violation of a clearly established right, respondent must plead sufficient factual matter to show that petitioners adopted and implemented the detention policies at issue not for a neutral, investigative reason but for the purpose of discriminating on account of race, religion, or national origin.

Respondent disagrees. He argues that, under a theory of "supervisory liability," petitioners can be liable for "knowledge and acquiescence in their subordinates' use of discriminatory criteria to make classification decisions among detainees." That is to say, respondent believes a supervisor's mere knowledge of his subordinate's discriminatory purpose amounts to the supervisor's violating the Constitution. We reject this argument. * * * [P]etitioners may not be held accountable for the misdeeds of their agents. * * * [E]ach Government official, his or her title notwithstanding, is only liable for his or her own misconduct. In the context of determining whether there is a violation of clearly established right to overcome qualified immunity, purpose rather than knowledge is required to impose *Bivens* liability on the subordinate for unconstitutional discrimination; the same holds true for an official charged with violations arising from his or her superintendent responsibilities.

IV

A

We turn to respondent's complaint. Under Federal Rule of Civil Procedure 8(a)(2), a pleading must contain a "short and plain statement of the claim showing that the pleader is entitled to relief." As the Court held in [*Bell Atlantic Corp. v.*] *Twombly*[, 550 U.S. 544 (2007)], the pleading standard Rule 8 announces does not require "detailed factual allegations," but it demands more than an unadorned, the-defendant-unlawfully-harmed-me accusation. A pleading that offers "labels and conclusions" or "a formulaic recitation of the elements of a cause of action will not do." Nor does a complaint suffice if it tenders "naked assertion[s]" devoid of "further factual enhancement."

To survive a motion to dismiss, a complaint must contain sufficient factual matter, accepted as true, to "state a claim to relief that is plausible on its face." A claim has facial plausibility when the plaintiff pleads factual content that allows the court to draw the reasonable inference that the defendant is liable for the misconduct alleged. The plausibility standard is not akin to a "probability requirement," but it asks for more than a sheer possibility that a defendant has acted unlawfully. Where a complaint pleads facts that are "merely consistent with" a defendant's liability, it "stops short of the line between possibility and plausibility of 'entitlement to relief.' "

Two working principles underlie our decision in *Twombly*. First, the tenet that a court must accept as true all of the allegations contained in a complaint is inapplicable to legal conclusions. Threadbare recitals of the elements of a cause of action, supported by mere conclusory statements, do not suffice. (Although for the purposes of a motion to dismiss we must take all of the factual allegations in the complaint as true, we "are not bound to accept as true a legal conclusion couched as a factual allegation.") Rule 8 marks a notable and generous departure from the hyper-technical, code-pleading regime of a prior era, but it does not unlock the doors of discovery for a plaintiff armed with nothing more than conclusions. Second, only a complaint that states a plausible claim for relief survives a motion to dismiss. Determining whether a complaint states a plausible claim for relief will * * * be a context-specific task that requires the reviewing court to draw on its judicial experience and common sense. But where the well-pleaded facts do not permit the court to infer more than the mere possibility of misconduct, the complaint has alleged—but it has not "show[n]"—"that the pleader is entitled to relief." Fed. R. Civ. P. 8(a)(2).

In keeping with these principles a court considering a motion to dismiss can choose to begin by identifying pleadings that, because they are no more than conclusions, are not entitled to the assumption of truth. While legal conclusions can provide the framework of a complaint, they must be supported by factual allegations. When there are well-pleaded factual allegations, a court should assume their veracity and then determine whether they plausibly give rise to an entitlement to relief.

Our decision in *Twombly* illustrates the two-pronged approach. There, we considered the sufficiency of a complaint alleging that incumbent telecommunications providers had entered an agreement not to compete and to forestall competitive entry, in violation of the Sherman Act, 15 U.S.C. § 1. Recognizing that § 1 enjoins only anticompetitive conduct "effected by a contract, combination, or conspiracy," the plaintiffs in *Twombly* flatly pleaded that the defendants "ha[d] entered into a contract, combination or conspiracy to prevent competitive entry . . . and ha[d] agreed not to compete with one another." The complaint also alleged that the defendants' "parallel course of conduct . . . to prevent competition" and inflate prices was indicative of the unlawful agreement alleged.

The Court held the plaintiffs' complaint deficient under Rule 8. In doing so it first noted that the plaintiffs' assertion of an unlawful agreement was a "legal conclusion" and, as such, was not entitled to the assumption of truth. Had the Court simply credited the allegation of a conspiracy, the plaintiffs would have stated a claim for relief and been entitled to proceed perforce. The Court next addressed the "nub" of the plaintiffs' complaint—the well-pleaded, nonconclusory factual allegation of parallel behavior—to determine whether it gave rise to a "plausible suggestion of conspiracy." Acknowledging that parallel conduct was consistent with an unlawful agreement, the Court nevertheless concluded that it did not plausibly suggest an illicit accord because it was not only compatible with, but indeed was more likely explained by, lawful, unchoreographed free-market behavior. Because the well-pleaded fact of parallel conduct, accepted as true, did not plausibly suggest an unlawful agreement, the Court held the plaintiffs' complaint must be dismissed.

B

Under *Twombly*'s construction of Rule 8, we conclude that respondent's complaint has not "nudged [his] claims" of invidious discrimination "across the line from conceivable to plausible."

We begin our analysis by identifying the allegations in the complaint that are not entitled to the assumption of truth. Respondent pleads that petitioners "knew of, condoned, and willfully and maliciously agreed to subject [him]" to harsh conditions of confinement "as a matter of policy, solely on account of [his] religion, race, and/or national origin and for no legitimate penological interest." The complaint alleges that Ashcroft was the "principal architect" of this invidious policy, and that Mueller was "instrumental" in adopting and executing it. These bare assertions, much like the pleading of conspiracy in *Twombly*, amount to nothing more than a "formulaic recitation of the elements" of a constitutional discrimination claim, namely, that petitioners adopted a policy " 'because of,' not merely 'in spite of,' its adverse effects upon an identifiable group." As such, the allegations are conclusory and not entitled to be assumed true. To be clear, we do not reject these bald allegations on the ground that they are unrealistic or nonsensical. * * * It is the conclusory nature of respondent's allegations, rather than their extravagantly fanciful nature, that disentitles them to the presumption of truth.

We next consider the factual allegations in respondent's complaint to determine if they plausibly suggest an entitlement to relief. The complaint alleges that "the [FBI], under the direction of Defendant Mueller, arrested and detained thousands of Arab Muslim men . . . as part of its investigation of the events of September 11." It further claims that "[t]he policy of holding post-September-11th detainees in highly restrictive conditions of confinement until they were 'cleared' by the FBI was approved by Defendants Ashcroft and Mueller in discussions in the weeks after September 11, 2001." Taken as true, these allegations are consistent with petitioners' purposefully designating detainees "of high interest" because of their race, religion, or national origin. But given more likely explanations, they do not plausibly establish this purpose.

The September 11 attacks were perpetrated by 19 Arab Muslim hijackers who counted themselves members in good standing of al Qaeda, an Islamic fundamentalist group. Al Qaeda was headed by another Arab Muslim—Osama bin Laden—and composed in large part of his Arab Muslim disciples. It should come as no surprise that a legitimate policy directing law enforcement to arrest and detain individuals because of their suspected link to the attacks would produce a disparate, incidental impact on Arab Muslims, even though the purpose of the policy was to target neither Arabs nor Muslims. On the facts respondent alleges the arrests Mueller oversaw were likely lawful and justified by his nondiscriminatory intent to detain aliens who were illegally present in the United States and who had potential connections to those who committed terrorist acts. As between that "obvious alternative explanation" for the arrests, and the purposeful, invidious discrimination respondent asks us to infer, discrimination is not a plausible conclusion.

But even if the complaint's well-pleaded facts give rise to a plausible inference that respondent's arrest was the result of unconstitutional discrimination, that inference alone would not entitle respondent to relief. * * * [R]espondent's complaint challenges neither the constitutionality of his arrest nor his initial detention in the MDC. Respondent's constitutional claims against petitioners rest solely on their ostensible "policy of holding post-September-11th detainees" in the ADMAX SHU once they were categorized as "of high interest." To prevail on that theory, the complaint must contain facts plausibly showing that petitioners purposefully adopted a policy of classifying post-September-11 detainees as "of high interest" because of their race, religion, or national origin.

This the complaint fails to do. Though respondent alleges that various other defendants, who are not before us, may have labeled him a person of "of high interest" for impermissible reasons, his only factual allegation against petitioners accuses them of adopting a policy approving "restrictive conditions of confinement" for post-September-11 detainees until they were " 'cleared' by the FBI." Accepting the truth of that allegation, the complaint does not show, or even intimate, that petitioners purposefully housed detainees in the ADMAX SHU due to their race, religion, or national origin. All it plausibly suggests is that the Nation's top law enforcement officers, in the aftermath of a devastating terrorist attack, sought to keep suspected terrorists in the most secure conditions available until the suspects could be cleared of terrorist activity. Respondent does not argue, nor can he, that such a motive would violate petitioners' constitutional obligations. He would need to allege more by way of factual content to "nudg[e]" his claim of purposeful discrimination "across the line from conceivable to plausible."

* * * [H]ere, as we have noted, petitioners cannot be held liable unless they themselves acted on account of a constitutionally protected characteristic. Yet respondent's complaint does not contain any factual allegation sufficient to plausibly suggest petitioners' discriminatory state of mind. His pleadings thus do not meet the standard necessary to comply with Rule 8.

* * *

C

* * *

Respondent offers three arguments that bear on our disposition of his case, but none is persuasive.

1

Respondent first says that our decision in *Twombly* should be limited to pleadings made in the context of an antitrust dispute. This argument is not supported by *Twombly* and is incompatible with the Federal Rules of Civil Procedure. * * * Our decision in *Twombly* expounded the pleading standard for "all civil actions," and it applies to antitrust and discrimination suits alike.

2

Respondent next implies that our construction of Rule 8 should be tempered where, as here, * * * "the district court * * * cabin[ed] discovery in such a way as to preserve" petitioners' defense of qualified immunity "as much as possible in anticipation of a summary judgment motion." We have held, however, that the question presented by a motion to dismiss a complaint for insufficient pleadings does not turn on the controls placed upon the discovery process.

Our rejection of the careful-case-management approach is especially important in suits where Government-official defendants are entitled to assert the defense of qualified immunity. The basic thrust of the qualified-immunity doctrine is to free officials from the concerns of litigation, including "avoidance of disruptive discovery." There are serious and legitimate reasons for this. If a Government official is to devote time to his or her duties, and to the formulation of sound and responsible policies, it is counterproductive to require the substantial diversion that is attendant to participating in litigation and making informed decisions as to how it should proceed. Litigation * * * exacts heavy costs in terms of efficiency and expenditure of valuable time and resources * * *. The costs * * * are only magnified when Government officials are charged with responding to * * * "a national and international security emergency unprecedented in the history of the American Republic."

* * *

* * * Because respondent's complaint is deficient under Rule 8, he is not entitled to discovery, cabined or otherwise.

3

Respondent finally maintains that the Federal Rules expressly allow him to allege petitioners' discriminatory intent "generally," which he equates with a conclusory allegation. It follows, respondent says, that his complaint is sufficiently well pleaded because it claims that petitioners discriminated against him "on account of [his] religion, race, and/or national origin and for no legitimate penological interest." Were we required to accept this allegation as true, respondent's complaint would survive petitioners' motion to dismiss. But the Federal Rules do not require courts to credit a complaint's conclusory statements without reference to its factual context.

* * *

V

We hold that respondent's complaint fails to plead sufficient facts to state a claim for purposeful and unlawful discrimination against petitioners. The Court of Appeals should decide in the first instance whether to remand to the District Court so that respondent can seek leave to amend his deficient complaint.

The judgment of the Court of Appeals is reversed, and the case is remanded for further proceedings consistent with this opinion.

* * *

JUSTICE SOUTER, with whom JUSTICE STEVENS, JUSTICE GINSBURG, and JUSTICE BREYER join, dissenting.

* * * The majority * * * misapplies the pleading standard under *Twombly* to conclude that the complaint fails to state a claim. I respectfully dissent * * *.

I

* * *

II

* * * Ashcroft and Mueller admit they are liable for their subordinates' conduct if they "had actual knowledge of the assertedly discriminatory nature of the classification of suspects as being 'of high interest' and they were deliberately indifferent to that discrimination." Iqbal alleges that after the September 11 attacks the Federal Bureau of Investigation (FBI) "arrested and detained thousands of Arab Muslim men," that many of these men were designated by high-ranking FBI officials as being " 'of high interest,' " and that in many cases, including Iqbal's, this designation was made "because of the race, religion, and national origin of the detainees, and not because of any evidence of the detainees' involvement in supporting terrorist activity." The complaint further alleges that Ashcroft was the "principal architect of the policies and practices challenged," and that Mueller "was instrumental in the adoption, promulgation, and implementation of the policies and practices challenged." According to the complaint, Ashcroft and Mueller "knew of, condoned, and willfully and maliciously agreed to subject [Iqbal] to these conditions of confinement as a matter of policy, solely on account of [his] religion, race, and/or national origin and for no legitimate penological interest." The complaint thus alleges, at a bare minimum, that Ashcroft and Mueller knew of and condoned the discriminatory policy their subordinates carried out. Actually, the complaint goes further in alleging that Ashcroft and Muller affirmatively acted to create the discriminatory detention policy. If these factual allegations are true, Ashcroft and Mueller were, at the very least, aware of the discriminatory policy being implemented and deliberately indifferent to it.

Ashcroft and Mueller argue that these allegations fail to satisfy the "plausibility standard" of *Twombly*. They contend that Iqbal's claims are implausible because such high-ranking officials "tend not to be personally involved in the specific actions of lower-level officers down the bureaucratic chain of command." But this response bespeaks a fundamental misunderstanding of the enquiry that *Twombly* demands. *Twombly* does not require a court at the motion-to-dismiss stage to consider whether the factual allegations are probably true. We made it clear, on the contrary, that a court must take the allegations as true, no matter how skeptical the court may be. * * *

Under *Twombly*, the relevant question is whether, assuming the factual allegations are true, the plaintiff has stated a ground for relief that is plausible. That is, in *Twombly*'s words, a plaintiff must "allege facts" that, taken as true, are "suggestive of illegal conduct." * * * Here, * * * the allegations in the complaint are neither confined to naked legal conclusions nor consistent with legal conduct. The complaint alleges that FBI officials discriminated against Iqbal solely on account of his race, religion, and national origin, and it alleges the knowledge and deliberate indifference that, by Ashcroft and Mueller's own admission, are sufficient to make them liable for the illegal action. Iqbal's complaint therefore contains "enough facts to state a claim to relief that is plausible on its face."

* * * [T]he majority discards the allegations discussed above with regard to Ashcroft and Mueller as conclusory, and is left considering only two statements in the complaint: that "the [FBI], under the direction of

Defendant Mueller, arrested and detained thousands of Arab Muslim men . . . as part of its investigation of the events of September 11," and that "[t]he policy of holding post-September-11th detainees in highly restrictive conditions of confinement until they were 'cleared' by the FBI was approved by Defendants Ashcroft and Mueller in discussions in the weeks after September 11, 2001." I * * * agree [with the majority] that [these] two allegations * * *, standing alone, do not state a plausible entitlement to relief for unconstitutional discrimination.

But these allegations do not stand alone * * *, for the complaint contains many allegations linking Ashcroft and Mueller to the discriminatory practices of their subordinates. * * *

* * * Iqbal's claim is not that Ashcroft and Mueller "knew of, condoned, and willfully and maliciously agreed to subject" him to a discriminatory practice that is left undefined; his allegation is that "they knew of, condoned, and willfully and maliciously agreed to subject" him to a particular, discrete, discriminatory policy detailed in the complaint. Iqbal does not say merely that Ashcroft was the architect of some amorphous discrimination, or that Mueller was instrumental in an ill-defined constitutional violation; he alleges that they helped to create the discriminatory policy he has described. Taking the complaint as a whole, it gives Ashcroft and Mueller " 'fair notice of what the . . . claim is and the grounds upon which it rests.' "

* * *

I respectfully dissent.

[Dissenting opinion by JUSTICE BREYER is omitted.]

NOTES AND QUESTIONS

1.   As discussed in *Iqbal*, Federal Rule of Civil Procedure 8(a)(2) states that a pleading must contain "a short and plain statement of the claim showing that the pleader is entitled to relief." Prior to *Twombly* (discussed in *Iqbal*), courts had interpreted this language liberally. In *Conley v. Gibson*, 355 U.S. 41 (1957), the Supreme Court held that "a complaint should not be dismissed for failure to state a claim unless it appears beyond doubt that the plaintiff can prove no set of facts in support of his claim which would entitle him to relief." *Id.* at 45–46. How, if at all, did the Supreme Court's *Twombly* and *Iqbal* decisions change this test?

2.   What was the precise pleading issue in *Iqbal*? How did the majority resolve the issue? What were the grounds of disagreement by the dissent? Which opinion is more persuasive? Notably, Justice Souter, who wrote the dissent in *Iqbal*, had previously written the majority opinion in *Twombly*. Yet, the majority in *Iqbal* found that *Twombly* compelled dismissal of the claims.

3.   Some scholars have warned that *Twombly* and *Iqbal* will have (and are already having) grave consequences with respect to the ability of plaintiffs

to bring civil lawsuits. *See, e.g.*, Mark Payne, *The Post-*Iqbal *State of Pleading: An Argument Opposing A Uniform National Pleading Regime*, 20 U. Miami Bus. L. Rev. 245 (2012) (arguing that the *Iqbal* pleading standard allows judges too much discretion in determining whether a claim is plausible); Michael Eaton, *The Key to the Courthouse Door: The Effect of* Ashcroft v. Iqbal *and the Heightened Pleading Standard*, 51 Santa Clara L. Rev. 299 (2011) (noting that the *Iqbal* pleading standard precludes even meritorious claims from going forward in some cases). Other commentators, however, have argued that the *Iqbal* decision will not have serious adverse consequences. *See, e.g.*, Stephen Brown, *Reconstructing Pleading:* Twombly, Iqbal, *and the Limited Role of the Plausibility Inquiry*, 43 Akron L. Rev. 1265 (2010) (arguing that criticisms of *Twombly* and *Iqbal* are unjustified because plaintiffs were already required to demonstrate that they were reasonably entitled to relief at the pleading stage); Adam McDonell Moline, *Nineteenth-Century-Principles for Twenty-First-Century Pleading*, 60 Emory L.J. 159 (2010) (asserting that the pleading standard announced in *Twombly* and *Iqbal* advances the interests of procedural fairness by promoting fair notice to defendants of the allegations against them).

4. Statistical studies have shown that *Twombly* and *Iqbal* have had some impact, but more studies are needed. *See, e.g.*, JOE CECIL ET AL., FED. JUDICIAL CTR., MOTIONS TO DISMISS FOR FAILURE TO STATE A CLAIM AFTER IQBAL: REPORT TO THE JUDICIAL CONFERENCE ADVISORY COMMITTEE ON CIVIL RULES (2011), *available at* http://www.fjc.gov/public/pdf.nsf/lookup/motion iqbal.pdf/$file/motioniqbal.pdf (determining that the probability of a motion to dismiss being filed in a given case had doubled from 2.9 to 5.8 percent following *Iqbal*, but that, in most types of cases, the rate at which motions to dismiss were granted had not been affected); Jonah Gelbach, *Locking the Doors to Discovery?: Assessing the Effects of* Twombly *and* Iqbal *on Access to Discovery*, 121 Yale L.J. 2270 (2012) (concluding that 15 to 21 percent of plaintiffs were negatively affected by the heightened pleading standard announced in *Iqbal*, either by not advancing to discovery or by not achieving a settlement).

5. In *Khalik v. United Air Lines*, 671 F.3d 1188 (10th Cir. 2012), the Tenth Circuit applied *Twombly* and *Iqbal* in the context of a woman's claims of workplace discrimination under Title VII (a federal law prohibiting discrimination or retaliation based on race, religion, national origin, or ethnic heritage); retaliation for taking time off for family and medical reasons under the Family and Medical Leave Act (FMLA); and violation of various state laws. According to the court: "To set forth a prima facie case of discrimination, a plaintiff must establish that (1) she is a member of a protected class, (2) she suffered an adverse employment action, (3) she qualified for the position at issue, and (4) she was treated less favorably than others not in the protected class." *Id.* at 1192. The court held that plaintiff's allegations were insufficient to state a claim because, apart from conclusory allegations, she alleged only that:

(1) Plaintiff is an Arab-American who was born in Kuwait; (2) Plaintiff's religion is Islam; (3) Plaintiff performed her job well; (4)

> Plaintiff was grabbed by the arm in the office; (5) Plaintiff complained internally about discrimination; (6) Plaintiff also complained internally about being denied FMLA leave; (7) Plaintiff complained about an email that described a criminal act; and (8) Defendant terminated Plaintiff's employment position.

Id. at 1193–94. What more did the plaintiff in *Khalik* need to include in her complaint?

By contrast, in *Keys v. Humana, Inc.*, 684 F.3d 605 (6th Cir. 2012), the Sixth Circuit held that an individual did state a plausible claim for relief based on employment discrimination. The plaintiff, an African American woman, alleged race discrimination under Title VII and other federal law. Plaintiff alleged that (1) she had been interviewed and hired for the position of Consultant Director, but her official offer was instead for the position of Consultant Leader, while Caucasian candidates received the correct title; (2) she was offered a compensation plan incentive of 15 percent, while the Caucasian candidates received an incentive of 25 percent; (3) a Caucasian male was appointed to support her, but gradually assumed her duties; (4) she was no longer invited to weekly sales meetings, while the Caucasian directors were invited; (5) she was demoted and placed on a performance improvement plan, despite meeting all performance goals; (6) ten to twelve other African American management-level employees were similarly placed on performance plans and then forced to resign or were terminated, while no Caucasian employees were placed on performance plans; and (7) she was later demoted again and then terminated. The district court dismissed the case for failure to state a claim. On appeal, the Sixth Circuit reversed, concluding:

> The Amended Complaint contains allegations that are neither speculative nor conclusory; it alleges facts that easily state a plausible claim. The Amended Complaint alleges Humana had a pattern or practice of discrimination against African American managers and professional staff in hiring, compensation, promotion, discipline, and termination. It details several specific events in each of those employment-action categories where Keys alleges she was treated differently than her Caucasian management counterparts; it identifies the key supervisors and other relevant persons by race and either name or company title; and it alleges that Keys and other African Americans received specific adverse employment actions notwithstanding satisfactory employment performances.

Id. at 610. Can these two cases be reconciled? If so, how?

6.   *Iqbal* involved a motion to dismiss for failure to state a claim upon which relief can be granted. Fed. R. Civ. P. 12(b)(6). Rule 12 permits various other types of defenses as well, including motions asserting lack of subject-matter jurisdiction, 12(b)(1); lack of personal jurisdiction, 12(b)(2); improper venue, 12(b)(3); insufficient process, 12(b)(4); insufficient service of process, 12(b)(5); and failure to join a required party, 12(b)(7). Other motions include a motion for judgment on the pleadings, 12(c), which is similar to a motion to

dismiss but is filed after an answer (see below); and a motion to strike "an insufficient defense or any redundant, immaterial, impertinent, or scandalous matter," 12(f).

7.   The responsive pleading is known as an "answer." The normal time for filing an answer is extended under Rule 12(a)(4) if defendant files a motion pursuant to Rule 12(b). The purpose of an answer is to admit or deny the allegations and to assert various defenses (including, among others, fraud, duress, release, and statute of limitations). *See* Fed. R. Civ. P. 8(b)–(c). An answer may also assert counterclaims (claims against the opposing party) and cross-claims (claims against a co-party).

8.   For discussions of the various pleading devices, *see, e.g.*, MARY KAY KANE, CIVIL PROCEDURE IN A NUTSHELL 103–06, 109–16 (7th ed. 2013). *See also* Amy St. Eve & Michael Zuckerman, *The Forgotten Pleading*, 7 Fed. Cts. L. Rev. 152 (2013) (detailed discussion of Rule 12 defenses and the answer).

F.   DISCOVERY

Before trial, parties participate in "discovery," a process through which the parties can gather information from each other (and from third parties) relevant to the claims and defenses in the case. Various discovery tools (discussed *infra*) exist to enable parties to gather oral testimony, written answers, and documents. The court is typically not actively involved in discovery. Instead, the parties generally communicate directly, exchanging discovery as authorized by the Federal Rules of Civil Procedure. Of course, if there are allegations of abuse or failure to comply with the discovery rules, the court may need to intervene. The following case involved such an intervention.

CINE FORTY-SECOND STREET THEATRE CORP. V. ALLIED ARTISTS PICTURES CORP.

United States Court of Appeals, Second Circuit, 1979
602 F.2d 1062

KAUFMAN, CHIEF JUDGE.

* * *

[This case] raises the following question: where a party, fully able to comply with a magistrate's order compelling discovery fails to do so due to a total dereliction of professional responsibility, amounting to gross negligence, may the district court in its discretion order a preclusion of evidence tantamount to the dismissal of a claim under Fed. R. Civ. P. 37? We conclude that it may.

I

Appellee Cine Forty-Second Street Theatre Corp. ("Cine"), has operated a movie theater in New York City's Times Square area since July

1974. It alleges that those owning neighboring theaters on West Forty-Second Street (the "exhibitors") attempted through abuse of City agency processes to prevent the opening of its theater. When this tactic was unsuccessful, Cine contends, the exhibitors entered into a conspiracy with certain motion picture distributors to cut off its access to first-run, quality films. Bringing suit on August 1, 1975, Cine claimed $3,000,000 in treble damages under the antitrust laws, and sought an injunction against the defendants' alleged anticompetitive practices.

On November 6, 1975, the eleven defendants served plaintiff with a set of consolidated interrogatories. Cine thereupon secured its adversaries' consent to defer discovery on the crucial issue of damages until it could retain an expert to review the rival exhibitors' box office receipts. Not until four months after the deadline upon which the parties had agreed, however, did Cine file its first set of answers to the remaining interrogatories. Moreover, even casual scrutiny reveals the patent inadequacy of these responses. Many were bare, ambiguous cross-references to general answers elsewhere in the responses. Highly specific questions concerning the design of Cine's theater were answered with architectural drawings that did not even purport to show the dimensions requested.

Although Cine now complains bitterly that these interrogatories amounted to pure harassment, it never moved to strike them as irrelevant or as harassing. Rather, it filed supplemental answers, which were similarly deficient, and then failed to obey two subsequent orders from Magistrate Gershon compelling discovery. At a hearing in October of 1977, the magistrate found Cine's disobedience to have been willful, and assessed $500 in costs against it. Soon afterwards, she further warned plaintiff that any further noncompliance would result in dismissal.

By the summer of 1977, as this conflict was coming to a head, Cine had still not retained the expert it claimed was necessary to respond to the damages interrogatories. Magistrate Gershon quite reasonably and leniently ordered Cine merely to produce a plan to answer, but this yielded no result. The magistrate then directed Cine to answer the damages interrogatories, admonishing its counsel that future nonfeasance would be viewed in light of past derelictions. Cine did file two sets of answers, one over two months late and both seriously deficient.

The responses omitted, *inter alia*, any information concerning significant time periods for which Cine claimed injury. Moreover, they failed to provide any indication as to the method of calculating a major portion of the alleged damages. Thereupon, at [a] * * * hearing held on September 7, 1978, Magistrate Gershon once again held off the imposition of final sanctions in these already over-protracted discovery proceedings and ordered the defects cured, on pain of dismissal of the complaint. Cine stood mute, neither appealing from, objecting to, nor complying with the order. On September 20, the defendants moved before the magistrate for dismissal of the complaint, citing plaintiff's failure to obey the order requiring responses on damages.

At a formal hearing on October 19, 1978, Cine's attorney argued that several months earlier he and defense counsel had reached an "understanding," pursuant to which a deposition of Cine's principal officer, Clark, would replace the answers at issue. Cine has never introduced any written evidence or corroborative testimony demonstrating the existence of such an understanding. In any case, the magistrate's subsequent oral order compelling answers to the interrogatories would have superseded it.

Accordingly, Magistrate Gershon found that Cine had no basis for assuming that the answers were not due on the dates set in her orders. After noting plaintiff's history of disobedience in the face of her own repeated warnings, the magistrate concluded that Cine's present non-compliance was willful. "[T]he plaintiff," she stated, "has decided when it will be cooperative and when it will not be cooperative, and that it does not have any right to do." She thereupon recommended to the district court that Cine be precluded from introducing evidence with respect to damages. This sanction was, of course, tantamount to a dismissal of Cine's damage claim, but left standing its claim for injunctive relief.

Judge Goettel, the district judge to whom Magistrate Gershon's order was submitted for approval, reacted to Cine's behavior as did Magistrate Gershon. He wrote, "[i]f there were ever a case in which drastic sanctions were justified, this is it." But Judge Goettel could not fully accept the magistrate's finding of willfulness. "[T]he actions of plaintiff's counsel," he concluded,

> were either willful or a total dereliction of professional responsibility. No other conclusion is possible. However, in the absence of a written direction, it is virtually impossible to establish that the attorney's action was in fact willful, rather than grossly negligent.

The district judge thus apparently believed it possible that Cine's counsel, confused as to the precise terms of Magistrate Gershon's oral orders, could have thought in good faith that the answers were not due. Action taken upon that baseless belief, however, was, at the very least, grossly negligent. The district court "regretfully" concluded that * * * it lacked the power, absent a finding of willfulness, to impose the extreme sanction recommended by the magistrate. Instead, the court merely assessed costs in the amount of $1,000. But, recognizing that he might have "misperceive[d] the controlling law of this circuit," Judge Goettel certified this interlocutory appeal on his own motion under 28 U.S.C. § 1292(b) [which authorizes interlocutory review in certain circumstances when the district court deems immediate review to be warranted].

On reargument, Judge Goettel expressed some doubt regarding the correctness of his prior decision. In light of plaintiff's subsequent response to the damages interrogatories, however, the court adhered to its earlier view.

II

The question before us is whether a grossly negligent failure to obey an order compelling discovery may justify the severest disciplinary measures available under Fed. R. Civ. P. 37. This rule provides a spectrum of sanctions. The mildest is an order to reimburse the opposing party for expenses caused by the failure to cooperate. More stringent are orders striking out portions of the pleadings, prohibiting the introduction of evidence on particular points and deeming disputed issues determined adversely to the position of the disobedient party. Harshest of all are orders of dismissal and default judgment.

These sanctions serve a threefold purpose. Preclusionary orders ensure that a party will not be able to profit from its own failure to comply. Rule 37 strictures are also specific deterrents and, like civil contempt, they seek to secure compliance with the particular order at hand. Finally, although the most drastic sanctions may not be imposed as "mere penalties," courts are free to consider the general deterrent effect their orders may have on the instant case and on other litigation, provided that the party on whom they are imposed is, in some sense, at fault.

Where the party makes good faith efforts to comply, and is thwarted by circumstances beyond his control—for example, a foreign criminal statute prohibiting disclosure of the documents at issue—an order dismissing the complaint would deprive the party of a property interest without due process of law. It would, after all, be unfair and irrational to prevent a party from being heard solely because of a nonculpable failure to meet the terms of a discovery order. Indeed, such measures would be gratuitous, for if the party is unable to obey there can be no effective deterrence, general or specific. Accordingly, "Rule 37 should not be construed to authorize dismissal of [a] complaint because of petitioner's noncompliance with a pretrial production order when it has been established that failure to comply has been due to inability, and not to willfulness, bad faith, or any fault of petitioner."

The lower court did not determine whether willfulness caused plaintiff's failure to respond. It was possible, Judge Goettel apparently believed, that Cine's counsel simply did not understand the exact requirements of the magistrate's unwritten order compelling discovery. If so, Cine's failure to answer the damages interrogatories might not rise to the level of "willfulness" or "bad faith" for both of these conditions imply a deliberate disregard of the lawful orders of the court. The question, then, is whether gross negligence amounting to a "total dereliction of professional responsibility," but not a conscious disregard of court orders, is properly embraced within * * * "fault" * * *.

Fault, of course, is a broad and amorphous concept, and the Courts of Appeals have had considerable difficulty construing it in this context. Indeed, one court defined "fault" by the apparent oxymoron "intentional negligence." Thus, commentators have opined that an element of willfulness or conscious disregard of the court's orders is a prerequisite to the harsher categories of Rule 37 sanctions. But the appellate cases commonly cited for this proposition hold only that dismissal is an abuse of discretion where failure to comply was not the result of the fault of any party.

* * * [P]lainly, if "fault" has any meaning not subsumed by "willfulness" and "bad faith," it must at least cover gross negligence of the type present in this case. * * *

* * *

In the final analysis, however, this question cannot turn solely upon a definition of terms. We believe that our view advances the basic purposes of Rule 37, while respecting the demands of due process. The principal objective of the general deterrent policy [of Supreme Court precedent] is strict adherence to the "responsibilities counsel owe to the Court and to their opponents." Negligent, no less than intentional, wrongs are fit subjects for general deterrence. And gross professional incompetence no less than deliberate tactical intransigence may be responsible for the interminable delays and costs that plague modern complex lawsuits. * * * The parties, and particularly their lawyers, must rise to the freedom granted by the Rules and cooperate in good faith both in question and response.

Considerations of fair play may dictate that courts eschew the harshest sanctions provided by Rule 37 where failure to comply is due to a mere oversight of counsel amounting to no more than simple negligence. But where gross professional negligence has been found—that is, where counsel clearly should have understood his duty to the court—the full range of sanctions may be marshalled. Indeed, in this day of burgeoning, costly and protracted litigation courts should not shrink from imposing harsh sanctions where, as in this case, they are clearly warranted.

A litigant chooses counsel at his peril, and here, as in countless other contexts, counsel's disregard of his professional responsibilities can lead to extinction of his client's claim.

Plaintiff urges that because it has at last filed answers to the damage interrogatories, it should be permitted to prove its losses at trial. But it forgets that sanctions must be weighed in light of the full record in the case. Furthermore, "[i]f parties are allowed to flout their obligations, choosing to wait to make a response until a trial court has lost patience with them, the effect will be to embroil trial judges in day-to-day supervision of discovery, a result directly contrary to the overall scheme of the federal discovery rules." Moreover, as we have indicated, compulsion of performance in the particular case at hand is not the sole function of Rule 37 sanctions. * * * [P]laintiff's hopelessly belated compliance should not be accorded great weight. Any other conclusion would encourage dilatory tactics, and compliance with discovery orders would come only when the backs of counsel and the litigants were against the wall.

In light of the fact that plaintiff, through its undeniable fault, has frozen this litigation in the discovery phase for nearly four years, we see no reason to burden the court below with extensive proceedings on remand. Judge Goettel's opinion makes it abundantly clear that but for his misinterpretation of the governing law in this circuit, he would have wholeheartedly adopted Magistrate Gershon's original recommendation. Accordingly, the judge's order declining to adopt the magistrate's recommendation that proof of damages be precluded is reversed.

[Concurring opinion by JUDGE OAKES is omitted.]

NOTES AND QUESTIONS

1.   What purpose does discovery serve? Why is there a need for each side to preview the other side's evidence before trial?

2.   What is the issue in the *Cine Forty-Second Street Theatre Corp.* case? How did the court of appeals resolve the case? Is the court of appeals' resolution of the case fair? How did Judge Goettel misconstrue the controlling law?

3.   The five principal discovery tools under the Federal Rules of Civil Procedure are (1) requests for documents, (2) requests for admissions, (3) interrogatories, (4) depositions, and (5) a mental or physical examination of a party. Document requests enable parties to obtain from their opponents a variety of documents, including writings, drawings, graphs, recordings, and other data compilations, or any relevant tangible object. Fed. R. Civ. P. 34. Requests for admission allow the parties to request that the opposing party agree to the truth of any relevant facts, points of law, or the genuineness of any described documents. Fed. R. Civ. P. 36. Interrogatories allow a party to ask the opposing party about any relevant and non-privileged matter and receive a written response. Fed. R. Civ. P. 33. Each party is limited to 25 interrogatories, absent court approval for additional interrogatories. Depositions allow a party to question under oath a person having relevant knowledge, regardless of whether that person is a party in the case. Depositions may be conducted orally or in writing. Fed. R. Civ. P. 30, 31. Only 10 depositions are allowed per party absent court approval for additional depositions. Finally, mental or physical exams of a party are authorized, but only when the party's "mental or physical condition * * * is in controversy." Fed. R. Civ. P. 35.

When the party receiving a discovery request views the request as overbroad, unfair, or as seeking irrelevant evidence, the party has the option of objecting to the request. If the parties cannot work out their disagreement, they may seek the court's involvement. Fed. R. Civ. P. 37. And, as *Cine Forty-Second Street Theatre Corp.* shows, Rule 37 can provide a basis for sanctions.

4. For additional discussion of the discovery process, *see* Paul Grimm & David Yellin, *A Pragmatic Approach to Discovery Reform: How Small Changes Can Make a Big Difference in Civil Discovery*, 64 S.C. L. Rev. 495 (2013) (discussing attorney dissatisfaction with civil discovery due to its broadness and the burden of providing extensive information, and proposing an approach that would limit discovery to information that is essential to proving claims and defenses, employing a cost-shifting provision for additional discovery requests, and establishing an obligation for the parties to cooperate during discovery); Ezra Siller, *The Origins of the Oral Deposition in the Federal Rules: Who's in Charge?*, 10 Seton Hall Circuit Rev. 43 (2013) (exploring the historical roots of discovery devices, focusing primarily on depositions, and noting that liberal discovery has decreased the need for civil trials by clarifying factual issues before trial).

5. Litigants can abuse discovery tools in a variety of ways, such as by failing to turn over discoverable material, failing to follow the timeline for discovery, or using discovery to delay litigation or incur unnecessary costs for the opposing party. As *Cine Forty-Second Street Theater Corp.* illustrates, courts can deal with these discovery violations in different ways. Sanctions are typically administered based on the type and severity of the violation. *See, e.g.*, *Reilly v. Natwest Markets Grp. Inc.*, 181 F.3d 253 (2d Cir. 1999) (affirming the application of sanctions in the form of prohibiting plaintiffs from calling two witnesses at trial when plaintiffs failed to make them available for deposition); *Hyde & Drath v. Baker*, 24 F.3d 1162 (9th Cir. 1994) (approving the application of sanctions by the district court in the form of attorneys' fees, costs, and dismissal of the action when the plaintiffs failed to appear for deposition); *but see Dondi Props. Corp. v. Commerce Sav. & Loan Ass'n*, 121 F.R.D. 284 (N.D. Tex. 1988) (declining to order sanctions when the plaintiffs' attorney failed to answer interrogatories, comply with court orders, and turn over documents, because the court did not want to punish the plaintiffs for their attorneys' discovery violations).

6. The broad discovery available in civil cases does not exist in the criminal context. *See* Chapters 7 and 8 (discussing discovery in criminal cases). One commentator notes three reasons why discovery in criminal cases is circumscribed: (1) more discovery would allow "defendants to develop effective perjured testimony" to respond to the prosecution's evidence; (2) expanded discovery could "permit witness intimidation"; and (3) the prosecution would not benefit because the Fifth Amendment protects defendants against "reciprocal disclosures." Robert Mosteller, *Exculpatory Evidence, Ethics, and the Road to the Disbarment of Mike Nifong: The Critical Importance of Full Open-File Discovery*, 15 Geo. Mason L. Rev. 257, 273 (2008). Do these three

reasons justify the narrow scope of discovery in criminal cases versus civil cases?

G. SUMMARY JUDGMENT

In the United States, most civil cases settle at some point. Some cases, however, do not settle and go to trial. Still other cases are resolved prior to trial through dispositive motions. Two important motions that defendants frequently file are motions for summary judgment (*see, e.g.,* Fed. R. Civ. P. 56) and motions to dismiss for failure to state a claim upon which relief can be granted (*see, e.g.,* Fed. R. Civ. P. 12(b)(6)). Both motions are designed to achieve efficiency by terminating—without a trial—cases that are factually or legally flawed.

A motion to dismiss under Rule 12(b)(6) tests the sufficiency of the complaint's allegations to establish the relief sought. The court treats the allegations of the complaint as true and determines whether those allegations set forth a legally cognizable claim.

Summary judgment under Rule 56 is a tool that, in certain circumstances, allows for the disposition of a case before trial on the ground that there is no material issue of fact for the factfinder to adjudicate. In the context of a motion for summary judgment, both sides are permitted to attach supporting evidence.

The case below discusses the contours of the summary judgment device. Although the wording of Rule 56 has changed somewhat since the case was decided, the decision remains an authoritative statement of the basic summary judgment principles.

CELOTEX CORP. V. CATRETT

Supreme Court of the United States, 1986
477 U.S. 317

JUSTICE REHNQUIST delivered the opinion of the Court.

* * *

Respondent commenced this lawsuit in September 1980, alleging that the death in 1979 of her husband, Louis H. Catrett, resulted from his exposure to products containing asbestos manufactured or distributed by 15 named corporations. Respondent's complaint sounded in negligence, breach of warranty, and strict liability. Two of the defendants filed motions challenging [personal] jurisdiction, and the remaining 13, including petitioner [Celotex], filed motions for summary judgment. Petitioner's motion * * * argued that summary judgment was proper because respondent had "failed to produce evidence that any [Celotex] product . . . was the proximate cause of the injuries alleged * * *." In particular, petitioner noted that respondent had failed to identify, in answering interrogatories * * *, any witnesses who could testify about the decedent's exposure to petitioner's asbestos products. In response to petitioner's * * * motion, respondent then produced three documents which she claimed "demonstrate that there is a genuine material factual dispute" as to whether the decedent had ever been exposed to petitioner's asbestos products. The three documents included a transcript of a deposition of the decedent, a letter from an official of one of the decedent's former employers whom petitioner planned to call as a trial witness, and a letter from an insurance company to respondent's attorney, all tending to establish that the decedent had been exposed to petitioner's asbestos products in Chicago during 1970–1971. Petitioner, in turn, argued that the three documents were inadmissible hearsay and thus could not be considered in opposition to the summary judgment motion.

In July 1982, almost two years after the commencement of the lawsuit, the District Court granted all of the motions filed by the various defendants. * * * [The Court of Appeals reversed.]

* * * Under [Federal Rule of Civil Procedure] 56(c), summary judgment is proper "if the pleadings, depositions, answers to interrogatories, and admissions on file, together with the affidavits, if any, show that there is no genuine issue as to any material fact and that the moving party is entitled to a judgment as a matter of law." * * * [T]he plain language of Rule 56(c) mandates the entry of summary judgment, after adequate time for discovery and upon motion, against a party who fails to make a showing sufficient to establish the existence of an element essential to that party's case, and on which that party will bear the burden of proof at trial. In such a situation, there can be "no genuine issue as to any material fact," since a complete failure of proof concerning an essential element of the nonmoving party's case necessarily renders all other facts immaterial. * * *

Of course, a party seeking summary judgment always bears the initial responsibility of informing the district court of the basis for its motion, and identifying those portions of "the pleadings, depositions, answers to interrogatories, and admissions on file, together with the affidavits, if any," which it believes demonstrate the absence of a genuine issue of material fact. But * * * we find no express or implied requirement in Rule 56 that the moving party support its motion with affidavits or other similar materials *negating* the opponent's claim. On the contrary, Rule 56(c), which refers to "the affidavits, *if any*" (emphasis added [by the Court]), suggests the absence of such a requirement. And if there were any doubt about the meaning of Rule 56(c) in this regard, such doubt is clearly removed by Rules 56(a) and (b), which provide that claimants and defendants, respectively, may move for summary judgment *"with or without supporting affidavits"* (emphasis added [by the Court]). The import of these subsections is that, regardless of whether the moving party accompanies its summary judgment motion with affidavits, the motion may, and should, be granted so long as whatever is before the district court demonstrates that the standard for the entry of summary judgment, as set forth in Rule 56(c), is satisfied. One of the principal purposes of the summary judgment rule is to isolate and dispose of factually unsupported claims or defenses, and we think it should be interpreted in a way that allows it to accomplish this purpose.

Respondent argues, however, that Rule 56(e), by its terms, places on the nonmoving party the burden of coming forward with rebuttal affidavits, or other specified kinds of materials, only in response to a motion for summary judgment "made and supported as provided in this rule." According to respondent's argument, since petitioner did not "support" its motion with affidavits, summary judgment was improper in this case. But as we have already explained, a motion for summary judgment may be made pursuant to Rule 56 "with or without supporting affidavits." In cases like the instant one, where the nonmoving party will bear the burden of proof at trial on a dispositive issue, a summary judgment motion may properly be made in reliance solely on the "pleadings, depositions, answers to interrogatories, and admissions on file." Such a motion, whether or not accompanied by affidavits, will be "made and supported as provided in this rule," and Rule 56(e) therefore requires the nonmoving party to go beyond the pleadings and by her own affidavits, or by the "depositions, answers to interrogatories, and admissions on file," designate "specific facts showing that there is a genuine issue for trial."

We do not mean that the nonmoving party must produce evidence in a form that would be admissible at trial in order to avoid summary judgment. Obviously, Rule 56 does not require the nonmoving party to depose her own witnesses. Rule 56(e) permits a proper summary judgment motion to be opposed by any of the kinds of evidentiary materials listed in Rule 56(c), except the mere pleadings themselves, and it is from this list that one would normally expect the nonmoving party to make the showing to which we have referred.

* * *

Respondent commenced this action in September 1980, and petitioner's motion was filed in September 1981. The parties had conducted discovery, and no serious claim can be made that respondent was in any sense "railroaded" by a premature motion for summary judgment. Any potential problem with such premature motions can be adequately dealt with under Rule 56(f), which allows a summary judgment motion to be denied, or the hearing on the motion to be continued, if the nonmoving party has not had an opportunity to make full discovery.

In this Court, respondent's brief and oral argument have been devoted as much to the proposition that an adequate showing of exposure to petitioner's asbestos products was made as to the proposition that no such showing should have been required. But the Court of Appeals [did not] address either the adequacy of the showing made by respondent in opposition to petitioner's motion for summary judgment, or the question whether such a showing, if reduced to admissible evidence, would be sufficient to carry respondent's burden of proof at trial. We think the Court of Appeals with its superior knowledge of local law is better suited than we are to make these determinations in the first instance.

The Federal Rules of Civil Procedure have for almost 50 years authorized motions for summary judgment upon proper showings of the lack of a genuine, triable issue of material fact. Summary judgment procedure is properly regarded not as a disfavored procedural shortcut, but rather as an integral part of the Federal Rules as a whole, which are designed "to secure the just, speedy and inexpensive determination of every action." Fed. R. Civ. P. 1. Before the shift to "notice pleading" accomplished by the Federal Rules, motions to dismiss a complaint or to strike a defense were the principal tools by which factually insufficient claims or defenses could be isolated and prevented from going to trial with the attendant unwarranted consumption of public and private resources. But with the advent of "notice pleading," the motion to dismiss seldom fulfills this function any more, and its place has been taken by the motion for summary judgment. Rule 56 must be construed with due regard not only for the rights of persons asserting claims and defenses that are adequately based in fact to have those claims and defenses tried to a jury, but also for the rights of persons opposing such claims and defenses to demonstrate in the manner provided by the Rule, prior to trial, that the claims and defenses have no factual basis.

The judgment of the Court of Appeals is accordingly reversed, and the case is remanded for further proceedings consistent with this opinion.

* * *

[Concurring opinion by JUSTICE WHITE is omitted.]

JUSTICE BRENNAN, with whom THE CHIEF JUSTICE and JUSTICE BLACKMUN join, dissenting.

This case requires the Court to determine whether Celotex satisfied its initial burden of production in moving for summary judgment on the ground that the plaintiff lacked evidence to establish an essential element of her case at trial. I do not disagree with the Court's legal analysis. The Court clearly rejects the [argument] that the defendant must provide affirmative evidence disproving the plaintiff's case. Beyond this, however, the Court has not clearly explained what is required of a moving party seeking summary judgment on the ground that the nonmoving party cannot prove its case. This lack of clarity is unfortunate: district courts must routinely decide summary judgment motions, and the Court's opinion will very likely create confusion. For this reason, even if I agreed with the Court's result, I would have written separately to explain more clearly the law in this area. However, because I believe that Celotex did not meet its burden of production under Federal Rule of Civil Procedure 56, I respectfully dissent from the Court's judgment.

I

[Justice Brennan summarized the basic summary judgment principles.]

II

* * * My disagreement with the Court concerns [not the basic summary judgment principles but] the application of th[o]se principles to the facts of this case.

Defendant Celotex sought summary judgment on the ground that plaintiff had "failed to produce" any evidence that her decedent had ever been exposed to Celotex asbestos. Celotex supported this motion with a two-page "Statement of Material Facts as to Which There is No Genuine Issue" and a three-page "Memorandum of Points and Authorities" which asserted that the plaintiff had failed to identify any evidence in responding to two sets of interrogatories propounded by Celotex and that therefore the record was "totally devoid" of evidence to support plaintiff's claim.

Approximately three months earlier, Celotex had filed an essentially identical motion. Plaintiff responded to this earlier motion by producing three pieces of evidence which she claimed "[a]t the very least ... demonstrate that there is a genuine factual dispute for trial:" (1) a letter from an insurance representative of another defendant describing asbestos products to which plaintiff's decedent had been exposed; (2) a letter from T.R. Hoff, a former supervisor of decedent, describing asbestos products to which decedent had been exposed; and (3) a copy of decedent's deposition from earlier workmen's compensation proceedings. Plaintiff also apparently indicated at that time that she intended to call Mr. Hoff as a witness at trial.

Celotex subsequently withdrew its first motion for summary judgment. However, as a result of this motion, when Celotex filed its second summary judgment motion, the record *did* contain evidence—including at least one witness—supporting plaintiff's claim. Indeed, counsel for Celotex admitted to this Court at oral argument that Celotex was aware of this evidence and of plaintiff's intention to call Mr. Hoff as a witness at trial when the second summary judgment motion was filed. Moreover, plaintiff's response to Celotex's second motion pointed to this evidence—noting that it had already been provided to counsel for Celotex in connection with the first motion—and argued that Celotex had failed to "meet its burden of proving that there is no genuine factual dispute for trial."

On these facts, there is simply no question that Celotex failed to discharge its initial burden of production. Having chosen to base its motion on the argument that there was no evidence in the record to support plaintiff's claim, Celotex was not free to ignore supporting evidence that the record clearly contained. Rather, Celotex was required, as an initial matter, to attack the adequacy of this evidence. Celotex's failure to fulfill this simple requirement constituted a failure to discharge its initial burden of production under Rule 56, and thereby rendered summary judgment improper.

* * *

[Dissenting opinion by JUSTICE STEVENS is omitted.]

NOTES AND QUESTIONS

1.   What test did the *Celotex* majority apply in determining whether summary judgment was appropriate? How does that approach differ from the approach applied by the court of appeals?

2.   How does the approach of the *Celotex* dissent differ from that of the majority? Which opinion is more persuasive?

3.   Summary judgment cases tend to be very fact-intensive. *See, e.g.,* *Perry v. Roy*, 782 F.3d 73 (1st Cir. 2015) (reversing grant of summary judgment in a civil rights action brought by a prisoner against prison nurses alleging deliberate indifference to his broken jaw because the following facts were disputed: (1) whether the prisoner could speak or open his mouth, (2) whether the prisoner said that he had a broken jaw and asked to go the hospital, (3) whether those facts and the prisoner's cut, pain, and bleeding amounted to a serious medical need, (4) whether the nurses' inspection of the prisoner's tooth, but not jaw, was sufficient to justify postponing treatment, (5) whether the prisoner asked to go to the hospital after passing out and being revived with smelling salts, (6) whether the nurse denied treatment after talking to a police officer who asked her to let the inmate sleep instead of providing treatment, (7) whether the prisoner denied having any pain, and (8) whether the injury was so obvious that anyone would have recognized the need for medical attention); *Jacobs v. N.C. Admin. Office of the Courts*, 780 F.3d 562 (4th Cir. 2015) (reversing grant of summary judgment in an employee's Americans with Disabilities Act claim (discrimination on the basis of a disability) when there were issues of material fact as to: (1) whether the employee was disabled, (2) whether the employee requested that the employer accommodate her disability by allowing her to work in a position with less interpersonal interaction, (3) whether the employer discharged the employee because of her disability or because of her request for accommodation, (4) whether the employee was otherwise qualified for the job, and (5) whether the employer was aware of the disability).

4.   In 2014, the U.S. Supreme Court twice addressed summary judgment issues in lawsuits under 42 U.S.C. § 1983 alleging use of excessive force by the

police. In *Tolan v. Cotton*, 572 U.S. ___, 134 S. Ct. 1861 (2014), Tolan alleged that, following a traffic stop, the police officer (defendant) forcefully grabbed and injured his mother, and that Tolan then told the officer to take his hands off of his mother. Tolan alleged that the officer then fired three shots at him without any verbal warning, permanently injuring him. The officer disputed the amount of force used against Tolan's mother, the nature of Tolan's response, and whether there was a verbal warning preceding the gunshots. The district court granted the officer's motion for summary judgment, holding that the officer was entitled to qualified immunity, and the Fifth Circuit affirmed. *See Iqbal, supra* (discussing qualified immunity). The Supreme Court reversed, holding that

> [b]y weighing the evidence and reaching factual inferences contrary to Tolan's competent evidence, the court below neglected to adhere to the fundamental principle that at the summary judgment stage, reasonable inferences should be drawn in favor of the nonmoving party.

Id. at 1868.

In *Plumhoff v. Rickard*, 572 U.S. ___, 134 S. Ct. 2012 (2014), an officer fired three shots at a car driven by the plaintiff during a high-speed chase. The district court denied the officer's summary judgment motion based on qualified immunity and the Sixth Circuit affirmed. The Supreme Court reversed. It held that summary judgment should have been granted because the officer's conduct did not violate the law, but even if it had the officers were entitled to qualified immunity. The Court explained:

> An official sued under § 1983 is entitled to qualified immunity unless it is shown that the official violated a statutory or constitutional right that was " 'clearly established' " at the time of the challenged conduct. And a defendant cannot be said to have violated a clearly established right unless the right's contours were sufficiently definite that any reasonable official in the defendant's shoes would have understood that he was violating it. * * *

Id. at 2023. Applying that standard, the Court concluded that the officer was entitled to summary judgment because there was no clearly established law that use of deadly force to stop a high-speed chase was unconstitutional.

What is the likely reason why motions for summary judgment are frequently filed in cases alleging excessive use of force by police?

5.   Commentators have debated whether summary judgment is useful or harmful. *Compare, e.g.*, Edward Brunet, *The Efficiency of Summary Judgment*, 43 Loy. U. Chi. L.J. 689 (2012) (explaining how summary judgment makes the litigation system more efficient by clarifying the factual and legal issues, ensuring the judge's involvement at an earlier stage of litigation, and increasing the bargaining power of non-moving parties for purposes of settlement if a motion is denied), *with* John Bronsteen, *Against Summary Judgment*, 75 Geo. Wash. L. Rev. 522 (2007) (asserting that the summary

judgment device should be eliminated because it discourages early settlement, deprives litigants of their right to trial, and results in pro-defendant bias).

6. Two other procedures that can result in termination of litigation should be mentioned. First, a default judgment can be entered against a defendant who "has failed to plead or otherwise defend[.]" Fed. R. Civ. P. 55(a)–(b). Second, in certain circumstances a plaintiff can voluntarily dismiss its case. *See* Fed. R. Civ. P. 41(a). *See generally* MARY KAY KANE, CIVIL PROCEDURE IN A NUTSHELL 178–83 (7th ed. 2013) (discussing both procedures).

H. TRIALS, APPEALS, AND ALTERNATIVE DISPUTE RESOLUTION

In the United States, most civil cases settle. *See* Jonathan Glater, *Study Finds Settling Is Better than Going to Trial*, N.Y. TIMES, Aug. 7, 2008, http://www.nytimes.com/2008/08/08/business/08law.html (an estimated 80 to 92 percent of all civil cases settle). *See also* Chapter 7 (explaining that most criminal cases result in plea bargains). In fact, trials have become so infrequent in many types of cases that many judges, practitioners, and scholars warn about the "vanishing trial." *See, e.g.*, Marc Galanter, *The Vanishing Trial: An Examination of Trials and Related Matters in Federal and State Courts*, 1 J. Empirical Legal Stud. 459 (2004) (noting that between 1962 and 2002, the proportion of civil cases that went to trial fell from 11.5 percent to 1.8 percent).

Nonetheless, cases do go to trial. Except in unusual circumstances, such as juvenile cases, trials are open to the public. In many civil cases, the parties are guaranteed a right to a jury trial. Indeed, as noted *supra*, the Seventh Amendment guarantees a jury trial right for most suits for money damages in federal court, and most states also afford such a right. Jury selection (known as voir dire) is an important skill of a trial lawyer. *See, e.g.*, Mark Bennett, *16 Simple Rules for Better Jury Selection*, THE JURY EXPERT (Jan. 1, 2010), http://www.thejuryexpert.com/2010/01/16–simple-rules-for-better-jury-selection/ (experienced attorney offering strategies for jury selection).

In addition to their advocacy role in jury selection, trial attorneys advocate for their clients throughout the trial—from opening statements to direct and cross examinations of witnesses, to closing arguments. Countless trial strategy books exist, including one by the author. ROBERT KLONOFF & PAUL COLBY, WINNING JURY TRIALS: TRIAL TACTICS AND SPONSORSHIP STRATEGIES (3d ed. 2007). Trials can be exciting events, and countless popular movies revolve around trial settings, including both civil and criminal cases. *E.g.*, RUNAWAY JURY (Regency Enterprises 2003); A CIVIL ACTION (Touchstone Pictures 1998); A TIME TO KILL (Regency Enterprises 1996); PHILADELPHIA (TriStar Pictures 1993); PRESUMED INNOCENT (Warner Bros. 1990); TO KILL A MOCKINGBIRD (Universal Int'l

Pictures 1962); and WITNESS FOR THE PROSECUTION (Edward Small Productions 1957).

A party that believes that the evidence is insufficient (or that some prejudicial error occurred) has a variety of remedies. In federal court, these include a motion for judgment as a matter of law and a motion for a new trial (Fed. R. Civ. P. 50; Fed. R. Civ. P. 59). *See, e.g.*, MARY KAY KANE, CIVIL PROCEDURE IN A NUTSHELL 207–17 (7th ed. 2013) (discussing these remedies).

Absent a special statute authorizing attorneys' fees for the prevailing party, the usual rule in the United States is that the losing party does not pay the attorneys' fees of the prevailing party. *See Alyeska Pipeline Serv. Co. v. Wilderness Soc'y*, 421 U.S. 240, 247 (1975) (discussing the "American Rule" whereby "the prevailing litigant is ordinarily not entitled to collect a reasonable attorneys' fee from the loser"). On the other hand, various out-of-pocket costs incurred by the prevailing party may be recoverable. *See* Fed. R. Civ. P. 54(d)(1) (generally authorizing costs other than attorneys' fees to the prevailing party); Fed. R. App. P. 39(e) (allowing various costs incurred on appeal by the prevailing party); 28 U.S.C. § 1920 (2012) (specifying costs that may be imposed, including court and transcript fees, printing costs, docket fees, and others).

There is also a right to appeal in most civil cases, at least to the first appellate court level (in the federal court, the U.S. Courts of Appeals). Appellate practice is a specialized area and is the subject of a separate course in many law schools. A host of issues arise in the appellate context, including: whether a non-final order is appealable (for example, an order denying a motion to dismiss); grounds for seeking emergency relief from the appellate court; rules for the form and content of a brief (a written document, often of substantial length, explaining why the party submitting the brief should prevail; rules governing oral argument; discretionary review by the highest court (the U.S. Supreme Court or the highest court of the state); and numerous other topics. For a concise overview of appellate issues in the federal context, *see* GREGORY CASTANIAS & ROBERT KLONOFF, FEDERAL APPELLATE PRACTICE AND PROCEDURE IN A NUTSHELL (2008).

One important issue involves the standard of review that the appellate court utilizes in reviewing a lower court judgment. As a general matter, findings of fact at the trial level may not be set aside by the appellate court unless they are "clearly erroneous." Fed. R. Civ. P. 52(a)(6); *Anderson v. Bessemer City*, 470 U.S. 564, 573 (1985) (finding of intentional discrimination is a fact subject to clearly erroneous review). On the other hand, appellate judges are experts in determining rules of law, and thus engage in de novo review on legal determinations, giving no deference to the trial court. *See, e.g., Salve Regina Coll. v. Russell*, 499 U.S. 225 (1991) (explaining that appellate judges devote their primary attention to reflecting on legal issues); *see also* Bryan Adamson, *Federal Rule of Civil*

Procedure 52(a) as an Ideological Weapon?, 34 Fla. St. U. L. Rev. 1025 (2007) (criticizing Rule 52(a) as being "malleable" and thus easily circumvented by appellate courts).

Many cases get resolved not by courts but through Alternative Dispute Resolution (ADR). ADR is a general term that encompasses an assortment of procedures to resolve disputes without a trial. ADR plays an important role in modern litigation because it "provides relief from an already overcrowded court docket." Mike Jay Garcia, *Key Trends in the Legal Profession*, 71 Fla. B.J. 16, 22 (May 1997). Two of the most commonly used forms of ADR are "mediation" and "arbitration."

Mediation is a process in which a person assists the parties in resolving a dispute. The mediator does not adjudicate anything but instead helps the parties to reach a resolution. An effective mediation enables the parties to "make[ ] free and informed choices as to process and outcome." AM. ARBITRATION ASS'N, AM. BAR ASS'N & ASS'N FOR CONFLICT RESOLUTION, THE MODEL STANDARDS OF CONDUCT FOR MEDIATORS (2005). Mediation is typically informal, and mediators use a number of different styles and approaches. *See, e.g.*, Samuel Imperati et al., *If Freud, Jung, Rogers, and Beck Were Mediators, Who Would the Parties Pick and What Are the Mediator's Obligations?*, 43 Idaho L. Rev. 643 (2007) (discussing various mediation approaches).

In contrast to mediation, arbitration is more like a court proceeding. Indeed, many arbitrators are retired judges. *See, e.g.*, JAMS, http://www.jamsadr.com/adr-arbitration/ (last visited Dec. 8, 2015) (noting that its arbitrators include retired federal and state court judges). In arbitration, each side presents its case to an arbitrator, who (unlike a mediator) has authority to make binding decisions. Ideally, arbitration occurs more promptly and inexpensively than a court proceeding, especially given that many U.S. courts are backlogged. *See* Jean Sternlight, *Introduction: Dreaming About Arbitration Reform*, 8 Nev. L.J. 1 (2007). The arbitration process is also intended to be less formal than a trial—eliminating or minimizing pre-hearing procedures, relaxing the rules of evidence, and allowing appeals in only limited circumstances. *See* David Schwartz, *If You Love Arbitration, Set it Free: How "Mandatory" Undermines "Arbitration"*, 8 Nev. L.J. 400 (2007) (discussing those characteristics but calling them an "idealization"). In recent years, however, some have criticized arbitrations as being protracted and expensive. *See, e.g.*, Joseph Daly & Suzanne Scheller, *Strengthening Arbitration by Facing its Challenges*, 28 Quinnipiac L. Rev. 67 (2009) (discussing the failure of arbitration to fulfill its promise of being faster and less expensive than litigation); Christine Newhall, *The AAA's War on Time and Cost*, 67 Disp. Resol. J. 20 (Oct. 2012) (discussing the American Arbitration Association's recent attempts to combat the increasing time and cost of arbitration).

Companies often use arbitration clauses in contracts with consumers. Arbitration clauses preclude bringing a lawsuit in court and require the consumer to resolve any dispute in arbitration. The use of arbitration clauses has become increasingly prevalent in recent years. As one article notes, arbitration clauses are becoming common in a wide variety of areas, such as cell phone contracts, cable TV contracts, employment agreements, car rental agreements, on-line transactions, and even in doctor-patient relationships. *See* Jessica Silver-Greenberg & Robert Gebeloff, *Arbitration Everywhere, Stacking the Deck of Justice*, N.Y. TIMES, Nov. 1, 2015, at A1. In many instances, arbitration clauses ban class action suits, making it unrealistic for consumers with small claims to pursue relief. One of the main difficulties in challenging such arbitration clauses as unfair or one-sided is that the Federal Arbitration Act (FAA) "embodies a strong federal policy favoring arbitration." Robert Klonoff, *The Decline of Class Actions*, 90 Wash. U. L. Rev. 729, 816 (2013). Recent Supreme Court cases have made it exceedingly difficult for consumers and others to challenge arbitration clauses. *See, e.g., DIRECTV, Inc. v. Imburgia*, 577 U.S. ___, 136 S. Ct. 463 (2015) (reversing a California court's refusal to enforce an arbitration clause and emphasizing that *Concepcion* is controlling law despite being a 5–4 decision); *Am. Express Co. v. Italian Colors Rest.*, 570 U.S. ___, 133 S. Ct. 2304 (2013) (reaffirming *Concepcion*, and holding that the FAA does not permit courts to ignore an arbitration clause waiving class actions even when the cost of arbitration would exceed the amount of the claim); *AT&T Mobility LLC v. Concepcion*, 563 U.S. 333 (2011) (holding that the savings clause of the FAA preempted state unconscionability laws).

Another controversial aspect of arbitration is the so-called captive arbitrator dilemma. When a company uses an arbitration clause, it is the company that chooses the arbitrator. If the arbitrator reaches decisions that are favorable to the consumer, the company will be less likely to use the arbitrator again. Studies show that companies are more likely to win in arbitration than at trial, and arbitrators who consistently find for businesses over consumers are more likely to get hired again. *See* JOSHUA FRANK, CENTER FOR RESPONSIBLE LENDING, STACKED DECK: A STATISTICAL ANALYSIS OF FORCED ARBITRATION 1–2 (2009). One report found, in a study of over 19,000 arbitration cases, that the business entity won more than 94% of the time. PUBLIC CITIZEN, THE ARBITRATION TRAP: HOW CREDIT CARD COMPANIES ENSNARE CONSUMERS 2 (2007).

For additional scholarly discussion of arbitration, *see, e.g.*, Richard Frankel, *The Arbitration Clause As Super Contract*, 91 Wash. U. L. Rev. 531 (2014) (arguing that courts should not favor arbitration, but rather should treat arbitration clauses like other contract provisions by requiring unambiguous language and allowing waiver when one party acts inconsistently with the arbitration clause); Theodore Eisenberg et al., *Arbitration's Summer Soldiers: An Empirical Study of Arbitration Clauses in Consumer and Nonconsumer Contracts*, 41 U. Mich. J.L. Reform 871 (2008) (concluding, based on empirical evidence, that corporate parties prefer litigation to arbitration in contracts with other corporations, but favor arbitration in consumer contracts, suggesting that corporations use arbitration clauses primarily to avoid consumer class action lawsuits); Theodore St. Antoine, *Mandatory Arbitration: Why It's Better Than It Looks*, 41 U. Mich. J.L. Reform 783 (2008) (concluding that arbitration may be a superior option to litigation for plaintiffs because it is less costly, more accessible, and yields comparable results).

I. REMEDIES

In both federal and state courts, numerous remedies are available. Monetary relief may consist of compensatory damages (to compensate a plaintiff for actual harm) and punitive damages (to punish a defendant for misconduct). A number of cases in this chapter and later chapters address requests for compensatory (and in some cases punitive) damages. Compensatory damages can address financial harm, personal injury, property damage, business loss, and a host of other types of damage. They are the primary vehicle for compensating injured parties. As one court has noted, "[t]he fundamental principle of damages is to restore the injured party, as nearly as possible, to the position he would have been in had it not been for the wrong of the other party." *United States v. Hatahley*, 257 F.2d 920, 923 (10th Cir. 1958). In some instances, proving damages can be challenging—for instance, when a plaintiff claims pain and suffering. Punitive damages are designed not to compensate the plaintiff but instead to punish defendants for especially egregious conduct. The Supreme Court has made clear that "grossly excessive" punitive damage awards violate the Fourteenth Amendment's Due Process Clause. *Pac. Mut. Life Ins. Co. v. Haslip*, 499 U.S. 1 (1991); Benjamin McMichael, Note, *Constitutional Limitations on Punitive Damages: Ambiguous Effects and Inconsistent Justifications*, 66 Vand. L. Rev. 961 (2013) (analyzing and critiquing Supreme Court's punitive damages jurisprudence).

There are also a variety of remedies that may be available in a particular case, with certain remedies being available even before judgment. Such remedies may include civil "arrest" of the defendant, "attachment" (seizure of property by a sheriff), "replevin" (recovery of property by the owner), "garnishment" (a court order directing payment of some or all of a person's salary to the person entitled to financial relief), and "sequestration" (taking possession of assets until a judgment is paid). Fed. R. Civ. P. 64(b). Prejudgment attachment of property can sometimes raise constitutional concerns. *See, e.g., Connecticut v. Doehr*, 501 U.S. 1 (1991) (Connecticut statute authorizing prejudgment attachment of real estate without prior notice or hearing (and with no requirement of posting a bond) violated the Due Process Clause of the Fourteenth Amendment).

One important remedy is an injunction. An injunction is an equitable device whereby a court can order a party to do something or refrain from doing something. Some injunctions (temporary restraining orders and preliminary injunctions) are ordered prior to judgment to require a party to take (or not take) specific action pending final judgment. A temporary restraining order is an emergency measure and in some instances can be issued without notice to the opposing party. A preliminary injunction, by contrast, is often intended to last until final judgment, and notice to the adverse party is required. *See, e.g.,* Fed. R. Civ. P. 65(a)–(b) (requiring notice for preliminary injunctions but not requiring notice for temporary restraining orders if specific requirements are met). Some injunctions are permanent in nature and are awarded as part of the judgment. Permanent injunctions have sometimes been used to grant structural relief, such as enforcing changes in prison conditions. The following case discusses the criteria for granting a permanent injunction.

eBAY INC. v. MERCEXCHANGE, L.L.C.

Supreme Court of the United States, 2006
547 U.S. 388

JUSTICE THOMAS delivered the opinion of the Court.

Ordinarily, a federal court considering whether to award permanent injunctive relief to a prevailing plaintiff applies the four-factor test historically employed by courts of equity. Petitioners eBay Inc. and Half.com, Inc., argue that this traditional test applies to disputes arising under the Patent Act, 35 U.S.C. §§ 1–376. We agree and, accordingly, vacate the judgment of the Court of Appeals.

I

Petitioner eBay operates a popular internet Web site that allows private sellers to list goods they wish to sell, either through an auction or at a fixed price. Petitioner Half.com, now a wholly owned subsidiary of eBay, operates a similar Web site. Respondent MercExchange, L.L.C., holds a number of patents, including a business method patent for an electronic market designed to facilitate the sale of goods between private individuals by establishing a central authority to promote trust among participants. MercExchange sought to license its patent to eBay and Half.com, as it had previously done with other companies, but the parties failed to reach an agreement. MercExchange subsequently filed a patent infringement suit against eBay and Half.com in the United States District Court for the Eastern District of Virginia. A jury found that MercExchange's patent was valid, that eBay and Half.com had infringed that patent, and that an award of damages was appropriate.

Following the jury verdict, the District Court denied MercExchange's motion for permanent injunctive relief. The Court of Appeals for the

Federal Circuit reversed, applying its "general rule that courts will issue permanent injunctions against patent infringement absent exceptional circumstances." We granted certiorari to determine the appropriateness of this general rule.

II

According to well-established principles of equity, a plaintiff seeking a permanent injunction must satisfy a four-factor test before a court may grant such relief. A plaintiff must demonstrate: (1) that it has suffered an irreparable injury; (2) that remedies available at law, such as monetary damages, are inadequate to compensate for that injury; (3) that, considering the balance of hardships between the plaintiff and defendant, a remedy in equity is warranted; and (4) that the public interest would not be disserved by a permanent injunction. The decision to grant or deny permanent injunctive relief is an act of equitable discretion by the district court, reviewable on appeal for abuse of discretion.

These familiar principles apply with equal force to disputes arising under the Patent Act. As this Court has long recognized, "a major departure from the long tradition of equity practice should not be lightly implied." Nothing in the Patent Act indicates that Congress intended such a departure. To the contrary, the Patent Act expressly provides that injunctions "may" issue "in accordance with the principles of equity."

To be sure, the Patent Act also declares that "patents shall have the attributes of personal property," § 261, including "the right to exclude others from making, using, offering for sale, or selling the invention," § 154(a)(1). According to the Court of Appeals, this statutory right to exclude alone justifies its general rule in favor of permanent injunctive relief. But the creation of a right is distinct from the provision of remedies for violations of that right. Indeed, the Patent Act itself indicates that patents shall have the attributes of personal property "[s]ubject to the provisions of this title," 35 U.S.C. § 261, including, presumably, the provision that injunctive relief "may" issue only "in accordance with the principles of equity," § 283.

This approach is consistent with our treatment of injunctions under the Copyright Act. Like a patent owner, a copyright holder possesses "the right to exclude others from using his property." Like the Patent Act, the Copyright Act provides that courts "may" grant injunctive relief "on such terms as it may deem reasonable to prevent or restrain infringement of a copyright." 17 U.S.C. § 502(a). And as in our decision today, this Court has consistently rejected invitations to replace traditional equitable considerations with a rule that an injunction automatically follows a determination that a copyright has been infringed.

Neither the District Court nor the Court of Appeals below fairly applied these traditional equitable principles in deciding respondent's motion for a permanent injunction. Although the District Court recited the traditional four-factor test, it appeared to adopt certain expansive principles suggesting that injunctive relief could not issue in a broad swath of cases. Most notably, it concluded that a "plaintiff's willingness to license its patents" and "its lack of commercial activity in practicing the patents" would be sufficient to establish that the patent holder would not suffer irreparable harm if an injunction did not issue. But traditional equitable principles do not permit such broad classifications. For example, some patent holders, such as university researchers or self-made inventors, might reasonably prefer to license their patents, rather than undertake efforts to secure the financing necessary to bring their works to market themselves. Such patent holders may be able to satisfy the traditional four-factor test, and we see no basis for categorically denying them the opportunity to do so. To the extent that the District Court adopted such a categorical rule, then, its analysis cannot be squared with the principles of equity adopted by Congress. The court's categorical rule is also in tension with *Continental Paper Bag Co. v. Eastern Paper Bag Co.*, 210 U.S. 405 (1908), which rejected the contention that a court of equity has no jurisdiction to grant injunctive relief to a patent holder who has unreasonably declined to use the patent.

In reversing the District Court, the Court of Appeals departed in the opposite direction from the four-factor test. The court articulated a "general rule," unique to patent disputes, "that a permanent injunction will issue once infringement and validity have been adjudged." The court further indicated that injunctions should be denied only in the "unusual" case, under "exceptional circumstances" and " 'in rare instances . . . to protect the public interest.' " Just as the District Court erred in its categorical denial of injunctive relief, the Court of Appeals erred in its categorical grant of such relief.

Because we conclude that neither court below correctly applied the traditional four-factor framework that governs the award of injunctive relief, we vacate the judgment of the Court of Appeals, so that the District Court may apply that framework in the first instance. In doing so, we take no position on whether permanent injunctive relief should or should not issue in this particular case, or indeed in any number of other disputes arising under the Patent Act. We hold only that the decision whether to grant or deny injunctive relief rests within the equitable discretion of the district courts, and that such discretion must be exercised consistent with traditional principles of equity, in patent disputes no less than in other cases governed by such standards.

Accordingly, we vacate the judgment of the Court of Appeals and remand the case for further proceedings consistent with this opinion.

[Concurring opinion by CHIEF JUSTICE ROBERTS, joined by JUSTICE SCALIA and JUSTICE GINSBURG, is omitted.]

NOTES AND QUESTIONS

1. What is a permanent injunction? What criteria must a party satisfy in seeking a permanent injunction?

2. In the *eBay* case, why was MercExchange seeking a permanent injunction?

3. The Supreme Court in *eBay* found that both the district court and the court of appeals had applied an incorrect analysis (in different ways). How did the district court err? How did the court of appeals err? What approach did the Supreme Court order the lower courts to apply on remand?

4. The *eBay* test has also been applied to preliminary injunctions, which are injunctions issued pending trial to prevent irreparable injury. As the Supreme Court has explained: "A plaintiff seeking a preliminary injunction must establish that he is likely to succeed on the merits, that he is likely to suffer irreparable harm in the absence of preliminary relief, that the balance of equities tips in his favor, and that an injunction is in the public interest." *Winter v. Nat. Res. Def. Council, Inc.*, 555 U.S. 7, 20 (2008). *See generally* Anthony DiSarro, *Freeze Frame: The Supreme Court's Reaffirmation of the Substantive Principles of Preliminary Injunctions*, 47 Gonz. L. Rev. 51 (2011–2012) (surveying Supreme Court law of preliminary injunctions and tracing the device back to equitable principles of English chancery courts).

5. For additional discussion on the effect of *eBay* on injunction law, *see, e.g.*, Jiarui Liu, *Copyright Injunctions After* eBay: *An Empirical Study*, 16 Lewis & Clark L. Rev. 215 (2012) (discussing the disconnect between the *eBay* decision and practical concerns of copyright law).

J. SANCTIONS

"Sanctions" are penalties that courts can impose on parties or attorneys for violations of court orders or rules. Sanctions can take many forms, including fines, restrictions at trial, and even dismissal of claims. Generally, the type of sanction applied will depend on the severity of the violation. The *Cine Forty-Second Street Theater Corp.* case discussed sanctions in the discovery context. The following case discusses sanctions under Fed. R. Civ. P. 11 in the context of a complaint that allegedly lacked evidentiary support.

GRYNBERG V. IVANHOE ENERGY, INC.

United States District Court, District of Colorado, 2009
663 F. Supp. 2d 1022

MILLER, DISTRICT JUDGE.

This matter is before me on Defendant Robert M. Friedland's ("Friedland") Motion for Sanctions. * * *

BACKGROUND

This case surrounds the Pungarayacu Tar Sands Heavy Oil Deposit (the "Pungarayacu Field") in the Nation of Ecuador ("Ecuador"). Essentially, Plaintiffs allege that Defendants conspired to acquire Plaintiffs' concessions to the Pungarayacu Field by unlawfully utilizing Plaintiffs' confidential technical analysis of the Pungarayacu Field and bribing Ecuadorian officials, including President Raphael Correa Delgado, to cancel Plaintiffs' concessions and, instead, award the concessions to Defendants. Friedland is the President, CEO, and Executive Chairman of Ivanhoe Energy, Inc. ("Ivanhoe"). Ivanhoe is the parent company of both Ivanhoe Energy Latin America, Inc. ("IELA") and Ivanhoe Energy Ecuador, Inc. ("IEE"), the company to which the Pungarayacu Field concessions were awarded. In the Original Complaint, Plaintiffs allege that Friedland was in Ecuador in March 2008 and had "started negotiations for the Plaintiffs' Pungarayacu deposit with the Government of Ecuador." The Original Complaint goes on to allege that Jose Fabricio Correa Delgado ("Correa")[1] "demanded and received cash and valuable gifts from his co-Defendants as his payment to expedite award of the Pungarayacu [Field] concession to the Ivanhoe Defendants." Plaintiffs further allege that [Friedland and other defendants violated various U.S. statutes by bribing Ecuadorian government officials].

* * *

On January 9, 2009, pursuant to Fed. R. Civ. P. 11(c)(2), Friedland sent Plaintiffs a copy of his Rule 11 motion which alleges that Plaintiffs did not have sufficient evidentiary support for some of the factual contentions included in the Original Complaint. Specifically, Friedland maintains that Plaintiffs' allegations that he traveled to Ecuador or bribed any Ecuadorian government officials are patently false and, therefore, could not have been supported by sufficient evidentiary basis as required by Fed. R. Civ. P. 11(b). Friedland submits a sworn affidavit stating that he has never traveled to Ecuador, has never met Correa, has never met with any Ecuadorian government officials, and has never bribed any government officials. After waiting the requisite twenty-one days under Fed. R. Civ. P. 11(c)(2), Friedland filed the current motion for sanctions on February 9, 2009. The motion seeks "sanctions against Mr. Grynberg[2] and Mr. Jatko"[3] jointly and severally in the form of "attorney fees and costs incurred in responding to the frivolous allegations in the Complaint." Friedland also requests that [various paragraphs] be struck from the Complaint.

---

[1]   Correa was previously a defendant in this lawsuit. However, I dismissed him from the case for lack of personal jurisdiction * * *.

[2]   Plaintiff Jack J. Grynberg ("Grynberg") verified the Original Complaint.

[3]   Roger A. Jatko ("Jatko") is one of the attorneys of record for the Plaintiffs in this action and the attorney that signed the Original Complaint.

On the same day that Friedland filed the Motion for Sanctions, Plaintiffs filed an Amended Complaint. * * * The Amended Complaint alters the specific allegations relating to Friedland, Correa, and the alleged bribery. Correa's involvement in the alleged bribery is completely excluded from the Amended Complaint which, instead, alleges simply that "access to President Raphael Correa Delgado" was the "key" to Defendants' acquisition of the concessions to the Pungarayacu Field but does not specify which government official provided the "access" to President Correa Delgado or accepted the bribes. With respect to Friedland, the Amended Complaint removes his name from the allegations, instead referring generally to "representatives of Ivanhoe" or "Defendants." * * *

STANDARD OF REVIEW

Federal Rule of Civil Procedure 11 provides that:

> By presenting to the court a pleading, written motion, or other paper . . . an attorney or unrepresented party certifies that to the best of the person's knowledge, information, and belief, formed after an inquiry reasonable under the circumstances * * * the factual contentions have evidentiary support or, if specifically so identified, will likely have evidentiary support after a reasonable opportunity for further investigation or discovery. . . .

Fed. R. Civ. P. 11(b). Essentially, "Rule 11 imposes a duty on attorneys to certify that they have conducted a reasonable inquiry and have determined that any papers filed with the court are well-grounded in fact, legally tenable, and 'not interposed for any improper purpose.'" *Cooter & Gell v. Hartmarx Corp.*, 496 U.S. 384, 393 (1990). The rule applies with equal force to the attorney who signs the document and any represented party who signs the document. *See Bus. Guides, Inc. v. Chromatic Communs. Enters.*, 498 U.S. 533, 543–44 (1991) ("It seems plain that the voluntary signature of a represented party, no less than the mandatory signature of an attorney, is capable of violating [Rule 11].")

With respect to violations, Rule 11 provides that "[i]f, after notice and a reasonable opportunity to respond, the court determines that Rule 11(b) has been violated, the court may impose an appropriate sanction on any attorney, law firm, or party that violated the rule or is responsible for the violation." Fed. R. Civ. P. 11(c)(1). Rule 11 sanctions may include, "if imposed on motion and warranted for effective deterrence, an order directing payment to the movant or part of all of the reasonable attorney's fees and other expenses directly resulting from the violation." Fed. R. Civ. P. 11(c)(4). However, imposition of sanctions under Rule 11 "must be limited to what suffices to deter repetition of the conduct or comparable conduct by others similarly situated." *Id.; see also Hutchinson v. Pfeil*, 208 F.3d 1180, 1183 (10th Cir. 2000) ("[I]n keeping with its 'ultimate goal of deterrence, rather than compensation,' Rule 11 'de-emphasizes monetary sanctions and discourages direct payouts to the opposing party.'" [citation omitted]).

DISCUSSION

In this case, Friedland seeks joint and several sanctions against Jatko, as the attorney who signed the Original Complaint, and Grynberg, as the represented party who verified the Original Complaint, for failure to ensure that the factual allegations in the Original Complaint had adequate evidentiary support. In response, Plaintiffs present no valid argument that they had adequate evidentiary support for the specific allegations made against Friedland in the Original Complaint. Rather, they allege that they based their factual allegations in the Original Complaint on statements by witnesses in Ecuador whom Plaintiffs are currently not willing or unable to reveal due to alleged safety concerns for the witnesses. Furthermore, Plaintiffs admit that "presently available witnesses may not now adequately support the precise identification of the Ivanhoe Energy, Inc. representatives who participated in the activities alleged in Plaintiffs' Verified Complaint. Notably, however, they do not allege that the confidential witnesses specifically named Friedland as the individual engaging in negotiations in Ecuador or bribing Ecuadorian government officials. Nor do Plaintiffs provide any additional detail regarding the statements of these witnesses such as how these witnesses became aware of the bribery, whether the witnesses were in a position to know the specific parties involved in the alleged bribery, or whether the witnesses were parties to the bribery or had merely heard rumors of the bribery. Therefore, I conclude that Plaintiffs have not demonstrated that they based their allegations concerning Friedland on sufficient evidentiary basis to avoid sanctions under Rule 11.

I note that Plaintiffs' filing of the Amended Complaint does not cure their violation of Rule 11. Rule 11 provides a "safe harbor" provision that requires the moving party to serve a copy of the motion on the alleged violator and allow the alleged violator twenty-one days in which to "withdraw[ ] or appropriately correct[ ]" the "challenged paper, claim, defense, contention, or denial." Fed. R. Civ. P. 11(c)(2). If the alleged violator remedies the alleged violation, the moving party is barred from filing the motion with the court. In this case, as Friedland served Plaintiffs on January 9, 2009, Plaintiffs' safe harbor period ended on January 30, 2009. Plaintiffs did not move to dismiss the complaint or file an amended complaint removing the specific allegations against Friedland during this time. As Rule 11 does not include a deadline for filing, Friedland was free to file the motion for sanctions at any time after January 30, 2009. He did so on February 9, 2009 at 11:28 a.m. MST. Some four hours later, at 3:45 p.m. MST, Plaintiffs filed the Amended Complaint removing the specific allegations against Friedland and instead generally referring to the "representatives of Ivanhoe" or "Defendants." As the Amended Complaint was filed outside of the safe harbor period, it did not cure the Rule 11 violations contained in the Original Complaint. Plaintiffs' suggestions that Friedland improperly filed his motion for sanctions *after* Plaintiffs cured the deficiencies by filing the Amended Complaint is plainly wrong.

[Plaintiffs argue] that Defendants are using the motion for sanctions to delay the proceedings in this Court or for intimidation * * *. Not only is there no deadline for filing the motion, the delay provided Plaintiffs with further opportunity to amend the complaint. Moreover, a ten-day delay * * * was certainly not a lengthy [one]. * * * With regard to Plaintiffs' claim that Friedland used the Rule 11 procedure as intimidation, a moving party is required under Rule 11 to send a copy of the motion to the opposing party prior to filing such motion with the court. These arguments do not persuade me that Plaintiffs should not be sanctioned.

Turning to possible sanctions, the ultimate goal of Rule 11 is deterrence as opposed to compensation for the moving party. Although one could arguably impose a penalty and a larger expense amount to deter Plaintiffs' actions in the future, I conclude that a sanction for the amount of the expenses incurred by Friedland in making his motion for sanctions is sufficient to promote the goal of deterrence, especially given Plaintiffs' filing of the Amended Complaint to correct the Original Complaint's deficiencies. Therefore, Friedland shall submit a description of the total amount of expenses, including attorneys' fees, incurred in responding to the Original Complaint and in making the motion for sanctions. * * *

Accordingly, it is ordered:

* * *

* * * Plaintiff Jack J. Grynberg and counsel Roger A. Jatko are sanctioned, jointly and severally, pursuant to Fed. R. Civ. P. 11(c) for a violation of Fed. R. Civ. P. 11(b)(3) in the amount of the total expenses, including attorneys' fees, incurred by Friedland in filing this motion for sanctions.

* * *

NOTES AND QUESTIONS

1.   What is the purpose of Federal Rule of Civil Procedure 11? What is the "safe harbor" and what purpose does it serve?

2.   What did the *Grynberg* court hold? Was the court correct in concluding that sanctions were justified? Did the court impose sufficiently onerous sanctions under the circumstances?

3.   In contrast to the discovery-based sanctions under Fed. R. Civ. P. 37 in *Cine Forty-Second Street Theatre Corp.*, discussed *supra*, the sanctions in *Grynberg* are under Fed. R. Civ. P. 11. Rule 37 sanctions are appropriate when an attorney fails to comply with the rules of discovery or the court's orders

regarding discovery. Rule 11 sanctions are appropriate, *inter alia*, when an attorney files a pleading that lacks evidentiary support.

4. For further discussion of Rule 11 sanctions, *see, e.g.*, Richard Johnson, *Integrating Legal Ethics & Professional Responsibility with Federal Rule of Civil Procedure 11*, 37 Loy. L.A. L. Rev. 819 (2004) (analyzing the relationship between Rule 11 and the rule of professional conduct that prohibits lawyers from filing baseless claims, and concluding that Rule 11 should be the primary tool for enforcing compliance with attorney ethical standards); Georgene Vairo, *Rule 11 and the Profession*, 67 Fordham L. Rev. 589 (1998) (arguing that Rule 11 has had positive effects by increasing pre-filing research and decreasing marginal pleadings or motions, but has also led to abuse by lawyers who file improper and unsupported Rule 11 motions).

K. PRIVILEGES

In a variety of circumstances, communications are protected from disclosure (and thus are "privileged"). A privilege may apply, for example, to communications between spouses, between a religious advisor (such as a priest) and an advisee, between a therapist and a patient, and between an attorney and a client. (*United States v. Nixon*, a case featured in Chapter 2, involved the scope of privilege for conversations between the President and his close advisors.) Protecting these various kinds of communications promotes full and uninhibited discussions. At the same time, invocation of a privilege may deprive the opposing party of important evidence. The following case discusses the attorney-client privilege in the corporate context. It also discusses a related doctrine known as the "work product" doctrine.

UPJOHN CO. V. UNITED STATES
Supreme Court of the United States, 1981
449 U.S. 383

JUSTICE REHNQUIST delivered the opinion of the Court.

We granted certiorari in this case to address important questions concerning the scope of the attorney-client privilege in the corporate context and the applicability of the work-product doctrine in proceedings to enforce tax summonses. With respect to the privilege question the parties and various *amici* have described our task as one of choosing between two "tests" which have gained adherents in the courts of appeals. We are acutely aware, however, that we sit to decide concrete cases and not abstract propositions of law. We decline to lay down a broad rule or series of rules to govern all conceivable future questions in this area, even were we able to do so. We can and do, however, conclude that the attorney-client privilege protects the communications involved in this case from compelled disclosure and that the work-product doctrine does apply in tax summons enforcement proceedings.

I

Petitioner Upjohn Co. manufactures and sells pharmaceuticals here and abroad. In January 1976 independent accountants conducting an audit of one of Upjohn's foreign subsidiaries discovered that the subsidiary made payments to or for the benefit of foreign government officials in order to secure government business. The accountants so informed petitioner, Mr. Gerard Thomas, Upjohn's Vice President, Secretary, and General Counsel. Thomas is a member of the Michigan and New York Bars, and has been Upjohn's General Counsel for 20 years. He consulted with outside counsel and R. T. Parfet, Jr., Upjohn's Chairman of the Board. It was decided that the company would conduct an internal investigation of what were termed "questionable payments." As part of this investigation the attorneys prepared a letter containing a questionnaire which was sent to "All Foreign General and Area Managers" over the Chairman's signature. The letter began by noting recent disclosures that several American companies made "possibly illegal" payments to foreign government officials and emphasized that the management needed full information concerning any such payments made by Upjohn. The letter indicated that the Chairman had asked Thomas, identified as "the company's General Counsel," "to conduct an investigation for the purpose of determining the nature and magnitude of any payments made by the Upjohn Company or any of its subsidiaries to any employee or official of a foreign government." The questionnaire sought detailed information concerning such payments. Managers were instructed to treat the investigation as "highly confidential" and not to discuss it with anyone other than Upjohn employees who might be helpful in providing the requested information. Responses were to be sent directly to Thomas. Thomas and outside counsel also interviewed the recipients of the questionnaire and some 33 other Upjohn officers or employees as part of the investigation.

On March 26, 1976, the company voluntarily submitted a preliminary report to the Securities and Exchange Commission [SEC] on Form 8-K disclosing certain questionable payments.* A copy of the report was simultaneously submitted to the Internal Revenue Service [IRS], which immediately began an investigation to determine the tax consequences of the payments. Special agents conducting the investigation were given lists by Upjohn of all those interviewed and all who had responded to the questionnaire. On November 23, 1976, the Service issued a summons pursuant to [federal law] demanding production of:

> All files relative to the investigation conducted under the supervision of Gerard Thomas to identify payments to employees of foreign governments and any political contributions made by the Upjohn Company or any of its affiliates since January 1, 1971

---

* A Form 8-K is a report whereby public companies reveal to the SEC material events that would be of interest to shareholders. [Ed.]

and to determine whether any funds of the Upjohn Company had been improperly accounted for on the corporate books during the same period.

The records should include but not be limited to written questionnaires sent to managers of the Upjohn Company's foreign affiliates, and memorandums or notes of the interviews conducted in the United States and abroad with officers and employees of the Upjohn Company and its subsidiaries.

The company declined to produce the documents specified in the second paragraph on the grounds that they were protected from disclosure by the attorney-client privilege and constituted the work product of attorneys prepared in anticipation of litigation. On August 31, 1977, the United States filed a petition seeking enforcement of the summons * * * in the United States District Court for the Western District of Michigan. That court adopted the recommendation of a Magistrate who concluded that the summons should be enforced. Petitioners appealed to the Court of Appeals for the Sixth Circuit which rejected the Magistrate's finding of a waiver of the attorney-client privilege, but agreed that the privilege did not apply "[t]o the extent that the communications were made by officers and agents not responsible for directing Upjohn's actions in response to legal advice . . . for the simple reason that the communications were not the 'client's.'" The court reasoned that accepting petitioners' claim for a broader application of the privilege would encourage upper-echelon management to ignore unpleasant facts and create too broad a "zone of silence." Noting that Upjohn's counsel had interviewed officials such as the Chairman and President, the Court of Appeals remanded to the District Court so that a determination of who was within the "control group" could be made. * * *

II

Federal Rule of Evidence 501 provides that "the privilege of a witness . . . shall be governed by the principles of the common law as they may be interpreted by the courts of the United States in light of reason and experience." The attorney-client privilege is the oldest of the privileges for confidential communications known to the common law. Its purpose is to encourage full and frank communication between attorneys and their clients and thereby promote broader public interests in the observance of law and administration of justice. The privilege recognizes that sound legal advice or advocacy serves public ends and that such advice or advocacy depends upon the lawyer's being fully informed by the client. * * * "The lawyer-client privilege rests on the need for the advocate and counselor to know all that relates to the client's reasons for seeking representation if the professional mission is to be carried out." And we [have] recognized the purpose of the privilege to be "to encourage clients to make full disclosure to their attorneys." This rationale for the privilege has long been recognized by the Court. * * * Admittedly[,] complications in the application of the privilege arise when the client is a corporation, which in theory is an artificial creature of the law, and not an individual; but this Court has assumed that the privilege applies when the client is a corporation, and the Government does not contest the general proposition.

The Court of Appeals, however, considered the application of the privilege in the corporate context to present a "different problem," since the client was an inanimate entity and "only the senior management, guiding and integrating the several operations . . . can be said to possess an identity analogous to the corporation as a whole." The first case to articulate the so-called "control group test" adopted by the court below, *Philadelphia v. Westinghouse Elec. Corp.*, 210 F. Supp. 483, 485 (E.D. Pa. 1962), reflected a similar conceptual approach:

> Keeping in mind that the question is, Is it the corporation which is seeking the lawyer's advice when the asserted privileged communication is made?, the most satisfactory solution, I think, is that if the employee making the communication, of whatever rank he may be, is in a position to control or even to take a substantial part in a decision about any action which the corporation may take upon the advice of the attorney, . . . then, in effect, *he is (or personifies) the corporation* when he makes his disclosure to the lawyer and the privilege would apply. (Emphasis supplied.)

Such a view, we think, overlooks the fact that the privilege exists to protect not only the giving of professional advice to those who can act on it but also the giving of information to the lawyer to enable him to give sound and informed advice. The first step in the resolution of any legal problem is ascertaining the factual background and sifting through the facts with an eye to the legally relevant. *See* ABA Code of Professional Responsibility, Ethical Consideration 4–1:

> A lawyer should be fully informed of all the facts of the matter he is handling in order for his client to obtain the full advantage of our legal system. It is for the lawyer in the exercise of his independent professional judgment to separate the relevant and important from the irrelevant and unimportant. The observance of the ethical obligation of a lawyer to hold inviolate the confidences and secrets of his client not only facilitates the full development of facts essential to proper representation of the client but also encourages laymen to seek early legal assistance.

In the case of the individual client the provider of information and the person who acts on the lawyer's advice are one and the same. In the corporate context, however, it will frequently be employees beyond the control group as defined by the court below—"officers and agents . . . responsible for directing [the company's] actions in response to legal advice"—who will possess the information needed by the corporation's lawyers. Middle-level—and indeed lower-level—employees can, by actions within the scope of their employment, embroil the corporation in serious legal difficulties, and it is only natural that these employees would have the relevant information needed by corporate counsel if he is adequately to advise the client with respect to such actual or potential difficulties. * * *

The control group test adopted by the court below thus frustrates the very purpose of the privilege by discouraging the communication of relevant information by employees of the client to attorneys seeking to render legal advice to the client corporation. The attorney's advice will also frequently be more significant to noncontrol group members than to those who officially sanction the advice, and the control group test makes it more difficult to convey full and frank legal advice to the employees who will put into effect the client corporation's policy.

The narrow scope given the attorney-client privilege by the court below not only makes it difficult for corporate attorneys to formulate sound advice when their client is faced with a specific legal problem but also threatens to limit the valuable efforts of corporate counsel to ensure their client's compliance with the law. In light of the vast and complicated array of regulatory legislation confronting the modern corporation, corporations, unlike most individuals, "constantly go to lawyers to find out how to obey the law," particularly since compliance with the law in this area is hardly an instinctive matter. The test adopted by the court below is difficult to apply in practice, though no abstractly formulated and unvarying "test" will necessarily enable courts to decide questions such as this with mathematical precision. But if the purpose of the attorney-client privilege is to be served, the attorney and client must be able to predict with some degree of certainty whether particular discussions will be protected. An uncertain privilege, or one which purports to be certain but results in widely varying applications by the courts, is little better than no privilege at all. The very terms of the test adopted by the court below suggest the unpredictability of its application. The test restricts the availability of the privilege to those officers who play a "substantial role" in deciding and directing a corporation's legal response. Disparate decisions in cases applying this test illustrate its unpredictability.

The communications at issue were made by Upjohn employees to counsel for Upjohn acting as such, at the direction of corporate superiors in order to secure legal advice from counsel. As the Magistrate found, "Mr. Thomas consulted with the Chairman of the Board and outside counsel and thereafter conducted a factual investigation to determine the nature and extent of the questionable payments *and to be in a position to give legal advice to the company with respect to the payments.*" (Emphasis supplied.) Information, not available from upper-echelon management, was needed to supply a basis for legal advice concerning compliance with securities and tax laws, foreign laws, currency regulations, duties to shareholders, and potential litigation in each of these areas. The communications concerned matters within the scope of the employees' corporate duties, and the employees themselves were sufficiently aware that they were being questioned in order that the corporation could obtain legal advice. The questionnaire identified Thomas as "the company's General Counsel" and referred in its opening sentence to the possible illegality of payments such as the ones on which information was sought. A statement of policy accompanying the questionnaire clearly indicated the legal implications of the investigation. The policy statement was issued "in order that there be no uncertainty in the future as to the policy with respect to the practices which are the subject of this investigation." It began "Upjohn will comply with all laws and regulations," and stated that commissions or payments "will not be used as a subterfuge for bribes or illegal payments" and that all payments must be "proper and legal." Any future agreements with foreign distributors or agents were to be approved "by a company attorney" and any questions concerning the policy were to be referred "to the company's General Counsel." This statement was issued to Upjohn employees worldwide, so that even those interviewees not receiving a questionnaire were aware of the legal implications of the interviews. Pursuant to explicit instructions from the Chairman of the Board, the communications were considered "highly confidential" when made, and have been kept confidential by the company. Consistent with the underlying purposes of the attorney-client privilege, these communications must be protected against compelled disclosure.

The Court of Appeals declined to extend the attorney-client privilege beyond the limits of the control group test for fear that doing so would entail severe burdens on discovery and create a broad "zone of silence" over corporate affairs. Application of the attorney-client privilege to communications such as those involved here, however, puts the adversary in no worse position than if the communications had never taken place. The privilege only protects disclosure of communications; it does not protect disclosure of the underlying facts by those who communicated with the attorney.

* * *

Here the Government was free to question the employees who communicated with Thomas and outside counsel. Upjohn has provided the IRS with a list of such employees, and the IRS has already interviewed some 25 of them. While it would probably be more convenient for the Government to secure the results of petitioner's internal investigation by simply subpoenaing the questionnaires and notes taken by petitioner's attorneys, such considerations of convenience do not overcome the policies served by the attorney-client privilege. * * *

Needless to say, we decide only the case before us, and do not undertake to draft a set of rules which should govern challenges to investigatory subpoenas. Any such approach would violate the spirit of Federal Rule of Evidence 501. While such a "case-by-case" basis may to some slight extent undermine desirable certainty in the boundaries of the attorney-client privilege, it obeys the spirit of the Rules. At the same time we conclude that the narrow "control group test" sanctioned by the Court of Appeals, in this case cannot * * * govern the development of the law in this area.

III

Our decision that the communications by Upjohn employees to counsel are covered by the attorney-client privilege disposes of the case so far as the responses to the questionnaires and any notes reflecting responses to interview questions are concerned. The summons reaches further, however, and Thomas has testified that his notes and memoranda of interviews go beyond recording responses to his questions. To the extent that the material subject to the summons is not protected by the attorney-client privilege as disclosing communications between an employee and counsel, we must reach the ruling by the Court of Appeals that the work-product doctrine does not apply to summonses issued [by the IRS].

The Government concedes, wisely, that * * * the work-product doctrine [applies] to IRS summonses. This doctrine was announced by the Court over 30 years ago in *Hickman v. Taylor*, 329 U.S. 495 (1947). In that case the Court rejected "an attempt, without purported necessity or justification, to secure written statements, private memoranda and personal recollections prepared or formed by an adverse party's counsel in the course of his legal duties." The Court noted that "it is essential that a lawyer work with a certain degree of privacy" and reasoned that if discovery of the material sought were permitted

> much of what is now put down in writing would remain unwritten. An attorney's thoughts, heretofore inviolate, would not be his own. Inefficiency, unfairness and sharp practices would inevitably develop in the giving of legal advice and in the preparation of cases for trial. The effect on the legal profession would be demoralizing. And the interests of the clients and the cause of justice would be poorly served.

* * *

* * * [T]he obligation imposed by a tax summons remains "subject to the traditional privileges and limitations." Nothing in the language of the [applicable federal statute] or [its] legislative history suggests an intent on the part of Congress to preclude application of the work-product doctrine. Rule 26(b)(3) codifies the work-product doctrine, and the Federal Rules of Civil Procedure are made applicable to summons enforcement proceedings by Rule 81(a)(3) [currently Rule 81(a)(5)]. While conceding the applicability of the work-product doctrine, the Government asserts that it has made a

sufficient showing of necessity to overcome its protections. The Magistrate apparently so found. The Government relies on the following language in *Hickman*:

> We do not mean to say that all written materials obtained or prepared by an adversary's counsel with an eye toward litigation are necessarily free from discovery in all cases. Where relevant and nonprivileged facts remain hidden in an attorney's file and where production of those facts is essential to the preparation of one's case, discovery may properly be had. . . . And production might be justified where the witnesses are no longer available or can be reached only with difficulty.

The Government stresses that interviewees are scattered across the globe and that Upjohn has forbidden its employees to answer questions it considers irrelevant. The above-quoted language from *Hickman*, however, did not apply to "oral statements made by witnesses . . . whether presently in the form of [the attorney's] mental impressions or memoranda." As to such material the Court did "not believe that any showing of necessity can be made under the circumstances of this case so as to justify production. . . . If there should be a rare situation justifying production of these matters petitioner's case is not of that type." Forcing an attorney to disclose notes and memoranda of witnesses' oral statements is particularly disfavored because it tends to reveal the attorney's mental processes.

Rule 26 accords special protection to work product revealing the attorney's mental processes. The Rule permits disclosure of documents and tangible things constituting attorney work product upon a showing of substantial need and inability to obtain the equivalent without undue hardship. This was the standard applied by the Magistrate. Rule 26 goes on, however, to state that "[i]n ordering discovery of such materials when the required showing has been made, the court shall protect against disclosure of the mental impressions, conclusions, opinions or legal theories of an attorney or other representative of a party concerning the litigation." Although this language does not specifically refer to memoranda based on oral statements of witnesses, the *Hickman* court stressed the danger that compelled disclosure of such memoranda would reveal the attorney's mental processes. It is clear that this is the sort of material the draftsmen of the Rule had in mind as deserving special protection. *See* Notes of Advisory Committee on 1970 Amendment to Rules, 28 U.S.C. App., p. 442 ("The subdivision . . . goes on to protect against disclosure the mental impressions, conclusions, opinions, or legal theories . . . of an attorney or other representative of a party. The *Hickman* opinion drew special attention to the need for protecting an attorney against discovery of memoranda prepared from recollection of oral interviews. The courts have steadfastly safeguarded against disclosure of lawyers' mental impressions and legal theories. . . .").

Based on the foregoing, some courts have concluded that *no* showing of necessity can overcome protection of work product which is based on oral statements from witnesses. Those courts declining to adopt an absolute rule have nonetheless recognized that such material is entitled to special protection.

We do not decide the issue at this time. It is clear that the Magistrate applied the wrong standard when he concluded that the Government had made a sufficient showing of necessity to overcome the protections of the work-product doctrine. The Magistrate applied the "substantial need" and "without undue hardship" standard articulated in the first part of Rule 26(b)(3). The notes and memoranda sought by the Government here, however, are work product based on oral statements. If they reveal communications, they are, in this case, protected by the attorney-client privilege. To the extent they do not reveal communications, they reveal the attorneys' mental processes in evaluating the communications. As Rule 26 and *Hickman* make clear, such work product cannot be disclosed simply on a showing of substantial need and inability to obtain the equivalent without undue hardship.

While we are not prepared at this juncture to say that such material is always protected by the work-product rule, we think a far stronger showing of necessity and unavailability by other means than was made by the Government or applied by the Magistrate in this case would be necessary to compel disclosure. Since the Court of Appeals thought that the work-product protection was never applicable in an enforcement proceeding such as this, and since the Magistrate whose recommendations the District Court adopted applied too lenient a standard of protection, we think the best procedure with respect to this aspect of the case would be to reverse the judgment of the Court of Appeals for the Sixth Circuit and remand the case to it for such further proceedings in connection with the work-product claim as are consistent with this opinion.

Accordingly, the judgment of the Court of Appeals is reversed, and the case remanded for further proceedings.

[Concurring opinion by CHIEF JUSTICE BURGER is omitted.]

NOTES AND QUESTIONS

1.   Why is the attorney-client privilege important? What unique attorney-client privilege issues arise in the context of a corporation?

2.   What is the work product doctrine? Why is the doctrine important? How does the work product doctrine differ from the attorney-client privilege?

3.   What did the Supreme Court in *Upjohn* hold with respect to the attorney-client privilege? Is the Court's analysis persuasive?

4.   What did the Supreme Court in *Upjohn* hold with respect to the work product doctrine? Is the Court's analysis persuasive?

5.   For further discussion of the attorney-client privilege and the work product doctrine, *see, e.g.*, Edward Imwinkelried, *The Validity of the 2010 Federal Rule of Civil Procedure 26 Amendment Governing the Waiver of Work Product Protection: Is the Work Product Doctrine an Evidentiary Privilege?*, 37 U. Dayton L. Rev. 279 (2012) (explaining the similarities and differences between the attorney-client privilege and the work product doctrine; among the similarities, both doctrines exclude evidence that may be reliable and relevant; among the differences, the attorney-client privilege must be asserted by the client, while the work product doctrine is a right attributed to both the client and the attorney); Douglas Richmond, *The Attorney-Client Privilege and Associated Confidentiality Concerns in the Post-Enron Era*, 110 Penn St. L. Rev. 381 (2005) (explaining that, to avoid waiver of the attorney-client privilege, attorneys must be aware of issues arising from technology, use of public relations consultants, cooperation with the government, and cooperation with insurance agencies, among other things).

L. CLASS ACTIONS AND OTHER MULTI-PARTY CASES

A class action is one of many devices in the United States to aggregate parties. Others include joinder (allowing, or sometimes requiring, parties to join in an action if their claims arise out of the same events or if the parties are raising questions of law or fact common to all plaintiffs, Fed. R. Civ. P. 19, 20); consolidation (allowing a court to combine actions pending in a particular court when they involve a common question of law or fact, Fed R. Civ. P. 42); intervention (allowing a party to intervene in an action when he has an interest in the outcome of the proceeding and his ability to pursue that interest would be impaired if he did not participate in the action, Fed. R. Civ. P. 24); interpleader (bringing multiple parties into a lawsuit when they have a shared stake in the subject of the litigation, Fed. R. Civ. P. 22); and impleader (allowing a defendant to bring a nonparty into an action when the nonparty is or may be liable to the defendant for the claim against him, Fed. R. Civ. P. 14). For an overview of those aggregation devices, *see* ROBERT KLONOFF, CLASS ACTIONS AND OTHER MULTI-PARTY LITIGATION IN A NUTSHELL 408–52 (4th ed. 2012).

Bankruptcy is another device that aggregates cases. When an individual files for bankruptcy, the petition automatically stays numerous types of lawsuits that may be pending against the debtor in state or federal court. The various claims against the debtor's estate are then consolidated in the bankruptcy court to ensure that the estate is divided among the creditors in an orderly and equitable way. *See id.* at 463–68.

Another important aggregation device, known as multidistrict litigation (MDL), enables a special court—the Judicial Panel on Multidistrict Litigation (JPML)—to transfer pending federal court cases "involving one or more common questions of fact" to a single federal judge for pretrial coordination. *See* 28 U.S.C. § 1407; KLONOFF, *supra*, at 455–60;

Edward Sherman, *The MDL Model for Resolving Complex Litigation if a Class Action is Not Possible*, 82 Tul. L. Rev. 2205 (2008). The MDL device can be used regardless of whether the cases are class actions or individual lawsuits. Many of the largest and most complex mass actions have been managed by judges designated by the JPML. *See, e.g.*, Jaime Dodge, *Facilitative Judging: Organizational Design in Mass-Multidistrict Litigation*, 64 Emory L.J. 329, 331 (2014) (noting that "fully one-third of all federal cases are MDL matters"). Those include many high-profile cases, such as the British Petroleum Deepwater Horizon Oil Spill case, the National Football League Concussion Injury case, and the Unintended Acceleration Litigation involving Toyota. *See* Amanda Robert, *Scholars Say MDL Filings Increase, Compete with Class Actions*, LEGALNEWSLINE (Mar. 22, 2013), http://legalnewsline.com/stories/510514916–scholars-say-mdl-filings-increase-compete-with-class-actions.

Of all the types of multi-party cases, the largest and most widely publicized cases are class actions. A class action is a representative suit in which one or more individuals sue on behalf of others similarly situated. To obtain class certification, plaintiffs must satisfy a number of strict requirements, including (among others) the existence of a sufficiently numerous class, adequate and typical class representatives to act on behalf of the class, and (as discussed in the following case), the existence of one or more common issues of law or fact. *See, e.g.*, KLONOFF, *supra*, at 23–25, 30–133. In most class actions, all similarly situated class members are automatically part of the case unless they affirmatively choose to opt out. For example, if a class is defined as "all owners of X Brand toasters," all such owners would be bound by any judgment—favorable or unfavorable—unless they affirmatively requested to be excluded by an announced deadline. Most states also have class action provisions, although the requirements sometimes differ from the federal requirements.

Unlike in many countries, class members in U.S. class actions typically do not pay any attorneys' fees or costs to class counsel unless the suit is successful. In many other countries, however, such "contingent fee" agreements are not permitted.

The following case involves claims of sex discrimination by female employees of Wal-Mart Stores, Inc., one of the world's largest companies. The issue is whether the case was properly brought as a class action.

WAL-MART STORES, INC. V. DUKES

Supreme Court of the United States, 2011
564 U.S. 338

JUSTICE SCALIA delivered the opinion of the Court.

We are presented with one of the most expansive class actions ever. The District Court and the Court of Appeals approved the certification of a class comprising about one and a half million plaintiffs, current and former female employees of petitioner Wal-Mart who allege that the discretion exercised by their local supervisors over pay and promotion matters violates Title VII by discriminating against women. * * *

* * *

I

A

Petitioner Wal-Mart is the Nation's largest private employer. It operates four types of retail stores throughout the country: Discount Stores, Supercenters, Neighborhood Markets, and Sam's Clubs. Those stores are divided into seven nationwide divisions, which in turn comprise 41 regions of 80 to 85 stores apiece. Each store has between 40 and 53 separate departments and 80 to 500 staff positions. In all, Wal-Mart operates approximately 3,400 stores and employs more than one million people.

Pay and promotion decisions at Wal-Mart are generally committed to local managers' broad discretion, which is exercised "in a largely subjective manner." Local store managers may increase the wages of hourly employees (within limits) with only limited corporate oversight. As for salaried employees, such as store managers and their deputies, higher corporate authorities have discretion to set their pay within pre-established ranges.

Promotions work in a similar fashion. Wal-Mart permits store managers to apply their own subjective criteria when selecting candidates as "support managers," which is the first step on the path to management. Admission to Wal-Mart's management training program, however, does require that a candidate meet certain objective criteria, including an above-average performance rating, at least one year's tenure in the applicant's current position, and a willingness to relocate. But except for those requirements, regional and district managers have discretion to use their own judgment when selecting candidates for management training. Promotion to higher office—*e.g.*, assistant manager, co-manager, or store manager—is similarly at the discretion of the employee's superiors after prescribed objective factors are satisfied.

B

The named plaintiffs in this lawsuit, representing the 1.5 million members of the certified class, are three current or former Wal-Mart employees who allege that the company discriminated against them on the basis of their sex by denying them equal pay or promotions, in violation of Title VII.

Betty Dukes began working at a Pittsburgh, California, Wal-Mart in 1994. She started as a cashier, but later sought and received a promotion to customer service manager. After a series of disciplinary violations, however, Dukes was demoted back to cashier and then to greeter. Dukes concedes she violated company policy, but contends that the disciplinary actions were in fact retaliation for invoking internal complaint procedures and that male employees have not been disciplined for similar infractions. Dukes also claims two male greeters in the Pittsburgh store are paid more than she is.

Christine Kwapnoski has worked at Sam's Club stores in Missouri and California for most of her adult life. She has held a number of positions, including a supervisory position. She claims that a male manager yelled at her frequently and screamed at female employees, but not at men. The manager in question "told her to 'doll up,' to wear some makeup, and to dress a little better."

The final named plaintiff, Edith Arana, worked at a Wal-Mart store in Duarte, California, from 1995 to 2001. In 2000, she approached the store manager on more than one occasion about management training, but was brushed off. Arana concluded she was being denied opportunity for advancement because of her sex. She initiated internal complaint procedures, whereupon she was told to apply directly to the district manager if she thought her store manager was being unfair. Arana, however, decided against that and never applied for management training again. In 2001, she was fired for failure to comply with Wal-Mart's timekeeping policy.

These plaintiffs, respondents here, do not allege that Wal-Mart has any express corporate policy against the advancement of women. Rather, they claim that their local managers' discretion over pay and promotions is exercised disproportionately in favor of men, leading to an unlawful disparate impact on female employees, *see* 42 U.S.C. § 2000e–2(k). And, respondents say, because Wal-Mart is aware of this effect, its refusal to cabin its managers' authority amounts to disparate treatment, *see* § 2000e–2(a). * * * *

* * *

Importantly for our purposes, respondents claim that the discrimination to which they have been subjected is common to *all* Wal-Mart's female employees. The basic theory of their case is that a strong and uniform "corporate culture" permits bias against women to infect, perhaps subconsciously, the discretionary decision-making of each one of Wal-Mart's thousands of managers—thereby making every woman at the company the victim of one common discriminatory practice. Respondents

---

*   Title VII provides remedies for both "disparate treatment," *i.e.*, intentional discrimination, as well as for "disparate impact," *i.e.*, where a facially non-discriminatory practice or policy nonetheless produces a discriminatory effect. [Ed.]

therefore wish to litigate the Title VII claims of all female employees at
Wal-Mart's stores in a nationwide class action.

C

* * * Under Rule 23(a), the party seeking certification must
demonstrate, first, that:

(1) the class is so numerous that joinder of all members is
impracticable,

(2) there are questions of law or fact common to the class,

(3) the claims or defenses of the representative parties are typical
of the claims or defenses of the class, and

(4) the representative parties will fairly and adequately protect
the interests of the class.

* * *

* * * [R]espondents moved the District Court to certify a plaintiff class
consisting of "[a]ll women employed at any Wal-Mart domestic retail store
at any time since December 26, 1998, who have been or may be subjected
to Wal-Mart's challenged pay and management track promotions policies
and practices." As evidence that there were * * * "questions of law or fact
common to" all the women of Wal-Mart, as Rule 23(a)(2) requires,
respondents relied chiefly on three forms of proof: statistical evidence about
pay and promotion disparities between men and women at the company,
anecdotal reports of discrimination from about 120 of Wal-Mart's female
employees, and the testimony of a sociologist, Dr. William Bielby, who
conducted a "social framework analysis" of Wal-Mart's "culture" and
personnel practices, and concluded that the company was "vulnerable" to
gender discrimination. * * *

[The district court certified a nationwide class of female Wal-Mart
employees. The Court of Appeals affirmed.]

* * *

II

* * *

A

The crux of this case is commonality—the rule requiring a plaintiff to
show that "there are questions of law or fact common to the class." Rule
23(a)(2).[5] * * * Commonality requires the plaintiff to demonstrate that the

---

[5] We have previously stated in this context that "[t]he commonality and typicality
requirements of Rule 23(a) tend to merge. Both serve as guideposts for determining whether under
the particular circumstances maintenance of a class action is economical and whether the named
plaintiff's claim and the class claims are so interrelated that the interests of the class members

class members "have suffered the same injury." * * * Their claims must depend upon a common contention—for example, the assertion of discriminatory bias on the part of the same supervisor. That common contention, moreover, must be of such a nature that it is capable of classwide resolution—which means that determination of its truth or falsity will resolve an issue that is central to the validity of each one of the claims in one stroke.

* * *

Rule 23 does not set forth a mere pleading standard. A party seeking class certification must affirmatively demonstrate his compliance with the Rule—that is, he must be prepared to prove that there are *in fact* sufficiently numerous parties, common questions of law or fact, etc. * * *

In this case, proof of commonality necessarily overlaps with respondents' merits contention that Wal-Mart engages in a *pattern or practice* of discrimination. That is so because, in resolving an individual's Title VII claim, the crux of the inquiry is "the reason for a particular employment decision," *Cooper v. Federal Reserve Bank of Richmond*, 467 U.S. 867, 876 (1984). Here respondents wish to sue about literally millions of employment decisions at once. Without some glue holding the alleged *reasons* for all those decisions together, it will be impossible to say that examination of all the class members' claims for relief will produce a common answer to the crucial question *why was I disfavored.*

B

* * * [There are two ways of demonstrating commonality in a case such as this one.] First, if the employer "used a biased testing procedure to evaluate both applicants for employment and incumbent employees, a class action on behalf of every applicant or employee who might have been prejudiced by the test clearly would satisfy the commonality and typicality requirements of Rule 23(a)." Second, "[s]ignificant proof that an employer operated under a general policy of discrimination conceivably could justify a class of both applicants and employees if the discrimination manifested itself in hiring and promotion practices in the same general fashion, such as through entirely subjective decision making processes." * * * The first manner * * * obviously has no application here; Wal-Mart has no testing procedure or other companywide evaluation method that can be charged with bias. The whole point of permitting discretionary decision-making is to avoid evaluating employees under a common standard.

---

will be fairly and adequately protected in their absence. Those requirements therefore also tend to merge with the adequacy-of-representation requirement, although the latter requirement also raises concerns about the competency of class counsel and conflicts of interest." *General Telephone Co. of Southwest v. Falcon*, 457 U.S. 147, 157–58 n.13 (1982). In light of our disposition of the commonality question, however, it is unnecessary to resolve whether respondents have satisfied the typicality and adequate representation requirements of Rule 23(a).

The second manner * * * requires "significant proof" that Wal-Mart "operated under a general policy of discrimination." That is entirely absent here. Wal-Mart's announced policy forbids sex discrimination, and * * * the company imposes penalties for denials of equal employment opportunity. The only evidence of a "general policy of discrimination" respondents produced was the testimony of Dr. William Bielby, their sociological expert. * * * Bielby testified that Wal-Mart has a "strong corporate culture," that makes it " 'vulnerable' " to "gender bias." He could not, however, "determine with any specificity how regularly stereotypes play a meaningful role in employment decisions at Wal-Mart. At his deposition . . . Dr. Bielby conceded that he could not calculate whether 0.5 percent or 95 percent of the employment decisions at Wal-Mart might be determined by stereotyped thinking." * * * Bielby's testimony does nothing to advance respondents' case. "[W]hether 0.5 percent or 95 percent of the employment decisions at Wal-Mart might be determined by stereotyped thinking" is the essential question on which respondents' theory of commonality depends. If Bielby admittedly has no answer to that question, we can safely disregard what he has to say. It is worlds away from "significant proof" that Wal-Mart "operated under a general policy of discrimination."

C

The only corporate policy that the plaintiffs' evidence convincingly establishes is Wal-Mart's "policy" of *allowing discretion* by local supervisors over employment matters. On its face, of course, that is just the opposite of a uniform employment practice that would provide the commonality needed for a class action; it is a policy *against having* uniform employment practices. It is also a very common and presumptively reasonable way of doing business—one that we have said "should itself raise no inference of discriminatory conduct," *Watson v. Fort Worth Bank & Trust*, 487 U.S. 977, 990 (1988).

To be sure, we have recognized that, "in appropriate cases," giving discretion to lower-level supervisors can be the basis of Title VII liability under a disparate-impact theory—since "an employer's undisciplined system of subjective decision making [can have] precisely the same effects as a system pervaded by impermissible intentional discrimination." But the recognition that this type of Title VII claim "can" exist does not lead to the conclusion that every employee in a company using a system of discretion has such a claim in common. To the contrary, left to their own devices most managers in any corporation—and surely most managers in a corporation that forbids sex discrimination—would select sex-neutral, performance-based criteria for hiring and promotion that produce no actionable disparity at all. * * * In such a company, demonstrating the invalidity of one manager's use of discretion will do nothing to demonstrate the invalidity of another's. A party seeking to certify a nationwide class will be unable to show that all the employees' Title VII claims will in fact depend on the answers to common questions.

Respondents have not identified a common mode of exercising discretion that pervades the entire company * * *. In a company of Wal-Mart's size and geographical scope, it is quite unbelievable that all managers would exercise their discretion in a common way without some common direction. * * *

The statistical evidence consists primarily of regression analyses performed by Dr. Richard Drogin, a statistician, and Dr. Marc Bendick, a labor economist. Drogin conducted his analysis region-by-region, comparing the number of women promoted into management positions with the percentage of women in the available pool of hourly workers. After considering regional and national data, Drogin concluded that "there are statistically significant disparities between men and women at Wal-Mart . . . [and] these disparities . . . can be explained only by gender discrimination." Bendick compared work-force data from Wal-Mart and competitive retailers and concluded that Wal-Mart "promotes a lower percentage of women than its competitors."

Even if they are taken at face value, these studies are insufficient to establish that respondents' theory can be proved on a classwide basis. * * * A regional pay disparity, for example, may be attributable to only a small set of Wal-Mart stores, and cannot by itself establish the uniform, store-by-store disparity upon which the plaintiffs' theory of commonality depends.

There is another, more fundamental, respect in which respondents' statistical proof fails. Even if it established (as it does not) a pay or promotion pattern that differs from the nationwide figures or the regional figures in *all* of Wal-Mart's 3,400 stores, that would still not demonstrate that commonality of issue exists. Some managers will claim that the availability of women, or qualified women, or interested women, in their stores' area does not mirror the national or regional statistics. And almost all of them will claim to have been applying some sex-neutral, performance-based criteria—whose nature and effects will differ from store to store. * * * Other than the bare existence of delegated discretion, respondents have identified no "specific employment practice"—much less one that ties all their 1.5 million claims together. Merely showing that Wal-Mart's policy of discretion has produced an overall sex-based disparity does not suffice.

Respondents' anecdotal evidence suffers from the same defects, and in addition is too weak to raise any inference that all the individual, discretionary personnel decisions are discriminatory. In *Teamsters v. United States*, 431 U.S. 324 (1977), in addition to substantial statistical evidence of company-wide discrimination, the Government (as plaintiff) produced about 40 specific accounts of racial discrimination from particular individuals. That number was significant because the company involved had only 6,472 employees, of whom 571 were minorities, and the class itself consisted of around 334 persons. The 40 anecdotes thus represented roughly one account for every eight members of the class. Moreover, the Court of Appeals noted that the anecdotes came from individuals "spread throughout" the company who "for the most part" worked at the company's operational centers that employed the largest numbers of the class members. Here, by contrast, respondents filed some 120 affidavits reporting experiences of discrimination—about 1 for every 12,500 class members—relating to only some 235 out of Wal-Mart's 3,400 stores. More than half of these reports are concentrated in only six States (Alabama, California, Florida, Missouri, Texas, and Wisconsin); half of all States have only one or two anecdotes; and 14 States have no anecdotes about Wal-Mart's operations at all. Even if every single one of these accounts is true, that would not demonstrate that the entire company "operate[s] under a general policy of discrimination," which is what respondents must show to certify a companywide class.

* * *

The judgment of the Court of Appeals is *Reversed.*

JUSTICE GINSBURG, with whom JUSTICE BREYER, JUSTICE SOTOMAYOR, and JUSTICE KAGAN join, [dissenting in relevant part].

* * * The Court * * * disqualifies the class at the starting gate, holding that the plaintiffs cannot cross the "commonality" line set by Rule 23(a)(2). * * *

I

A

Rule 23(a)(2) establishes a preliminary requirement for maintaining a class action: "[T]here are questions of law or fact common to the class." The Rule "does not require that all questions of law or fact raised in the litigation be common;" indeed, "[e]ven a single question of law or fact common to the members of the class will satisfy the commonality requirement." A "question" is ordinarily understood to be "[a] subject or point open to controversy." American Heritage Dictionary 1483 (3d ed. 1992). Thus, a "question" "common to the class" must be a dispute, either of fact or of law, the resolution of which will advance the determination of the class members' claims.[3]

B

The District Court, recognizing that "one significant issue common to the class may be sufficient to warrant certification," found that the

---

[3] The Court suggests Rule 23(a)(2) must mean more than it says. If the word "questions" were taken literally, the majority asserts, plaintiffs could pass the Rule 23(a)(2) bar by "[r]eciting . . . questions" like "Do all of us plaintiffs indeed work for Wal-Mart?" Sensibly read, however, the word "questions" means disputed issues, not any utterance crafted in the grammatical form of a question.

plaintiffs easily met that test. Absent an error of law or an abuse of discretion, an appellate tribunal has no warrant to upset the District Court's finding of commonality. The District Court certified a class of "[a]ll women employed at any Wal-Mart domestic retail store at any time since December 26, 1998." The named plaintiffs, led by Betty Dukes, propose to litigate, on behalf of the class, allegations that Wal-Mart discriminates on the basis of gender in pay and promotions. They allege that the company "[r]eli[es] on gender stereotypes in making employment decisions such as . . . promotion[s] [and] pay." Wal-Mart permits those prejudices to infect personnel decisions, the plaintiffs contend, by leaving pay and promotions in the hands of "a nearly all male managerial workforce" using "arbitrary and subjective criteria." Further alleged barriers to the advancement of female employees include the company's requirement, "as a condition of promotion to management jobs, that employees be willing to relocate." Absent instruction otherwise, there is a risk that managers will act on the familiar assumption that women, because of their services to husband and children, are less mobile than men.

Women fill 70 percent of the hourly jobs in the retailer's stores but make up only "33 percent of management employees." "[T]he higher one looks in the organization the lower the percentage of women." The plaintiffs' "largely uncontested descriptive statistics" also show that women working in the company's stores "are paid less than men in every region" and "that the salary gap widens over time even for men and women hired into the same jobs at the same time."

The District Court identified "systems for . . . promoting in-store employees" that were "sufficiently similar across regions and stores" to conclude that "the manner in which these systems affect the class raises issues that are common to all class members." The selection of employees for promotion to in-store management "is fairly characterized as a 'tap on the shoulder' process," in which managers have discretion about whose shoulders to tap. Vacancies are not regularly posted; from among those employees satisfying minimum qualifications, managers choose whom to promote on the basis of their own subjective impressions.

Wal-Mart's compensation policies also operate uniformly across stores, the District Court found. * * * The District Court reviewed means Wal-Mart used to maintain a "carefully constructed . . . corporate culture," such as frequent meetings to reinforce the common way of thinking, regular transfers of managers between stores to ensure uniformity throughout the company, monitoring of stores "on a close and constant basis," and "Wal-Mart TV," "broadcas[t] . . . into all stores."

The plaintiffs' evidence, including class members' tales of their own experiences, suggests that gender bias suffused Wal-Mart's company culture. Among illustrations, senior management often refer to female associates as "little Janie Qs." One manager told an employee that "[m]en are here to make a career and women aren't." A committee of female Wal-Mart executives concluded that "[s]tereotypes limit the opportunities offered to women."

Finally, the plaintiffs presented an expert's appraisal to show that the pay and promotions disparities at Wal-Mart "can be explained only by gender discrimination and not by . . . neutral variables." Using regression analyses, their expert, Richard Drogin, controlled for factors including, *inter alia*, job performance, length of time with the company, and the store where an employee worked. The results, the District Court found, were sufficient to raise an "inference of discrimination."

C

The District Court's identification of a common question, whether Wal-Mart's pay and promotions policies gave rise to unlawful discrimination, was hardly infirm. The practice of delegating to supervisors large discretion to make personnel decisions, uncontrolled by formal standards, has long been known to have the potential to produce disparate effects. Managers, like all humankind, may be prey to biases of which they are unaware.[6] The risk of discrimination is heightened when those managers are predominantly of one sex, and are steeped in a corporate culture that perpetuates gender stereotypes.

* * *

We have held that "discretionary employment practices" can give rise to Title VII claims, not only when such practices are motivated by discriminatory intent but also when they produce discriminatory results. *See Watson v. Fort Worth Bank & Trust*, 487 U.S. 977, 988, 991 (1988). In *Watson*, as here, an employer had given its managers large authority over promotions. An employee sued the bank under Title VII, alleging that the "discretionary promotion system" caused a discriminatory effect based on race. Four different supervisors had declined, on separate occasions, to promote the employee. Their reasons were subjective and unknown. The employer, we noted "had not developed precise and formal criteria for evaluating candidates"; "[i]t relied instead on the subjective judgment of supervisors."

Aware of "the problem of subconscious stereotypes and prejudices," we held that the employer's "undisciplined system of subjective decision-

---

[6] An example vividly illustrates how subjective decision-making can be a vehicle for discrimination. Performing in symphony orchestras was long a male preserve. Goldin and Rouse, *Orchestrating Impartiality: The Impact of "Blind" Auditions on Female Musicians*, 90 Am. Econ. Rev. 715, 715–16 (2000). In the 1970's orchestras began hiring musicians through auditions open to all comers. Reviewers were to judge applicants solely on their musical abilities, yet subconscious bias led some reviewers to disfavor women. Orchestras that permitted reviewers to see the applicants hired far fewer female musicians than orchestras that conducted blind auditions, in which candidates played behind opaque screens.

making" was an "employment practic[e]" that "may be analyzed under the disparate impact approach."

The plaintiffs' allegations state claims of gender discrimination in the form of biased decision-making in both pay and promotions. The evidence reviewed by the District Court adequately demonstrated that resolving those claims would necessitate examination of particular policies and practices alleged to affect, adversely and globally, women employed at Wal-Mart's stores. Rule 23(a)(2), setting a necessary but not a sufficient criterion for class-action certification, demands nothing further.

II

* * *

Wal-Mart's delegation of discretion over pay and promotions is a policy uniform throughout all stores. The very nature of discretion is that people will exercise it in various ways. A system of delegated discretion, *Watson* held, is a practice actionable under Title VII when it produces discriminatory outcomes. A finding that Wal-Mart's pay and promotions practices in fact violate the law would be the first step in the usual order of proof for plaintiffs seeking individual remedies for company-wide discrimination. *Teamsters v. United States*, 431 U.S. 324, 359 (1977). That each individual employee's unique circumstances will ultimately determine whether she is entitled to backpay or damages, § 2000e–5(g)(2)(A) (barring backpay if a plaintiff "was refused . . . advancement . . . for any reason other than discrimination"), should not factor into the Rule 23(a)(2) determination.

* * *

The Court errs in [its] Rule 23(a) commonality inquiry. I therefore cannot join Part II of the Court's opinion.

NOTES AND QUESTIONS

1.   Why is the class action device useful? How does it achieve efficiencies? What dangers does it pose?

2.   As noted at the outset of this section, numerous requirements must be satisfied before a class action can be certified. A key requirement, at issue in *Dukes*, is that the case must contain common issues of law or fact. This requirement is often referred to as "commonality." Why is it sensible to require the existence of common questions of law or fact before allowing a class action?

3.   In some types of class actions, especially those seeking monetary relief, plaintiffs must show not just commonality but also that "questions of law or fact common to class members predominate over questions affecting only individual class members." Fed. R. Civ. P. 23(b)(3). That requirement is known as the "predominance" requirement. *See* ROBERT KLONOFF, CLASS ACTIONS AND OTHER MULTI-PARTY LITIGATION IN A NUTSHELL 112–24 (4th ed.

2012). Why would the class action rules impose such a rigorous requirement? In a portion of her dissent not reproduced above, Justice Ginsburg accused the majority of conflating commonality and predominance. *See Dukes, supra*, at 2565 ("The Court blends Rule 23(a)(2)'s threshold criterion with the more demanding criteria of Rule 23(b)(3).").

4.   What was the factual setting in which the commonality requirement presented itself in *Dukes*? What were plaintiffs' arguments about why commonality was satisfied? What did Wal-Mart argue as to why commonality was not satisfied?

5.   How did the Court rule on the commonality question? What was its reasoning? On what grounds did the dissent differ from the majority? Which approach is more persuasive?

6.   Commentators have criticized the Supreme Court's approach to commonality in *Dukes. See, e.g.*, Robert Klonoff, *The Decline of Class Actions*, 90 Wash. U. L. Rev. 729, 776 (2013) ("The majority decision in *Dukes* cannot be squared with the text, structure, or history of Rule 23(a)(2). Nothing in the text of Rule 23(a)(2), or in the Advisory Committee Notes thereto, requires that the common question be central to the outcome."); A. Benjamin Spencer, *Class Actions, Heightened Commonality, and Declining Access to Justice*, 93 B.U. L. Rev. 441 (2013) (urging the Supreme Court to reconsider the heightened commonality standard announced in *Dukes* and return to the wording of Rule 23).

7.   One leading jurist, Richard Posner of the U.S. Court of Appeals for the Seventh Circuit has noted on behalf of the court: "The class action is a worthwhile supplement to conventional litigation procedure, but it is controversial and embattled, in part because it is frequently abused." *Eubank v. Pella Corp.*, 753 F.3d 718, 719 (7th Cir. 2014). In *Eubank*, window buyers brought a class action against the window manufacturers. The parties reached a settlement that was approved by the district court; however, various class members objected to the settlement and appealed. The appellate court held that the district court erred in approving the settlement. Among other things, the lawyer representing the class had a conflict of interest and was being investigated for unethical behavior in another matter. Also, the settlement guaranteed large attorneys' fees but class members did not fare well—and indeed, they were not guaranteed any award at all.

8.   For further reading on class actions, *see* PRINCIPLES OF THE LAW OF AGGREGATE LITIGATION (Am. Law Inst. 2010) (providing guidance on structuring and resolving class actions and other aggregate litigation); Robert Klonoff, *The Decline of Class Actions, supra* (identifying the significant limits that courts have placed on plaintiffs' ability to bring class actions and urging courts to return to a more balanced approach); John Coffee, Jr., *Rethinking the Class Action: A Policy Primer on Reform*, 62 Ind. L.J. 625 (1987) (explaining that class members sometimes have different and competing interests); Arthur Miller, *Of Frankenstein Monsters and Shining Knights: Myth, Reality, and the*

"Class Action Problem", 92 Harv. L. Rev. 664 (1979) (defending the class action device against its critics and providing an historical perspective).

M. ISSUE AND CLAIM PRECLUSION

The purpose of a lawsuit is to resolve a dispute. For the legal system to operate fairly, a judgment must have finality. This means that once the litigation achieves an outcome and all appeals are exhausted, the losing party cannot start over as if nothing had happened. "In our system of jurisprudence the usual rule is that merits of a legal claim once decided in a court of competent jurisdiction are not subject to redetermination in another forum." *Kremer v. Chem. Const. Corp.*, 456 U.S. 461 (1982). The concept of finality, known as res judicata, refers to two types of preclusion of relitigation: (1) "issue preclusion," which is sometimes referred to as collateral estoppel, and (2) "claim preclusion," which is sometimes referred to as res judicata (a term that also refers broadly to both issue and claim preclusion).

Issue preclusion applies when one discrete issue within a claim has already been adjudicated in another case. Claim preclusion applies when a party has raised, or could have raised, the claim at issue in a previous lawsuit. Together, these two doctrines promote fairness and efficiency. As the Supreme Court has stated: "To preclude parties from contesting matters that they have had a full and fair opportunity to litigate protects their adversaries from the expense and vexation attending multiple lawsuits, conserves judicial resources, and fosters reliance on judicial action by minimizing the possibility of inconsistent decisions." *Montana v. United States*, 440 U.S. 147 (1979).

As the above discussion reveals, an important distinction between claim and issue preclusion is that claim preclusion can apply even if the claim was not actually raised (but could have been), whereas issue preclusion applies only to issues that were actually adjudicated in the earlier action. The rationale for such a broad scope of claim preclusion is to avoid piecemeal litigation:

> [A] party seeking to enforce a claim * * * must present to the court * * * all the grounds upon which he expects a judgment in his favor. He is not at liberty to * * * present only a portion of the grounds upon which special relief is sought, and leave the rest to be presented in a second suit, if the first fail. There would be no end to litigation if such a practice were permissible.

Stark v. Starr, 94 U.S. 477, 485 (1876).

The following case addresses the doctrine of claim preclusion.

PAVON V. SWIFT TRANSPORTATION CO., INC.

Court of Appeals for the Ninth Circuit, 1999
192 F.3d 902

FLETCHER, CIRCUIT JUDGE.

Swift Transportation Company, Inc. ("Swift") appeals the district court's judgment, following a jury trial, in favor of Fernando Pavon in Pavon's wrongful discharge action * * * arising when Pavon was terminated after complaining about ongoing racial harassment in his job as a diesel mechanic at Swift. * * * We * * * affirm.

FACTS AND PROCEDURAL BACKGROUND

Pavon was hired by Swift in November, 1994. Pavon is a United States citizen of Hispanic origin, born in Honduras. While working at his post in February, 1995, Pavon was subjected to racial slurs and harassment by his co-worker, Kevin Sterle. Sterle's harassment of Pavon included calling him "beaner," "fucking Mexican," "wet back," "spic," "illiterate," and "stupid." Sterle also taunted Pavon with comments like "go home," and "go back to Colombia," and threatening to turn him in to immigration.

Pavon complained several times to his shop foreman and supervisor, Ted Staley, about Sterle's remarks. Staley reported Pavon's complaints to his superior, Mark Janszen. The harassment continued on a near-daily basis. Pavon complained directly to Janszen, who issued Pavon a disciplinary warning. After meeting with Pavon and Sterle, Janszen decided to transfer Pavon to a separate workstation, the Fuel Shop. The transfer was not accompanied by a loss of pay or benefits, but Pavon saw it as a demotion and disciplinary action, because the Fuel Shop was a station to which new and inexperienced employees were normally assigned.

After Pavon's transfer, Sterle continued to search out Pavon and to taunt him with racial slurs. Plaintiff again complained to his supervisors. Janszen prepared disciplinary notices relating to Pavon. Larry Sampson, a colleague of Pavon's at Swift, advised Pavon to contact the company recruiter, Don Diggins, and Ron Rodriguez at company headquarters in Phoenix. Pavon could not reach Diggins, but did contact Rodriguez. Pavon followed the latter's advice to start keeping a notebook of what was going on. Despite having been told of Pavon's complaints by Sampson, Diggins took no action to interview Pavon or to investigate the allegations.

On July 5, 1995, Pavon was called into a meeting with Janszen and Diggins. Pavon continued to object to the company's discipline of him and its refusal to remedy the ongoing racial harassment. Diggins asked Pavon, "Do you know who Martin Luther King was? Remember what happened to him?" Pavon returned to work after the meeting. Later that day, he was terminated.

Following his termination, Pavon lost $1,218 in wages in a two-week period before he secured comparable employment. On September 18, 1995, Pavon filed a complaint in Multnomah County District Court seeking unpaid wages. That action was dismissed following settlement by the parties. On October 2, 1995, Pavon filed this action in federal district court under [various federal and state laws]. Defendant's motion for summary judgment, based on the ground that the action was claim-precluded because it involved issues that could have been raised in the state court action, was denied. Following a three-day jury trial, judgment was entered in favor of Pavon. As total economic damages for all four of his claims, he was awarded $1,218. In addition, * * * he was awarded $250,000 in noneconomic damages and $300,000 in punitive damages. * * * Swift appealed.

DISCUSSION

Claim Preclusion

Swift [argues] that all of Pavon's employment-related claims form a single transaction for purposes of claim preclusion. We review res judicata-claim preclusion claims de novo. Because the underlying judgment was rendered in an Oregon state court, we must apply Oregon's rules of claim preclusion.

* * *

Upon review of Oregon law, we find that Pavon's federal suit was not barred by his state wage penalty action. Oregon law focuses on the transaction at issue in the state and federal cases and gives preclusive effect to all claims against the defendant that were available to the plaintiff arising from that transaction. "The expression 'transaction, or series of connected transactions,' is not capable of a mathematically precise definition; it invokes a pragmatic standard to be applied with attention to the facts of the cases." [The Oregon Supreme Court has] listed the following criteria as relevant to the transaction inquiry: time, space, origin of the harm, subjective or objective motivation, convenience, and similar acts. We agree with the district court that there is not enough similarity of facts or claims underlying the federal and state claims for claim preclusion to apply. As the district court explained, Pavon's state court action was a wage penalty claim which required proof of unpaid wages and failure to pay within thirty days, and a payroll penalty claim involving the absence of authorization for a payroll deduction. His federal court action, in contrast, involves proof of an allegedly hostile work environment, plaintiff's complaints to management, defendant's alleged failure to take effective remedial action and retaliation against plaintiff for his complaints, defendant's termination of plaintiff, and the connection between the termination and plaintiff's membership in a protected class.

Showing discriminatory intent was an essential element of the federal claims, but not of the state claims. Pavon did need to show in his state court action that Swift's failure to pay him his final wages was "willful" in order to recover. However, under the statute, "willful" means "merely that the thing done or omitted to be done was done or omitted intentionally." Showing "willfulness" in the state proceedings required different witnesses, and different evidence than what was required to show discriminatory intent in federal court. While the events that gave rise to the federal claims were connected to those that gave rise to the wage claims, we find that aspects of the state and federal claims did not "*necessarily* overlap any complete litigation of another," and that therefore, under Oregon law, Swift's defense of claim preclusion would fail.

* * *

Affirmed.

NOTES AND QUESTIONS

1. What was at issue in Pavon's first lawsuit? What was the result of that lawsuit? What was at issue in the lawsuit here?

2. Is the court persuasive in holding that claim preclusion did not apply? Is there any suggestion in the court's opinion that the earlier court could not have adjudicated the discrimination claims? If such claims could have been brought, what was the rationale of the court in holding that the plaintiff was not barred from bringing them in a later lawsuit? Could the egregious treatment of the plaintiff account for the court's willingness to hold that the discrimination lawsuit was not precluded by the earlier lawsuit?

3. For additional cases discussing preclusion, *see, e.g., B & B Hardware, Inc. v. Hargis Indus., Inc.*, 575 U.S. ___, 135 S. Ct. 1293 (2015) (holding that an adjudication by an administrative agency can have preclusive effect in a subsequent suit brought in court); *Kremer v. Chem. Constr. Corp.*, 456 U.S. 461 (1982) (holding in an employment discrimination case that claim preclusion was appropriate when a state court had previously upheld a state agency's determination that the discrimination claim at issue was meritless).

4. For further discussion of issue and claim preclusion, *see, e.g.*, Edward Cavanagh, *Issue Preclusion in Complex Litigation*, 29 Rev. Litig. 859 (2010) (discussing unique preclusion issues that arise in class actions and other complex cases); Graham Lilly, *The Symmetry of Preclusion,* 54 Ohio St. L.J. 289 (1993) (arguing in favor of a broad application of preclusion to ensure uniformity and predictability).

CHAPTER 4

CONTRACTS

■ ■ ■

The law of contracts focuses on the rules governing agreements between two or more parties. To create a valid and enforceable contract, the parties must satisfy a number of requirements. This chapter focuses on the key requirements (and a number of related topics).

A. OFFER AND ACCEPTANCE

To form a contract, one party must make an offer and another party must accept the offer. This section addresses the complications that can arise in determining whether an offer and acceptance were made, and thus whether an enforceable contract exists.

LEONARD V. PEPSICO, INC.
United States District Court, S.D. New York, 1999
88 F. Supp. 2d 116

WOOD, DISTRICT JUDGE.

Plaintiff brought this action seeking, among other things, specific performance of an alleged offer of a Harrier Jet, featured in a television advertisement for defendant's "Pepsi Stuff" promotion. Defendant has moved for summary judgment * * *. For the reasons stated below, defendant's motion is granted.

I. Background

This case arises out of a promotional campaign conducted by defendant, the producer and distributor of the soft drinks Pepsi and Diet Pepsi. The promotion, entitled "Pepsi Stuff," encouraged consumers to collect "Pepsi Points" from specially marked packages of Pepsi or Diet Pepsi and redeem these points for merchandise featuring the Pepsi logo. Before introducing the promotion nationally, defendant conducted a test of the promotion in the Pacific Northwest from October 1995 to March 1996. A Pepsi Stuff catalog was distributed to consumers in the test market, including Washington State. Plaintiff is a resident of Seattle, Washington. While living in Seattle, plaintiff saw the Pepsi Stuff commercial that he contends constituted an offer of a Harrier Jet.

A. The Alleged Offer

Because whether the television commercial constituted an offer is the central question in this case, the Court will describe the commercial in detail. The commercial opens upon an idyllic, suburban morning, where the chirping of birds in sun-dappled trees welcomes a paperboy on his morning route. As the newspaper hits the stoop of a conventional two-story house, the tattoo of a military drum introduces the subtitle, "MONDAY 7:58 AM." The stirring strains of a martial air mark the appearance of a well-coiffed teenager preparing to leave for school, dressed in a shirt emblazoned with the Pepsi logo, a red-white-and-blue ball. While the teenager confidently preens, the military drumroll again sounds as the subtitle "T-SHIRT 75 PEPSI POINTS" scrolls across the screen. Bursting from his room, the teenager strides down the hallway wearing a leather jacket. The drumroll sounds again, as the subtitle "LEATHER JACKET 1450 PEPSI POINTS" appears. The teenager opens the door of his house and, unfazed by the glare of the early morning sunshine, puts on a pair of sunglasses. The drumroll then accompanies the subtitle "SHADES 175 PEPSI POINTS." A voiceover then intones, "Introducing the new Pepsi Stuff catalog," as the camera focuses on the cover of the catalog. (The "Catalog").

The scene then shifts to three young boys sitting in front of a high school building. The boy in the middle is intent on his Pepsi Stuff Catalog, while the boys on either side are each drinking Pepsi. The three boys gaze in awe at an object rushing overhead, as the military march builds to a crescendo. The Harrier Jet is not yet visible, but the observer senses the presence of a mighty plane as the extreme winds generated by its flight create a paper maelstrom in a classroom devoted to an otherwise dull physics lesson. Finally, the Harrier Jet swings into view and lands by the side of the school building, next to a bicycle rack. Several students run for cover, and the velocity of the wind strips one hapless faculty member down to his underwear. While the faculty member is being deprived of his dignity, the voiceover announces: "Now the more Pepsi you drink, the more great stuff you're gonna get."

The teenager opens the cockpit of the fighter and can be seen, helmetless, holding a Pepsi. "[L]ooking very pleased with himself," the teenager exclaims, "Sure beats the bus," and chortles. The military drumroll sounds a final time, as the following words appear: "HARRIER FIGHTER 7,000,000 PEPSI POINTS." A few seconds later, the following appears in more stylized script: "Drink Pepsi—Get Stuff." With that message, the music and the commercial end with a triumphant flourish.

Inspired by this commercial, plaintiff set out to obtain a Harrier Jet. Plaintiff explains that he is "typical of the 'Pepsi Generation' . . . he is young, has an adventurous spirit, and the notion of obtaining a Harrier Jet appealed to him enormously." Plaintiff consulted the Pepsi Stuff Catalog. The Catalog features youths dressed in Pepsi Stuff regalia or enjoying

Pepsi Stuff accessories, such as "Blue Shades" ("As if you need another reason to look forward to sunny days."), "Pepsi Tees" ("Live in 'em. Laugh in 'em. Get in 'em."), "Bag of Balls" ("Three balls. One bag. No rules."), and "Pepsi Phone Card" ("Call your mom!"). The Catalog specifies the number of Pepsi Points required to obtain promotional merchandise. The Catalog includes an Order Form which lists, on one side, fifty-three items of Pepsi Stuff merchandise redeemable for Pepsi. Conspicuously absent from the Order Form is any entry or description of a Harrier Jet. The amount of Pepsi Points required to obtain the listed merchandise ranges from 15 (for a "Jacket Tattoo" ("Sew 'em on your jacket, not your arm.")) to 3300 (for a "Fila Mountain Bike" ("Rugged. All-terrain. Exclusively for Pepsi.")). It should be noted that plaintiff objects to the implication that because an item was not shown in the Catalog, it was unavailable.

The rear foldout pages of the Catalog contain directions for redeeming Pepsi Points for merchandise. These directions note that merchandise may be ordered "only" with the original Order Form. The Catalog notes that in the event that a consumer lacks enough Pepsi Points to obtain a desired item, additional Pepsi Points may be purchased for ten cents each; however, at least fifteen original Pepsi Points must accompany each order.

Although plaintiff initially set out to collect 7,000,000 Pepsi Points by consuming Pepsi products, it soon became clear to him that he "would not be able to buy (let alone drink) enough Pepsi to collect the necessary Pepsi Points fast enough." Reevaluating his strategy, plaintiff "focused for the first time on the packaging materials in the Pepsi Stuff promotion," and realized that buying Pepsi Points would be a more promising option. Through acquaintances, plaintiff ultimately raised about $700,000.

B. Plaintiff's Efforts to Redeem the Alleged Offer

On or about March 27, 1996, plaintiff submitted an Order Form, fifteen original Pepsi Points, and a check for $700,008.50. Plaintiff appears to have been represented by counsel at the time he mailed his check; the check is drawn on an account of plaintiff's first set of attorneys. At the bottom of the Order Form, plaintiff wrote in "1 Harrier Jet" in the "Item" column and "7,000,000" in the "Total Points" column. In a letter accompanying his submission, plaintiff stated that the check was to purchase additional Pepsi Points "expressly for obtaining a new Harrier jet as advertised in your Pepsi Stuff commercial."

On or about May 7, 1996, defendant's fulfillment house rejected plaintiff's submission and returned the check, explaining that:

> The item that you have requested is not part of the Pepsi Stuff collection. It is not included in the catalogue or on the order form, and only catalogue merchandise can be redeemed under this program.

The Harrier jet in the Pepsi commercial is fanciful and is simply included to create a humorous and entertaining ad. We apologize for any misunderstanding or confusion that you may have experienced and are enclosing some free product coupons for your use.

Plaintiff's previous counsel responded on or about May 14, 1996, as follows:

Your letter of May 7, 1996 is totally unacceptable. We have reviewed the video tape of the Pepsi Stuff commercial . . . and it clearly offers the new Harrier jet for 7,000,000 Pepsi Points. Our client followed your rules explicitly. . . .

This is a formal demand that you honor your commitment and make immediate arrangements to transfer the new Harrier jet to our client. If we do not receive transfer instructions within ten (10) business days of the date of this letter you will leave us no choice but to file an appropriate action against Pepsi. . . .

This letter was apparently sent onward to the advertising company responsible for the actual commercial, BBDO New York ("BBDO"). In a letter dated May 30, 1996, BBDO Vice President Raymond E. McGovern, Jr., explained to plaintiff that:

I find it hard to believe that you are of the opinion that the Pepsi Stuff commercial ("Commercial") really offers a new Harrier Jet. The use of the Jet was clearly a joke that was meant to make the Commercial more humorous and entertaining. In my opinion, no reasonable person would agree with your analysis of the Commercial.

On or about June 17, 1996, plaintiff mailed a similar demand letter to defendant.

* * *

[After several years of "jurisdictional and procedural wrangling,"] PepsiCo moved for summary judgment pursuant to Fed. R. Civ. P. 56. * * *

II. Discussion

A. The Legal Framework

1. Standard for Summary Judgment

* * * To prevail on a motion for summary judgment, the moving party * * * must show that there are no such genuine issues of material fact to be tried, and that he or she is entitled to judgment as a matter of law. * * *

* * *

The question of whether or not a contract was formed is appropriate for resolution on summary judgment. * * * "Summary judgment is proper

when the 'words and actions that allegedly formed a contract [are] so clear themselves that reasonable people could not differ over their meaning.' "
* * *

* * *

B. Defendant's Advertisement Was Not An Offer

1. Advertisements as Offers

The general rule is that an advertisement does not constitute an offer. The Restatement (Second) of Contracts explains that:

> Advertisements of goods by display, sign, handbill, newspaper, radio or television are not ordinarily intended or understood as offers to sell. The same is true of catalogues, price lists and circulars, even though the terms of suggested bargains may be stated in some detail. It is of course possible to make an offer by an advertisement directed to the general public, but there must ordinarily be some language of commitment or some invitation to take action without further communication.

Restatement (Second) of Contracts § 26 cmt. b (1979). * * *

An advertisement is not transformed into an enforceable offer merely by a potential offeree's expression of willingness to accept the offer through, among other means, completion of an order form. * * * [A]dvertisements and order forms are "mere notices and solicitations for offers which create no power of acceptance in the recipient." * * * Under these principles, plaintiff's letter of March 27, 1996, with the Order Form and the appropriate number of Pepsi Points, constituted the offer. There would be no enforceable contract until defendant accepted the Order Form and cashed the check.

The exception to the rule that advertisements do not create any power of acceptance in potential offerees is where the advertisement is "clear, definite, and explicit, and leaves nothing open for negotiation"; in that circumstance, "it constitutes an offer, acceptance of which will complete the contract." *Lefkowitz v. Great Minneapolis Surplus Store*, 251 Minn. 188, 86 N.W.2d 689, 691 (1957). In *Lefkowitz*, defendant had published a newspaper announcement stating: "Saturday 9 AM Sharp, 3 Brand New Fur Coats, Worth to $100.00, First Come First Served $1 Each." Mr. Morris Lefkowitz arrived at the store, dollar in hand, but was informed that under defendant's "house rules," the offer was open to ladies, but not gentlemen. The court ruled that because plaintiff had fulfilled all of the terms of the advertisement and the advertisement was specific and left nothing open for negotiation, a contract had been formed.

The present case is distinguishable from *Lefkowitz*. First, the commercial cannot be regarded in itself as sufficiently definite, because it specifically reserved the details of the offer to a separate writing, the

Catalog. The commercial itself made no mention of the steps a potential offeree would be required to take to accept the alleged offer of a Harrier Jet. The advertisement in *Lefkowitz*, in contrast, "identified the person who could accept." Second, even if the Catalog had included a Harrier Jet among the items that could be obtained by redemption of Pepsi Points, the advertisement of a Harrier Jet by both television commercial and catalog would still not constitute an offer. * * * [T]he absence of any words of limitation such as "first come, first served," renders the alleged offer sufficiently indefinite that no contract could be formed. "A customer would not usually have reason to believe that the shopkeeper intended exposure to the risk of a multitude of acceptances resulting in a number of contracts exceeding the shopkeeper's inventory." There was no such danger in *Lefkowitz*, owing to the limitation "first come, first served."

The Court finds, in sum, that the Harrier Jet commercial was merely an advertisement. The Court now turns to the line of cases upon which plaintiff rests much of his argument.

REWARDS AS OFFERS

In opposing the present motion, plaintiff largely relies on a different species of unilateral offer, involving public offers of a reward for performance of a specified act. * * * The most venerable of these precedents is the case of *Carlill v. Carbolic Smoke Ball Co.*, 1 Q.B. 256 (Court of Appeal, 1892), a quote from which heads plaintiff's memorandum of law: "[I]f a person chooses to make extravagant promises . . . he probably does so because it pays him to make them, and, if he has made them, the extravagance of the promises is no reason in law why he should not be bound by them." *Carbolic Smoke Ball*, 1 Q.B. at 268 (Bowen, L.J.).

Long a staple of law school curricula, *Carbolic Smoke Ball* owes its fame not merely to "the comic and slightly mysterious object involved," but also to its role in developing the law of unilateral offers. The case arose during the London influenza epidemic of the 1890s. Among other advertisements of the time, for Clarke's World Famous Blood Mixture, Towle's Pennyroyal and Steel Pills for Females, Sequah's Prairie Flower, and Epp's Glycerine Jube-Jubes, appeared solicitations for the Carbolic Smoke Ball. The specific advertisement that Mrs. Carlill saw, and relied upon, read as follows:

> 100 £ reward will be paid by the Carbolic Smoke Ball Company to any person who contracts the increasing epidemic influenza, colds, or any diseases caused by taking cold, after having used the ball three times daily for two weeks according to the printed directions supplied with each ball. 1000 £ is deposited with the Alliance Bank, Regent Street, showing our sincerity in the matter.

> During the last epidemic of influenza many thousand carbolic smoke balls were sold as preventives against this disease, and in

no ascertained case was the disease contracted by those using the carbolic smoke ball.

"On the faith of this advertisement," Mrs. Carlill purchased the smoke ball and used it as directed, but contracted influenza nevertheless. The lower court held that she was entitled to recover the promised reward.

Affirming the lower court's decision, Lord Justice Lindley began by noting that the advertisement was an express promise to pay £ 100 in the event that a consumer of the Carbolic Smoke Ball was stricken with influenza. The advertisement was construed as offering a reward because it sought to induce performance, unlike an invitation to negotiate, which seeks a reciprocal promise. As Lord Justice Lindley explained, "advertisements offering rewards . . . are offers to anybody who performs the conditions named in the advertisement, and anybody who does perform the condition accepts the offer." Because Mrs. Carlill had complied with the terms of the offer, yet contracted influenza, she was entitled to £ 100.

* * *

Other "reward" cases underscore the distinction between typical advertisements, in which the alleged offer is merely an invitation to negotiate for purchase of commercial goods, and promises of reward, in which the alleged offer is intended to induce a potential offeree to perform a specific action, often for noncommercial reasons. * * *

In the present case, the Harrier Jet commercial did not direct that anyone who appeared at Pepsi headquarters with 7,000,000 Pepsi Points on the Fourth of July would receive a Harrier Jet. Instead, the commercial urged consumers to accumulate Pepsi Points and to refer to the Catalog to determine how they could redeem their Pepsi Points. The commercial sought a reciprocal promise, expressed through acceptance of, and compliance with, the terms of the Order Form. * * * Plaintiff states that he "noted that the Harrier Jet was not among the items described in the catalog, but this did not affect [his] understanding of the offer." It should have.

Carbolic Smoke Ball itself draws a distinction between the offer of reward in that case, and typical advertisements, which are merely offers to negotiate. * * *

Because the alleged offer in this case was, at most, an advertisement to receive offers rather than an offer of reward, plaintiff cannot show that there was an offer made in the circumstances of this case.

C. An Objective, Reasonable Person Would Not Have Considered the Commercial an Offer

Plaintiff's understanding of the commercial as an offer must also be rejected because the Court finds that no objective person could reasonably have concluded that the commercial actually offered consumers a Harrier Jet.

1. Objective Reasonable Person Standard

In evaluating the commercial, the Court must not consider defendant's subjective intent in making the commercial, or plaintiff's subjective view of what the commercial offered, but what an objective, reasonable person would have understood the commercial to convey.

If it is clear that an offer was not serious, then no offer has been made[.]

An obvious joke, of course, would not give rise to a contract. On the other hand, if there is no indication that the offer is "evidently in jest," and that an objective, reasonable person would find that the offer was serious, then there may be a valid offer.

2. Necessity of a Jury Determination

[The court rejected plaintiff's argument] that summary judgment is improper because the question of whether the commercial conveyed a sincere offer can be answered only by a jury. * * *

* * * [In the court's view,] [t]his case * * * presents a question of whether there was an offer to enter into a contract, requiring the Court to determine how a reasonable, objective person would have understood defendant's commercial. Such an inquiry is commonly performed by courts on a motion for summary judgment.

3. Whether the Commercial Was "Evidently Done In Jest"

Plaintiff's insistence that the commercial appears to be a serious offer requires the Court to explain why the commercial is funny. Explaining why a joke is funny is a daunting task; as the essayist E.B. White has remarked, "Humor can be dissected, as a frog can, but the thing dies in the process. . . ." The commercial is the embodiment of what defendant appropriately characterizes as "zany humor."

First, the commercial suggests, as commercials often do, that use of the advertised product will transform what, for most youth, can be a fairly routine and ordinary experience. The military tattoo and stirring martial music, as well as the use of subtitles in a Courier font that scroll terse messages across the screen, such as "MONDAY 7:58 AM," evoke military and espionage thrillers. The implication of the commercial is that Pepsi Stuff merchandise will inject drama and moment into hitherto unexceptional lives. The commercial in this case thus makes the exaggerated claims similar to those of many television advertisements: that by consuming the featured clothing, car, beer, or potato chips, one will become attractive, stylish, desirable, and admired by all. A reasonable viewer would understand such advertisements as mere puffery, not as statements of fact; and refrain from interpreting the promises of the commercial as being literally true.

Second, the callow youth featured in the commercial is a highly improbable pilot, one who could barely be trusted with the keys to his parents' car, much less the prize aircraft of the United States Marine Corps. Rather than checking the fuel gauges on his aircraft, the teenager spends his precious preflight minutes preening. The youth's concern for his coiffure appears to extend to his flying without a helmet. Finally, the teenager's comment that flying a Harrier Jet to school "sure beats the bus" evinces an improbably insouciant attitude toward the relative difficulty and danger of piloting a fighter plane in a residential area, as opposed to taking public transportation.

Third, the notion of traveling to school in a Harrier Jet is an exaggerated adolescent fantasy. In this commercial, the fantasy is underscored by how the teenager's schoolmates gape in admiration, ignoring their physics lesson. The force of the wind generated by the Harrier Jet blows off one teacher's clothes, literally defrocking an authority figure. As if to emphasize the fantastic quality of having a Harrier Jet arrive at school, the Jet lands next to a plebeian bike rack. This fantasy is, of course, extremely unrealistic. No school would provide landing space for a student's fighter jet, or condone the disruption the jet's use would cause.

Fourth, the primary mission of a Harrier Jet, according to the United States Marine Corps, is to "attack and destroy surface targets under day and night visual conditions." The jet is designed to carry a considerable armament load, including Sidewinder and Maverick missiles. As one news report has noted, "Fully loaded, the Harrier can float like a butterfly and sting like a bee—albeit a roaring 14-ton butterfly and a bee with 9,200 pounds of bombs and missiles." In light of the Harrier Jet's well-documented function in attacking and destroying surface and air targets, armed reconnaissance and air interdiction, and offensive and defensive anti-aircraft warfare, depiction of such a jet as a way to get to school in the morning is clearly not serious even if, as plaintiff contends, the jet is capable of being acquired "in a form that eliminates [its] potential for military use."

Fifth, the number of Pepsi Points the commercial mentions as required to "purchase" the jet is 7,000,000. To amass that number of points, one would have to drink 7,000,000 Pepsis (or roughly 190 Pepsis a day for the next hundred years—an unlikely possibility), or one would have to purchase approximately $700,000 worth of Pepsi Points. The cost of a Harrier Jet is roughly $23 million dollars, a fact of which plaintiff was aware when he set out to gather the amount he believed necessary to accept the alleged offer. Even if an objective, reasonable person were not aware of this fact, he would conclude that purchasing a fighter plane for $700,000 is a deal too good to be true.

Plaintiff argues that a reasonable, objective person would have understood the commercial to make a serious offer of a Harrier Jet because there was "absolutely no distinction in the manner" in which the items in the commercial were presented. Plaintiff also relies upon a press release highlighting the promotional campaign, issued by defendant, in which "[n]o mention is made by [defendant] of humor, or anything of the sort." These arguments suggest merely that the humor of the promotional campaign was tongue in cheek. * * * In light of the obvious absurdity of the commercial, the Court rejects plaintiff's argument that the commercial was not clearly in jest.

* * *

D. The Alleged Contract Does Not Satisfy the Statute of Frauds

The absence of any writing setting forth the alleged contract in this case provides an entirely separate reason for granting summary judgment. Under the New York Statute of Frauds,

> a contract for the sale of goods for the price of $500 or more is not enforceable by way of action or defense unless there is some writing sufficient to indicate that a contract for sale has been made between the parties and signed by the party against whom enforcement is sought or by his authorized agent or broker.

* * *

* * * The commercial is not a writing; plaintiff's completed order form does not bear the signature of defendant, or an agent thereof; and to the extent that plaintiff seeks discovery of any contracts between defendant and its advertisers, such discovery would be unavailing: plaintiff is not a party to, or a beneficiary of, any such contracts. Because the alleged contract does not meet the requirements of the Statute of Frauds, plaintiff has no claim for breach of contract or specific performance.

* * *

III. Conclusion

* * *

* * * For the reasons stated above, the Court grants defendant's motion for summary judgment. * * *

NOTES AND QUESTIONS

1.   The U.S. Court of Appeals for the Second Circuit affirmed the decision in *Leonard* "for substantially the reasons stated in Judge Wood's opinion." *Leonard v. PepsiCo, Inc.*, 210 F.3d 88 (2d Cir. 2000). The precise issue in the *Leonard* case was whether the court should grant defendant's motion for summary judgment. Summary judgment is discussed in detail in Chapter 3.

2. *Leonard* involved issues of state contract law, but the case was adjudicated in federal court. This was possible based on "diversity jurisdiction." Diversity jurisdiction is discussed in Chapter 3. Because Leonard and PepsiCo were citizens of different states and the lawsuit was for a Harrier Jet, worth well over $75,000, the parties satisfied the requirements for diversity jurisdiction. Thus, PepsiCo was entitled to remove the case, which was originally brought in state court, to federal court. Why would PepsiCo have wanted the case to be heard in federal court rather than in state court?

3. Restatements of the Law, such as the Restatement of Contracts referenced in *Leonard*, are scholarly works created by the American Law Institute, a private organization whose mission is to clarify and improve the law. *See* American Law Institute, *About ALI*, http://www.ali.org/index. cfm?fuseaction=about.overview. The Restatements summarize basic principles of law regarding a variety of subjects. Although the Restatements do not have the force of law, they are highly influential and are frequently cited by courts, attorneys, and scholars. For more information on Restatements and on the American Law Institute generally, *see, e.g.*, Brooklyn Law School Library, *Restatements of the Law: A How to Guide: An Introduction to the Restatements*, http://guides.brooklaw.edu/restatements.

4. The *Leonard* court rejected plaintiff's suit on several grounds. What were those grounds? Which is most persuasive? How is this case distinguishable from *Lefkowitz*? How is this case distinguishable from *Carbolic Smoke Ball*? What is the basis for the court's "Statute of Frauds" ruling?

5. Could plaintiff in *Leonard* have reasonably believed that he would prevail in the event of a trial? If not, what was his likely motivation in filing suit? *See, e.g.*, Benjamin Sunshine & Víctor Abel Pereyra, *Access-to-Justice v. Efficiency: An Empirical Study of Settlement Rates After* Twombly & Iqbal, 2015 U. Ill. L. Rev. 357 (2015) (discussing high percentage of cases that settle).

6. A classic case involving whether an offer was made in jest is *Lucy v. Zehmer*, 196 Va. 493, 84 S.E.2d 516 (1954). In that case, Zehmer and Lucy, while consuming liquor in a restaurant, discussed a tract of land owned by Zehmer. Lucy said, " 'I bet you wouldn't take $50,000.00 for that place.' " *Id.* at 495, 84 S.E.2d at 518. Zehmer responded, " 'Yes, I would too; you wouldn't give fifty.' " *Id.* Lucy said he would indeed give that amount, and instructed Zehmer to draw up an agreement. Zehmer did so on the back of a restaurant check, but tore it up because Lucy noted that Mrs. Zehmer would also have to sign it. Zehmer then wrote out another agreement and had Mrs. Zehmer (who had entered the restaurant) sign it as well. In all, the discussion about the sale of the land lasted about 30–40 minutes. When Lucy later made arrangements for his attorney to examine the title, Zehmer stated that he did not intend to go through with the deal. Zehmer argued, in a suit brought by Lucy to enforce the contract, that Zehmer had acted in jest and was intoxicated at the time. The trial court found for Zehmer, but the West Virginia high court reversed. It concluded that Zehmer's undisclosed belief that the agreement was made in jest did not nullify Lucy's reasonable belief that an agreement had been reached. Moreover, the facts did not indicate that Zehmer and Lucy were so

intoxicated that they did not understand what they were doing. Thus, the court held that Lucy was entitled to purchase the land for the agreed-upon price of $50,000. Can *Lucy v. Zehmer* be reconciled with *Leonard*? If so, on what basis? Is the result in the *Lucy* case fair?

7.   The precise remedy in *Lucy v. Zehmer* was "specific performance." *See* Restatement (Second) of Contracts § 357, cmt. a (1981) (specific performance means that a party must "render the performance that he promised"); Restatement (Second) of Contracts § 359 (1981) (noting that "[s]pecific performance or an injunction will not be ordered if damages would be adequate to protect the expectation interest of the injured party"). Why is specific performance a logical remedy in the context of a real estate transaction? *Cf.* Tanya Marsh, *Sometimes Blackacre Is A Widget: Rethinking Commercial Real Estate Contract Remedies*, 88 Neb. L. Rev. 635 (2010) (discussing the unique status of land in contract law and arguing that, while specific performance is generally appropriate in land contracts, some land is not unique, such as some commercial real estate properties, and specific performance is unnecessary).

8.   Another instructive case is *Kolodziej v. Mason*, 774 F.3d 736 (11th Cir. 2014). In that case, an attorney representing a criminal defendant stated during the trial that he would "pay * * * a million dollars" to anyone who could disprove his client's alibi that he could not have traveled from the Atlanta airport to a nearby hotel in only 28 minutes. *Id.* at 739. A law student, believing that this was a valid offer, successfully traveled from the airport to the hotel in 28 minutes. When the student sued for payment of the $1 million, both the trial court and the court of appeals held that it was not objectively reasonable for the student to believe that the challenge was an offer. The Eleventh Circuit found it "neither prudent nor permissible to impose contractual liability for offhand remarks or grandstanding," particularly in the context of a criminal trial. *Id.* at 746. Based on *Leonard* and *Lucy*, was this decision correct?

9.   Traditional concepts of offer and acceptance have had to adjust to modern technology. For a discussion of how technology has impacted the formation of contracts, *see* Valerie Watnick, *The Electronic Formation of Contracts and the Common Law "Mailbox Rule,"* 56 Baylor L. Rev. 175 (2004) (discussing contracts made online and arguing that the "mailbox rule"—the principle that an offer is accepted as soon as the acceptance is placed in the mail rather than when the acceptance is received—should apply to electronic contract formation because the traditional purposes of certainty and ease of contracting from a distance continue to apply).

10.   For additional discussion of the doctrines of offer and acceptance, *see* Shawn Bayern, *Offer and Acceptance in Modern Contract Law: A Needless Concept*, 103 Cal. L. Rev. 67 (2015) (arguing that principles of offer and acceptance are outdated and should be replaced with a standard that considers the parties' actions both before and after the offer and acceptance to determine whether the parties created a contract); Melvin Eisenberg, *Expression Rules in Contract Law and Problems of Offer and Acceptance*, 82 Cal. L. Rev. 1127 (1994) (noting that some offer and acceptance doctrines, such as the principle that advertisements are presumptively not offers, do not comport with modern

understandings); Peter Meijes Tiersma, *The Language of Offer and Acceptance: Speech Acts and the Question of Intent*, 74 Cal. L. Rev. 189 (1986) (arguing that the key to determining if there is an offer and acceptance is whether the speaker intended to create an understanding of offer or acceptance in the listener).

B. CONSIDERATION

In addition to an offer and an acceptance, parties must also exchange "consideration" to form a contract. Consideration is something of value, such as money or a promise to perform a service. This section explores the doctrine of consideration in the context of a romantic relationship.

WILLIAMS V. ORMSBY
Supreme Court of Ohio, 2012
131 Ohio St.3d 427, 966 N.E.2d 255

LANZINGER, JUSTICE.

We are asked to determine whether merely resuming a romantic relationship by moving into a home with another can serve as consideration for a contract. We hold that it cannot.

I. Factual Background

This case arises in the context of a nonmarital relationship between Amber Williams, the appellee, and Frederick Ormsby, the appellant. In May 2004, Frederick moved into Amber's house on Hardwood Hollow in Medina to which she had received title through her divorce settlement. Frederick began making the mortgage payments in August and paid the 2004 property taxes. He eventually paid the remaining mortgage balance of approximately $310,000. In return, Amber gave Frederick title to the property by executing a quitclaim deed dated December 15, 2004, that was recorded the same day.

Although the couple had planned to marry, they canceled their plans in January 2005 when Frederick's divorce did not occur. They did, however, continue to live together. After a disagreement in March 2005, Amber left the house, and Frederick obtained a restraining order against her. As a result of this separation, Amber and Frederick signed a document dated March 24, 2005, to immediately sell the Medina house and allocate the proceeds.

Two months later, the couple tried to reconcile and attended couples counseling. Amber refused to move back into the house with Frederick unless he granted her an undivided one-half interest in the property. On June 2, 2005, they signed a second document, purportedly making themselves "equal partners" in the Medina house and, among other things, providing for property disposition in the event that their relationship ended. Amber then returned to the house, and the couple resumed their relationship. But by April 2007, they were living in separate areas of the house, and although they tried counseling again, Amber ended the relationship in September 2007. The two continued living in separate areas of the house until Frederick left in April 2008.

The next month, Amber and Frederick filed suit against each other in two separate actions, which the trial court consolidated. Amber sought either specific performance of the contract that she alleged was created in June 2005 to give her a half-interest in the property or damages stemming from breach of that contract. In his complaint, Frederick alleged causes of action for quiet title and unjust enrichment or quantum meruit [reasonable payment for services performed] and sought a declaratory judgment that both the March 2005 and June 2005 documents are invalid for lack of consideration. He also alleged causes of action for breach of contract, partition [dividing up the property], and contribution if either or both agreements were held valid.

Both parties filed motions for summary judgment. On April 16, 2009, the trial court determined that the March 2005 agreement was supported by consideration but that the June 2005 agreement was not. The court granted judgment to Frederick on Amber's complaint and held that title to the property was vested in him exclusively. Amber was granted judgment on Frederick's causes of action for contribution and unjust enrichment. The trial court ruled that the only issue remaining for trial was whether Frederick was entitled to damages for any possible breach of the March 2005 contract.

Over the next several months, the parties amended their pleadings and attempted to dismiss various claims. A judgment [was later entered, and] * * * Amber appealed.

The [court of appeals] reversed the trial court's judgment, concluding that under the facts of this case, "moving into a home with another and resuming a relationship can constitute consideration sufficient to support a contract." [It] also held that the June 2005 contract was not conditioned upon marriage, and thus, the consideration had not failed.

Frederick appealed, and we accepted jurisdiction on his sole proposition of law: "Moving into a home with another and resuming a romantic relationship cannot serve as legal consideration for a contract; love and affection are insufficient consideration for a contract."

II. Legal Analysis

We must first note that the proposition accepted does not refer broadly to all circumstances of cohabitation. As we have held, "[t]he essential elements of 'cohabitation' are (1) sharing of familial or financial responsibilities and (2) consortium." In the case before us, the issue is only whether the emotional aspect of resuming a relationship by moving in together can serve as consideration for a contract—separate and apart from the sharing of financial resources and obligations.

Although the dissenting opinion takes a rather cynical view of the relationship between the parties and seems to liken it to a business transaction allowing Amber to avoid her creditors, we disagree. Speculation and innuendo are not evidence. While it is not surprising that there was no longer any love or affection between the parties at the time of their depositions, both Amber and Frederick agreed that they began a romantic relationship on April 30, 2004, moved in together the next month, became engaged in July 2004, separated in March 2005, and in June 2005, reunited and "plan[ned] to be married." Furthermore, although there was some evidence that Amber had some outstanding financial obligations from her divorce at the time Frederick moved into the house, there is absolutely no evidence that she was unable or unwilling to meet those obligations.

Frederick contends that the only consideration offered for the June 2005 agreement was resuming a romantic relationship, which cannot serve as consideration for a contract. He argues that to enforce such a contract is the same as enforcing a contract to make a gift in consideration of love and affection.

Amber counters that the March 2005 agreement was novated, *i.e.*, legally substituted, by the June 2005 agreement and that Frederick received a benefit that he bargained for. She maintains that the June 2005 agreement was supported by consideration.

A.   General Contract Principles

We have stated, " 'A contract is generally defined as a promise, or a set of promises, actionable upon breach. Essential elements of a contract include an offer, acceptance, contractual capacity, consideration (the bargained for legal benefit and/or detriment), a manifestation of mutual assent and legality of object and of consideration.' "

1.   The need for consideration

In this case, we are concerned with the legal enforceability of the June 2005 writing, for a contract is not binding unless supported by consideration.

Consideration may consist of either a detriment to the promisee or a benefit to the promisor. A benefit may consist of some right, interest, or profit accruing to the promisor, while a detriment may consist of some forbearance, loss, or responsibility given, suffered, or undertaken by the promisee.

We also have a long-established precedent that courts may not inquire into the adequacy of consideration, which is left to the parties as " 'the sole judges of the benefits or advantages to be derived from their contracts.' " [The court quotes case law for the principle that "[g]ratuitous promises are not consideration."] But whether there is consideration at all is a proper question for a court.

2. Novation

Amber argues that the June 2005 agreement is a valid novation of the March 2005 agreement. "A contract of novation is created where a previous valid obligation is extinguished by a new valid contract, accomplished by substitution of parties or of the undertaking, with the consent of all the parties, and based on valid consideration." A novation can never be presumed but must be evinced by a clear and definite intent on the part of all the parties to the original contract to completely negate the original contract and enter into the second.

Because a novation is a new contract, it too must meet all the elements of a contract. Therefore, even if the June 2005 document is a novation of the original March 2005 agreement, it must be supported by consideration.

3. Distinction between contract and gift

The trial court concluded that the June 2005 agreement was nothing more than a written gratuitous promise because there was no consideration for that agreement. In fact, the requirement for consideration is what distinguishes a contract from a gift. The essential elements of an *inter vivos* gift are (1) an intention on the part of the donor to transfer the title and right of possession to the donee, (2) delivery by the donor to the donee, (3) relinquishment of ownership, dominion, and control over the gift by the donor, and (4) acceptance by the donee. Therefore, a gift is a voluntary transfer by the donor to the donee without any consideration or compensation.

Even if we were to construe the June 2005 agreement as a promise to make a gift of one-half interest in the property, we must still examine whether there is consideration, because even a written promise to make a gift is not binding on the promisor if the promise lacks consideration.

B. The Agreements

To be enforceable between the parties, therefore, the agreements must be supported by consideration. Although the enforceability of the March agreement is not before us, the terms of both documents signed by the parties will be summarized.

1. The March 2005 agreement

The trial court found that in March 2005, the parties executed a valid, written contract supported by mutual consideration. This agreement provided that the Hardwood Hollow house would be sold, with the first $324,000 of the proceeds to Frederick and the balance to Amber. Both Frederick and Amber specified their separate rights to reside at the subject property until it was sold. Under the March 2005 agreement, Amber assumed responsibility for the real estate taxes if the property was not sold in two months. The two also were to equally share the costs necessary to operate and maintain the house as long as both were living there. This agreement also detailed who was responsible for certain bills and repairs to the residence.

The March 2005 agreement also provided an alternative plan whereby Frederick could pay Amber the difference between $324,000 and the fair market value of the property, and Amber would then vacate the residence.

2.   The June 2005 agreement

With respect to the second document, signed in June 2005, the trial court found that the writing was not a valid contract, because there was no consideration to support it. The June document, which asserted the March contract to be void, stated that "for valuable consideration," the parties agree that although titled solely in Frederick's name, the house was owned jointly by Frederick and Amber and that they were equal partners. In addition, Amber's name would be placed on the deed at a time she specified, and she could file a lien against the house for her share of the property until it was retitled. This writing required Frederick to pay all expenses on the property, including taxes and insurance. If the house was sold, Amber and Frederick would divide the proceeds from the sale after expenses were paid. Finally, if their relationship ended and they chose not to sell the house, Frederick could elect to keep the house and pay Amber for her share of the property or to leave the house to Amber after being paid for his share.

C.   The Court of Appeals' Opinion

[Discussion omitted.]

D.   Love and Affection Are Not Consideration for a Contract

* * * [O]ur decision in *Flanders v. Blandy*, 45 Ohio St. 108, 12 N.E. 321 (1887), is instructive on whether moving into the home with another while engaging in a romantic relationship is consideration for the formation of a contract. In *Flanders*, a father had intended to give his daughter certain bonds worth $2,000 in addition to interest. But the daughter did not receive the bonds as a gift, because they were never delivered to her. Her father then delivered to her a written promise to pay her $2,000 with interest in lieu of the bonds. Upon her father's death, the daughter sought to enforce the written promise, but we held that her father's promise to give her the value of the bonds was not enforceable as a contract, because that promise lacked consideration.

We stated that a gift required a transfer to take effect "for the reason that, there being no consideration therefor, no action will lie to enforce it." * * * Thus, for more than a century, love and affection alone have not been recognized as consideration for a contract.

E.   The June 2005 Document—A Failed Contract and Novation

The court of appeals * * * conclude[d] that consideration supported the June 2005 document: " * * * [B]y resuming the relationship, [Amber] agreed to undertake a way of life that entailed among other things 'providing companionship, and fulfilling each other's needs, financial, emotional, physical, and social, as best as [she was] able,' as well as foregoing other romantic possibilities." Nevertheless, the record does not show evidence of this statement. * * *

Although the June document states that the agreement was made "for valuable consideration," it does not specify what the consideration is. The document does not refer to "fulfilling each other's needs, financial, emotional, physical, and social." The court of appeals supplied those terms on its own. And unlike the March 2005 agreement, which contains mutual obligations and benefits (*i.e.*, both parties had a right to reside at the property and, equally shared costs necessary to maintain the house, with Amber being responsible for real estate taxes starting the second half of 2004), the June 2005 document requires Frederick to pay all expenses, taxes, and insurance costs. Nonetheless, the court of appeals relied on Amber's reply to a question of whether she had paid Frederick or given him anything of value in exchange for the June 2005 agreement. She stated, "I didn't pay him anything, no. I thought what was of value was the fact that we were sharing all sorts of things. He had my love. He had—I shared my assets with him, too. We were living together as a couple." But this vague statement falls short of establishing that she shared her assets as consideration for the June 2005 agreement and appears to refer to how she had previously shared her assets before entering into the June agreement.

Rather, the evidence demonstrates that the only consideration offered by Amber for the June 2005 agreement was her resumption of a romantic relationship with Frederick. There is no detriment to Amber in the June 2005 document, only benefit. Essentially, this agreement amounts to a gratuitous promise by Frederick to give Amber an interest in property based solely on the consideration of her love and affection. Therefore, the June 2005 document is not an enforceable contract, because it fails for want of consideration.

Amber argues, and the dissent agrees, that the voiding of the March agreement in the June document was consideration for the June agreement, and thus Amber contends that the June agreement amounted to a novation. * * * But a novation is effective only when a previous valid obligation is extinguished by a *new valid contract*. In order to qualify as a novation, the June agreement must be a valid contract in its own right *before* it can be used to void the March agreement.

Amber had been living in the house for more than seven years, having lived there with her husband and having retained the residence as part of the property division in their divorce. Despite having transferred legal ownership to Frederick in December 2004, Amber already had the contractual right to reside in the property by virtue of the March 2005 contract, which had required her to vacate the guest bedroom and bath to accommodate Frederick. She was also to have been granted upon the sale of the residence the net proceeds of the sale after Frederick received $324,000. It was Amber's demand that she be given an equal property interest in the house before she would move back in and resume her romantic relationship with Frederick—there was no consideration.

Because there is no consideration for the June agreement, it cannot extinguish the existing obligations established under the March agreement. Therefore, the June document was not an enforceable novation of the March 2005 agreement.

We hold that merely moving into a home with another while engaging in a romantic relationship is not consideration for the formation of a contract. To hold otherwise would open the door to palimony claims and invite a number of evidentiary problems.

* * *

PFEIFER, JUSTICE, concurring in part and dissenting in part.

* * *

The majority seems to have chased a red herring ("love and affection") all the way upstream until it reached a dry creek bed. Love and affection were not offered in consideration of the June 2005 contract. Although the contract refers to a contemplated marriage, it never mentions love and affection.

The record is replete with shadings and innuendo that there was no love and affection between the parties. The record includes statements that suggest or allege that Williams and Ormsby were searching for a way to continue living well without engaging in full-time work, that Williams was seeking to both delude and elude creditors, that Williams's name may have been fraudulently signed on the quitclaim deed or that the person who notarized her signature did so without being present when Williams signed, that domestic-violence charges had been filed, and that each had promised not to accuse the other of domestic violence. That Williams wouldn't move back into the house until Ormsby signed the agreement, which he wrote, was not offered as consideration and was not consideration. It was a simple fact of life—a fact that is outside the contract and is of no relevance.

The resolution of this case should be straightforward. Among the consideration that Williams and Ormsby offered for the second agreement was the voiding of the first agreement, which denied to each of them rights that the first agreement granted. That either or both of them offered additional consideration is beside the point because we consider only the existence of consideration, not its adequacy.

Amber Williams and Frederick Ormsby entered into two contracts. The first was entered into in March 2005 "FOR VALUABLE CONSIDERATION that is mutually agreed upon" but unstated. * * * Williams, Ormsby, their respective attorneys, the trial court, the court of appeals, and this court all agree that the March 2005 agreement is a valid, binding contract. The second contract was entered into in June 2005 "FOR VALUABLE CONSIDERATION that is mutually agreed upon" but unstated. * * * The exact same consideration language is used in both contracts—yet it is sufficient in one instance but not in the other. The parties are the same, the subject matter is the same, the consideration is stated the same way—but this court concludes that there is no consideration for the second contract.

The first clause of the June 2005 contract resolves the issue before us. It states: "FOR VALUABLE CONSIDERATION that is mutually agreed upon, the AGREEMENT deems all other agreements concerning the items stated below to be null and void * * *." Could it be more clear? The March 2005 contract required that the house be sold and entitled Williams to, among other things, sales proceeds in excess of $324,000 and to live in the house until its sale. In consideration for giving up those rights, Williams entered into the June 2005 contract, which entitled her to different rights. How can it be argued that by voiding a contract that entitled her to specific rights, Williams was not offering consideration for the June 2005 contract, which entitled her to different rights? For instance, under the March agreement, if the property sold for $650,000, Williams would be entitled to $326,000; under the June agreement, she would be entitled to $325,000. If the property sold for $1,000,000, under the March agreement, Williams would get $726,000; under the June agreement, she would get $500,000. In that scenario, the March agreement benefits her considerably. Under the June contract, she also gives up the right to get proceeds from an immediate sale. Ormsby, meanwhile, under the June agreement does not have to vacate the house or pay Williams her equity portion to remain there—obligations of his under the March agreement. Under the June agreement, Ormsby gains more control over the timing of any sale of the house. For these benefits, he forfeits some equity in the house.

I am convinced that Williams and Ormsby offered consideration for the second contract. * * *

NOTES AND QUESTIONS

1.   What purpose does the consideration requirement serve? Under the *Williams* court's opinion, is love and affection deemed consideration for a contract?

2.   The enforceability of the March 2005 contract was not before the Ohio Supreme Court. Rather, the issue was whether there was consideration for the June 2005 agreement, which (if valid) would have extinguished the obligations created by the March 2005 contract. What did the Ohio Supreme Court hold on that question, and what was its reasoning?

3.   On what basis did the dissent disagree with the majority? Which opinion, the majority or the dissent, is more persuasive?

4.   When a couple divorces, one spouse often has to pay "alimony" to support his or her former spouse. Alimony is defined as: "[a] court-ordered allowance that one spouse pays to the other spouse for maintenance and support while they are separated, while they are involved in a matrimonial lawsuit, or after they are divorced." Black's Law Dictionary (10th ed. 2014). The term "palimony"—mentioned at the end of *Williams v. Ormsby*—was introduced in *Marvin v. Marvin*, 557 P.2d 106, 18 Cal.3d 660 (1976), to describe alimony-type agreements between individuals who were never married. In that case, actor Lee Marvin had allegedly promised to support his mistress for the rest of her life. After the two had cohabited for seven years, however, the relationship ended, prompting the mistress to sue for support. The trial court dismissed the claim, and the court of appeals affirmed. On appeal, the California Supreme Court reversed, holding that the mistress stated a claim for breach of an express promise. The appellate court therefore remanded the case for further proceedings.

Should an individual be legally obligated to support a girlfriend or boyfriend, who was not a spouse, after the relationship dissolves? Commentators disagree on this question. *Compare, e.g.*, Kaiponanea Matsumura, *Public Policing of Intimate Agreements*, 25 Yale J.L. & Feminism 159 (2013) (criticizing the failure of courts to enforce agreements between non-married intimate partners, because such nonenforcement impairs the ability to contract on matters of domestic relations and introduces uncertainty with respect to topics such as child rearing and support), *with* Lynn Wardle, *Marriage and Other Domestic Relationships: Comparative and Critical Equality Analysis of Differences in Form and Substance*, 26 J. Civ. Rts. & Econ. Dev. 663 (2012) (arguing against conferring legal rights on nontraditional relationships because doing so would undermine traditional family and child-rearing values underlying marriage). *See also* Ann Laquer Estin, *Ordinary Cohabitation*, 76 Notre Dame L. Rev. 1381 (2001) (examining case law following *Marvin* and noting that courts have not generally recognized rights based on cohabitation, despite the significant increase in non-marital cohabitation).

5.   For scholarly perspectives on the pros and cons of requiring consideration to enforce a contract, *see, e.g.*, Peter Linzer, *Consider Consideration*, 44 St. Louis U. L.J. 1317 (2000) (arguing that the consideration doctrine does not work well because it leaves some intended promises unenforced, and proposing the elimination of consideration in various types of contracts); Val Ricks, *The Sophisticated Doctrine of Consideration*, 9 Geo. Mason L. Rev. 99 (2000) (arguing that the consideration requirement should

be applied with flexibility, as it was when the doctrine originated in the 16th century).

C. DUTY TO READ

In contract law, there is a presumption that contracting parties have read the documents that establish the contract and knowingly agreed to all of the terms contained therein. That presumption, known as the "duty to read," will sometimes mean that parties who failed to read the terms of a contract are treated as if they had read and understood those terms. The following case addresses these issues.

JAMES V. MCDONALD'S CORP.
United States Court of Appeals, Seventh Circuit, 2005
417 F.3d 672

RIPPLE, CIRCUIT JUDGE.

Linda James * * * alleg[es] state law contract and tort claims against McDonald's Corporation, Simon Marketing, Inc. and the owner-operators of two McDonald's restaurants (collectively "McDonald's"). * * * The district court granted McDonald's motion to compel Ms. James to arbitrate her claims and to stay judicial proceedings pending the outcome of arbitration. Ms. James did not pursue arbitration; instead, nearly a year later, she asked the district court to reconsider its order. The district court denied the motion and later dismissed the case for failure to prosecute. Ms. James has appealed. For the reasons set forth in the following opinion, we now affirm the judgment of the district court.

I

BACKGROUND

A.

In 2001, McDonald's was promoting sales of its food products by sponsoring a game called "Who Wants to be a Millionaire." Ms. James obtained a game card in May of 2001 when she purchased an order of french fries at the drive-thru window of a McDonald's restaurant in Franklin, Kentucky. She believed the game card to be a grand prize winner worth one million dollars. In order to redeem her prize, Ms. James sent in the original game card to the McDonald's redemption center. On June 14, 2001, however, the redemption center sent her a letter explaining that, "[t]hrough security codes on your Game Card we have been able to determine that it is a Low-level Prize Game Card. Low-level prizes included food prizes and $1 to $5 in cash."

In August 2001, the Federal Bureau of Investigation arrested eight employees of Simon Marketing who allegedly had stolen the winning game cards from the "Who Wants to be a Millionaire" game and another

McDonald's promotion. Ms. James filed suit alleging that McDonald's induced her to purchase its food products by the chance to win the "Who Wants to be a Millionaire" game when it knew that, due to the theft of winning game cards, the odds of winning were less than represented. She also alleged that, as part of its fraud scheme, McDonald's had used a false pretense to refuse to honor her winning game card.

McDonald's filed a motion to compel Ms. James to arbitrate her claims. It relied on an arbitration clause contained in the rules for the "Who Wants to be a Millionaire" game ("Official Rules"), which stated:

> Except where prohibited by law, as a condition of participating in this Game, participant agrees that (1) any and all disputes and causes of action arising out of or connected with this Game, or any prizes awarded, shall be resolved individually, without resort to any form of class action, and exclusively by final and binding arbitration under the rules of the American Arbitration Association and held at the AAA regional office nearest the participant; (2) the Federal Arbitration Act shall govern the interpretation, enforcement and all proceedings at such arbitration; and (3) judgment upon such arbitration award may be entered in any court having jurisdiction.

McDonald's presented evidence, credited by the district court, that the Official Rules were posted openly in participating restaurants. The rules were posted near the food counter, on the back of in-store tray liners and near the drive-thru window. Also, the french fry cartons to which game cards were affixed had language directing participants to see the Official Rules for details.

B.

On February 4, 2003, the district court granted McDonald's motion to compel Ms. James to arbitrate her claims. Applying Kentucky law, the district court concluded that Ms. James could not avoid the arbitration clause by claiming that she never saw or read the Official Rules. Next, the court determined that arbitration, not the court, was the appropriate forum for resolving Ms. James's claim that the arbitration clause should not be enforced because McDonald's fraudulently had induced her to participate in the game. * * * Finally, the district court found unavailing Ms. James's claim that it should not enforce the arbitration clause because the costs of arbitration were prohibitive. * * *

* * *

II

ANALYSIS

A. Standard of Review

We review a district court's decision, under the Federal Arbitration Act ("FAA"), to compel parties to arbitrate their disputes de novo. We review the district court's findings of fact for clear error.

B. Arbitration

Ms. James contends that the district court erred by ordering her to submit her claims to arbitration * * * [because] she did not enter into a valid agreement to arbitrate her claims. * * *

* * *

The FAA provides that a "written provision in any . . . contract . . . to settle by arbitration" any future controversy arising out of such contract "shall be valid, irrevocable, and enforceable, save upon such grounds as exist at law or in equity for the revocation of any contract." 9 U.S.C. § 2.1. The FAA was designed "to reverse the longstanding judicial hostility to arbitration agreements . . . and to place [them] on the same footing as other contracts." Any doubts with respect to arbitrability therefore should be resolved in favor of arbitration.

However, a party can be compelled to arbitrate only those matters that she has agreed to submit to arbitration. In deciding whether the parties agreed to arbitrate a certain matter, federal courts generally should rely on state contract law governing the formation of contracts.

Ms. James contends that she should not be forced to arbitrate her claims because she never entered into an agreement to arbitrate her dispute. She submits that she was not aware of the Official Rules, much less that the rules deprived her of a jury trial. For the same reasons, Ms. James contends that, if there was an agreement to arbitrate, it is unconscionable and should not be enforced. To support her position, Ms. James submits that one cannot assume that she knew of, and accepted, the arbitration clause in the Official Rules simply because she ate at a McDonald's restaurant. She maintains that customers cannot be expected to read every container of food they purchase in order to know that they are entering a contract. Rather, she submits that it was McDonald's burden to assure her understanding of, and willingness to be bound by, the arbitration provision.

Certainly, as Ms. James urges, a contract includes only terms on which the parties have agreed. However, one of the things that Ms. James agreed to by participating in the "Who Wants to be a Millionaire" game was to follow the game's rules in order to win the promised prize. As a general rule, a participant in a prize-winning contest must comply with the terms of the contest's rules in order to form a valid and binding contract with the contest promoter. The promoter's obligation is limited by the terms of the offer, including the conditions and rules of the contest that are made public.

Ms. James challenges the district court's reliance on Kentucky case law that provides that a party who had the opportunity to read a contract, but did not, is bound by the contract terms. Ms. James insists that these cases are inapposite because they involve contracts that were negotiated and signed by the parties. Instead, she relies on *Oakwood Mobile Homes, Inc. v. Sprowls*, 82 S.W.3d 193, 199 (Ky. 2002), which held that an employee could not validly agree to arbitrate without "actual notice" of the employer's arbitration policy. The district court's ruling is not inconsistent with *Oakwood*, however, because the court found that the Official Rules were "clearly and undisputably identified to [Ms. James] as being part of the contest." It is axiomatic that a contest normally has rules regarding eligibility to win the promised prize. Moreover, Ms. James cannot claim, on the one hand, that a valid contract obligates McDonald's to redeem her prize and, on the other hand, argue that no contract binds her to the contest rules. A contest participant cannot pick and choose among the terms and conditions of the contest; the rules stand or fall in their entirety.

Outside the promotional-contest context, this court has held that parties are bound to an arbitration provision even if they did not read the provision. * * *

* * * [Here, t]o require McDonald's cashiers to recite to each and every customer the fourteen pages of the Official Rules, and then have each customer sign an agreement to be bound by the rules, would be unreasonable and unworkable. The Official Rules were identified to Ms. James as part of the contest, and that identification is sufficient in this case to apprise her of the contents of the rules.

* * *

Conclusion

* * * [W]e affirm the judgment of the district court.

NOTES AND QUESTIONS

1.   What is arbitration? Why would McDonald's have included an arbitration clause in the rules for the "Who Wants to be a Millionaire" game? Why is the arbitration clause central to the outcome of the *James* case? Arbitration is discussed in detail in Chapter 3.

2.   Why did the *James* court reject Ms. James's arguments? Is the court's decision fair? What arguments can be made in support of Ms. James's position?

3.   Based on the *James* court's decision, has Ms. James lost her chance to recover the money that she sought? Despite the arbitration clause, could she

have pursued a monetary remedy had she done so in a timely fashion? What should she have done?

4. The duty to read is often criticized in the context of standard form contracts between companies and consumers on the ground that there is frequently an imbalance of power—a sophisticated business entity versus an unsophisticated consumer. For critical analyses of the duty to read in the consumer context, *see, e.g.*, Ian Ayres & Alan Schwartz, *The No-Reading Problem in Consumer Contract Law*, 66 Stan. L. Rev. 545 (2014) (arguing that the enforceability of contract terms should be based on the typical consumer's understanding of the contract); Wayne Barnes, *Toward A Fairer Model of Consumer Assent to Standard Form Contracts: In Defense of Restatement Subsection 211(3)*, 82 Wash. L. Rev. 227, 227 (2007) (arguing in favor of the adoption of Section 211 of the Restatement (Second) of Contracts, which would void terms of a contract if "the [merchant] has reason to believe that the [consumer] would not [assent] if he knew that the writing contained a particular term"). The related concept of unconscionability—a doctrine that prevents the enforcement of contracts when there is an unfair imbalance of power—is discussed in Section E of this chapter.

D. DUTY AND BREACH

When parties form a contract, each agrees to do something, and that obligation is a party's "duty" under the contract. When a party fails to perform his duty, he violates the terms of the contract and commits a "breach." Under contract law, breaches are treated in a variety of ways, with the remedy typically depending on the type of duty involved. These issues are discussed in the case below.

RAYMOND WEIL, S.A. V. THERON
United States District Court, S.D. New York, 2008
585 F. Supp. 2d 473

MCMAHON, DISTRICT JUDGE.

Plaintiff Raymond Weil, S.A. filed this suit against defendants Charlize Theron and Denver & Delilah Films, Inc. seeking damages for alleged breaches of an endorsement contract and for fraud.

Before this Court are the parties' cross motions for summary judgment. Raymond Weil moves for judgment in its favor on its claim for breach of contract. Theron and Denver & Delilah Films move for summary judgment dismissing all the claims asserted against them.

* * *

I. BACKGROUND

Unless otherwise indicated, the following facts are undisputed.

A. The Parties

1. Plaintiff Raymond Weil

Raymond Weil ("RW") is a Swiss corporation, with its general place of business in Geneva, Switzerland. It manufactures and sells high-end luxury watches in countries around the globe.

2. Defendant Charlize Theron

Charlize Theron ("Theron") is an Oscar-winning actress and entertainer.

3. Defendant Denver & Delilah Films, Inc.

Denver and Delilah Films ("DDF") is a California corporation owned and operated by Theron. It acts as both a film production company and a so-called "loan-out" corporation. A loan-out corporation enters into agreements whereby Theron (the "Artist") renders services of various kinds to third-parties (*i.e.* is "loaned out" to them).

B. The Agreement

On or about May 17, 2005, Raymond Weil entered into an agreement (the "Agreement") with DDF, whereby RW agreed to pay to DDF three million dollars in exchange for the use of Theron's image in a world-wide print media advertising campaign for Raymond Weil's "Shine" watch collection.

For our purposes, the relevant provisions of the Agreement are as follows:

Paragraph 8. Exclusivity

As of the signing of this Agreement, Artist [Theron] commits not to wear publicly any other watches other than RW watches during the Term. Additionally, Artist hereby agrees that during the Term she shall not endorse or advertise watches or jewelry for any other person, entity or company. Furthermore, Artist agrees that she will not endorse or advertise watches or jewelry for any other person, entity or company, including for charity. . . .

Notwithstanding the foregoing, RW acknowledges and agrees that Artist is permitted to wear jewelry of her choice in public and to awards shows during the Term.

Additionally, Artist may be asked to wear non-RW watches as part of her performance in a feature film and/or television show and that such action by Artist shall not be deemed a breach by Artist, provided however, no merchandising or commercial tie-in campaign shall be allowed in connection with non-RW watches utilizing her name, voice and/or likeness in connection with such film or television show that is released and/or broadcast during the Term.

This contract does not prevent RW from using other artists or celebrities to endorse its products. However, RW agrees that Artist shall be the sole female artist to endorse RW during the Term in Europe and the United States

In the event of a breach of the Agreement by either party, the Agreement provides that:

No party shall have the right to terminate this Agreement or sue for breach of this Agreement until it gives written notice of the alleged breach to the other party and a period of five (5) business days (in the country wherein the breach occurred) to cure the breach and such period elapses without such cure, unless the breach is of such a nature that it cannot be cured. In that case, termination or suit may proceed immediately. . . .

The term of Agreement ran from the date of the "publication of the October 2005 issue of major print media through December 31, 2006." * * * [E]ither party could elect to renew [the Agreement], and if the other party agreed, the term of the Agreement would be extended for an additional fifteen months. If the parties did not both agree to renew on the same terms and conditions, the Agreement would expire at the end of 2006.

The Agreement contained a very limited non-compete. If RW offered to renew on the same terms and conditions but Theron declined, then Theron agreed not to endorse or advertise any brand of watch, and any watches or jewelry produced by an enumerated list of high-end watch brands, for a period of for one year, or until the end of 2007.

The Agreement was signed by both parties. Theron signed the document "On behalf of Denver & Delilah Films (Artist)." Olivier Bernheim ("Bernheim"), Raymond Weil's CEO, signed "On behalf of Raymond Weil (RW)."

Neither party sought to exercise the extension option under the Agreement. Instead, the parties opened negotiations in the spring of 2006 about terms for a new agreement. According to Bernheim, RW did not seek to extend the terms of the old deal because there were terms RW wanted to modify if it went forward with Theron. However, negotiations broke off in August 2006 and no new deal was signed.

The original Agreement was allowed to expire on December 31, 2006.

Since RW had not sought to extend the Agreement, Theron's one year non-compete was never triggered.

II. THE INSTANT ACTION

RW sued Theron and DDF (collectively, "Defendants") on February 5, 2007, well after the Agreement had expired by its terms. It alleged that Theron had breached the agreement on several occasions during its term, and that Defendants had fraudulently induced RW to enter into the Agreement in the first place. RW sought to recover all sums previously paid to Theron under the Agreement, as well as all monies expended by RW for the Shine watch advertising campaign, all monies paid to Defendants by competing manufacturers to promote their products, and such other damages as may appropriately be awarded in a case of this nature

Defendants filed an answer denying the allegations in the complaint * * *.

A. Alleged Breaches of the Agreement

In the Complaint, Plaintiff alleged four instances of breach of the Agreement. RW has since abandoned two of the four * * *. The [remaining] two * * * are described more fully below.

1. The Montblanc Incident

Montblanc sells luxury goods, primarily writing instruments, but also watches, leather goods and, more recently, women's jewelry. In the fall of 2006, Montblanc launched a line of silver jewelry. As a promotional device for this launch, Montblanc partnered with the Entertainment Industry Foundation ("EIF"), a charity. EIF promised to secure the participation of a celebrity to be part of Montblanc's advertising campaign, in exchange for a donation to EIF from Montblanc. Theron agreed to appear in a promotional piece for EIF, which would identify Montblanc as the sponsor. In exchange, Montblanc agreed to pay EIF two-hundred and fifty thousand dollars. This agreement was never reduced to writing. Nonetheless, Theron participated in a photo shoot with the purpose of creating an image for the venture.

After looking at test Polaroid photographs of Theron wearing a Montblanc necklace during the photo shoot, Montblanc decided to photograph the actress without jewelry and then later superimpose a necklace, believing that this would produce this most in-focus image of both Theron and the Montblanc necklace. The finished product was incorporated into an approximately fourteen foot high poster

Montblanc believed that it had received permission through EIF to display that poster of Theron with the Montblanc necklace draped over her forearm at the 2006 Salon International de La Haute Horlogerie ("SIHH") in Switzerland. The SIHH is a prestigious watch and jewelry trade show and exhibition, lasting six days, at which a select number of jewelers and watch makers display their new products. From about April 3, 2006 to April 5, 2006, the poster was hanging up at the Montblanc booth. According to

Montblanc, the image was only displayed inside [the] booth, such that it was not visible to visitors passing by and was exposed only in one key entrance area. Nonetheless, the poster was up and people at the SIHH undoubtedly saw it.

After the poster had been on display for about two or three days, RW notified DDF that defendants were in breach of paragraph 8 of the Agreement. DDF immediately mobilized its lawyers, who persuaded Montblanc to take the poster down. The poster was removed sometime between fourteen and thirty-six hours later—within the five day cure period provided for in the Agreement.

As far as the court knows, RW made no effort to terminate the Agreement once the poster was removed.

2.   The South by Southwest Film Conference and Festival

On March 14, 2006, Theron attended a screening of East of Havana, a documentary film Ms. Theron produced through DDF, at the South by Southwest Film Festival ("SXSW"), an annual, regional film festival held in Austin, Texas. Theron, together with the producers of other films featured at the festival, participated in a panel discussion before an audience that included members of the public and professional photographers. Theron wore a Christian Dior ("Dior") watch to the press conference—a decision she now calls "regrettable."

Theron is one of the world's most beautiful women—she has even been named "The Sexiest Woman Alive" by Esquire Magazine—and many photographs were taken of her during the press conference. Some of those photographs showed Theron wearing the Dior watch, and some of those photos were posted to a website called "Wireimage"—essentially a clearing house for professional photographers. When someone sees an image on Wireimage that he wants to use, he downloads it and pays a fee, which is split between the photographer and the proprietors of Wireimage. Once a photographer has uploaded an image to Wireimage, she does not control, or necessarily even know, who will subsequently use the image or how. The celebrity depicted apparently knows even less.

One of several third parties to download the image of Theron wearing the Dior watch was LVMH Watch and Jewelry USA, another maker of luxury goods and the owner of Dior watches. LVMH submitted the image to Tourneau LLC "Tourneau," a prominent retailer and manufacturer of high-end watches. Tourneau is among the leading retailers of almost every brand of watch it carries based upon annual volume. Tourneau carries both RW and Dior watches in its inventory

Tourneau publishes an in-store annual called the *Tourneau Times*, which is mailed to about one hundred thousand, high-spending Tourneau customers and is made available free of charge in Tourneau retail locations. The October 2006 *Tourneau Times* ran a photograph taken at the SXSW

Festival depicting Theron wearing the Christian Dior watch on her wrist. The photograph of Theron in the Dior watch appeared on page fifteen of the publication in the "Star Watch" section, over a caption that reads, "Charlize Theron wears Dior." RW became aware of the image of Theron in the *Tourneau Times* in November of 2006.

In the same issue of the *Tourneau Times* RW ran an advertisement [of] RW Shine watches featuring the model Telma Thormasdittor. At the time the magazine appeared, DDF claims it had not relaxed the prohibition against RW's use of other female artists in *print* advertising, although it had granted RW permission to use other female artists in certain indoor and outdoor durable transparency or "duratrans" advertising. Thus, the use of the photographs of Thelma Thormasdittor is at least arguably a breach of RW's covenant not to use any other female artists to endorse its products in Europe and the United States during the term of the Agreement. However, Defendants have not asserted a counterclaim to this effect.

* * *

DISCUSSION

As noted above, RW now moves for partial summary judgment on its breach of contract claim and Defendants move for summary judgment on RW's claims for breach of contract and for fraud. * * *

I.   STANDARD OF REVIEW

Under [Fed. R. Civ. P.] 56(c), summary judgment is properly granted when "the pleadings, depositions, answers to interrogatories and admissions on file, together with the affidavits, if any, show that there is no issue as to any material fact and that the moving party is entitled to judgment as a matter of law." * * *

* * *

Since this Court's jurisdiction is based on the diversity of the parties, New York State substantive law applies.

II.   PLAINTIFF'S FRAUD CLAIM IS DISMISSED

[The court found no evidence to support a fraud claim.]

III. PLAINTIFF'S BREACH OF CONTRACT CLAIM IS DISMISSED ONLY IN PART

A.   Theron's Motion for Summary Judgment Dismissing her as a Party is Denied

The parties dispute whether Theron was properly named a party defendant in this lawsuit. Defendants argue that the only contracting party was DDF, and that Theron signed the Agreement with RW solely in her capacity as an agent of DDF, not in her own right. They urge that it was not possible for Theron to breach the contract, and they move for summary judgment dismissing her as a party defendant on those claims.

Under New York law, "an agent signing an agreement on his principal's behalf, will not be found personally liable under the terms of the agreement unless there is a clear and explicit evidence of the agent's intention to substitute or superadd his personal liability for, or to, that of his principal." To determine whether an agent signing on behalf of a corporation will nonetheless be found personally liable, New York courts and other courts in this Circuit applying New York law, have considered various iterations of the following factors: (1) the length of the contract; (2) the placement of the liability clause relative to the signature line; (3) the appearance of the signatory's name in the agreement itself; (4) the nature of the negotiation that surrounded the contract; and (5) the signatory's role in the company.

* * *

* * * [D]espite Theron's contention that she did not intend to become personally bound by the Agreement, this is patently not a situation where "a single sentence in a lengthy contract created a trap for an unwary agent" warranting against the possibility of individual liability. Applying the factors discussed above, it is obvious that Theron cannot be dismissed as a defendant on the breach of contract claim. She was not an unwary agent signing on behalf of a principal, but the very object of the Agreement agreeing (albeit through the medium of a personal services corporation) to lend HER celebrity to RW. Theron is the owner of DDF and therefore exercises considerable control over its corporate decisions. The agreement was only ten pages long, and Theron marked every page with her initials. Indeed, Theron even testified that she personally participated in the negotiations for the contract.

Additionally, the title of the Agreement is "Denver & Delilah Films, Inc. (Lender) for the Services of Charlize Theron (Artist) 2005–2006 Agreement with Raymond Weil (RW)" (Agreement at title line) and the only services under the Agreement are to be provided by "Artist" (Theron). At the end of the Agreement, just above the signature block, it states, "[t]his agreement shall bind and inure to the benefit of Artist [Theron]." * * * Theron signed "on behalf of Denver & Delilah Films (Artist)." That is, she signed on behalf of both the corporation and herself individually, not just in her capacity as president of the corporation. Her signature is not followed by the addition of any corporate title. The conclusion is inescapable that the parties intended Theron to be bound personally and that she signed the Agreement in both her corporate and personal capacities.

Theron's motion for summary judgment dismissing her as a party defendant (at least on the breach of contract claim) is denied.

B. Defendants' Motion for Summary Judgment as to the Montblanc Incident is Granted

The display of the poster of Theron holding the Montblanc necklace at the SIHH, a prestigious watch and jewelry trade show, constituted a breach of the Agreement between RW, Theron and DDF. While the parties dispute exactly what Theron knew about the final image used in the poster, it is clear from the record that Theron loaned her image to a purpose that was forbidden under the Agreement—to promote and advertise Montblanc silver jewelry. The fact that the image was to be used for charitable purposes does not excuse Defendants' breach, because paragraph 8 of the Agreement specifically states that Theron will not "endorse or advertise watches or jewelry for any other person, entity or company, *including for charity*" during the term of the Agreement. (Agreement ¶ 8) (emphasis added [by the court]).

However, the Agreement permitted a breaching party to cure within five days [relevant language quoted in Part IB, *supra*] and the breach—the public display of the poster with Theron's image and the necklace at an event promoting Montblanc products—was, in fact, remediated within five days after RW notified DDF of the breach. Therefore, RW's claim for breach of contract on this score must be dismissed.

* * *

The point of drafting a contract with a cure period provision is to allow the parties, in the event of breach, to correct their course and maintain the promises in their contract. * * *

RW argues that the cure provision is irrelevant, because the breach was of the incurable variety. It notes that the people who saw the poster while it was hanging cannot "un-see it." RW misidentifies the breach. It is not the act of viewing the poster by third parties that constitutes the breach—third parties are not bound by the Agreement and so cannot breach it. It is, rather, Theron's participation in Montblanc's advertising campaign and charitable promotion that breaches the contract. That breach is perfectly curable, as demonstrated by the fact that the breach was cured: the poster was taken down. This satisfied RW at the time; Bernheim, the company's CEO, testified at his deposition that he considered the removal of the Montblanc poster to be an adequate cure of the breach. In view of Bernheim's admission, it is difficult to see why RW persists in arguing that Theron's breach is actionable. It is not.

Defendants' cross motion for summary judgment dismissing the breach of contract claim insofar as it is predicated on the Montblanc incident is granted. RW's motion for summary judgment on this issue is denied.

C.   Plaintiff's Motion for Summary Judgment as to the Dior Watch Incident Is Granted in Part

By wearing a Christian Dior watch at a film festival, Theron breached her covenant not to "wear publicly any other watches other than RW." Theron recognizes as much, calling her decision to wear the watch "regrettable." It was more than "regrettable"; it was a clear breach of the Agreement.

Defendants' contention that Theron only wore the Dior watch for "about one hour of the fifteen month contract term" is an obvious effort to render the breach immaterial. But clearly it was not: Theron was photographed wearing the watch; the photographs ended up on the internet, where they were sold to a competitor of RW, which made sure that they were used to promote its products. Since the essence of the contract is Theron's agreeing to represent RW exclusively during the term of the Agreement, a breach, however fleeting, that resulted in the use of Theron's image in connection with another manufacturer's watch cannot be deemed immaterial.

Theron cannot hide behind the fact that she had no control over what the photographers did with the pictures they took at the panel discussion, or of the use that customers of the web site made of photographs they purchased. Her breach was wearing the watch. Subsequent uses over which she had no control are relevant, not to the issue of breach, but to the issue of damages.

Moreover, it was foreseeable to Theron—a famous movie star—that photographs of her would be made available for purchase and that they might appear in publications. Her lack of involvement in what happened with the pictures does not mean she is not culpable for any damage they caused to RW.

Therefore, RW's motion for partial summary judgment on the issue of liability for breach is granted to the extent of the claim arising out of the Dior watch incident and its subsequent use, and Defendants' motion for summary judgment on that claim on the issue of actual breach is denied.

* * *

NOTES AND QUESTIONS

1.   What was the agreement in *Raymond Weil*? Why would the parties enter into such an agreement?

2.   What was Theron's argument for being dismissed as a party defendant? How did the court rule and why? What is the governing rule with respect to whether an agent is liable for signing a contract on a principal's behalf?

3.   What was the court's ruling with respect to the display of the poster of Theron holding a Montblanc necklace at the trade show? Is the ruling fair?

4.   What was the court's ruling with respect to the Dior watch display at a film festival? Is the ruling fair?

5.   In *Knelman v. Middlebury College*, 898 F. Supp. 2d 697 (D. Vt. 2012), *aff'd*, 570 F. App'x 66 (2d Cir. 2014), a college athlete sued his college and hockey coach based on the athlete's dismissal from the hockey team during his junior year. The dismissal was largely based on the fact that Knelman had left an alumni banquet early. The banquet was in honor of the 50th anniversary of the hockey team's winning season, and many alumni were present, so all team members were expected to attend. A week before the banquet, Knelman asked his coach how long the banquet would last because he wanted to have dinner with his parents. The coach indicated that the banquet would last about two and a half hours. Knelman left the banquet after two and a half hours, approximately thirty minutes before the banquet actually concluded. The coach found out that Knelman had left the banquet early and suspended him for the season.

Knelman argued, based on the Middlebury College student handbook, that the coach could not arbitrarily remove him from the team because the handbook guaranteed that any discipline would go through a Community Judicial Board. The district court, however, found that the handbook did not explicitly regulate coaching decisions, such as removing a player from the team. The handbook governed only specified misconduct, such as non-academic misconduct, academic dishonesty, and plagiarism. Accordingly, even though the handbook created certain contractual duties on the part of the college, the court found that the coach and the college did not breach those duties. The U.S. Court of Appeals for the Second Circuit affirmed. It noted that while the coach's "decision to bar Knelman from the team for the remainder of the season was arguably harsh, there was no breach of contract." 570 F. App'x at 68. Based on the above summary, does the outcome of this case appear to be fair? What kind of contractual rights should student athletes have with respect to the universities they attend?

6.   For additional perspectives on the concepts of duty and breach, *see, e.g.*, Amy Cohen, *Reviving* Jacob and Youngs, Inc. v. Kent: *Material Breach Doctrine Reconsidered*, 42 Vill. L. Rev. 65 (1997) (noting that the law punishes only material breaches and arguing that a breach is more egregious (and thus more likely to be material) when the breaching party has acted in bad faith); Eric Andersen, *A New Look at Material Breach in the Law of Contracts*, 21 U.C. Davis L. Rev. 1073 (1988) (arguing that whether a breach is material should be based on whether the breach is so egregious that the only appropriate remedy is to cancel the contract; such an approach would protect the victim of the breach, but would allow the contract to proceed for minor breaches and thus would not impose unnecessary costs on the party in breach); Steven Burton, *Breach of Contract and the Common Law Duty to Perform in Good Faith*, 94 Harv. L. Rev. 369 (1980) (explaining that the duty to perform in good faith prohibits the party who has the discretion to determine various aspects

of the contract—such as timing, quantity, or price—from taking unfair advantage of the other party).

E. UNCONSCIONABILITY AND DURESS

Some contracts—even with valid offers, acceptances, and consideration—may be unenforceable because of unequal bargaining power. "Unconscionability" is the principle that a court may decline to enforce a contract when it is unfair, either because of procedural abuses when the contract was negotiated, or because of substantive unfairness in the resulting contract. Alternatively, a party may be relieved from performance because he was under duress when he entered into the contract. This section explores the contours of unconscionability and duress.

BOSE CORP. V. EJAZ

United States Court of Appeals, First Circuit, 2013
732 F.3d 17

LYNCH, CHIEF JUDGE.

Plaintiff Bose Corporation won summary judgment on its breach of contract and trademark claims against defendant Salman Ejaz. Ejaz admitted to selling home theater systems manufactured by Bose for use in the United States to customers in other countries, selling them across international markets to take advantage of higher retail prices abroad. Bose asserted that Ejaz sold its American products in Australia without Bose's consent even though he had signed a settlement agreement promising not to do so after he had made similar sales in Europe. Ejaz appeals, and we affirm.

I.

Because this case comes to us following Bose's motion for summary judgment, we recite the facts in the light most favorable to Ejaz.

Ejaz first began selling Bose products online through eBay as early as 2005. He was not an authorized reseller or distributor of Bose products. Rather, he sought to take advantage of the fact that the price of electronics can vary significantly between different countries, and would buy electronics in one country and resell them in another. Products sold in this way are known as "gray market goods" because the goods themselves are legitimate and unaltered products of the claimed manufacturer, but they are sold outside of their intended retail markets.

Throughout 2005 and 2006, Ejaz sold Bose products designed for use in the United States to customers in other countries, mostly in Europe. Bose soon became aware of Ejaz's activities and approached him in late 2006 with threats of legal action. At that time, Bose indicated that Ejaz could be liable for roughly $250,000 for trademark infringement based on his unauthorized sales of Bose products. Bose then went on to offer a settlement: in essence, Bose would drop all of its existing legal claims against Ejaz, including a suit that it had already filed in the United Kingdom, and in exchange, Ejaz would not sell Bose products without Bose's permission.

Negotiations over the settlement were tense. Ejaz chose to be unrepresented and later stated that he found the tactics Bose's lawyers used "very pressurizing, very intimidating." He was recently married, and he and his wife were "anxious to resolve the dispute." Ejaz felt as though Bose's lawyers were implicitly suggesting throughout the negotiations that he would go to jail if he did not reach an agreement with Bose, although he never claims such threats of criminal prosecution were actually made. By January of 2007, Ejaz agreed to settle the claims.

The agreement was executed through two documents. First, the parties agreed to the terms of a written Settlement Agreement. The Settlement Agreement released all of Bose's preexisting claims, including those not related to the U.K. lawsuit, and prohibited Ejaz from selling Bose products anywhere in the world without Bose's prior consent. It further provided that Ejaz would owe Bose $50,000 in liquidated damages for every violation of the Settlement Agreement. Ejaz signed the Settlement Agreement on January 27, 2007. Bose signed it on February 26, 2007, and it took effect on that date. Second, the Settlement Agreement included a Consent Order, to be filed in the British High Court of Justice. The Consent Order was filed with that court on February 23, 2007, and issued by that court on March 9, 2007. The Consent Order terminated the U.K. lawsuit in exchange for Ejaz's promise to stop selling Bose products in the European Union.

Not long after executing the Settlement Agreement, Ejaz violated it. As he wrote in an email, "greed got [the] better of [him]," and he started selling Bose products in Australia. In response, Bose initiated the present case. Bose sought damages against Ejaz for breach of the Settlement Agreement on seven occasions. It also added [a trademark infringement claim].

After discovery, Bose moved for summary judgment. Ejaz opposed the motion, claiming that there were a number of disputed material facts relating to several contract defenses. * * *

* * *

* * * [T]he district court granted summary judgment in favor of Bose on its breach of contract * * * claims. Ejaz now appeals. He argues that the Settlement Agreement, or at least its liquidated damages provision, is unenforceable, and that the district court erred in holding him liable under

it on summary judgment. * * * We reject these claims and affirm the grant of summary judgment.

II.

* * *

According to Section 8.4 of the Settlement Agreement, "interpretation and performance of [the] Agreement" is governed by Massachusetts law. Under Massachusetts law, a breach of contract claim requires the plaintiff to show that (1) a valid contract between the parties existed, (2) the plaintiff was ready, willing, and able to perform, (3) the defendant was in breach of the contract, and (4) the plaintiff sustained damages as a result. Ejaz contests only two elements of Bose's case: whether a valid contract existed and whether the contract's liquidated damages clause is enforceable.

A. Contract Validity

Ejaz offers [several] arguments to explain why the Settlement Agreement is not a valid contract. * * *

* * *

Unconscionability as Defense to the Contract

Ejaz claims that Bose's lawyers used heavy-handed tactics to get him, unrepresented by counsel, to sign the Settlement Agreement. Unconscionability is an affirmative defense, placing the burden of proof on Ejaz. Under Massachusetts law, unconscionability requires a "two-part inquiry," in which the defendant must prove both "procedural" and "substantive" unconscionability.

The evidence does not show substantive unconscionability as to the making of the contract here. * * * Contracts are substantively unconscionable if they show a "gross disparity" in consideration that makes them facially unfair. The record in this case shows that, at the time he signed the agreement, Ejaz understood that he would be relieved of legal liability that could have reached $250,000 in the U.K. litigation alone. Because the financial benefit for him was at least a quarter of a million dollars in liability avoided, no reasonable factfinder could conclude that Ejaz has met his burden of proof in his attempt to establish unconscionability.

Duress

Duress is an affirmative defense for which Ejaz must prove three elements: "(1) he has been the victim of some unlawful or wrongful act or threat; (2) the act or threat deprived him of his free or unfettered will; and (3) due to the first two factors, he was compelled to make a disproportionate exchange of values." Ejaz contends that Bose acted wrongfully by pressuring and intimidating him using what he says he perceived as threats of jail time, and that Bose's attorneys violated the Massachusetts Rules of Professional Conduct by advising him, as an unrepresented party, to sign the Settlement Agreement. These actions, he claims, constituted duress.

Ejaz mischaracterizes the facts of this case. Bose's lawyers approached him, a savvy internet businessman with total annual eBay sales near $75,000 and growing quickly, to offer a settlement agreement to avoid a lawsuit. Those lawyers, according to Ejaz, told him that there could be "repercussions" to his actions, which Ejaz took to mean criminal sanctions. However, Ejaz does not assert that Bose actually made threats, as opposed to statements that he subjectively interpreted to be threatening. Indeed, as he described the exchange in his deposition, Bose's lawyer "might have said [something] along the lines that people do end up going to jail but I don't remember him exactly saying that, but behind the words was that implication. Or at least I felt that way." Ejaz later stated in his affidavit: "I do not remember the precise words that they used about the consequences of not signing the agreement, but what I understood from those conversations is that I could face penalties of as much as $250,000 and possible imprisonment if I did not agree to what they were asking." None of these statements show that Ejaz was ever actually threatened or that Bose's counsel delivered any threats; rather, they show only that Ejaz believed he could potentially face legal penalties due to his unlawful sales. This is far from the "unlawful or wrongful act or threat," required to establish a duress defense.

More importantly, Ejaz has provided no basis to believe that the statements by Bose's counsel "deprived him of his free or unfettered will," and forced him to sign the contract. Instead, the facts show that Ejaz was able to review the proposed agreement at his own pace, was free to seek advice from others (and actually did seek advice from his wife), and voluntarily signed and returned it. As long as the option to reject the contract remained, Ejaz did not act under duress.

* * *

[The court also held that the district court correctly granted summary judgment to Bose on the trademark infringement claim.]

* * * [T]he district court's decision is AFFIRMED.

NOTES AND QUESTIONS

1. What were Ejaz's unconscionability and duress arguments? How did the court rule on each argument? Should Ejaz have been allowed to avoid his contract with Bose?

2. In *Spring Lake NC, LLC v. Holloway*, 110 So. 3d 916 (Fla. Dist. Ct. App. 2013), *review denied*, 134 So. 3d 446 (Fla. 2014), an elderly woman signed a contract upon entering a rehabilitation facility. The woman was 92 years old,

had only a fourth grade education, and was often confused. Moreover, the contract's terms were technical and complicated. Nonetheless, the court held that the contract was enforceable because there was no evidence that the rehabilitation facility staff had used improper methods or misled the woman. The court determined that a literal "meeting of the minds" was not necessary to enter into a binding contract, stating: "Our modern economy simply could not function if a 'meeting of the minds' required individualized understanding of all aspects of the typical standardized contract that is now signed without any expectation that the terms will actually be negotiated between the parties." *Id.* at 918. Instead, the court relied on an objective view of whether a contract had been formed, and noted that "the law must address abuses in standardized contracts by rules other than the 'meeting of the minds.'" *Id.* Should a "meeting of the minds" have been required in that case? What about a requirement of basic understanding?

3. As in *Holloway*, most courts evaluate contracts based on objective indicators, rather than on the particular characteristics and circumstances of the parties involved. Commentators are divided on the merits of that approach. *See, e.g.*, Wayne Barnes, *The Objective Theory of Contracts*, 76 U. Cin. L. Rev. 1119 (2008) (discussing the history of the objective theory of contracts and arguing that contract doctrines that are not objective should be eliminated); Richard Barnes, *Rediscovering Subjectivity in Contracts: Adhesion and Unconscionability*, 66 La. L. Rev. 123 (2005) (arguing that the objective rule is inappropriate in some circumstances, such as when there has been a subjective misunderstanding between the contracting parties); Joseph Perillo, *The Origins of the Objective Theory of Contract Formation and Interpretation*, 69 Fordham L. Rev. 427 (2000) (arguing that the objective theory has always dominated contract law, as courts "since time immemorial" relied on the written terms of contracts).

4. As noted in *Bose Corp.*, there are two broad types of unconscionability: procedural unconscionability and substantive unconscionability. As one court has explained:

> Substantive unconscionability concerns the legality and fairness of the contract terms themselves. * * * The substantive analysis focuses on such issues as whether the contract terms are commercially reasonable and fair, the purpose and effect of the terms, the one-sidedness of the terms, and other similar public policy concerns. Procedural unconscionability goes beyond the mere facial analysis of the contract and examines the particular factual circumstances surrounding the formation of the contract, including the relative bargaining strength, sophistication of the parties, and the extent to which either party felt free to accept or decline terms demanded by the other.

Cordova v. World Fin. Corp. of N.M., 146 N.M. 256, 262–63, 208 P.3d 901, 907–08 (2009). Courts are most likely to find a contract unconscionable when there are elements of both procedural and substantive unconscionability. *Id.* at 263, 208 P.3d at 908.

5.   What factors should courts consider in determining whether a contract is unconscionable? The Uniform Commercial Code (U.C.C.), a model code that governs the sale of goods, describes the test for unconscionability as follows: "The basic test is whether, in the light of the general commercial background and the commercial needs of the particular trade or case, the clauses involved are so one-sided as to be unconscionable under the circumstances existing at the time of the making of the contract." U.C.C. § 2–302, cmt. 1 (2012). Some form of the U.C.C. has been adopted by all 50 states.

6.   The Restatement (Second) of Contracts provides a detailed discussion of unconscionability:

> A bargain is not unconscionable merely because the parties to it are unequal in bargaining position, nor even because the inequality results in an allocation of risks to the weaker party. But gross inequality of bargaining power, together with terms unreasonably favorable to the stronger party, may confirm indications that the transaction involved elements of deception or compulsion, or may show that the weaker party had no meaningful choice, no real alternative, or did not in fact assent or appear to assent to the unfair terms. Factors which may contribute to a finding of unconscionability in the bargaining process include the following: belief by the stronger party that there is no reasonable probability that the weaker party will fully perform the contract; knowledge of the stronger party that the weaker party will be unable to receive substantial benefits from the contract; [and] knowledge of the stronger party that the weaker party is unable to reasonably protect his interests by reason of physical or mental infirmities, ignorance, illiteracy or inability to understand the language of the agreement, or similar factors.

Restatement (Second) of Contracts § 208, cmt. d (1981). A number of courts have adopted the Restatement guidance. *See, e.g., In re Marriage of Shanks*, 758 N.W.2d 506 (Iowa 2008); *Miller v. Cotter*, 448 Mass. 671, 863 N.E.2d 537 (2007); *Vockner v. Erickson*, 712 P.2d 379 (Alaska 1986). Other courts have adopted different formulations, but the criteria largely overlap with the Restatement guidance. *See, e.g., Jenkins v. First Am. Cash Advance of Ga., LLC*, 400 F.3d 868 (11th Cir. 2005) (also focusing on procedural and substantive unconscionability).

7.   Should it matter whether an individual is subjectively incapable of understanding a contractual term? For example, if an individual cannot read or speak English, should he still be bound by the terms (written in English) of a contract that he has signed? In *Carmona v. Lincoln Millennium Car Wash, Inc.*, 226 Cal.App.4th 74 (2014), employees who only spoke Spanish and could not read English were presented with a contract that included a provision requiring that all disputes be resolved by arbitration, not through in-court litigation. The employees were told to "take it or leave it," with little time to review the document. Although the arbitration clause was translated into Spanish, other parts of the contract—including a confidentiality agreement (spanning a page and a half) and an enforceability provision—were only

available in English. The employees challenged the arbitration provision, claiming that the clause was unconscionable. The court found that the contract was unenforceable on procedural unconscionability grounds because the employees were not able to negotiate the terms of the contract and believed that they would not be allowed to work if they refused to sign the contract. The court also found the contract unenforceable based on substantive unconscionability because the employers had rights under the contract that were denied to the employees. For example, the arbitration agreement was found "lacking in mutuality [because] it required arbitration only for the claims of the weaker party [the employee] but a choice of forums for the claims of the stronger party [the employer]." *Id.* at 86. Did the *Carmona* court reach the correct result by finding procedural and substantive unconscionability? On what grounds is that case distinguishable from *Ejaz?*

8.   For scholarly discussion of the unconscionability doctrine, *see, e.g.,* Melissa Lonegrass, *Finding Room for Fairness in Formalism—The Sliding Scale Approach to Unconscionability,* 44 Loy. U. Chi. L.J. 1 (2012) (advocating that a finding of unconscionability should be permissible when there are strong elements of procedural unconscionability, even if the elements of substantive unconscionability are weak, and vice versa, thereby allowing a more nuanced analysis of subjective assent in the context of standard-form contracts); Evelyn Brown, *The Uncertainty of U.C.C. Section 2–302: Why Unconscionability Has Become A Relic,* 105 Com. L.J. 287 (2000) (arguing that the flexibility of the unconscionability doctrine, under both the Restatement and the U.C.C., is both an advantage and a drawback because courts need flexibility in determining when to enforce or reject contracts based on equitable grounds, but at the same time the disparate outcomes can lead to uncertainty).

9.   For additional reading on the duress doctrine, *see, e.g.,* Nancy Kim, *Situational Duress and the Aberrance of Electronic Contracts,* 89 Chi.-Kent L. Rev. 265 (2014) (proposing a contractual defense of "situational duress" that would account for the increased coerciveness of contracting online in situations when digital content is blocked until a consumer accepts the terms of a contract); Grace Giesel, *A Realistic Proposal for the Contract Duress Doctrine,* 107 W. Va. L. Rev. 443 (2005) (arguing that the current doctrine of contract duress is fundamentally flawed, and offering a new framework).

F. DUTY TO DISCLOSE

The "duty to disclose" typically arises in the real estate context. Under the common law doctrine of "caveat emptor," there is no duty to disclose property defects. Recently, however, courts have found that there may be a duty to disclose in some contexts, particularly when the seller has information that may be difficult for the buyer to discover. The following case illustrates one such example.

STAMBOVSKY V. ACKLEY

Supreme Court, Appellate Division, First Department, New York, 1991
572 N.Y.S.2d 672, 169 A.D.2d 254

RUBIN, JUSTICE.

Plaintiff, to his horror, discovered that the house he had recently contracted to purchase was widely reputed to be possessed by poltergeists, reportedly seen by defendant seller and members of her family on numerous occasions over the last nine years. Plaintiff promptly commenced this action seeking rescission of the contract of sale. [The New York] Supreme Court [trial division] reluctantly dismissed the complaint, holding that plaintiff has no remedy at law in this jurisdiction.

The unusual facts of this case, as disclosed by the record, clearly warrant a grant of equitable relief to the buyer who, as a resident of New York City, cannot be expected to have any familiarity with the folklore of the Village of Nyack. Not being a "local," plaintiff could not readily learn that the home he had contracted to purchase is haunted. Whether the source of the spectral apparitions seen by defendant seller are parapsychic or psychogenic, having reported their presence in both a national publication ("Readers' Digest") and the local press (in 1977 and 1982, respectively), defendant is estopped to deny their existence and, as a matter of law, the house is haunted. More to the point, however, no divination is required to conclude that it is defendant's promotional efforts in publicizing her close encounters with these spirits which fostered the home's reputation in the community. In 1989, the house was included in a five-home walking tour of Nyack and described in a November 27th newspaper article as "a riverfront Victorian (with ghost)." The impact of the reputation thus created goes to the very essence of the bargain between the parties, greatly impairing both the value of the property and its potential for resale. The extent of this impairment may be presumed for the purpose of reviewing the disposition of this motion to dismiss the cause of action for rescission and represents merely an issue of fact for resolution at trial.

While [this court agrees] with [the trial court] that the real estate broker, as agent for the seller, is under no duty to disclose to a potential buyer the phantasmal reputation of the premises and that, in his pursuit of a legal remedy for fraudulent misrepresentation against the seller, plaintiff hasn't a ghost of a chance, I am nevertheless moved by the spirit of equity to allow the buyer to seek rescission of the contract of sale and recovery of his down payment. New York law fails to recognize any remedy for damages incurred as a result of the seller's mere silence, applying instead the strict rule of caveat emptor. Therefore, the theoretical basis for granting relief, even under the extraordinary facts of this case, is elusive if not ephemeral.

* * *

From the perspective of a person in the position of plaintiff herein, a very practical problem arises with respect to the discovery of a paranormal phenomenon: "Who you gonna' call?" as the title song to the movie "Ghostbusters" asks. Applying the strict rule of caveat emptor [let the buyer beware] to a contract involving a house possessed by poltergeists conjures up visions of a psychic or medium routinely accompanying the structural engineer and Terminix [insect and pest control] man on an inspection of every home subject to a contract of sale. It portends that the prudent attorney will establish an escrow account lest the subject of the transaction come back to haunt him and his client—or pray that his malpractice insurance coverage extends to supernatural disasters. In the interest of avoiding such untenable consequences, the notion that a haunting is a condition which can and should be ascertained upon reasonable inspection of the premises is a hobgoblin which should be exorcised from the body of legal precedent and laid quietly to rest.

It has been suggested by a leading authority that the ancient rule which holds that mere non-disclosure does not constitute actionable misrepresentation "finds proper application in cases where the fact undisclosed is patent, or the plaintiff has equal opportunities for obtaining information which he may be expected to utilize, or the defendant has no reason to think that he is acting under any misapprehension[.]" Prosser, *Law of Torts* § 106, at 696 (4th ed., 1971). However, with respect to transactions in real estate, New York adheres to the doctrine of caveat emptor and imposes no duty upon the vendor to disclose any information concerning the premises unless there is a confidential or fiduciary relationship between the parties or some conduct on the part of the seller which constitutes "active concealment[.]" Normally, some affirmative misrepresentation or partial disclosure is required to impose upon the seller a duty to communicate undisclosed conditions affecting the premises.

Caveat emptor is not so all-encompassing a doctrine of common law as to render every act of non-disclosure immune from redress, whether legal or equitable. "In regard to the necessity of giving information which has not been asked, the rule differs somewhat at law and in equity, and while the law courts would permit no recovery of *damages* against a vendor, because of mere concealment of facts *under certain circumstances*, yet if the vendee refused to complete the contract because of the concealment of a material fact on the part of the other, equity would refuse to compel him so to do, because equity only compels the specific performance of a contract which is fair and open, and in regard to which all material matters known to each have been communicated to the other[.]" Even as a principle of law, long before exceptions were embodied in statute law, the doctrine was held inapplicable to contagion among animals, adulteration of food, and insolvency of a maker of a promissory note and of a tenant substituted for another under a lease. Common law is not moribund. *Ex facto jus oritur* (law arises out of facts). Where fairness and common sense dictate that an exception should be created, the evolution of the law should not be stifled by rigid application of a legal maxim.

The doctrine of caveat emptor requires that a buyer act prudently to assess the fitness and value of his purchase and operates to bar the purchaser who fails to exercise due care from seeking the equitable remedy of rescission. For the purposes of the instant motion to dismiss the action * * *, plaintiff is entitled to every favorable inference which may reasonably be drawn from the pleadings, specifically, in this instance, that he met his obligation to conduct an inspection of the premises and a search of available public records with respect to title. It should be apparent, however, that the most meticulous inspection and the search would not reveal the presence of poltergeists at the premises or unearth the property's ghoulish reputation in the community. Therefore, there is no sound policy reason to deny plaintiff relief for failing to discover a state of affairs which the most prudent purchaser would not be expected to even contemplate.

The case law in this jurisdiction dealing with the duty of a vendor of real property to disclose information to the buyer is distinguishable from the matter under review. The most salient distinction is that existing cases invariably deal with the physical condition of the premises, defects in title, liens against the property, expenses or income, and other factors affecting its operation. No case has been brought to this court's attention in which the property value was impaired as the result of the reputation created by information disseminated to the public by the seller (or, for that matter, as a result of possession by poltergeists).

Where a condition which has been created by the seller materially impairs the value of the contract and is peculiarly within the knowledge of the seller or unlikely to be discovered by a prudent purchaser exercising due care with respect to the subject transaction, nondisclosure constitutes a basis for rescission as a matter of equity. Any other outcome places upon the buyer not merely the obligation to exercise care in his purchase but rather to be omniscient with respect to any fact which may affect the bargain. No practical purpose is served by imposing such a burden upon a purchaser. To the contrary, it encourages predatory business practice and offends the principle that equity will suffer no wrong to be without a remedy.

Defendant's contention that the contract of sale, particularly the merger or "as is" clause, bars recovery of the buyer's deposit is unavailing. Even an express disclaimer will not be given effect where the facts are peculiarly within the knowledge of the party invoking it. Moreover, a fair reading of the merger clause reveals that it expressly disclaims only representations made with respect to the physical condition of the premises and merely makes general reference to representations concerning "any other matter or things affecting or relating to the aforesaid premises." As broad as this language may be, a reasonable interpretation is that its effect is limited to tangible or physical matters and does not extend to paranormal phenomena. Finally, if the language of the contract is to be construed as broadly as defendant urges to encompass the presence of poltergeists in the house, it cannot be said that she has delivered the premises "vacant" in accordance with her obligation under the provisions of the contract rider.

* * *

In the case at bar, defendant seller deliberately fostered the public belief that her home was possessed. Having undertaken to inform the public at large, to whom she has no legal relationship, about the supernatural occurrences on her property, she may be said to owe no less a duty to her contract vendee. It has been remarked that the occasional modern cases which permit a seller to take unfair advantage of a buyer's ignorance so long as he is not actively misled are "singularly unappetizing." Where, as here, the seller not only takes unfair advantage of the buyer's ignorance but has created and perpetuated a condition about which he is unlikely to even inquire, enforcement of the contract (in whole or in part) is offensive to the court's sense of equity. Application of the remedy of rescission, within the bounds of the narrow exception to the doctrine of caveat emptor set forth herein, is entirely appropriate to relieve the unwitting purchaser from the consequences of a most unnatural bargain.

* * *

* * * [T]he * * * cause of action seeking rescission of the contract [is] reinstated * * *.

* * *

SMITH, JUSTICE [with whom MILONAS, JUSTICE, joins], dissenting.

I would affirm the dismissal of the complaint by the motion court.

* * *

"It is settled law in New York that the seller of real property is under no duty to speak when the parties deal at arm's length. The mere silence of the seller, without some act or conduct which deceived the purchaser, does not amount to a concealment that is actionable as a fraud. The buyer has the duty to satisfy himself as to the quality of his bargain pursuant to the doctrine of caveat emptor, which in New York State still applies to real estate transactions."

The parties herein were represented by counsel and dealt at arm's length. This is evidenced by the contract of sale which, *inter alia*, contained various riders and a specific provision that all prior understandings and agreements between the parties were merged into the contract, that the contract completely expressed their full agreement and that neither had relied upon any statement by anyone else not set forth in the contract.

There is no allegation that defendants, by some specific act, other than the failure to speak, deceived the plaintiff. Nevertheless, a cause of action may be sufficiently stated where there is a confidential or fiduciary relationship creating a duty to disclose and there was a failure to disclose a material fact, calculated to induce a false belief. However, plaintiff herein has not alleged and there is no basis for concluding that a confidential or fiduciary relationship existed between these parties to an arm's length transaction such as to give rise to a duty to disclose. In addition, there is no allegation that defendants thwarted plaintiff's efforts to fulfill his responsibilities fixed by the doctrine of caveat emptor.

Finally, if the doctrine of caveat emptor is to be discarded, it should be for a reason more substantive than a poltergeist. The existence of a poltergeist is no more binding upon the defendants than it is upon this court.

Based upon the foregoing, the motion court properly dismissed the complaint.

NOTES AND QUESTIONS

1. What were the buyer's arguments in *Stambovsky* for seeking to rescind the contract? How did the court rule? Why did the dissent disagree with the majority? Which opinion is more persuasive?

2. The court suggested that its decision was based on principles of equity. Normally, the doctrine of caveat emptor would control. What were the unusual facts here that, in the majority's view, made the invocation of caveat emptor unfair?

3. Courts sometimes deny real property damages based on later-discovered defects. For example, in *Behar v. Glickenhaus Westchester Development, Inc.*, 996 N.Y.S.2d 678, 122 A.D.3d 784 (App. Div. 2014), a New York intermediate appellate court affirmed the trial court's decision to deny damages to homeowners who bought property next to a golf course. The homeowners alleged that Glickenhaus had violated its duty to disclose the fact that the property could be damaged by golf balls. The court held, however, that without active concealment, Glickenhaus had "no duty to disclose any information regarding the premises under the doctrine of caveat emptor" in arm's length negotiations. *Behar*, 122 A.D.3d at 786, 996 N.Y.S.2d at 680. Moreover, the court found that the risk of golf balls damaging the property was one that plaintiffs could have ascertained. Based on *Behar* and *Stambovsky*, what types of problems should property sellers be required to disclose? How diligent must property buyers be in investigating potential problems with real estate they are purchasing? Should buyers be able to recover whenever the property is not what they subjectively expected?

4. For scholarly discussion of the duty to disclose, *see, e.g.*, Alan Weinberger, *Let the Buyer Be Well Informed?—Doubting the Demise of Caveat Emptor*, 55 Md. L. Rev. 387 (1996) (arguing that statutorily-mandated

disclosure statements required in many states do not benefit buyers or sellers because such statements increase the difficulty and cost of selling a home); Frona Powell, *The Seller's Duty to Disclose in Sales of Commercial Property*, 28 Am. Bus. L.J. 245 (1990) (arguing that, although parties to a commercial real estate transaction are presumed to be sophisticated, the duty to disclose should apply to commercial property as well as residential property (based on principles of good faith and fair dealing)).

G. PROMISSORY ESTOPPEL

Sometimes a court will find that, even if a contract has not been formed, it would be unfair to allow a party who made a promise to escape liability. This doctrine, known as "promissory estoppel," allows courts to enforce a promise (not constituting a contract) when one party has reasonably relied on the promise and would be damaged if the promise were not enforced. The following case illustrates the difficult facts that courts must address in deciding whether to invoke promissory estoppel.

ALDEN V. PRESLEY
Supreme Court of Tennessee, 1982
637 S.W.2d 862

FONES, JUSTICE.

This is an action against the estate of Elvis Presley to enforce a gratuitous promise to pay off the mortgage on plaintiff's home made by decedent but not consummated prior to his death.

The trial court denied recovery but the Court of Appeals found that plaintiff had relied upon the promise to her detriment and awarded plaintiff judgment on the theory of promissory estoppel.

I.

Plaintiff alleged that she relied to her detriment on a promise made by the decedent to pay off the mortgage indebtedness on plaintiff's home. Defendant did not deny a promise was made by decedent but contended that plaintiff's continued reliance upon that promise following decedent's death constituted an unreasonable and unjustified action on her part, and furthermore, that any damage done to plaintiff occurred as a result of affirmative action taken by her despite her knowledge of decedent's death and with full knowledge that decedent's executor had denied legal liability to fulfill the promise.

Plaintiff, Jo Laverne Alden, is the mother of Ginger Alden, the former girlfriend of the late Elvis Presley. Presley was a singer of great renown throughout the world and a man of substantial wealth. In January of 1977, Presley became engaged to Ginger Alden. He was quite generous to several members of the Alden family including Ginger and her mother, the plaintiff. Gifts to plaintiff included the funds for landscaping the lawn and installing a swimming pool for the Alden home. Due to his close relationship with plaintiff's daughter, Presley also became aware of plaintiff's desire to obtain a divorce from her husband. Presley offered to pay all expenses incurred in the divorce proceeding, including furnishing plaintiff an attorney; to advance plaintiff money to purchase her husband's equity in the Alden home; and to pay off the remaining mortgage indebtedness on the Alden home.

As a result of these promises, plaintiff filed for divorce on the grounds of irreconcilable differences. On August 1, 1977, a property settlement agreement was executed in which plaintiff paid her husband $5,325.00 for his equity in return for a deed conveying all of his interest in the home to plaintiff plus a release of the husband from all further liability upon the mortgage indebtedness on the Alden home. The mortgage indebtedness at the time of the execution of the settlement agreement was in the sum of $39,587.66, and it is this amount which is the subject of the present suit, all the other gifts and promises to plaintiff having been fulfilled.

On August 16, 1977, Presley died suddenly leaving unpaid the mortgage indebtedness on the Alden home. On August 25, 1977, Drayton Beecher Smith, II, an attorney for the Presley estate, informed plaintiff that the estate would not assume liability for the mortgage indebtedness.

Plaintiff filed the present suit on February 14, 1978, to enforce the promise made by decedent to pay the home mortgage. On March 3, 1978, Smith informed plaintiff he could no longer represent her in the divorce action since he was serving as an attorney for decedent's estate. Plaintiff failed to employ new counsel and the divorce action was dismissed for failure to prosecute.

Plaintiff re-filed her divorce action in April 1978, upon the same grounds and sought approval of the property settlement agreement executed in August, 1977, in conjunction with the original divorce suit. The divorce was granted in April, 1980, on the grounds of irreconcilable differences, and the property settlement was approved by the court. Plaintiff did not disclose to the court in the divorce case that decedent's estate had informed her it was not their intention to pay the mortgage on the Alden home.

In the instant case, the trial court held that decedent did make a promise unsupported by consideration to plaintiff, that no gift was consummated for failure of delivery, that plaintiff and her husband suffered no detriment as she "wound up much better off after their association with Elvis A. Presley than either would have been if he had never made any promise to Jo Laverne Alden," and that plaintiff did not rely upon the promise since her divorce petition was filed subsequent to the present suit and subsequent to being told that decedent's estate would not accept legal responsibility for decedent's promise.

The Court of Appeals concurred in the trial court finding that there was no gift for failure of delivery * * *.

However, the Court of Appeals reversed the remainder of the trial court's decision by adopting and applying the doctrine of promissory estoppel * * *.

We concur in the reasoning of the trial court and Court of Appeals' findings that decedent did not make a gift of the money necessary to pay off the mortgage * * *. We find it unnecessary to address the question of whether or not Tennessee recognizes the doctrine of promissory estoppel because plaintiff has failed * * * to prove essential elements of promissory estoppel, to-wit: detrimental reliance, and a loss suffered as a result of detrimental reliance.

II.

The Court of Appeals relied upon definitions of promissory estoppel found in the Restatement of Contracts and L. Simpson's, *Law of Contracts.* Since these works present representative definitions of promissory estoppel we quote with approval from the Court of Appeals' opinion as follows:

A concise statement concerning promissory estoppel is found in Restatement of Contracts, Section 90, as follows:

A promise which the promisor should reasonably expect to induce action or forbearance of a definite and substantial character on the part of the promisee and which does induce such action or forbearance is binding if injustice can be avoided only by enforcement of the promise.

A more thorough examination of the doctrine, its elements and limitations is set forth in L. Simpson, *Law of Contracts* § 61 (2d ed. 1965); to-wit:

Detrimental action or forbearance by the promisee in reliance on a gratuitous promise, within limits constitutes a substitute for consideration, or a sufficient reason for enforcement of the promise without consideration. This doctrine is known as promissory estoppel. A promisor who induces substantial change of position by the promisee in reliance on the promise is estopped to deny its enforceability as lacking consideration. The reason for the doctrine is to avoid an unjust result, and its reason defines its limits. No injustice results in refusal to enforce a gratuitous promise where the loss suffered in reliance is negligible, nor where the promisee's action in reliance was unreasonable or unjustified by the promise. The limits of promissory estoppel are: (1) the detriment suffered in reliance must be substantial in an economic sense; (2) the substantial loss to the promisee in acting in reliance must have been foreseeable by the promisor; (3) the promisee must have acted reasonabl[y] in justifiable reliance on the promise as made.

* * *

IV.

The residence of the Aldens and the mortgage indebtedness thereon was obviously subject to such disposition as alimony, as the circumstances of the parties justified at the time that the divorce was granted, April 1980.

Mrs. Alden did not inform the court that the estate had denied legal responsibility for the mortgage indebtedness, after she had entered into the property settlement agreement, but instead, affirmatively sought approval of the property settlement agreement. Beyond question, she was entitled to relief from that portion of the property settlement agreement wherein she assumed the mortgage indebtedness, upon revealing to the divorce court that she agreed to assume the mortgage only because decedent promised to pay it off gratuitously, but that the estate denied liability subsequent to the execution of the property settlement agreement. She was represented by counsel and must be charged with the knowledge that those facts constituted a change of circumstances that, as a matter of law, entitled her to relief from that portion of the agreement.

In this action plaintiff has shown that decedent's promise induced her to assume a $39,587 mortgage as part of a property settlement agreement dated August 1, 1977. However, the property settlement agreement was not binding upon plaintiff or her husband until approved by the court and the estate's denial of liability for decedent's gratuitous promise before submission of the agreement to the court removed the element of detrimental reliance from the factual scenario of this case. It follows, plaintiff's reliance on the promise after August 25, 1977, was not reasonably justified and she suffered no loss as a result of justifiable reliance.

The judgment of the Court of Appeals is reversed and this case is dismissed. * * *

NOTES AND QUESTIONS

1.   What is promissory estoppel? What purpose does that doctrine promote?

2.   What did the Tennessee Supreme Court rule in *Alden* with respect to promissory estoppel? How did its approach differ from that of the court of appeals? Which approach is more justified based on the facts of the case and on principles of fairness?

3. Would plaintiff's case have been stronger had she secured the promise from Elvis Presley in writing? How would the gratuitous nature of the promise have complicated even a written promise?

4. If one were able to ask Elvis what he wanted, what would he likely have said? Should that kind of speculation enter into the resolution of the *Alden* case?

5. One of the most famous promissory estoppel cases (from more than a century ago) is *Ricketts v. Scothorn*, 57 Neb. 51, 77 N.W. 365 (1898). In that case, a grandfather promised his granddaughter $2,000 to induce her not to work outside of the home. The granddaughter sued her grandfather's estate for fulfillment of that obligation. The court held that, because the granddaughter relied on her grandfather's promise and left her job, his estate was estopped (prohibited) from arguing lack of consideration and was required to pay the granddaughter the amount promised. As the court explained: "Having intentionally influenced the plaintiff to alter her position for the worse on the faith of the note being paid when due, it would be grossly inequitable to permit the maker, or his executor, to resist payment on the ground that the promise was given without consideration." *Id.* at 58, 77 N.W. at 367.

In a recent case, *Bouton v. Byers*, 50 Kan. App. 2d 35, 321 P.3d 780 (2014), a court faced a similar issue when a father (Byers) induced his daughter (Bouton) to leave her career as a law professor with the promise that he would bequeath land to her that was worth more than $1 million. Byers later sold the land, rather than leaving it for his daughter to inherit. Bouton sued her father, seeking damages for the lost land based on a theory of promissory estoppel. The district court granted summary judgment in favor of Byers, finding that (1) Byers could not have reasonably predicted that Bouton would leave her job based on the promise, and (2) it was unreasonable for Bouton to leave her job based on the promise. The appellate court reversed and remanded the case for trial, holding that Bouton could have reasonably relied on Byers's promise and that Byers could have anticipated that reliance, making summary judgment inappropriate. As the court noted: "Byers made a promise that reasonably could have induced Bouton to abandon an excellent job to come work at the ranch. Although Byers later became disenchanted with Bouton's handling of the ranch work, justice might fairly be construed to hold him to the inducement he offered to get Bouton to leave her professorship in the first place." *Id.* at 48, 321 P.3d at 791. Thus, the granddaughter in *Ricketts* won in full on appeal, and Bouton was given a chance to prove her claim at trial.

Why were the claims by Bouton and the granddaughter in *Ricketts* kept alive while Alden's claim was dismissed? Can *Alden* be reconciled with *Ricketts* and *Bouton*?

6. In discussing the definition of promissory estoppel, the court in *Alden* referred to § 90 of the Restatement of Contracts. The inclusion of the promissory estoppel doctrine in § 90 of the Restatement (First) of Contracts in 1932 was a watershed event that gave great prominence to the doctrine of promissory estoppel. *See, e.g.*, Marco Jimenez, *The Many Faces of Promissory*

Estoppel: An Empirical Analysis Under the Restatement (Second) of Contracts, 57 UCLA L. Rev. 669, 674 (2010) (characterizing the inclusion of § 90 in the 1932 Restatement as "the most important event in twentieth century American contract law"). Promissory estoppel remains a core topic in every contracts course in U.S. law schools.

7.   For additional discussions of promissory estoppel, including conflicting empirical studies, *see id.* (examining more than 300 promissory estoppel cases adjudicated between 1981 and 2008 and concluding that promissory estoppel claims have a slightly higher rate of success than do traditional breach of contract claims); Juliet Kostritsky, *The Rise and Fall of Promissory Estoppel or Is Promissory Estoppel Really as Unsuccessful as Scholars Say It Is: A New Look at the Data*, 37 Wake Forest L. Rev. 531 (2002) (surveying five years of cases and arguing that promissory estoppel continues to be an important theory of contract law); Robert Hillman, *Questioning the "New Consensus" on Promissory Estoppel: An Empirical and Theoretical Study*, 98 Colum. L. Rev. 580 (1998) (analyzing a sample of promissory estoppel cases and concluding that the theory rarely leads to recovery; author offers various possible explanations for this lack of success, including the possibility that courts disfavor the doctrine); Phuong Pham, *The Waning of Promissory Estoppel*, 79 Cornell L. Rev. 1263 (1994) (concluding that promissory estoppel arguments are not usually successful, and arguing that this lack of success underscores a preference by courts for the traditional bargain theory of contract law).

H. DAMAGES

After a court has determined that there is an enforceable contract that was breached (or that promissory estoppel is justified), it must determine the appropriate remedy. The court will typically award damages designed to make each party "whole," thereby compensating the plaintiff for the damage caused by the breach. As a general rule, damages designed to punish a party for its breach are *not* recoverable for breach of contract. The following case reveals one court's calculation of contract damages.

KENFORD CO., INC. V. COUNTY OF ERIE

Court of Appeals of New York, 1989
540 N.Y.S.2d 1, 537 N.E.2d 176

MOLLEN, JUDGE.*

This appeal arises out of breach of contract litigation spanning 18 years and involving the proposed construction and operation of a domed stadium facility in the County of Erie. The issue is whether the plaintiff Kenford Company, Inc. (Kenford) is entitled to recover damages against the defendant County of Erie (County) for the loss of anticipated

---

*   Designated pursuant to N.Y. Constitution, Article VI, § 2 [designation of a substitute judge because of a recusal or disqualification].

appreciation in the value of the land which Kenford owned in the periphery of the proposed stadium site. Under the circumstances of this case, we conclude that Kenford is not entitled to recovery on this claim since there is no evidence to support a determination that the parties contemplated, prior to or at the time of the contract, assumption by the County of liability for these damages.

By way of background, the County of Erie adopted enabling legislation in May 1968 authorizing it to finance and construct a domed sports stadium in the vicinity of the City of Buffalo. The County, simultaneously, adopted a resolution authorizing a $50 million bond resolution for the purpose of financing the construction of the proposed stadium. In December 1968, Kenford, through its president and sole shareholder, Edward H. Cottrell, submitted an offer to the County with regard to the stadium project. By its terms, Kenford, which had acquired options on various parcels of land located in the Town of Lancaster in Erie County, proposed to sell a portion of that land to the County as a site for the stadium facility. Although the County initially expressed interest in Kenford's proposal, it eventually declined the offer. Kenford, however, pursued the matter and thereafter engaged the services of [former Texas politician] Roy Hofheinz, who had been instrumental in the development of the Houston Astrodome. Kenford then approached the County with a new offer. By its terms, Kenford was to donate to the County the land upon which the stadium was to be built, in exchange for which the County was to permit Hofheinz and Cottrell, who had formed the management company of Dome Stadium, Inc. (DSI), to lease or manage the proposed stadium facility.

In June 1969, the County adopted a resolution accepting Kenford's new offer, after which the parties engaged in contract negotiations. During this period of time, Cottrell, as agent for Kenford, exercised his options on several parcels of land located in the Town of Lancaster. On August 8, 1969, the County, Kenford and DSI executed a contract which provided, in pertinent part, that Kenford would donate 178 acres of land located in the Town of Lancaster to the County for use in construction of the stadium and necessary access roadways. In consideration therefor, the County agreed to commence construction of the stadium within 12 months. The County also agreed to negotiate a 40-year lease with DSI for the operation of the facility which was to provide, *inter alia*, that the County would receive, as its consideration, lease revenues of not less than $63.75 million over the 40-year term to be comprised of (1) all tax revenues received by the County generated by the operation of the stadium site area; (2) rental payments from DSI; and (3) increased real property taxes resulting from increased assessments and other tax revenues received from or generated by "the peripheral lands and development thereof." The term "peripheral lands" was defined as "those lands presently owned, contracted for or hereinafter acquired by Edward H. Cottrell or Kenford, and located within the area of the Town of Lancaster." If a mutually satisfactory lease could not be agreed upon within three months of the contract signing, the County and DSI were to execute a 20-year management agreement which was annexed to the contract.[1]

Following execution of the contract, the County solicited construction bids for the proposed stadium. The bids received by the County indicated that the proposed project would cost approximately $72 million which was $22 million in excess of the County's prior bond resolution. Although efforts were made to seek an increase in the appropriation for the stadium, those efforts were unsuccessful and, in January 1971, the County adopted a resolution terminating the contract with Kenford and DSI. Kenford's subsequent attempts to procure alternate financing for the proposed stadium facility proved futile.

In June 1971, Kenford and DSI instituted the instant breach of contract action and sought specific performance thereof, or, in the alternative, damages in the amount of $90 million.[2] Following the award of summary judgment in favor of the plaintiffs on the issue of liability, the matter was set down for a trial on the issue of damages. The damage trial lasted approximately nine months and resulted in a jury award to Kenford [among other damages to Kenford and DSI] in the sum of $18 million for its lost appreciation in the value on its property located on the periphery of the proposed stadium site * * *.

On appeal, * * * the majority of the Appellate Division determined [in relevant part] that Kenford's loss of land appreciation was both a foreseeable and certain damage for which it was entitled to recover. The majority, however, found that the award was based upon improper appraisal evidence provided by the Kenford's expert who assumed that the property in question would be improved with, among other things, a theme park, office buildings and a golf course. The court ruled that the proper measure of damage was the value of the land as raw acreage following the construction of the proposed stadium less the value of the land when purchased. Two Justices dissented on the issue of Kenford's right to recover damages for anticipated land appreciation and took the position that these damages were not foreseeable and, in any event, were inherently speculative and, therefore, not recoverable.

[The court describes various appellate proceedings prior to retrial.]

* * *

* * * [T]he retrial on the issue of damages for Kenford's loss of anticipated land appreciation ensued and the jury awarded Kenford the sum of $6.5 million. The Appellate Division affirmed the jury award. * * *

---

[1] Despite extensive negotiations, the County and DSI never agreed upon a satisfactory 40-year lease agreement.

[2] The plaintiffs were later granted permission to increase the ad damnum clause [damages limit] to $495 million.

It is well established that in actions for breach of contract, the nonbreaching party may recover general damages which are the natural and probable consequence of the breach. "[I]n order to impose on the defaulting party a further liability * * *, such unusual or extraordinary damages must have been brought within the contemplation of the parties as the probable result of a breach at the time of or prior to contracting[.]" *Chapman v. Fargo*, 223 N.Y. 32, 36, 119 N.E. 76 (1918); *Hadley v. Baxendale*, 9 Exch. 341, 156 Eng. Rep. 145 (1854); McCORMICK, DAMAGES § 138, at 562 (1935). In determining the reasonable contemplation of the parties, the nature, purpose and particular circumstances of the contract known by the parties should be considered, as well as "what liability the defendant fairly may be supposed to have assumed consciously, or to have warranted the plaintiff reasonably to suppose that it assumed, when the contract was made."

In the case before us, it is beyond dispute that at the time the contract was executed, all parties thereto harbored an expectation and anticipation that the proposed domed stadium facility would bring about an economic boom in the County and would result in increased land values and increased property taxes. This expectation is evidenced by the terms of the provision of the parties' contract requiring the County and DSI to undertake negotiations of a lease which would provide for specified revenues to be derived from, *inter alia*, the increased taxes on the peripheral lands. We cannot conclude, however, that this hope or expectation of increased property values and taxes necessarily or logically leads to the conclusion that the parties contemplated that the County would assume liability for Kenford's loss of anticipated appreciation in the value of its peripheral lands if the stadium were not built. * * * "[T]he provisions in the contract providing remedy for a default do not suggest or provide for such a heavy responsibility on the part of the County. In the absence of any provision for such an eventuality, *the commonsense rule to apply is to consider what the parties would have concluded had they considered the subject.* The evidence here fails to demonstrate that liability for loss of profits over the length of the contract would have been in the contemplation of the parties at the relevant time."

Similarly, there is no provision in the contract between Kenford and the County, nor is there any evidence in the record to demonstrate that the parties, at any relevant time, reasonably contemplated or would have contemplated that the County was undertaking a contractual responsibility for the lack of appreciation in the value of Kenford's peripheral lands in the event the stadium was not built. This conclusion is buttressed by the fact that Kenford was under no contractual obligation to the County to acquire or maintain ownership of any land surrounding the 178 acres it was required to donate to the County. Although the County was aware that Kenford had acquired and intended to further acquire peripheral lands, this knowledge, in and of itself, is insufficient, as a matter of law, to impose liability on the County for the loss of anticipated appreciation in the value of those lands since the County never contemplated at the time of the contract's execution that it assumed legal responsibility for these damages upon a breach of the contract. * * * "[B]are notice of special consequences which might result from a breach of contract, unless under such circumstances as to imply that it formed the basis of the agreement, would not be sufficient [to impose liability for special damages.]" *See also Czarnikow-Rionda Co. v. Federal Sugar Ref. Co.*, 255 N.Y. 33, 173 N.E. 913 (1930) (the defendant supplier of sugar was not made aware at the time of the contract that the plaintiff purchaser could not acquire sugar on the open market and, therefore, was not liable for the plaintiff's special damages arising out of the breach of contract); *Baldwin v. U.S. Tel. Co.*, 45 N.Y. 744 (1871) (the defendant telegraph company was not liable for special damages caused by delay in delivery of message since it was without notice or information indicating that extraordinary care or speed of delivery was necessary); *Hadley v. Baxendale, supra* (the common carrier was not liable for the loss of profits at the plaintiffs' flour mill since the carrier, who knew that the mill was closed, was not aware that the mill's continued operation was dependent solely on prompt delivery of the mill's broken shaft).

Undoubtedly, Kenford purchased the peripheral lands in question with the hope of benefiting from the expected appreciation in the value of those lands once the stadium was completed and became operational. In doing so, Kenford voluntarily and knowingly assumed the risk that, if the stadium were not built, its expectations of financial gain would be unrealized. There is no indication that either Kenford or the County reasonably contemplated at the time of the contract that this risk was assumed, either wholly or partially, by the County. To hold otherwise would lead to the irrational conclusion that the County, in addition to promising to build the domed stadium, provided a guarantee that if for any reason the stadium were not built, Kenford would still receive all the hoped for financial benefits from the peripheral lands it anticipated to receive upon the completion of the stadium. According to Kenford's version of the facts, Kenford was to realize all of its anticipated gains with or without the stadium. Clearly, such a result is illogical and without any basis whatsoever in the record.

Thus, the constant refrain which flows throughout the legion of breach of contract cases dating back to the leading case of *Hadley v. Baxendale* provides that damages which may be recovered by a party for breach of contract are restricted to those damages which were reasonably foreseen or contemplated by the parties during their negotiations or at the time the contract was executed. The evident purpose of this well-accepted principle of contract law is to limit the liability for unassumed risks of one entering into a contract and, thus, diminish the risk of business enterprise. In the case before us, although Kenford obviously anticipated and expected that it would reap financial benefits from an anticipated dramatic increase in the value of its peripheral lands upon the completion of the proposed domed stadium facility, * * * there is no indication whatsoever that the County reasonably contemplated at any relevant time that it was to assume liability for Kenford's unfulfilled land appreciation expectations in the event that the stadium was not built. Thus, under the principles set forth in *Hadley v. Baxendale* and its progeny of cases in this State, Kenford is not entitled to recovery * * * for its lost appreciation in the value of its peripheral lands caused by the County's breach of the parties' contract.

* * *

NOTES AND QUESTIONS

1. What is the rule of damages in *Hadley v. Baxendale*? Is the rule a sensible one?

2. What injury did Kenford allege? Why did the court hold that Kenford could not recover its damages? Is the outcome fair based on the facts of the case?

3. As mentioned in the introduction to this section, courts generally do not award punitive damages for breach of contract. Such damages may be awarded, however, if they are specifically permitted by statute. *See Wood v. Foremost Ins. Co.*, 477 F.3d 1027 (8th Cir. 2007) (discussing Missouri's Vexatious Refusal to Pay Claim statute, which allows for the recovery of additional, punitive damages when insurance companies refuse to pay valid claims).

4. Liquidated damage provisions can be used to simplify breach of contract scenarios by allowing the parties to determine in advance what damages are appropriate in the event of a breach. Nonetheless, whether the damages provisions are enforceable depends on the precise facts of a case. For example, in *Garden Ridge, L.P. v. Advance International, Inc.*, 403 S.W.3d 432 (Tex. App. 2013), Garden Ridge, a home decoration store, ordered inflatable snowmen decorations from Advance International ("Advance"). Advance produced two types of snowmen decorations, one that waved and one that held a banner. Garden Ridge placed two orders for the waving snowmen and no orders for the banner snowmen. When Advance sent one shipment of waving snowmen and one shipment of banner snowmen, Garden Ridge refused to pay for the shipments and attempted to enforce a liquidated damages provision based on Advance's violation of the contract. Garden Ridge claimed damages of approximately $90,000. Notwithstanding that claim, Garden Ridge admitted that it made approximately $113,000 in profits from the snowmen sales and would not have made more money had it received both shipments of waving snowmen. The trial court granted a motion for directed verdict against Garden Ridge based on the lack of evidence of damages. On appeal, the Texas Court of Appeals affirmed, explaining: "The test for determining whether a provision is valid and enforceable as liquidated damages is (1) if the damages for the prospective breach of the contract are difficult to measure; and (2) the

stipulated damages are a reasonable estimate of actual damages." *Id.* at 440. Because Garden Ridge had no actual damages, the court concluded that the "provisions are unenforceable as penalties under the UCC because they fixed unreasonably large liquidated damages." *Id.* at 441.

By contrast, in *Kent State University v. Ford*, 26 N.E.3d 868 (Ohio Ct. App. 2015), Kent State University included a liquidated damages provision in its employment contract with Gene Ford, the head basketball coach. In the 2008 employment contract, the clause read:

> GENE A. FORD recognizes that his promise to work for the UNIVERSITY for the entire term of this four (4) year Contract is of the essence of this Contract with the UNIVERSITY. GENE A. FORD also recognizes that the UNIVERSITY is making a highly valuable investment in his continued employment by entering into this Contract and its investment would be lost were he to resign or otherwise terminate his employment with the UNIVERSITY prior to the expiration of this Contract. Accordingly, he will pay to the UNIVERSITY as liquidated damages an amount equal to his base and supplemental salary, multiplied by the number of years (or portion(s) thereof) remaining on the Contract.

Id. at 870. In 2010, Ford and the university renewed the contract for a five-year term, including the same damages provision. In 2011, however, Ford accepted a coaching position at another university and left Kent State. Subsequently, Kent State brought a claim against Ford for breach of contract. The liquidated damages provision required Ford, in the event of a breach, to pay his total salary—which was $300,000 in 2010—multiplied by the four years remaining in his contract, for a total of $1.2 million. The coach argued that the amount was unreasonable and designed to punish him for breaching the contract. (Because liquidated damages provisions are designed to reflect actual damages, they cannot include punitive damages. *See* Restatement (Second) of Contracts § 356 (1981).) The court held that the liquidated damages were reasonable because the university would need to recruit a new coach and otherwise make up for the loss of Ford. Moreover, the court found that the liquidated damages provision was designed to award only actual damages. Is $1.2 million too large of a recovery? Does it make sense that Kent State could recover damages under a liquidated damages provision, but Garden Ridge could not?

5.   For further discussion of liquidated damages, *see, e.g.*, Michael Pressman, *The Two-Contract Approach to Liquidated Damages: A New Framework for Exploring the Penalty Clause Debate*, 7 Va. L. & Bus. Rev. 651 (2013) (arguing that contracts containing liquidated damages should be viewed as contracts that include two alternative outcomes: performance or payment of a stipulated sum of money); Charles Goetz & Robert Scott, *Liquidated Damages, Penalties and the Just Compensation Principle: Some Notes on an Enforcement Model and a Theory of Efficient Breach*, 77 Colum. L. Rev. 554 (1977) (arguing that, assuming a fair bargaining process, liquidated damages

provisions can be the most efficient method of insuring against the consequences of a breach).

6.   For additional discussion of contract damages, *see, e.g.*, Mara Kent, *The Common-Law History of Non-Economic Damages in Breach of Contract Actions Versus Willful Breach of Contract Actions*, 11 Tex. Wesleyan L. Rev. 481 (2005) (exploring the practice of awarding non-economic damages, such as for mental or emotional distress, and arguing that the current lack of uniformity in awarding such damages should be replaced by a foreseeability standard, under which parties would be liable for non-economic damages that were reasonably foreseeable); David Barnes, *The Net Expectation Interest in Contract Damages,* 48 Emory L.J. 1137 (1999) (arguing for contract damages based on a "net expectation" theory, which would put the party in the position it would have been in had the party in breach performed).

CHAPTER 5

TORTS

■ ■ ■

The focus of torts is on conduct that causes injury and entitles the victim to seek damages. Some torts involve intentional conduct; some involve negligence; and some involve liability without fault (strict liability). In some instances, the conduct may warrant not only a tort suit, but also a criminal prosecution. A course on torts, however, is concerned mainly with civil liability (although, at times, cases involving criminal prosecutions are instructive).

A. INTENTIONAL TORTS

As the name suggests, an "intentional tort" is an intentional, wrongful act that one person commits against another. Acting with intent means either that "the actor desires to cause consequences of his act, or that he believes that the consequences are substantially certain to result from it." Restatement (Second) of Torts § 8A (1965). Intentional torts can be distinguished from torts alleging "negligence" or "strict liability"—which, as discussed later in this chapter, do not require a showing of intent. This section addresses a variety of intentional torts.

1. ASSAULT AND BATTERY

The tort of assault involves an imminent threat of harm. The tort of battery involves actual physical harm. The following case discusses the contours of these torts. The case is somewhat unusual because it involves elements of contract law as well. In the case, the defendant, Oxnard Hospitality Enterprises, had an insurance policy with the plaintiff, Mount Vernon Fire Insurance Company, through which Mount Vernon agreed to indemnify Oxnard from any liability stemming from certain types of harm and damage on the premises. The insurance contract, however, contained a provision that excluded coverage stemming from assaults or batteries that involved "wrongful physical contact." The issue in the case was whether the conduct at issue fell under that exclusion.

MOUNT VERNON FIRE INSURANCE CORP. V. OXNARD HOSPITALITY ENTERPRISE, INC.

Court of Appeal, Second District, Division 3, California, 2013
219 Cal.App.4th 876, 162 Cal.Rptr.3d 211

CROSKEY, JUSTICE.

This appeal involves the interpretation of the term "physical contact" in an insurance liability policy's "Assault or Battery" exclusion [from coverage]. Appellant, Roberta Busby (Busby) sued her employer, Oxnard Hospitality Enterprise, Inc., and others (collectively, Oxnard), for negligence after she sustained serious bodily injuries when a third party threw a glass full of a flammable liquid on her and set her on fire (underlying action). The trial court entered a $10 million stipulated judgment [an agreed-upon judgment without a trial] in Busby's favor against Oxnard.

In the instant action, Mount Vernon Fire Insurance Company (Insurer), the liability insurer for Oxnard, sought a declaratory judgment that it had no duty to indemnify Oxnard (and/or its owners), nor to pay any claim of Busby * * * arising from this incident. Insurer relied entirely on the policy's "Assault or Battery" exclusion. Based on that exclusion, the trial court granted Insurer's motion for summary judgment.

After a review of the record and the policy's provisions, we affirm. The term "battery," as used in that exclusion, is defined as *physical contact with another without consent* (italics added). We reject Busby's argument that such definition requires a direct "body-to-body" contact. Instead, we conclude that it necessarily includes a striking or touching as occurred in this case.

FACTUAL AND PROCEDURAL BACKGROUND

Busby, a nightclub dancer, suffered bodily injury on Oxnard's premises shortly after she had completed her shift when a patron of the nightclub threw flammable liquid on her and then set her on fire. Her assailant was later convicted of aggravated mayhem and torture. In the underlying action, Busby sued Oxnard and others for negligent failure to provide adequate security. * * *

* * *

While the underlying action was pending, the Insurer brought the instant action for declaratory relief. It sought a judgment declaring that it had no duty under the policy to pay any damages * * * [because of] the "Assault or Battery" exclusion in the liability policy issued to Oxnard. That endorsement excluded coverage for "all 'bodily injury' . . . arising out of 'assault' or 'battery' * * *."

The underlying action was resolved by a stipulated judgment against Oxnard in the amount of $10 million. * * * Oxnard assigned all of its rights against Insurer to Busby.

Subsequently, in the instant action, Insurer filed a motion for summary judgment against Busby [based on the exclusion]. In Busby's opposition to Insurer's motion for summary judgment, she argued that the exclusion's definition of battery required actual "body-to-body" physical contact. Since that admittedly did not occur here, she contends that the exclusion did not apply and thus there *was* coverage under the policy. * * *

* * *

The trial court agreed with Insurer and granted its motion. Busby * * * filed a timely notice of appeal.

* * *

DISCUSSION

1. Standard of Review

"We determine de novo whether a triable issue of material fact exists * * *."

2. The "Assault or Battery" Exclusion Bars Coverage

a. Analysis of the Exclusionary Language

The exclusion at issue, in relevant parts, provides the following. "This insurance does not apply to: Any claim, demand or 'suit' based on 'assault' or 'battery', or out of any act or omission in connection with the prevention or suppression of any 'assault' or 'battery', including the use of reasonable force to protect persons or property, whether caused by . . . an insured . . . [or] patrons. . . . Further, no coverage is provided for any claim, demand or suit in which the underlying operative facts constitute 'assault' or 'battery'. This exclusion applies to all 'bodily injury' . . . arising out of 'assault' or 'battery' . . . including but not limited to 'assault' or 'battery' arising out of or caused in whole or in part by negligence. . . . 'Assault' means the threat or use of force on another that causes that person to have apprehension of imminent harmful or offensive conduct, whether or not the threat or use of force is alleged to be negligent, intentional or criminal in nature. 'Battery' means negligent or intentional physical contact with another without consent that results in physical or emotional injury."

Apart from the endorsement's inclusive language, the tort of battery generally is not limited to direct body-to-body contact. In fact, the commentary to the Restatement Second of Torts clearly states that the "[m]eaning of 'contact with another's person'" does not require that one "should bring any part of his own body in contact with another's person. . . . [One] is liable [for battery] in this Section if [one] throws a substance, such as water, upon the other. . . ." * * *

b.   The Exclusion Is Not Ambiguous

We have no trouble concluding that the exclusion at issue is free from ambiguity. * * *

"The principal rule of contract interpretation is to give effect to the parties' intent as expressed in the terms of the contract. Insurance policy terms are treated no differently and will be given the 'objectively reasonable' meaning a lay person would ascribe to them." * * *

Applying those principles to this case leaves no question that the policy's definition of battery extends to the intentional attack made on Busby. Had her assailant struck Busby with a closed fist, there could be no argument that such a striking was not a "battery" under Oxnard's policy. Could the answer be any different if that fist contained a glass container that was used to strike Busby? Certainly no reasonable person would make such an argument. How, then, could or should the result be any different if the glass container were filled, as in this case, with a flammable substance used to set Busby afire? * * *

* * *

* * * [T]he exclusion's definition of battery as "physical contact with another" does not distinguish between directly striking an individual and striking an individual through an intermediary object.

c.   Our Analysis is Consistent with Other Jurisdictions

Persuasive federal and New York cases also apply the common law definition of battery to "Assault or Battery" exclusions. In fact, New York common law relevantly defines "battery" as intentional wrongful *physical contact* with another person without consent. * * * When New York courts apply the common law definition to an "Assault or Battery" exclusion, they do not distinguish between a battery from "body-to-body" contact and a battery from an object set in motion by the defendant's action. For example, in *Mark McNichol Enterprises, Inc. v. First Financial Ins. Co.*, 284 A.D.2d 964, 726 N.Y.S.2d 828 (2001), the court held that the insurer had no duty to indemnify the insured because the battery exclusion barred coverage in an action in which a "patron in the tavern was injured when she was struck in the face by a beer bottle that had been thrown during a fight. . . ." The decision implies that "physical contact" does not require skin-to-skin contact and includes contact with objects set in motion (*i.e.*, thrown bottles).

* * * [T]he insurance policy at issue here does not provide coverage for Busby's damages * * *.

* * *

The judgment against Busby * * * is affirmed. * * *

NOTES AND QUESTIONS

1. What is the precise issue in the *Mount Vernon Fire Insurance Corp.* case? How did the court resolve the issue? Who stood to benefit from a judgment that the assault and battery exclusion did not bar coverage?

2. Why would insurance policies, such as the one in the case, exclude claims based on assault and battery?

3. Is the court persuasive in holding that physical contact is not limited to face-to-face contact?

4. The Restatement (Second) of Torts § 13 (1965) states that a person is liable for battery if "(a) he acts intending to cause a harmful or offensive contact with the person of the other or a third person, or an imminent apprehension of such a contact, and (b) a harmful contact with the person of the other directly or indirectly results." One issue that has arisen under this definition is whether battery requires both intent to cause bodily contact and intent to cause harm or offense (*i.e.*, dual intent) or whether it is sufficient that the defendant intends a bodily contact that turns out to be either harmful or offensive (*i.e.*, single intent). *See, e.g.*, Nancy Moore, *Intent and Consent in the Tort of Battery: Confusion and Controversy*, 61 Am. U.L. Rev. 1585 (2012) (noting the inconsistent application of the "intent" element by courts). The most recent draft of the Restatement of Torts has attempted to clarify the ambiguity, and has advocated for the "single intent" approach. *See* Restatement (Third) of Torts: Intentional Torts to Persons § 101 (2015). Another issue is whether consent is an affirmative defense (*i.e.*, a defense that the defendant must prove) or whether lack of consent is an essential element of the plaintiff's claim (*i.e.*, an element the plaintiff must prove). *See* Moore, *supra* (noting the inconsistent application of the "consent" element by courts).

5. Plaintiffs often bring assault and battery claims in the same lawsuit. Nonetheless, the two torts differ in an important way: Battery is committed when a person *actually* causes an intentional harmful or offensive contact with a person; a person is liable for assault, however, when "(a) he acts intending to cause a harmful or offensive contact with the person of the other or a third person, or an imminent apprehension of such a contact, and (b) the other is *thereby put in such imminent apprehension.*" Restatement (Second) of Torts § 21 (1965) (emphasis added). Thus, assault does not require actual contact, but only an imminent apprehension of such contact (*e.g.*, a threat of harmful contact).

6. Under what is commonly referred to as the "eggshell skull" doctrine, the defendant takes the victim as he finds him. In other words, if the plaintiff had a thin skull such that even a slight knock on his head causes severe injury, the defendant is liable for such injury (assuming intent or negligence is shown). *See, e.g.*, *Figueroa-Torres v. Toledo-Davila*, 232 F.3d 270 (1st Cir. 2000) (in case involving wrongful death suit against a police officer who had kicked and punched the plaintiff in the stomach during an arrest, police officer was liable for the plaintiff's death resulting from a ruptured spleen even when the plaintiff had a preexisting condition involving a diseased and enlarged spleen);

Castillo v. Young, 272 Neb. 240, 720 N.W.2d 40 (2006) (finding that the plaintiff was entitled to an eggshell skull jury instruction in a negligence action when a car accident aggravated the plaintiff's preexisting jaw condition). It is important to note, however, that courts often reject the application of the eggshell skull doctrine to pre-existing *mental* rather than *physical* conditions. *See, e.g., Munn v. Algee*, 924 F.2d 568 (5th Cir. 1991) (victim involved in auto accident refused to accept blood transfusions as a result of her religious beliefs and later died of blood loss; court held that the eggshell skull doctrine did not apply because the victim's religious beliefs were a pre-existing mental rather than physical condition). Some scholars have questioned the fairness of this distinction. *See, e.g.*, J. Stanley McQuade, *The Eggshell Rule and Related Problems in Recovery for Mental Harm in the Law of Torts*, 24 Campbell L. Rev. 1 (2001) (arguing that it is inequitable to allow an eggshell skull rule for physical harms but not for mental or emotional harms (which can often be serious and long-lasting)). Should the eggshell skull doctrine apply equally to both physical and mental harms?

2. FALSE IMPRISONMENT

A claim of false imprisonment arises when one person has been unlawfully confined against his will. The following case discusses such a claim.

SHARP V. CLEVELAND CLINIC

Court of Appeals of Ohio, Eleventh District, Trumbull County, 2008
176 Ohio App.3d 226, 891 N.E.2d 809

CANNON, JUDGE.

Appellant, Brianna Sharp, R.N., appeals the judgment entered by the Trumbull County Court of Common Pleas. The trial court entered summary judgment in favor of appellee, the Cleveland Clinic.

Sharp is a registered nurse, and she began working at the Cleveland Clinic in that capacity in March 2006. On several occasions in April and May 2006, Sharp was counseled by her supervisors about documentation errors regarding narcotic medications. Due to the documentation errors, certain amounts of narcotic medications were unaccounted for. One instance of improper documentation occurred when Sharp removed three 100-milligram doses of Fentanyl, a narcotic, during a single shift. Each time, however, she administered only 25 milligrams of the drug to each of the three patients. The remaining 75 milligrams of each dose were not properly documented as being wasted and were not otherwise accounted for.

On May 24, 2006, during her shift, Sharp was called into a meeting with Nurse Manager Rosslyn Van Den Bossche, Assistant Nurse Manager Rick Haire, and Kevin Peterca, a representative from the Employee Assistance Program. Haire informed Sharp that there were suspicions that she was possessing and/or using controlled substances. Sharp denied using any drugs and consented to a drug test, in order to clear her name. Sharp and Van Den Bossche walked to the emergency room at the Cleveland Clinic for the purpose of the drug test.

In the emergency room, blood and urine samples were collected from Sharp. Sharp acknowledged that there was nothing unusual with the actual collection methods of these samples. After the samples were collected, Sharp and Van Den Bossche waited in the emergency room for several minutes. Sharp asked if she could go home. Van Den Bossche told Sharp that she was free to leave, but that she was not permitted to drive her car. Sharp asked what would happen if she tried to leave in her car on her own, and the charge nurse in the emergency room told her that she would be arrested. Sharp eventually called her boyfriend, who lived in Trumbull County, and he agreed to drive to Cleveland to pick her up.

At some point, Van Den Bossche's shift ended, and another nurse was sent to the emergency room to continue the one-on-one observation of Sharp. Thereafter, Sharp requested permission to go to her car to retrieve some personal belongings. Sharp was told that she was not allowed to walk to her car. Then, two Cleveland Clinic police officers arrived in the emergency room and told Sharp that there was a police car waiting outside to take her to her car. Sharp and her supervisor got into the back of the police car, and a female police officer drove Sharp to her car. Sharp retrieved her personal items, and the police officer drove Sharp and her supervisor back to the emergency room.

After returning to the emergency room, Sharp asked to have a cigarette. One of the police officers told her she could go outside to smoke, but that she had to stay in a certain area. In addition, her supervisor went outside with her.

Eventually, Sharp's boyfriend arrived and picked her up. They went to a local restaurant for dinner. Afterwards, Sharp retrieved her car from the parking garage and drove to her home in Trumbull County.

Although the drug tests were negative, Sharp's employment was terminated due to her performance.

Sharp filed a complaint against the Cleveland Clinic alleging five causes of action[, including false imprisonment] * * *.

The Cleveland Clinic filed a motion for summary judgment in regard to all of the claims in Sharp's complaint. * * * The trial court granted the Cleveland Clinic's motion * * *.

Sharp raises the following assignments of error:

[1.] The trial court erred in holding that the acts of appellee police officers did not constitute false imprisonment.

[2.] The trial court erred in its holding that appellant was free to move about with no threat of force sufficient to invoke false imprisonment.

* * *

False imprisonment occurs when a person confines another intentionally without privilege and against her consent within a limited area for any appreciable time, however short. "The essence of the tort is depriving someone of his or her liberty without lawful justification."

The focus of this matter is whether Sharp was ever confined by any Cleveland Clinic employees. "Confinement consists of a 'total detention or restraint upon [the plaintiff's] freedom of locomotion, imposed by force or threats.'" Since a threat may constitute confinement, the lack of physical force does not defeat a false-imprisonment claim.

We will individually address the events of May 24, 2006, to determine whether any of them amount to confinement.

Regarding the drug tests themselves, Sharp was not confined. When an individual voluntarily agrees to be in a certain place, that individual is not confined, since she is not held against her will. Sharp voluntarily submitted to the tests and stated in her deposition that the tests were conducted in a standard manner. Therefore, she was not confined during the tests.

Sharp stated that she waited in the emergency room after the tests were conducted. When she asked if she could leave, she was informed that she was free to leave, but that she was not permitted to drive her car. Sharp was informed that she would be arrested if she tried to leave in her own car. * * *

* * *

* * * [T]he Cleveland Clinic's prohibition against Sharp driving was reasonable under the circumstances. The Cleveland Clinic had reason to believe that Sharp was diverting narcotics for her personal use and, as a result, was under the influence of narcotics during the relevant time period. Thus, the employees of the Cleveland Clinic had reasonable concerns regarding Sharp's ability to safely operate a motor vehicle. Further, * * * Sharp was not prohibited from leaving the Cleveland Clinic; she was prohibited only from driving her car. * * * Sharp could have called a taxi, taken public transportation, or called a friend for a ride. In fact, Sharp called her boyfriend for a ride, and she left the emergency room with him. Since Sharp was free to leave the emergency room, she was not confined during that time.

Sharp was under one-on-one observation with a supervisor from the nursing department while she was in the emergency room. * * * The Cleveland Clinic had a right to supervise its employee on its premises.

Again, Sharp voluntarily agreed to the drug tests, and the fact that her supervisor was monitoring her during that time does not transform her voluntary actions into confinement. Neither of the supervisors from the nursing department physically prohibited or threatened Sharp from leaving the Cleveland Clinic campus after the drug tests. At most, the nurse supervisors informed Sharp that she was not permitted to drive her personal vehicle. However, as noted above, this restriction does not amount to confinement.

Sharp argues that the fact that police officers were present in the emergency room escalated the situation into one of confinement. We disagree. The evidence suggests that the officers appeared in response to Sharp's request to retrieve personal items from her car. The officers were employed by the Cleveland Clinic and had a right to be in the emergency room. Also, the fact that Sharp was ordered by the officers on where she should stand when she smoked a cigarette does not amount to confinement.

Finally, we will address the incident in which Sharp was driven by a Cleveland Clinic police officer to her car. Sharp contends that she should have been permitted to walk to her car, which was several blocks away. As the Cleveland Clinic notes, Sharp had requested to leave in her car on multiple occasions, so the employees in the emergency room could have reasonably believed that Sharp's request to walk to her car was a pretext to her driving home in her car. In order to accommodate Sharp's request to retrieve items out of her personal car, the Cleveland Clinic provided a female police officer to drive Sharp to her car. The fact that Sharp was in a police car does not, *per se*, equal confinement. This is especially true in this case, since the officer did not threaten or touch Sharp, Sharp's nursing supervisor rode in the vehicle with her, and the trip was facilitated to accommodate Sharp. If Sharp did not want to ride in the police car, she could have easily forgone the trip and left her personal items, a garage door opener and dirty dishes, in her car. In fact, since Sharp sneaked into the parking garage after dinner and retrieved her car, it was not essential that she get the personal items at the time she did. Accordingly, Sharp was not confined when she voluntarily rode in the police car, which was provided by the Cleveland Clinic to accommodate Sharp's personal request.

At no time on May 24, 2006 was Sharp confined by employees of the Cleveland Clinic. * * * [Thus,] the trial court did not err by entering summary judgment in favor of the Cleveland Clinic on Sharp's false-imprisonment claim.

* * *

O'TOOLE, JUDGE, dissenting.

I respectfully dissent.

* * * Nurse Sharp agreed to drug tests following the accusation that she was diverting narcotics. The clinic may be said to have possessed a

privilege, therefore, to limit or confine her movements in some fashion until those tests were completed. However, it points to no authority allowing it to limit Nurse Sharp's movements once the tests were completed. Rather, it falls back on the assertion that those limitations were justified by the suspicion that she was on drugs and thus could not operate her vehicle safely.

The reasoning is tautological. The clinic points to no evidence by a qualified expert—such as a physician or drug-addiction specialist—that Nurse Sharp exhibited behavioral characteristics typical of a person on narcotics and incapable of driving safely. The suspicion of drug use was founded on the discrepancies in her recordkeeping, not her behavior. If founded on the latter, one reasonably might ask how the clinic could allow Nurse Sharp to work for half a shift the day of this incident before pulling her off the floor. In concluding that the clinic had reasonable cause to prevent Nurse Sharp from driving following the conclusion of her voluntary drug tests, the majority * * * weighs the evidence, rather than construing it in her favor.

Similarly, I would find that a genuine issue of material fact exists regarding whether Nurse Sharp was falsely imprisoned following the appearance of the clinic's police in the emergency room. An implied threat of the use of force to limit a person's freedom of movement is sufficient to establish a claim for false imprisonment. * * * [T]he threat to call the police or security, or the appearance of police or security at the scene of a dispute, necessarily implies that force will be used.

* * * In this case, there was only evidence that Nurse Sharp's recordkeeping was poor and that she was nervous. These facts might—or might not—indicate that she was diverting narcotics for personal use. The resolution of factual disputes requires trial by jury, not disposition in summary proceedings.

I would reverse the judgment and remand this matter for trial.

NOTES AND QUESTIONS

1.   What was the basis of plaintiff's argument that the Cleveland Clinic committed false imprisonment? How did the Ohio Supreme Court rule? On what basis did the dissent disagree with the majority? Which opinion is more persuasive—the majority or the dissent?

2.   Could the Cleveland Clinic have addressed its concerns in a less intrusive and threatening way? If so, how?

3.   The Restatement (Second) of Torts § 42 (1965) states that a person is "not liable for false imprisonment unless the person being restrained knows of the confinement *or is harmed by it*." (Emphasis added.) Under that test, even if an individual is unaware that he has been confined, he may have a cause of action for false imprisonment if he suffered harm as a result of any

confinement. *See, e.g.*, William Prosser, *False Imprisonment: Consciousness of Confinement*, 55 Colum. L. Rev. 847 (1955) (listing examples of individuals who might be unaware of false imprisonment, such as small children, intoxicated people, delirious people, or sick and unconscious people).

4.   False imprisonment claims frequently turn on whether there is a safe and reasonable means to escape the confinement. If such a means of escape exists, the claim will likely fail. For example, in *Richardson v. Costco Wholesale Corp.*, 169 F. Supp. 2d 56 (D. Conn. 2001), a district court concluded that walking through an emergency exit door is a reasonable means of escape, even if such escape would sound off an alarm and might result in employee discipline. Moreover, even the possibility of a complete loss of employment resulting from an escape is unlikely to render a viable escape route unreasonable. *See, e.g.*, *Maietta v. United Parcel Serv., Inc.*, 749 F. Supp. 1344, 1367 (D.N.J. 1990) (concluding that an employee's concern that he would lose his job if he left an interview with company investigators was insufficient to render the available escape route unreasonable), *aff'd*, 932 F.2d 960 (3d Cir. 1991). By contrast, if a means of escape would jeopardize an individual's safety or compromise his personal dignity, that means of escape will likely be deemed unreasonable. *See, e.g.*, *State v. C.V.C.*, 153 Wis.2d 145, 450 N.W.2d 463 (1989) (finding, in the analogous context of a criminal charge of false imprisonment, that a means of escape was unreasonable when the victim was threatened with immediate violence if she attempted to escape); *Peterson v. Sorlien*, 299 N.W.2d 123 (Minn. 1980) (recognizing that a danger or threat of bodily or material harm may render a means of escape unreasonable).

5.   Because of qualified immunity (discussed in Chapter 3), law enforcement officers are often shielded from false imprisonment and other tort claims as long as their conduct was within the scope of their duty and was not manifestly unjustified. *See, e.g.*, *Abbott v. Sangamon Cnty.*, 705 F.3d 706, 723 (7th Cir. 2013) (holding that a false imprisonment claim brought under federal statute could not proceed against a sheriff's deputy who had wrongfully arrested a woman because, while the officer was ultimately mistaken about the grounds leading to arrest, a "reasonable mind" could interpret the deputy's actions as justified at the time of the arrest).

6.   Some commentators have argued that civil remedies should be enhanced for domestic violence because existing remedies are inadequate. *See, e.g.*, Camille Carey, *Domestic Violence Torts: Righting a Civil Wrong*, 62 U. Kan. L. Rev. 695 (2014) (asserting that states should legislate more expansive domestic violence tort causes of action to supplement the current false imprisonment actions). What unique problems arise in the domestic violence context?

3.   INTENTIONAL INFLICTION OF EMOTIONAL DISTRESS

Although many torts entitle a plaintiff to seek damages for mental or emotional harm, a special tort claim exists that is designed exclusively to address severe emotional distress. "Intentional infliction of emotional distress" (IIED) is committed when someone intentionally causes another person to suffer serious mental or emotional harm. The following case discusses an IIED claim.

QUAKER PETROLEUM CHEMICALS CO. v. WALDROP
Court of Appeals of Texas, San Antonio, 2002
75 S.W.3d 549

GREEN, JUSTICE.

Quaker Petroleum Chemicals Company ("Quaker") appeals a jury verdict awarding damages to Linda Tuttle Waldrop and Jane McCord for * * * intentional infliction of emotional distress in relation to a chemical spill occurring in Hallettsville, Texas. Because the evidence is legally insufficient to support the verdict, we * * * reverse the trial court's judgment as to Waldrop and McCord, and render judgment in favor of Quaker.

BACKGROUND

Dave Edmonds stored chemicals for Quaker in plastic drums in a warehouse in Hallettsville. Edmonds allowed Linda and Louis Tuttle, neighbors to the warehouse, to store a meat freezer in the warehouse. When Linda Tuttle went into the warehouse in October 1990, she noticed a sharp smell. She quickly retrieved meat from the freezer and left, but later that day, she went to the emergency room, complaining of respiratory problems. The smell was traced to a leaking plastic drum. After the spill, Quaker representative Rick Talley visited the warehouse. Talley talked to Jane McCord, another neighbor to the warehouse, and told her that if anyone was thinking of suing Quaker over the spill, Quaker would countersue. Talley made similar comments to Linda. Talley paid Linda and her husband for medical bills and inconvenience after they signed a letter stating they would not bring suit for damages directly or indirectly related to the spill.

Four months later, while Jane was at a church Valentine's Day party, she overheard Edmonds discussing with another parishioner how things would go a lot more smoothly if "there wasn't a lot of sue-happy people around." After these comments and others like them, Jane and her husband spoke to the preacher, who advised them to change religion classes. After Jane's brother-in-law died and her son was diagnosed with a serious illness, she asked that her family's name be added to the church prayer list. After she made the request, Edmonds told Jane that "when bad things happen to good people, it's because they're not living their life right and that it's a punishment from God." After the comments, Jane and Linda, along with their families, joined new churches because "Mr. Edmonds was a gossip person, he * * * was worse than a woman. But his voice was loud and it was big and he was in good with the preacher, so he just put—put all of us down and just got real ugly and they were spreading rumors and it was just—it hurt a lot." In October 1992, the families brought suit against Quaker alleging negligence for the spill. Two years later, they amended their petition to add the claim of intentional infliction of emotional distress (IIED), relying on the statements made by Talley and Edmonds.

At trial, the jury found Quaker liable to * * * Linda, Jane, and Jane's son for IIED. Quaker appeals * * *.

SUFFICIENCY OF THE EVIDENCE

Quaker claims * * * [that] the evidence is legally insufficient to support the jury findings of * * * IIED. * * *

We review * * * the evidence in the light most favorable to the jury findings * * *.

* * *

Intentional Infliction of Emotional Distress

* * * To sustain an IIED claim, a plaintiff must prove: (1) the acts were intentional or reckless; (2) the conduct was extreme and outrageous; (3) the acts caused the plaintiff emotional distress; and (4) the distress suffered was severe. The threshold issue for the trial court is whether the conduct in question may reasonably be regarded as extreme and outrageous.

In recognizing the IIED claim, the supreme court adopted section 46 of the [Restatement (Second) of Torts]:

> It has not been enough that the defendant has acted with an intent which is tortious or even criminal, or that he has intended to inflict emotional distress, or even that his conduct has been characterized by "malice," or a degree of aggravation which would entitle the plaintiff to punitive damages for another tort.

Rather, the conduct must be "so outrageous in character, and so extreme in degree, as to go beyond all possible bounds of decency, and to be regarded as atrocious, and utterly intolerable in a civilized community." Mere insults, indignities, threats, annoyances, petty oppressions, or other trivialities do not rise to the level of extreme and outrageous conduct.

Linda and Jane sought IIED damages based on the comments made by Quaker employees and on the chemical spill, itself. Although we do not comment on the appropriateness of Talley's and Edmonds's conduct, we cannot hold that their statements rise to the level of extreme and outrageous conduct. Further, an IIED claim based on Quaker's handling of the spill fails for lack of intentionality. In [*Standard Fruit & Vegetable Co., Inc. v. Johnson*, 985 S.W.2d 62 (Tex. 1998)], the Texas Supreme Court held that a plaintiff could not recover damages for IIED after witnessing a truck driver drive a tractor-trailer rig into a parade:

> [W]e hold that a claim for intentional infliction of emotional distress cannot be maintained when the risk that emotional distress will result is merely incidental to the commission of some other tort. In the present case, Marshall's conduct, even if reckless, involved a primary risk of physical injury or death. * * *

The court emphasized that IIED * * * should not be extended to circumvent the limitations placed on the recovery of mental anguish damages under more established tort doctrines. To allow Linda and Jane to recover IIED damages based upon the chemical spill would circumvent the limitations placed on the recovery of mental anguish damages on a negligence or gross negligence claim. * * *

CONCLUSION

* * * We * * * render judgment in favor of Quaker * * *.

NOTES AND QUESTIONS

1.   What are the elements of IIED? Why is the burden on the plaintiff such a high one?

2.   Although the plaintiff has a high burden in establishing the elements of IIED, that tort is different from many other intentional torts because it allows a claim against a defendant who "recklessly" causes severe emotional distress to the plaintiff. *See* Restatement (Second) of Torts § 46 (1965) ("One who by extreme and outrageous conduct intentionally *or recklessly* causes severe emotional distress to another is subject to liability for such emotional distress, and if bodily harm to the other results from it, for such bodily harm." (Emphasis added.)) "Recklessness" is not as exacting a test as "intent," but it is more exacting than "negligence."

3.   What was the plaintiffs' theory of IIED in *Waldrop*? How did the court rule? What was the court's main concern in refusing to permit recovery for IIED under the facts of the case?

4.   The Restatement (Second) of Torts § 46 (1965) and a number of states allow for an IIED claim in limited circumstances stemming from harm inflicted on third persons. Usually, those types of claims are brought when a person suffers severe emotional distress after witnessing harm to an immediate family member. For example, in *Bevan v. Fix*, 42 P.3d 1013 (Wyo. 2002), the Wyoming Supreme Court held that a plaintiff who could hear her mother being physically beaten in another room could maintain an action for IIED against the mother's attacker. Similarly, in *Courtney v. Courtney*, 186 W.Va. 597, 413 S.E.2d 418 (1991), the West Virginia Supreme Court held that a child could bring an IIED claim after he suffered distress from witnessing his stepfather verbally and physically assault his mother. Most courts require that, to bring an IIED claim involving harm to a third party, the plaintiff must have witnessed the harm in person. One scholar, however, has advocated for a relaxed view of that requirement in certain contexts. *See* Mary Kate Kearney, *Child Witnesses of Domestic Violence: Third Party Recovery for Intentional*

Infliction of Emotional Distress, 47 Loy. L. Rev. 283 (2001) (advocating for a relaxed standard in the context of domestic violence cases because some children may suffer IIED from domestic violence even if they are not always present during instances of familial abuse). Should a plaintiff's presence be required in cases involving harm to a third person? More generally, should recovery be allowed at all in IIED cases based on harm to third parties?

5. A claim for IIED contains multiple elements that must be established, but as the *Waldrop* case indicates, the tort often hinges on the element of "outrageousness." Various authorities suggest that courts, in assessing the outrageousness, should look at any special relationship between the parties, *see* Restatement (Second) of Torts § 46 cmt. e (1965); any position of authority the defendant has over the victim, *see, e.g., Akers v. Alvey*, 338 F.3d 491 (6th Cir. 2003) (finding that repeated sexual advances, lewd jokes, inappropriate gestures, and repeated sexual comments by a male supervisor to his female employee was sufficiently outrageous to survive a motion for summary judgment); as well as the defendant's knowledge that the victim is peculiarly susceptible to emotional distress, *see, e.g., Subbe-Hirt v. Baccigalupi*, 94 F.3d 111 (3d Cir. 1996) (finding conduct sufficiently outrageous to survive a motion for summary judgment when an employer had knowledge of an employee's fragile emotional state yet repeatedly subjected the employee to unnecessarily stressful employment tasks). The element of outrageousness, however, is inherently fact-specific. *See, e.g.,* Daniel Givelber, *The Right to Minimum Social Decency and the Limits of Evenhandedness: Intentional Infliction of Emotional Distress by Outrageous Conduct*, 82 Colum. L. Rev. 42, 74–75 (1982) (stating that the tort of IIED has "defie[d] consistent definition" because "[c]ourts are literally left to their own devices to figure out whether conduct qualifies as outrageous").

6. As illustrated in *Snyder v. Phelps*, 562 U.S. 443 (2011), discussed in Chapter 2, IIED claims may sometimes clash with First Amendment freedom of speech rights. In *Snyder*, the U.S. Supreme Court reversed an IIED judgment because it held that the defendant's "distressing" speech, *i.e.,* protesting at a military funeral (which the attendees found offensive), was protected under the First Amendment. Some scholars have criticized *Snyder* as an unnecessary erosion of common law IIED claims. *See, e.g.,* Benjamin Zipursky, Snyder v. Phelps, *Outrageousness, and the Open Texture of Tort Law*, 60 DePaul L. Rev. 473, 519 (2011) (arguing that *Snyder* was erroneously decided, and stating: "The question is not whether the state may regulate or prohibit this type of speech. It is whether the state may permit accountability and individual recovery when one person has emotionally harmed another under such circumstances"); Mark Strasser, *Funeral Protests, Privacy, and the Constitution: What Is Next After* Phelps?, 61 Am. U. L. Rev. 279 (2011) (arguing that *Snyder* failed to explain the extent of First Amendment protections in the context of private speech and asserting that the opinion raised more questions than it answered).

4. LIBEL, SLANDER, AND INVASION OF PRIVACY

A claim for "libel" or "slander" exists when the plaintiff's reputation is damaged by a defendant's wrongful conduct. The following case discusses a claim of libel, as well as the related tort of invasion of privacy.

ROMAINE V. KALLINGER
Supreme Court of New Jersey, 1988
109 N.J. 282, 537 A.2d 284

HANDLER, JUSTICE.

More than ten years ago Joseph Kallinger and his son went on a criminal rampage in Pennsylvania and New Jersey. The offenses were vicious, involving physical threats and sexual abuse of victims during the course of robberies of suburban homes. Kallinger murdered his victims on three occasions. In 1983, approximately eight years after Kallinger and his son had been apprehended, the defendant Simon & Schuster Publishing Inc. published a book entitled "*The Shoemaker*," written by the defendant Flora Rheta Schreiber, depicting the life and crimes of Joseph Kallinger. The book gave rise to this litigation.

The plaintiffs, Randi Romaine, Edwina Wiseman, Retta Romaine Welby, and Frank Welby, were victims of Kallinger, whose criminal acts against them resulted in the murder of a young woman, Maria Fasching. Plaintiffs sued the defendants Kallinger, Elizabeth Kallinger, his wife, Schreiber, Simon & Schuster, and Paul J. Giblin, claiming to have been legally injured by defamatory and offensively intrusive statements relating to these crimes contained in "*The Shoemaker*." Plaintiffs sought in separate counts the award of compensatory and punitive damages based respectively on libel and invasion of privacy by being cast in a false light; they also claimed that their privacy had been invaded through the unreasonable publication of private facts. * * *

Defendants Simon & Schuster and Schreiber filed motions for summary judgment seeking dismissal of the action. * * * The trial court granted defendants' motion for summary judgment with respect to the defamation and privacy claims. * * *

Plaintiffs filed a notice of appeal. In an unpublished opinion, the Appellate Division affirmed the dismissal of the defamation and privacy claims * * *. Plaintiffs then filed a petition for certification, which was granted by this Court.

I.

The factual context of this litigation is important. Ms. Schreiber, the author of "*The Shoemaker*," is a professor at the City University of New York, John Jay College of Criminal Justice. Although she has no formal training as a psychologist, Ms. Schreiber has written extensively about psychological subjects, and has focused on the problem of child abuse in her work. She is the author of *Sybil*, a study of a woman who suffered from a multiple-personality disorder.

According to defendants, Professor Schreiber's work is an in-depth study of the psychological make-up of a killer. Specifically, the book explores the relationship between the abuse suffered by Kallinger as a child and the psychotic behavior that led to his criminal acts. *"The Shoemaker"* received a significant amount of critical praise and Schreiber was named "Author of the Year" by the American Society of Journalists and Authors in 1985 in recognition of her work.

The complaint focuses on a chapter of *"The Shoemaker"* called "The Hunting Knife." The chapter, which consists of twenty-one pages out of a total of 423, describes the murder of Maria Fasching on January 8, 1975, in Leonia, New Jersey. The chapter relates that Kallinger and his son broke into the home of Mr. and Mrs. DeWitt Romaine. Eight people, who were in the home, were held hostage by Kallinger and his son. Kallinger ordered several of them to remove their clothes, and tied them up. He committed acts of personal abuse and physical degradation on two of the women. While this was occurring, Maria Fasching, a friend of one of the victims, the plaintiff Randi Romaine, came into the house. She was also captured by Kallinger. He directed Ms. Fasching, a nurse, to perform an act of sexual mutilation on plaintiff Frank Welby, who was tied up and helpless. When she refused to do so, he killed her by slashing her throat several times. About one-half of the chapter is devoted to Kallinger's own recollections of the murder, obtained by Schreiber during interviews with him; these recollections are presented to indicate the extent that Kallinger's acts were the product of his mental illness. The balance of the chapter consists of the re-creation of the murder, as derived from testimony offered at Kallinger's trial by the survivors of the incident.

On the second page of "The Hunting Knife" chapter this passage appears relating the circumstances leading up to Maria Fasching's visit to the Romaine house:

> 2:45 p.m. A black Volkswagen parked in front of the tan stucco house. A slender woman, whose name was Maria Fasching, turned off the ignition, put the key into the pocket of her imitation fur coat, and stepped gracefully out of her car. She was five feet two inches tall, had brown shoulder-length hair, brown eyes, and a round face with full lips. She was engaged to be married, and, already a licensed practical nurse, she looked forward to becoming an RN.

> A militant women's libber, Maria Fasching was famous among her friends for her battles on behalf of the weak and downtrodden. She would always try to rescue someone a bully had attacked, and she could not tolerate racists.

Maria thought of herself as a "free spirit." She resisted anything that she considered a restriction on her freedom. She cared for cats that had been hit by cars and for birds with broken wings.

Today, Maria Fasching was on the four-to-midnight shift at Hackensack Hospital, and she wore her nurse's uniform under her coat. In the morning Maria's friend Randi Romaine, who lived in the stucco house, had called Maria and asked her to drop over for coffee. The two women had not seen each other for a long time, for, between hospital duties and preparations for her wedding, Maria's schedule was full.

At first Maria said that she couldn't visit because she had to go to a wake. The wake, however, was only for an acquaintance. Randi and her twin sister, Retta, had been Maria's friends since they were all in the first grade. Besides, Maria was eager for news from Randi about a junkie they both knew who was doing time in prison. Finally, Maria changed her mind. She didn't go to the wake, but drove her Volkswagen to the two-story tan stucco house at 124 Glenwood Avenue, the house of Mr. and Mrs. Dewitt Romaine.

According to plaintiffs, one sentence in the passage falsely depicts the reason for Ms. Fasching's visit: "Besides, Maria was eager for news from Randi about a junkie they both knew who was doing time in prison." This sentence, it is claimed, is defamatory as a matter of law and constitutes a false-light invasion of privacy. The chapter's general narration of the criminal events, from which this passage is taken, is in turn the basis for plaintiffs' invasion of privacy by unreasonable publication of private facts claim.

II.

Plaintiff Randi Romaine asserts that the particular sentence is defamatory as a matter of law, or alternatively, that the statement's defamatory content was at least a question for the jury. She claims this sentence falsely accuses her of criminality or associations with criminals. Plaintiff also contends that the false accusation was particularly damaging because it injured Ms. Romaine's professional reputation as a drug counselor and a social worker, interfering with her ability to obtain future employment.

A defamatory statement is one that is false and "injurious to the reputation of another" or exposes another person to "hatred, contempt or ridicule" or subjects another person to "a loss of the good will and confidence" in which he or she is held by others.

The threshold issue in any defamation case is whether the statement at issue is reasonably susceptible of a defamatory meaning. This question is one to be decided first by the court. In making this determination, the court must evaluate the language in question "according to the fair and natural meaning which will be given it by reasonable persons of ordinary intelligence." In assessing the language, the court must view the publication as a whole and consider particularly the context in which the statement appears.

If a published statement is susceptible of one meaning only, and that meaning is defamatory, the statement is libelous as a matter of law. Conversely, if the statement is susceptible of only a non-defamatory meaning, it cannot be considered libelous, justifying dismissal of the action. However, in cases where the statement is capable of being assigned more than one meaning, one of which is defamatory and another not, the question of whether its content is defamatory is one that must be resolved by the trier of fact.

Certain kinds of statements denote such defamatory meaning that they are considered defamatory as a matter of law. A prime example is the false attribution of criminality. Relying essentially on this example of defamation, plaintiff Randi Romaine contends in this case that the published offending statement must be considered libelous *per se*. According to Ms. Romaine, the sentence has only a defamatory meaning, in that it accuses her of having engaged in criminal conduct or having associated with criminals relating to drugs.

The trial court concluded, and the Appellate Division agreed, that only the most contorted reading of the offending language could lead to the conclusion that it accuses plaintiff of illegal drug use or criminal associations. We concur in the determinations of the courts below. A reasonable and fair understanding of the statement simply does not yield an interpretation that the plaintiff was or had been in illegal possession of drugs or otherwise engaging in any illegal drug-related activity.

At most, the sentence can be read to imply that plaintiff knew a junkie. Even if we assume that a commonly accepted and well-understood meaning of the term "junkie" is "a narcotics peddler or addict," the statement still does not suggest either direct or indirect involvement by plaintiff herself in any criminal drug-related activities. Absent exceptional circumstances, the mere allegation that plaintiff knows a criminal is not defamatory as a matter of law.

Beyond the language itself, we are satisfied that the statement in its contextual setting cannot fairly and reasonably be invested with any defamatory meaning. Maria Fasching, we note, is described in the chapter as a person who had compassion for others and who would care for less fortunate persons. The reasonable meaning of the critical sentence that is implied from this context is that Ms. Fasching's interest in the "junkie" stemmed from sympathy and compassion, not from any predilection toward or involvement in criminal drug activity. As extended to Randi Romaine, the only fair inference to be drawn from the larger context is that Ms.

Romaine shared her friend's feelings, attitudes and interests, and that her own interest in the junkie was similar to that of Ms. Fasching's.

We note the further contention that this statement had a defamatory meaning because it implied that the only reason for Ms. Fasching's visit to the Romaine home was her "interest" in news about a "junkie." A review of the full text, however, indicates that there were several reasons for the visit, only one of which was Ms. Fasching's interest in the "junkie." The lower courts soundly rejected this contention.

We conclude that the statement is not defamatory as a matter of law and accordingly uphold the ruling of the lower court on this point.

III.

Plaintiffs claim that the publication of the statement invaded their privacy by placing them in a false light. They allege that because it implies criminal conduct or associations with drug users on their part, the statement thus casts them in a false light that is highly offensive to a reasonable person. The trial court's dismissal of this count of the complaint was upheld by the Appellate Division.

It is accepted in New Jersey that a cause of action exists for invasions of privacy involving "publicity that unreasonably places the other in a false light before the public." Liability for this form of privacy invasion is found when

> [o]ne . . . gives publicity to a matter concerning another that places the other before the public in a false light [and]
>
> (a) the false light in which the other was placed would be highly offensive to a reasonable person, and
>
> (b) the actor had knowledge of or acted in reckless disregard as to the falsity of the publicized matter and the false light in which the other would be placed.

[Restatement (Second) of Torts § 652E.]

There are differing interests protected by the law of defamation and the law of privacy, which account for the substantive gradations between these torts. The interest protected by the duty not to place another in a false light is that of the individual's peace of mind, *i.e.*, his or her interest "in not being made to appear before the public in an objectionable false light or false position, or in other words, otherwise than as he is." "The action for defamation," on the other hand, "is to protect a person's interest in a good reputation. . . ." Nevertheless, despite analytical distinctions, there is a conceptual affinity between the causes of action based on these two theories. As with the requirement in defamation actions that the matter publicized be untrue, a fundamental requirement of the false light tort is that the disputed publicity be in fact false, or else "at least have the capacity to give rise to a false public impression as to the plaintiff."

However, unlike a defamation claim, it is not necessary in false-light actions that the material that casts plaintiff in a false light also injure her standing in the community.

The publicized material in a false-light claim must constitute a "major misrepresentation of [plaintiff's] character, history, activities or beliefs." Thus, there can be no recovery for false-light invasion of privacy unless it is shown that the publicity at issue was of a character "highly offensive to a reasonable person." This protection of privacy does not extend to the "hypersensitive person"; the material publicized "must be something that would be objectionable to the ordinary person under the circumstances."

As with defamation claims, it is for the court first to determine whether the criticized matter is capable of the meaning assigned to it by plaintiff, and whether that meaning is highly offensive to a reasonable person. In making this determination, the court "should not consider words or elements in isolation, but should view them in the context of the whole article to determine if they constitute an invasion of privacy."

We concur in this case with the trial court's analysis of the criticized statement and the court's determination that it could not reasonably be construed to constitute an accusation of illegal drug use; nor, as we have pointed out, is it reasonably susceptible of an interpretation denoting that any of the plaintiffs associated with illegal drug users or traffickers. Because the sentence does not carry the meaning ascribed to it by plaintiffs, it cannot be found to be highly offensive to a reasonable person, and it could not have cast plaintiffs in a false light.

Furthermore, the subject matter of the criticized sentence constitutes only a minor or insubstantial portion of the overall text. For this additional reason, any inaccuracies or false statements contained in that material cannot fairly be regarded as highly offensive to a reasonable person as a matter of law.

Not even the most strained reading of the sentence reveals a meaning that in any way concerns the plaintiffs other than Randi Romaine or places them in a false or meretricious light. To the extent that these plaintiffs may be viewed as asserting a "relational right of privacy," no plausible basis for such a cause of action can be gleaned from the record.

Accordingly, we conclude that the lower courts properly determined that plaintiffs had failed as a matter of law to demonstrate that the particular passage tortiously invaded their protectable privacy interests by placing them in a false light.

IV.

Plaintiffs contend that the chapter "The Hunting Knife" publicizes matters pertaining to their private lives in a manner offensive to a reasonable person. They thus claim a cause of action based upon the invasion of privacy by the unreasonable publication of private facts. In making this claim, plaintiffs concede that the chapter is an accurate and truthful depiction of the events that occurred on January 8, 1975. However, they contend that their criminal victimization, personal degradation, and physical abuse at the hands of Kallinger occurred in private, and that disclosure of the details of these crimes eight years after their occurrence is highly offensive.

The invasion of privacy by unreasonable publication of private facts occurs when it is shown that "the matters revealed were actually private, that dissemination of such facts would be offensive to a reasonable person, and that there is no legitimate interest of the public in being apprised of the facts publicized."

It is important to stress that this privacy tort permits recovery for *truthful* disclosures. For this reason the recognition of such a tort creates significant potential for conflict with the guarantees contained in the first amendment of the Constitution. This constitutional dimension explains the stringency of the requirements that must be met in order successfully to establish this privacy-invasion cause of action.

The critical chapter describes the painful treatment, the humiliation, and abuse that the plaintiffs suffered at the hands of Kallinger. Such publicity is likely traumatic and profoundly disturbing for plaintiffs and would be highly offensive to a reasonable person because it exposes to the public eye the suffering and degradation that they were forced to endure. However, plaintiffs' appeal fails because the facts revealed are not private, and even if they were private, they are of legitimate concern to the public and so privileged under the "newsworthiness" exception to the "unreasonable publication of private facts" claim.

The determination as to whether published facts are actually private constitutes the first key element of this cause of action. If the facts are public information, even though they relate to matters of individual privacy, they cannot for these purposes be considered "private." The court must first determine then whether the published facts were in the public domain, and hence not private facts.

Public records that recount or disclose particular facts may serve to place such facts in the public arena and thus bar a claim for publication of private facts. While the term "public records" is not self-defining, we need not in this case determine the extent to which particular official governmental records place facts in the public domain. Here, the facts complained of were contained in non-confidential official court records of the Kallinger trial.

* * *

Plaintiffs also contend that recovery should not be barred in this case because eight years passed between the crimes depicted in *"The*

Shoemaker" and the publication of the book. This argument is unpersuasive. * * * [C]ourts * * * have found a privilege to disseminate matters contained in public court records despite the passage of a significant period of time.

This claim is related to the additional argument made by defendants that the information that was published in *"The Shoemaker"* was newsworthy and therefore its publication was privileged. If facts cannot otherwise be considered "private," then a determination of their "newsworthiness" is obviated. However, if the critical facts are private, publication of those facts would not constitute an actionable invasion of privacy if they are "newsworthy" and thus a matter of legitimate public concern.

The "newsworthiness" defense in privacy-invasion tort actions is available to bar recovery where the subject matter of the publication is one in which the public has a legitimate interest. A publication is commonly understood to be "newsworthy" when it contains an " 'indefinable quality of information' that arouses the public's interest and attention."

In addition, once a matter is found to be within the sphere of public interest, otherwise private facts that are related to the subject may also be considered "newsworthy," and therefore publishable. Further, the newsworthiness defense in this context often encompasses information pertaining to individuals who have not actively or consciously sought, or who have scrupulously avoided, publicity. However, there must be an appropriate nexus between the plaintiff and the matter that is newsworthy or of legitimate public interest.

The events that occurred in the Romaine home on January 8, 1975, were newsworthy and matters of legitimate public concern. These events were the subject of widespread and intense publicity when they occurred. Extensive contemporaneous publicity of this sort is a strong indication that the subject is one that is clearly newsworthy. Moreover, the facts surrounding the commission of a crime are subjects of legitimate public concern. This concern extends to victims and other individuals who unwillingly become involved in the commission of a crime or its prosecution.

The contention of plaintiffs that the publicized matter is stale or remote may suggest that the publicized information was not "newsworthy" or a matter of legitimate public concern, and therefore recovery ought not be barred. The news value and public interest in criminal events are not abated by the passage of time. Most courts that have addressed the effect of the passage of time on the public interest have concluded that a lapse of time does not dilute newsworthiness or lessen the legitimacy of the public's concern.

* * *

In sum, we conclude that the trial court properly dismissed plaintiffs' unreasonable publicity claim. The facts reported in *"The Shoemaker"* were in the public domain, newsworthy, and matters of legitimate public concern. Thus, their publication is entitled to protection.

V.

For the reasons set forth in this opinion, we affirm the judgment below.

O'HERN, JUSTICE, dissenting.

* * *

It may be that there is a quite innocent or rational explanation for the author's reference to Ms. Romaine's association with a "junkie." That reference may be a mere mistake and thus might be insulated from liability in the context of this work, which is intended to explore matters that are reasonably to be regarded as within the public interest. Because this case comes to us on a motion for summary judgment, however, we must assume the worst scenario for the offenders: that they deliberately misstated this element of the narrative. I suspect that such a scenario is far from reality, but because of the procedural posture of the case I must dissent from the holding that no jury could find that the reference to an innocent victim of crime as an associate of a convicted "junkie" reduced her esteem in the community or placed her in a false light before the public.

NOTES AND QUESTIONS

1. Who was suing for libel in *Romaine*? What was her theory? How did the court rule?

2. Who was suing for invasion of privacy? What were the theories underlying that claim?

3. How did the court rule on each of the claims? Is there any merit in the dissent's view that the libel and invasion of privacy (false light) claims should have gone to a jury instead of being dismissed?

4. As noted by the court in *Romaine*, courts have established several types of statements that are defamatory *per se*, meaning that the statement is so likely to cause injury to reputation that actual proof of harm is not required to recover compensation. Defamation *per se* generally consists of false statements that link the plaintiff to a criminal act, a repugnant disease, a matter adversely affecting the person's ability to work in a profession, or gross sexual misconduct. *See, e.g., Carey v. Piphus*, 435 U.S. 247, 262 n.18 (1978) (stating that "[t]he essence of libel *per se* is the publication in writing of false statements that tend to injure a person's reputation"); *Giant Screen Sports v. Can. Imperial Bank of Commerce*, 553 F.3d 527 (7th Cir. 2009) (holding that an incorrect statement that disparaged a company's financial integrity was defamatory *per se* when the declarant knew that the statement was false); *Gordon v. Boyles*, 99 P.3d 75 (Colo. App. 2004) (finding that an incorrect

statement that a police officer had committed criminal offenses and had an extramarital affair were defamatory *per se*).

5.   Another issue that often arises in defamation cases is the size of the community in which the plaintiff was defamed. As one court has explained, "[n]o falsehood is thought about or even known by all the world." It is enough that the defamation would tend to prejudice a plaintiff in the eyes of a *"substantial and respectable minority." Jews For Jesus, Inc. v. Rapp*, 997 So.2d 1098, 1115 (Fla. 2008) (emphasis added). *See also id.* (reasoning that a plaintiff may have a viable defamation claim if she suffered injury in her "personal, social, official, or business relations"); *Burns v. McGraw-Hill Broadcasting Co.*, 659 P.2d 1351 (Colo. 1983) (finding that viewers of a news broadcast constituted a substantial and respectable minority of the community); *Farnsworth v. Hyde*, 266 Or. 236, 512 P.2d 1003 (1973) (finding that a defamatory passage published in a book may have harmed the plaintiff in a substantial and respectable minority of the community where he resided).

6.   *Romaine* also involved an action for "unreasonable publication of private facts." As the *Romaine* court indicated, an action for invasion of privacy cannot be maintained when the subject matter of the publicity is a matter of "legitimate concern to the public." That principle stems from the U.S. Supreme Court's decision in *Cox Broadcasting Co. v. Cohn*, 420 U.S. 469 (1975), where the Court held that the U.S. Constitution prohibits states from imposing sanctions for the publication of truthful information contained in official court records open to public inspection. *See also The Fla. Star v. B.J.F.*, 491 U.S. 524 (1989) (finding that the imposition of damages stemming from a newspaper's publication of the name of a sexual assault victim violated the First Amendment; the Court reasoned that the information was obtained lawfully from a police report, the identification of the victim was accurate, and the state law imposing liability was not narrowly tailored to satisfy strict scrutiny).

7.   Although *Romaine* did not involve major public figures or celebrities, invasion of privacy claims are prevalent among celebrities. A tort claim is a viable remedy for invasion of privacy, but many states have also adopted legislation to reinforce the privacy protection of celebrities. For a detailed look at California's "Anti-Paparazzi statute," *see* Note, *Privacy, Technology, and the California "Anti-Paparazzi" Statute*, 112 Harv. L. Rev. 1367 (1999).

8.   Like other topics discussed in this chapter, the tort of defamation has been forced to adapt to the internet era. Not surprisingly, defamation claims have become more prevalent as a result of internet forums and other online discussion groups. Corporations, small businesses, and private individuals have all attempted to use defamation lawsuits to deter online publication of negative information. Because it is often difficult to determine the author of anonymous online content, those lawsuits have sometimes been called "John Doe suits." Some scholars have raised concerns about those types of lawsuits and have identified ways for courts to protect such online discourse as legitimate public opinion. *See, e.g.*, Lyrissa Barnett Lidsky, *Silencing John Doe: Defamation & Discourse in Cyberspace*, 49 Duke L.J. 855, 945–46 (2000) (discussing need for an "opinion privilege," *i.e.*, a privilege "for statements that

do not imply assertions of objective facts"). Some scholars, however, have expressed concern that there must be swift and efficient recourse for online communications that damage reputations. *See, e.g.*, David Hallett, *How to Destroy a Reputation and Get Away With It: The Communication Decency Act Examined: Do the Policies and Standards Set Out in the Digital Millennium Copyright Act Provide a Solution for a Person Defamed Online?*, 41 IDEA 259 (2001) (arguing that business owners need protection against online defamation and asserting that Congress and the courts need to implement approaches that will protect defamed individuals).

5. TRESPASS

The preceding tort claims have discussed intentional harm aimed directly at a person. Tort claims, however, can also be brought for wrongs committed against property. The following case discusses a claim of trespass, where a plaintiff alleges that the defendant wrongly intruded onto the plaintiff's property.

CONNOLLEY V. OMAHA PUBLIC POWER DISTRICT
Supreme Court of Nebraska, 1970
185 Neb. 501, 177 N.W.2d 492

KOKJER, JUSTICE.

The plaintiff was injured by electricity when a metal flagpole he was helping to lower came in contact with a wire of defendant's transmission line. He claims that defendant is liable for his damages because the wire, at the point of contact, hung over the property of plaintiff's family 54/100ths of a foot. No negligence on the part of defendant was proved. The claim for recovery is based on the asserted trespass of defendant upon the property. When the evidence was completed, defendant moved for * * * a dismissal of the case. The motion was sustained * * *. Plaintiff appealed.

The evidence, construed most favorably to plaintiff, * * * sustains the trespass. The power line had been constructed along the east line of the property in the year 1930. Plaintiff's father bought the lot in the year 1959. He started to construct a house on it in 1962. Some work was done the same year on the line but the location of the wires had not been changed between the time the house was constructed and the date of the accident on July 3, 1965. Plaintiff's father testified that he believed they had moved into the house in March 1964.

Shortly before July 3, 1965, plaintiff's father had poured a concrete base rising 6 to 8 inches above the ground, and included therein a hole in which to insert a flagpole. The base was 2.61 feet west of the west wire of the transmission line and 3.15 feet west of the east property line. The wire at that point on April 15, 1967, was 30.24 feet above the ground. The plaintiff's father had assembled a flag pole by taking a section of pipe, inserting a smaller pipe into it, bolting them together, then inserting a still smaller pipe into that one and bolting them together. The length of the finished flagpole was 33 feet, 5 inches.

On July 3, 1965, plaintiff, plaintiff's father, and a neighbor placed the butt end of the flagpole against the concrete base. Taking hold of the outer end, they walked toward the base, lifting the outer end of the pole higher as they walked, until it was vertical, and then slipped the butt end into the hole in the base. The neighbor went home and plaintiff's uncle then arrived. It was discovered that the pulley rope to which the flag was to be attached was too high to be reached, and they decided to take the pole down and cut off some of the bottom of it. The three of them took hold of the pole and, after lifting it up out of the hole, set it on top of the concrete base.

On direct examination plaintiff's father testified as follows: "Q. Go ahead and tell the Jury then what happened. A. I don't know what happened after that hit us or the length of time, I wouldn't know this, but evidently if it had struck that wire up there, which that evidently is what it did, then we fell away to the ground unconscious."

On cross-examination plaintiff's father testified as follows: "Q. And as you stood there, was there any particular length of time went by before this accident occurred? A. It was a very short while, very, very short while after we had it out of the socket that it made contact with, I would imagine, the electric wire. Q. Well, there is no doubt in your mind but what the electric wire was contacted is there? A. No doubt, no sir."

An electric shock injured plaintiff severely and also injured his father and uncle to a degree not disclosed by the record.

Both plaintiff and his father admitted they knew that it was dangerous to contact an electric wire. They knew the wires were there but as they proceeded to erect the flagpole they paid no attention to them and did not discuss the possibility of danger.

An engineer testified that on April 15, 1967, somewhat over a year and 9 months after the incident he, with the assistance of two boys, by use of a transit, a method known as triangulation, and trigonometry, determined that on that date the westernmost wire of the transmission line hung 54/100ths of a foot, a little more than 6 inches, inside the property line.

Later, plaintiff, a minor, by his mother and next friend, filed this suit against defendant to recover for his injuries.

Plaintiff's attorneys had evidently decided that the facts would not sustain a suit against the defendant for any negligence on its part; and that if plaintiff were to recover at all, it would have to be on the theory that defendant had trespassed upon the property of plaintiff's family. They asked the court to require the defendant to pay for plaintiff's damages on the following theories:

(1) A trespasser on land is subject to liability or bodily harm caused to the possessor thereof, or to the members of his household, by the trespass, irrespective of whether the trespasser's conduct is such as would subject him to liability were he not a trespasser.

(2) Trespass and negligence are distinguishable. To recover against a trespasser, it is not necessary to prove negligence.

(3) Neither contributory negligence nor assumption of risk constitutes a defense in an action for trespass.

(4) Proximate cause is ordinarily a question for the jury. It is that cause which is an efficient agent in producing a given result. Where several causes concur to produce a certain result, either may be termed a proximate cause if it is an efficient cause of the result in question.

The district court sustained one other of plaintiff's theories and held there was a reasonable inference of trespass, but held that plaintiff's case based on trespass to real estate, anciently referred to as trespass *quare clausum fregit*, had to rest on proof that the injury complained of was the immediate and direct result of the trespass, and this proof was lacking. The district court also held that, even construing the action as one for negligence, anciently referred to as trespass on the case, it would be defeated by negligence of plaintiff and his father which were the proximate cause of the injuries.

Since nearly every violation of one's rights was anciently considered a trespass, there are literally hundreds of cases dealing with *trespass vi et armis, trespass de bonis asportatis, trespass quare clausum fregit*, trespass on the case, and so forth. In many of the reported cases the distinctions are blurred, and a negligence case may be treated loosely as one for trespass. The opinions frequently commingled the theories.

Generally speaking, trespass on the case lies for an injury resulting from a wrongful act other than physical force, or for an injury resulting from nonfeasance or negligence, or for an injury which is a consequential, as distinguished from a direct or immediate, result of the wrongful act.

Such would be an action for injuries contributed to by an electric company's negligence in permitting wires to sag so the wind might blow them and cause a dangerous condition; or to construct their lines too low or too close to a place where contact with any person or thing could be reasonably expected.

An injury is considered as immediate and therefore remediable by an action of trespass, as distinguished from trespass on the case, only when it is directly occasioned by, and is not merely a consequence resulting from, the act complained of.

Such would be an act directly damaging a person's house or garden or trees during line construction, and perhaps initially energizing a new line into a home without providing an adequate transformer, so that by that act excessively high voltages would burn out appliances, cause a fire, or personally injure the home owner's family.

The difficulty in applying the correct rules in this area of the law is summarized in [a legal encyclopedia] as follows:

> Case and trespass are clearly distinguishable, although the distinction is somewhat subtle and sometimes difficult of application. As ordinarily stated, the distinction is that where the injury resulting from a particular act is direct and immediate, trespass is the proper remedy, but that where it is not direct, but merely consequential, the proper remedy is case. * * * [B]ut it has been suggested that the true gist of the distinction intended lies not so much in the proximate or remote character of the damage as in the primary or secondary nature of the trespass.

> While theoretically the distinction between the actions of case and trespass is clear and well settled, yet it is one which is often difficult to apply to the facts and circumstances of particular cases.

> * * * "The probability of injury resulting from the act done, under the circumstances of the particular case, is an element to be considered in determining the directness of the injury as affecting the proper form of action."

* * *

Plaintiff herein proposes a rule which would make a power district or other proprietor of an electric transmission line an insurer for all time of a property owner and his family so long as the transmission line hangs over the property to any degree, even though it is constructed and maintained without negligence. Such a rule would require payment of damages regardless of any reckless, negligent, or even willful act of the property owner and his family. There is no sound basis in reason, statute, or applicable case law for such a rule.

Plaintiff claims that the district court erred in not submitting the question of proximate cause to the jury. It is true that ordinarily this is a jury question. Could it be in this case where: (1) Defendant cannot be held liable, in any event, on the theory of trespass for an act which was not a direct, immediate, or primary result of the injury; and (2) there is no proof whatever of any negligence on the part of the defendant? We think not.

* * * Under the facts of this case, the district court was correct in not submitting the question of proximate cause to the jury.

The judgment of the district court was correct and it is affirmed.

* * *

SPENCER, JUSTICE, dissenting.

I am not in agreement with the majority opinion herein * * *.

The base for the flagpole was constructed on and 3.15 feet from the east lot line of the property. The defendant owned, maintained, and operated an electrical distribution line on North Seventy-eighth Street in Omaha, Nebraska, which runs north and south in the parkway along the east side of the Connolley property but has no connection to that property. The west wire of said line is conceded to be .54 feet into the Connolley property. For the purposes of this case, it must be conceded that the defendant had no right by consent, prescription, easement, or otherwise to maintain the west wire over or upon the Connolley property. The electrical energy carried at the time of the accident was 13,000 volts. It is undisputed that there were no warning signs showing that this line carried a dangerous charge of electricity or that this highly energized wire was protruding over the property. This line did not serve the Connolley property. It was served with electricity by a transmission line behind the house from a line which comes off a pole in the southwest corner of the property.

Other than the participants, the only eyewitness was one Emil John Torres who testified that he lives four lots south of the Connolleys, or approximately 400 feet away, and that he did not know them personally. At the time of the accident he was in his front yard and noticed some people in the Connolley front yard who were holding something straight up in the air, approximately vertical. About the same instant he noticed a yellow flash in the vicinity of the west wire. The flash was directly above what he saw the people holding. The flash was yellow like an arc, and was plainly visible.

There is only one issue presented in this appeal: Did the trial court err in sustaining defendant's motion for a directed verdict, thereby removing from the jury the question of the proximate cause of the plaintiff's injury? * * *

There can be no question the defendant is a trespasser on the property involved herein. A taking of land for public use without authorization is a trespass.

We are concerned here with what is described as a continuing trespass. A trespass may be committed by the continued presence on the land of a structure, chattel, or other thing which the actor or his predecessor in legal interest has placed on the land. The actor's failure to remove from land in the possession of another a structure, chattel, or other thing which he has tortiously erected or placed on the land constitutes a continuing trespass for the entire time during which the thing is wrongfully on the land.

In the instant case, the wire overhanging the property of plaintiff's parents is constantly energized and the trespass was active and operative at the moment of plaintiff's injury. The Restatement rule on the extent of a trespasser's liability for harm is as follows: "A trespass on land subjects the trespasser to liability for physical harm to the possessor of the land at the time of the trespass, or to the land or to his things, or to members of his household or to their things, caused by any act done, activity carried on, or condition created by the trespasser, irrespective of whether his conduct is such as would subject him to liability were he not a trespasser." Restatement (Second) of Torts § 162 (1965).

This is not a case where we can assume that the Connolleys lost control of the pole and that it fell eastward onto the offending wire. The evidence which we must consider herein is otherwise. The reasonable inference from the testimony of the only disinterested eyewitness is that the electricity arced or jumped from the wire to the pole. This must be considered in connection with the plaintiff's testimony that the pole was straight up and down at the time he was knocked unconscious. When the parties were knocked to the ground, the pole fell. The marks on the pole * * * would indicate that the pole could have slid along the wire when it fell, after electricity jumped the gap between the wire and the pole. Defendant's crew foreman on cross-examination admitted that after the initial contact further contact might have been made between the pole and the wire.

Plaintiff's father was erecting the flagpole on his own property. The base he prepared for it was located more than 3 feet from the east lot line. If the defendant's wire had not been over his property but in the parkway adjoining it, we would have an entirely different situation. * * * We cannot separate the accident herein from defendant's trespass. Even if we assume negligence on the part of plaintiff's father, it still took the trespass to produce the injury.

The plaintiff herein testified that he had no occasion to look up at the wires; that he had never paid any attention to them; and even if he had, he would not have known what they were. This testimony should be considered in connection with the fact that the plaintiff's home was not served with electricity from these wires but from one coming into the home from the rear. Further, he had a right to be where he was at the time of the accident; he was engaged in assisting his father in a family project wholly upon his parent's property. Defendant's wire was suspended over this property without right.

* * * On the facts herein, it must be assumed that plaintiff had no knowledge of the extremely dangerous character of the wire. Even if plaintiff had specifically observed the wire, there is a serious question as

to whether a child of his years and experience would realize the danger. Also, he might have assumed it to be further away than it actually was. It is of interest that defendant's crew foreman, who had considerable experience in such matters, placed the wire as 4 feet from the base of the pole. * * * "A high-voltage power line is one of the most dangerous things known to man. Not only is the current deadly, but the ordinary person has no means of knowing whether any particular wire is carrying a deadly current or is harmless" * * *.

Defendant was unlawfully maintaining a dangerous energized wire over the property on which plaintiff resided. Plaintiff's injury arose out of this unauthorized invasion of that property. This continuous trespass is at the very least a proximate cause of plaintiff's injury.

* * *

NOTES AND QUESTIONS

1. What was plaintiff's theory of recovery in *Connolley*? What was the advantage of a trespass action over one for negligence?

2. How did the majority rule? What was the rationale of the dissent? Based on the facts of the case, is the dissent correct that defendant's trespass was the proximate cause of plaintiff's injury?

3. *Connolley* illustrates that property interests do not end at the mere physical ground or structures on a plot of land. As the Restatement (Second) of Torts § 159 (1965) notes: "[T]respass may be committed on, beneath, or above the surface of the earth." For example, a landowner may establish trespass by proving that a cave extended underneath his land. *See, e.g., Edwards v. Lee*, 230 Ky. 375, 19 S.W.2d 992 (1929). Similarly, a landowner may pursue a trespass action against an intruder floating or fishing on a private, non-navigable stream running over a landowner's property. *See, e.g., People v. Emmert*, 198 Colo. 137, 597 P.2d 1025 (1979).

4. As *Connolley* shows, a landowner has an interest in the airspace above his property. An action for trespass against a passing airplane is theoretically possible, but the Restatement places significant limitations on trespass via a passing aircraft. As the Restatement (Second) of Torts § 159 (1965) notes: "Flight by aircraft in the air space above the land of another is a trespass if, *but only if*, it enters into the immediate reaches of the air space next to the land and it interferes substantially with the other's use and enjoyment of his land" (emphasis added). In addressing where the line should be drawn in determining the "immediate reaches" of airspace, the Restatement states: "In the ordinary case, flight at 500 feet or more above the surface is not within the 'immediate reaches,' while flight within 50 feet, which interferes with actual use, clearly is, and flight within 150 feet, which also so interferes, may present a question of fact." *Id.* at cmt. 1.

5. Although trespass is an ancient doctrine concerning property rights, trespass claims are potentially viable with respect to evolving forms of

technology. *See, e.g., eBay, Inc. v. Bidder's Edge, Inc.*, 100 F. Supp. 2d 1058 (N.D. Cal. 2000) (finding that a website could be liable for trespass for using robotic search mechanisms to access eBay's website without consent or authorization); *CompuServ, Inc. v. Cyber Promotions, Inc.*, 962 F. Supp. 1015 (S.D. Ohio 1997) (finding that burdening internet users with spam and junk email was actionable as a trespass). Some scholars, however, have maintained that the tort of trespass is ill suited to internet technology. *See, e.g.*, R. Clifton Merrell, *Trespass to Chattels in the Age of the Internet*, 80 Wash. U.L.Q. 675 (2002) (arguing that applying traditional trespass doctrine to the internet would pose a danger to the internet's continued growth because it would inhibit the sharing of information); Laura Quilter, *The Continuing Expansion of Cyberspace Trespass to Chattels*, 17 Berkeley Tech. L.J. 421, 443 (2002) (arguing that applying traditional doctrines of trespass to the internet "poses a real threat to the fundamental activities underlying the internet," and concluding that courts and legislatures should treat cyberspace cases differently from traditional property because the internet does not have the same characteristics as traditional property). Other commentators, however, believe the trespass is broad enough to cover various internet-related claims without specially-created elements. *See, e.g.*, Peter Winn, *The Guilty Eye: Unauthorized Access Trespass and Privacy*, 62 Bus. Law 1395 (2007) (arguing that traditional trespass doctrine is flexible enough to cover computer-related trespass claims).

6.   Because trespass claims revolve mainly around property rights, the topic will be addressed further in Chapter 6 of this textbook.

6.   ADDITIONAL INTENTIONAL TORT DOCTRINES

a.   Trespass to Chattels: In addition to the doctrine of trespass to land presented in *Connolley*, there is also a claim known as "trespass to chattels." Essentially, a trespass to chattels is a temporary interference with a person's property other than land. As the Restatement (Second) of Torts § 217 (1965) states: "A trespass to a chattel may be committed by intentionally (a) dispossessing another of the chattel, or (b) using or intermeddling with a chattel in the possession of another." *See, e.g., Register.Com, Inc. v. Verio, Inc.*, 356 F.3d 393 (2d Cir. 2004) (holding that a plaintiff could sustain an action for trespass to chattels when the functioning of its computer system was impaired by automated software that the defendant used to invade the plaintiff's computer system); *cf. Intel Corp. v. Hamidi*, 30 Cal.4th 1342, 71 P.3d 296 (2003) (holding that a plaintiff could not establish a trespass to chattels claim after receiving numerous unwanted emails because there was no evidence that the unwanted emails damaged the computer or impaired the functioning of the email system).

b.   Conversion: Another tort claim involving property other than land is known as conversion. Conversion is essentially a tort action for theft. As the Restatement (Second) of Torts § 222A (1965) states:

"Conversion is an intentional exercise of dominion or control over a chattel which so seriously interferes with the right of another to control it that the actor may justly be required to pay the other the full value of the chattel." In determining the seriousness of the interference, the Restatement instructs courts to examine "(a) the extent and duration of the actor's exercise of dominion or control; (b) the actor's intent to assert a right in fact inconsistent with the other's right of control; (c) the actor's good faith; (d) the extent and duration of the resulting interference with the other's right of control; (e) the harm done to the chattel; [and] (f) the inconvenience and expense caused to the other." *Id. See, e.g., Buzzell v. Citizens Auto. Fin., Inc.*, 802 F. Supp. 2d 1014 (D. Minn. 2011) (holding that the plaintiff could establish a claim of conversion when the defendant wrongfully repossessed and sold the plaintiff's vehicle); *Wiseman v. Schaffer*, 115 Idaho 557, 768 P.2d 800 (Idaho Ct. App. 1989) (holding that the plaintiffs (a husband and wife) had satisfied the elements for conversion when, without their consent, the defendant towed their vehicle to a location where it was later stolen). Conversion issues often arise in property law courses as well as torts courses (*see* Chapter 6).

    c.   **Fraud:** If an individual suffers harm from another individual's fraudulent conduct, that individual may have a claim (known as fraud) to recover damages. According to the Restatement (Second) of Torts § 526 (1965): "A misrepresentation is fraudulent if the maker (a) knows or believes that the matter is not as he represents it to be, (b) does not have the confidence in the accuracy of his representation that he states or implies, or (c) knows that he does not have the basis for his representation that he states or implies." *See, e.g., Follo v. Florindo*, 185 Vt. 390, 970 A.2d 1230 (2009) (holding that a buyer of a business could maintain an action for fraud against the seller when the seller misrepresented the business' profits during the sale); *cf. Parker v. Fla. Bd. of Regents ex rel. Fla. State Univ.*, 724 So.2d 163 (Fla. Dist. Ct. App. 1998) (holding that the plaintiff could not establish a claim for fraud because he failed to establish that the defendant had misrepresented the information at issue in bad faith).

    d.   **Defenses to Intentional Torts:** There are many common law and statutory defenses to intentional torts, but the major defenses are: *self-defense* (the defendant reasonably believed his actions were necessary to prevent imminent harm to himself), *see, e.g., Tatman v. Cordingly*, 672 P.2d 1286 (Wyo. 1983) (holding that the defendant had established a claim of self-defense in an action against him for battery after he struck the plaintiff during a fight that the plaintiff started); *defense of others* (the defendant reasonably believed his actions were necessary to defend another person from imminent harm), *see, e.g., Brown v. State*, 675 N.Y.S.2d 611, 250 A.D.2d 796 (N.Y. App. Div. 1998) (holding that a police officer had established a claim of defense of others in a lawsuit against him when he shot the plaintiff after the plaintiff had lunged at another police officer with a weapon); and *necessity* (the defendant caused damage to property out of a necessity to protect a public or private interest, such as damaging property to prevent a greater harm), *see, e.g.*, *Steele v. City of Houston*, 603 S.W.2d 786, 792 (Tex. 1980) (stating that "[u]ncompensated destruction of property has been occasionally justified by reason of war, riot, pestilence or other great public calamity," and allowing the defendant to argue a necessity defense when the defendant (a police department) set fire to the plaintiff's house in an effort to recapture dangerous escaped convicts who were hiding in the house). A necessity defense is treated differently depending on whether the tortfeasor was protecting a public or private interest. If the tortfeasor was protecting a public interest (*i.e.*, the interests of the community at large), the defense is a complete bar to liability. Restatement (Second) of Torts § 196 (1965). If, however, the defendant was acting to protect his own private interest, he will likely have to compensate a plaintiff for any actual damage caused to the plaintiff's property. *Id.* § 197.

B. NEGLIGENCE

Unlike the intentional torts discussed in Section A of this chapter, an action for negligence does not require intentional wrongdoing by the defendant. Typically, a plaintiff bringing a claim for negligence must establish five elements: (1) the defendant owed the plaintiff a duty of care, (2) the defendant breached the duty of care, (3) the defendant's breach caused the plaintiff a legally recognized harm, (4) the plaintiff's harm was the proximate cause of the defendant's conduct, and (5) the harm can be remedied with monetary damages. Restatement (Third) of Torts: Liability for Physical & Emotional Harm § 6 cmt. b (2012). The elements are often shortened to: (1) duty, (2) breach, (3) cause in fact, (4) proximate cause, and (5) damages. The following materials discuss some of the issues that arise in negligence lawsuits.

1. DUTY OF CARE

In a negligence case, the first inquiry is whether the defendant owed a "duty of care" to the plaintiff. The following case discusses that issue.

WESTMINSTER PRESBYTERIAN CHURCH OF MUNCIE V. YONGHONG CHENG

Court of Appeals of Indiana, 2013
992 N.E.2d 859

VAIDIK, JUDGE.

* * *

After the death of their four-month-old son while under the care of a babysitter recommended by a pastor at their church, Yonghong Cheng and Hongjun Niu ("June") (collectively, "the Chengs") brought suit against

Westminster Presbyterian Church ("Westminster") for wrongful death [and other claims] * * *.

* * * [W]e find that there was no duty of care * * * in this case * * *.

FACTS AND PROCEDURAL HISTORY

Westminster, located in Muncie, Indiana, has approximately 425 members. Dr. Gary Cox is the Pastor, and Kristofer Holroyd is the Associate Pastor. There is also a Chinese Christian fellowship at Westminster that uses the facility, but it has its own pastor, worship service, and fellowship time.

The Chengs began attending Westminster in 2005. They attended Westminster's regular Sunday services and June sang in the choir; they were not members of the Chinese Christian fellowship. Their son, Matthew, was born in September 2009, and due to their fears Matthew would contract the flu, Matthew and Yonghong would usually stay home from services on Sundays.

Around January 1, 2010, June got a job with Love's Tax Service and was expected to start on January 4, resulting in a search for a babysitter for Matthew. June contacted Joy Wegener, a woman she knew through Bible study at Westminster, and asked if she would babysit. Wegener initially agreed, but she later changed her mind and called June to decline. Wegener mentioned Tina Byrd as a possible alternative, telling June that Byrd was also from Westminster. Wegener gave Byrd's phone number to June, and June called and left a message for her that day. However, June was still hoping that Wegener would change her mind, so she went over to Wegener's house to talk to her. Wegener still declined; she then called another woman from Westminster who also declined. At this point, according to June, Wegener called Holroyd and told him that "June is here trying to find child care for Matthew." However, according to Holroyd, Wegener told him that her "Chinese friend" was looking for someone to babysit her baby and asked him if he knew anyone to recommend. Holroyd said "Tina is taking babies." Wegener then asked Holroyd if any college students from Westminster could babysit, and Holroyd said he would send out an email to check. Holroyd testified he did not know that June was with Wegener at the time of the call, and he did not mention that a baby had died while in Byrd's care just two months before. Holroyd also did not think that he was making a recommendation to anyone to use Byrd as a babysitter, nor did he consider the phone call to be one seeking pastoral advice.

Before June left Wegener's house, Byrd called back and indicated that she could babysit Matthew. Byrd asked June how old Matthew was and whether he was on formula, and she told June that if she decided to hire her, Byrd would email her a list of things to bring. Byrd also told June that she could start the next day, January 4. June did not hire Byrd at this time;

she discussed the matter with Yonghong and called Byrd later to let her know that they were going to hire her. June said that they would be able to pay Byrd $80 per week, and Byrd agreed to the amount. June did not do any other research on Byrd, and Byrd gave June no more information.

About two months before, however, in mid-October 2009, Byrd started babysitting the baby of another family from Westminster. On November 3, 2009, Byrd put him down for a nap and the baby died. When the baby was discovered, he was unresponsive in his crib, so Byrd and her daughter called 911 and Byrd performed CPR. The baby's death was ruled by the coroner to be "a case of Sudden Unexpected Infant Death (SUID)," with the official manner of death being "undetermined." Byrd was questioned by the police and the Indiana Department of Child Services, but she was never charged. The baby's death was well-known within the Westminster community.

After the baby's death, Byrd did not think she would babysit again. However, Byrd's father had helped her financially after she got divorced, and he passed away shortly after the baby's death. Byrd's ex-husband was also behind on child-support payments, so Byrd returned to babysitting in order to start earning money again.

Byrd began babysitting Matthew on January 4, 2010. The first day, June took Matthew to Byrd's house, staying for thirty to forty minutes to feed him before going to work. Around 12:30 or 1:00 p.m., Byrd called June, telling her she "couldn't do it," so June called Yonghong to pick Matthew up from Byrd's house. Byrd said that Matthew "kept on crying" and that she could not handle it and did not want to babysit anymore. When Yonghong picked Matthew up, Byrd suggested that they try bottle feeding him, and that when Matthew was ready, they could try having her babysit him again. The Chengs worked on weaning Matthew off of breast feeding, and the next week they dropped him back off at Byrd's house without issue.

On January 19, 2010, June dropped Matthew off at Byrd's house. At 2:15 that afternoon, when Matthew was sleeping, Byrd left the house to pick up her daughter from school and make another stop, leaving Matthew alone in the house. She had checked on Matthew about ten minutes before she left, and he seemed to be asleep on his side. Byrd's nineteen-year-old daughter, Kassey, worked at a preschool about five minutes from the house, and she was expected home soon after the school let out around 2:00 p.m. When Byrd returned home with her other daughter, Kataryna, Kassey was already there. Kataryna went into the room where Matthew had been sleeping and found him dead in the crib. Byrd started CPR and 911 was called. June was not notified about Matthew's death until she came to Byrd's house to pick him up and was met by Byrd's son who told her, "your baby died." Byrd was questioned by the police and initially lied about her whereabouts that afternoon, as well as how she positioned Matthew for his nap. As a result, Byrd pled guilty to obstruction of justice.

Dr. Cox first learned of Matthew's death around 3:00 p.m. that day, and he and his wife first went to the police station where Byrd was. They then went to the hospital where the Chengs were, along with Holroyd and another Westminster member. Dr. Cox believed that the Chengs were part of the Chinese Christian fellowship, but he did not see anyone from the Chinese ministry there, so he advised the hospital chaplain that he was their pastor and prayed for the Chengs. While at the hospital, Dr. Cox described June's condition as: "In all my years of pastoral ministry, I have never seen someone that visibly distraught, wailing ... she was inconsolable at that time." Dr. Cox then drove the Chengs to their house and left at their request so that they could grieve as a family. Dr. Cox also gave the Chengs his phone number, telling them that he would call the next day, which he never did.

* * *

An autopsy was performed on Matthew, and his cause of death was determined to be "Sudden Unexplained Infant Death (SUID), cause undetermined. The autopsy report also stated that "[r]isk factors identified for his death include prematurity, prone sleeping position, and death under uncertain household circumstances."

On March 15, the Chengs filed their wrongful death complaint against Westminster and Byrd. Eight months later, they filed an amended complaint, adding [other counts]. * * * The trial court denied [summary judgment on the wrongful death claim]. * * *

* * * Westminster asked the trial court to certify its order for interlocutory appeal, which the trial court did. This Court accepted jurisdiction * * *.

DISCUSSION AND DECISION

* * *

* * * We hold that the trial court * * * err[ed] in denying Westminster's summary-judgment motion on the claim[ ] for wrongful death * * *.

I.   Negligence

* * *

* * * In order to impose a duty at common law, the court must balance (1) the relationship between the parties, (2) the reasonable foreseeability of the harm to the person injured, and (3) public policy concerns. * * * [A] balancing of the [three] factors * * * shows that Westminster did not owe a duty of care to the Chengs * * *.

A.   Relationship Between the Parties

It is clear that there was some relationship between the parties involved in this case. Holroyd, an Associate Pastor at Westminster, provided Byrd's name to the Chengs through Wegener as a potential babysitter for Matthew. This interaction is sufficient to create a relationship between the two parties.

The Chengs, however, contend that this created the pastor-parishioner relationship—one that this Court has said creates a fiduciary/confidential relationship. Regardless of whether Holroyd was aware that June was with Wegener during the phone conversation in which he provided Byrd's name as a potential babysitter, it is clear that there was no special pastor-parishioner relationship created in this situation.

The fact that Holroyd was a pastor, standing alone, does not create a fiduciary relationship between him and the Chengs. "[W]hether a special relationship exists is fact sensitive and dependent on the level of interaction or dependency between the parties that surpasses what is common or usual." * * *

In this case, the relevant facts show that there was no special relationship created. June received the information about Byrd through an intermediary, Wegener, rather than directly and confidentially from Holroyd. There is also no showing that this advice from Holroyd was special counseling that June was dependent on him for; rather this was readily available public information that she could have received from any number of people. The information sought was also general in nature, as Holroyd was asked if he knew of anyone to recommend as a babysitter and not specifically about Byrd and her qualifications as a babysitter. Finally, we note that the nature of the inquiry was personal and not related to the church, as childcare was not a ministry of Westminster and its pastors. Therefore, * * * there is nothing to indicate that the level of interaction and dependency between June and Holroyd was great enough to trigger a special pastor-parishioner relationship that the Chengs contend gives rise to Westminster's liability.

B.   Reasonable Foreseeability of the Harm

* * * [H]arm is foreseeable if "the person actually harmed was a foreseeable victim and . . . the type of harm actually inflicted was reasonably foreseeable." In this case, Matthew's death, while tragic, was not reasonably foreseeable.

Matthew died from "Sudden Unexplained Infant Death (SUID), cause undetermined." While the autopsy provided risk factors for Matthew's death, the cause of death could not be definitively determined or explained. With no answers as to how or why Matthew died, we cannot say that he was a foreseeable victim or that his death was reasonably foreseeable. There was nothing about Byrd's house that the coroner was able to point to that caused Matthew's death, so Byrd babysitting Matthew did not foreseeably place him in danger of dying.

The Chengs also contend that Holroyd had a duty to warn them about the death of the baby that happened two months before Matthew was placed under Byrd's care. While another baby had died while under Byrd's care just a few months before Matthew, the cause of that death was also ruled to be "a case of Sudden Unexpected Infant Death (SUID)," with the official manner of death being "undetermined." By its very name, the death therefore was unexpected, and the reason for the death was undetermined. We cannot say that Westminster should have known that another baby was likely to die from SUID while in Byrd's care. Therefore, it would not be reasonable to impose a duty on Holroyd to warn future parents that a child had previously died in Byrd's care from SUID.

C.   Public Policy Concerns

The public policy concerns at issue here are great. Society has an expectation that liability will attach for certain actions, but not for mere recommendations that are freely and frequently given as a part of daily life. Wegener called Holroyd and asked him if he knew anyone to recommend for child care. In this situation, no one would expect that a recommendation given by a church's associate pastor would subject the church to potential liability if the recommendation given results in any sort of harm. In order to assume a duty, the defendant "must have specifically and deliberately undertaken the duty." That deliberation is noticeably absent in a case such as this, where Holroyd was contacted and asked for advice; Westminster did not deliberately set out to undertake the duty of insuring the safety of a child under Byrd's care. We therefore cannot say that it would be fair to place such a burden on the recommender.

* * *

* * * [W]e conclude that Westminster did not owe a duty to the Chengs * * *. We therefore reverse and remand with instructions that the trial court enter summary judgment in favor of Westminster on the Chengs' wrongful-death claim.

* * *

NOTES AND QUESTIONS

1.   What was the Chengs' theory of negligence? Why did the court reject the Chengs' theory?

2.   Is the *Westminster* court's ruling a fair one? What arguments can be made against it?

3.   Contrary to the intentional torts discussed earlier in this chapter, negligence actions generally arise out of conduct that is unintentional. As the Restatement (Second) of Torts § 282 (1965) states: "[N]egligence is conduct which falls below the standard established by law for the protection of others

against unreasonable risk of harm. It does not include conduct recklessly [or intentionally] disregardful of an interest of others."

4. As the *Westminster* case exemplifies, one of the key issues in a negligence case is whether the defendant had a duty to exercise a certain degree of care to ensure the plaintiff's safety. Although *Westminster* found that no duty of care existed for the pastor who had recommended the babysitter, courts frequently take an expansive view in assessing duty of care. *See, e.g., Novak v. Capital Mgmt. & Dev. Corp.*, 452 F.3d 902 (D.C. Cir. 2006) (holding that a dance club had duty to protect patrons from an attack in an alley outside the only exit from the club); *Marla H. v. Knox Cnty.*, 361 S.W.3d 518 (Tenn. Ct. App. 2011) (finding that a guest lecturer at a local school owed a duty of care to the school students to protect them from emotional or mental harm that might occur after showing graphic photographs of dead bodies during his presentation); *Marshall v. Burger King Corp.*, 222 Ill.2d 422, 856 N.E.2d 1048 (2006) (holding that a fast food restaurant had a duty to protect customers from unreasonable risk of physical harm posed by an out-of-control car that crashed into the restaurant); *Lugtu v. Cal. Highway Patrol*, 110 Cal.Rptr.2d 528, 28 P.3d 249 (2001) (finding that a police officer had duty to exercise reasonable care for the safety of persons who were stopped by the officer during a traffic stop, and that this duty included an obligation not to expose them to unreasonable risk of injury by third parties who were driving past the stop); *Ortega v. Kmart Corp.*, 114 Cal.Rptr.2d 470, 36 P.3d 11 (2001) (finding that a supermarket owed a duty to a store patron who had slipped and injured himself on milk that had been spilled at the supermarket); *Landis v. Rockdale Cnty.*, 206 Ga.App. 876, 427 S.E.2d 286 (Ga. App. Ct. 1992) (holding that a police officer owed a duty of care to the general public to prevent a noticeably intoxicated driver from continuing to drive).

5. *Westminster* dealt with a defendant's potential duty to warn parents about the prior conduct of a third-party babysitter. Although the *Westminster* court failed to impose such a duty on the church, there are some situations where a duty may be imposed on an actor to control a third party's conduct. *See, e.g.*, Restatement (Second) of Torts § 316 (1965) (asserting that a parent has a duty to control a minor child so as to prevent the child from intentionally harming others if the harm caused was foreseeable and preventable with supervision); *Maroon v. Dept. of Mental Health*, 411 N.E.2d 404 (Ind. Ct. App. 1980) (holding, in a case involving a citizen who was killed by an escaped prisoner, that the State owed a duty to exercise reasonable care in its control of patients of the Department of Mental Health). Is it fair to impose a duty of care on third-party actors who do not directly cause harm? How should that duty be imposed in the context of medical professionals, who often give care to violent and mentally ill patients? *See, e.g.*, Jacqueline Johnson, *A Proposal to Adopt a Professional Judgment Standard of Care in Determining the Duty of a Psychiatrist to Third Persons*, 62 U. Colo. L. Rev. 237 (1991) (surveying various approaches among jurisdictions regarding professional liability for the acts of mentally ill patients and arguing that an objective standard of reasonableness should be employed). The concept of third-party liability will be discussed later in this chapter in the context of the doctrine of respondeat superior.

2. BYSTANDER DUTIES

Although a duty of care generally imposes a duty to *refrain* from causing an unreasonable risk of harm (*i.e.*, a person *must not* engage in conduct that poses a risk of harm to other), some situations impose an "affirmative" duty to act to prevent harm (*i.e.*, a person *must* engage in an *affirmative action* to prevent harm). The following case discusses the "bystander rule" and the potential duty to render aid to harmed individuals.

PODIAS V. MAIRS

Superior Court of New Jersey, Appellate Division, 2007
394 N.J.Super. 338, 926 A.2d 859

PARRILLO, JUDGE.

At issue is whether passengers in a car may, in certain circumstances, owe a duty to a pedestrian struck by a driver who is either unwilling or unable to seek emergency aid or assistance himself. Plaintiff Sevasti Podias, Administratrix of the estate of decedent Antonios Podias (Podias), appeals from the summary judgment dismissal of his wrongful death and survivorship action against defendants Andrew K. Swanson, Jr. and Kyle Charles Newell, which concluded that defendants owed decedent no such duty * * *. We * * * reverse.

* * * In the evening of September 27, 2002 and early morning hours of September 28, eighteen-year old Michael Mairs was drinking beer at the home of a friend Thomas Chomko. He eventually left with two other friends, defendants Swanson and Newell, both also eighteen years of age, to return to Monmouth University where all three were students. Mairs was driving. Swanson was in the front passenger seat and Newell was seated in the rear of the vehicle where he apparently fell asleep. It was raining and the road was wet.

At approximately 2:00 a.m., while traveling southbound in the center lane of the Garden State Parkway, Mairs lost control of the car, struck a motorcycle driven by Antonios Podias, and went over the guardrail. All three exited the vehicle and "huddled" around the car. Swanson saw Podias lying in the roadway and because he saw no movement and heard no sound, told Mairs and Newell that he thought Mairs had killed the cyclist. At that time, there were no other cars on the road, or witnesses for that matter.

Even though all three had cell phones, no one called for assistance. Instead they argued about whether the car had collided with the motorcycle. And, within minutes of the accident, Mairs called his girlfriend on Newell's cell phone since his was lost when he got out of the car. Swanson also used his cell phone, placing seventeen calls in the next one-and-one-half hours. Twenty-six additional calls were made from Newell's cell phone in the two-and-one-half hours after the accident, the first just three minutes post-accident and to Matawan, where Chomko resides. None of these, however, were emergency assistance calls. As Swanson later explained: "I didn't feel responsible to call the police." And Newell just "didn't want to get in trouble."

After about five or ten minutes, the trio all decided to get back in the car and leave the scene. Swanson directed, "we have to get to an exit." Upon their return to the car, Swanson instructed Mairs "not to bring up his name or involve him in what occurred" and "don't get us [Swanson and Newell] involved, we weren't there." The three then drove south on the parkway for a short distance until Mairs's car broke down. Mairs pulled over and waited in the bushes for his girlfriend to arrive, while Swanson and Newell ran off into the woods, where Newell eventually lost sight of Swanson. Before they deserted him, Swanson again reminded Mairs that "there was no need to get [Swanson and Newell] in trouble. . . ." Mairs thought Swanson was "just scared" and that both defendants were concerned about Mairs "drinking and driving." Meanwhile, a motor vehicle operated by Patricia Uribe ran over Podias, who died as a result of injuries sustained in these accidents.

In the ensuing investigation, when State Police located Mairs hours after the accident, Mairs claimed that he was alone in the car. He also denied striking the motorcycle, seemingly unaware of any impact despite being told otherwise by Swanson. At the time, the police officers observed that Mairs "manifested symptoms of alcohol consumption and intoxication." Indeed, when blood was drawn at 5:12 a.m., more than three hours after the accident and well after his last drink at Chomko's house, Mairs's blood alcohol level was .085. It was not until months afterwards that Mairs admitted that defendants were passengers in the car on the evening of the accident and that he had lied to the police because "he was doing what his friends asked him to do." Consequently, when defendants were separately interviewed three months after the accident, they each confirmed the police officers' initial observations. Newell told State Police that Mairs appeared intoxicated from "[t]he way he was acting" and "the odor of his breath." "He had a wobble walk and his speech was slurred a little." Swanson attributed the accident to "[f]irst and foremost, Mike's intoxication." Swanson also claimed that Mairs threatened to leave him at the scene after he told Mairs he had struck the motorcycle and possibly killed the cyclist.

Plaintiff, individually and on behalf of decedent's estate, filed a complaint against several defendants, all of whom save Swanson and Newell, either settled or were found liable after jury trial. Following discovery, defendants Swanson and Newell moved for summary judgment, which the motion judge granted, * * * finding [that] defendants had no legal duty to volunteer emergency assistance to one whose injury they neither caused nor substantially assisted another in bringing about. As to the latter, the judge reasoned:

> I find that the Plaintiff has not established sufficient facts to permit a rational factfinder to resolve any dispute in issue in favor of the Plaintiff concerning the actions of Mr. Newell and Mr. Swanson that would indicate a concert[ed] action. Even assuming that [Newell and Swanson] individually should have known of the duty of Mr. Mairs to call the police, there is absolutely no testimony that either [one] encouraged Mairs not to call the police and to leave the scene of the accident or * * * substantially assist[ed] Mr. Mairs in that endeavor. Assistance and encouragement require active and purposeful conduct in order to be liable * * *.

Plaintiff appeals, arguing that * * * defendants owed a duty to decedent which a jury could reasonably find was breached in this instance, and further, * * * a jury could reasonably find that defendants substantially assisted another in his breach of a direct duty.

(i)

* * * Ordinarily, * * * mere presence at the commission of [a] wrong, or failure to object to it, is not enough to charge one with responsibility inasmuch as there is no duty to take affirmative steps to interfere. Because of this reluctance to countenance "inaction" as a basis of liability, the common law "has persistently refused to impose on a stranger the moral obligation of common humanity to go to the aid of another human being * * *, even if the other is in danger of losing his life." Thus, the common law rule * * * relieves a bystander from any obligation to provide affirmative aid or emergency assistance, even if the bystander has the ability to help. The underlying rationale for what has come to be known as the "innocent bystander rule" seems to be that by "passive inaction," defendant has made the injured party's situation no worse, and has merely failed to benefit him by interfering in his affairs.

Of course, exceptions are as longstanding as the rule. For instance, if one already has a pre-existing legal duty to render assistance, * * * either by statute or "public calling" * * *, then it is that duty which impels him to act, for which omission he may be liable. So too, at common law, those under no pre-existing duty may nevertheless be liable if they choose to volunteer emergency assistance for another but do so negligently.

Over the years, liability for inaction has been gradually extended still further to a "limited group of relations, in which custom, public sentiment, and views of social policy have led courts to find a duty of affirmative action." Thus, a duty to render assistance may either be "contractual, relational or transactional." In New Jersey, courts have recognized that the existence of a relationship between the victim and one in a position to provide aid may create a duty to render assistance. * * *

To establish liability, * * * such relationships need not be limited to those where a pre-existing duty exists, or involving economic ties, or dependent on the actor's status as, for instance, a landowner or business owner. Rather, it may only be necessary "to find some definite relation between the parties of such a character that social policy justifies the imposition of a duty to act." So, for instance, the general duty which arises in many relations to take reasonable precautions for the safety of others may include the obligation to exercise control over the conduct of third persons with dangerous propensities.

So too, even though the defendant may be under no obligation to render assistance himself, he is at least required to take reasonable care that he does not prevent others from giving it. In other words, there may be liability for interfering with the plaintiff's opportunity of obtaining assistance. And even where the original danger was created by innocent conduct, involving no fault on the part of the defendant, there may be a duty to make a reasonable effort to give assistance and avoid further harm where the prior innocent conduct has created an unreasonable risk of harm to the plaintiff. * * *

* * * [T]he extension of liability based on these and other "relational" features mirrors evolving notions of duty, which are no longer tethered to rigid formalisms or static historical classifications. This progression is not surprising. The assessment of duty necessarily includes an examination of the relationships between and among the parties. The fundamental question is "whether the plaintiff's interests are entitled to legal protection against the defendant's conduct." In this regard, the determination of the existence of duty is ultimately a question of fairness and public policy * * *."

The duty determination, which is a judicial one, involves a complex analysis that weighs and balances several related factors * * *.

* * *

Specifically, "[f]oreseeability of the risk of harm is the foundational element in the determination of whether a duty exists." Foreseeability, in turn, is based on the defendant's knowledge of the risk of injury. * * *

Also included in the analysis is "an assessment of the defendant's 'responsibility for conditions creating the risk of harm' and an analysis of whether the defendant had sufficient control, opportunity, and ability to have avoided the risk of harm." And ultimately, there is public policy, which "must be determined in the context of contemporary circumstances and considerations."

Governed by these principles, we are satisfied that the summary judgment record admits of sufficient facts from which a reasonable jury could find defendants breached a duty which proximately caused the victim's death. In the first place, the risk of harm, even death, to the injured victim lying helpless in the middle of a roadway, from the failure of defendants to summon help or take other precautionary measures was readily and clearly foreseeable. Not only were defendants aware of the risk of harm created by their own inaction, but were in a unique position to know of the risk of harm posed by Mairs's own omission in that regard, as well as Mairs's earlier precipatory conduct in driving after having consumed alcohol. Even absent any encouragement on their part, defendants had special reason to know that Mairs would not himself summon help, but instead illegally depart the scene of a hit-and-run accident, either intentionally or because of an inability to fulfill a duty directly owed the victim, thereby further endangering the decedent's safety.

Juxtaposed against the obvious foreseeability of harm is the relative ease with which it could have been prevented. All three individuals had cell phones and in fact used them immediately before and after the accident for their own purposes, rather than to call for emergency assistance for another in need. The ultimate consequence wrought by the harm in this case—death—came at the expense of failing to take simple precautions at little if any cost or inconvenience to defendants. Indeed, in contrast to Mairs's questionable ability to appreciate the seriousness of the situation, defendants appeared lucid enough to comprehend the severity of the risk and sufficiently in control to help avoid further harm to the victim. In other words, defendants had both the opportunity and ability to help prevent an obviously foreseeable risk of severe and potentially fatal consequence.

In our view, given the circumstances, the imposition of a duty upon defendants does not offend notions of fairness and common decency and is in accord with public policy. * * * [D]efendants here were far more than innocent bystanders or strangers to the event. On the contrary, the instrumentality of injury in this case was operated for a common purpose and the mutual benefit of defendants, and driven by someone they knew to be exhibiting signs of intoxication. Although Mairs clearly created the initial risk, at the very least the evidence reasonably suggests defendants acquiesced in the conditions that may have helped create it and subsequently in those conditions that further endangered the victim's safety. Defendants therefore bear some relationship not only to the primary wrongdoer but to the incident itself. It is this nexus which distinguishes this case from those defined by mere presence on the scene without more, and therefore implicates policy considerations simply not pertinent to the latter.

(ii)

Even assuming no independent duty to take affirmative action, at the very least defendants were obligated, in our view, not to prevent Mairs from exercising his direct duty of care. In this regard, traditional tort theory recognizes vicarious liability for concerted tortious action. Concerted action may be either by agreement (conspiracy) or substantial assistance (aiding and abetting). These two bases of liability correspond generally to the first two subsections in the Restatement (Second) of Torts, § 876 (1979) (1979 Restatement) on "Persons Acting in Concert":

> For *harm resulting* to a third person from the *tortious conduct* of another, one is *subject to liability* if he
>
> (a) does a tortious act in concert with the other or pursuant to a common design with him [conspiracy], or
>
> (b) knows *that the other's conduct constitutes a breach of duty and gives substantial assistance or encouragement to the other so to conduct himself* [aiding-abetting], or
>
> (c) gives substantial assistance to the other in accomplishing a tortious result and his own conduct, separately considered, constitutes a breach of duty to the third person.

Thus, "aiding-abetting" focuses on whether a defendant knowingly gave "substantial assistance" to someone engaged in wrongful conduct, not on whether the defendant *agreed* to join the wrongful conduct.

Of course, how much assistance is substantial enough is fact-sensitive. The 1979 Restatement lists five factors:

> the nature of the act encouraged, the amount of assistance given by the defendant, his presence or absence at the time of the tort, his relation to the other [tortfeasor] and his state of mind[.]

Additionally, * * * [one court has] provided a sixth factor, the duration of the assistance provided.

Vicarious liability does not have to be based on *acts* of assistance but may rest on inaction, or on words of encouragement. "Advice or encouragement to act operates as a moral support to a tortfeasor and if the act encouraged is known to be tortious it has the same effect upon the liability of the adviser as participation or physical assistance." Thus, suggestive words that plant the seeds of or fuel negligent action may be enough to create joint liability. * * *

* * *

Applying the Restatement's factors to the facts * * *, we conclude a jury may reasonably find defendants' assistance was "substantial." Whether the principal wrongdoer was either impaired or entirely coherent, it is reasonable to infer that at the very least defendants collaborated in, verbally supported, or approved his decision to leave the scene, and at most actively convinced Mairs to flee as a means of not getting caught. The record reasonably admits that defendants feared apprehension. Mairs had just engaged in wrongful conduct causing injury to another under circumstances from which defendants evidently desired to disassociate. Defendants were aware of Mairs's role in the tortious activity and took affirmative steps in the immediate aftermath to conceal their involvement in the event. Indeed, Swanson supposedly told Mairs not to disclose their names and participation and Mairs complied "because he was doing what his friends told him to do." After five or ten minutes of arguing, there was agreement to depart without calling for assistance. Thereafter, Swanson directed Mairs to the nearest parkway exit and when the car broke down, defendants ran into the woods. The entire aftermath of the incident betrays an orchestrated scheme among the three to avoid detection not only by taking no action to prevent further harm to the victim, but by affirmatively abandoning the scene, practically guaranteeing his death. Whether Mairs was especially vulnerable to defendants' pleas because of a mental condition weakened by alcohol or whether he was simply encouraged by defendants' "group" mentality of escaping accountability, a jury could reasonably find * * * defendants' assistance substantial enough to justify civil liability * * * on an aiding and abetting theory.

(iii)

We formulate today no rule of general application since the question of duty remains one of judicial balancing of the mix of factors peculiar to each case. We also stress the narrowness of the issue before us. As we understand plaintiff's claim, defendants, while riding as passengers in a third person's car, are not liable to another run over by the car even though they may know or have reason to know the driver was unable to operate the vehicle in a reasonably careful and prudent manner. Rather, plaintiff's claim of actionable negligence * * * is based on [defendants'] alleged breach of a duty arising thereafter in the accident's aftermath to take emergency action to prevent further harm to the helpless victim. On this score, we mention the original danger created by third party conduct not to suggest defendants' liability therefor, but only insofar as it might have created an unreasonable risk of *further* harm to the already injured victim, of which defendants were aware and had the opportunity and ability to help prevent, and to illustrate defendants' connection to the entire episode, which, as part of a common undertaking, transcended that of the innocent bystander or uninvolved stranger who is otherwise shielded from liability for failing to summon emergency aid.

It is the degree of defendants' involvement, coupled with the serious peril threatening imminent death to another that might have been avoided with little effort and inconvenience, suggested by the evidence, that in our view creates a sufficient relation to impose a duty of action. Of course, it still remains a question of fact whether the primary wrongdoer was able to exercise reasonable care to summon emergency assistance or was prevented from doing so by defendants; whether, on the other hand, defendants knew or had reason to know that Mairs was unable or unwilling to do so, and thereafter were in a position to have influenced the outcome; whether the decision to abandon the victim was otherwise Mairs's alone or the result of encouragement, cooperation or interference from defendants; and finally, if the latter, whether the assistance was substantial enough to support a finding of liability. The facts here are certainly not such that all reasonable persons must draw the same conclusion. We cannot say that upon any version of the facts there is no duty.

Reversed and remanded.

NOTES AND QUESTIONS

1. The trial court in *Podias* found against plaintiff, holding that defendants had no duty to render emergency assistance. On what grounds did the appellate court reverse?

2. According to the court of appeals, "the common law rule imposes 'no independent duty of rescue at all' and relieves a bystander from any obligation to provide affirmative aid or emergency assistance, even if the bystander has the ability to help." Does the appellate court's decision adhere to that rule?

3. Although the *Podias* court acknowledged that there was no common law duty for a bystander to render assistance, it also recognized many scenarios in which a bystander may be liable for failing to provide assistance. What are these situations? Which, if any, applied in *Podias*?

4. The Restatement (Third) of Torts: Liability for Physical & Emotional Harm § 40 (2012) has adopted a broad scope of so-called "special relationships" that may pose an affirmative duty to render aid in some circumstances. Those special relationships include: "(1) a common carrier with its passengers; (2) an innkeeper with its guests; (3) a business or other possessor of land that holds its premises open to the public with those who are lawfully on the premises; (4) an employer with its employees who, while at work, are (a) in imminent danger, or (b) injured or ill and thereby rendered helpless; (5) a school with its students; (6) a landlord with its tenants; and (7) a custodian with those in its custody, if (a) the custodian is required by law to take custody or voluntarily takes custody of the other, and (b) the custodian has a superior ability to protect the other." This broad scope of special relationships has been the subject of criticism. *See, e.g.*, Victor Schwartz & Christopher Appel, *Reshaping the Traditional Limits of Affirmative Duties Under the Third Restatement of Torts*, 44 J. Marshall L. Rev. 319 (2011) (arguing that courts should hesitate to adopt § 40 of the Restatement 3d because that provision opens the door to unprecedented and unexpected liability). Is the Restatement justified in urging expansion of liability to ensure maximum assistance in dire circumstances?

5. In an interesting application of bystander duties, a New Jersey appellate court held in 2013 that "a person sending text messages has a duty not to text someone who is driving if the texter knows, or has special reason to know, the recipient will view the text while driving." *Kubert v. Best*, 432 N.J.

Super. 495, 507, 75 A.3d 1214, 1221 (N.J. Super. Ct. App. Div. 2013). The *Kubert* case dealt with a scenario where a fatal car crash occurred when a driver lost control of a vehicle while reading a text message. Although one might question the imposition of such a duty (on the sender of the message), the court placed a high burden in establishing that the duty is in fact created. The court reasoned that to breach such a duty, the sender must know (or have special reason to know) that the driver will read the message while driving and thereby become distracted. The court indicated that a showing of prior experiences in which the recipient responded to a text message while driving may demonstrate knowledge or special reason to know. Although the *Kubert* court held that no duty was triggered in the case because the defendant did not know whether the driver would read the message, the court does indicate a willingness to expand bystander duties in the context of cell phone technology. For a detailed discussion of the *Kubert* case, *see* Blair Keltner, *Texters Beware: Analyzing the Court's Decision in* Kubert v. Best, *75 A.3d 1214 (N.J. Super. Ct. App. Div. 2013)*, 39 S. Ill. U. L.J. 125 (2014) (concluding that, because the majority's criteria will rarely be met, the result in *Kubert* is a useless and wrongly conceived duty of care).

3. BREACH OF DUTY

Once it is determined that a "duty of care" existed at the time of the incident, the next question is whether the defendant's actions breached that duty of care. The following case discusses the inquiry involved in determining whether a duty of care was breached. The case also introduces the concept of proximate cause, which is discussed further in a later section.

RODDEY V. WAL-MART STORES EAST, LP
Court of Appeals of South Carolina, 2012
400 S.C. 59, 732 S.E.2d 635

FEW, CHIEF JUDGE.

Alice Hancock died in an automobile crash as she drove away from the Wal-Mart in Lancaster. She was being chased by Derrick Jones, an employee of U.S. Security Associates, Inc., which provided security in the Wal-Mart parking lot pursuant to a contract with Wal-Mart. Wal-Mart management had advised Jones that a passenger in Hancock's vehicle attempted to steal merchandise from the store, and they instructed him to get the vehicle's license tag number. At trial, the court directed a verdict for Wal-Mart, and the jury returned a defense verdict [for] Jones and U.S. Security. Hancock's estate appeals the decision to direct a verdict in favor of Wal-Mart. We affirm.

I. FACTS AND PROCEDURAL HISTORY

On the night of June 20, 2006, Hancock drove to Wal-Mart with her sister, Donna Beckham. Hancock entered the store with Beckham but later returned to her vehicle in the parking lot. While Hancock waited in the car, Beckham attempted to shoplift several items from the store by placing them in plastic bags. As Beckham testified at trial, "I then went and got a bag and went and put some pants into the bag[.] I shouldn't have done it."

Hope Rollings, one of the store's customer service managers, saw Beckham do this. Rollings alerted fellow manager Shaun Cox and several other employees that Beckham was attempting to steal merchandise. Rollings then walked outside to speak with Jones, who was on duty in his company truck. As Rollings and Jones spoke, Cox used a handheld radio to tell them that Beckham was headed towards one of the exits. Rollings went back inside, and Jones drove to the exit. Jones testified he asked over the radio what he should do, as he did not have the authority to detain Beckham. He was told to "try to delay her. Try to talk to her until we can get out there."

As Beckham approached the exit with the bags of merchandise, a Wal-Mart greeter asked to see her receipt. Beckham told the greeter Hancock had the receipt in the car. She testified, "I told her that my sister had it but that was a lie." Beckham then put down the bags and walked out of the store. Jones saw Beckham and spoke to her briefly. Beckham testified Jones screamed at her. Beckham began running towards Hancock's car. Jones followed her in his truck but did not physically detain her. Hancock saw Beckham, pulled out of her parking space, and drove down a lane of the parking lot towards Beckham. Jones drove into the lane, blocking Hancock's vehicle. While Hancock's car was still moving, Beckham jumped into the back seat. As Beckham later testified, she told Hancock to "get them the hell out of here." Hancock put her car in reverse, backed up at a high speed, struck a median in the parking lot, turned around, and drove towards the exit of the parking lot. Jones followed behind her.

As these events unfolded, Cox walked to the main entrance of the store and radioed to Jones, "Get her tag number." According to Jones, he received instructions over the radio from Cox and Rollings to get the license tag information from Hancock's vehicle. Jones testified, "And I'm on the walkie-talkie, telling them, I can't see this license plate tag number, and they're about to leave the parking lot." A Wal-Mart employee replied, "Man, well, you got to do what you got to do. You need to get that license plate number." These instructions by Wal-Mart personnel violated Wal-Mart's policy for investigating and detaining suspected shoplifters, which provided:

> NEVER pursue a fleeing Suspect more than approximately 10 feet beyond the point you are located when the Suspect begins to run to avoid detention. Ten feet is about three long steps. This limitation applies both inside and outside the facility.

> NEVER pursue a Suspect who is in a moving vehicle.

NEVER pursue a Suspect off the Facility's property.

NEVER use a moving vehicle to pursue a Suspect.

TERMINATE the pursuit of a Suspect, if the Suspect begins to enter a vehicle.

LET THE SUSPECT GO, rather than continue a pursuit that is likely to injure or cause harm to someone.

As Hancock left the parking lot and drove onto a highway, she ran a stop sign and a stop light, nearly getting into an accident. In violation of his training and U.S. Security policy, Jones left the parking lot and pursued Hancock and Beckham onto the highway. According to Jones, Hancock drove up an onramp, "almost slamm[ing] into the back of another lady's car" and missing it by swerving to the left. Jones testified he lost Hancock and Beckham at that point, and he did not find them again until he saw her vehicle's hazard lights flashing off of the side of the road. However, Beckham testified Jones stayed close behind them. Crouching in the back seat, she periodically looked up over the seat and saw Jones driving "on [their] bumper" and flashing the high-beams on his truck. After about two miles, Hancock told Beckham "he's still on our ass," and then Beckham heard and felt a bump. Hancock's car left the road and crashed. Hancock died at the scene.

Travis Roddey, the personal representative of Hancock's estate, sued Wal-Mart, U.S. Security, and Jones for negligence. At trial, the court granted Wal-Mart's motion for a directed verdict. The jury found Hancock was 65% at fault and U.S. Security and Jones were 35% at fault.* Roddey filed a motion * * * seeking a new trial as to all defendants on the basis that the court erred in directing a verdict for Wal-Mart. The court denied the motion.

II.   How the Panel Votes to Affirm

Wal-Mart asserted three grounds for its directed verdict motion: (1) Roddey presented no evidence Wal-Mart breached its duty of care; (2) Wal-Mart's actions were not the proximate cause of Hancock's death as a matter of law because Jones's and Hancock's actions were not foreseeable; and (3) Hancock's fault in causing her own death was more than 50% as a matter of law. The trial court granted the motion on the first two grounds, stating "I . . . find that there is insufficient evidence that Wal-Mart was negligent, or even if [it was] there is a lack of proximate cause [in] that the events were not foreseeable." As to the third ground, the court stated it was "[un]able to find as a matter of law that Hancock was more than 50 percent [at fault]."

---

* The legal doctrine of comparing the negligence of the defendant with that of the plaintiff is examined in detail in a later section of this chapter on comparative and contributory negligence. Under South Carolina law, if a plaintiff is more than 50 percent at fault, then the plaintiff is not entitled to recover. [Ed.]

Judge Huff and I believe the trial court erred in finding there was insufficient evidence of Wal-Mart's negligence and in finding Jones's and Hancock's actions were not foreseeable. However, I vote to affirm because I believe Hancock was more than 50% at fault. As Judge Short explains in his concurring opinion, he votes to affirm because he believes the trial court correctly found no proximate cause as a matter of law. As Judge Huff explains in his dissent, he would reverse and remand for a new trial as to Wal-Mart.

III. Evidence of Wal-Mart's Negligence

Cox and Rollings's instructions that Jones get the tag number of Hancock's vehicle, including the command "do what you got to do," violated the Wal-Mart policy designed to prevent injuries and deaths caused by fleeing suspects. A defendant's violation of its own safety policies is some evidence of negligence. Therefore, the trial court should not have directed a verdict on the basis that there was insufficient evidence of negligence.

IV. Foreseeability of Hancock's Actions

The purpose of Wal-Mart's policy is to prevent injury or death resulting from negligent or reckless driving in pursuit of a suspect. * * * Therefore, the danger that a fleeing suspect or the security officer chasing her might drive negligently or recklessly and injure the suspect or someone else is not simply foreseeable—it is the very reason Wal-Mart adopted the policy in the first place. I disagree that Jones's and Hancock's actions were not foreseeable to Wal-Mart.

V. Hancock's Fault

There are two reasons this court should hold that Hancock was more than 50% at fault and on that basis affirm the directed verdict in favor of Wal-Mart. First, the jury's factual determination of how fault should be apportioned between Hancock, Jones, and U.S. Security is binding on Roddey even though Wal-Mart's actions were not included in the jury's analysis. Second, the trial court should have directed a verdict for Wal-Mart on the ground that Hancock was more than 50% at fault as a matter of law.

a. Effect of the Jury's Apportionment of Fault

In his post-trial motion, Roddey stated his theory of the case is that the "car accident was due less to the decedent's actions and more to (1) Wal-Mart's decision to encourage Derrick Jones to chase the decedent by vehicle, and (2) Jones's actions during the chase—flashing his lights and driving on the decedent's bumper." The specific allegations in Roddey's complaint were that Wal-Mart was liable in three ways: (1) it was vicariously liable for Jones's actions; (2) it failed to properly supervise Jones; and (3) it "improperly advised or instructed" Jones to follow Hancock and obtain her license tag information. None of these allegations can possibly result in liability against Wal-Mart, now that the jury has found Hancock to be 65% at fault in the accident.

With respect to the first allegation, Roddey claims Jones was Wal-Mart's agent, and therefore Wal-Mart is vicariously liable for his conduct. Roddey's right to recover from Wal-Mart under this claim depends entirely on whether Jones was liable. In other words, because Wal-Mart's liability is derivative of Jones's liability, the jury's finding that Jones was only 35% at fault forecloses the liability of Wal-Mart.

Roddey's other two allegations involve acts and omissions by Wal-Mart. Roddey argues that because the jury apportioned fault only between Hancock, Jones, and U.S. Security, Wal-Mart's conduct, if considered by the jury, could have reduced Hancock's proportion of fault to the point that her negligence was not greater than that of all the defendants. In many cases involving multiple tortfeasors, the negligence of a tortfeasor absent from the case could affect the relative fault of the plaintiff. In this case, however, Wal-Mart's conduct cannot reduce Hancock's proportion of fault.

The jury's comparison of fault necessarily involved an examination of the actions taken by the two participants in the chase—Hancock and Jones—and a determination of how their actions contributed to Hancock's death. Evidence was presented that Hancock drove through the parking lot towards Beckham as she ran from the store, did not stop the car as Beckham jumped into it, backed up in the parking lot at a high rate of speed, hit a concrete median, ran a stop sign and a stop light as she turned onto a public highway, swerved through traffic, and narrowly avoided two collisions with other cars. There was also evidence that Jones blocked Hancock's car, pursued her through the parking lot, left his assigned area, followed Hancock's car onto the highway, drove "on [the] bumper" of Hancock's car on the highway, flashed his headlights, and possibly made contact with Hancock's car. Whatever Jones's and Hancock's motivation may have been for taking those actions, it was the actions themselves that proximately caused the crash that killed Hancock. The jury already considered all of those actions, and it determined Hancock's actions made her 65% at fault.

Even under Roddey's theory of the case, Wal-Mart's conduct merely provides some explanation of what motivated Jones's actions. Wal-Mart's negligence could affect how much of the remaining 35% of fault is attributable to Jones, for if Jones was motivated by Wal-Mart's improper actions, arguably he would bear less of the fault for Hancock's death. However, Wal-Mart's actions can have no effect on Hancock's fault. Wal-Mart obviously did not advise or instruct Hancock to flee, nor did it enable her actions by failing to adequately supervise her. There is no evidence in the record that Hancock knew anything about what Wal-Mart told Jones. Therefore, Wal-Mart's alleged conduct could not have reduced Hancock's proportion of fault in the way it could have reduced that of Jones. Even if the jury had been permitted to consider Wal-Mart in its apportionment of fault, Wal-Mart's conduct could not have affected the jury's determination that Hancock was 65% at fault.

Because Wal-Mart's conduct could not have reduced Hancock's fault, Roddey is bound by the jury's finding that she was 65% at fault, and the trial court's decision to grant Wal-Mart a directed verdict could not have prejudiced Roddey. Therefore, I believe we must affirm.

b. Hancock's Fault as a Matter of Law

I would also affirm on the basis that no reasonable jury could have concluded Hancock was 50% or less at fault. Beckham testified Hancock "had no idea I was going in there to steal." However, the evidence is overwhelming that once Beckham "jumped" into the back seat of Hancock's moving car, Hancock was aware that she was fleeing a crime scene. Rather than testifying Hancock did not know they were fleeing the Wal-Mart, Beckham testified she commanded Hancock to "get them the hell out of here." Viewing all the evidence in the light most favorable to Roddey, no reasonable jury could have concluded Hancock's fault was not greater than the fault of the defendants, even including Wal-Mart. * * *

VI. Conclusion

The trial court's decision to direct a verdict in favor of Wal-Mart is affirmed.

SHORT, JUDGE, concurring in a separate opinion.

I agree the trial court's order should be affirmed. I write separately because I would decline to rule on whether Wal-Mart breached its duty to Hancock and whether Hancock was more than 50% at fault. Rather, I affirm because even when viewing the evidence in the light most favorable to Roddey, I find Wal-Mart was entitled to a directed verdict on the proximate cause element of Roddey's negligence action based on the unforeseeability of Jones's actions. * * *

* * *

* * * I conclude Roddey failed to establish legal cause sufficient to submit the question to the jury. "Proximate cause requires proof of both causation in fact and legal cause." "Legal cause is proved by establishing foreseeability." The test of foreseeability is whether the injury is the natural and probable consequence of the alleged negligent act. "Where the injury complained of is not reasonably foreseeable there is no liability." Where intervening acts occur, the original wrongdoer may be liable despite intervening acts if the intervening acts are foreseeable, or if not foreseeable, if the original wrongdoer's acts " 'would have caused the loss in natural course.' "

* * * [I]t was not foreseeable to Wal-Mart that Jones would leave the parking lot and continue pursuit for several miles while flashing his high-beams and aggressively following Hancock as she ran a stop sign and a stop light and drove onto a highway. I would affirm the trial court's finding that Wal-Mart was entitled to directed verdict based on the lack of foreseeability of Jones's actions.

HUFF, JUDGE, dissenting.

I respectfully dissent. While I agree with Chief Judge Few that there is evidence of Wal-Mart's negligence in this matter that was foreseeable, I do not agree that the jury's finding that Hancock was 65% negligent renders Hancock 65% negligent as a matter of law, and that this jury finding is binding on Roddey as to his cause of action against Wal-Mart, considering that Wal-Mart's negligence was not factored into the jury's determination. Further, I disagree with Judge Short's determination that Wal-Mart was entitled to a directed verdict because there was no proximate cause as a matter of law. Accordingly, I would reverse and remand for a new trial against Wal-Mart.

* * *

ANALYSIS

NEGLIGENCE AND PROXIMATE CAUSE

As to Judge Short's concurring opinion, I believe the issues of Wal-Mart's negligence and proximate cause should have been submitted to the jury. * * *

* * *

1. Negligence

* * *

* * * [V]iewed in the light most favorable to Roddey, there is evidence from which the jury could determine that Wal-Mart employees violated their own policies * * *. While a jury could very well conclude, based upon the evidence presented, that Wal-Mart employees merely requested Jones speak with Beckham and simply made a singular request for Jones to obtain the tag number of Hancock's vehicle while he was safely in a position to do so, and these actions were permitted by Wal-Mart's guidelines and policies, there was evidence presented from which a jury could also reasonably conclude Wal-Mart was negligent in deviating from its guidelines and policies in this instance. * * * [T]here is evidence from which a jury could reasonably conclude that Wal-Mart employees directed Jones, on more than one occasion, to obtain Hancock's tag number, that they did so while observing Jones pursue Beckham and Hancock in his patrol vehicle, and they observed the reckless driving of Hancock and Jones in the parking lot, *yet they continued to instruct Jones to obtain the tag number* *after Jones warned, not just that the women were leaving the parking lot, but that he and the women were leaving the parking lot.* Thus, there is evidence from which a jury could reasonably conclude that Wal-Mart employees acquiesced in, and possibly instructed, Jones's improper pursuit of the women in violation of the Private Security Contractors guidelines. Additionally, * * * there is evidence from which a jury could find Wal-Mart employees instructed Jones to do something their policy strictly prohibited the employees themselves from doing. Accordingly, there is sufficient evidence of Wal-Mart's negligence such that the matter was a question for the jury.

2.   Proximate Cause

* * *

* * * [T]here was evidence presented that, despite Wal-Mart's knowledge of the aggressive and reckless driving manners of Hancock and Jones and in spite of being advised both vehicles were leaving the property, Wal-Mart continued to instruct Jones to obtain the tag number. Notably, Roddey's expert witness in the area of pursuit, [Jeffrey] Albert, testified concerning the effects of vehicular pursuit on those being pursued, and specifically opined that had Jones stayed in the parking lot and not pursued Hancock's vehicle, it was highly unlikely the crash would have taken place. Thus, there is evidence that "but for" these actions by Wal-Mart, the accident would not have occurred.

With respect to foreseeability, there was evidence presented that the accident was a foreseeable consequence of Wal-Mart's instructions to Jones, which were in violation of Wal-Mart's established policies and guidelines, such that the matter should have been submitted to the jury. * * *

Additionally, I do not believe, considered in a light most favorable to Roddey, that as a matter of law Jones's actions were independent intervening acts which could not have been foreseen by Wal-Mart, or that Wal-Mart's acts were only a remote cause that did nothing more than furnish the condition or give rise to the occasion by which the injury was made possible * * *.

JURY FINDING AS TO HANCOCK'S NEGLIGENCE

As to Chief Judge Few's majority opinion, I do not believe that Wal-Mart's liability in this matter is strictly derivative of Jones's and/or USSA's liability such that the jury's finding that Jones was only 35% at fault foreclosed any additional liability on the part of Wal-Mart. * * * [W]hile a jury could very well find Hancock was still 65% negligent after considering Wal-Mart's potential liability, it could conceivably find, after factoring in any negligence by Wal-Mart, that Hancock was less than 50% at fault. I believe this is a question for the jury * * *. Accordingly, I would reverse the directed verdict in favor of Wal-Mart and remand for a new trial as to Wal-Mart alone.

NOTES AND QUESTIONS

1.   Wal-Mart was the obvious target of the Hancock estate, given its enormous assets to pay a judgment. Such a defendant is sometimes referred to as a "deep pocket" defendant. Given the various participants in the events that culminated in Hancock's death, was Wal-Mart more or less culpable that the others who were involved?

2.   This case illustrates that even a relatively simple fact pattern can lead to a variety of views by appellate court judges. What was the rationale of Chief Judge Few? To what extent did Judge Huff agree with that rationale? What was the rationale of Judge Short? On what grounds did Judge Huff dissent? Which opinion is most persuasive and why?

3.   The case addresses not only breach of duty but also proximate cause. Proximate cause is addressed further later in this chapter.

4.   The determination of negligence depends on the specific facts of the case. For example, with respect to the standard of care that an actor owes to another (assuming a duty is established), the Restatement (Second) of Torts § 283 (1965) states: "[T]he standard of conduct to which [an actor] must conform to avoid being negligent is that of a reasonable man under like circumstances." Although the Restatement's standard aims to assess every situation through the eyes of a "reasonable person," is that standard fair in every situation? Some commentators contend that it is not. *See, e.g.*, Charles Korsmo, *Lost in Translation: Law, Economics, and Subjective Standards of Care in Negligence Law*, 118 Penn St. L. Rev. 285, 336 (2013) (discussing anomalies that arise in applying the reasonable person test to "unusually skilled" or "unusually unskilled" people). A number of courts hold that if an actor has special skills or knowledge, those skills or knowledge must be taken into account in determining whether the actor has behaved as a reasonably careful person under the circumstances. For example, in *Levi v. Southwest Louisiana Electric Membership Co-op.*, 542 So.2d 1081 (La. 1989), the Louisiana Supreme Court reasoned that an electric company should have used its superior knowledge, skill, and experience in electrical safety to reduce the hazards caused by a hanging high-voltage power line. In this situation, a "reasonable person" is one with the same knowledge and skills as the defendant.

Issues also arise when the defendant is a minor. In that situation, courts are generally willing to assess the "reasonable person" standard from the standpoint of a reasonably careful minor of the same age and experience. *See, e.g., Bragan ex rel. Bragan v. Symanzik*, 263 Mich. App. 324, 328, 687 N.W.2d 881, 884 (2004) ("Minors are required only to exercise 'that degree of care which a *reasonably careful minor* of the age, mental capacity and experience' of other similarly situated minors would exercise under the circumstances."). It is important to note, however, that if a minor is engaged in a "high-risk activity," many courts hold that the minor's age and inferior experience should *not* be considered in the reasonableness analysis. For example, in *Stevens v. Veenstra*, 226 Mich. App. 441, 573 N.W.2d 341 (1997), the Michigan Court of Appeals held that a 14-year-old student driver who was involved in an accident during his first driver's education lesson should be held to the same standard as an experienced driver. As the court reasoned: "[S]ome activities are so dangerous that risk must be borne by [the] beginner rather than the innocent victims, and lack of competence is no excuse." *Id.* at 446. Is this treatment of student drivers fair? Is it sensible to distinguish between routine activities and "high-risk activities" when dealing with defendants who are minors?

5.   In *United States v. Carroll Towing Co.*, 159 F.2d 169 (2d Cir. 1947), a famous American jurist, Judge Learned Hand, articulated a simple test for determining whether a defendant's conduct should be considered a breach of the standard of care. Under Judge Hand's formulation, where B is the burden or precaution that one must undertake to avoid harm, P is the probability that harm will occur, and L is the magnitude of the potential harm (or loss), the precaution should be undertaken if the following is true:

$$B < PL$$

Under this formula, if there is a high probability (P) of a large harm (L), then a great burden (B) should be undertaken to prevent such an incident. On the other hand, if there is only a small probability of a small loss, then a lesser burden is acceptable. If the defendant fails to satisfy the burden of precaution that is appropriate in the case, then a breach may be found. The Learned Hand formula, while not embodied in formal statutory law, has become a common formula among law students and practicing attorneys to address whether a jury or a court may find a breach. Lawyers frequently explain the "B < PL" formula to the jury during arguments at trial. For a discussion and application of the Learned Hand formula for breach, *see, e.g.*, Eric Johnson, *Negligence's X Factor*, 2012 Cardozo L. Rev. de novo 318, *available at* http://www.cardozolaw review.com/content/denovo/johnson_2012_318.pdf. The "B < PL" formula is sometimes used by appellate courts in discussing the issue of breach. *See, e.g.*, *Bodin v. City of Stanwood*, 130 Wash.2d 726, 927 P.2d 240 (1996) (both majority and dissenting opinions note that the B < PL analysis is often part of a court's determination of breach).

6.   In some situations where an actor's conduct constitutes a violation of law, "breach" of the standard of care may be presumed as a matter of law. That concept is known as negligence *per se*. Generally, the determination of negligence *per se* involves a two-part test: "An actor is negligent if, without excuse, the actor violates a statute that is designed to protect against the type of accident the actor's conduct causes, and if the accident victim is within the class of persons the statute is designed to protect." Restatement (Third) of Torts: Liability for Physical & Emotional Harm § 14 (2012). For example, if a driver violates a traffic law by failing to yield to a pedestrian in a crosswalk and strikes the pedestrian, the driver will be considered negligent *per se* because the driver broke a traffic law that was designed to protect against the precise kind of harm that occurred (*i.e.*, a vehicle hitting a pedestrian). *See,*

e.g., Jenkins v. Wolf, 911 A.2d 568 (Pa. Super. Ct. 2006) (plaintiff was entitled to a negligence *per se* instruction when she was walking in a crosswalk and the driver failed to yield and struck her).

4. EMERGENCY DOCTRINE

The reasonable person standard in determining breach provides for broad flexibility depending on the circumstances. Courts have recognized that an act taken in an emergency situation should be given more protection from tort liability than one taken in a non-emergency situation. The following case arises in the context of an emergency.

TARNAVSKA V. MANHATTAN & BRONX SURFACE TRANSIT OPERATING AUTHORITY

Supreme Court, Appellate Division, Second Department New York, 2013
966 N.Y.S.2d 171, 106 A.D.3d 1079

[All judges concurred in an unassigned opinion.]

In an action to recover damages for personal injuries, the plaintiff appeals from an order of the Supreme Court [trial court], Kings County * * * which granted the defendants' motion for summary judgment dismissing the complaint.

* * *

The plaintiff allegedly sustained injuries when she was thrown to the floor after the bus in which she was riding stopped short to avoid a collision with a vehicle that, without signaling, had suddenly cut in front of it to make a left turn.

The "emergency doctrine holds that those faced with a sudden and unexpected circumstance, not of their own making, that leaves them with little or no time for reflection or reasonably causes them to be so disturbed that they are compelled to make a quick decision without weighing alternative courses of conduct, may not be negligent if their actions are reasonable and prudent in the context of the emergency."

Here, the defendants established their prima facie entitlement to judgment as a matter of law by submitting evidence demonstrating that the defendant bus driver was confronted with a sudden and unexpected circumstance not of her own making and that, under the circumstances, her actions were reasonable and prudent in response to the emergency. In opposition, the plaintiff's speculative and conclusory assertions failed to raise a triable issue of fact.

Accordingly, the [trial court] properly granted the defendants' motion for summary judgment dismissing the complaint.

NOTES AND QUESTIONS

1.   What is the emergency doctrine? What is the rationale of the doctrine? Did the *Tarnavska* court correctly apply the doctrine here?

2.   The emergency doctrine gives a defendant a possible way to shield itself from liability for negligence. Indeed, some courts hold that the emergency doctrine may preclude or lessen liability even in cases of negligence *per se*. *See, e.g., Totsky v. Riteway Bus Serv., Inc.*, 233 Wis. 2d 371, 607 N.W.2d 637 (2000) (relying on the emergency doctrine to excuse a bus driver's negligence *per se* for failing to stop at a stop sign because of an icy road). *But see* Robert Blomquist, *The Trouble with Negligence Per Se*, 61 S.C. L. Rev. 221, 259 (2009) (criticizing *Totsky* on the ground that "it seems to warp the concept of an excused emergency to allow a motorist to avoid civil liability for violating a statute simply because the road at the intersection was icy").

3.   It is important to note that the emergency doctrine is not a complete defense for defendants in every scenario. As the Supreme Court of Kentucky stated in *Regenstreif v. Phelps*, 142 S.W.3d 1, 4 (Ky. 2004): "The sudden emergency doctrine does not excuse fault; it defines the conduct to be expected of a prudent person in an emergency situation." Thus, a person will not be relieved of all consequences of his actions simply because an emergency existed; instead, a court will recognize that reasonable people will act with less care during an emergency and will impose a lower standard of what was "reasonable" in the situation.

4.   For additional applications of the emergency doctrine, *see, e.g., Ferrer v. Harris*, 55 N.Y.2d 285, 434 N.E.2d 231 (1982) (holding that the emergency doctrine lowered the applicable standard of care when a four-year-old unexpectedly ran in front of the defendant's vehicle from between two parked cars); *Lockhart v. List*, 542 Pa. 141, 665 A.2d 1176 (1995) (holding that the emergency doctrine lowered the applicable standard of care when a driver went around a curve on the highway and struck a garbage truck that was unexpectedly parked diagonally across her lane of travel).

5.   PROXIMATE CAUSE/FORESEEABILITY

Even if a defendant (1) owes a duty of care, and (2) breaches that duty of care, the court or jury must also determine whether that the defendant's breach of the duty was the "proximate cause" of the plaintiff's injury (*i.e.*, whether plaintiff's injury was caused by the defendant's breach and whether the injury was a foreseeable consequence of the defendant's breach). Those issues were touched upon in *Roddey v. Wal-Mart Stores East, LP*, and are discussed further in the following case.

LUCERO V. HOLBROOK

Supreme Court of Wyoming, 2012
2012 WY 152, 288 P.3d 1228

VOIGT, JUSTICE.

Nanette Holbrook, the appellee, left her car unattended with the motor running in her private driveway while she briefly returned to her home to retrieve her pocketbook. In the interim, Colbey Emms (Emms), a methamphetamine user, stole her vehicle. Emms later got into a high-speed chase with the police, which ended when the car he was driving collided with a vehicle driven by Katrina Lucero (Lucero), one of the appellants, and mother of EL and IL, also appellants. Lucero filed a complaint on behalf of herself and her children alleging that the appellee breached a duty to them of due care by leaving her car unattended with the keys in the ignition. The district court granted the appellee's motion for summary judgment on the basis that no duty was owed to the appellants * * * and that the appellee's leaving of her keys in her car with the motor running was not the proximate cause of the accident. We affirm.

* * *

FACTS

On the morning of December 18, 2009, the appellee got into her car, started the engine, and pulled the car out of her garage and onto her driveway as she was preparing to leave her home to go to work. She soon realized that she had forgotten her purse and returned to her home to retrieve it, leaving the car doors unlocked and engine running. Within approximately three minutes, the appellee returned to the driveway only to find the car missing. She quickly returned to the house and called 911 to report that her car had been stolen.

The appellee testified that she did not see anyone suspicious in the vicinity of her driveway at the time that she had returned to the house. Nevertheless, Emms stole her vehicle during the appellee's brief absence. The police located Emms driving the stolen vehicle and made contact with Emms who then attempted to flee. This evolved into a high-speed chase. The chase ended soon after Emms collided with Lucero, who was driving with her two children, ages six months and five years, to her mother's house. Lucero and her children suffered serious injuries. Emms was under the influence of methamphetamine at the time of the accident.

The appellants filed a complaint in district court alleging that the appellee, by leaving the keys in the ignition of her unattended vehicle, was negligent and that such negligence was the proximate cause of the injuries incurred by the appellants. In response, the appellee filed a motion for summary judgment which the district court granted * * *.

* * *

DISCUSSION

Negligence occurs when one fails to act as would a reasonable person of ordinary prudence under like circumstances. More specifically, to establish negligence, the following must be shown:

> (1) The defendant owed the plaintiff a duty to conform to a specified standard of care, (2) the defendant breached the duty of care, (3) the defendant's breach of the duty of care proximately caused injury to the plaintiff, and (4) the injury sustained by the plaintiff is compensable by money damages.

Duty and breach of duty must be established before addressing causation and the tortfeasor's responsibility for any harm suffered. "Elements (1) and (2), duty and breach of duty, address whether the conduct of the alleged tortfeasor was in fact negligent. Element (3), proximate cause, is considered only after negligence is first established to determine whether the tortfeasor should be legally responsible for his negligence." Proximate cause addresses the scope of a defendant's liability and is a question of fact for the factfinder, and less appropriate for a summary judgment action.

[The court first held that Holbrook owed no duty to Lucero and her children under the circumstances of the case.]

* * *

* * * [E]ven if we recognized the existence of a duty, there simply is no proximate cause connection between the acts of the appellee and the harm to the appellants.

> In order for proximate cause to exist, "the accident or injury must be the natural and probable consequence of the act of negligence." In fact, "[t]he ultimate test of proximate cause is foreseeability of injury. In order to qualify as a legal cause, the conduct must be a substantial factor in bringing about the plaintiff's injuries."

* * *

* * * [I]f the conduct is "that cause which in natural and continuous sequence, unbroken by a sufficient intervening cause produces the injury, without which the result would not have occurred," it must be identified as a substantial factor in bringing about the harm. If, however, it created only a condition or occasion for the harm to occur then it would be regarded as a remote, not a proximate, cause, and would not be a substantial factor in bringing about the harm. * * *

* * *

The appellants argue that the appellee easily could have removed her keys from the ignition before returning to her house and that imposing a duty on the appellee to that extent would not impose a substantial burden.

The burden that this factor addresses is not, however, the effortlessness in removing the keys, but rather the burden that will result from imposing a duty not to leave the motor running temporarily in a vehicle parked in one's driveway. It must be remembered that the imposition of a duty not to leave the motor running in a vehicle in one's driveway would apply across the board, and would create potential liability for every person in Wyoming who, on a cold winter day, starts his or her car to warm it up and defrost the windshield before driving upon the public highways.

* * *

Our task here is to determine whether the interest of the appellants who have "suffered invasion [were] entitled to legal protection at the hands of the" appellee. We conclude that, under the facts presented * * *, the acts of the appellee were not the proximate cause of the appellants' harm. The district court properly granted summary judgment.

* * *

NOTES AND QUESTIONS

1.   What was the proximate cause issue in *Lucero*? How did the Wyoming Supreme Court rule?

2.   What arguments can be made against the *Lucero* court's ruling on proximate cause?

3.   A proximate causation analysis is broken down into two distinct parts: "cause-in-fact" and "legal cause." *See, e.g.*, Amelia Buragas, *Proximate Cause: Limiting Liability Along the Chain of Causation*, 102 Ill. B.J. 88 (2014) (explaining the difference between cause-in-fact and legal cause, and noting that cause-in-fact focuses on whether the defendant actually caused an injury, while legal cause focuses on foreseeability). Foreseeability is often the main issue in a negligence case—*i.e.*, is the injury "a type that a reasonable person would see as the likely result of his or her conduct[?]"*Id.* at 89.

4.   It is important to note that the "eggshell skull" doctrine, discussed in the assault and battery section, applies with equal force in negligence actions. If the *type* of injury was foreseeable as a result of the defendant's negligent conduct, the defendant may be liable for the full extent of that injury under the eggshell skull doctrine. For example, if it was foreseeable that someone might hit his or her head (a type of injury) on a negligently repaired awning, the defendant may be liable for the full extent of the injury (*e.g.*, even severe head injuries caused by a rare medical condition). Proximate cause assesses the foreseeability of the *type* of injury suffered; the eggshell skull doctrine makes the defendant fully liable for the full *extent* of a foreseeable type of injury.

5.   A landmark case involving proximate cause is *Palsgraf v. Long Island Railroad Co.*, 248 N.Y. 339, 162 N.E. 99 (1928). As Judge Cardozo summarized the *Palsgraf* facts:

Plaintiff was standing on a platform of defendant's railroad after buying a ticket to go to Rockaway Beach. A train stopped at the station, bound for another place. Two men ran forward to catch it. One of the men reached the platform of the car without mishap, though the train was already moving. The other man, carrying a package, jumped aboard the car, but seemed unsteady as if about to fall. A guard on the car, who had held the door open, reached forward to help him in, and another guard on the platform pushed him from behind. In this act, the package was dislodged, and fell upon the rails. It was a package of small size, about fifteen inches long, and was covered by a newspaper. In fact it contained fireworks, but there was nothing in its appearance to give notice of its contents. The fireworks when they fell exploded. The shock of the explosion threw down some scales at the other end of the platform many feet away. The scales struck the plaintiff, causing injuries * * *. *Id.* at 340–41, 162 N.E. at 99.

The court held that the plaintiff could not recover from the railroad for her injuries because "there was nothing in the situation to suggest to the most cautious mind that the parcel wrapped in newspaper would spread wreckage through the station." *Id.* at 345, 162 N.E. at 101. Because of the unusual circumstances of the case—and the fact that the decision was written by one of the most respected jurists in U.S. history (who later served on the U.S. Supreme Court)—*Palsgraf* is widely studied in U.S. law schools. Not surprisingly, it has also been the subject of extensive scholarly analysis. *Compare, e.g.*, Joseph Little, Palsgraf *Revisited (Again)*, 6 Pierce L. Rev. 75 (2007) (defending *Palsgraf*'s approach and arguing that, while the standard the court adopted is based on judicial discretion, the approach is effective because it allows precise tailoring based on the facts of each case), *with* William Prosser, Palsgraf *Revisited*, 52 Mich. L. Rev. 1 (1953) (expressing concern about the vague and unpredictable test articulated by *Palsgraf*).

6. Cases raising proximate cause issues often involve unusual facts. For example, in *Leavitt v. Brockton Hosp., Inc.*, 454 Mass. 37, 907 N.E.2d 213 (2009), a third party struck the patrol car of the plaintiff, a police officer, when the officer was responding to the scene of a separate accident, causing the officer to suffer permanent physical injuries. In the separate accident, a hospital patient had been struck by a vehicle while he was walking home from a procedure at the hospital. The officer alleged that the hospital breached a duty by not escorting the patient home (as was apparently hospital protocol) and that the hospital's actions led to his own injuries that he suffered while responding to that accident. The court held, *inter alia*, that the hospital was not liable because the officer's injuries fell outside the scope of the hospital's foreseeable risk. In *Hale v. Brown*, 287 Kan. 320, 197 P.3d 438 (2007), a motorist's automobile was rear-ended while she was waiting in traffic for a single-car accident to be cleared. The motorist sued the driver involved in the single-car accident (and the driver's employer) for negligence. The trial court granted defendants' motion to dismiss and held—in a decision affirmed by the Kansas Supreme Court—that it was not foreseeable that someone would be

injured 35 minutes later by the negligence of a third driver distracted by the commotion. In *Mellen v. Lane*, 377 S.C. 261, 659 S.E.2d 236 (S.C. Ct. App. 2008), the defendant "shoved" the plaintiff in the back during a verbal confrontation at a bar. The shove led to a large fight at the bar, and during that fight someone other than the defendant struck the plaintiff in the head with a bottle, causing him injuries. The court held that the shove in the back was the proximate cause of the plaintiff's injury from the bottle because the larger fight and subsequent injury could have been reasonably foreseen by the defendant. As these cases demonstrate, proximate cause cases are very fact-specific.

6. DEFENSE TO NEGLIGENCE: COMPARATIVE FAULT AND CONTRIBUTORY NEGLIGENCE

If a plaintiff establishes a defendant's negligence, the question often arises whether the plaintiff was negligent as well. If the defendant can show that the plaintiff's own negligence contributed to the harm, the defendant may have a partial or complete defense to liability. This defense is known either as "contributory negligence" or "comparative negligence" depending on the jurisdiction. The following cases discuss this defense.

VICK V. PANKEY

Court of Appeal of Louisiana, 2009
15 So.3d 1199

STEWART, JUDGE.

Defendant/Appellant, Barry J. Pankey, is appealing a judgment rendered in favor of Plaintiffs/Appellees, Alan S. Vick and Amy Vick. For the reasons stated herein, we affirm the trial court's judgment.

FACTS

On August 18, 2004, both parties attended a mud track automobile race at the Calhoun Mud Bowl in Calhoun, Louisiana. A physical altercation ensued between Barry Pankey, his brother Terry Pankey, and Mr. Vick. Mr. Vick alleges that he was attacked without provocation, while Barry and Terry Pankey contend that Mr. Vick was intoxicated and provoked the fight. The Pankey brothers contend that Mr. Vick threw the first punch at Terry Pankey. Because Mr. Vick initiated the fight, Barry Pankey argues that he was acting in self-defense as to any role he may have had in this incident.

As a result of the altercation, Mr. Vick sustained several injuries, including multiple shattered facial bones requiring six titanium plates and 27 screws to be surgically installed in his face, as well as broken orbital bones, a broken nose and a broken palate. He also was rendered blind for two weeks after the accident. His mouth was wired for months and he could not eat solid foods for over six weeks. Mr. Vick testified that he incurred approximately $46,000.00 in medical expenses related to the treatment of the injuries he sustained from the altercation. Further, he was unable to work [for several weeks].

After reviewing a video recording of the altercation, the trial court ruled in favor of the Vicks. According to the trial court, the video showed Terry Pankey attempting to punch Mr. Vick. Then, Barry Pankey punched Mr. Vick in the face with his fists. Mr. Vick was "backing up" or "retreating" the entire time. The trial court found that the video clearly showed Mr. Vick attempting a "defensive effort" as best he could. When Mr. Vick fell to the ground, Barry Pankey continued to batter him. The trial court determined that "insults and intoxication alone provide no legal escape from liability caused by a beating such as this." Even if Mr. Vick was the physical aggressor, the degree of force used by the Pankey brothers to repel any such aggression was totally out of proportion to what was necessary to stop Mr. Vick. The Pankey brothers' actions were excessive.

The Vicks were awarded $44,918.40 in medical expenses, $6,300.00 in lost wages, $250,000.00 in general damages, and $6,000.00 in loss of consortium to Mrs. Vick. * * * Barry Pankey now appeals.

LAW AND DISCUSSION

Comparative Fault

* * * Pankey alleges that the trial court erroneously ignored the intentional acts of the plaintiff and failed to reduce the amount of damages accordingly.

* * *

The factors to be considered by the courts in determining the percentages of fault are the nature of the conduct of each party at fault and the extent of the causal relation between the conduct and the damages. In assessing the nature of the conduct of the parties, various factors may influence the degree of fault assigned, including: (1) whether the conduct resulted from inadvertence or involved an awareness of danger, (2) how great a risk was created by the conduct, (3) the significance of what was sought by the conduct, (4) the capacities of the actor, whether superior or inferior, and (5) any extenuating circumstances which might require the actor to proceed in haste, without proper thought.

Nonetheless, Louisiana's aggressor doctrine precludes tort recovery where the plaintiff acts in such a way as to provoke a reasonable person to use physical force in fear or anticipation of further injury at the hand of the aggressor plaintiff, unless the person retaliating has used excessive force to repel the aggression.

The issues of which party was the aggressor and whether excessive force was used in repelling the attack are questions of fact that must be determined from the peculiar facts and circumstances of each case. * * *

Various factors relied upon by the courts to determine the reasonableness of the actions of the party being attacked are the character and reputation of the attacker, the belligerence of the attacker, a large difference in size and strength between the parties, an overt act by the attacker, threats of serious bodily harm, and the impossibility of a peaceful retreat.

The video shows Terry Pankey, at the very least, attempting to punch Mr. Vick. Then, Barry Pankey punched Mr. Vick several times in the face. Mr. Vick is backing away from Barry Pankey the entire time. Even when Mr. Vick fell to the ground, Barry Pankey continued to punch him.

Barry Pankey argues that the evidence introduced at trial is compelling in showing that Mr. Vick's actions and behavior made him the provocateur in the fight, and that his actions leading up to the fight were intentional and rise far beyond mere negligence. He further testified that the intentional acts and belligerence of Mr. Vick, as well as his obscene language, were the initial catalyst of the subsequent fight. For these reasons, Pankey urges that the trial court failed to apportion fault to Mr. Vick, whose intentional wrongdoing was a contributing factor and substantial cause of his injuries.

The trial court determined that "insults and intoxication alone fail to provide a legal escape from liability caused by a beating such as this." Even if Barry Pankey was provoked by Mr. Vick as he alleges, he clearly responded in a manner that was inappropriate and unnecessarily excessive under the circumstances. This determination is clearly supported by the record. The trial court was correct in finding that Barry and Terry Pankey were 100% at fault for the injuries suffered by Mr. Vick. Therefore, we find that this assignment of error is meritless.

* * *

YOUNG V. STATE

Supreme Court of Alaska, 1971
491 P.2d 122

ERWIN, JUSTICE.

This is an appeal by Frank Young from the adverse decision of the trial court sitting without a jury. We affirm.

In 1963, the State of Alaska let a construction contract to Peter Kiewit Sons' Company for the construction of a highway to Chena Hot Springs, north of Fairbanks. The contract specifications required Peter Kiewit Sons' Company to construct completed bridge approaches, the bridges themselves to be contracted for separately by the state.

On September 12, 1964, Edward Krivak and appellant Young, his passenger, drove in Krivak's car to the area where the road construction began. A moveable barricade had been erected marking the end of the public highway and the beginning of the construction zone. Although several signs were posted along the road and on the barricade itself warning that the road was under construction and closed, Young and Krivak proceeded past the barricade intending to drive to Young's cabin located adjacent to the hot springs.

Several miles down the road, Krivak drove toward a new bridge approach at approximately 35 miles per hour and realized too late that there was no bridge beyond. He veered to the left, ran off the road and down the embankment and, as a result, Young suffered injury. At trial, Young argued that the state and the contractor were negligent in failing to post signs at hazardous points along the route and in failing to lock the barricade in order to prevent access to the road.

* * * [T]he trial judge found that adequate warning signs had been posted and a barricade erected, and that Young had seen the signs and knew the road was closed, having been over the road several times in the past while it was under construction. * * *

The appellant's argument on appeal focuses on the concluding sentences of the lower court's opinion[, in which the court said that "plaintiff's travel beyond the noted warnings and knowledge of the construction area beyond led directly to the injury he suffered and would bar his recovery."]

* * *

Young argues that the lower court mistakenly applied the contributory negligence standard governing a driver's conduct to a passenger without any control over the vehicle. Appellant reasons that since it would not have been negligent for a passenger to doze, watch the scenery, or read a map, he was under no duty to keep a lookout or to warn the driver of particular hazards on the road. We think that this argument, although persuasive on the surface, misconstrues the lower court's holding. The court found the plaintiff contributorily negligent not for his failure to warn the driver of the particular hazards involved in approaching the bridge at a high rate of speed, but rather for agreeing to travel on the road under construction, with knowledge of the dangers involved.

It is clear that this is a proper case for application of the contributory negligence defense. The [Restatement (Second) of Torts § 463 (1965)] defines contributory negligence as "conduct on the part of the plaintiff which falls below the standard to which he should conform for his own protection, and which is a legally contributing cause co-operating with the negligence of the defendant in bringing about the plaintiff's harm." Restatement § 466 provides that plaintiff's contributory negligence may be either:

a) an intentional and unreasonable exposure of himself to danger created by the defendant's negligence, of which danger the plaintiff knows or has reason to know, or

b) conduct which, in respects other than those stated in Clause (a), falls short of the standard to which a reasonable man should conform in order to protect himself from harm.

The contributory negligence at issue here, of course, is of the former variety, sometimes referred to by the court as "voluntary assumption of risk." The Restatement sets out the following example of this type of contributory negligence:

[I]f a plaintiff rides in an automobile knowing that the driver is drunk, ignorant of driving, or habitually reckless or careless, or that the machine has insufficient brakes or headlights, he ordinarily cannot recover against the defendant through whose negligence an accident occurs if the drunkenness, incompetence or carelessness of the driver or the bad condition of the vehicle is a contributing factor in bringing about the accident. [Restatement (Second) of Torts § 466, cmt. e (1965).]

It is well established that in certain circumstances a person can be contributorily negligent by merely agreeing to be a passenger in a vehicle.

* * * [I]f a plaintiff voluntarily and unreasonably assumes a negligently created risk, his conduct amounts to contributory negligence and he is barred from recovery. * * * [W]e think there was sufficient evidence [in] the record so that the court's finding of contributory negligence was not "clearly erroneous."

A more troublesome aspect of the lower court's opinion is its apparent failure to find the defendants negligent before reaching the issue of the plaintiff's contributory negligence. * * * [T]he court stated:

* * * Even if the defendants were to be found negligent under any theory, *and the court does not make a finding in this regard,* plaintiff's travel beyond the noted warnings and knowledge of the construction area beyond lead directly to the injury he suffered and would bar his recovery . . . (emphasis added [by the court]).

* * *

* * * Thus, the question arises: Is it proper for a court to bar a plaintiff's recovery by finding contributory negligence without first deciding whether the defendant was negligent?

The well-established rule is stated by the California Supreme Court in *O'Keefe v. South End Rowing Club,* 64 Cal.2d 729, 51 Cal.Rptr. 534, 547, 414 P.2d 830, 843 (1966):

The question of the plaintiff's contributory negligence is a matter of defense, to be litigated, if at all, only after the plaintiff has proved the elements of his case, including the defendant's duty and breach thereof.

Doctrinally, contributory negligence presupposes negligence for which the defendant is responsible, and for which recovery would be allowed but for the concurrence of contributory negligence. In the absence of actionable negligence, contributory negligence cannot exist. Further, as a matter of policy, it is inappropriate to allow the trial court to use the contributory negligence defense to sidestep difficult proximate cause issues, or, as here, to avoid troublesome issues regarding the duty owed by the defendant which can be resolved only by an intricate balancing of public policy considerations. It might lead to excessive use of this disfavored defense.[11]

Finally, it is clear that the practice utilized by the court below may lead to unnecessary new trials in cases where this court disagrees on appeal with the lower court's finding of contributory negligence. For example, if, in this case, we were to hold that there was no contributory negligence, a new trial on the issue of defendant's negligence would be required since the trial court made no finding in that regard.

Therefore, although this court has in the past approved the above practice, we deem it appropriate to announce a different rule for the future. * * * [T]he trial court should make a finding on the issue of negligence before reaching the issue of contributory negligence. In this way, we may avoid a piecemeal approach to litigation which might result in successive retrials.

The judgment is affirmed.

NOTES AND QUESTIONS

1.   What is comparative negligence? What was Pankey's argument in the *Vick* case for reducing the amount of damages awarded in the trial court? How did the Louisiana Court of Appeal rule? Is the result reached by the Louisiana appellate court a fair one?

2.   What is contributory negligence? Why does the defense presuppose the existence of negligence? What was the contributory negligence issue in *Young*? How did the Alaska Supreme Court rule? Why is it important for a court to decide negligence before deciding contributory negligence?

3.   Unlike contributory negligence, which bars recovery for a negligence action if the plaintiff was also negligent to *any* extent, comparative negligence compares the fault of the two parties and apportions damages in direct proportion to the amount of fault. For example, a plaintiff who is 40% responsible for an accident could recover 60% of his losses in a comparative

---

[11] This danger is aggravated by the rule that plaintiff's contributory negligence, no matter how slight in relation to defendant's negligence, will bar recovery.

negligence jurisdiction but no damages in a contributory negligence jurisdiction. The vast majority of states (all but Alabama, Maryland, North Carolina, and Virginia) have some form of comparative negligence. At the federal level, the U.S. Supreme Court has endorsed comparative negligence in the maritime context. *See United States v. Reliable Transfer Co., Inc.*, 421 U.S. 397 (1975).

4. In a "pure" comparative negligence jurisdiction, the plaintiff would be permitted to recover for a percentage of damages regardless of the percent of his fault (*e.g.*, a plaintiff could recover 1% of his losses even if he was 99% at fault). Some jurisdictions, however, employ what is known as "modified" comparative negligence, where a plaintiff cannot recover if his fault is 50% or more (though some jurisdictions—like South Carolina (*see Roddey, supra*)— place the cutoff at 51% or more). Many courts have criticized this "modified" approach to comparative negligence. As the Michigan Supreme Court noted when it adopted a pure comparative negligence standard: "Is the person who is 49% negligent that much more deserving than the one who is 51% negligent?" *Placek v. City of Sterling Heights*, 405 Mich. 638, 661, 275 N.W.2d 511, 519 (1979). As between "pure" and "modified" comparative negligence, which approach makes the most sense?

5. Another defense that is often related to contributory and comparative negligence is "assumption of the risk." According to the Restatement (Second) of Torts § 496A (1965): "A plaintiff who voluntarily assumes a risk of harm arising from the negligent or reckless conduct of the defendant cannot recover for such harm." That assumption can be either by an express agreement or implied by the plaintiff's conduct. As the Restatement also states: "[A] plaintiff who fully understands a risk of harm to himself or his things caused by the defendant's conduct or by the condition of the defendant's land or chattels, and who nevertheless voluntarily chooses to enter or remain, or to permit his things to enter or remain within the area of that risk, under circumstances that manifest his willingness to accept it, is not entitled to recover for harm within that risk." *Id.* § 496C. For an application of the doctrine, *see, e.g., De Amiches v. Popczun*, 35 Ohio St.2d 180, 299 N.E.2d 265 (1973) (the plaintiff had known about a hole in a driveway for over a year and chose to take an icy and slippery path around the hole, causing her to fall and injure her ankle when she slipped on the ice; court held that the landowner was not liable for the injury, because the plaintiff voluntarily assumed the risk by choosing a path she knew to be icy and dangerous); *Southwick v. S.S. Mullen, Inc.*, 19 Utah 2d 430, 432 P.2d 56 (1967) (a cameraman visited a construction blasting site to document the blasting procedure and chose to work from a dangerous area without consulting with the construction crew; the court held that the cameraman knew of the risks and had a duty to protect himself).

6. The foregoing cases in this section have involved claims of ordinary negligence. Some plaintiffs, however, are forced to meet the higher standard of "gross negligence." Gross negligence claims typically involve "a reckless disregard of safety or an indifference to the consequences" of actions. *Howard v. Chimps, Inc.*, 251 Or. App. 636, 649, 284 P.3d 1181, 1189 (2012). In assessing

that standard, most courts analyze gross negligence under a two-pronged test involving both an objective and subjective element. As the Texas Supreme Court reasoned in *U-Haul Int'l Inc. v. Waldrip*, 380 S.W.3d 118, 137 (Tex. 2012):

> Plaintiffs must prove by clear and convincing evidence that (1) when viewed objectively from the defendant's standpoint at the time of the event, the act or omission involved an extreme degree of risk, considering the probability and magnitude of the potential harm to others and (2) the defendant had actual, subjective awareness of the risk involved, but nevertheless proceeded with conscious indifference to the rights, safety, or welfare of others.

In *Waldrip*, the court held that the plaintiff, who was injured when a rental truck rolled over him after the parking brake failed, could not show that the defendant was *subjectively* aware of the dangerous condition posed by the faulty parking brake and thus plaintiff could not demonstrate gross negligence. Does the subjective component make sense? Or does it simply encourage defendants to remain ignorant of potentially dangerous conditions?

One common situation where gross negligence must be shown is when a signed release of liability from negligent or careless acts precludes a claim based on ordinary negligence. *See, e.g., Howard, supra* (intern at defendant's chimpanzee sanctuary, who had signed a waiver releasing defendant for acts of negligence, could not recover after being attacked by a chimpanzee because she could not show gross negligence). There are several other situations where gross negligence may come into play. For example, gross negligence is the standard that many state laws require in evaluating medical malpractice claims involving emergency medical services. *See, e.g., Johnson v. Omondi*, 294 Ga. 74, 751 S.E.2d 288 (2013) (requiring the plaintiff to meet the gross negligence standard when bringing an action for injuries sustained during medical services in the hospital's emergency department). Similarly, some state laws require gross negligence to be shown where police cause injury to motorists while pursuing a third party who is violating the law. *See, e.g., Norris v. Zambito*, 135 N.C.App. 288, 520 S.E.2d 113 (N.C. Ct. App. 1999) (requiring the plaintiff to meet the gross negligence standard when bringing an action for injuries sustained when a police officer crashed into the plaintiff's vehicle while pursuing a criminal suspect). For further discussion of gross negligence, *see, e.g.*, Patrick Martin, *The BP Spill and the Meaning of "Gross Negligence or Willful Misconduct"*, 71 La. L. Rev. 957 (2011) (explaining that the factor that transforms "ordinary negligence" into "gross negligence" is the defendant's subjective awareness that he is acting in a manner that threatens injury to others); Randolph Stuart Sergent, *Gross, Reckless, Wanton and Indifferent: Gross Negligence in Maryland Civil Law*, 30 U. Balt. L. Rev. 1 (2000) (detailing the history of the gross negligence standard and listing several situations where the standard is sometimes applied, including torts cases seeking punitive damages and some product liability disputes).

C. STRICT LIABILITY

In certain cases, courts apply a "strict liability" standard of fault. If strict liability applies, the defendant will be responsible for any harm he has caused even if he was not negligent. The following case addresses strict liability.

WILEY V. SANDERS

Court of Appeal of Louisiana, Second Circuit, 2003
850 So.2d 771

DREW, JUDGE.

In this drowning case, plaintiff appeals a judgment granting defendants' motion for a directed verdict. We affirm.

FACTS

Vernon Sanders is the owner of a nine-acre tract of land located in Columbia, Louisiana. The property contained a pond that Vernon had constructed for fishing and swimming. On June 13, 1992, he was working on a construction job in Shreveport. His wife joined him there because he was unable to return home for the weekend. Left at home was their 18-year-old son, Samuel. That evening, Samuel Sanders had invited a few people over to his family's home, but more showed up, eventually swelling the gathering to approximately 20 to 30 people. Many of the guests were in the pond. Among them was 19-year-old Robert Wiley. Sometime after midnight, the partygoers were unable to find Robert Wiley when it was noticed that he was missing. That morning after sunrise, Robert Wiley's body was discovered in the pond. He had apparently drowned.

On June 11, 1993, Claymon Wiley, Robert's mother, filed suit against Vernon Sanders and State Farm, his homeowner's liability insurer. Mrs. Wiley died on March 27, 1998. Mrs. Wiley's daughter, Aisha Moore, in her capacity as administratrix of her mother's succession, was substituted as plaintiff in June of 1999.

* * *

Trial on the merits was held on August 27, 2002. Defendants moved for a directed verdict after the plaintiff concluded her case. The trial court granted the motion[, reasoning] * * * that the pond was not unreasonably dangerous, and there was no evidence establishing negligence or breach of duty by Vernon. Plaintiff appealed.

DISCUSSION

Plaintiff is attempting to recover under theories of both negligence and strict liability. The owner of property may be held liable to a person injured on the property under a negligence theory if there is a defect on the property which causes the injury, and the owner knew or should have known of the existence of the defect. In addition, at the time of the drowning, a property owner could also be held liable under a theory of strict liability to any person injured because of an unreasonably dangerous condition on the property.

Under strict liability, it is the defendant's legal relationship with the property containing a defect that gives rise to a duty. However, the finding of the existence of a defect alone is not sufficient to establish liability. "[A property owner] cannot be held responsible for all injuries resulting from any risk posed by his [property], only those caused by an unreasonable risk of harm to others." The absence of an unreasonably dangerous condition of the property implies the absence of a duty.

Under either theory, negligence or strict liability, the plaintiff must prove that the defendant had custody * * * of the thing which caused the damage, that the thing contained a defect (a condition posing an unreasonable risk of harm to the plaintiff), and that this defective condition caused the plaintiff's injuries.

When determining whether a risk is unreasonable, a court is to balance the likelihood and magnitude of the harm and the utility of the thing, while also taking into account a broad range of social, moral, and economic factors including the cost to the defendant of avoiding the risk and the social utility of the plaintiff's conduct when the accident occurred. Justice and social utility are guideposts, with consideration given to individual and societal rights and obligations.

The pond was constructed by Vernon, who, as a qualified heavy machine operator, had previously assisted in the construction of ponds. He described the pond as being saucer-shaped and having a tapered surface from the pond edges to the center, such that it gradually became deeper toward the middle. He believed that a 6 foot tall individual could walk within 10 feet of the middle and the water would still not be over his head, and if he wanted to continue across the pond, all he had to do was to take two or three "bounce" steps and he would return to a depth where he could walk the remainder of the way. According to Aisha Moore, her brother (the decedent) was 6-feet tall. Samuel estimated that the pond was 8 feet deep in the middle.

There was no fence around the pond, nor were there any markers or signs designating the various depths of the pond. The only artificial light provided for the pond was from a light in the front yard of the house, and this light only illuminated part of the pond. Vernon estimated that the pond was located approximately 40 to 45 yards from the rear of his home; Samuel believed it was between 60 and 80 yards. Richard Morgan, an acquaintance of Samuel, testified that on the night of the drowning, there was enough natural light for him to see the other people out in the pond.

The water source for the pond was rainfall. Vernon described the pond water as murky, but he thought that a person could see the bottom until the pond water was stirred up from individuals entering the pond. Morgan described the water in the pond as muddy or murky. Morgan also found the bank and pond bottom to be slippery. The pond was cleaned every 12 to 18 months, and the area around the pond was regularly mowed.

Vernon did not feel that there was any need to provide a lifeguard because his children were able to swim. He assumed that everyone who went near the pond would exercise good judgment, and he generally told guests not to get in the pond if they could not swim. Life preservers were hung on the outside of a shed that Vernon testified was located approximately 120 feet from the pond. Samuel estimated that the shed was 80 to 100 yards away from the pond, and he did not think the life preservers were noticeable unless a person went near the shed.

A prominent feature of the pond was a floating dock containing a diving board. The dock was sometimes anchored at the pond's center. According to Vernon, the dock was constructed essentially the same on both its top and bottom, permitting the dock to still be used, even for diving, when it was turned over. Vernon did not believe the dock was unsafe when upside-down. The diving board would be underwater when the dock was in the upside-down position. On the night of the drowning, the dock was pulled up onto the bank at times, and at other times it was anchored 10 feet from the shore.

Richard Morgan testified that he left work at 10:00 p.m. on the night of the drowning. He then went to the residence of Dale Tucker in order to pick up Robert Wiley, who was attending a gathering at Mr. Tucker's residence. Morgan estimated that he arrived there at 10:30 p.m., and then left with Robert Wiley 10 minutes later. Morgan witnessed Robert Wiley drinking beer there and taking a couple of beer bottles with him when he left. Morgan and Robert Wiley stopped at a gas station before continuing on their journey to Samuel's party. Morgan related that he and Robert Wiley had been at the Samuel's residence the prior evening, and had been told by Samuel to return the next day. Vernon testified that he was unaware of the party, and he added that his children had never previously had a party when either he or his wife was not present.

Morgan testified that upon arriving at the Sanders' property, he and Robert Wiley first went to the home for a few minutes before heading to the pond. Morgan watched Robert Wiley remove his outer clothing and enter the water. He never saw Robert Wiley leave the water. Morgan recalled seeing Robert Wiley playing in the water. When asked what he meant by "playing," Morgan explained:

> We was just splashing the water and everybody just, just talking and jumping up, you know, people playing and pushing on each, you know, pushing on each other, you know. . . .

Morgan stated that Robert Wiley was hanging on the side of the dock without any apparent problem the last time he saw him. He did not think Robert Wiley was in any discomfort or was unable to care for himself at the time. Morgan testified that Robert Wiley did not seem anxious or uncomfortable in the water, and he seemed to be enjoying himself. Morgan did not hear any splashes indicating someone was in trouble, and he did not hear anyone cry for help. Morgan stayed in waist-deep water or near the bank while in the pond. He did not want to venture any farther out because he did not know how to swim. Morgan estimated that there were 30 people in the water or on the bank.

Samuel admitted consuming 12 beers that evening, but he denied serving alcohol to those gathered at his family's property. He recalled seeing Robert Wiley three or four times that evening at the house before later seeing him enter the pond in knee-deep water. Samuel believed that it was around midnight the last time he saw Robert Wiley. He recalled that at the time he was leaning on the upside-down dock and Robert Wiley was wading toward the dock in waist-deep water. Samuel was unsure whether the dock was along the pond's bank or 10 feet out when he last saw Robert Wiley. Samuel estimated that around 8 to 10 people were with him at the dock. He also testified that 5 to 10 people were in the pond at that time, and they were grouped in a small area, enabling him to see them.

Samuel stated that after he and the others had been hanging around the dock for approximately 30 minutes, they began leaving the water and heading back to the house. Shortly thereafter, Morgan asked Samuel if he had seen Robert Wiley. Those present began searching for Robert Wiley on land and then in the pond for 10 minutes. After the land was searched again and Robert Wiley had still not been found, the police were summoned. Robert Wiley's body was discovered that morning after daybreak.

Samuel testified that he was told Robert Wiley's body was discovered 15 feet from the bank and 30 feet to the right of the dock. Samuel estimated that this would have been in 4 feet of water. Aisha Moore viewed her brother's body several hours after learning of his death. She testified that his body was covered in mud with mud packed on his face, his hands were clasped like he was grabbing for something, and he had mud under his fingernails. She also saw a knot on his right temple. The death certificate listed drowning as the cause of death. Dr. Alfredo Suarez performed a second autopsy on June 23, 1992. He concluded in his report that the "presence of hemorrhage in the inner ear favor[ed] drowning as the cause of death."

Plaintiff argues that the "totality of the circumstances of the pond" presented an unreasonably dangerous condition. The totality of circumstances is in reference to the muddy or murky nature of the water, and the lack of direct artificial lighting, nearby life-preservers, and signs warning of the pond's depth.

We disagree that the pond in question was unreasonably dangerous to this 19-year-old. There were no obstacles or hazards along the bottom of the pond that would have endangered Robert Wiley or anyone else in the pond. The pond was sloped and did not contain any sudden drop-offs. The only danger presented by the pond was that it contained water. Such a danger would have been open and obvious to Robert Wiley when he entered the pond. The evidence established that Robert Wiley spent his initial moments in the pond without difficulty. Without question, Robert Wiley was in the best position to avoid this accident by not entering the water in the first place if he was unable to swim.

Because the pond did not present an unreasonably dangerous condition, the issue is then framed as whether Vernon breached a duty to act as a reasonable man. A homeowner has a duty to act as a reasonable man and to guard against unreasonable risks of injury to guests. The test to determine whether a breach of a landowner's duty has occurred is whether, in the management of his property, he has acted as a reasonable man in view of the probability of injury to others.

* * *

The evidence in this matter failed to establish that Vernon breached any duty owed to Robert Wiley. * * * Vernon was not even present on the date of the drowning, as he was out-of-town at the time, with no knowledge of the party, apparently organized by his 18-year-old son, Samuel, at his home. Moreover, * * * had [Wiley] exercised reasonable care, [he] should have observed that he could drown in a pond filled with water. "[A] landowner is not liable for an injury resulting from a condition which should have been observed by an individual in the exercise of reasonable care."

* * *

After reviewing this record in a light most favorable to plaintiff, we [conclude that] * * * the trial court did not err in granting the motion for a directed verdict.

NOTES AND QUESTIONS

1.   What is the difference between negligence and strict liability? What is the advantage for a plaintiff in suing for strict liability as opposed to negligence?

2.   What was the strict liability issue in *Wiley*? How did the Louisiana Court of Appeal rule?

3.   As *Wiley* illustrates, the question whether a condition is readily observable (or open and obvious) is frequently a critical inquiry in strict

liability cases alleging an unreasonably dangerous condition of land. Consistent with *Wiley*, many other courts have also held that imposing strict liability is improper when the allegedly dangerous feature is easily observable to a reasonable passerby. *See, e.g., Handy v. City of Kenner*, 97 So.3d 539 (La. Ct. App. 2012) (finding that a stairwell on which patron struck his head was an open and obvious condition that did not present an unreasonable risk of harm).

4.   In *Spano v. Perini Corp*, 25 N.Y.2d 11, 250 N.E.2d 31 (1969), the plaintiffs' property was damaged by explosive shockwaves when the Perini Corporation had (without negligence) used dynamite in a blasting operation near the plaintiffs' property. The court held that explosive blasting is an ultra-hazardous activity to which strict liability must be imposed. The *Spano* court imposed liability on the defendant despite the absence of negligence on defendant's part. Courts have applied strict liability to numerous other types of ultra-hazardous activities. *See, e.g., Interfaith Cmty. Org. v. Honeywell Int'l, Inc.*, 263 F. Supp. 2d 796 (D.N.J. 2003) (improper disposal and failure to remove a hazardous chemical at a property was an ultra-hazardous and abnormally dangerous activity subjecting the defendant to strict liability), *aff'd*, 399 F.3d 248 (3d Cir. 2005); *Koos v. Roth*, 293 Or. 670, 652 P.2d 1255 (1982) (use of a "field burning" agricultural tactic to burn a field of old crops was an ultra-hazardous activity subject to strict liability); *Cities Serv. Co. v. State*, 312 So.2d 799 (Fla. Ct. App. 1975) (maintaining a dam that held back billions of gallons of phosphate chemical slime behind a wall was an ultra-hazardous activity subject to strict liability). On the other hand, courts have shown unwillingness to find the initial manufacturers of hazardous materials strictly liable for accidents that occur during the shipping of those materials. *See, e.g., Ind. Harbor Belt R.R. Co. v. Am. Cyanamid Co.*, 916 F.2d 1174 (7th Cir. 1990) (finding that chemical manufacturing company, which manufactured a toxic chemical that was shipped through a densely populated area in a railway tanker, was not strictly liable for consequences of a spill during shipping). As Judge Posner wrote for the Seventh Circuit in the *American Cyanamid Co.* case: "[T]he manufacturer of a product is not considered to be engaged in an abnormally dangerous activity merely because the product becomes dangerous when it is handled or used in some way after it leaves his premises, even if the danger is foreseeable." *Id.* at 1181. In different types of cases, however, a products manufacturer *will* face strict liability under products liability law for selling defective and unreasonably dangerous products. *See* note 5 below.

Most courts take the position that whether an activity is "ultra-hazardous" or "abnormally dangerous" is a question for the court, not the jury, to decide. *See, e.g., Bella v. Aurora Air, Inc.*, 279 Or. 13, 566 P.2d 489 (1977); *Langan v. Valicopters, Inc.*, 88 Wash.2d 855, 567 P.2d 218 (1977). Does that approach make sense? Should it be up to the jury (as opposed to the judge) to decide whether an activity is "ultra-hazardous" or "abnormally dangerous" within that particular community?

5. The strict liability standard is also used in many products liability cases where a consumer alleges that a manufacturer's product was unreasonably dangerous and caused injury. In a strict liability products case, a plaintiff generally has to establish five elements: "(1) the defendant was engaged in the business of selling the product; (2) the product was in a defective condition unreasonably dangerous to the consumer or user; (3) the defect caused the injury for which compensation was sought; (4) the defect existed at the time of the sale; and (5) the product was expected to and did reach the consumer without substantial change in condition." *Potter v. Chicago Pneumatic Tool Co.*, 241 Conn. 199, 214, 694 A.2d 1319, 1330 (1997); *see also* Restatement (Second) of Torts § 402A (1965). If the plaintiff can establish all five elements, the manufacturer will be held strictly liable for any injury caused by its product, regardless of whether there was any negligence during the manufacturing process. For a detailed account of the history of products liability law, *see* Kyle Graham, *Strict Products Liability at 50: Four Histories*, 98 Marq. L. Rev. 555 (2014) (discussing the history of products liability law since the 1960s).

D. RESPONDEAT SUPERIOR

Respondeat superior is a Latin phrase that means "let the master answer." In a respondeat superior case, the plaintiff attempts to hold the defendant liable for the conduct of a subordinate under the defendant's control. Usually, respondeat superior claims arise in cases seeking to hold an employer responsible for the conduct of an employee who was acting in the course of employment. The following case involves a respondeat superior claim.

HINMAN V. WESTINGHOUSE ELECTRIC CO.
Supreme Court of California, 1970
2 Cal.3d 956, 471 P.2d 988

PETERS, JUSTICE.

In this action for damages for personal injuries, plaintiff Eugene C. Hinman, and intervener, City of Los Angeles, appeal from a judgment for defendant Westinghouse Electric Company entered after a jury verdict * * *.

Plaintiff, a Los Angeles policeman, was standing on the center divider of a freeway inspecting a possible road hazard when he was struck by a car driven by Frank Allen Herman, an employee of defendant Westinghouse. As a result of the accident he received permanent injuries. The city paid his medical expenses and disability pension.

At the time of the accident, Herman was employed by Westinghouse as an elevator constructor's helper and was returning home from work from a job site. He had been working for Westinghouse for about four months. His work was assigned from the Westinghouse office. He did not go to the office before or after work but instead went from home directly to the job site and after work returned home from the job site. The particular job on which Herman was working was not completed at the time of the accident, and he would ordinarily return to the job site until the job was completed or he was told not to return.

The union contracts under which Herman worked provided for the payment of "carfare" and travel time in certain circumstances depending on the location of the job site in relation to the Los Angeles City Hall. As to this job, which was 15 to 20 miles from the city hall, Herman received an hour and a half per day as his roundtrip travel time and $1.30 for his travel expense. The employer had no control over the method or route of transportation used by Herman.

The trial judge refused instructions that Herman was acting within the scope of his employment at the time of the accident and instead instructed the jury that whether he was acting within the scope of his employment depended upon a number of factors including among others "whether his conduct was authorized by his employer, either expressly or impliedly; the nature of the employment, its object and the duties imposed thereby; whether the employee was acting in his discharge thereof; whether his conduct occurred during the performance of services for the benefit of the employer, either directly or indirectly, or of himself; whether his conduct, even though not expressly or impliedly authorized, was an incidental event connected with his assigned work; and many other things besides the time and place of performance of his duties as an employee."

After the jury returned its verdict in favor of Westinghouse * * *, the trial judge inquired, as "a matter of information only," if the jury found negligence on the part of Herman. The foreman responded in the affirmative to that question and also the further question as to whether the jury's decision related to scope of employment.

Although earlier authorities sought to justify the respondeat superior doctrine on such theories as "control" by the master of the servant, the master's "privilege" in being permitted to employ another, the third party's innocence in comparison to the master's selection of the servant, or the master's "deep pocket" to pay for the loss, "the modern justification for vicarious liability is a rule of policy, a deliberate allocation of a risk. The losses caused by the torts of employees, which as a practical matter are sure to occur in the conduct of the employer's enterprise, are placed upon that enterprise itself, as a required cost of doing business. They are placed upon the employer because, having engaged in an enterprise which will, on the basis of past experience, involve harm to others through the torts of employees, and sought to profit by it, it is just that he, rather than the innocent injured plaintiff, should bear them; and because he is better able to absorb them, and to distribute them, through prices, rates or liability insurance, to the public, and so to shift them to society, to the community at large." * * *

* * * [T]he modern and proper basis of vicarious liability of the master is not his control or fault but the risks incident to his enterprise. "We are not here looking for the master's fault but rather for risks that may fairly be regarded as typical of or broadly incidental to the enterprise he has undertaken. * * * Further, we are not looking for that which can and should reasonably be avoided, but with the more or less inevitable toll of a lawful enterprise."

Similarly, California cases have long recognized that the employer's responsibility for the torts of his employee extends beyond his actual or possible control of the servant to injuries which are "risks of the enterprise." * * * "The principal justification for the application of the doctrine of respondeat superior in any case is the fact that the employer may spread the risk through insurance and carry the cost thereof as part of his costs of doing business." Thus, it must be deemed settled in California that in accordance with the principal justification for the doctrine, the employer's liability extends to the risks inherent in or created by the enterprise.

The cases which have considered recovery against the master for accidents occurring within the scope and during the period of employment have established a general rule of liability with a few exceptions for cases where the employee has substantially deviated from his duties for personal purposes. In the instant case, the employee was on company time and was engaged in the very conduct contemplated by the employer.

Liability of the employer may not be avoided on the basis of the "going and coming" rule. Under the "going and coming" rule, an employee going to and from work is ordinarily considered outside the scope of employment so that the employer is not liable for his torts. The "going and coming" rule is sometimes ascribed to the theory that the employment relationship is "suspended" from the time the employee leaves until he returns, or that in commuting he is not rendering service to his employer. Nevertheless, there are exceptions to the rule.

Thus in *Harvey v. D & L Construction Co.*, 251 Cal.App.2d 48 (1967), the court reversed a nonsuit for the employer where it was shown that because of the remote site of the construction project, the employer had asked the employee to recruit other employees, one such employee was riding at the time of the accident, and the employer was furnishing the gas for the trip to the employee's home. Similarly, in *Richards v. Metropolitan Life Ins. Co.*, 19 Cal.2d 236, 120 P.2d 650 (1941), liability of the employer to an innocent third party was recognized from the time that an outside salesman left his home to see clients outside the office, and where his work involved both office work and field work; it was held immaterial whether he was proceeding to his office or to see some of his customers elsewhere.

In *Boynton v. McKales*, 139 Cal.App.2d 777, 294 P.2d 733 (1956), the employer was held liable where the injury occurred while the employee was driving home from a company banquet.

Liability of an employer to an innocent third party for an accident occurring on the way to work was upheld in *Breland v. Traylor Eng. etc., Co.*, 52 Cal.App.2d 415, 126 P.2d 455 (1942), where the employer had sent the employee to California from Pennsylvania to help construct a kiln, traveling and subsistence allowances were paid by the employer while the employee was traveling to California, and the employer paid five cents a mile for use of the car from the employee's temporary home to the job site. The court reasoned that under this showing it could be inferred that the employer "impliedly agreed" that the employee should be deemed to be acting in the course and scope of his employment while going to and coming from work.

In *Kobe v. Industrial Acc. Comm.*, 35 Cal.2d 33, 215 P.2d 736 (1950), * * * the court reasoned that, although the employment relationship is ordinarily suspended when the employee is going or coming, "the employer may agree, either expressly or impliedly, that the relationship shall continue during the period of 'going and coming,' in which case the employee is entitled to the protection of the act during that period. Such an agreement may be inferred from the fact that the employer furnishes transportation to and from work as an incident to the employment. It seems equally clear that such an agreement may also be inferred from the fact that the employer compensates the employee for the time consumed in traveling to and from work."

The above cases indicate that exceptions will be made to the "going and coming" rule where the trip involves an incidental benefit to the employer, not common to commute trips by ordinary members of the work force. The cases also indicate that the fact that the employee receives personal benefits is not determinative when there is also a benefit to the employer.

There is a substantial benefit to an employer in one area to be permitted to reach out to a labor market in another area or to enlarge the available labor market by providing travel expenses and payment for travel time. It cannot be denied that the employer's reaching out to the distant or larger labor market increases the risk of injury in transportation. In other words, the employer, having found it desirable in the interests of his enterprise to pay for travel time and for travel expenses and to go beyond the normal labor market or to have located his enterprise at a place remote from the labor market, should be required to pay for the risks inherent in his decision.

We are satisfied that, where, as here, the employer and employee have made the travel time part of the working day by their contract, the employer should be treated as such during the travel time, and it follows that so long as the employee is using the time for the designated purpose, to return home, the doctrine of respondeat superior is applicable. It is unnecessary to determine the appropriate rule to be applied if the employee had used the time for other purposes. We also need not decide now whether the mere payment of travel expenses without additional payment for the travel time of the employee * * * reflects a sufficient benefit to the employer so that he should bear responsibility to innocent third parties for the risks inherent in the travel.

The facts relating to the applicability of the doctrine of respondeat superior are undisputed in the instant case, and we conclude that as a matter of law the doctrine is applicable and that the trial court erred in its instructions in leaving the issue as one of fact to the jury.

* * *

The judgment is reversed. * * *

NOTES AND QUESTIONS

1.   What is respondeat superior? What are the policy reasons for the doctrine?

2.   What was the issue in *Hinman*? How did the California Supreme Court rule? What facts were crucial to the court's decision?

3.   With advances in technology, employees are often able to work at unusual times and in unusual places. For example, an employee may participate in a conference call while on an airplane, in an automobile, or at the beach. How far should the scope of employment for respondeat superior extend? Scholars and judges have debated that question. *See, e.g.*, Isaac Hof, *Wake-Up Call: Eliminating the Major Roadblock that Cell Phone Driving Creates for Employer Liability*, 84 Temp. L. Rev. 701 (2012) (urging states to modify respondeat superior rules to allow courts to expand liability in negligence cases that involve employees on cell phones). In *Miller v. American Greetings Corp.*, 161 Cal.App.4th 1055, 1063, 74 Cal.Rptr.3d 776, 783 (Cal. Ct. App. 2008), the California Court of Appeal addressed the problem of cell phone use by describing a "continuum":

> We envision the link between respondeat superior and most work-related cell phone calls while driving as falling along a continuum. Sometimes the link between the job and the accident will be clear, as when an employee is on the phone for work at the moment of the accident. Oftentimes, the link will fall into a gray zone, as when an employee devotes some portion of his time and attention to work calls during the car trip so that the journey cannot be fairly called entirely personal. But sometimes, as [in this case], the link is *de minimis*—one call of less than one minute 8 or 9 minutes before an accident while traveling on a personal errand of several miles' duration heading neither to nor from a worksite. When that happens, we find no respondeat superior as a matter of law.

Is the court's "continuum" approach a sensible one? Why or why not?

4. For further scholarly discussion of respondeat superior, *see, e.g.*, Lisa Hawke, *Municipal Liability and Respondeat Superior: An Empirical Study and Analysis*, 38 Suffolk U. L. Rev. 831 (2005) (analyzing respondeat superior in the context of municipal employees and advocating for an expanded doctrine of respondeat superior in that context); Charles Davant IV, *Employer Liability for Employee Fraud: Apparent Authority or Respondeat Superior?*, 47 S.D.L. Rev. 554 (2002) (arguing that respondeat superior should be unavailable when an employee is accused of defrauding the plaintiff unless the plaintiff reasonably believed that he was dealing directly with the employer at the time of the fraud); David Culp, *Corporate Irresponsibility: A Return to the Back of the Bus*, 30 Cal. W. L. Rev. 93 (1993) (analyzing respondeat superior in the context of federal race discrimination claims, and arguing that employers should be held liable for the racially-discriminatory acts of their employees).

E. THE TORT REFORM DEBATE

Many politicians and legal scholars have advocated for reform to improve the current U.S. tort system. Many others, however, have voiced support for the current system. The following article discusses some of the competing arguments.

THE ARGUMENTS FOR AND AGAINST TORT REFORM

Christy Rakoczy, The Legal Finance Journal, June 24, 2013.

Documentaries like HBO's *Hot Coffee* have drawn more attention to the field of tort litigation and tort reform * * *, but the battle for and against tort reform has been raging for years. The *Hot Coffee* documentary takes a look at the case of Stella Liebeck, an Albuquerque woman who famously sued McDonald's for spilling hot coffee on herself. The case became a cause celebre for corporations and others to argue that jury awards and so-called "frivolous lawsuits" were out of control in the US.

Indeed, the documentary points out the debate about tort reform. On the one side are experts who believe that tort laws ensure that plaintiffs can pursue rewards in cases where they have been injured, ensuring that [defendants] are held accountable for their actions. On the other side of the debate are corporations, insurance carriers and other experts, who claim that tort laws need to be reformed because they allow plaintiffs to pursue so called "jackpot justice" for profit. As HBO's *Hot Coffee* notes, corporations spend considerable [public relations] dollars ensuring that their view of "frivolous court cases" is seen by the general public.

What Is Tort Reform?

Tort reform involves making changes to the tort law system that place caps on the amount of damages that people who file a civil lawsuit can recover. Civil lawsuits are filed for many types of personal injuries, from medical malpractice to car accidents to defective products.

When a civil lawsuit is filed, plaintiffs can collect both economic damages (such as medical bills and lost wages) as well as compensatory damages (money for things like pain and suffering and emotional distress or loss of companionship). Plaintiffs can also pursue punitive damages, which are specifically created to deter defendants from engaging in risky or negligent behavior again.

Tort reform places a limit on the amount of non-economic damages that can be received. In other words, the amount of pain and suffering that a person may be awarded by a jury is capped. These caps are set by individual state laws and, when they exist, the amounts and types of cases that they apply to can vary.

Arguments for Tort Reform

Arguments for tort reform primarily revolve around medical malpractice torts. In many medical malpractice cases, damages awards are very high, especially in cases of wrongful death or situations where a baby or mother is injured during the birthing process. These high damage awards increase medical malpractice insurance premiums for doctors.

The cost of the high medical malpractice insurance premiums is passed on to individuals using the health care system. A doctor who has to pay high malpractice insurance premiums, it is argued, will need to charge more to provide his services. The patients, and the system as a whole, thus have to pay. By capping medical malpractice damages, the belief is that the savings from lower malpractice premiums will be passed on to consumers, lowering the cost of health care.

Another argument is that doctors may be influenced by the risk of civil lawsuits and the potential for high damages and may begin to make medical decisions based not just on what is best for the patient, but instead on what is best for avoiding litigation. It is argued, for example, that doctors may recommend cesarean sections more often than they otherwise would do because this can reduce potential liability as they can claim that they did everything they could for the patient and used all medical tools at their disposal.

Finally, there is a concern that there will be a shortage of doctors in some fields as a result of potential tort liability and high medical malpractice premiums. Of particular concern is the field of obstetrics, where high damage awards are a serious risk.

Arguments Against Tort Reform

There are also equally compelling arguments against the concept of capping damages. In fact, tort damage caps are actually prohibited in [some] state constitutions. One of the main arguments against tort reform is that it is unfair to the patient. Why should a person who is harmed be less-than-fully compensated for all that he or she has been through? Sometimes, injuries can be especially painful and gruesome. Some of these injuries can be permanent. If the purpose of tort law is to make a plaintiff whole, how can it be fair to arbitrarily cap the amount that a person can receive?

Another argument is that the principle of tort reform violates Constitutional rights. A jury is vested with the responsibility of hearing cases, making decisions and determining an appropriate damage award. Tort damage caps limit the power of the jury, perhaps in an inappropriate way.

Finally, one of the purposes of civil liability is to make people accountable for their actions. A doctor who is negligent or a company [that] makes a defective product should be responsible for paying for the cost of what they have done. The fear of civil lawsuits can help ensure that they do behave in a careful manner and that they take steps to avoid doing harm and making themselves subject to a lawsuit. How can something that urges additional care for people's health be bad?

NOTES AND QUESTIONS

1.   Are caps on damages in tort suits a good idea? Should damages for pain and suffering be available in tort suits? What about punitive damages? Should the answers to these questions depend on whether the conduct in question was intentional, reckless, or merely negligent?

2.   As the above article notes, the McDonald's "Hot Coffee" case has become a symbol to many of what is wrong with the U.S. tort system. But the facts are somewhat complicated. The 79-year-old woman in the case suffered third-degree burns over 16 percent of her body, was hospitalized for eight days, and needed long-term skin grafting and other treatment. Under its corporate policy, McDonald's served its coffee at between 180 and 190 degrees Fahrenheit (82 to 88 degrees Celsius), and the plaintiff offered evidence that there had been other victims of burns from McDonald's coffee. The jury awarded the plaintiff $160,000 in compensatory damages and $2.7 million in punitive damages. The $2.7 million punitive damages figure was arrived at based on two days' worth of daily coffee revenues from McDonald's (the daily coffee revenues for the corporation were approximately $1.34 million). The judge presiding over the case ultimately reduced the punitive damages award to $480,000. After trial, the parties eventually settled the case for an undisclosed amount, rumored to be less than $600,000. Kevin Cain, *And Now, the Rest of the Story . . . The McDonald's Coffee Lawsuit*, 11 J. Consumer & Com. L. 14 (2007). Based on the above facts, did the U.S. tort system work properly? Or does the case demonstrate the need for tort reform?

CHAPTER 6

PROPERTY

■ ■ ■

The law of property covers a wide array of topics, ranging from traditional forms of property—such as real property (land) and personal property—to new forms of intellectual property and intangible assets. Modern principles of property law often stem from ancient concepts of ownership, but the law in the United States has consistently adapted to accommodate new and evolving forms of property. From controversial nineteenth century ownership rights over African slaves—*see The Antelope*, 23 U.S. 66 (1825) (discussing the property rights that a slave trader may have over African slaves)—to complex forms of modern property such as DNA information and internet websites, principles of property law have played a large role in U.S. jurisprudence. This chapter provides a basic foundation of U.S. property law.

A. NON-PHYSICAL PROPERTY

The first inquiry in a property dispute is whether the subject of the dispute constitutes a legally recognizable "property" interest. Although many property disputes deal with generally accepted forms of property, such as real estate or tangible objects, the following case illustrates that property issues can arise in less conventional settings.

KREMEN V. COHEN

United States Court of Appeals, Ninth Circuit, 2002
337 F.3d 1024

KOZINSKI, CIRCUIT JUDGE.

We decide whether Network Solutions may be liable for giving away a registrant's domain name on the basis of a forged letter.

Background

"Sex on the internet?," they all said. "*That*'ll never make any money." But computer-geek-turned-entrepreneur Gary Kremen knew an opportunity when he saw it. The year was 1994; domain names were free for the asking, and it would be several years yet before Henry Blodget and hordes of eager NASDAQ day traders would turn the internet into the Dutch tulip craze of our times. With a quick e-mail to the domain name registrar Network Solutions, Kremen became the proud owner of sex.com.

He registered the name to his business, Online Classifieds, and listed himself as the contact.

Con man Stephen Cohen, meanwhile, was doing time for impersonating a bankruptcy lawyer. He, too, saw the potential of the domain name. Kremen had gotten it first, but that was only a minor impediment for a man of Cohen's boundless resource and bounded integrity. Once out of prison, he sent Network Solutions what purported to be a letter he had received from Online Classifieds. It claimed the company had been "forced to dismiss Mr. Kremen," but "never got around to changing our administrative contact with the internet registration, and now our Board of directors has decided to *abandon* the domain name sex.com." Why was this unusual letter being sent via Cohen rather than to Network Solutions directly? It explained:

> Because we do not have a direct connection to the internet, we request that you notify the internet registration on our behalf, to delete our domain name sex.com. Further, we have no objections to your use of the domain name sex.com and this letter shall serve as our authorization to the internet registration to transfer sex.com to your corporation.

Despite the letter's transparent claim that a company called "*Online* Classifieds" had no internet connection, Network Solutions made no effort to contact Kremen. Instead, it accepted the letter at face value and transferred the domain name to Cohen. When Kremen contacted Network Solutions some time later, he was told it was too late to undo the transfer. Cohen went on to turn sex.com into a lucrative online porn empire.

And so began Kremen's quest to recover the domain name that was rightfully his. He sued Cohen and several affiliated companies in federal court, seeking return of the domain name and disgorgement of Cohen's profits. The district court found that the letter was indeed a forgery and ordered the domain name returned to Kremen. It also told Cohen to hand over his profits * * *. It awarded $40 million in compensatory damages and another $25 million in punitive damages.

Kremen, unfortunately, has not had much luck collecting his judgment. The district court froze Cohen's assets, but Cohen ignored the order and wired large sums of money to offshore accounts. His real estate property, under the protection of a federal receiver, was stripped of all its fixtures—even cabinet doors and toilets—in violation of another order. The court commanded Cohen to appear and show cause why he shouldn't be held in contempt, but he ignored that order, too. The district judge finally took off the gloves—he declared Cohen a fugitive from justice, signed an arrest warrant and sent the U.S. Marshals after him.

Then things started getting *really* bizarre. Kremen put up a "wanted" poster on the sex.com site with a mug shot of Cohen, offering a $50,000 reward to anyone who brought him to justice. Cohen's lawyers responded with a motion to vacate the arrest warrant. They reported that Cohen was under house arrest in Mexico and that gunfights between Mexican authorities and would-be bounty hunters seeking Kremen's reward money posed a threat to human life. The district court rejected this story as "implausible" and denied the motion. Cohen, so far as the record shows, remains at large.

Given his limited success with the bounty hunter approach, it should come as no surprise that Kremen seeks to hold someone else responsible for his losses. That someone is Network Solutions, the exclusive domain name registrar at the time of Cohen's antics. Kremen sued it for mishandling his domain name, invoking four theories * * *. [One of those theories] is that he has a property right in the domain name sex.com, and Network Solutions committed the tort of conversion by giving it away to Cohen. * * *

The district court granted summary judgment in favor of Network Solutions on all claims. * * *

* * *

* * * [With respect to conversion,] [t]he court agreed that sex.com was Kremen's property. It concluded, though, that it was intangible property to which the tort of conversion does not apply. * * *

Kremen appeals * * *.

[The court rejected two of Kremen's theories and did not reach the fourth one, finding that the third theory (conversion) was dispositive.]

* * *

Conversion

* * * To establish [the] tort [of conversion], a plaintiff must show "ownership or right to possession of property, wrongful disposition of the property right and damages." The preliminary question, then, is whether registrants have property rights in their domain names. Network Solutions all but concedes that they do. * * *

Property is a broad concept that includes "every intangible benefit and prerogative susceptible of possession or disposition." We apply a three-part test to determine whether a property right exists: "First, there must be an interest capable of precise definition; second, it must be capable of exclusive possession or control; and third, the putative owner must have established a legitimate claim to exclusivity." Domain names satisfy each criterion. Like a share of corporate stock or a plot of land, a domain name is a well-defined interest. Someone who registers a domain name decides where on the internet those who invoke that particular name—whether by typing it into their web browsers, by following a hyperlink, or by other means—are sent. Ownership is exclusive in that the registrant alone makes that decision. Moreover, like other forms of property, domain names are valued, bought and sold, often for millions of dollars * * *.

Finally, registrants have a legitimate claim to exclusivity. Registering a domain name is like staking a claim to a plot of land at the title office. It informs others that the domain name is the registrant's and no one else's. Many registrants also invest substantial time and money to develop and promote websites that depend on their domain names. Ensuring that they reap the benefits of their investments reduces uncertainty and thus encourages investment in the first place, promoting the growth of the internet overall.

Kremen therefore had an intangible property right in his domain name, and a jury could find that Network Solutions "wrongful[ly] dispos[ed] of" that right to his detriment by handing the domain name over to Cohen. The district court nevertheless rejected Kremen's conversion claim. It held that domain names, although a form of property, are intangibles not subject to conversion. This rationale derives from a distinction tort law once drew between tangible and intangible property: Conversion was originally a remedy for the wrongful taking of another's lost goods, so it applied only to tangible property. Virtually every jurisdiction, however, has discarded this rigid limitation to some degree. Many courts ignore or expressly reject it. Others reject it for some intangibles but not others. The Restatement, for example, recommends the following test:

> (1) Where there is conversion of a document in which intangible rights are merged, the damages include the value of such rights.
>
> (2) One who effectively prevents the exercise of intangible rights of the kind customarily *merged in a document* is subject to a liability similar to that for conversion, even though the document is not itself converted.

Restatement (Second) of Torts § 242 (1965) (emphasis added [by the court]). An intangible is "merged" in a document when, "by the appropriate rule of law, the right to the immediate possession of a chattel and the power to acquire such possession is *represented by* [the] document," or when "an intangible obligation [is] *represented by* [the] document, which is regarded as equivalent to the obligation." *Id.* cmt. a (emphasis added [by the court]). The district court applied this test and found no evidence that Kremen's domain name was merged in a document.

The court assumed that California follows the Restatement on this issue. Our review, however, revealed that "there do not appear to be any California cases squarely addressing whether the 'merged with' requirement is a part of California law." * * *

We conclude that * * * California does not follow the Restatement's strict requirement that some document must actually represent the owner's intangible property right. On the contrary, courts routinely apply the tort to intangibles without inquiring whether they are merged in a document and, while it's often possible to dream up *some* document the intangible is connected to in some fashion, it's seldom one that represents the owner's property interest. * * *

Were it necessary to settle the issue once and for all, we would * * * hold that conversion is "a remedy for the conversion of every species of personal property." But we need not do so to resolve this case. Assuming *arguendo* that California retains some vestigial merger requirement, it is clearly minimal, and at most requires only *some* connection to a document or tangible object—not representation of the owner's intangible interest in the strict Restatement sense.

Kremen's domain name falls easily within this class of property. He argues that the relevant document is the Domain Name System, or "DNS"—the distributed electronic database that associates domain names like sex.com with particular computers connected to the internet. We agree that the DNS is a document (or perhaps more accurately a collection of documents). That it is stored in electronic form rather than on ink and paper is immaterial. It would be a curious jurisprudence that turned on the existence of a *paper* document rather than an electronic one. Torching a company's file room would then be conversion while hacking into its mainframe and deleting its data would not. That is not the law, at least not in California.

The DNS also bears some relation to Kremen's domain name. We need not delve too far into the mechanics of the internet to resolve this case. It is sufficient to observe that information correlating Kremen's domain name with a particular computer on the internet must exist somewhere in some form in the DNS; if it did not, the database would not serve its intended purpose. Change the information in the DNS, and you change the website people see when they type "www.sex.com."

Network Solutions quibbles about the mechanics of the DNS. It points out that the data corresponding to Kremen's domain name is not stored in a single record, but is found in several different places: The components of the domain name ("sex" and "com") are stored in two different places, and each is copied and stored on several machines to create redundancy and speed up response times. Network Solutions' theory seems to be that intangibles are not subject to conversion unless they are associated only with a *single* document.

Even if Network Solutions were correct that there is no single record in the DNS architecture with which Kremen's intangible property right is associated, that is no impediment under California law. A share of stock, for example, may be evidenced by more than one document. A customer list is protected, even if it's recorded on index cards rather than a single piece of paper. Audio recordings may be duplicated, and confidential information and regulatory filings may be photocopied. Network Solutions' "single document" theory is unsupported.

Network Solutions also argues that the DNS is not a document because it is refreshed every twelve hours when updated domain name information is broadcast across the internet. This theory is even less persuasive. A document doesn't cease being a document merely because it is often updated. If that were the case, a share registry would fail whenever shareholders were periodically added or dropped, as would an address file whenever business cards were added or removed. Whether a document is updated by inserting and deleting particular records or by replacing an old file with an entirely new one is a technical detail with no legal significance.

Kremen's domain name is protected by California conversion law, even on the grudging reading we have given it. Exposing Network Solutions to liability when it gives away a registrant's domain name on the basis of a forged letter is no different from holding a corporation liable when it gives away someone's shares under the same circumstances. We have not "creat[ed] new tort duties" in reaching this result. We have only applied settled principles of conversion law to what the parties and the district court all agree is a species of property.

The district court supported its contrary holding with several policy rationales, but none is sufficient grounds to depart from the common law rule. The court was reluctant to apply the tort of conversion because of its strict liability nature. This concern rings somewhat hollow in this case because the district court effectively exempted Network Solutions from liability to Kremen altogether, whether or not it was negligent. Network Solutions made no effort to contact Kremen before giving away his domain name, despite receiving a facially suspect letter from a third party. A jury would be justified in finding it was unreasonably careless.

We must, of course, take the broader view, but there is nothing unfair about holding a company responsible for giving away someone else's property even if it was not at fault. Cohen is obviously the guilty party here, and the one who should in all fairness pay for his theft. But he's skipped the country, and his money is stashed in some offshore bank account. Unless Kremen's luck with his bounty hunters improves, Cohen is out of the picture. The question becomes whether Network Solutions should be open to liability for its decision to hand over Kremen's domain name. Negligent or not, it was Network Solutions that gave away Kremen's property. Kremen never did anything. It would not be unfair to hold Network Solutions responsible and force *it* to try to recoup its losses by chasing down Cohen. This, at any rate, is the logic of the common law, and we do not lightly discard it.

The district court was worried that "the threat of litigation threatens to stifle the registration system by requiring further regulations by [Network Solutions] and potential increases in fees." Given that Network Solutions' "regulations" evidently allowed it to hand over a registrant's domain name on the basis of a facially suspect letter without even contacting him, "further regulations" don't seem like such a bad idea. And the prospect of higher fees presents no issue here that it doesn't in any other context. A bank could lower its ATM fees if it didn't have to pay security guards, but we doubt most depositors would think that was a good idea.

The district court thought there were "methods better suited to regulate the vagaries of domain names" and left it "to the legislature to fashion an appropriate statutory scheme." The legislature, of course, is always free (within constitutional bounds) to refashion the system that courts come up with. But that doesn't mean we should throw up our hands and let private relations degenerate into a free-for-all in the meantime. We apply the common law until the legislature tells us otherwise. And the common law does not stand idle while people give away the property of others.

The evidence supported a claim for conversion, and the district court should not have rejected it.

* * *

NOTES AND QUESTIONS

1. How does the *Kremen* court define property? What does the court conclude with respect to the internet domain name at issue?

2. How did the district court in *Kremen* rule on the conversion issue? How did the court of appeals rule? Which court's rationale is more persuasive?

3. As the Ninth Circuit noted in *Kremen*, property is a broad concept that encompasses even intangible possessory interests. Accordingly, the issue of what constitutes property has arisen in a variety of circumstances. *See, e.g.*, *M.C. Multi-Family Dev., L.L.C. v. Crestdale Assocs., Ltd.*, 124 Nev. 901, 193 P.3d 536 (2008) (holding that a contractor's license held by a real estate developer was a protected intangible property interest); *Creveling v. Treser*, 245 F. App'x 575 (9th Cir. 2007) (holding that even though a member of an Indian tribe had a right to fish in a stream on his property, the member failed to demonstrate a property interest in fish that the state removed from a canal upstream of his property); *G.S. Rasmussen & Assocs., Inc. v. Kalitta Flying Serv., Inc.*, 958 F.2d 896 (9th Cir. 1992) (holding that an aeronautical engineer's exclusive Federal Aviation Administration certification, which permitted him to make an approved design change to an aircraft, was a protected intangible property interest).

4.   The *Kremen* case involved a dispute over an internet domain name. Similar property issues have arisen with respect to social media accounts. *See, e.g., Eagle v. Morgan*, No. 11-4303, 2013 WL 943350 (E.D. Pa. Mar. 12, 2013) (holding that the plaintiff could not support a sufficient property interest in her "LinkedIn" account when the plaintiff brought an action for conversion for interference with her use of the account); *PhoneDog v. Kravitz*, 2011 WL 5415612 (N.D. Cal. Nov. 8, 2011) (holding that the plaintiff could avoid dismissal as a matter of law on a conversion claim after allegedly being denied access to a property interest in a "Twitter" account). On the other hand, some scholars have argued that traditional property claims may not be the most viable legal theory for pursuing social media-related claims. *See, e.g.,* Zoe Argento, *Whose Social Network Account? A Trade Secret Approach to Allocating Rights*, 19 Mich. Telecomm. & Tech. L. Rev. 201 (2013) (arguing that social media account holders should not try to create a new species of personal property, but rather, that trade secret law (*e.g.*, that a secret password for access to an account is a trade secret) is a more suitable basis for seeking relief); Michelle Hull, *Sports Leagues' New Social Media Policies: Enforcement Under Copyright Law and State Law*, 34 Colum. J.L. & Arts 457 (2011) (noting that copyright law may be a viable option to protect social media rights). Should property rights extend to social media accounts in the same way that they extend to domain names?

B. OWNERSHIP

Once it is established that the subject of a dispute is indeed a legally recognizable "property" interest, the next inquiry involves determining who "owns" the property. The following case deals with a dispute over ownership rights.

MOORE V. THE REGENTS OF THE UNIVERSITY OF CALIFORNIA

Supreme Court of California, En Banc, 1990
51 Cal.3d 120, 793 P.2d 479

PANELLI, JUSTICE.

I.   INTRODUCTION

We granted review in this case to determine whether plaintiff has stated a cause of action against his physician and other defendants for using his cells in potentially lucrative medical research without his permission. * * *

II. FACTS

* * * [W]e briefly summarize the pertinent factual allegations of the * * * complaint.

The plaintiff is John Moore (Moore), who underwent treatment for hairy-cell leukemia at the Medical Center of the University of California at

Los Angeles (UCLA Medical Center). The five defendants are: (1) Dr. David W. Golde (Golde), a physician who attended Moore at UCLA Medical Center; (2) the Regents of the University of California (Regents), who own and operate the university; (3) Shirley G. Quan, a researcher employed by the Regents; (4) Genetics Institute, Inc. (Genetics Institute); and (5) Sandoz Pharmaceuticals Corporation and related entities (collectively Sandoz).

Moore first visited UCLA Medical Center on October 5, 1976, shortly after he learned that he had hairy-cell leukemia. After hospitalizing Moore and "withdr[awing] extensive amounts of blood, bone marrow aspirate, and other bodily substances," Golde confirmed that diagnosis. At this time all defendants, including Golde, were aware that "certain blood products and blood components were of great value in a number of commercial and scientific efforts" and that access to a patient whose blood contained these substances would provide "competitive, commercial, and scientific advantages."

On October 8, 1976, Golde recommended that Moore's spleen be removed. Golde informed Moore "that he had reason to fear for his life, and that the proposed splenectomy operation . . . was necessary to slow down the progress of his disease." Based upon Golde's representations, Moore signed a written consent form authorizing the splenectomy.

Before the operation, Golde and Quan "formed the intent and made arrangements to obtain portions of [Moore's] spleen following its removal" and to take them to a separate research unit. Golde gave written instructions to this effect on October 18 and 19, 1976. These research activities "were not intended to have . . . any relation to [Moore's] medical . . . care." However, neither Golde nor Quan informed Moore of their plans to conduct this research or requested his permission. Surgeons at UCLA Medical Center, [who are not] defendants, removed Moore's spleen on October 20, 1976.

Moore returned to the UCLA Medical Center several times between November 1976 and September 1983. He did so at Golde's direction and based upon representations "that such visits were necessary and required for his health and well-being, and based upon the trust inherent in and by virtue of the physician-patient relationship. . . ." On each of these visits Golde withdrew additional samples of "blood, blood serum, skin, bone marrow aspirate, and sperm." On each occasion Moore travelled to the UCLA Medical Center from his home in Seattle because he had been told that the procedures were to be performed only there and only under Golde's direction.

"In fact, [however,] throughout the period of time that [Moore] was under [Golde's] care and treatment, . . . the defendants were actively involved in a number of activities which they concealed from [Moore]. . . ." Specifically, defendants were conducting research on Moore's cells and planned to "benefit financially and competitively . . . [by exploiting the cells] and [their] exclusive access to [the cells] by virtue of [Golde's] on-going physician-patient relationship. . . ."

Sometime before August 1979, Golde established a cell line from Moore's T-lymphocytes.[2] On January 30, 1981, the Regents applied for a patent on the cell line, listing Golde and Quan as inventors. "[B]y virtue of an established policy . . . , [the] Regents, Golde, and Quan would share in any royalties or profits . . . arising out of [the] patent." The patent issued on March 20, 1984, naming Golde and Quan as the inventors of the cell line and the Regents as the assignee of the patent.

The Regents' patent also covers various methods for using the cell line to produce lymphokines. Moore admits in his complaint that "the true clinical potential of each of the lymphokines . . . [is] difficult to predict, [but] . . . competing commercial firms in these relevant fields have published reports in biotechnology industry periodicals predicting a potential market of approximately $3.01 Billion Dollars by the year 1990 for a whole range of [such lymphokines]. . . ."

With the Regents' assistance, Golde negotiated agreements for commercial development of the cell line and products to be derived from it. Under an agreement with Genetics Institute, Golde "became a paid consultant" and "acquired the rights to 75,000 shares of common stock." Genetics Institute also agreed to pay Golde and the Regents "at least $330,000 over three years, including a pro-rata share of [Golde's] salary and fringe benefits, in exchange for . . . exclusive access to the materials and research performed" on the cell line and products derived from it. On June 4, 1982, Sandoz "was added to the agreement," and compensation payable to Golde and the Regents was increased by $110,000. "[T]hroughout this period, . . . Quan spent as much as 70 [percent] of her time working for [the] Regents on research" related to the cell line.

Based upon these allegations, Moore attempted to state 13 causes of action [including conversion]. * * * The superior court [found] * * * the entire complaint insufficient * * *.

---

[2]   A T-lymphocyte is a type of white blood cell. T-lymphocytes produce lymphokines, or proteins that regulate the immune system. Some lymphokines have potential therapeutic value. If the genetic material responsible for producing a particular lymphokine can be identified, it can sometimes be used to manufacture large quantities of the lymphokine through the techniques of recombinant DNA [combing DNA from different sources].

While the genetic code for lymphokines does not vary from individual to individual, it can nevertheless be quite difficult to locate the gene responsible for a particular lymphokine. Because T-lymphocytes produce many different lymphokines, the relevant gene is often like a needle in a haystack. Moore's T-lymphocytes were interesting to the defendants because they overproduced certain lymphokines, thus making the corresponding genetic material easier to identify. * * *

Cells taken directly from the body (primary cells) are not very useful for these purposes. Primary cells typically reproduce a few times and then die. One can, however, sometimes continue to use cells for an extended period of time by developing them into a "cell line," a culture capable of reproducing indefinitely. This is not, however, always an easy task. * * *

* * * [T]he Court of Appeal reversed, holding that the complaint [stated] a cause of action for conversion. * * *

III. DISCUSSION

A. Breach of Fiduciary Duty and Lack of Informed Consent

[The court held "that a physician who is seeking a patient's consent for a medical procedure must, in order to satisfy his fiduciary duty and to obtain the patient's informed consent, disclose personal interests unrelated to the patient's health, whether research or economic, that may affect his medical judgment."]

[With respect to Dr. Golde, the court held that "Moore plainly asserts that Golde concealed an economic interest in the postoperative procedures. Therefore, * * * the allegations state a cause of action for breach of fiduciary duty or lack of informed consent." With respect to the remaining defendants, who are not physicians and thus do not stand in a fiduciary relationship with Moore, the court held that "if any of these defendants is to be liable for breach of fiduciary duty or performing medical procedures without informed consent, it can only be on account of Golde's acts and on the basis of a recognized theory of secondary liability, such as respondeat superior."* The court thus determined that issues involving those defendants should first be addressed on remand.]

* * *

B. Conversion

Moore also attempts to characterize the invasion of his rights as a conversion—a tort that protects against interference with possessory and ownership interests in personal property. He theorizes that he continued to own his cells following their removal from his body, at least for the purpose of directing their use, and that he never consented to their use in potentially lucrative medical research. Thus, * * * defendants' unauthorized use of his cells constitutes a conversion. As a result of the alleged conversion, Moore claims a proprietary interest in each of the products that any of the defendants might ever create from his cells or the patented cell line.

No court, however, has ever in a reported decision imposed conversion liability for the use of human cells in medical research. While that fact does not end our inquiry, it raises a flag of caution. * * *

* * * [W]e should be hesitant to "impose [new tort duties] when to do so would involve complex policy decisions," especially when such decisions are more appropriately the subject of legislative deliberation and resolution. * * *

---

*   The doctrine of respondeat superior (holding an employer liable for the employee's actions) is covered in Chapter 5. [Ed.]

* * * [W]e first consider whether the tort of conversion clearly gives Moore a cause of action under existing law. We do not believe it does. * * * [We then] consider next whether it is advisable to extend the tort to this context.

1.   Moore's Claim Under Existing Law

"To establish a conversion, plaintiff must establish an actual interference with his *ownership* or *right of possession*. . . . Where plaintiff neither has title to the property alleged to have been converted, nor possession thereof, he cannot maintain an action for conversion."

* * *

Neither the Court of Appeal's opinion, the parties' briefs, nor our research discloses a case holding that a person retains a sufficient interest in excised cells to support a cause of action for conversion. We do not find this surprising * * *. [S]pecialized statutes, not the law of conversion, [are what] courts ordinarily should and do look [to] for guidance on the disposition of human biological materials.

Lacking direct authority for importing the law of conversion into this context, Moore relies * * * primarily on decisions addressing privacy rights. One line of cases involves unwanted publicity. [But those decisions did not rely] on property law. * * * [And o]nly property can be converted.

Not only are the wrongful-publicity cases irrelevant to the issue of conversion, but the analogy to them seriously misconceives the nature of the genetic materials and research involved in this case. Moore * * * argues that "[i]f the courts have found a sufficient proprietary interest in one's persona, how could one not have a right in one's own genetic material, something far more profoundly the essence of one's human uniqueness than a name or a face?" However, * * * the goal and result of defendants' efforts has been to manufacture lymphokines. Lymphokines, unlike a name or a face, have the same molecular structure in every human being and the same, important functions in every human being's immune system. Moreover, the particular genetic material which is responsible for the natural production of lymphokines, and which defendants use to manufacture lymphokines in the laboratory, is also the same in every person; it is no more unique to Moore than the number of vertebrae in the spine or the chemical formula of hemoglobin.

Another privacy case offered by analogy to support Moore's claim establishes only that patients have a right to refuse medical treatment. * * * Yet one may earnestly wish to protect privacy and dignity without accepting the extremely problematic conclusion that interference with those interests amounts to a conversion of personal property. * * *

The next consideration that makes Moore's claim of ownership problematic is California statutory law, which drastically limits a patient's control over excised cells. Pursuant to Health and Safety Code section 7054.4, "[n]otwithstanding any other provision of law, recognizable anatomical parts, human tissues, anatomical human remains, or infectious waste following conclusion of scientific use shall be disposed of by interment, incineration, or any other method determined by the state department [of health services] to protect the public health and safety." Clearly the Legislature did not specifically intend this statute to resolve the question of whether a patient is entitled to compensation for the nonconsensual use of excised cells. A primary object of the statute is to ensure the safe handling of potentially hazardous biological waste materials. Yet one cannot escape the conclusion that the statute's practical effect is to limit, drastically, a patient's control over excised cells. By restricting how excised cells may be used and requiring their eventual destruction, the statute eliminates so many of the rights ordinarily attached to property that one cannot simply assume that what is left amounts to "property" or "ownership" for purposes of conversion law.

* * *

Finally, the subject matter of the Regents' patent—the patented cell line and the products derived from it—cannot be Moore's property. This is because the patented cell line is both factually and legally distinct from the cells taken from Moore's body. Federal law permits the patenting of organisms that represent the product of "human ingenuity," but not naturally occurring organisms. Human cell lines are patentable because "[l]ong-term adaptation and growth of human tissues and cells in culture is difficult—often considered an art . . . ," and the probability of success is low. It is this *inventive effort* that patent law rewards, not the discovery of naturally occurring raw materials. Thus, Moore's allegations that he owns the cell line and the products derived from it are inconsistent with the patent, which constitutes an authoritative determination that the cell line is the product of invention. * * *

2. Should Conversion Liability Be Extended?

* * *

There are three reasons why [conversion liability should not be extended]. First, a fair balancing of the relevant policy considerations counsels against extending the tort. Second, problems in this area are better suited to legislative resolution. Third, the tort of conversion is not necessary to protect patients' rights. * * *

Of the relevant policy considerations, two are of overriding importance. The first is protection of a competent patient's right to make autonomous medical decisions. * * * This policy weighs in favor of providing a remedy to patients when physicians act with undisclosed motives that may affect their professional judgment. The second * * * is that we not threaten with disabling civil liability innocent parties who are engaged in socially useful activities, such as researchers who have no reason to believe that their use of a particular cell sample is, or may be, against a donor's wishes.

* * *

* * * [A]n examination of the relevant policy considerations suggests an appropriate balance: Liability based upon existing disclosure obligations, rather than an unprecedented extension of the conversion theory, protects patients' rights of privacy and autonomy without unnecessarily hindering research.

To be sure, the threat of liability for conversion might help to enforce patients' rights indirectly. This is because physicians might be able to avoid liability by obtaining patients' consent, in the broadest possible terms, to any conceivable subsequent research use of excised cells. Unfortunately, to extend the conversion theory would utterly sacrifice the other goal of protecting innocent parties. Since conversion is a strict liability tort [*i.e.*, negligence or mistake is no excuse,] it would impose liability on all those into whose hands the cells come, whether or not the particular defendant participated in, or knew of, the inadequate disclosures that violated the patient's right to make an informed decision. * * *

Research on human cells plays a critical role in medical research. This is so because researchers are increasingly able to isolate naturally occurring, medically useful biological substances and to produce useful quantities of such substances through genetic engineering. These efforts are beginning to bear fruit. Products developed through biotechnology that have already been approved for marketing in this country include treatments and tests for leukemia, cancer, diabetes, dwarfism, hepatitis-B, kidney transplant rejection, emphysema, osteoporosis, ulcers, anemia, infertility, and gynecological tumors, to name but a few.

The extension of conversion law into this area will hinder research by restricting access to the necessary raw materials. Thousands of human cell lines already exist in tissue repositories * * *. These repositories respond to tens of thousands of requests for samples annually. Since the patent office requires the holders of patents on cell lines to make samples available to anyone, many patent holders place their cell lines in repositories to avoid the administrative burden of responding to requests. At present, human cell lines are routinely copied and distributed to other researchers for experimental purposes, usually free of charge. This exchange of scientific materials, which still is relatively free and efficient, will surely be compromised if each cell sample becomes the potential subject matter of a lawsuit.

To expand liability by extending conversion law into this area would have a broad impact. The House Committee on Science and Technology of the United States Congress found that "49 percent of the researchers at medical institutions surveyed used human tissues or cells in their research." * * *

* * *

* * * [T]he theory of liability that Moore urges us to endorse threatens to destroy the economic incentive to conduct important medical research. If the use of cells in research is a conversion, then with every cell sample a researcher purchases a ticket in a litigation lottery. Because liability for conversion is predicated on a continuing ownership interest, "companies are unlikely to invest heavily in developing, manufacturing, or marketing a product when uncertainty about clear title exists." In our view, * * * "[i]t is not unreasonable to conclude * * * that the imposition of a harsher test for liability would not further the public interest in the development and availability of these important products."

* * *

If the scientific users of human cells are to be held liable for failing to investigate the consensual pedigree of their raw materials, we believe the Legislature should make that decision. * * *

Finally, there is no pressing need to impose a judicially created rule of strict liability, since enforcement of physicians' disclosure obligations will protect patients against the very type of harm with which Moore was threatened. So long as a physician discloses research and economic interests that may affect his judgment, the patient is protected from conflicts of interest. Aware of any conflicts, the patient can make an informed decision to consent to treatment, or to withhold consent and look elsewhere for medical assistance. * * *

For these reasons, we hold that the allegations of Moore's third amended complaint state a cause of action for breach of fiduciary duty or lack of informed consent, but not conversion.

* * *

[Concurring opinion by JUSTICE ARABIAN is omitted.]

[Concurring and dissenting opinion by JUSTICE BROUSSARD is omitted.]

MOSK, JUSTICE, dissenting.

I dissent.

* * * For convenience I shall discuss the six premises of the majority's conclusion in the order in which they appear.

1.

The majority first take the position that Moore has no cause of action for conversion under existing law because he retained no "ownership interest" in his cells after they were removed from his body. * * *

* * *

The [majority notes] that "no reported judicial decision supports Moore's claim * * *." Neither, however, is there any reported decision rejecting such a claim. * * *

The majority * * * [also] conclude[s] in effect that in the present case we should also "look for guidance" to the Legislature rather than to the law of conversion. Surely this argument is out of place in an opinion of the highest court of this state. * * * [T]he law of conversion is a creature of the common law. * * * Although the Legislature may of course speak to the subject, in the common law system the primary instruments of this evolution are the courts * * *."

Especially is this true in the field of torts. * * *

* * *

2.

The majority's second reason for doubting that Moore retained an ownership interest in his cells after their excision is that "[section 7054.4] ... drastically limits a patient's control over excised cells." * * * I do not believe section 7054.4 supports the * * * majority.

First, * * * the statute does not authorize the principal use that defendants claim the right to make of Moore's tissue, i.e., its commercial exploitation. * * *

By its terms, section 7054.4 permits only "scientific use" of excised body parts and tissue before they must be destroyed. * * * It would stretch the English language beyond recognition * * * to say that commercial exploitation of the kind and degree alleged here is * * * a usual and ordinary meaning of the phrase "scientific use."

* * * Under [Moore's] allegations, defendants Dr. David W. Golde and Shirley G. Quan were not only scientists, they were also full-fledged entrepreneurs: the complaint repeatedly declares that they appropriated Moore's tissue in order "to further defendants' independent research and commercial activities and promote their economic, financial and competitive interests." The complaint also alleges that defendant Regents of the University of California (hereafter Regents) actively assisted the individual defendants in applying for patent rights and in negotiating with bioengineering and pharmaceutical companies to exploit the commercial potential of Moore's tissue. Finally, the complaint alleges in detail the contractual arrangements between the foregoing defendants and defendants Genetics Institute, Inc., and Sandoz Pharmaceuticals Corporation, giving the latter companies exclusive rights to exploit that commercial potential while providing substantial financial benefits to the individual defendants * * *. To exclude such traditionally commercial

activities from the phrase "scientific use" * * * gives the phrase its usual and ordinary meaning * * *.

Secondly, even if section 7054.4 does permit defendants' commercial exploitation of Moore's tissue under the guise of "scientific use," it does not follow that * * * the statute "eliminates so many of the rights ordinarily attached to property" that what remains does not amount to "property" or "ownership" for purposes of the law of conversion.

The concepts of property and ownership in our law are extremely broad. * * * " 'The term 'property' is sufficiently comprehensive to include every species of estate, real and personal, and everything which one person can own and transfer to another. It extends to every species of right and interest capable of being enjoyed as such upon which it is practicable to place a money value.' "

Being broad, the concept of property is also abstract: rather than referring directly to a material object such as a parcel of land or the tractor that cultivates it, the concept of property is often said to refer to a "bundle of rights" that may be exercised with respect to that object—principally the rights to possess the property, to use the property, to exclude others from the property, and to dispose of the property by sale or by gift. * * * But the same bundle of rights does not attach to all forms of property. For a variety of policy reasons, the law limits or even forbids the exercise of certain rights over certain forms of property. For example, both law and contract may limit the right of an owner of real property to use his parcel as he sees fit.[6] Owners of various forms of personal property may likewise be subject to restrictions on the time, place, and manner of their use. Limitations on the disposition of real property, while less common, may also be imposed. Finally, some types of personal property may be sold but not given away, while others may be given away but not sold, and still others may neither be given away nor sold.

In each of the foregoing instances, the limitation or prohibition diminishes the bundle of rights that would otherwise attach to the property, yet what remains is still deemed in law to be a protectable property interest. * * * Moore * * * retained valuable rights in that tissue. Above all, at the time of its excision he at least had *the right to do with his own tissue whatever the defendants did with it: i.e.,* he could have contracted with researchers and pharmaceutical companies to develop and exploit the vast commercial potential of his tissue and its products. * * *

---

[6]   Zoning or nuisance laws, or covenants running with the land or equitable servitudes, or condominium declarations, may prohibit certain uses of the parcel or regulate the number, size, location, etc., of buildings an owner may erect on it. Even if rental of the property is a permitted use, rent control laws may limit the benefits of that use. * * * Historic preservation laws may prohibit an owner from demolishing a building on the property, or even from altering its appearance. And endangered species laws may limit an owner's right to develop the land from its natural state.

3.

The majority's third and last reason for their conclusion that Moore has no cause of action for conversion under existing law is that "the subject matter of the Regents' patent—the patented cell line and the products derived from it—cannot be Moore's property." The majority then offer a dual explanation: "This is because the patented cell line is *factually* and *legally* distinct from the cells taken from Moore's body." Neither branch of the explanation withstands analysis.

* * * For present purposes no distinction can be drawn between Moore's cells and the Mo cell line. It appears that the principal reason for establishing a cell line is not to "improve" the quality of the parent cells but simply to extend their life indefinitely, in order to permit long-term study and/or exploitation of the qualities already present in such cells. The complaint alleges that Moore's cells naturally produced certain valuable proteins in larger than normal quantities; indeed, that was why defendants were eager to culture them in the first place. * * *

Second, the majority assert in effect that Moore cannot have an ownership interest in the Mo cell line because defendants patented it. The majority's point wholly fails to meet Moore's claim that he is entitled to compensation for defendants' unauthorized use of his bodily tissues *before* defendants patented the Mo cell line * * *.

Nor did the issuance of the patent in 1984 necessarily have the drastic effect that the majority contend. To be sure, the patent granted defendants the exclusive right to make, use, or sell the invention for a period of 17 years. But Moore * * * seeks to show that he is entitled * * * to some share in the profits that defendants have made and will make from their commercial exploitation of the Mo cell line. * * * [N]o one can question Moore's crucial contribution to the invention* * *: but for the cells of Moore's body taken by defendants, *there would have been no Mo cell line.* * * *

Nevertheless the majority conclude that the patent somehow cut off all Moore's rights * * *. The majority cite no authority for this unfair result, and I cannot believe it is compelled by the general law of patents * * *. I am aware that "patients and research subjects who contribute cells to research will not be considered inventors." Nor is such a person, strictly speaking, a "joint inventor" [under federal law]. But he does fall within the spirit of the law[, which] * * * "guarantees that all who contribute in a substantial way to a product's development benefit from the reward that the product brings."

* * * "[T]he policy reasons that inform joint inventor patents should also apply to cell donors. * * * By providing the researchers with unique raw materials, * * * the donors become necessary contributors to the product." * * *

Under this reasoning, * * * the law of patents would not be a bar to Moore's assertion of an ownership interest in his cells * * *.

4.

Having concluded—mistakenly, in my view—that Moore has no cause of action for conversion under existing law, the majority next consider whether to "extend" the conversion cause of action to this context. * * *

* * *

The majority begin their analysis by stressing the obvious facts that research on human cells plays an increasingly important role in the progress of medicine * * *. Yet it does not necessarily follow that * * * application of the law of conversion to this area "will hinder research * * *."

To begin with, if the relevant exchange of scientific materials was ever "free and efficient," it is much less so today. Since biological products of genetic engineering became patentable in 1980, human cell lines have been amenable to patent protection * * *. Among those who have taken advantage of this development, of course, are the defendants herein: * * * defendants Golde and Quan obtained a patent on the Mo cell line in 1984 and assigned it to defendant Regents. With such patentability has come a drastic reduction in the formerly free access of researchers to new cell lines and their products * * *.

An even greater force for restricting the free exchange of new cell lines and their products has been the rise of the biotechnology industry and the increasing involvement of academic researchers in that industry. * * *

In their turn, the biotechnological and pharmaceutical companies demanded and received exclusive rights in the scientists' discoveries * * *.

Secondly, to the extent that cell cultures and cell lines may still be "freely exchanged," *e.g.*, for purely research purposes, it does not follow that the researcher who obtains such material must necessarily remain ignorant of any limitations on its use: by means of appropriate recordkeeping, the researcher can be assured that the source of the material has consented to his proposed use of it, and hence that such use is not a conversion. * * *

* * *

* * * The majority claim that a conversion cause of action threatens to "destroy the economic incentive" to conduct the type of research here in issue, but it is difficult to take this hyperbole seriously. * * * [W]ith proper recordkeeping the researcher acquires not a litigation-lottery ticket but the information he needs precisely in order to avoid litigation. * * * [And] the risk at hand is not of a multiplicity of actions: * * * here [the harm] can be suffered by only one person—the original source of the research material that began that process. * * *

In any event, * * * our society acknowledges a profound ethical imperative to respect the human body as the physical and temporal expression of the unique human persona. * * * [Exploitation] arises wherever scientists or industrialists claim, as defendants claim here, the right to appropriate and exploit a patient's tissue for their sole economic benefit—the right, in other words, to freely mine or harvest valuable physical properties of the patient's body * * *.

* * * [Moreover], [o]ur society values fundamental fairness in dealings between its members, and condemns the unjust enrichment of any member at the expense of another. * * * In the case at bar, for example, the complaint alleges that the market for the kinds of proteins produced by the Mo cell line was predicted to exceed $3 billion by 1990. These profits are currently shared exclusively between the biotechnology industry and the universities that support that industry. * * *

There is, however, a third party to the biotechnology enterprise—the patient who is the source of the blood or tissue from which all these profits are derived. * * * [H]is contribution to the venture is absolutely crucial: * * * but for the cells of Moore's body taken by defendants there would have been no Mo cell line at all. * * *

There will be such equitable sharing if the courts recognize that the patient has a legally protected property interest in his own body and its products * * *.

* * *

5.

The majority's second reason for declining to extend the conversion cause of action to the present context is that "the Legislature should make that decision." * * * The fact that the Legislature may intervene * * *, however, does not in the meanwhile relieve the courts of their duty of enforcing—or if need be, fashioning—an effective judicial remedy for the wrong here alleged. * * *

* * *

6.

The majority's final reason for refusing to recognize a conversion cause of action on these facts is that "there is no pressing need" to do so because [a claim exists based on nondisclosure]. * * *

* * *

I disagree * * * with the majority's * * * conclusion that in the present context a nondisclosure cause of action is an adequate * * * substitute for a conversion cause of action. In my view the nondisclosure cause of action falls short [for several reasons].

* * *

[To begin with, the nondisclosure] remedy is largely illusory. * * * There are two barriers to recovery. First, "the patient must show that if he or she had been informed of all pertinent information, he or she would have declined to consent to the procedure in question." * * *

The second barrier to recovery is still higher * * *: he must also prove that in the same circumstances *no reasonably prudent person* would have given such consent. * * *

* * * [I]t may be difficult for a plaintiff to prove that no reasonably prudent person would have consented to the proposed treatment if the doctor had disclosed the particular risk of physical harm that ultimately caused the injury. This is because in many cases the potential benefits of the treatment to the plaintiff clearly outweigh the undisclosed risk of harm. But that imbalance will be even greater in the kind of nondisclosure action that the majority now contemplate: here we deal not with a risk of physical injuries such as a stroke, but with the possibility that the doctor might later use some of the patient's cast-off tissue for scientific research or the development of commercial products. Few if any judges or juries are likely to believe that disclosure of such a possibility of research or development would dissuade a reasonably prudent person from consenting to the treatment. For example, in the case at bar no trier of fact is likely to believe that if defendants had disclosed their plans for using Moore's cells, no reasonably prudent person in Moore's position—*i.e.*, a leukemia patient suffering from a grossly enlarged spleen—would have consented to the routine operation that saved or at least prolonged his life. * * * In this context, accordingly, the threat of suit on a nondisclosure cause of action is largely a paper tiger.

[Moreover,] the nondisclosure cause of action is inadequate [because] it fails to solve half the problem before us: it gives the patient only the right to *refuse* consent, *i.e.*, the right to prohibit the commercialization of his tissue; it does not give him the right to *grant* consent to that commercialization on the condition that he share in its proceeds. * * *

* * * [T]he patient can say no, but he cannot say yes and expect to share in the proceeds of his contribution. Yet, * * * there are sound reasons of ethics and equity to recognize the patient's right to participate in such benefits. * * *

[In addition,] the nondisclosure cause of action fails to reach a major class of potential defendants: all those who are outside the strict physician-patient relationship with the plaintiff. Thus the majority concede that here only defendant Golde, the treating physician, can be directly liable to Moore on a nondisclosure cause of action * * *. As to [the other] defendants, the majority can offer Moore only a slim hope of recovery: if they are to be liable on a nondisclosure cause of action * * * "it can only be on account of

Golde's acts and on the basis of a recognized theory of secondary liability, such as respondeat superior." * * *

To the extent that a plaintiff such as Moore is unable to plead or prove a satisfactory theory of secondary liability, the nondisclosure cause of action will thus be inadequate to reach a number of parties to the commercial exploitation of his tissue. * * * [S]ome or all of those parties may well have participated more in, and profited more from, such exploitation than the particular physician with whom the plaintiff happened to have a formal doctor-patient relationship at the time.

* * *

I would affirm the decision of the Court of Appeal * * *.

NOTES AND QUESTIONS

1.   The majority and dissent in *Moore* take sharply different views. What is the majority's rationale for rejecting the conversion claim? How does the dissent respond? Which arguments are more persuasive?

2.   In an opinion not reproduced above, Justice Arabian concurred in the majority's result, but echoed Justice Mosk's concerns about the moral dimension of the case. As Justice Arabian stated: "Plaintiff has asked us to * * * regard the human vessel—the single most venerated and protected subject in any civilized society—as equal with the basest commercial commodity." *Moore*, 51 Cal.3d 120, 148, 793 P.2d 479, 497 (Arabian, J., concurring). Should the majority have paid more attention to the moral issues in the case?

3.   *Moore* has generated extensive commentary and is often viewed as the foundation for current property law litigation involving genetic information. *See, e.g.*, Michelle Huckaby Lewis, *Laboratory Specimens and Genetic Privacy: Evolution of Legal Theory*, 41 J.L. Med. & Ethics 65 (2013) (surveying post-*Moore* cases involving genetic information claims and concluding that, while property law claims have not fared well since *Moore*, plaintiffs alleging an unlawful invasion of privacy have had some success); Meredith Render, *The Law of the Body*, 62 Emory L.J. 549 (2013) (supporting the logic of *Moore*'s holding but arguing that a special "law of the body" is needed to address the unique nature of property rights of a person's body); Bridget Crawford, *Our Bodies, Our (Tax) Selves*, 31 Va. Tax Rev. 695, 708 (2012) (stating that "[t]he determination that Mr. Moore's cells were not property was * * * unnecessary to the court's decision," and asserting that the court could have simplified its holding by concluding that Moore's cells had no financial value because they were useless until they were developed); Michelle Goodwin, *Rethinking Legislative Consent Law?*, 5 DePaul J. Health Care L. 257, 300 (2002) (asserting that the outcome in *Moore* may have stemmed from the court's "reticence to open a potential floodgate of litigation" by extending the tort of conversion to the medical context).

4.   Although the U.S. Supreme Court declined to review the California Supreme Court's *Moore* decision, *see* 499 U.S. 936 (1991), it did grant review on two cases many years later to assess analogous issues. First, in *Mayo Collaborative Services v. Prometheus Laboratories, Inc.*, 566 U.S. ___, 132 S. Ct. 1289 (2012), the Supreme Court unanimously invalidated Prometheus Laboratories' patent that granted the company exclusive rights to the drug testing process used to treat gastrointestinal diseases. The Court reasoned that "[l]aws of nature, natural phenomena, and abstract ideas are not patentable." *Id.* at 1293 (internal quotation omitted). One year later, the Court relied on *Mayo* in deciding *Association for Molecular Pathology v. Myriad Genetics, Inc.*, 569 U.S. ___, 133 S. Ct. 2107 (2013). In that case, the Myriad Genetics Company isolated certain genetic mutations that indicated whether a patient was at a higher risk for breast cancer. Myriad applied for, and was granted, a patent on the genes. The Association for Molecular Pathology (among other parties) filed suit, arguing that granting a patent to Myriad violated the Patent Act (35 U.S.C. § 101) because the isolated genes were products of nature. Myriad argued that because it isolated the genes, those genes were no longer in their natural state and thus the patent was proper. The Supreme Court unanimously disagreed with Myriad's argument, and held that naturally occurring gene sequences and their derivative products are not eligible for patents under the Patent Act. The Court further held, however, that synthetically created gene sequences that do not naturally occur in nature *are* eligible for patents under the Act.

Both *Mayo* and *Myriad Genetics* are patent cases, not property cases, but the issues certainly overlap with property rights questions. Indeed, the *Myriad Genetics* case has generated significant scholarly commentary regarding property rights. *See, e.g.*, James Dawkins, *Intellectual Property—Patents— Isolated Human Genes are a Product of Nature and Therefore Not Patent Eligible*, 44 Cumb. L. Rev. 527, 540 (2013–2014) (supporting the Court's holding in *Myriad Genetics* and stating: "Like sunlight and saltwater, genes existed for millions of years prior to the existence of humanity and—also like sunlight and saltwater—genes should not be owned"); Jill Fraley, *The Jurisprudence of Nature: The Importance of Defining What is "Natural"*, 63 Cath. U. L. Rev. 917, 951 (2014) (noting that defining what is a "product of nature" is a complex scientific task, and concluding that after *Myriad Genetics* the "language of property rights provides insights and guideposts that may more efficiently and reliably allow us to navigate the process of formally defining 'nature' ").

C. RULE OF CAPTURE

In determining the extent of ownership rights, it is often important to consider how the person came into possession of the property. Although many forms of property are purchased, traded, or inherited, some forms of property are "captured." The following case discusses the "rule of capture" and how it relates to ownership rights.

POPOV V. HAYASHI

Superior Court, San Francisco County, California, 2002
2002 WL 31833731

MCCARTHY, JUDGE.

FACTS

In 1927, Babe Ruth hit sixty home runs. That record stood for thirty-four years until Roger Maris broke it in 1961 with sixty-one home runs. Mark McGwire hit seventy in 1998. On October 7, 2001, at PacBell Park in San Francisco, Barry Bonds hit number seventy-three. That accomplishment set a record which, in all probability, will remain unbroken for years into the future.

The event was widely anticipated and received a great deal of attention.

The ball that found itself at the receiving end of Mr. Bonds's bat garnered some of that attention. Baseball fans in general, and especially people at the game, understood the importance of the ball. It was worth a great deal of money[1] and whoever caught it would bask, for a brief period of time, in the reflected fame of Mr. Bonds.

With that in mind, many people who attended the game came prepared for the possibility that a record setting ball would be hit in their direction. Among this group were plaintiff Alex Popov and defendant Patrick Hayashi. They were unacquainted at the time. Both men brought baseball gloves, which they anticipated using if the ball came within their reach.

They, along with a number of others, positioned themselves in the arcade section of the ballpark. This is a standing room only area located near right field. It is in this general area that Barry Bonds hits the greatest number of home runs. The area was crowded with people on October 7, 2001 and access was restricted to those who held tickets for that section.

Barry Bonds came to bat in the first inning. With nobody on base and a full count, Bonds swung at a slow knuckleball. He connected. The ball sailed over the right-field fence and into the arcade.

Josh Keppel, a cameraman who was positioned in the arcade, captured the event on videotape. Keppel filmed much of what occurred from the time Bonds hit the ball until the commotion in the arcade had subsided. He was standing very near the spot where the ball landed and he recorded a significant amount of information critical to the disposition of this case.

In addition to the Keppel tape, seventeen * * * witnesses testified as to what they saw after the ball came into the stands. The testimony of these witnesses varied on many important points. Some of the witnesses had a good vantage point and some did not. Some appeared disinterested in the

---

[1]   It has been suggested that the ball might sell for something in excess of $1,000,000.

outcome of the litigation and others had a clear bias. Some remembered the events well and others did not. Some were encumbered by prior inconsistent statements which diminished their credibility.

The factual findings in this case are the result of an analysis of the testimony of all the witnesses as well as a detailed review of the Keppel tape. Those findings are as follows:

When the seventy-third home run ball went into the arcade, it landed in the upper portion of the webbing of a softball glove worn by Alex Popov. While the glove stopped the trajectory of the ball, it is not at all clear that the ball was secure. Popov had to reach for the ball and in doing so, may have lost his balance.

Even as the ball was going into his glove, a crowd of people began to engulf Mr. Popov. He was tackled and thrown to the ground while still in the process of attempting to complete the catch. Some people intentionally descended on him for the purpose of taking the ball away, while others were involuntarily forced to the ground by the momentum of the crowd.

Eventually, Mr. Popov was buried face down on the ground under several layers of people. At one point he had trouble breathing. Mr. Popov was grabbed, hit and kicked. People reached underneath him in the area of his glove. Neither the tape nor the testimony is sufficient to establish which individual members of the crowd were responsible for the assaults on Mr. Popov.

The videotape clearly establishes that this was an out of control mob, engaged in violent, illegal behavior. * * *

Mr. Popov intended at all times to establish and maintain possession of the ball. At some point the ball left his glove and ended up on the ground. It is impossible to establish the exact point in time that this occurred or what caused it to occur.

Mr. Hayashi was standing near Mr. Popov when the ball came into the stands. He, like Mr. Popov, was involuntarily forced to the ground. He committed no wrongful act. While on the ground he saw the loose ball. He picked it up, rose to his feet and put it in his pocket.

Although the crowd was still on top of Mr. Popov, security guards had begun the process of physically pulling people off. Some people resisted those efforts. One person argued with an official and another had to be pulled off by his hair.

Mr. Hayashi kept the ball hidden. He asked Mr. Keppel to point the camera at him. At first, Mr. Keppel did not comply and Mr. Hayashi continued to hide the ball. Finally after someone else in the crowd asked Mr. Keppel to point the camera at Mr. Hayashi, Mr. Keppel complied. It was only at that point that Mr. Hayashi held the ball in the air for others to see. Someone made a motion for the ball and Mr. Hayashi put it back in

PROPERTY

CH. 6

his glove. It is clear that Mr. Hayashi was concerned that someone would take the ball away from him and that he was unwilling to show it until he was on videotape. Although he testified to the contrary, that portion of his testimony is unconvincing.

Mr. Popov eventually got up from the ground. He made several statements while he was on the ground and shortly after he got up which are consistent with his claim that he had achieved some level of control over the ball and that he intended to keep it. Those statements can be heard on the audio portion of the tape. When he saw that Mr. Hayashi had the ball he expressed relief and grabbed for it. Mr. Hayashi pulled the ball away. Security guards then took Mr. Hayashi to a secure area of the stadium.

It is important to point out what the evidence did not and could not show. Neither the camera nor the * * * witnesses were able to establish whether Mr. Popov retained control of the ball as he descended into the crowd. Mr. Popov's testimony on this question is inconsistent on several important points, ambiguous on others and, on the whole, unconvincing. We do not know when or how Mr. Popov lost the ball.

Perhaps the most critical factual finding of all is one that cannot be made. We will never know if Mr. Popov would have been able to retain control of the ball had the crowd not interfered with his efforts to do so. Resolution of that question is the work of a psychic, not a judge

LEGAL ANALYSIS

Plaintiff has pled causes of actions for conversion, trespass to chattel, injunctive relief and constructive trust.

Conversion is the wrongful exercise of dominion over the personal property of another. There must be actual interference with the plaintiff's dominion. Wrongful withholding of property can constitute actual interference even where the defendant lawfully acquired the property. If a person entitled to possession of personal property demands its return, the unjustified refusal to give the property back is conversion.

The act constituting conversion must be intentionally done. There is no requirement, however, that the defendant know that the property belongs to another or that the defendant intends to dispossess the true owner of its use and enjoyment. Wrongful purpose is not a component of conversion.

The injured party may elect to seek either specific recovery of the property or monetary damages.

Trespass to chattel, in contrast, exists where personal property has been damaged or where the defendant has interfered with the plaintiff's use of the property. Actual dispossession is not an element of the tort of trespass to chattel.

In the case at bar, Mr. Popov is not claiming that Mr. Hayashi damaged the ball or that he interfered with Mr. Popov's use and enjoyment of the ball. He claims instead that Mr. Hayashi intentionally took it from him and refused to give it back. There is no trespass to chattel. If there was a wrong at all, it is conversion.

Conversion does not exist, however, unless the baseball rightfully belongs to Mr. Popov. One who has neither title nor possession, nor any right to possession, cannot sue for conversion. The deciding question in this case then, is whether Mr. Popov achieved possession or the right to possession as he attempted to catch and hold on to the ball.

The parties have agreed to a starting point for the legal analysis. Prior to the time the ball was hit, it was possessed and owned by Major League Baseball. At the time it was hit it became intentionally abandoned property. The first person who came in possession of the ball became its new owner.

The parties fundamentally disagree about the definition of possession. In order to assist the court in resolving this disagreement, four distinguished law professors participated in a forum to discuss the legal definition of possession.[17] The professors also disagreed.

The disagreement is understandable. Although the term possession appears repeatedly throughout the law, its definition varies depending on the context in which it is used. Various courts have condemned the term as vague and meaningless.

This level of criticism is probably unwarranted.

While there is a degree of ambiguity built into the term possession, that ambiguity exists for a purpose. Courts are often called upon to resolve conflicting claims of possession in the context of commercial disputes. A stable economic environment requires rules of conduct which are understandable and consistent with the fundamental customs and practices of the industry they regulate. Without that, rules will be difficult to enforce and economic instability will result. Because each industry has different customs and practices, a single definition of possession cannot be applied to different industries without creating havoc.

This does not mean that there are no central principles governing the law of possession. It is possible to identify certain fundamental concepts that are common to every definition of possession.

Professor Bernhardt has recognized that "[p]ossession requires both physical control over the item and an intent to control it or exclude others from it. But these generalizations function more as guidelines than as

---

[17]   They are Professor Brian Gray [U.C. Hastings]; Professor Roger Bernhardt [Golden Gate]; Professor Paul Finkelman [Tulsa]; and Professor Jan Stiglitz [California Western].

direct determinants of possession issues. Possession is a blurred question of law and fact."

Professor [Ray Andrews] Brown argues [in his treatise] that "[t]he orthodox view of possession regards it as a union of the two elements of the physical relation of the possessor to the thing, and of intent. This physical relation is the actual power over the thing in question, the ability to hold and make use of it. But a mere physical relation of the possessor to the thing in question is not enough. There must also be manifested an intent to control it."

The task of this court is to use these principles as a starting point to craft a definition of possession that applies to the unique circumstances of this case.

We start with the observation that possession is a process which culminates in an event. The event is the moment in time that possession is achieved. The process includes the acts and thoughts of the would be possessor which lead up to the moment of possession.

The focus of the analysis in this case is not on the thoughts or intent of the actor. Mr. Popov has clearly evidenced an intent to possess the baseball and has communicated that intent to the world. The question is whether he did enough to reduce the ball to his exclusive dominion and control. Were his acts sufficient to create a legally cognizable interest in the ball?

Mr. Hayashi argues that possession does not occur until the fan has complete control of the ball. Professor Gray suggests the following definition [hereafter "Gray's Rule"]: "A person who catches a baseball that enters the stands is its owner. A ball is caught if the person has achieved complete control of the ball at the point in time that the momentum of the ball and the momentum of the fan while attempting to catch the ball ceases. A baseball, which is dislodged by incidental contact with an inanimate object or another person, before momentum has ceased, is not possessed. Incidental contact with another person is contact that is not intended by the other person. The first person to pick up a loose ball and secure it becomes its possessor."

Mr. Popov argues that this definition requires that a person seeking to establish possession must show unequivocal dominion and control, a standard rejected by several leading cases. Instead, he offers the perspectives of Professor Bernhardt and Professor Finkelman, who suggest that possession occurs when an individual intends to take control of a ball and manifests that intent by stopping the forward momentum of the ball whether or not complete control is achieved.

Professors Finkelman and Bernhardt have correctly pointed out that some cases recognize possession even before absolute dominion and control is achieved. Those cases require the actor to be actively and ably engaged in efforts to establish complete control. Moreover, such efforts must be significant and they must be reasonably calculated to result in unequivocal dominion and control at some point in the near future.

This rule is applied in cases involving the hunting or fishing of wild animals or the salvage of sunken vessels. The hunting and fishing cases recognize that a mortally wounded animal may run for a distance before falling. The hunter acquires possession upon the act of wounding the animal, not the eventual capture. Similarly, whalers acquire possession by landing a harpoon, not by subduing the animal.

In the salvage cases, an individual may take possession of a wreck by exerting as much control "as its nature and situation permit." Inadequate efforts, however, will not support a claim of possession. Thus, a "sailor cannot assert a claim merely by boarding a vessel and publishing a notice, unless such acts are coupled with a then present intention of conducting salvage operations, and he immediately thereafter proceeds with activity in the form of constructive steps to aid the distressed party."

These rules are contextual in nature. They are crafted in response to the unique nature of the conduct they seek to regulate. Moreover, they are influenced by the custom and practice of each industry. The reason that absolute dominion and control is not required to establish possession in the cases cited by Mr. Popov is that such a rule would be unworkable and unreasonable. The "nature and situation" of the property at issue does not immediately lend itself to unequivocal dominion and control. It is impossible to wrap one's arms around a whale, a fleeing fox, or a sunken ship.

The opposite is true of a baseball hit into the stands of a stadium. Not only is it physically possible for a person to acquire unequivocal dominion and control of an abandoned baseball, but fans generally expect a claimant to have accomplished as much. The custom and practice of the stands creates a reasonable expectation that a person will achieve full control of a ball before claiming possession. There is no reason for the legal rule to be inconsistent with that expectation. Therefore Gray's Rule is adopted as the definition of possession in this case.

The central tenant of Gray's Rule is that the actor must retain control of the ball after incidental contact with people and things. Mr. Popov has not established by a preponderance of the evidence that he would have retained control of the ball after all momentum ceased and after any incidental contact with people or objects. Consequently, he did not achieve full possession.

That finding, however, does not resolve the case. The reason we do not know whether Mr. Popov would have retained control of the ball is not because of incidental contact. It is because he was attacked. His efforts to establish possession were interrupted by the collective assault of a band of wrongdoers.[34]

A decision which ignored that fact would endorse the actions of the crowd by not repudiating them. Judicial rulings, particularly in cases that receive media attention, affect the way people conduct themselves. This case demands vindication of an important principle. We are a nation governed by law, not by brute force.

As a matter of fundamental fairness, Mr. Popov should have had the opportunity to try to complete his catch unimpeded by unlawful activity. To hold otherwise would be to allow the result in this case to be dictated by violence. That will not happen.

For these reasons, the analysis cannot stop with the valid observation that Mr. Popov has not proved full possession.

The legal question presented at this point is whether an action for conversion can proceed where the plaintiff has failed to establish possession or title. It can. An action for conversion may be brought where the plaintiff has title, possession or the right to possession.

Here Mr. Popov seeks, in effect, a declaratory judgment that he has either possession or the right to possession. In addition he seeks the remedies of injunctive relief and a constructive trust. These are all actions in equity. A court sitting in equity has the authority to fashion rules and remedies designed to achieve fundamental fairness.

Consistent with this principle, the court adopts the following rule. Where an actor undertakes significant but incomplete steps to achieve possession of a piece of abandoned personal property and the effort is interrupted by the unlawful acts of others, the actor has a legally cognizable pre-possessory interest in the property. That pre-possessory interest constitutes a qualified right to possession which can support a cause of action for conversion.

Possession can be likened to a journey down a path. Mr. Popov began his journey unimpeded. He was fast approaching a fork in the road. A turn in one direction would lead to possession of the ball—he would complete the catch. A turn in the other direction would result in a failure to achieve possession—he would drop the ball. Our problem is that before Mr. Popov got to the point where the road forked, he was set upon by a gang of bandits, who dislodged the ball from his grasp.

---

[34] Professor Gray has suggested that the way to deal with this problem is to demand that Mr. Popov sue the people who assaulted him. This suggestion is unworkable for a number of reasons. First, it was an attack by a large group of people. It is impossible to separate out the people who were acting unlawfully from the people who were involuntarily pulled into the mix. Second, in order to prove damages related to the loss of the ball, Mr. Popov would have to prove that but for the actions of the crowd he would have achieved possession of the ball. As noted earlier, this is impossible.

Recognition of a legally protected pre-possessory interest vests Mr. Popov with a qualified right to possession and enables him to advance a legitimate claim to the baseball based on a conversion theory. Moreover it addresses the harm done by the unlawful actions of the crowd.

It does not, however, address the interests of Mr. Hayashi. The court is required to balance the interests of all parties.

Mr. Hayashi was not a wrongdoer. He was a victim of the same bandits that attacked Mr. Popov. The difference is that he was able to extract himself from their assault and move to the side of the road. It was there that he discovered the loose ball. When he picked up and put it in his pocket he attained unequivocal dominion and control.

If Mr. Popov had achieved complete possession before Mr. Hayashi got the ball, those actions would not have divested Mr. Popov of any rights, nor would they have created any rights to which Mr. Hayashi could lay claim. Mr. Popov, however, was able to establish only a qualified pre-possessory interest in the ball. That interest does not establish a full right to possession that is protected from a subsequent legitimate claim.

On the other hand, while Mr. Hayashi appears on the surface to have done everything necessary to claim full possession of the ball, the ball itself is encumbered by the qualified pre-possessory interest of Mr. Popov. At the time Mr. Hayashi came into possession of the ball, it had, in effect, a cloud on its title.

An award of the ball to Mr. Popov would be unfair to Mr. Hayashi. It would be premised on the assumption that Mr. Popov would have caught the ball. That assumption is not supported by the facts. An award of the ball to Mr. Hayashi would unfairly penalize Mr. Popov. It would be based on the assumption that Mr. Popov would have dropped the ball. That conclusion is also unsupported by the facts.

Both men have a superior claim to the ball as against all the world. Each man has a claim of equal dignity as to the other. We are, therefore, left with something of a dilemma.

Thankfully, there is a middle ground.

The concept of equitable division was fully explored in a [1983 Fordham Law Review] article authored by Professor R.H. Helmholz * * *. Professor Helmholz addressed the problems associated with rules governing finders of lost and mislaid property. For * * * reasons not directly relevant [here], Helmholz suggested employing the equitable remedy of division to resolve competing claims between finders of lost or mislaid property and the owners of land on which the property was found.

There is no reason * * * that the same remedy cannot be applied [here], where issues of property, tort and equity intersect.

The concept of equitable division has its roots in ancient Roman law. As Helmholz points out, it is useful in that it "provides an equitable way to resolve competing claims which are equally strong." Moreover, "[i]t comports with what one instinctively feels to be fair."

* * *

Application of the principle of equitable division is illustrated in the case of *Keron v. Cashman*, 33 A. 1055 (1896). In that case, five boys were walking home along a railroad track in the city of Elizabeth New Jersey. The youngest of the boys came upon an old sock that was tied shut and contained something heavy. He picked it up and swung it. The oldest boy took it away from him and beat the others with it. The sock passes from boy to boy. Each controlled it for a short time. At some point in the course of play, the sock broke open and out spilled $775 as well as some rags, cloths and ribbons.

The court noted that possession requires both physical control and the intent to reduce the property to one's possession. Control and intent must be concurrent. None of the boys intended to take possession until it became apparent that the sock contained money. Each boy had physical control of the sock at some point before that discovery was made.

Because none could present a superior claim of concurrent control and intent, the court held that each boy was entitled to an equal share of the money. * * *

Here, the issue is not intent, or concurrence. Both men intended to possess the ball at the time they were in physical contact with it. The issue, instead, is the legal quality of the claim. With respect to that, neither can present a superior argument as against the other.

Mr. Hayashi's claim is compromised by Mr. Popov's pre-possessory interest. Mr. Popov cannot demonstrate full control. Albeit for different reasons, they stand before the court in exactly the same legal position as did the five boys. Their legal claims are of equal quality and they are equally entitled to the ball.

The court therefore declares that both plaintiff and defendant have an equal and undivided interest in the ball. Plaintiff's cause of action for conversion is sustained only as to his equal and undivided interest. In order to effectuate this ruling, the ball must be sold and the proceeds divided equally between the parties.

The parties are ordered to * * * come to an agreement as to how to implement this decision. * * *

The court retains jurisdiction to issue orders consistent with this decision. The ball is to remain in the custody of the court until further order.

NOTES AND QUESTIONS

1. The *Popov* court attempted to achieve an equitable result in a difficult case. Did it succeed?

2. What other options were available to the court for resolving the case? Would any of those alternatives have been preferable from a fairness standpoint?

3. The *Popov* court concluded that Popov and Hayashi were co-owners of the famous baseball. Neither party appealed the case. Instead, the two men put the baseball up for auction in New York City, and the ball sold for $450,000. By contrast, the baseball from the previous record-setting home run by Mark McGwire sold for $3.2 million. Popov and Hayashi were understandably disappointed with the auction price. As Hayashi told a reporter, "After legal fees, I guess it will be a wash." Ira Berkow, *73rd Home Run Ball Sells for $450,000*, N.Y. TIMES, June 26, 2003, http://www.nytimes.com/2003/06/26/sports/baseball–73rd-home-run-ball-sells-for–450000.html.

4. The *Popov* case addressed the common law "rule of capture." Another famous (and much older) rule of capture case is *Pierson v. Post*, 3 Cai. R. 175 (N.Y. 1805), which involved a dispute over who had legal title to a fox. Post had spent significant effort chasing and pursuing the fox, but Pierson ultimately killed it and carried it out of the forest. Post subsequently claimed legal title to the fox as a result of his significant effort in pursing the fox. New York's highest court disagreed with Post, and held that merely pursuing an animal does not result in legal title. The court held that, to claim title, a party must "capture" the animal by either killing it or mortally wounding it. The court in *Popov* deviated slightly from a pure "rule of capture" doctrine in favor of a more equitable "pre-possessory interest" approach. Would *Popov* have been decided differently under the approach in *Pierson v. Post*?

5. The rule of capture has proven controversial in natural resources cases. As the Eleventh Circuit noted in *State of Alabama v. U.S. Department of Interior*, 84 F.3d 410, 413 (1996):

> The problem with the rule of capture is that it encourages a tract owner to build wells near his border so as to drain not only the reserves underlying his own tract, but also the reserves underlying a neighboring tract. * * * Each tract owner then has an incentive virtually to race to drain the reservoir as quickly as possible to capture as much oil or gas as he can. The result is (1) economic waste in drilling unnecessary wells; (2) a corresponding heightened risk of damage to the environment; and (3) physical waste of the oil or gas itself * * *.

Based on such concerns, many jurisdictions have abandoned the rule of capture in the natural resources context and instead have adopted the "reasonable use" or "correlative rights" doctrine—whereby a landowner can make use of the resources beneath his property as long as such use does not unreasonably interfere with his neighbor's reasonable use of the same resource. *See, e.g.,*

Bristor v. Cheatham, 75 Ariz. 227, 255 P.2d 173 (1953) (adopting the "reasonable use" doctrine); *Evans v. City of Seattle*, 182 Wash. 450, 458, 47 P.2d 984, 987 (1935) (same). Which approach is preferable: the traditional rule of capture or the reasonable use doctrine?

D. ADVERSE POSSESSION

Once a person establishes ownership of property, that person is generally free to transfer and sell the property as he pleases. But property may also change owners without an express transfer or sale. The following case discusses the doctrine of "adverse possession," under which someone can gain legal ownership of property by adversely "possessing" a parcel of land for a specified period of time.

NOME 2000 V. FAGERSTROM

Supreme Court of Alaska, 1990
799 P.2d 304

MATTHEWS, CHIEF JUSTICE.

This appeal involves a dispute over a tract of land measuring approximately seven and one-half acres, overlooking the Nome River (hereinafter the disputed parcel). Record title to a tract of land known as mineral survey 1161, which includes the disputed parcel, is held by Nome 2000.

On July 24, 1987, Nome 2000 filed suit to eject Charles and Peggy Fagerstrom from the disputed parcel. The Fagerstroms counterclaimed that through their use of the parcel they had acquired title by adverse possession.

A jury trial ensued and, at the close of the Fagerstroms' case, Nome 2000 moved for a directed verdict on two grounds. First, it maintained that the Fagerstroms' evidence of use of the disputed parcel did not meet the requirements of the doctrine of adverse possession. Alternatively, Nome 2000 maintained that the requirements for adverse possession were met only as to the northerly section of the parcel and, therefore, the Fagerstroms could not have acquired title to the remainder. The trial court denied the motion. After Nome 2000 presented its case, the jury found that the Fagerstroms had adversely possessed the entire parcel. The court then entered judgment in favor of the Fagerstroms.

On appeal, Nome 2000 contests the trial court's denial of its motion for a directed verdict and the sufficiency of the evidence in support of the jury verdict. * * *

I. FACTUAL BACKGROUND

The disputed parcel is located in a rural area known as Osborn. During the warmer seasons, property in Osborn is suitable for homesites and subsistence and recreational activities. During the colder seasons, little or no use is made of Osborn property.

Charles Fagerstrom's earliest recollection of the disputed parcel is his family's use of it around 1944 or 1945. At that time, he and his family used an abandoned boy scout cabin present on the parcel as a subsistence base camp during summer months. Around 1947 or 1948, they moved their summer campsite to an area south of the disputed parcel. However, Charles and his family continued to make seasonal use of the disputed parcel for subsistence and recreation.

In 1963, Charles and Peggy Fagerstrom were married and, in 1966, they brought a small quantity of building materials to the north end of the disputed parcel. They intended to build a cabin.

In 1970 or 1971, the Fagerstroms used four cornerposts to stake off a twelve acre, rectangular parcel * * *. The northeast and southeast stakes were located on or very near mineral survey 1161. The northwest and southwest stakes were located well to the west of mineral survey 1161. The overlap constitutes the disputed parcel. The southeast stake disappeared at an unknown time.

Also around 1970, the Fagerstroms built a picnic area on the north end of the disputed parcel. The area included a gravel pit, beachwood blocks as chairs, firewood and a 50-gallon barrel for use as a stove.

About mid-July 1974, the Fagerstroms placed a camper trailer on the north end of the disputed parcel. The trailer was leveled on blocks and remained in place through late September. Thereafter, until 1978, the Fagerstroms parked their camper trailer on the north end of the disputed parcel from early June through September. The camper was equipped with food, bedding, a stove and other household items.

About the same time that the Fagerstroms began parking the trailer on the disputed parcel, they built an outhouse and a fish rack on the north end of the parcel. Both fixtures remained through the time of trial in their original locations. The Fagerstroms also planted some spruce trees, not indigenous to the Osborn area, in 1975–76.

During the summer of 1977, the Fagerstroms built a reindeer shelter on the north end of the disputed parcel. The shelter was about 8x8 feet wide, and tall enough for Charles Fagerstrom to stand in. Around the shelter, the Fagerstroms constructed a pen which was 75 feet in diameter and 5 feet high. The shelter and pen housed a reindeer for about six weeks and the pen remained in place until the summer of 1978.

During their testimony, the Fagerstroms estimated that they were personally present on the disputed parcel from 1974 through 1978, "every other weekend or so" and "[a] couple times during the week . . . if the weather was good." When present they used the north end of the parcel as a base camp while using the entire parcel for subsistence and recreational purposes. Their activities included gathering berries, catching and drying fish and picnicking. Their children played on the parcel. The Fagerstroms also kept the property clean, picking up litter left by others.

While so using the disputed parcel, the Fagerstroms walked along various paths which traverse the entire parcel. The paths were present prior to the Fagerstroms' use of the parcel and, according to Peggy Fagerstrom, were free for use by others in connection with picking berries and fishing. On one occasion, however, Charles Fagerstrom excluded campers from the land. They were burning the Fagerstroms' firewood.

* * *

During the summer of 1978, the Fagerstroms put a cabin on the north end of the disputed parcel. Nome 2000 admits that from the time that the cabin was so placed until the time that Nome 2000 filed this suit, the Fagerstroms adversely possessed the north end of the disputed parcel. Nome 2000 filed its complaint on July 24, 1987.

II. DISCUSSION

A.

The Fagerstroms' claim of title by adverse possession is governed by [Alaska statutory law], which provides for a ten-year limitations period for actions to recover real property. Thus, if the Fagerstroms adversely possessed the disputed parcel, or any portion thereof, for ten consecutive years, then they have acquired title to that property. Because the Fagerstroms' use of the parcel increased over the years, and because Nome 2000 filed its complaint on July 24, 1987, the relevant period is July 24, 1977 through July 24, 1987.

We recently described the elements of adverse possession as follows: "In order to acquire title by adverse possession, the claimant must prove, by clear and convincing evidence, . . . that for the statutory period 'his use of the land was continuous, open and notorious, exclusive and hostile to the true owner.'" The first three conditions—continuity, notoriety and exclusivity—describe the physical requirements of the doctrine. The fourth condition, hostility, is often imprecisely described as the "intent" requirement.

On appeal, Nome 2000 argues that as a matter of law the physical requirements are not met absent "significant physical improvements" or "substantial activity" on the land. Thus, according to Nome 2000, only when the Fagerstroms placed a cabin on the disputed parcel in the summer of 1978 did their possession become adverse. For the prior year, so the argument goes, the Fagerstroms' physical use of the property was insufficient because they did not construct "significant structure[s]" and their use was only seasonal. Nome 2000 also argues that the Fagerstroms' use of the disputed parcel was not exclusive because "[o]thers were free to pick the berries, use the paths and fish in the area." We reject these arguments.

Whether a claimant's physical acts upon the land are sufficiently continuous, notorious and exclusive does not necessarily depend on the existence of significant improvements, substantial activity or absolute exclusivity. Indeed, this area of law is not susceptible to fixed standards because the quality and quantity of acts required for adverse possession depend on the *character* of the land in question. Thus, the conditions of continuity and exclusivity require only that the land be used for the statutory period as an average owner of similar property would use it. Where, as in the present case, the land is rural, a lesser exercise of dominion and control may be reasonable.

The character of the land in question is also relevant to the notoriety requirement. Use consistent with ownership which gives visible evidence of the claimant's possession, such that the reasonably diligent owner "could see that a hostile flag was being flown over his property," is sufficient. Where physical visibility is established, community repute is also relevant evidence that the true owner was put on notice.[7]

Applying the foregoing principles to this case, we hold that the jury could reasonably conclude that the Fagerstroms established, by clear and convincing evidence, continuous, notorious and exclusive possession for ten years prior to the date Nome 2000 filed suit. We point out that we are concerned only with the first year, the summer of 1977 through the summer of 1978, as Nome 2000 admits that the requirements of adverse possession were met from the summer of 1978 through the summer of 1987.

The disputed parcel is located in a rural area suitable as a seasonal homesite for subsistence and recreational activities. This is exactly how the Fagerstroms used it during the year in question. On the premises throughout the entire year were an outhouse, a fish rack, a large reindeer pen (which, for six weeks, housed a reindeer), a picnic area, a small quantity of building materials and some trees not indigenous to the area. During the warmer season, for about 13 weeks, the Fagerstroms also placed a camper trailer on blocks on the disputed parcel. The Fagerstroms and their children visited the property several times during the warmer season to fish, gather berries, clean the premises, and play. In total, their conduct and improvements went well beyond "mere casual and occasional trespasses" and instead "evince[d] a purpose to exercise exclusive dominion over the property." That others were free to pick berries and fish is consistent with the conduct of a hospitable landowner, and undermines neither the continuity nor exclusivity of their possession.

---

[7]   The function of the notoriety requirement is to afford the true owner an opportunity for notice. However, actual notice is not required; the true owner is charged with knowing what a reasonably diligent owner would have known.

With respect to the notoriety requirement, a quick investigation of the premises, especially during the season which it was best suited for use, would have been sufficient to place a reasonably diligent landowner on notice that someone may have been exercising dominion and control over at least the northern portion of the property. Upon such notice, further inquiry would indicate that members of the community regarded the Fagerstroms as the owners. Continuous, exclusive, and notorious possession were thus established.

* * *

Having concluded that the Fagerstroms established the elements of adverse possession, we turn to the question whether they were entitled to the entire disputed parcel. Specifically, the question presented is whether the jury could reasonably conclude that the Fagerstroms adversely possessed the southerly portion of the disputed parcel.

Absent color of title, only property actually possessed may be acquired by adverse possession. Here, from the summer of 1977 through the summer of 1978, the Fagerstroms' only activity on the southerly portion of the land included use of the pre-existing trails in connection with subsistence and recreational activities, and picking up litter. They claim that these activities, together with their placement of the cornerposts, constituted actual possession of the southerly portion of the parcel. Nome 2000 argues that this activity did not constitute actual possession and, at most, entitled the Fagerstroms to an easement by prescription across the southerly portion of the disputed parcel.*

Nome 2000 is correct. The Fagerstroms' use of the trails and picking up of litter, although perhaps indicative of adverse use, would not provide the reasonably diligent owner with visible evidence of another's exercise of dominion and control. To this, the cornerposts add virtually nothing. Two of the four posts are located well to the west of the disputed parcel. Of the two that were allegedly placed on the parcel in 1970, the one located on the southerly portion of the parcel disappeared at an unknown time. The Fagerstroms maintain that because the disappearing stake was securely in place in 1970, we should infer that it remained for a "significant period." Even if we draw this inference, we fail to see how two posts on a rectangular parcel of property can, as the Fagerstroms put it, constitute "[t]he objective act of taking physical possession" of the parcel. The two posts simply do not serve to mark off the boundaries of the disputed parcel and, therefore, do not evince an exercise of dominion and control over the entire parcel. Thus, we conclude that the superior court erred in its denial of Nome 2000's motion for a directed verdict as to the southerly portion. This case is remanded to the trial court, with instructions to determine the extent of the Fagerstroms' acquisition in a manner consistent with this opinion.

---

* The concept of an easement is discussed in the next section of this chapter. [Ed.]

* * *

Affirmed in part, reversed in part, and remanded.

NOTES AND QUESTIONS

1.   What is the purpose of the adverse possession doctrine?

2.   What did the Alaska Supreme Court hold in *Fagerstrom*? Is the decision (which gives something to each side) fair?

3.   Under the statute involved in *Fagerstrom*, a party must "adversely possess" property in Alaska for a period of ten years before he can attempt to claim legal title to the land. States have adopted a variety of time periods for an adverse possession claim. *See, e.g.*, Kan. Stat. Ann. § 60–503 (15 years); N.J. Stat. Ann. § 2A:14–30 (30 years). Moreover, some states impose additional requirements before a claim of adverse possession can be established. For example, some states require (in addition to a specified period of possession) a payment of property taxes or a deed to the land for a specified period of time. *See, e.g.*, Cal. Civ. Proc. Code § 325 (requiring adverse possession for at least five years plus payment of taxes on the land for the five year period); N.M. Stat. Ann. § 37–1–22 (requiring a period of at least ten years plus a document or deed to the land). If these types of heightened requirements had been mandatory in Alaska, the Fagerstroms would not have had a claim. Many scholars have supported legislation that requires a heightened showing beyond basic possession. *See, e.g.*, Matthew Sipe, *Jagged Edges*, 124 Yale L.J. 853 (2014) (arguing that heightened adverse possession criteria should be adopted because of the increasingly reliable recording systems for determining who owns a parcel of land); Kristine Cherek, *From Trespasser to Homeowner: The Case Against Adverse Possession in the Post-Crash World*, 20 Va. J. Soc. Pol'y & L. 271 (2012) (arguing to the same effect).

4.   Adverse possession has ancient roots. *See* Brian Gardiner, *Squatters' Rights and Adverse Possession*, 8 Ind. Int'l & Comp. L. Rev. 119, 123 n.18 (1997) (discussing adverse possession under the 2250 B.C. Code of Hammurabi). Despite the doctrine's historic pedigree, however, some scholars have questioned the modern use of the doctrine. *See, e.g.*, Jeffrey Evans Stake, *The Uneasy Case for Adverse Possession*, 89 Geo. L.J. 2419, 2435, 2473 (2001) (stating that "adverse possession [has] been undermined by modern surveying and record-keeping technology" and asserting that "there is little justification today for legal rules that force the use of land"); John Sprankling, *An Environmental Critique of Adverse Possession*, 79 Cornell L. Rev. 816 (1994) (arguing that the modern doctrine of adverse possession wrongfully encourages economic exploitation and degradation of rural and sparsely settled regions). Another commentator, however, believes that the doctrine remains valid, and has even advocated shortening of the adverse possession period. *See* Gardiner, *supra* (arguing for relaxed adverse possession requirements as a means of enhancing the efficient use of property, clarifying title, and increasing access to property).

E. EASEMENTS

A full transfer of ownership is one way to gain the right to use a certain piece of property, but a person can obtain the right to *use* someone else's property without having full ownership rights. That concept is known as an "easement." There are several different types of easements within property law, all of which grant the right to the easement holder to legally use someone else's property in a certain, limited manner.

An easement can be expressly granted, sold, and purchased just like any other property interest. There are, however, other ways in which a court may grant an easement to a particular party. The following materials survey the various types of easements.

1. PRESCRIPTIVE EASEMENTS

An easement-related doctrine akin to adverse possession is "prescriptive easement." A prescriptive easement constitutes the adverse "use" of an easement for the statutorily defined period of time. Restatement (Third) of Property (Servitudes) § 2.17 (2000). There is one major distinction between a prescriptive easement and an adverse possession claim: a prescriptive easement does not require exclusivity. The reason for not requiring exclusive use is that several parties may enjoy similar servitudes in the same land without conflict (*e.g.*, easements to use roads). For example, in *Interior Trails Preservation Coalition v. Swope*, 115 P.3d 527 (Alaska 2005), private owners purchased property that featured a pathway to a hiking trail that had been used for many years by local hikers. After the private owners attempted to foreclose any further use of the pathway, a nonprofit group sought to establish a public prescriptive easement to allow public use of the pathway to access the hiking trails. The Supreme Court of Alaska held that the nonprofit organization could maintain an action for prescriptive easement to use the pathway if the organization could establish continuous use by the general public for the statutory period of ten years.

2. EASEMENTS BY NECESSITY

"Easements by necessity" are usually granted only in the limited circumstances in which a property becomes landlocked by other parcels of land (thus resulting in no access to the landlocked parcel by its owner). In this situation, a court may grant an easement by necessity to give the landlocked property owner a right of ingress and egress across adjacent properties to ensure that the landlocked owner can access his property. If an easement by necessity is granted, the easement holder will have the legal right to travel across another's property to access his own property.

3. EASEMENTS IMPLIED BY PRIOR USE

An "easement implied by prior use" often arises in situations where an owner holds a single piece of property but decides to sever the property into multiple parcels (which are then sold to different owners), creating a situation where one severed parcel may need to be used for the efficient use of another severed parcel. These types of easements often arise in cases where a single property with a single driveway is split and sold into two properties that each continue to use that same single driveway. This may perhaps result in a situation where one parcel owns part of the driveway, and the other owns the rest. In this scenario, although a party may not have legal title to the entire driveway, that party may seek an easement to use the whole driveway. For example, in *Granite Properties Ltd. Partnership v. Manns*, 117 Ill.2d 425, 512 N.E.2d 1230 (1987), a single parcel was developed into multiple parcels, each of which was sold separately. The original parcel had an access driveway that was used for the entire property, but when the property was severed the driveway was divided into different segments that each fell on different property lines. When one owner attempted to forbid another owner from using his portion of the driveway, the court granted an easement based on the prior use doctrine.

Easements implied by prior use may seem similar to easements by necessity, but the two are not identical. Easements by necessity will only be granted when there is an absolute necessity to cross another's land to access property (*i.e.*, a landlocked parcel). Without the easement by necessity, the landowner would have absolutely no ability (via ground travel) to legally access his property. Easements implied by prior use, on the other hand, require a showing less than absolute necessity. *See, e.g., Manns, supra* (the parcel in question was not truly landlocked, and the owner *could* have created another driveway from another access point on the property, but the court held that an implied easement to use the pre-existing driveway was the more equitable remedy).

Easements implied by prior use may arise in a variety of situations. *See, e.g., West End Props. Ass'n of Camp Mineola, Inc. v. Anderson*, 823 N.Y.S.2d 412, 32 A.D.3d 928 (N.Y. App. Div. 2006) (implied easement granted when a private road had been previously used for access to a beach and there was no alternative access to the beach in existence); *Bear Island Water Ass'n, Inc. v. Brown*, 125 Idaho 717, 874 P.2d 528 (1994) (holding that a property owner was not entitled to an easement to use an existing water well when there was nothing stopping the landowner from simply drilling another well); *Motel 6, Inc. v. Pfile*, 718 F.2d 80 (3d Cir. 1983) (holding that a motel was entitled to an implied easement to use a sewer treatment plant when it had been using the sewer openly and notoriously for an extensive period of time).

4. EASEMENTS BY ESTOPPEL

"Easement by estoppel" may occur when a landowner grants permission to a third party to use his land for a specified purpose for an extended period of time. (The required time period is not usually codified in property statutes, but courts typically use periods comparable to the period required for adverse possession. *See, e.g.*, *Kovach v. Gen. Tel. Co.*, 340 Pa. Super. 144, 489 A.2d 883 (Pa. Super. Ct. 1985) (20 years was sufficient); *Dick v. Shannon*, 596 S.W.2d 79 (Mo. Ct. App. 1980) (15 years was sufficient)). When this permission is granted and the third party relies on this permission for an extensive period, the landowner may be barred from later revoking this permission. For example, in *Holbrook v. Taylor*, 532 S.W.2d 763 (Ky. 1976), the plaintiffs purchased a tract of land and were granted permission by the defendant to use a road on the defendant's property to access the tract. Relying on the defendant's permission, the plaintiffs made considerable improvements to the roadway and built a residence at the end of the roadway. When the defendant attempted to revoke access to the roadway, the plaintiffs asserted a claim for easement by estoppel. The court accepted the argument, holding that because the plaintiffs had (with defendant's permission) engaged in significant repairs to the roadway and had relied on the roadway to build a house, the plaintiffs' license to use the roadway could not be revoked.

5. THE "APPURTENANT" VS. "IN GROSS" LEGAL DISTINCTION

Another issue that sometimes arises in disputes is whether a particular easement is considered an "appurtenant" or "in gross" easement. An appurtenant easement is an easement that is tied directly to the land, no matter who uses the easement. Restatement (Third) of Property (Servitudes) § 1.5 (2000). Conversely, an easement in gross applies exclusively to one particular party, and can only be exercised by that specific party. *Id.* Two cases illustrate the distinction. In *Skeen v. Boyles*, 146 N.M. 627, 213 P.3d 531 (N.M. Ct. App. 2009), the court held that an easement for a ranch owner to use a water well on the defendant's property was an appurtenant agreement that applied to *all* subsequent owners of the ranch, not just the original owner. The New Mexico court held that the easement should be considered "appurtenant" because it would be beneficial to all future users of the property. By contrast, in *Champaign National Bank v. Illinois Power Co.*, 125 Ill.App.3d 424, 465 N.E.2d 1016 (Ill. Ct. App. 1984), an Illinois appellate court held that an easement granted to an electrical company to access railroad property for maintenance work was a valid easement in gross that granted access only to the electrical company and its subsidiaries. The court held that the easement should be considered "in gross" because it would only be beneficial to a single party (the electrical company)—the only party using the easement to perform maintenance.

F. TRESPASS

Once a person has established ownership rights over a parcel of property, that owner is generally entitled to exclude others from the property. As discussed in Chapter 5, a person can bring an action for trespass against a person who wrongfully enters his land. The following case discusses the doctrine of trespass in the context of property rights.

JACQUE V. STEENBERG HOMES, INC.

Supreme Court of Wisconsin, 1997
209 Wis.2d 605, 563 N.W.2d 154

BABLITCH, JUSTICE.

Steenberg Homes had a mobile home to deliver. Unfortunately for Harvey and Lois Jacque (the Jacques), the easiest route of delivery was across their land. Despite adamant protests by the Jacques, Steenberg plowed a path through the Jacques' snow-covered field and via that path, delivered the mobile home. Consequently, the Jacques sued Steenberg Homes for intentional trespass. At trial, Steenberg Homes conceded the intentional trespass, but argued that no compensatory damages had been proved, and that punitive damages could not be awarded without compensatory damages. Although the jury awarded the Jacques $1 in nominal damages and $100,000 in punitive damages, the circuit court set aside the jury's award of $100,000. The court of appeals affirmed * * *. We * * * reverse and remand for reinstatement of the punitive damage award.

I.

The relevant facts follow. Plaintiffs, Lois and Harvey Jacques, are an elderly couple, now retired from farming, who own roughly 170 acres near Wilke's Lake in the town of Schleswig. The defendant, Steenberg Homes, Inc. (Steenberg), is in the business of selling mobile homes. In the fall of 1993, a neighbor of the Jacques purchased a mobile home from Steenberg. Delivery of the mobile home was included in the sales price.

Steenberg determined that the easiest route to deliver the mobile home was across the Jacques' land. Steenberg preferred transporting the home across the Jacques' land because the only alternative was a private road which was covered in up to seven feet of snow and contained a sharp curve which would require sets of "rollers" to be used when maneuvering the home around the curve. Steenberg asked the Jacques on several separate occasions whether it could move the home across the Jacques' farm field. The Jacques refused. The Jacques were sensitive about allowing others on their land because they had lost property valued at over $10,000 to other neighbors in an adverse possession action in the mid-1980's. Despite repeated refusals from the Jacques, Steenberg decided to sell the mobile home, which was to be used as a summer cottage, and delivered it on February 15, 1994.

On the morning of delivery, Mr. Jacque observed the mobile home parked on the corner of the town road adjacent to his property. He decided to find out where the movers planned to take the home. The movers, who were Steenberg employees, showed Mr. Jacque the path they planned to take with the mobile home to reach the neighbor's lot. The path cut across the Jacques' land. Mr. Jacque informed the movers that it was the Jacques' land they were planning to cross and that Steenberg did not have permission to cross their land. He told them that Steenberg had been refused permission to cross the Jacques' land.

One of Steenberg's employees called the assistant manager, who then came out to the Jacques' home. In the meantime, the Jacques called and asked some of their neighbors and the town chairman to come over immediately. Once everyone was present, the Jacques showed the assistant manager an aerial map and plat book of the township to prove their ownership of the land, and reiterated their demand that the home not be moved across their land.

At that point, the assistant manager asked Mr. Jacque how much money it would take to get permission. Mr. Jacque responded that it was not a question of money; the Jacques just did not want Steenberg to cross their land. Mr. Jacque testified that he told Steenberg to "[F]ollow the road, that is what the road is for." Steenberg employees left the meeting without permission to cross the land.

At trial, one of Steenberg's employees testified that, upon coming out of the Jacques' home, the assistant manager stated: "I don't give a ____ what [Mr. Jacque] said, just get the home in there any way you can." The other Steenberg employee confirmed this testimony and further testified that the assistant manager told him to park the company truck in such a way that no one could get down the town road to see the route the employees were taking with the home. The assistant manager denied giving these instructions, and Steenberg argued that the road was blocked for safety reasons.

The employees, after beginning down the private road, ultimately used a "bobcat" to cut a path through the Jacques' snow-covered field and hauled the home across the Jacques' land to the neighbor's lot. One employee testified that upon returning to the office and informing the assistant manager that they had gone across the field, the assistant manager reacted by giggling and laughing. The other employee confirmed this testimony. The assistant manager disputed this testimony.

When a neighbor informed the Jacques that Steenberg had, in fact, moved the mobile home across the Jacques' land, Mr. Jacque called the Manitowoc County Sheriff's Department. After interviewing the parties and observing the scene, an officer from the sheriff's department issued a $30 citation to Steenberg's assistant manager.

The Jacques commenced an intentional tort action * * * seeking compensatory and punitive damages from Steenberg. [After the jury rendered its verdict, the trial court set aside the jury's $100,000 punitive damages award.] * * *

This case presents three issues: (1) whether an award of nominal damages for intentional trespass to land may support a punitive damage award and, if so; (2) whether the law should apply to Steenberg or should only be applied prospectively; and * * * (3) [if the law is applied to Steenberg,] whether the $100,000 in punitive damages awarded by the jury is excessive.

* * *

II.

Before the question of punitive damages in a tort action can properly be submitted to the jury, the circuit court must determine, as a matter of law, that the evidence will support an award of punitive damages. * * *

Steenberg argues that, as a matter of law, punitive damages could not be awarded by the jury because punitive damages must be supported by an award of compensatory damages and here the jury awarded only nominal * * * damages. The Jacques contend that the rationale supporting the compensatory damage award requirement is inapposite when the wrongful act is an intentional trespass to land. We agree with the Jacques.

* * *

* * * The rationale for the compensatory damage requirement [as a general rule of punitive damages] is that if the individual cannot show actual harm, he or she has but a nominal interest, hence, society has little interest in having the unlawful, but otherwise harmless, conduct deterred * * *.

However, whether nominal damages can support a punitive damage award in the case of an intentional trespass to land has never been squarely addressed by this court. Nonetheless, Wisconsin law is not without reference to this situation. * * *

* * *

* * * [I]n * * * establishing punitive damages in this state, this court [has] recognized that in certain situations of trespass, the actual harm is not in the damage done to the land, which may be minimal, but in the loss of the individual's right to exclude others from his or her property, and the court [has] implied that this right may be punished by a large damage award despite the lack of measurable harm.

* * * The Jacques argue that both the individual and society have significant interests in deterring intentional trespass to land, regardless of the lack of measurable harm that results. We agree * * *.

We turn first to the individual landowner's interest in protecting his or her land from trespass. * * * [A] private landowner's right to exclude others from his or her land is "one of the most essential sticks in the bundle of rights that are commonly characterized as property." * * *

* * *

* * * Harvey and Lois Jacque have the right to tell Steenberg Homes and any other trespasser, "No, you cannot cross our land." But that right has no practical meaning unless protected by the State. * * *

* * * Because a legal right is involved, the law recognizes that actual harm occurs in every trespass. The action for intentional trespass to land is directed at vindication of the legal right. The law infers some damage from every direct entry upon the land of another. * * * Thus, * * * the nominal damage award represents the recognition that, although immeasurable in mere dollars, actual harm has occurred.

The potential for harm resulting from intentional trespass also supports an exception to * * * [the compensatory damage requirement]. A series of intentional trespasses * * * can threaten the individual's very ownership of the land. The conduct of an intentional trespasser, if repeated, might ripen into prescription or adverse possession and, as a consequence, the individual landowner can lose his or her property rights to the trespasser.

In sum, the individual has a strong interest in excluding trespassers from his or her land. Although only nominal damages were awarded to the Jacques, Steenberg's intentional trespass caused actual harm. We turn next to society's interest in protecting private property from the intentional trespasser.

Society has an interest in punishing and deterring intentional trespassers beyond that of protecting the interests of the individual landowner. Society has an interest in preserving the integrity of the legal system. Private landowners should feel confident that wrongdoers who trespass upon their land will be appropriately punished. When landowners have confidence in the legal system, they are less likely to resort to "self-help" remedies. * * *

People expect wrongdoers to be appropriately punished. Punitive damages have the effect of bringing to punishment types of conduct that, though oppressive and hurtful to the individual, almost invariably go unpunished by the public prosecutor. * * * If punitive damages are not allowed in a situation like this, what punishment will prohibit the intentional trespass to land? * * *

In sum, * * * we hold that nominal damages may support a punitive damage award in an action for intentional trespass to land.

* * *

III.

[The court held that, in order to prevent injustice, its opinion would apply to Steenberg's conduct.]

* * *

IV.

Finally, we consider whether the jury's $100,000 punitive damage award to the Jacques is excessive. * * *

The award of punitive damages * * * is entirely within the discretion of the jury. Notwithstanding the jury's broad discretion, the circuit court has the power to reduce the amount of punitive damages to an amount that it determines is fair and reasonable. * * * A jury's punitive damage award will not be disturbed unless the verdict is so clearly excessive as to indicate passion and prejudice. * * *

The Due Process Clause prohibits the court from imposing a " 'grossly excessive' " punishment on a tortfeasor. *BMW of N. Am., Inc. v. Gore*, 517 U.S. 559 (1996). * * *

* * * [There are] three factors [under *Gore* that] a court must consider * * *: (1) the degree of reprehensibility of the conduct; (2) the disparity between the harm or potential harm suffered by the plaintiff and the punitive damage award; and (3) the difference between this remedy and the civil or criminal penalties authorized or imposed in comparable cases.

* * * The most important indicium of the reasonableness of a punitive damage award is the degree of reprehensibility of the defendant's conduct. * * *

Steenberg's intentional trespass reveals an indifference and a reckless disregard for the law, and for the rights of others. At trial, Steenberg took an arrogant stance, arguing essentially that yes, we intentionally trespassed on the Jacques' land, but we cannot be punished for that trespass because the law protects us. We reject that position. We are further troubled by Steenberg's utter disregard for the rights of the Jacques. Despite numerous unambiguous refusals by the Jacques to allow Steenberg access to their land, Steenberg delivered the mobile home across the Jacques' land.

Furthermore, these deceitful acts were egregious; Steenberg Homes acted deviously. After the conversation in the Jacques' kitchen, the Jacques, their neighbors, and the town chairman were satisfied that the matter was resolved, and Steenberg would not trespass on the Jacques' land. Nevertheless, the Steenberg employees testified that as they walked out of the Jacques' home, the assistant manager told them to use any means to deliver the mobile home. This conduct is reprehensible. We conclude that the degree of reprehensibility of Steenberg's conduct supports the imposition of a substantial punitive award.

We now turn to the * * * disparity between the harm or potential harm suffered by the Jacques and the punitive damage award.

* * *

When compensatory damages are awarded, we consider the ratio of compensatory to punitive damages. This is so because compensatory damages represent the actual harm inflicted on the plaintiff. However, when nominal damages support a punitive damage award, use of a multiplier is of dubious assistance because the nominal damage award may not reflect the actual harm caused. If it did, the breathtaking 100,000 to 1 ratio of this case could not be upheld. However, in the proper case, a $1 nominal damage award may properly support a $100,000 punitive damage award where a much larger compensatory award might not. This could include situations where egregious acts result in injuries that are hard to detect or noneconomic harm that is difficult to measure. In these instances, as in the case before us, a mathematical bright line between the constitutional and the unconstitutional would turn the concept of punitive damages on its head.

Finally, * * * we compare the punitive damage award and the civil or criminal penalties that could be imposed for comparable misconduct. * * *

We consider this factor largely irrelevant in the present case because the "conduct at issue" here was scarcely that contemplated by the legislative action. Steenberg received a citation for trespass to land * * *. The maximum penalty * * * is $1000. Steenberg's egregious conduct could scarcely have been contemplated by the legislature when it enacted this statute which provides a penalty for simply "entering or remaining" on the land of another. Here, not only did Steenberg Homes illegally enter and remain on the Jacques' land, first they plowed a path across the Jacques' field, then they transported a mobile home over the path. Furthermore, the statute failed to deter Steenberg's egregious misconduct. And we see no reason why the legislative penalty for simple trespass will deter future conduct by Steenberg. Without punitive damages, Steenberg has a financial incentive to trespass again.

Our concern for deterrence is guided by our recognition of the nature of Steenberg's business. Steenberg sells and delivers mobile homes. It is, therefore, likely that they will again be faced with what was, apparently for them, a dilemma. Should they trespass and pay the forfeiture, which in this case was $30? Or, should they take the more costly course and obey the law? Today we alleviate the uncertainty for Steenberg Homes. We feel certain that the $100,000 will serve to encourage the latter course by removing the profit from the intentional trespass.

* * *

In conclusion, we hold that when nominal damages are awarded for an intentional trespass to land, punitive damages may, in the discretion of the jury, be awarded. * * * [We also] hold that the $100,000 punitive damages awarded by the jury is not excessive. * * *

Reversed and remanded with directions.

NOTES AND QUESTIONS

1. What was the theory of the lawsuit in *Jacque*? Why would the jury have concluded that punitive damages were justified? What did the circuit court do with the jury's award? What did the Wisconsin Supreme Court hold? Which approach is most persuasive?

2. What are punitive damages? Punitive damages have been discussed in Chapter 4 and Chapter 5.

3. Although trespass claims usually arise in the context of a civil lawsuit against a party for compensation, such claims have become increasingly relevant in criminal cases as well. For example, in *United States v. Jones*, 565 U.S. ___, 132 S. Ct. 945 (2012) (also discussed in Chapter 7), the Supreme Court held that the warrantless installation of a Global Positioning System (GPS) tracking device on a vehicle to monitor the vehicle's movements constituted an impermissible search under the Fourth Amendment. The Court reasoned that the defendant had a property interest in his vehicle, and that by placing the device on the defendant's vehicle, the police impermissibly trespassed on his private property. *See also Florida v. Jardines*, 565 U.S. ___, 133 S. Ct. 1409 (2013) (citing *Jones* and holding that law enforcement's warrantless use of a drug sniffing dog on the front porch of the defendant's home was a trespassory invasion of the curtilage of the home that violated the Fourth Amendment).

4. As shown in *Jacque*, an owner traditionally has had a broad right to exclude others from any private property he holds, even if no harm would be caused by the trespass. *Accord* Restatement (Second) of Torts § 163 (1965). Commentators have disagreed over the wisdom of this approach. *Compare, e.g.,* John Martinez, *Bikinis and Efficient Trespass Law*, 2013 Utah L. Rev. OnLaw 290 (2013) (arguing that a pure right to exclude (even absent interference with use or damage to property) promotes judicial efficiency by creating a bright line rule for guidance), *with* Ben Depoorter, *Fair Trespass*, 111 Colum. L. Rev. 1090 (2011) (arguing for a "fair use" approach that would consider: (1) the nature and character of the trespass; (2) the nature of the protected property; (3) the amount and substantiality of the trespass; and (4) the impact of the trespass on the owner's property interest). Which approach is preferable?

5. In *State v. Shack*, 58 N.J. 297, 277 A.2d 369 (1971), the New Jersey Supreme Court adopted a flexible approach in the context of a criminal charge of trespass. In that case, the defendants (the alleged trespassers) worked for two government-supported nonprofit organizations that provided health and legal services to migrant farm workers. The defendants went to a local farm (where several migrant farm workers lived and worked) and requested to visit the living quarters to provide medical and legal services to the farmworkers.

The owner of the farm refused to allow the defendants to consult with the workers outside of his presence and called the police. The defendants were subsequently convicted of criminal trespass. The New Jersey Supreme Court reversed the conviction, reasoning: "[T]he employer may not deny the worker his privacy or interfere with his opportunity to live with dignity and to enjoy associations customary among our citizens." *Id.* at 308, 277 A.2d at 374. Is the New Jersey Supreme Court's approach persuasive? If so, should the same approach apply in the civil context?

6.   Another concept that arises in trespass claims involves a "continuing trespass." In that situation, a property owner will typically seek an injunction from the court to stop the trespass from continuing indefinitely. For example, in *Amaral v. Cuppels*, 64 Mass. App. Ct. 85, 831 N.E.2d 915 (2005), the plaintiff bought a home that was located on the edge of a private golf course and claimed, in a trespass action against the golf course, that over a five-year period approximately 1,800 golf balls had struck her home and damaged her property. The plaintiff requested an injunction to stop the activity. The court agreed that an injunction was appropriate, even though the plaintiff bought the home on the golf course after the course had been operating for almost 20 years. The court reasoned that "coming to a trespass" (*i.e.*, purchasing a property when a trespass or nuisance already exists) does not bar a claim to enjoin an ongoing trespass. Is that approach fair?

G. NUISANCE

As discussed in the previous section, when an owner has established full rights over a parcel of property, that owner is generally entitled to exclude others from the property and be free from trespass onto the property. In addition to being free from physical trespass, however, an owner is also entitled to full and fair enjoyment of their property without significant interference from outsiders. Even if a physical trespass does not occur, when someone or something interferes with another's enjoyment of their property, the property owner may have a legal action for abatement (cessation) of a "nuisance." The following case involves a nuisance action.

BEATTY V. WASHINGTON METROPOLITAN AREA TRANSIT AUTHORITY

United States Court of Appeals, District of Columbia Circuit, 1988
860 F.2d 1117

RE, CHIEF JUDGE.

Appellant, Lorraine A. Beatty, brought this action claiming damages for * * * nuisance resulting from the operation of subway trains by appellee, Washington Metropolitan Area Transit Authority (WMATA). She appeals from an order of the United States District Court for the District of Columbia, which granted WMATA's motion for summary judgment. Having concluded that the * * * nuisance [was] permanent in nature, the district court held that the action was barred by the three-year statute of limitations.

Beatty contends that the district court erred in granting summary judgment because there is a factual dispute as to whether the nuisance is permanent or continuing.

* * *

On the record presented, we hold that there are genuine issues of material fact * * *. Accordingly, the grant of summary judgment by the district court is reversed, and the case is remanded.

I.   BACKGROUND

Beatty is the owner of a house located on the corner of Girard and Ninth Streets, N.E., Washington, D.C. WMATA is an agency and instrumentality of Maryland, Virginia, and the District of Columbia empowered to plan, develop, finance and operate a regional transit system pursuant to the WMATA Compact. Beatty's house, in which she has lived since 1952, is situated across the street from a retaining wall, which separates the Metrorail "B" Route (Red Line) from Ninth Street. This section of the Red Line, which runs 65 to 80 feet from Beatty's house, opened for service on February 6, 1978, after "test trains" were run along that route for several weeks prior to its opening.

In a letter to WMATA dated February 2, 1978, Beatty complained that the vibrations caused by the passing trains caused damage to her house. Specifically, she stated that the walls cracked, and that, whenever the trains passed by, the cabinets and dishes shook.

On January 31, 1986, Beatty sued WMATA, seeking $200,000 in damages under each count for damage to real property, trespass to realty, and nuisance. In her complaint, Beatty alleged that the vibrations from passing trains "caused and will continue to cause excessive cracking and spalling of the plaster and walls and ceiling of the house," and, thus, "greatly reduced its value." Stating that the "nuisance has been of a continuous nature," Beatty also alleged that the vibrations constituted a nuisance which deprived her "of the peaceful enjoyment of her home."

In her deposition and answers to WMATA's interrogatories, Beatty stated that the damage began in 1978, and became very severe in 1983 when she noticed that "a hole developed on one ceiling and ... cracks throughout the entire house." In her answer to interrogatories she stated that the "basement block foundation of the house developed cracks between January 12, 1985 and the present." Her deposition noted that the vibrations vary, stating that, "during the rush hour it is worse and then non-rush hour they don't go as fast and they don't run quite as often." In her deposition she also stated that, in addition to structural damage to her house, china has fallen from her china closet: "when you open the door my dishes have fallen to the floor and broken."

* * * WMATA moved for summary judgment. * * * [T]he district court concluded that the trespass and nuisance were "of a permanent nature," [and thus] it held that the statute of limitations began to run when Beatty "knew of the injury that would befall her."

* * * Beatty subsequently moved for reconsideration[,] * * * maintain[ing] that the nuisance was not permanent, but temporary or continuing, since it was abatable. Hence, she contended that the cause of action was not barred by the statute of limitations. In support of her motion, Beatty referred to a report prepared by Dr. George Wilson of Wilson, Ihrig & Associates, Inc., WMATA's acoustical consultant, which stated that the vibrations could be reduced by various methods. The district court held that Beatty did not justify her failure to present Dr. Wilson's report to the court prior to the decision granting summary judgment. Hence, * * * the district court denied Beatty's motion for reconsideration.

II. THE GRANT OF SUMMARY JUDGMENT

[The court discussed the standard for summary judgment under Fed. R. Civ. P. 56(c).]

III. BEATTY'S CLAIM OF NUISANCE

Nuisance, an ancient and fertile tort, is defined by the Restatement as "an interference with the interest in the private use and enjoyment of the land. . . ." Restatement (Second) of Torts § 821D cmt. d (1977). In nuisance actions it is important, for statute of limitations purposes, to ascertain whether the invasion or interference is "permanent" or "continuing."

In general terms a permanent nuisance may be defined as one of such a character, and existing under such circumstances, that it will be reasonably certain to continue indefinitely in the future. If the invasion is deemed to be "permanent," there is but one cause of action, and the statute of limitations commences to run from the time the invasion began, or when it became known to the aggrieved party.

A temporary or continuing nuisance is one which is "abatable," or, also, one which is intermittent or periodical. For statute of limitations purposes, the distinction between a permanent or continuing nuisance is crucial because, if the invasion is deemed "temporary" or "continuing," a new cause of action arises with each new invasion or injury. Here, since the district court concluded, as a matter of law, that the nuisance was permanent, it held that the action was barred by the statute of limitations * * *.

In granting summary judgment for WMATA, the district court stated that "[w]hether trespass is 'permanent' or 'continuing' is determined primarily by looking at the physical permanence of the source of the property invasion and the value of the source of the invasion to the community and the likelihood that the invasion could be enjoined." In construing the terms "permanent" and "continuing," the district court cited *L'Enfant Plaza East, Inc. v. John McShain, Inc.*, 359 A.2d 5 (D.C.1976). In *L'Enfant*, the District of Columbia Court of Appeals considered whether the encroachment of a building's footing into adjoining property was a permanent or continuing trespass. In determining permanency the court adopted three factors set forth in Professor Dobbs's text on Remedies [D. Dobbs, *Remedies* § 5.4 (1973)]:

> (1) is the source of the invasion physically permanent, *i.e.*, is it likely, in the nature of things, to remain indefinitely? (2) is the source of the invasion the kind of thing an equity court would refuse to abate by injunction because of its value to the community or because of relations between the parties? (3) which party seeks the permanent or prospective measure of damages?

The court concluded that since the footing of the building could be removed "without undue difficulty . . . it was not likely to remain indefinitely," and, thus, was a continuing trespass.

The district court, in this case, stated that " * * * the Metrorail system is likely to remain in place indefinitely." WMATA states that the district court properly applied * * * the factors of *L'Enfant* for permanency. According to WMATA, the permanency of the Metrorail system and its great value to the community are unquestioned, and, therefore, the first two factors * * * support a finding of permanence. Beatty, however, contends that WMATA's argument ignores the fact "that the instant case does not involve an 'encroachment' at all," but "recurrent vibrations emanating from outside [her] property. . . ."

The district court concluded that the vibrations were of a permanent nature, stating, "[v]ibrations are an inevitable incident of any subway or train system," and "they are going to continue so long as Metrorail trains operate." While vibrations may be inevitable, vibrations of such intensity that they cause damage to a house 65 to 80 feet from the train tracks might not be held to be an inevitable incident of the Metrorail system.

Support for Beatty's contention that the vibrations are continuing, even though the Metrorail is a permanent structure, may be found in Professor Dobbs's analysis of the relevant factors to determine permanency. Professor Dobbs notes that "[i]f the nuisance arises out of the particular way in which [an] operation is carried out, and present technology demonstrates that the operation can be changed at reasonable expense to avoid the nuisance, then the nuisance is not physically permanent at all because we would predict a substantial change as likely."

The explanation is pertinent since Beatty maintains that the vibrations are not permanent because they can be abated or reduced. Furthermore, Beatty stresses that "abatement of the nuisance in this case does not require anything extraordinary or drastic such as terminating Metrorail service on the Redline." It was in support of this contention that Beatty submitted, on her motion for reconsideration, the report of Dr. George Wilson, which described several methods by which the vibrations could be abated or reduced. In denying Beatty's motion for reconsideration, the district court stated that the "plaintiff seriously misconstrues the meaning of 'abatable,' " in maintaining that if "the nuisance and trespass are subject to correction," they are "not properly denominated 'permanent.' " In the view of the district court, "[a]n abatable nuisance or trespass is *not* one subject to any amelioration, . . . the inquiry on this point is restricted to whether the trespass or nuisance is 'abatable by a proceeding in equity.' " Consequently, it concluded that it "cannot but find that equity would not restrain so important an activity as public transit operation."

Since the benefits that public transit offers to the community are not in issue, the question is not whether equity will "restrain so important an activity." The question, rather, is whether the nuisance resulting from its operation is permanent, as a matter of law, for statute of limitations purposes. Having concluded that the nuisance was not "abatable" by a proceeding in equity, the district court held that the nuisance was permanent * * *. On the question of abatability, * * * Dr. Wilson's report sets forth proposals that would reduce the vibrations without terminating transit service. The proposals, which would appear obvious, are: (1) "slow the speed of the trains as they pass station 184 + 00"; (2) "vibration isolate the house"; (3) "provide an underground isolation barrier parallel to the retaining wall."

Whether it was possible to abate the nuisance was a crucial question of fact. To assume that a nuisance is abatable only if it can be completely terminated or removed does violence to the law of nuisance. Although the word is derived from the French "abattre," which means to beat down or pull down, it also means to lessen, diminish, decrease or moderate. Indeed, it has been stated that an abatable nuisance is "one which is practically susceptible of being suppressed . . . [it] does not necessarily mean that, in order to abate a nuisance, the structure or thing which has caused the injurious results should be destroyed."

The view that the exercise of equitable jurisdiction would require the termination of a valuable public service misconceives the beneficial role of equity and the flexible remedies that it has fashioned. * * *

In cases of nuisance, for centuries, courts of equity have resolved the conflicting interests of property owners, and have struck a balance to allow the reasonable enjoyment of their property. These actions were used as an early method of town planning, and helped regulate the advent of new industries and occupations. They illustrate the value of the flexible remedies fashioned in nuisance cases, and the ability of equity to resolve disputes between adjacent property owners in an accommodating, and practical manner. * * *

* * *

Many examples can be found of the beneficial role of the courts, exercising the traditional powers of courts of equity, in resolving disputes which assure parties the reasonable enjoyment of their property. * * *

* * * [A]batement does not necessarily mean total cessation or termination of the challenged activity. Rather, it implies a wise exercise of discretion which considers and balances all of the pertinent factors, including, of course, the equities of the parties and the rights of the public. * * *

* * *

An important distinction not mentioned by the district court is that nuisances may be classified for two distinct purposes, one for the assessment of damages, and the other for the application of the statute of limitations. The court, in determining the statute of limitations may be influenced by different considerations than in determining proper damages. Hence, a nuisance may be classified as "permanent" for the purpose of assessing damages, and as "continuing" for statute of limitations purposes. The Supreme Court applied this dual standard in *Harrisonville v. W.S. Dickey Clay Mfg. Co.*, 289 U.S. 334 (1933), when it awarded a permanent measure of damages, yet found the nuisance was not permanent for the purpose of the statute of limitations.

In *Harrisonville*, owners of a farm, near a sewage disposal plant operated by the city, complained that a drain pipe that discharged pollutants into a stream on the property, was a nuisance, and sought damages as well as injunctive relief. The Court held that the nuisance was "continuous or recurrent" in nature. The Court, however, denied the plaintiffs injunctive relief noting that "[w]here an important public interest would be prejudiced, the reasons for denying the injunction may be compelling." The Court, however, emphatically rejected the City's argument that plaintiffs' action was time barred because the nuisance was permanent in nature. The court found "no occasion to determine the scope of the doctrine of permanent nuisance as applied" * * * since the nuisance could at all times be removed, and thus "[b]eing so terminable, pollution of the creek cannot be deemed to be a permanent nuisance as of the date of the installation of the disposal plant. . . ."

The case law reveals that there is no single, all-inclusive rule to determine whether a nuisance is continuing or permanent, and that each case must be decided on its specific facts. It is well settled, however, that * * * questions of fact must be determined by the trier of facts. Consequently, the grant of summary judgment by the district court was inappropriate.

* * *

V. CONCLUSION

* * * [T]he district court's grant of summary judgment is reversed * * *.

NOTES AND QUESTIONS

1.   What is a nuisance? What was the claimed nuisance in the *Beatty* case? How did the nuisance issue relate to WMATA's argument that the lawsuit was barred by the statute of limitations? How did the appellate court rule? Is the court's reasoning sound?

2.   What is a permanent nuisance? How does it differ from a temporary or continuing nuisance?

3.   A landmark nuisance case is *Boomer v. Atlantic Cement Co.*, 26 N.Y.2d 219, 257 N.E.2d 870 (1970). In that case, Atlantic Cement Company operated an industrial cement plant in upstate New York. Nearby residents complained of loud noises, smoke, dirt, and vibrations that emanated from the plant into a nearby neighborhood. They filed suit seeking to shut down the operation of the cement plan as a nuisance. The New York Court of Appeals (the State's highest court) held that the proper approach was to grant relief "conditioned on the payment of permanent damages to plaintiffs which would compensate them for the total economic loss to their property present and future caused by defendant's operations." *Id.* at 225, 257 N.E.2d at 316–17. Thus, the court allowed the cement plant to continue to operate, but held that it had to compensate the plaintiffs for the loss in value of their property as a result of the nuisance. The court held that because the concrete plant was an economically valuable resource to the community (investment in the plant exceeded $45 million and more than 300 people worked there), shutting down the plant would be economically and socially wasteful. Accordingly, the court found that awarding damages, as opposed to shutting down the source of the nuisance, was the more appropriate remedy. This approach has come to be known as the "comparative nuisance" approach, whereby a court will not enjoin an activity when the economic or social value of that activity outweighs the harm caused by the nuisance. The dissent in the case expressed concern that the majority's approach allowed a party to violate established property rights of others as long as it paid a fee for its conduct.

4.   Some scholars support the approach in *Boomer*. *See, e.g.*, Jeff Lewin, *Boomer and the American Law of Nuisance: Past, Present, and Future*, 54 Alb. L. Rev. 189, 291 (1990) (arguing that the court in *Boomer* correctly embraced the doctrine of "comparative nuisance" because that doctrine is "consistent with our notions of corrective justice and with the goal of economic efficiency"). Other scholars, however, have expressed concerns about the *Boomer* approach. *See, e.g.*, Joel Dobris, Boomer *Twenty Years Later: An Introduction, With Some Footnotes About "Theory"*, 54 Alb. L. Rev. 171, 182 (1990) (analyzing *Boomer* and recognizing that "[t]here is always a concern * * * that permanent damages will fail to monetize future health damage, or fail to inspire further efforts at nuisance abatement by the particular defendant"). Is the majority's

approach in *Boomer* the most socially desirable approach? Or should the court have required the shutdown of the plant?

5. The law of nuisance is premised on the Latin phrase, *"Sic utere tuo ut alienum non laedas,"* meaning, "So use your own as not to injure another's property." As the term implies, a nuisance claim can be brought for a broad array of interferences with the use or enjoyment of land. *See, e.g., Scribner v. Summers*, 84 F.3d 554 (2d Cir. 1996) (involving a metal disposal company that leaked hazardous chemical waste onto private property); *Aristides v. Foster*, 901 N.Y.S.2d 688, 73 A.D.3d 1105 (N.Y. App. Div. 2010) (involving the operation of a convenience store, where vehicles blocked access to plaintiff's house, caused pollution and noise from idling semi-trucks, and caused loitering and disturbances near the house); *JP Morgan Chase Bank v. Whitmore*, 838 N.Y.S.2d 142, 41 A.D.3d 433 (N.Y. App. Div. 2007) (involving extreme noise caused by exhaust fans in a condominium complex, which prevented residents from using their decks and sleeping in certain parts of the complex).

6. Although the concept of a nuisance is broad, courts have imposed some limits on the doctrine. For example, in *Fontainebleau Hotel Corp. v. Forty-Five Twenty-Five, Inc.*, 114 So.2d 357 (Fla. Dist. Ct. App. 1959), a Florida court held that a landowner could not claim a nuisance when a neighbor blocked the free flow of light and air across his land. In that case, the Fontainebleau Hotel began construction on a 14-story addition to its building that, when complete, would cast a shadow over the neighboring Eden Roc Hotel's cabana, pool, and beach areas. The Eden Roc Hotel moved to enjoin the construction, but the court denied relief, reasoning that there was no legal right to unobstructed light from an adjacent property. Although most states have followed *Fontainebleau*, the Supreme Court of Wisconsin distinguished the case in *Prah v. Maretti*, 108 Wis.2d 223, 321 N.W.2d 182 (1982). The *Prah* court held that a claim of private nuisance could be maintained where the proposed construction would interfere with the plaintiff's access to sunlight that was used for solar energy. The Wisconsin court reasoned that "[i]n this case the plaintiff seeks to protect access to sunlight, not for aesthetic reasons or as a source of illumination but as a source of energy." *Id.* at 236, 321 N.W.2d at 190. Is this distinction persuasive?

7. There is an important distinction between a public and a private nuisance. As the Supreme Court of Connecticut has explained: "Public nuisance law is concerned with the interference with a public right, and cases in this realm typically involve conduct that allegedly interferes with the public health and safety. Private nuisance law, on the other hand, is concerned with conduct that interferes with an individual's private right to the use and enjoyment of his or her land." *Pestey v. Cushman*, 259 Conn. 345, 357, 788 A.2d 496, 505 (2002). In *Pestey*, the court affirmed a jury verdict that a strong manure odor emanating from a dairy farm onto an adjacent private property was a private nuisance because the conduct did not pose a danger to public safety or health; rather, the conduct merely affected the enjoyment of land by a small group of landowners. The determination whether a nuisance is public or private can be important. For instance, a person challenging a public

nuisance (as opposed to a private nuisance) might not have standing to sue if he is merely a member of the public at large and cannot establish special damages. Moreover, a private nuisance might entitle the affected property owner to individual damages, whereas the remedy for a public nuisance could involve governmental enforcement leading to criminal or civil penalties. *See generally* Keith Hylton, *The Economics of Public Nuisance Law and the New Enforcement Actions*, 18 Sup. Ct. Econ. Rev. 43 (2010).

8.   It is sometimes difficult to distinguish between claims of trespass and nuisance. Professors Prosser and Keeton provide a useful discussion. They note, by way of example, that trespass involves "walking across [someone's] lawn," whereas nuisance involves "establishing a bawdy house next door." W. PAGE KEETON ET AL., PROSSER AND KEETON ON THE LAW OF TORTS 622 (5th ed. 1984).

H. PUBLIC TRUST

Although property ownership rights are generally assigned to a particular person or entity, some types of property are deemed to be owned by the public as a whole. This concept is known as the "public trust doctrine." Common forms of property subject to the public trust doctrine are tidelands and navigable waters that are open for public use. When dealing with those types of property, members of the general public can, in certain circumstances, sue to ensure that their rights are not significantly curtailed. The following case discusses the contours of the public trust doctrine.

CENTER FOR BIOLOGICAL DIVERSITY, INC. v. FPL GROUP, INC.

Court of Appeal, First District, Division 3, California, 2008
166 Cal.App.4th 1349, 83 Cal.Rptr.3d 588

POLLAK, JUSTICE.

Plaintiffs, the Center for Biological Diversity, Inc. and Peter Galvin (collectively CBD), appeal from the dismissal of their cause of action, which alleged that defendant owners and operators of wind turbine electric generators in the Altamont Pass Wind Resource Area in Alameda and Contra Costa Counties are, by the operation of their wind turbines, responsible for killing and injuring raptors and other birds in violation of the public trust doctrine. The trial court dismissed their action * * * on the ground that private parties are not entitled to bring an action for the violation of the public trust doctrine arising from the destruction of wildlife. We conclude that the trial court properly dismissed this particular action, although we qualify its broad holding and reject even broader assertions advanced by defendants in support of its ruling. Wildlife, including birds, is considered to be a public trust resource of all the people of the state, and private parties have the right to bring an action to enforce the public trust.

Nonetheless, in other proceedings of which we take judicial notice, the public agencies responsible for protecting these trust resources have taken action to do so. The proper means to challenge the adequacy of those measures is by [a] request for * * * appropriate relief brought against those agencies. Permitting the action to proceed as presented would require the court to make complex and delicate balancing judgments without the benefit of the expertise of the agencies responsible for protecting the trust resources and would threaten redundancy at best and inconsistency at worst.

BACKGROUND

In 1980, in response to federal legislation intended to encourage the development of alternative energy sources, the State Energy Resources Conservation and Development Commission (California Energy Commission) created the Altamont Pass Wind Resource Area. Since 1981 and prior to September 2005, Alameda County issued 46 use permits to operate private wind energy generation facilities in the approximately 40,000-acre Alameda County portion of this area. Plaintiffs' amended complaint alleges that there are currently more than 5,000 wind turbine generators operating in Altamont Pass. The amended complaint alleges that since the generators were first erected, "it has been known that in the process of generating electricity the Altamont Pass wind turbine generators kill and injure eagles, hawks, falcons, owls, and other raptors, as well as non-raptor birds. . . . Since the 1980's, the . . . generators . . . have killed tens of thousands of birds, including between 17,000 and 26,000 raptors—more than a thousand Golden Eagles, thousands of hawks, and thousands of other raptors." Further, the complaint alleges that "the vast majority" of the generators are inefficient and obsolete and that current state-of-the art generators would produce many times more electricity per generator and destroy far fewer birds. Although "defendants have repeatedly announced various plans to replace their obsolete, first-generation wind turbine generators . . . with large state-of-the art turbines . . . , [they] have never implemented any of these repowering plans, except for one small wind turbine generator replacement project involving just 31 turbines. Defendants expect to continue using the vast majority of the obsolete, first-generation wind turbine generators at Altamont Pass for 10 or more additional years."

Plaintiffs allege that * * * defendants' "destruction of California wildlife is a violation of the public trust" and pray for declaratory and injunctive relief. On October 12, 2006, the superior court [dismissed the claim] * * * on the ground that "[n]o statutory or common law authority supports a cause of action by a private party for violation of the public trust doctrine arising from the destruction of wild animals." [This appeal followed.]

* * *

DISCUSSION

The public trust doctrine applies to wildlife, including raptors and other birds.

Defendants' first line of defense is that the public trust doctrine applies only to tidelands and navigable waters, and has no application to wildlife. While the public trust doctrine has evolved primarily around the rights of the public with respect to tidelands and navigable waters, the doctrine is not so limited. * * * "Whatever the doctrine may have meant in Roman law, in medieval continental Europe, or in English law, the courts in this country have treated the public trust largely as a public property right of access to certain public trust natural resources for various public purposes."

The California Supreme Court has unequivocally embraced and expanded the scope of the public trust doctrine insofar as it relates to tidal and navigable bodies of water. * * * "Although early cases expressed the scope of the public's right in tidelands as encompassing navigation, commerce and fishing, the permissible range of public uses is far broader, including the right to hunt, bathe or swim, and the right to preserve the tidelands in their natural state as ecological units for scientific study." * * *

* * *

* * * [I]t has long been recognized that wildlife are protected by the public trust doctrine. "Because wildlife are generally transient and not easily confined, through the centuries and across societies they have been held to belong to no one and therefore to belong to everyone in common." Older decisions articulate this concept in property terms * * *. In *Ex parte Maier*, 103 Cal. 476, 37 P. 402 (1894), * * * the California Supreme Court observed, "The wild game within a state belongs to the people in their collective, sovereign capacity * * *." The United States Supreme Court subsequently cited this "well-considered opinion" in support of "[t]he common ownership, and its resulting responsibility in the state" * * *. *Geer v. Connecticut*, 161 U.S. 519, 527, 529 (1896), overruled [on other grounds] in *Hughes v. Oklahoma*, 441 U.S. 322 (1979). * * *

* * * "The whole ownership theory [recognizes] * * * the importance to its people that a State have power to preserve and regulate the exploitation of an important resource." * * * But " * * * the public trust doctrine [still] commands that the state not abdicate its duty to preserve and protect the public's interest in common natural resources."

Thus, * * * it is clear that the public trust doctrine encompasses the protection of undomesticated birds and wildlife. * * * Their protection and preservation is a public interest that is now recognized in numerous state and federal statutory provisions.

In *Environmental Protection and Information Center v. California Department of Forestry & Fire Protection*, 44 Cal.4th 459, 80 Cal.Rptr.3d 28, 187 P.3d 888 (2008) (*EPIC*), the California Supreme Court * * * referred to "two distinct public trust doctrines"—"the common law doctrine, which involves the government's 'affirmative duty to take the public trust into account in the planning and allocation of water resources'" and "a public trust duty derived from statute * * *." The court * * * stated that "the duty of government agencies to protect wildlife is primarily statutory." For purposes of deciding the issues presented in this case, it matters not whether the obligations imposed by the public trust are considered to be derived from the common law or from statutory law, or from both. Either way, public agencies must consider the protection and preservation of wildlife although * * * the contours of that obligation are, "[g]enerally speaking," defined by statute. What must be determined here is whether members of the public have the right to enforce that obligation and, if so, whether they may do so in an action against private parties who are adversely affecting trust property.

Members of the public may enforce the public trust.

* * * [T]he [California] Supreme Court reiterated that "any member of the general public . . . has standing to raise a claim of harm to the public trust." [*National Audubon Society v. Superior Court*, 33 Cal.3d 419, 431 n.11, 658 P.2d 709, 716 n.11 (Cal. 1983).] Nonetheless, defendants argue and the trial court held that * * * standing * * * applies only to actions to enforce "the traditional public trust interest in navigable and tidal waters and tidelands." * * * As the defendants argue and the trial court acknowledged, most of the cases recognizing wildlife as public trust property are actions brought by governmental agencies in the exercise of their police powers. * * *

While * * * the public trust over wildlife thus far has been enforced only in actions brought by public entities, there is no reason in principle why members of the public should be denied standing to maintain an appropriate action. The statement in *National Audubon Society* recognizing the standing of members of the public applied without qualification to "a claim of harm to the public trust." * * *

The concept of a public trust over natural resources unquestionably supports exercise of the police power by public agencies. But the public trust doctrine also places a *duty* upon the government to protect those resources. * * *

The interests encompassed by the public trust undoubtedly are protected by public agencies * * *. Nonetheless, the public retains the right to bring actions to enforce the trust when the public agencies fail to discharge their duties. Many of the cases establishing the public trust doctrine * * * have been brought by private parties to prevent agencies of government from abandoning or neglecting the rights of the public with respect to resources subject to the public trust. * * *

A claim for breach of the public trust must be brought against the responsible public agencies.

We thus reject the conclusion of the trial court that private parties may not invoke the public trust doctrine "beyond the traditional public trust interest in navigable and tidal waters and tidelands." That is not to say, however, that plaintiffs are entitled to maintain this action in the manner they have framed it. The defect in the present complaint is not that it seeks to enforce the public trust, but that it is brought against the wrong parties. Plaintiffs have brought this action against the windmill operators whose actions they allege are destroying natural resources protected by the public trust. Plaintiffs have not proceeded against the County of Alameda, which has authorized the use of the wind turbine generators, or against any agency such as the California Department of Fish and Game that has been given the statutory responsibility of protecting the affected natural resources. * * *

Under traditional trust concepts, plaintiffs, viewed as beneficiaries of the public trust, are not entitled to bring an action against those whom they allege are harming trust property. The trustee charged with the responsibility to implement and preserve the trust alone has the right to bring such an action. "[W]here a trustee cannot or will not enforce a valid cause of action that the trustee ought to bring against a third person, a trust beneficiary may seek judicial compulsion against the trustee." * * * Thus, analogizing this action to the enforcement of a traditional trust agreement, the action must be brought against the appropriate representative of the state as the trustee of the public trust.

The necessity for proceeding against the appropriate public agencies is supported by more than analogy. * * * [T]he [public trust] doctrine places on the state the responsibility to enforce the trust. If the appropriate state agencies fail to do so, members of the public may seek to compel the agency to perform its duties, but neither members of the public nor the court may assume the task of administering the trust. * * *

The amended complaint in this case is * * * an attempt to [circumvent] the expertise that has been brought to bear on the subject in the permit proceedings before the Alameda County authorities. * * * [I]n considering the applications to extend the conditional use permits, the county received input from a specially created Wind Power Working Group that included representatives from the California Department of Fish and Game and the United States Fish and Wildlife Service, and the California Energy Commission, the California Attorney General, expert consultants and others. The extended permits were granted subject to additional conditions designed to reduce avian mortality, and further measures are contemplated to study and to improve the mitigation measures in the future. * * *

As indicated above, plaintiffs have the right to insist that the state * * * protect and preserve public trust property, including raptors and other wildlife. * * * [T]he environmental values protected by the public trust doctrine "deserve to be taken into account. * * *." However, these are not the only interests that must be considered. A delicate balancing of the conflicting demands for energy and for the protection of other environmental values must be made. * * *

There unquestionably is a strong public interest in utilizing wind power as a source of energy. Since 1980 there has been a federal Wind Energy Systems Act designed to foster the development of wind power. Congress has declared that "the widespread use of wind energy systems to supplement and replace conventional methods for the generation of electricity and mechanical power would have a beneficial effect upon the environment." The Altamont Pass Wind Resource Area has been so designated by the California Energy Commission * * *.

The Alameda County Board of Supervisors, with the advice and cooperation of numerous other agencies, has attempted to strike a balance between the generation of clean renewable energy with wind turbines and the protection of raptors and other birds adversely affected by the turbines. A challenge to the permissibility of defendants' conduct must be directed to the agencies that have authorized the conduct. * * *

* * * The specification of conditions best designed to accommodate the conflicting environmental and energy concerns presented by the operation of wind turbines is both highly complex and value laden. Expertise from many disciplines is necessary to evaluate a myriad of alternatives and must be brought to bear in striking a reasonable balance. Moreover, * * * we are still on the upward slope of the learning curve in generating energy by the use of wind power.

Intervention by the courts, other than by exercising oversight over the administrative process and ensuring that proper standards are applied, not only would threaten duplication of effort and inconsistency of results, but would require the courts to perform an ongoing regulatory role as technology evolves and conditions change. * * *

* * *

We do not gainsay plaintiffs' concern for the protection of the raptors and other birds that are suffering in large numbers from the operation of the wind turbines in the Altamont Pass. However, * * * the responsible public agencies have not ignored this concern * * *. The courts are available to review the responses of those agencies, but they are not available to supersede their role in the regulatory process.

DISPOSITION

The judgment is affirmed.

NOTES AND QUESTIONS

1.   What is the harm that plaintiffs in *Center for Biological Diversity* seek to stop?

2.   What is the public trust doctrine? In the *Center for Biological Diversity* court's view, does the doctrine apply to wildlife or only to tidelands and navigable waterways?

3.   What is the court's reasoning in *Center for Biological Diversity*? Is that reasoning (and the court's disposition) persuasive? Under the public trust doctrine, as construed in *Center for Biological Diversity*, can private parties bring suit against the person or persons who caused the harm? If not, who are the appropriate defendants?

4.   In *National Audubon Society v. Superior Court*, cited in *Center for Biological Diversity*, the National Audubon Society claimed that the Los Angeles Department of Public Works violated the public trust doctrine by diverting four streams that fed into Mono Lake and that were to be used as a water supply for Los Angeles. The California Supreme Court acknowledged that both of the competing interests at stake were exceedingly strong. Los Angeles had an important interest in providing an essential resource to the citizens of the city, but the public also had a pressing interest in the preservation of the lake. Ultimately, the court decided that a study should be undertaken to pinpoint a solution that would minimize harm to both interests. Eleven years later, in 1994, the California State Water Resources Control Board determined that the lake had to be restored to a level of 6,392 feet above sea level, a rise of approximately 20 feet from its historic low. The board found that this result was the proper way to maintain the public trust of the lake while still retaining water rights for Los Angeles. *National Audubon Society* is considered a leading case in environmental law. *See, e.g.*, Craig Anthony Arnold, *Working Out an Environmental Ethic: Anniversary Lessons From Mono Lake*, 4 Wyo. L. Rev. 1 (2004) (asserting that *National Audubon Society* offers a case study in achieving environmental conservation); Michael Blumm & Thea Schwartz, *Mono Lake and the Evolving Public Trust in Western Water*, 37 Ariz. L. Rev. 701, 703 (1995) (stating that *National Audubon Society* "ranks in the top ten of American environmental law decisions").

5.   The public trust doctrine has been the subject of significant commentary in the context of climate change. *See, e.g.*, Patrick McGinley, *Climate Change and the Public Trust Doctrine*, 65 Planning & Environmental Law No. 8 (2013) (discussing the evolution of the public trust doctrine in climate change cases and concluding that it is unclear whether the doctrine can have a meaningful impact on climate change reform); Robin Kundis Craig, *Adapting to Climate Change: The Potential Role of State Common-Law Public Trust Doctrines*, 34 Vt. L. Rev. 781, 781 (2010) (stating that the public trust

doctrine may be an excellent vehicle to protect aquatic resources and ecosystems from the dangers of climate change).

I. IMPLIED WARRANTY OF HABITABILITY

Once a person establishes ownership rights over real property, that person is generally free to lease or rent that property to another person. The owner is referred to as the landlord and the renter is referred to as the tenant. When this type of relationship is created, the landlord owes various duties to the tenant. One such duty is the "implied warranty of habitability," which requires a landlord to maintain a rented living space in sanitary and habitable conditions. The following case discusses the implied warranty of habitability.

JAVINS V. FIRST NATIONAL REALTY CORP.
United States Court of Appeals, District of Columbia Circuit, 1970
428 F.2d 1071

WRIGHT, CIRCUIT JUDGE.

These cases present the question whether housing code violations which arise during the term of a lease have any effect upon the tenant's obligation to pay rent. The [District of Columbia landlord-tenant court] ruled [that] proof of such violations [was] inadmissible when proffered as a defense to an eviction action for nonpayment of rent. The District of Columbia Court of Appeals [the local appellate court] upheld this ruling.

Because of the importance of the question presented, we granted appellants' petitions for leave to appeal.* We now reverse * * *.

I.

The facts revealed by the record are simple. By separate written leases, each of the appellants rented an apartment in a three-building apartment complex in Northwest Washington known as Clifton Terrace. The landlord, First National Realty Corporation, [sued in landlord-tenant court] * * * seeking possession on the ground that each of the appellants had defaulted in the payment of rent due for the month of April. The tenants, appellants here, admitted that they had not paid the landlord any rent for April [1966]. However, they alleged [approximately 1500] violations of the Housing Regulations as "an equitable defense or [a] claim by way of recoupment or set-off in an amount equal to the rent claim" * * *.

* * *

---

* At the time of the *Javins* decision, the U.S. Court of Appeals in D.C. had authority to review decisions of the local appellate court, the D.C. Court of Appeals. That situation changed in 1970 by an act of Congress (effective as of February 1, 1971). Appeals from the D.C. Court of Appeals now go directly to the U.S. Supreme Court. [Ed.]

II.

Since, in traditional analysis, a lease was the conveyance of an interest in land, courts have usually utilized the special rules governing real property transactions to resolve controversies involving leases. However, * * * "the body of private property law * * *, more than almost any other branch of law, has been shaped by distinctions whose validity is largely historical." Courts have a duty to reappraise old doctrines in the light of the facts and values of contemporary life—particularly old common law doctrines which the courts themselves created and developed. * * * "The continued vitality of the common law * * * depends upon its ability to reflect contemporary community values and ethics."

The assumption of landlord-tenant law, derived from feudal property law, that a lease primarily conveyed to the tenant an interest in land may have been reasonable in a rural, agrarian society; it may continue to be reasonable in some leases involving farming or commercial land. * * * But in the case of the modern apartment dweller, the value of the lease is that it gives him a place to live. The city dweller who seeks to lease an apartment on the third floor of a tenement has little interest in the land 30 or 40 feet below, or even in the bare right to possession within the four walls of his apartment. When American city dwellers, both rich and poor, seek "shelter" today, they seek a well-known package of goods and services—a package which includes not merely walls and ceilings, but also adequate heat, light and ventilation, serviceable plumbing facilities, secure windows and doors, proper sanitation, and proper maintenance.

* * *

Ironically, however, the rules governing the construction and interpretation of "predominantly contractual" obligations in leases have too often remained rooted in old property law.

Some courts have realized that certain of the old rules of property law governing leases are inappropriate for today's transactions. * * * [C]ourts have [thus] been gradually introducing more modern precepts of contract law in interpreting leases. * * *

In our judgment the trend toward treating leases as contracts is wise and well considered. Our holding in this case reflects a belief that leases of urban dwelling units should be interpreted and construed like any other contract.

III.

Modern contract law has recognized that the buyer of goods and services in an industrialized society must rely upon the skill and honesty of the supplier to assure that goods and services purchased are of adequate quality. In interpreting most contracts, courts have sought to protect the legitimate expectations of the buyer and have steadily widened the seller's responsibility for the quality of goods and services through implied warranties of fitness and merchantability. Thus without any special agreement a merchant will be held to warrant that his goods are fit for the ordinary purposes for which such goods are used and that they are at least of reasonably average quality. Moreover, if the supplier has been notified that goods are required for a specific purpose, he will be held to warrant that any goods sold are fit for that purpose. These implied warranties have become widely accepted and well established features of the common law, supported by the overwhelming body of case law. Today most states as well as the District of Columbia have codified and enacted these warranties into statute, as to the sale of goods, in the Uniform Commercial Code.

Implied warranties of quality have not been limited to cases involving sales. The consumer renting a chattel, paying for services, or buying a combination of goods and services must rely upon the skill and honesty of the supplier to at least the same extent as a purchaser of goods. Courts have not hesitated to find implied warranties of fitness and merchantability in such situations. In most areas product liability law has moved far beyond "mere" implied warranties running between two parties in privity with each other.

The rigid doctrines of real property law have tended to inhibit the application of implied warranties to transactions involving real estate. Now, however, courts have begun to hold sellers and developers of real property responsible for the quality of their product. For example, builders of new homes have recently been held liable to purchasers for improper construction on the ground that the builders had breached an implied warranty of fitness. In other cases courts have held builders of new homes liable for breach of an implied warranty that all local building regulations had been complied with. And * * * very recent decisions and commentary suggest the possible extension of liability to parties other than the immediate seller for improper construction of residential real estate.

Despite this trend * * *, many courts have been unwilling to imply warranties of quality, specifically a warranty of habitability, into leases of apartments. Recent decisions have offered no convincing explanation for their refusal; rather they have relied without discussion upon the old common law rule that the lessor is not obligated to repair unless he covenants to do so in the written lease contract. * * * In our judgment, the old no-repair rule cannot coexist with the obligations imposed on the landlord by a typical modern housing code, and must be abandoned in favor of an implied warranty of habitability. In the District of Columbia, the standards of this warranty are set out in the Housing Regulations.

IV.

A.

In our judgment the common law itself must recognize the landlord's obligation to keep his premises in a habitable condition. This conclusion is compelled by three separate considerations. First, * * * the old rule was based on certain factual assumptions which are no longer true * * *. Second, * * * the consumer protection cases discussed above require that the old rule be abandoned in order to bring residential landlord-tenant law into harmony with the principles on which those cases rest. Third, * * * the nature of today's urban housing market also dictates abandonment of the old rule.

The common law rule absolving the lessor of all obligation to repair originated in the early Middle Ages. Such a rule was perhaps well suited to an agrarian economy; the land was more important than whatever small living structure was included in the leasehold, and the tenant farmer was fully capable of making repairs himself. * * *

Court decisions in the late 1800's began to recognize that the factual assumptions of the common law were no longer accurate in some cases. For example, the common law, since it assumed that the land was the most important part of the leasehold, required a tenant to pay rent even if any building on the land was destroyed. Faced with such a rule and the ludicrous results it produced, in 1863 [New York's highest court] declined to hold that an upper story tenant was obliged to continue paying rent after his apartment building burned down. The court * * * pointed out that the urban tenant had no interest in the land, only in the attached building.

Another line of cases created an exception to the no-repair rule for short-term leases of furnished dwellings. * * *

These as well as other similar cases demonstrate that some courts began some time ago to question the common law's assumptions that the land was the most important feature of a leasehold and that the tenant could feasibly make any necessary repairs himself. Where those assumptions no longer reflect contemporary housing patterns, the courts have created exceptions to the general rule that landlords have no duty to keep their premises in repair.

It is overdue for courts to admit that these assumptions are no longer true with regard to all urban housing. Today's urban tenants, the vast majority of whom live in multiple dwelling houses, are interested, not in the land, but solely in "a house suitable for occupation." Furthermore, today's city dweller usually has a single, specialized skill unrelated to maintenance work; he is unable to make repairs like the "jack-of-all-trades" farmer who was the common law's model of the lessee. Further, unlike his agrarian predecessor who often remained on one piece of land for his entire life, urban tenants today are more mobile than ever before. A tenant's tenure in a specific apartment will often not be sufficient to justify efforts at repairs. In addition, the increasing complexity of today's dwellings renders them much more difficult to repair than the structures of earlier times. In a multiple dwelling repair may require access to equipment and areas in the control of the landlord. Low and middle income tenants, even if they were interested in making repairs, would be unable to obtain any financing for major repairs since they have no long-term interest in the property.

Our approach to the common law of landlord and tenant ought to be aided by principles derived from the consumer protection cases referred to above. In a lease contract, a tenant seeks to purchase from his landlord shelter for a specified period of time. The landlord sells housing as a commercial businessman and has much greater opportunity, incentive and capacity to inspect and maintain the condition of his building. Moreover, the tenant must rely upon the skill and bona fides of his landlord at least as much as a car buyer must rely upon the car manufacturer. In dealing with major problems, such as heating, plumbing, electrical or structural defects, the tenant's position corresponds precisely with "the ordinary consumer who cannot be expected to have the knowledge or capacity or even the opportunity to make adequate inspection of mechanical instrumentalities, like automobiles, and to decide for himself whether they are reasonably fit for the designed purpose."

Since a lease contract specifies a particular period of time during which the tenant has a right to use his apartment for shelter, he may legitimately expect that the apartment will be fit for habitation for the time period for which it is rented. We point out that in the present cases there is no allegation that appellants' apartments were in poor condition or in violation of the housing code at the commencement of the leases. Since the lessees continue to pay the same rent, they were entitled to expect that the landlord would continue to keep the premises in their beginning condition during the lease term. It is precisely such expectations that the law now recognizes as deserving of formal, legal protection.

Even beyond the rationale of traditional products liability law, the relationship of landlord and tenant suggests further compelling reasons for the law's protection of the tenants' legitimate expectations of quality. The inequality in bargaining power between landlord and tenant has been well documented. Tenants have very little leverage to enforce demands for better housing. Various impediments to competition in the rental housing market, such as racial and class discrimination and standardized form leases, mean that landlords place tenants in a take it or leave it situation. The increasingly severe shortage of adequate housing further increases the landlord's bargaining power and escalates the need for maintaining and improving the existing stock. Finally, the findings by various studies of the social impact of bad housing has led to the realization that poor housing is detrimental to the whole society, not merely to the unlucky ones who must suffer the daily indignity of living in a slum.

Thus [we conclude] that the old common law rule imposing an obligation upon the lessee to repair during the lease term was really never intended to apply to residential urban leaseholds. Contract principles established in other areas of the law provide a more rational framework for the apportionment of landlord-tenant responsibilities; they strongly suggest that a warranty of habitability be implied into all contracts for urban dwellings.

B.

We believe, in any event, that the District's housing code requires that a warranty of habitability be implied in the leases of all housing that it covers. The housing code—formally designated the Housing Regulations of the District of Columbia—was established and authorized by the Commissioners of the District of Columbia on August 11, 1955. Since that time, the code has been updated * * * numerous [times]. The * * * Regulations provide a comprehensive regulatory scheme setting forth in some detail: (a) the standards which housing in the District of Columbia must meet; (b) which party, the lessor or the lessee, must meet each standard; and (c) a system of inspections, notifications and criminal penalties. The Regulations themselves are silent on the question of private remedies.

Two previous decisions of this court, however, have held that the Housing Regulations create legal rights and duties enforceable in tort by private parties. * * *

* * * [I]t is clear not only that the housing code creates privately enforceable duties * * * but that the basic validity of every housing contract depends upon substantial compliance with the housing code at the beginning of the lease term. * * *

* * * [S]erious failure to comply with [the housing code] before the lease term begins renders the contract void. We think it untenable to find that [the housing code regulations have] no effect on the contract after it has been signed. To the contrary, by signing the lease the landlord has undertaken a continuing obligation to the tenant to maintain the premises in accordance with all applicable law.

This principle of implied warranty is well established. Courts often imply relevant law into contracts to provide a remedy for any damage caused by one party's illegal conduct. * * *

We * * * [hold] that the housing code must be read into housing contracts—a holding also required by the purposes and the structure of the code itself. The duties imposed by the Housing Regulations may not be waived or shifted by agreement if the Regulations specifically place the duty upon the lessor. Criminal penalties are provided if these duties are ignored. * * * Yet official enforcement of the housing code has been far from uniformly effective. Innumerable studies have documented the desperate condition of rental housing in the District of Columbia and in the nation. * * *

We therefore hold that the Housing Regulations imply a warranty of habitability, measured by the standards which they set out, into leases of all housing that they cover.

V.

In the present cases, the landlord sued for possession for nonpayment of rent. Under contract principles, however, the tenant's obligation to pay rent is dependent upon the landlord's performance of his obligations, including his warranty to maintain the premises in habitable condition. In order to determine whether any rent is owed to the landlord, the tenants must be given an opportunity to prove the housing code violations alleged [by the tenants] * * *.

At trial, the finder of fact must make two findings: (1) whether the alleged violations existed during the period for which past due rent is claimed, and (2) what portion, if any or all, of the tenant's obligation to pay rent was suspended by the landlord's breach. If no part of the tenant's rental obligation is found to have been suspended, then a judgment for possession may issue forthwith. On the other hand, if the jury determines that the entire rental obligation has been extinguished by the landlord's total breach, then the action for possession on the ground of nonpayment must fail.

The jury may find that part of the tenant's rental obligation has been suspended but that part of the unpaid back rent is indeed owed to the landlord. In these circumstances, no judgment for possession should issue if the tenant agrees to pay the partial rent found to be due. If the tenant refuses to pay the partial amount, a judgment for possession may then be entered.

The judgment of the District of Columbia Court of Appeals is reversed and the cases are remanded for further proceedings consistent with this opinion.

So ordered.

CIRCUIT JUDGE ROBB concurs in the result and in Parts IV-B and V of the opinion.

NOTES AND QUESTIONS

1.   What did the U.S. Court of Appeals for the D.C. Circuit hold in *Javins*? Is the court's approach persuasive?

2. What is the significance of the fact that the D.C. Circuit applied contract law to the dispute, as opposed to real estate law?

3. As *Javins* demonstrates, a breach of the implied warranty of habitability is often a defense for tenants who do not pay their rent. In this context, the implied warranty of habitability is usually asserted in what is known as a "constructive eviction" defense. In constructive eviction cases, the tenant often claims that the residence has become so unusable that the situation should be treated as an eviction, for which payment of rent is not required. For example, in *Minjak Co. v. Randolph*, 528 N.Y.S.2d 554, 140 A.D.2d 245 (N.Y. App. Div. 1988), two-thirds of the tenant's commercial rental space was unusable due to ongoing renovations, and the remaining one-third of the space was lacking essential services. The tenants abandoned the space and refused to pay rent. When the landlord sued for back rent, the tenants alleged constructive eviction. The court agreed with the tenant, finding that the doctrine of constructive eviction applied.

4. Although the doctrine of constructive eviction is often related to the implied warranty of habitability, a constructive eviction may be asserted in other situations as well. For example, in *Blackett v. Olanoff*, 371 Mass. 714, 358 N.E.2d 817 (1977), a landlord refused to address persistent noise complaints, and one tenant ultimately moved out and refused to pay rent. When the landlord sued the tenant for back rent, the tenant claimed constructive eviction. The court agreed with the tenants, holding that the landlord had violated the tenant's "implied covenant of quiet enjoyment" and that the defense of constructive eviction was properly asserted. Much like the implied warranty of habitability, the warranty of quiet enjoyment is implied in every landlord-tenant relationship.

5. The implied warranty of habitability has been extensively litigated since *Javins*. Professor Donald Campbell has reviewed the case law in his article, *Forty (Plus) Years After the Revolution: Observations on the Implied Warranty of Habitability*, 35 U. Ark. Little Rock L. Rev. 793 (2013). As he explains, conditions affecting mere aesthetics of the leased premises—such as leaky water faucets, unpainted or cracked walls, or defective blinds—will not constitute a breach of the implied warranty of habitability. Moreover, one-time deficiencies in a leased premise—such as a single outbreak of mold—are unlikely to constitute a breach of the implied warranty if resolved in a timely manner. Finally, defective conditions outside of the premises—such as defects in parking structures or outside walkways—are unlikely to constitute a breach of the implied warranty. Cases finding uninhabitable premises usually involve severe unsanitary conditions or noxious odors, structural problems, a lack of essential amenities (clean water, heat, electricity, etc.), or extensive rodent and insect infestation. *See id.* at 813–20.

J. TAKINGS

Although private property owners usually have exclusive rights to transfer or retain a piece of property at their own will, in some situations, the government may take a piece of property and dedicate it to public use. This remedy is often referred to as a "taking," and this type of taking can occur even if the property owner does not consent to the transfer. These types of takings are subject to some regulation, however. The Fifth Amendment states that private property shall not "be taken for public use * * * without just compensation." The central dispute in many takings cases is whether the government is taking the property for an actual "public use," and also whether the government has provided the property owner with "just compensation" for the taking. The following case discusses the Fifth Amendment requirement that the property be taken for a "public use."

KELO V. CITY OF NEW LONDON

Supreme Court of the United States, 2005
545 U.S. 469

JUSTICE STEVENS delivered the opinion of the Court.

In 2000, the city of New London approved a development plan that, in the words of the Supreme Court of Connecticut, was "projected to create in excess of 1,000 jobs, to increase tax and other revenues, and to revitalize an economically distressed city, including its downtown and waterfront areas." In assembling the land needed for this project, the city's development agent has purchased property from willing sellers and proposes to use the power of eminent domain to acquire the remainder of the property from unwilling owners in exchange for just compensation. The question presented is whether the city's proposed disposition of this property qualifies as a "public use" within the meaning of the Takings Clause of the Fifth Amendment to the Constitution.[1]

I

The city of New London (hereinafter City) sits at the junction of the Thames River and the Long Island Sound in southeastern Connecticut. Decades of economic decline led a state agency in 1990 to designate the City a "distressed municipality." In 1996, the Federal Government closed the Naval Undersea Warfare Center, which had been located in the Fort Trumbull area of the City and had employed over 1,500 people. In 1998, the City's unemployment rate was nearly double that of the State, and its population of just under 24,000 residents was at its lowest since 1920.

These conditions prompted state and local officials to target New London, and particularly its Fort Trumbull area, for economic revitalization. To this end, respondent New London Development Corporation (NLDC), a private nonprofit entity established some years earlier to assist the City in planning economic development, was

---

[1] "[N]or shall private property be taken for public use, without just compensation." U.S. CONST. amend. V. That Clause is made applicable to the States by the Fourteenth Amendment.

reactivated. In January 1998, the State authorized a $5.35 million bond issue to support the NLDC's planning activities and a $10 million bond issue toward the creation of a Fort Trumbull State Park. In February, the pharmaceutical company Pfizer Inc. announced that it would build a $300 million research facility on a site immediately adjacent to Fort Trumbull; local planners hoped that Pfizer would draw new business to the area, thereby serving as a catalyst to the area's rejuvenation. After receiving initial approval from the city council, the NLDC continued its planning activities and held a series of neighborhood meetings to educate the public about the process. In May, the city council authorized the NLDC to formally submit its plans to the relevant state agencies for review. Upon obtaining state-level approval, the NLDC finalized an integrated development plan focused on 90 acres of the Fort Trumbull area.

The Fort Trumbull area is situated on a peninsula that juts into the Thames River. The area comprises approximately 115 privately owned properties, as well as the 32 acres of land formerly occupied by the naval facility (Trumbull State Park now occupies 18 of those 32 acres). The development plan encompasses seven parcels. Parcel 1 is designated for a waterfront conference hotel at the center of a "small urban village" that will include restaurants and shopping. This parcel will also have marinas for both recreational and commercial uses. A pedestrian "riverwalk" will originate here and continue down the coast, connecting the waterfront areas of the development. Parcel 2 will be the site of approximately 80 new residences organized into an urban neighborhood and linked by public walkway to the remainder of the development, including the state park. This parcel also includes space reserved for a new U.S. Coast Guard Museum. Parcel 3, which is located immediately north of the Pfizer facility, will contain at least 90,000 square feet of research and development office space. Parcel 4A is a 2.4-acre site that will be used either to support the adjacent state park, by providing parking or retail services for visitors, or to support the nearby marina. Parcel 4B will include a renovated marina, as well as the final stretch of the riverwalk. Parcels 5, 6, and 7 will provide land for office and retail space, parking, and water-dependent commercial uses.

The NLDC intended the development plan to capitalize on the arrival of the Pfizer facility and the new commerce it was expected to attract. In addition to creating jobs, generating tax revenue, and helping to "build momentum for the revitalization of downtown New London," the plan was also designed to make the City more attractive and to create leisure and recreational opportunities on the waterfront and in the park.

The city council approved the plan in January 2000, and designated the NLDC as its development agent in charge of implementation. The city council also authorized the NLDC to purchase property or to acquire property by exercising eminent domain in the City's name. The NLDC successfully negotiated the purchase of most of the real estate in the 90-acre area, but its negotiations with petitioners failed. As a consequence, in November 2000, the NLDC initiated the condemnation proceedings that gave rise to this case.

II

Petitioner Susette Kelo has lived in the Fort Trumbull area since 1997. She has made extensive improvements to her house, which she prizes for its water view. Petitioner Wilhelmina Dery was born in her Fort Trumbull house in 1918 and has lived there her entire life. Her husband Charles (also a petitioner) has lived in the house since they married some 60 years ago. In all, the nine petitioners own 15 properties in Fort Trumbull—4 in parcel 3 of the development plan and 11 in parcel 4A. Ten of the parcels are occupied by the owner or a family member; the other five are held as investment properties. There is no allegation that any of these properties is blighted or otherwise in poor condition; rather, they were condemned only because they happen to be located in the development area.

In December 2000, petitioners brought this action in the New London Superior Court. They claimed, among other things, that the taking of their properties would violate the "public use" restriction in the Fifth Amendment. After a 7-day bench trial, the Superior Court granted a permanent restraining order prohibiting the taking of the properties located in parcel 4A (park or marina support). It, however, denied petitioners relief as to the properties located in parcel 3 (office space).

After the Superior Court ruled, both sides took appeals to the Supreme Court of Connecticut. That court held, over a dissent, that all of the City's proposed takings were valid. * * *

* * *

We granted certiorari to determine whether a city's decision to take property for the purpose of economic development satisfies the "public use" requirement of the Fifth Amendment.

III

Two polar propositions are perfectly clear. On the one hand, it has long been accepted that the sovereign may not take the property of *A* for the sole purpose of transferring it to another private party *B*, even though *A* is paid just compensation. On the other hand, it is equally clear that a State may transfer property from one private party to another if future "use by the public" is the purpose of the taking; the condemnation of land for a railroad with common-carrier duties is a familiar example. Neither of these propositions, however, determines the disposition of this case.

As for the first proposition, the City would no doubt be forbidden from taking petitioners' land for the purpose of conferring a private benefit on a particular private party. Nor would the City be allowed to take property under the mere pretext of a public purpose, when its actual purpose was to bestow a private benefit. The takings before us, however, would be executed pursuant to a "carefully considered" development plan. The trial judge and all the members of the Supreme Court of Connecticut agreed that there was no evidence of an illegitimate purpose in this case. Therefore, * * * the City's development plan was not adopted "to benefit a particular class of identifiable individuals."

On the other hand, this is not a case in which the City is planning to open the condemned land—at least not in its entirety—to use by the general public. Nor will the private lessees of the land in any sense be required to operate like common carriers, making their services available to all comers. But although such a projected use would be sufficient to satisfy the public use requirement, this "Court long ago rejected any literal requirement that condemned property be put into use for the general public." Indeed, while many state courts in the mid-19th century endorsed "use by the public" as the proper definition of public use, that narrow view steadily eroded over time. Not only was the "use by the public" test difficult to administer (*e.g.*, what proportion of the public need have access to the property? at what price?), but it proved to be impractical given the diverse and always evolving needs of society. Accordingly, when this Court began applying the Fifth Amendment to the States at the close of the 19th century, it embraced the broader and more natural interpretation of public use as "public purpose." Thus, in a case upholding a mining company's use of an aerial bucket line to transport ore over property it did not own, Justice Holmes's opinion for the Court stressed "the inadequacy of use by the general public as a universal test." *Strickley v. Highland Boy Gold Mining Co.*, 200 U.S. 527, 531 (1906). We have repeatedly and consistently rejected that narrow test ever since.

The disposition of this case therefore turns on the question whether the City's development plan serves a "public purpose." Without exception, our cases have defined that concept broadly, reflecting our longstanding policy of deference to legislative judgments in this field.

In *Berman v. Parker*, 348 U.S. 26 (1954), this Court upheld a redevelopment plan targeting a blighted area of Washington, D. C., in which most of the housing for the area's 5,000 inhabitants was beyond repair. Under the plan, the area would be condemned and part of it utilized for the construction of streets, schools, and other public facilities. The remainder of the land would be leased or sold to private parties for the purpose of redevelopment, including the construction of low-cost housing.

The owner of a department store located in the area challenged the condemnation, pointing out that his store was not itself blighted and arguing that the creation of a "better balanced, more attractive community" was not a valid public use. Writing for a unanimous Court, Justice Douglas refused to evaluate this claim in isolation, deferring instead to the legislative and agency judgment that the area "must be planned as a whole" for the plan to be successful. The Court explained that "community redevelopment programs need not, by force of the Constitution, be on a piecemeal basis—lot by lot, building by building." The public use underlying the taking was unequivocally affirmed * * *.

In *Hawaii Housing Authority v. Midkiff*, 467 U.S. 229 (1984), the Court considered a Hawaii statute whereby fee title was taken from lessors and transferred to lessees (for just compensation) in order to reduce the concentration of land ownership. We unanimously upheld the statute and rejected the Ninth Circuit's view that it was "a naked attempt on the part of the state of Hawaii to take the property of A and transfer it to B solely for B's private use and benefit." * * * [W]e concluded that the State's purpose of eliminating the "social and economic evils of a land oligopoly" qualified as a valid public use. * * *

* * *

Viewed as a whole, our jurisprudence has recognized that the needs of society have varied between different parts of the Nation, just as they have evolved over time in response to changed circumstances. * * * For more than a century, our public use jurisprudence has wisely eschewed rigid formulas and intrusive scrutiny in favor of affording legislatures broad latitude in determining what public needs justify the use of the takings power.

IV

Those who govern the City were not confronted with the need to remove blight in the Fort Trumbull area, but their determination that the area was sufficiently distressed to justify a program of economic rejuvenation is entitled to our deference. The City has carefully formulated an economic development plan that it believes will provide appreciable benefits to the community, including—but by no means limited to—new jobs and increased tax revenue. As with other exercises in urban planning and development, the City is endeavoring to coordinate a variety of commercial, residential, and recreational uses of land, with the hope that they will form a whole greater than the sum of its parts. To effectuate this plan, the City has invoked a state statute that specifically authorizes the use of eminent domain to promote economic development. Given the comprehensive character of the plan, the thorough deliberation that preceded its adoption, and the limited scope of our review, it is appropriate for us * * * to resolve the challenges of the individual owners, not on a piecemeal basis, but rather in light of the entire plan. Because that plan unquestionably serves a public purpose, the takings challenged here satisfy the public use requirement of the Fifth Amendment.

To avoid this result, petitioners urge us to adopt a new bright-line rule that economic development does not qualify as a public use. * * * [N]either precedent nor logic supports petitioners' proposal. Promoting economic development is a traditional and long-accepted function of government. There is, moreover, no principled way of distinguishing economic development from the other public purposes that we have recognized. * * *

Petitioners contend that using eminent domain for economic development impermissibly blurs the boundary between public and private takings. Again, our cases foreclose this objection. Quite simply, the government's pursuit of a public purpose will often benefit individual private parties. * * *

It is further argued that without a bright-line rule nothing would stop a city from transferring citizen A's property to citizen B for the sole reason that citizen B will put the property to a more productive use and thus pay more taxes. Such a one-to-one transfer of property, executed outside the confines of an integrated development plan, is not presented in this case. While such an unusual exercise of government power would certainly raise a suspicion that a private purpose was afoot, the hypothetical cases posited by petitioners can be confronted if and when they arise. They do not warrant the crafting of an artificial restriction on the concept of public use.

Alternatively, petitioners maintain that for takings of this kind we should require a "reasonable certainty" that the expected public benefits will actually accrue. Such a rule, however, would represent an even greater departure from our precedent. "When the legislature's purpose is legitimate and its means are not irrational, our cases make clear that empirical debates over the wisdom of takings—no less than debates over the wisdom of other kinds of socioeconomic legislation—are not to be carried out in the federal courts." * * * A constitutional rule that required postponement of the judicial approval of every condemnation until the likelihood of success of the plan had been assured would unquestionably impose a significant impediment to the successful consummation of many such plans.

Just as we decline to second-guess the City's considered judgments about the efficacy of its development plan, we also decline to second-guess the City's determinations as to what lands it needs to acquire in order to effectuate the project. * * *

In affirming the City's authority to take petitioners' properties, we do not minimize the hardship that condemnations may entail, notwithstanding the payment of just compensation. We emphasize that nothing in our opinion precludes any State from placing further restrictions on its exercise of the takings power. Indeed, many States already impose "public use" requirements that are stricter than the federal baseline. Some of these requirements have been established as a matter of state constitutional law, while others are expressed in state eminent domain statutes that carefully limit the grounds upon which takings may be exercised. * * * This Court's authority, however, extends only to determining whether the City's proposed condemnations are for a "public use" within the meaning of the Fifth Amendment * * *. Because over a century of our case law interpreting that provision dictates an affirmative answer to that question, we may not grant petitioners the relief that they seek.

The judgment of the Supreme Court of Connecticut is affirmed.

[Concurring opinion by JUSTICE KENNEDY is omitted.]

JUSTICE O'CONNOR, with whom THE CHIEF JUSTICE, JUSTICE SCALIA, and JUSTICE THOMAS join, dissenting.

* * *

Today the Court abandons [a] long-held, basic limitation on government power. Under the banner of economic development, all private property is now vulnerable to being taken and transferred to another private owner, so long as it might be upgraded—*i.e.*, given to an owner who will use it in a way that the legislature deems more beneficial to the public—in the process. To reason, as the Court does, that the incidental public benefits resulting from the subsequent ordinary use of private property render economic development takings "for public use" is to wash out any distinction between private and public use of property—and thereby effectively to delete the words "for public use" from the Takings Clause of the Fifth Amendment. Accordingly I respectfully dissent.

I

* * *

* * * Petitioners maintain that the Fifth Amendment prohibits the NLDC from condemning their properties for the sake of an economic development plan. Petitioners are not holdouts; they do not seek increased compensation, and none is opposed to new development in the area. Theirs is an objection in principle: They claim that the NLDC's proposed use for their confiscated property is not a "public" one for purposes of the Fifth Amendment. While the government may take their homes to build a road or a railroad or to eliminate a property use that harms the public, say petitioners, it cannot take their property for the private use of other owners simply because the new owners may make more productive use of the property.

II

* * * [W]e have read the Fifth Amendment's language to impose two distinct conditions on the exercise of eminent domain: "[T]he taking must be for a 'public use' and 'just compensation' must be paid to the owner."

These two limitations * * * ensure stable property ownership by providing safeguards against excessive, unpredictable, or unfair use of the government's eminent domain power * * *.

While the Takings Clause presupposes that government can take private property without the owner's consent, the just compensation requirement spreads the cost of condemnations and thus "prevents the public from loading upon one individual more than his just share of the burdens of government." The public use requirement, in turn, imposes a more basic limitation, circumscribing the very scope of the eminent domain power: Government may compel an individual to forfeit her property for the *public's* use, but not for the benefit of another private person. This requirement promotes fairness as well as security.

Where is the line between "public" and "private" property use? We give considerable deference to legislatures' determinations about what governmental activities will advantage the public. But were the political branches the sole arbiters of the public-private distinction, the Public Use Clause would amount to little more than hortatory fluff. An external, judicial check on how the public use requirement is interpreted, however limited, is necessary if this constraint on government power is to retain any meaning.

Our cases have generally identified three categories of takings that comply with the public use requirement, though it is in the nature of things that the boundaries between these categories are not always firm. Two are relatively straightforward and uncontroversial. First, the sovereign may transfer private property to public ownership—such as for a road, a hospital, or a military base. Second, the sovereign may transfer private property to private parties, often common carriers, who make the property available for the public's use—such as with a railroad, a public utility, or a stadium. * * * [Third,] we have allowed that, in certain circumstances and to meet certain exigencies, takings that serve a public purpose also satisfy the Constitution even if the property is destined for subsequent private use.

This case [raises] * * * the hard question of when a purportedly "public purpose" taking meets the public use requirement. It presents an issue of first impression: Are economic development takings constitutional? I would hold that they are not. We are guided by two precedents * * *. In *Berman* [*v. Parker*, 348 U.S. 26 (1954)], we upheld takings within a blighted neighborhood of Washington, D.C. The neighborhood had so deteriorated that, for example, 64.3% of its dwellings were beyond repair. It had become burdened with "overcrowding of dwellings," "lack of adequate streets and alleys," and "lack of light and air." Congress had determined that the neighborhood had become "injurious to the public health, safety, morals, and welfare" and that it was necessary to "eliminat[e] all such injurious conditions by employing all means necessary and appropriate for the purpose," including eminent domain. Mr. Berman's department store was not itself blighted. Having approved of Congress's decision to eliminate the harm to the public emanating from the blighted neighborhood, however, we did not second-guess its decision to treat the neighborhood as a whole rather than lot-by-lot.

In [*Hawaii Housing Authority v.*] *Midkiff*, [467 U.S. 229 (1984),] we upheld a land condemnation scheme in Hawaii whereby title in real property was taken from lessors and transferred to lessees. At that time, the State and Federal Governments owned nearly 49% of the State's land, and another 47% was in the hands of only 72 private landowners. Concentration of land ownership was so dramatic that on the State's most urbanized island, Oahu, 22 landowners owned 72.5% of the fee simple titles. The Hawaii Legislature had concluded that the oligopoly in land ownership was "skewing the State's residential fee simple market, inflating land prices, and injuring the public tranquility and welfare," and therefore enacted a condemnation scheme for redistributing title.

* * *

The Court's holdings in *Berman* and *Midkiff* were true to the principle underlying the Public Use Clause. In both those cases, the extraordinary, precondemnation use of the targeted property inflicted affirmative harm on society—in *Berman* through blight resulting from extreme poverty and in *Midkiff* through oligopoly resulting from extreme wealth. And in both cases, the relevant legislative body had found that eliminating the existing property use was necessary to remedy the harm. * * * Here, in contrast, New London does not claim that Susette Kelo's and Wilhelmina Dery's well-maintained homes are the source of any social harm. Indeed, it could not so claim without adopting the absurd argument that any single-family home that might be razed to make way for an apartment building, or any church that might be replaced with a retail store, or any small business that might be more lucrative if it were instead part of a national franchise, is inherently harmful to society and thus within the government's power to condemn.

* * *

The Court protests that it does not sanction the bare transfer from A to B for B's benefit. It suggests two limitations * * *. First, it maintains a role for courts in ferreting out takings whose sole purpose is to bestow a benefit on the private transferee—without detailing how courts are to conduct that complicated inquiry. * * *

Even if there were a practical way to isolate the motives behind a given taking, the gesture toward a purpose test is theoretically flawed. If it is true that incidental public benefits from new private use are enough to ensure the "public purpose" in a taking, why should it matter * * * what inspired the taking in the first place?

[Second,] * * * [t]he logic of today's decision is that eminent domain may only be used to upgrade—not downgrade—property. * * * [T]his constraint has no realistic import. For who among us can say she already makes the most productive or attractive possible use of her property? The specter of condemnation hangs over all property. Nothing is to prevent the State from replacing any Motel 6 with a Ritz-Carlton, any home with a shopping mall, or any farm with a factory.

The Court also puts special emphasis on facts peculiar to this case: The NLDC's plan is the product of a relatively careful deliberative process; it proposes to use eminent domain for a multipart, integrated plan rather than for isolated property transfer; it promises an array of incidental benefits (even esthetic ones), not just increased tax revenue; it comes on the heels of a legislative determination that New London is a depressed municipality. But none [of the facts] * * * blunt[s] the force of today's holding. If legislative prognostications about the secondary public benefits of a new use can legitimate a taking, there is nothing in the Court's rule * * * to prohibit property transfers generated with less care, that are less comprehensive, that happen to result from less elaborate process, whose only projected advantage is the incidence of higher taxes, or that hope to transform an already prosperous city into an even more prosperous one.

Finally, * * * the Court suggests that property owners should turn to the States, who may or may not choose to impose appropriate limits on economic development takings. This is an abdication of our responsibility. States play many important functions in our system of dual sovereignty, but compensating for our refusal to enforce properly the Federal Constitution (and a provision meant to curtail state action, no less) is not among them.

* * *

* * * [T]he fallout from this decision will not be random. The beneficiaries are likely to be those citizens with disproportionate influence and power in the political process, including large corporations and development firms. As for the victims, the government now has license to transfer property from those with fewer resources to those with more. The [Founding Fathers] cannot have intended this perverse result. * * *

I would hold that the takings in both Parcel 3 and Parcel 4A are unconstitutional, reverse the judgment of the Supreme Court of Connecticut, and remand for further proceedings.

[Dissenting opinion by JUSTICE THOMAS is omitted.]

NOTES AND QUESTIONS

1. What is the issue in *Kelo*? What did the majority hold? On what grounds did the dissent disagree?

2. *Kelo* has generated significant commentary; some is favorable, but much is unfavorable. For a sample of the diverse commentary, *see* John Kieran Murphey, *Constitutional Corporatism: The Public Use Clause as a Means of*

Corporate Welfare, 2 U. Balt. J. Land & Dev. 91, 91 (2013) (asserting that "[s]tate and local governments, which are meant to serve and protect the * * * interests of their respective constituents, are instead serving and protecting the financial interests of the well-connected"); John Zuch, Kelo v. City of New London: *Despite the Outcry, the Decision is Firmly Supported by Precedent— However, Eminent Domain Critics Still Have Gained Ground*, 38 U. Mem. L. Rev. 187, 221 (2007) (concluding that *Kelo* "is firmly supported by over 100 years of precedent"); Charles Cohen, *Eminent Domain After* Kelo v. City of New London: *An Argument for Banning Economic Development Takings*, 29 Harv. J.L. & Pub. Pol'y 491, 497 (2006) (arguing that takings for economic development are an "abuse of existing property owners" and that there should be a complete ban of takings for such development). Retired Justice Stevens, the author of *Kelo*, has acknowledged that the Court's opinion has generated significant hostility, but argues that "the popularity and policy wisdom of that decision may be an issue for the political branches * * * but not * * * for the Supreme Court." John Paul Stevens, Kelo, *Popularity, and Substantive Due Process*, 63 Ala. L. Rev. 941, 954 (2012).

3.   Although *Kelo* had the effect of broadening the power of government to utilize its eminent domain power, some scholars argue that the decision has in fact spawned a legislative counter movement that has actually restricted eminent domain power. *See, e.g.*, Gregory Robson, Kelo v. City of New London: *Its Ironic Impact on Takings Authority*, 44 Urb. Law. 865 (2012) (noting that all but three states passed legislation in response to the case within one year of the Court's decision); Daniel Cole, *Why* Kelo *is Not Good News for Local Planners and Developers*, 22 Ga. St. U.L. Rev. 803 (2006) (noting that the political backlash that followed *Kelo* has made municipal development and redevelopment substantially more difficult to accomplish).

4.   The motive behind the taking of property in *Kelo* was to clear the way for economic rejuvenation. As of 2015, however, the 90-acre property taken in connection with the *Kelo* case remains undeveloped and vacant. In response to the vacancy, the Mayor of New London, Connecticut signed an agreement in 2015 to build a park on the property to recognize the victims of the eminent domain. *See* Ilya Somin, *New London May Build a "Memorial Park" Honoring Victims of Eminent Domain on the Former Site of the Kelo House*, WASH. POST, Apr. 1, 2015, http://www.washingtonpost.com/news/volokh-conspiracy/wp/2015/04/01/new-london-may-build-a-memorial-park-on-former-site-of-the-kelo-house/ (discussing the vacancy of the lot in 2015 as well as plans for a memorial park).

5.   In *Loretto v. Teleprompter Manhattan CATV Corp.*, 458 U.S. 419 (1982), a New York law authorized private cable television companies to install small cable boxes on the side of New York apartment buildings. The law stated that landlords could not interfere with the installation and could not demand payment from the cable company in excess of $1. A group of landlords brought a class action lawsuit against the State, contending that the law constituted an uncompensated taking. The Supreme Court agreed. As the majority stated: "[W]hen the 'character of the governmental action' is a permanent physical

occupation of property, our cases uniformly have found a taking to the extent of the occupation, without regard to whether the action achieves an important public benefit or has only minimal economic impact on the owner." *Id.* at 434–35. Can *Loretto* be reconciled with *Kelo*?

6.　A taking does not have to be permanent to be subject to compensation under the Takings Clause. In *Arkansas Game & Fish Commission v. United States*, 568 U.S. ___, 133 S. Ct. 511 (2012), the Supreme Court held that government-induced flooding to alleviate excess water accumulation behind a dam could potentially constitute a temporary taking when the deviated stream water temporarily deprived landowners of the use of their property. Determining compensation in temporary takings cases has proven difficult for some courts, and the topic has generated significant commentary. *See, e.g.,* Laura Powell, Comment, *The Parcel as a Whole: Defining the Relevant Parcel in Temporary Regulatory Takings Cases*, 89 Wash. L. Rev. 151 (2014) (noting that courts often have trouble defining the portion of the property subject to compensation in temporary takings cases, and arguing that the courts should consider the owner's investment in the property in determine fair compensation); Daniel Siegel & Robert Meltz, *Temporary Takings: Settled Principles and Unresolved Questions*, 11 Vt. J. Envtl. L. 479 (2010) (surveying cases on temporary takings and concluding that setting compensation is difficult because each case is fact-specific).

7.　Although Takings Clause cases usually involve the government's taking of real property, the Takings Clause applies to *any* form of property taken by the government. For example, in *Horne v. Department of Agriculture*, 576 U.S. ___, 135 S. Ct. 2419 (2015), the Supreme Court held that a federal program that permitted the Department of Agriculture to reserve a percentage of the yearly California raisin crop (in an effort to stabilize the market price of the raisins) constituted a taking, thus requiring the government to compensate the raisin farmers. That was so even though farmers were given a portion of the proceeds of reserves that were actually sold. The Court reasoned that the program deprived the farmers of their right to possess and use a portion of their crop. As the Court stated: "The Government's 'actual taking of possession and control' of the reserve raisins gives rise to a taking as clearly 'as if the Government held full title and ownership' * * *." *Id.* at 2428. Accordingly, the government was required to compensate the raisin farmers for the portion of the crop that was taken for the reserve program.

Furthermore, the Takings Clause even applies to some forms of intangible property, such as a person's labor or services. For example, in *Ex parte Brown*, 393 S.C. 214, 711 S.E.2d 899 (2011), the government appointed a lawyer to represent a defendant charged with multiple felony charges. The lawyer spent significant time on the case and repeatedly requested (unsuccessfully) to withdraw because the value of his work was well in excess of the state's $3500 statutory cap on state-appointed attorneys' fees. The lawyer claimed that not awarding him more than the statutory cap constituted a taking of services without compensation. The South Carolina Supreme Court agreed, holding that under the Takings Clause, "the attorney's services constitute property entitling the attorney to just compensation." *Id.* at 216, 711 S.E.2d at 900.

It should also be noted that because an easement is considered to be a property interest (albeit a non-possessory interest), the Fifth Amendment requires the government to compensate an easement holder if it attempts to cancel that easement to support a public use. *See, e.g., United States v. Va. Elec. & Power Co.*, 365 U.S. 624 (1961) (holding that the government was required to compensate the possessor a "water flowage easement" when the government revoked the easement to build a dam). Similarly, the Fifth Amendment requires the government to compensate a property owner when the government compels the owner to *create* an easement for public use on the owner's property. *See, e.g., Nollan v. Cal. Coastal Comm'n*, 483 U.S. 825 (1987) (holding that a state was required to compensate a landowner when it in essence required a public easement across the landowner's beachfront property).

8.   A complication in takings analysis results when the government seizes property in furtherance of its "police powers." For example, in *AmeriSource Corp. v. United States*, 525 F.3d 1149 (Fed. Cir. 2008), the government seized drugs of a pharmaceuticals distributor and retained the drugs as evidence in criminal proceedings against a third party. By the time the government returned the property to the distributor, the drugs had expired and were useless. The pharmaceuticals distributor alleged a Fifth Amendment taking and demanded just compensation, but the Federal Circuit disagreed. The court held that since the drugs were seized and retained pursuant to government's police power, the property was not taken for "public use" and did not fall under the Takings Clause. *See also Kam-Almaz v. United States*, 682 F.3d 1364 (Fed. Cir. 2012) (finding no Fifth Amendment taking when the content on the plaintiff's laptop was inadvertently destroyed while being used in a police investigation). The notion of "takings" under the police power is a controversial topic. *See, e.g.*, Patrick Galasso, *The Innocent's Property: A New Approach to Takings in Criminal Jurisprudence*, 23 Fed. Circuit B.J. 283 (2013) (arguing that uncompensated police takings reinforce distrust of law enforcement); D. Benjamin Barros, *The Police Power and the Takings Clause*, 58 U. Miami L. Rev. 471 (2004) (arguing that takings analysis should not focus on the character of the government's action, but rather on whether the government took an owner's property).

9.   Another category of takings should also be mentioned—"regulatory takings." These are not takings in the traditional sense that the government seizes property and converts it to public use; rather, they deal with government regulations that allegedly deprive an owner of an economically viable use of private property. For example, in *Penn Central Transportation Co. v. New York City*, 438 U.S. 104 (1978), the Supreme Court reviewed a New York City regulation that precluded Penn Central from constructing an office building on top of the Grand Central Train Station. Penn Central contended that the regulation amounted to a Fifth Amendment Taking because the regulation deprived it of the use of its property for a profitable purpose. The Court rejected

Penn Central's claim, holding that the regulation was a reasonable protection of the public interest and that a mere diminution in property value did not constitute a *per se* taking. In *Lucas v. South Carolina Coast Council*, 505 U.S. 1003 (1992), however, the Court held that a regulation that imposed a complete deprivation of *all* economic value did constitute a taking under the Fifth Amendment. In *Lucas*, the plaintiff purchased two residential lots on the Isle of Palms in South Carolina. He had intended to build homes on the lots, but before he could begin construction, South Carolina enacted a law that precluded the plaintiff from constructing permanent habitable structures on the land. The Supreme Court held that South Carolina was required to pay just compensation to Lucas for the regulation. As the Court stated: "[W]hen the owner of real property has been called upon to sacrifice *all* economically beneficial uses in the name of the common good, that is, to leave his property economically idle, he has suffered a taking." *Id.* at 1019 (emphasis in original).

CHAPTER 7

CRIMINAL PROCEDURE

∎ ∎ ∎

Criminal procedure, the subject of this chapter, is closely linked to criminal law, the subject of the next chapter. The two subjects, however, are distinct. Criminal law addresses the conduct that constitutes a crime and the range of possible punishment for such crimes. Criminal procedure, by contrast, focuses on the procedures that apply during a criminal prosecution. A major focus of criminal procedure is on the various provisions of the U.S. Constitution that are designed to protect the rights of criminal defendants.

A.   SEARCH AND SEIZURE (FOURTH AMENDMENT)

The Fourth Amendment to the U.S. Constitution provides: "The right of the people to be secure in their persons, houses, papers, and effects, against unreasonable searches and seizures, shall not be violated, and no warrants shall issue, but upon probable cause, supported by oath or affirmation, and particularly describing the place to be searched, and the persons or things to be seized." The Supreme Court has addressed Fourth Amendment issues in many cases. Some of the key cases are featured below.

1.   STOP AND FRISK

The Fourth Amendment's prohibition of "unreasonable searches and seizures" is phrased broadly. Thus, courts are frequently called upon to define the types of searches or seizures that are "reasonable" or "unreasonable." The following case is a landmark decision discussing investigative stops by police.

TERRY V. OHIO
Supreme Court of the United States, 1968
392 U.S. 1

CHIEF JUSTICE WARREN delivered the opinion of the Court.

This case presents serious questions concerning the role of the Fourth Amendment in the confrontation on the street between the citizen and the policeman investigating suspicious circumstances.

Petitioner Terry was convicted of carrying a concealed weapon and sentenced to the statutorily prescribed term of one to three years in the penitentiary. Following the denial of a pretrial motion to suppress, the prosecution introduced in evidence two revolvers and a number of bullets seized from Terry and a codefendant, Richard Chilton, by Cleveland Police Detective Martin McFadden. At the hearing on the motion to suppress this evidence, Officer McFadden testified that while he was patrolling in plain clothes in downtown Cleveland at approximately 2:30 in the afternoon of October 31, 1963, his attention was attracted by two men, Chilton and Terry, standing on the corner of Huron Road and Euclid Avenue. He had never seen the two men before, and he was unable to say precisely what first drew his eye to them. However, he testified that he had been a policeman for 39 years and a detective for 35 and that he had been assigned to patrol this vicinity of downtown Cleveland for shoplifters and pickpockets for 30 years. He explained that he had developed routine habits of observation over the years and that he would "stand and watch people or walk and watch people at many intervals of the day." He added: "Now, in this case when I looked over they didn't look right to me at the time."

His interest aroused, Officer McFadden took up a post of observation in the entrance to a store 300 to 400 feet away from the two men. * * * He saw one of the men leave the other one and walk southwest on Huron Road, past some stores. The man paused for a moment and looked in a store window, then walked on a short distance, turned around and walked back toward the corner, pausing once again to look in the same store window. He rejoined his companion at the corner, and the two conferred briefly. Then the second man went through the same series of motions, strolling down Huron Road, looking in the same window, walking on a short distance, turning back, peering in the store window again, and returning to confer with the first man at the corner. The two men repeated this ritual alternately between five and six times apiece—in all, roughly a dozen trips. At one point, while the two were standing together on the corner, a third man approached them and engaged them briefly in conversation. This man then left the two others and walked west on Euclid Avenue. Chilton and Terry resumed their measured pacing, peering, and conferring. After this had gone on for 10 to 12 minutes, the two men walked off together, heading west on Euclid Avenue, following the path taken earlier by the third man.

By this time Officer McFadden had become thoroughly suspicious. He testified that after observing [that conduct], he suspected the two men of "casing a job, a stick-up," and that he considered it his duty * * * to investigate further. He added that he feared "they may have [had] a gun." Thus, Officer McFadden followed Chilton and Terry and saw them stop in front of Zucker's store to talk to the same man who had conferred with them earlier on the street corner. Deciding that the situation was ripe for direct action, Officer McFadden approached the three men, identified himself as a police officer and asked for their names. * * * He was not acquainted with any of the three men by name or by sight, and he had received no information concerning them from any other source. When the men "mumbled something" in response to his inquiries, Officer McFadden grabbed petitioner Terry, spun him around so that they were facing the other two, with Terry between McFadden and the others, and patted down the outside of his clothing. In the left breast pocket of Terry's overcoat Officer McFadden felt a pistol. He reached inside the overcoat pocket, but was unable to remove the gun. At this point, keeping Terry between himself and the others, the officer ordered all three men to enter Zucker's store. As they went in, he removed Terry's overcoat completely, removed a .38-caliber revolver from the pocket and ordered all three men to face the wall with their hands raised. Officer McFadden proceeded to pat down the outer clothing of Chilton and the third man, Katz. He discovered another revolver in the outer pocket of Chilton's overcoat, but no weapons were found on Katz. The officer testified that he only patted the men down to see whether they had weapons, and that he did not put his hands beneath the outer garments of either Terry or Chilton until he felt their guns. So far as appears from the record, he never placed his hands beneath Katz' outer garments. Officer McFadden seized Chilton's gun, asked the proprietor of the store to call a police wagon, and took all three men to the station, where Chilton and Terry were formally charged with carrying concealed weapons.

On the motion to suppress the guns the prosecution took the position that they had been seized following a search incident to a lawful arrest. The trial court rejected [the] theory * * * that Officer McFadden had had probable cause to arrest the men before he patted them down for weapons. However, the court denied the defendants' motion on the ground that Officer McFadden * * * "had reasonable cause to believe * * * that the defendants were conducting themselves suspiciously, and some interrogation should be made of their action." Purely for his own protection, the court held, the officer had the right to pat down the outer clothing of these men * * *.

After the court denied their motion to suppress, Chilton and Terry waived jury trial and pleaded not guilty. The court adjudged them guilty, and the Court of Appeals * * * affirmed. The Supreme Court of Ohio dismissed their appeal * * *. We granted certiorari * * *. We affirm the conviction.

I.

* * *

"No right is held more sacred, or is more carefully guarded, by the common law, than the right of every individual to the possession and control of his own person, free from all restraint or interference of others, unless by clear and unquestionable authority of law."

* * * Of course, the specific content and incidents of this right must be shaped by the context in which it is asserted. * * * Unquestionably petitioner was entitled to the protection of the Fourth Amendment as he walked down the street in Cleveland. * * * The question is whether in all the circumstances of this on-the-street encounter, his right to personal security was violated by an unreasonable search and seizure.

* * *

On the one hand, it is frequently argued that in dealing with the rapidly unfolding and often dangerous situations on city streets the police are in need of an escalating set of flexible responses, graduated in relation to the amount of information they possess. For this purpose it is urged that distinctions should be made between a "stop" and an "arrest" (or a "seizure" of a person), and between a "frisk" and a "search." Thus, it is argued, the police should be allowed to "stop" a person and detain him briefly for questioning upon suspicion that he may be connected with criminal activity. Upon suspicion that the person may be armed, the police should have the power to "frisk" him for weapons. If the "stop" and the "frisk" give rise to probable cause to believe that the suspect has committed a crime, then the police should be empowered to make a formal "arrest," and a full incident "search" of the person. This scheme is justified in part upon the notion that a "stop" and a "frisk" amount to a mere "minor inconvenience and petty indignity," which can properly be imposed upon the citizen in the interest of effective law enforcement on the basis of a police officer's suspicion.

On the other side the argument is made that the authority of the police must be strictly circumscribed * * *. The heart of the Fourth Amendment, the argument runs, is a severe requirement of specific justification for any intrusion upon protected personal security, coupled with a highly developed system of judicial controls to enforce upon the agents of the State the commands of the Constitution. Acquiescence by the courts in the compulsion inherent in the field interrogation practices at issue here, it is urged, would constitute an abdication of judicial control over, and indeed an encouragement of, substantial interference with liberty and personal security by police officers * * *.

In this context we approach the issues in this case mindful of the limitations of the judicial function in controlling the myriad daily situations in which policemen and citizens confront each other on the street. * * * [I]n our system evidentiary rulings provide the context in which the judicial process of inclusion and exclusion approves some conduct as comporting with constitutional guarantees and disapproves other actions by state agents. A ruling admitting evidence in a criminal trial, we recognize, has the necessary effect of legitimizing the conduct which produced the evidence, while an application of the exclusionary rule withholds the constitutional imprimatur.

The exclusionary rule has its limitations, however, as a tool of judicial control. It cannot properly be invoked to exclude the products of legitimate police investigative techniques * * *. Moreover, in some contexts the rule is ineffective as a deterrent. Street encounters between citizens and police officers are incredibly rich in diversity. They range from wholly friendly exchanges of pleasantries or mutually useful information to hostile confrontations of armed men involving arrests, or injuries, or loss of life. * * * Doubtless some police "field interrogation" conduct violates the Fourth Amendment. But a stern refusal by this Court to condone such activity does not necessarily render it responsive to the exclusionary rule. Regardless of how effective the rule may be where obtaining convictions is an important objective of the police, it is powerless to deter invasions of constitutionally guaranteed rights where the police either have no interest in prosecuting or are willing to forgo successful prosecution in the interest of serving some other goal.

Proper adjudication of cases in which the exclusionary rule is invoked demands a constant awareness of these limitations. The wholesale harassment by certain elements of the police community, of which minority groups, particularly Negroes, frequently complain, will not be stopped by the exclusion of any evidence from any criminal trial. Yet a rigid and unthinking application of the exclusionary rule, in futile protest against practices which it can never be used effectively to control, may exact a high toll in human injury and frustration of efforts to prevent crime. No judicial opinion can comprehend the protean variety of the street encounter, and we can only judge the facts of the case before us. Nothing we say today is to be taken as indicating approval of police conduct outside the legitimate investigative sphere. Under our decision, courts still retain their traditional responsibility to guard against police conduct which is over-bearing or harassing, or which trenches upon personal security without the objective evidentiary justification which the Constitution requires. * * *

Having thus roughly sketched the perimeters of the constitutional debate * * *, we turn our attention to the quite narrow question * * * before us: whether it is always unreasonable for a policeman to seize a person and subject him to a limited search for weapons unless there is probable cause for an arrest. * * *

II.

Our first task is to establish at what point in this encounter the Fourth Amendment becomes relevant. That is, we must decide whether and when Officer McFadden "seized" Terry and whether and when he conducted a "search." There is some suggestion in the use of such terms as "stop" and "frisk" that such police conduct is outside the purview of the Fourth Amendment because neither action rises to the level of a "search" or "seizure" within the meaning of the Constitution. We emphatically reject this notion. It is quite plain that the Fourth Amendment governs "seizures" of the person which do not eventuate in a trip to the station house and prosecution for crime—"arrests" in traditional terminology. It must be recognized that whenever a police officer accosts an individual and restrains his freedom to walk away, he has "seized" that person. And it is nothing less than sheer torture of the English language to suggest that a careful exploration of the outer surfaces of a person's clothing all over his or her body in an attempt to find weapons is not a "search." Moreover, it is simply fantastic to urge that such a procedure performed in public by a policeman while the citizen stands helpless, perhaps facing a wall with his hands raised, is a "petty indignity." It is a serious intrusion upon the sanctity of the person, which may inflict great indignity and arouse strong resentment, and it is not to be undertaken lightly.

The danger in the logic which proceeds upon distinctions between a "stop" and an "arrest," or "seizure" of the person, and between a "frisk" and a "search" is twofold. It seeks to isolate from constitutional scrutiny the initial stages of the contact between the policeman and the citizen. And by suggesting a rigid all-or-nothing model of justification and regulation * * *, it obscures the utility of limitations upon the scope, as well as the initiation, of police action as a means of constitutional regulation. * * * The scope of the search must be "strictly tied to and justified by" the circumstances which rendered its initiation permissible.

The distinctions of classical "stop-and-frisk" theory thus serve to divert attention from the central inquiry under the Fourth Amendment—the reasonableness in all the circumstances of the particular governmental invasion of a citizen's personal security. "Search" and "seizure" are not talismans. We therefore reject the notions that the Fourth Amendment does not come into play at all as a limitation upon police conduct if the officers stop short of something called a "technical arrest" or a "full-blown search."

In this case there can be no question, then, that Officer McFadden "seized" petitioner and subjected him to a "search" when he took hold of him and patted down the outer surfaces of his clothing. We must decide whether at that point it was reasonable for Officer McFadden to have interfered with petitioner's personal security as he did. * * *

III.

If this case involved police conduct subject to the Warrant Clause of the Fourth Amendment, we would have to ascertain whether "probable cause" existed to justify the search and seizure which took place. However, that is not the case. We do not retreat from our holdings that the police must, whenever practicable, obtain advance judicial approval of searches and seizures through the warrant procedure, or that in most instances failure to comply with the warrant requirement can only be excused by exigent circumstances. But we deal here with an entire rubric of police conduct—necessarily swift action predicated upon the on-the-spot observations of the officer on the beat * * *. [T]he conduct involved in this case must be tested by the Fourth Amendment's general proscription against unreasonable searches and seizures.

* * * In order to assess the reasonableness of Officer McFadden's conduct * * *, it is necessary "first to focus upon the governmental interest which allegedly justifies official intrusion upon the constitutionally protected interests of the private citizen" * * *. And in justifying the particular intrusion the police officer must be able to point to specific and articulable facts which, taken together with rational inferences from those facts, reasonably warrant that intrusion. * * * And in making that assessment it is imperative that the facts be judged against an objective standard: would the facts available to the officer at the moment of the seizure or the search "warrant a man of reasonable caution in the belief" that the action taken was appropriate? Anything less would invite intrusions upon constitutionally guaranteed rights * * *. If subjective good faith alone were the test, the protections of the Fourth Amendment would evaporate * * *.

Applying these principles to this case, we consider first the nature and extent of the governmental interests involved. One general interest is of course that of effective crime prevention and detection * * *. It was this legitimate investigative function Officer McFadden was discharging when he decided to approach petitioner and his companions. He had observed Terry, Chilton, and Katz go through a series of acts, each of them perhaps innocent in itself, but which taken together warranted further investigation. * * * It would have been poor police work indeed for an officer of 30 years' experience in the detection of thievery from stores in this same neighborhood to have failed to investigate this behavior further.

The crux of this case, however, is not the propriety of Officer McFadden's taking steps to investigate petitioner's suspicious behavior, but rather, whether there was justification for McFadden's invasion of Terry's personal security by searching him for weapons in the course of that investigation. * * * Certainly it would be unreasonable to require that police officers take unnecessary risks in the performance of their duties. * * * [E]very year in this country many law enforcement officers are killed in the line of duty, and thousands more are wounded. Virtually all of these deaths and a substantial portion of the injuries are inflicted with guns and knives.

In view of these facts, we cannot blind ourselves to the need for law enforcement officers to protect themselves and other prospective victims of violence in situations where they may lack probable cause for an arrest. When an officer is justified in believing that the individual whose suspicious behavior he is investigating at close range is armed and presently dangerous to the officer or to others, it would appear to be clearly unreasonable to deny the officer the power to take necessary measures to determine whether the person is in fact carrying a weapon and to neutralize the threat of physical harm.

We must still consider, however, the nature and quality of the intrusion on individual rights which must be accepted if police officers are to be conceded the right to search for weapons in situations where probable cause to arrest for crime is lacking. Even a limited search of the outer clothing for weapons constitutes a severe, though brief, intrusion upon cherished personal security, and it must surely be an annoying, frightening, and perhaps humiliating experience. Petitioner contends that such an intrusion is permissible only incident to a lawful arrest, either for a crime involving the possession of weapons or for a crime the commission of which led the officer to investigate in the first place. However, this argument must be closely examined.

Petitioner does not argue that a police officer should refrain from making any investigation of suspicious circumstances until such time as he has probable cause to make an arrest; nor does he deny that police officers in properly discharging their investigative function may find themselves confronting persons who might well be armed and dangerous. Moreover, he does not say that an officer is always unjustified in searching a suspect to discover weapons. Rather, he says it is unreasonable for the policeman to take that step until such time as the situation evolves to a point where there is probable cause to make an arrest. When that point has been reached, petitioner would concede the officer's right to conduct a search of the suspect for weapons, fruits or instrumentalities of the crime, or "mere" evidence, incident to the arrest.

There are two weaknesses in this line of reasoning however. First, it fails to take account of traditional limitations upon the scope of searches, and thus recognizes no distinction in purpose, character, and extent between a search incident to an arrest and a limited search for weapons. The former, although justified in part by the acknowledged necessity to protect the arresting officer from assault with a concealed weapon, is also justified on other grounds, and can therefore involve a relatively extensive exploration of the person. A search for weapons in the absence of probable cause to arrest, however, must, like any other search, be strictly circumscribed by the exigencies which justify its initiation. Thus it must be limited to that which is necessary for the discovery of weapons which might be used to harm the officer or others nearby, and may realistically be characterized as something less than a "full" search, even though it remains a serious intrusion.

A second, and related, objection to petitioner's argument is that it assumes that the law of arrest has already worked out the balance between the particular interests involved here—the neutralization of danger to the policeman in the investigative circumstance and the sanctity of the individual. But this is not so. An arrest is a wholly different kind of intrusion upon individual freedom from a limited search for weapons, and the interests each is designed to serve are likewise quite different. An arrest is the initial stage of a criminal prosecution. It is intended to vindicate society's interest in having its laws obeyed, and it is inevitably accompanied by future interference with the individual's freedom of movement, whether or not trial or conviction ultimately follows. The protective search for weapons, on the other hand, constitutes a brief, though far from inconsiderable, intrusion upon the sanctity of the person. * * * Moreover, a perfectly reasonable apprehension of danger may arise long before the officer is possessed of adequate information to justify taking a person into custody for the purpose of prosecuting him for a crime. * * *

[We] conclude that there must be a narrowly drawn authority to permit a reasonable search for weapons for the protection of the police officer, where he has reason to believe that he is dealing with an armed and dangerous individual, regardless of whether he has probable cause to arrest the individual for a crime. The officer need not be absolutely certain that the individual is armed; the issue is whether a reasonably prudent man in the circumstances would be warranted in the belief that his safety or that of others was in danger. And in determining whether the officer acted reasonably in such circumstances, due weight must be given, not to his inchoate and unparticularized suspicion or "hunch," but to the specific reasonable inferences which he is entitled to draw from the facts in light of his experience.

IV.

We must now examine the conduct of Officer McFadden in this case * * *. He had observed Terry, together with Chilton and another man, acting in a manner he took to be preface to a "stick-up." We think on the facts and circumstances Officer McFadden detailed before the trial judge a reasonably prudent man would have been warranted in believing petitioner was armed and thus presented a threat to the officer's safety while he was investigating his suspicious behavior. The actions of Terry and Chilton were consistent with McFadden's hypothesis that these men were contemplating a daylight robbery—which, it is reasonable to assume, would be likely to involve the use of weapons—and nothing in their conduct from the time he first noticed them until the time he confronted them and identified himself as a police officer gave him sufficient reason to negate that hypothesis. Although the trio had departed the original scene, there was nothing to indicate abandonment of an intent to commit a robbery at some point. Thus, when Officer McFadden approached the three men gathered before the display window at Zucker's store he had observed enough to make it quite reasonable to fear that they were armed * * *. We cannot say his decision * * * to seize Terry and pat his clothing for weapons was the product of a volatile or inventive imagination, or was undertaken simply as an act of harassment; the record evidences the tempered act of a policeman who in the course of an investigation had to make a quick decision as to how to protect himself and others from possible danger, and took limited steps to do so.

The manner in which the seizure and search were conducted is, of course, as vital a part of the inquiry as whether they were warranted at all. * * *

We need not develop at length in this case, however, the limitations which the Fourth Amendment places upon a protective seizure and search for weapons. These limitations will have to be developed in the concrete factual circumstances of individual cases. Suffice it to note that such a search, unlike a search without a warrant incident to a lawful arrest, is not justified by any need to prevent the disappearance or destruction of evidence of crime. The sole justification of the search in the present situation is the protection of the police officer and others nearby, and it must therefore be confined in scope to an intrusion reasonably designed to discover guns, knives, clubs, or other hidden instruments for the assault of the police officer.

The scope of the search in this case presents no serious problem in light of these standards. Officer McFadden patted down the outer clothing of petitioner and his two companions. He did not place his hands in their pockets or under the outer surface of their garments until he had felt weapons, and then he merely reached for and removed the guns. He never did invade Katz' person beyond the outer surfaces of his clothes, since he discovered nothing in his patdown which might have been a weapon. Officer McFadden confined his search strictly to what was minimally necessary to learn whether the men were armed and to disarm them once he discovered the weapons. * * *

V.

We conclude that the revolver seized from Terry was properly admitted in evidence against him. At the time he seized petitioner and searched him for weapons, Officer McFadden had reasonable grounds to believe that petitioner was armed and dangerous, and it was necessary for the protection of himself and others to take swift measures to discover the true facts and neutralize the threat of harm if it materialized. * * * [This] search is a reasonable [one] under the Fourth Amendment, and any weapons seized may properly be introduced in evidence * * *.

Affirmed.

[Concurring opinions by JUSTICE HARLAN and JUSTICE WHITE are omitted.]

JUSTICE DOUGLAS, dissenting.

I agree that petitioner was "seized" within the meaning of the Fourth Amendment. I also agree that frisking petitioner and his companions for guns was a "search." But it is a mystery how that "search" and that "seizure" can be constitutional by Fourth Amendment standards, unless there was "probable cause" to believe that (1) a crime had been committed or (2) a crime was in the process of being committed or (3) a crime was about to be committed.

* * *

The infringement on personal liberty of any "seizure" of a person can only be "reasonable" under the Fourth Amendment if we require the police to possess "probable cause" before they seize him. Only that line draws a meaningful distinction between an officer's mere inkling and the presence of facts within the officer's personal knowledge which would convince a reasonable man that the person seized has committed, is committing, or is about to commit a particular crime. * * *

To give the police greater power than a magistrate is to take a long step down the totalitarian path. * * *

There have been powerful hydraulic pressures throughout our history that bear heavily on the Court to water down constitutional guarantees and give the police the upper hand. That hydraulic pressure has probably never been greater than it is today.

Yet if the individual is no longer to be sovereign, if the police can * * * "seize" and "search" him in their discretion, we enter a new regime. The decision to enter it should be made only after a full debate by the people of this country.

NOTES AND QUESTIONS

1.   What were the suspicious facts that led Officer McFadden to investigate and approach Terry and his companions?

2.   What did the Court hold with respect to the search of Terry? Was the State of Ohio entitled to use the gun seized from Terry as evidence at trial? Why did Justice Douglas disagree with the majority?

3.   Under the Court's decision, what legitimate reasons might an officer have to search someone even in the absence of probable cause to make an arrest?

4.   The *Terry* opinion mentions that the defendants pursued a "motion to suppress" the evidence against them in the trial court. In a criminal case, a "motion to suppress" evidence is a request the defendant makes to the court to exclude certain evidence from trial because it was obtained through unlawful means by the police. If the court deems that the evidence in question stemmed from unlawful or unconstitutional police action, all evidence derived from that unlawful action will, in most instances, be "suppressed" and cannot be used by the prosecution at trial. The concept of excluding unlawfully obtained evidence from trial has come to be known as the "exclusionary rule." A seminal case

discussing the exclusionary rule is *Mapp v. Ohio*, 367 U.S. 643 (1961), where the Supreme Court held that the rule applies not only in federal criminal cases, but in state criminal cases as well. Moreover, the Supreme Court has affirmed that the exclusionary rule applies to *any* evidence stemming from an unconstitutional police action, including evidence that was indirectly discovered as a result of the unconstitutional action. *See, e.g., Wong Sun v. United States*, 371 U.S. 471 (1963). The Supreme Court has often referred to evidence indirectly stemming from unlawful police action as "fruit of the poisonous tree," *id.* at 488, meaning that if the search itself was unlawful, all evidence stemming from that search is unlawful as well. In *Wong Sun*, for example, because the arrest of the defendant was unlawful, incriminatory statements made by him at the time of the unlawful arrest were inadmissible against him. In addition, narcotics seized from a third person based on the defendant's statement were also "fruit of the poisonous tree" and could not be used against the defendant.

The exclusionary rule was designed to deter misconduct by the police. In 2006, the Supreme Court observed: "The exclusionary rule as we know it is an entirely American legal creation. * * * [T]he automatic exclusionary rule applied in our courts is still 'universally rejected' by other countries." *Sanchez-Llamas v. Oregon*, 548 U.S. 331, 343–44. But that situation is changing. *See, e.g.*, Jenia Iontcheva Turner, *The Exclusionary Rule as a Symbol of the Rule of Law*, 67 SMU L. Rev. 821 (2014) (noting that the exclusionary rule has been adopted in many modern legal systems in South America, Europe, and Asia).

Although the exclusionary rule is a powerful rule, the Supreme Court has crafted a number of exceptions to it over the years. *See, e.g., Murray v. United States*, 487 U.S. 533 (1988) (holding that illegally discovered evidence is admissible if it is later obtained by independent means untainted by the initial illegality); *United States v. Leon*, 468 U.S. 897 (1984) (creating a "good faith exception" to the exclusionary rule and holding that evidence derived from a search was admissible when police conducted a search of the defendant's home with an approved warrant, but the warrant later turned out to be faulty because of an error by the judge who approved it); *Nix v. Williams*, 467 U.S. 431 (1984) (creating an "inevitable discovery exception" to the exclusionary rule and holding that unconstitutionally obtained evidence is admissible if the prosecution can prove that police would have inevitably discovered the evidence through lawful means).

5. The term *"Terry* stop" is now widely used by courts to describe a stop based on "reasonable suspicion." Since *Terry* was decided, the concept of "reasonable suspicion" has been a heavily litigated area of criminal procedure. The Supreme Court has adopted a relatively broad definition of "reasonable suspicion." In *Navarette v. California*, 572 U.S. ___, 134 S. Ct. 1683 (2014), the Court addressed the issue of whether a *Terry* stop can be initiated based purely on an anonymous and uncorroborated report of criminal activity. In the case, an anonymous caller contacted law enforcement dispatch through a 911 (emergency) telephone line and advised them that a silver Ford pickup truck had run the anonymous caller's vehicle off the roadway. The caller provided a

specific model of the truck, the license plate number, and a precise location where the alleged incident occurred. An officer responded to the vicinity and located the silver Ford truck driving on the highway near the reported location. He followed the truck for five minutes, but did not observe anything suspicious. Nonetheless, after that five-minute period, he initiated a *Terry* stop of the vehicle to investigate the alleged incident reported by the anonymous caller. Upon approaching the stopped vehicle, the officer smelled marijuana coming from the trunk. In a search of the trunk, the he found 30 pounds of marijuana and arrested the vehicle's occupants. The defendants moved to suppress the marijuana evidence, arguing that the initial *Terry* stop was not justified by lawful reasonable suspicion. The trial court denied the motion, the defendants pleaded guilty to drug offenses, and the California appellate court affirmed.

A divided U.S. Supreme Court affirmed. Justice Thomas's opinion for the majority reasoned that even if the officers did not personally observe any suspicious conduct, the reasonable suspicion standard allows an officer to rely on second-hand information to initiate a *Terry* stop as long as the officer reasonably believed that the information was reliable. The majority cited several factors that supported the anonymous tip's reliability: (1) the information came from an eyewitness driver who specifically described being run off the road; (2) the short time frame between the call and the alleged incident minimized the chance that the driver had fabricated the story; and (3) the caller used a 911 dispatch system, which deters false reports by allowing officers to trace fraudulent calls back to the caller. Accordingly, the Court held that it was reasonable for officers to assume that the anonymous information was reliable. The *Terry* stop, the Court held, was justified to investigate the possibility that the driver was intoxicated.

Justice Scalia dissented, noting: "After today's opinion all of us on the road, and not just drug dealers, are at risk of having our freedom of movement curtailed on suspicion of drunkenness, based upon a phone tip, true or false, of a single instance of careless driving." *Id.* at 1697. Are Justice Scalia's concerns valid? Or did the majority correctly rule based on the facts and circumstances presented by the anonymous caller?

6.   Can a *Terry* stop be constitutionally justified if the officer's suspicion is based on the officer's own mistaken reading of the law? In *Heien v. North Carolina*, 574 U.S. ___, 135 S. Ct. 530 (2014), the Supreme Court upheld the constitutionality of a stop in that situation. In *Heien*, a police officer observed a vehicle driving with a broken brake light, and he initiated a *Terry* stop to investigate what he believed was an infraction. In fact, however, the driver was in full compliance with the North Carolina traffic statute, which required him to have only a single working brake light (which he did). Chief Justice Roberts's opinion for the Court held that an officer's reasonable mistake of fact or law does not render a *Terry* seizure unconstitutional. Here, the relevant North Carolina traffic statute contained equivocal language, and there was no available precedent interpreting the statutory provision's vague terms. Accordingly, the Court held that the officer's mistaken interpretation that Heien was in violation of the statute was objectively reasonable. The Court was

careful to note, however, that its opinion was based narrowly on "objectively reasonable" mistakes of law, and that an officer may not justify a *Terry* stop based on a "sloppy" or incomplete reading of the law. *Id.* at 539–40. Justice Sotomayor dissented. In her view, "an officer's mistake of law, no matter how reasonable, cannot support the individualized suspicion necessary to justify a seizure under the Fourth Amendment." *Id.* at 547. Given the limits of the majority opinion, is Justice Sotomayor persuasive in urging a bright line rule?

7.   Not surprisingly, some scholars have been critical of *Navarette* and *Heien. See, e.g.,* Case Note, *Fourth Amendment—Search and Seizure— Anonymous Tips and Suspected Drunk Driving*—Navarette v. California, 128 Harv. L. Rev. 231, 240 (2014) (characterizing *Navarette* as an unwise expansion of the *Terry* doctrine, and concluding that the case "heralds unwarranted curtailment of Fourth Amendment protections"); John Whitehead, *Is Ignorance of the Law an Excuse for Police to Violate the Fourth Amendment?*, 9 N.Y.U. J. L. & Liberty 108, 118 (2015) (criticizing *Heien* and arguing that it creates a "dangerous double standard" whereby citizens but not law enforcement are held accountable for mistakes of law).

8.   Law enforcement's use of *Terry* stops has also created controversy regarding allegations of racial and economic profiling—*i.e.*, that police in several areas of the country have used *Terry* stops in a disparate fashion against minority racial and economic groups. As Professor David Harris points out in his article, *Factors for Reasonable Suspicion: When Black and Poor Means Stopped and Frisked*, 69 Ind. L.J. 659 (1994), under *Terry* law enforcement officers are routinely allowed to stop someone based purely on the observation of evasive behavior in a "high crime" neighborhood. As Professor Harris reveals, that practice disproportionately affects racial and economic minorities, who often comprise a higher percentage of the population in those types of designated "high crime" neighborhoods. Professor Harris contends that "[r]eplacing the current regime with a rule that requires more for reasonable suspicion than a high crime location plus [walking away from the police] is the minimum that must be done to restore some balance to inner-city law enforcement." *Id.* at 688. Is evasive behavior, coupled with presence in a high crime area, the type of reasonable suspicion that justifies a *Terry* stop? Or is Professor Harris correct that more indications of criminality should be required?

9.   Despite the willingness of the Court to expand the *Terry* doctrine, the Court has also placed some limits on what police may do during a *Terry* stop. For example, in *Rodriguez v. United States*, 575 U.S. ___, 135 S. Ct. 1609 (2015) the Court held that, absent reasonable suspicion, police may not extend a detention during a traffic stop for the purpose of having a drug-sniffing dog walk around the vehicle a number of times. The Court reasoned that unless an officer has reasonable suspicion that the driver of the vehicle may have illegal drugs, the officer cannot prolong a routine traffic stop to conduct further searches or investigation. Once the purpose of the initial stop (*e.g.*, completing the minimal investigation for the traffic infraction) has been satisfied, the officer must end the *Terry* stop.

2. FOURTH AMENDMENT AND MODERN TECHNOLOGY

With constantly evolving technology, modern law enforcement officials now possess advanced tools to deter criminal activity. Accordingly, U.S. courts have had to address how these new technologies intersect with the protections guaranteed by the Constitution. The following case analyzes Fourth Amendment protections in the context of cell phones.

RILEY V. CALIFORNIA

Supreme Court of the United States, 2014
573 U.S. ___, 134 S. Ct. 2473

CHIEF JUSTICE ROBERTS delivered the opinion of the Court.

These two cases raise a common question: whether the police may, without a warrant, search digital information on a cell phone seized from an individual who has been arrested.

I

A

In the first case, petitioner David Riley was stopped by a police officer for driving with expired registration tags. In the course of the stop, the officer also learned that Riley's license had been suspended. The officer impounded Riley's car, pursuant to department policy, and another officer conducted an inventory search of the car. Riley was arrested for possession of concealed and loaded firearms when that search turned up two handguns under the car's hood.

An officer searched Riley incident to the arrest and found items associated with the "Bloods" street gang. He also seized a cell phone from Riley's pants pocket. According to Riley's uncontradicted assertion, the phone was a "smart phone," a cell phone with a broad range of other functions based on advanced computing capability, large storage capacity, and internet connectivity. The officer accessed information on the phone and noticed that some words (presumably in text messages or a contacts list) were preceded by the letters "CK"—a label that, he believed, stood for "Crip Killers," a slang term for members of the Bloods gang.

At the police station about two hours after the arrest, a detective specializing in gangs further examined the contents of the phone. The detective testified that he "went through" Riley's phone "looking for evidence, because . . . gang members will often video themselves with guns or take pictures of themselves with the guns." Although there was "a lot of stuff" on the phone, particular files that "caught [the detective's] eye" included videos of young men sparring while someone yelled encouragement using the moniker "Blood." The police also found photographs of Riley standing in front of a car they suspected had been involved in a shooting a few weeks earlier.

Riley was ultimately charged, in connection with that earlier shooting, with firing at an occupied vehicle, assault with a semiautomatic firearm, and attempted murder. The State alleged that Riley had committed those crimes for the benefit of a criminal street gang, an aggravating factor that carries an enhanced sentence. Prior to trial, Riley moved to suppress all evidence that the police had obtained from his cell phone. He contended that the searches of his phone violated the Fourth Amendment, because they had been performed without a warrant and were not otherwise justified by exigent circumstances. The trial court rejected that argument. At Riley's trial, police officers testified about the photographs and videos found on the phone, and some of the photographs were admitted into evidence. Riley was convicted on all three counts and received an enhanced sentence of 15 years to life in prison.

The California Court of Appeal affirmed.

The California Supreme Court denied Riley's petition for review, and we granted certiorari.

B

In the second case, a police officer performing routine surveillance observed respondent Brima Wurie make an apparent drug sale from a car. Officers subsequently arrested Wurie and took him to the police station. At the station, the officers seized two cell phones from Wurie's person. The one at issue here was a "flip phone," a kind of phone that is flipped open for use and that generally has a smaller range of features than a smart phone. Five to ten minutes after arriving at the station, the officers noticed that the phone was repeatedly receiving calls from a source identified as "my house" on the phone's external screen. A few minutes later, they opened the phone and saw a photograph of a woman and a baby set as the phone's wallpaper. They pressed one button on the phone to access its call log, then another button to determine the phone number associated with the "my house" label. They next used an online phone directory to trace that phone number to an apartment building.

When the officers went to the building, they saw Wurie's name on a mailbox and observed through a window a woman who resembled the woman in the photograph on Wurie's phone. They secured the apartment while obtaining a search warrant and, upon later executing the warrant, found and seized 215 grams of crack cocaine, marijuana, drug paraphernalia, a firearm and ammunition, and cash.

Wurie was charged with distributing crack cocaine, possessing crack cocaine with intent to distribute, and being a felon in possession of a firearm and ammunition. He moved to suppress the evidence obtained from the search of the apartment, arguing that it was the fruit of an unconstitutional search of his cell phone. The District Court denied the motion. Wurie was convicted on all three counts and sentenced to 262 months in prison.

A divided panel of the First Circuit reversed [and vacated Wurie's convictions]. * * *

We granted certiorari.

II

* * *

As the text [of the Fourth Amendment] makes clear, [its] "ultimate touchstone * * * is 'reasonableness.' " * * * "Where a search is undertaken by law enforcement officials to discover evidence of criminal wrongdoing, . . . reasonableness generally requires the obtaining of a judicial warrant." Such a warrant ensures that the inferences to support a search are "drawn by a neutral and detached magistrate * * *." In the absence of a warrant, a search is reasonable only if it falls within a specific exception to the warrant requirement.

The two cases before us concern the reasonableness of a warrantless search incident to a lawful arrest. * * * [It is] well accepted that such a search constitutes an exception to the warrant requirement. Indeed, the label "exception" is something of a misnomer in this context, as warrantless searches incident to arrest occur with far greater frequency than searches conducted pursuant to a warrant.

Although the existence of the exception for such searches has been recognized for a century, its scope has been debated for nearly as long. That debate has focused on the extent to which officers may search property found on or near the arrestee. Three related precedents set forth the rules governing such searches:

The first, *Chimel v. California*, 395 U.S. 752 (1969), laid the groundwork for most of the existing search incident to arrest doctrine. Police officers in that case arrested Chimel inside his home and proceeded to search his entire three-bedroom house, including the attic and garage. In particular rooms, they also looked through the contents of drawers.

The Court crafted the following rule for assessing the reasonableness of a search incident to arrest:

> When an arrest is made, it is reasonable for the arresting officer to search the person arrested in order to remove any weapons that the latter might seek to use in order to resist arrest or effect his escape. * * * In addition, it is entirely reasonable for the arresting officer to search for and seize any evidence on the arrestee's person in order to prevent its concealment or destruction. . . . There is ample justification, therefore, for a search of the

arrestee's person and the area 'within his immediate control'—construing that phrase to mean the area from within which he might gain possession of a weapon or destructible evidence.

The extensive warrantless search of Chimel's home did not fit within this exception, because it was not needed to protect officer safety or to preserve evidence.

Four years later, in *United States v. Robinson*, 414 U.S. 218 (1973), the Court applied the *Chimel* analysis in the context of a search of the arrestee's person. A police officer had arrested Robinson for driving with a revoked license. The officer conducted a patdown search and felt an object that he could not identify in Robinson's coat pocket. He removed the object, which turned out to be a crumpled cigarette package, and opened it. Inside were 14 capsules of heroin.

* * * This Court * * * reject[ed] the notion that "case-by-case adjudication" was required to determine "whether or not there was present one of the reasons supporting the authority for a search of the person incident to a lawful arrest." * * * [A] "custodial arrest of a suspect based on probable cause is a reasonable intrusion under the Fourth Amendment; that intrusion being lawful, a search incident to the arrest requires no additional justification."

The Court thus concluded that the search of Robinson was reasonable even though there was no concern about the loss of evidence, and the arresting officer had no specific concern that Robinson might be armed. In doing so, the Court did not draw a line between a search of Robinson's person and a further examination of the cigarette pack found during that search. * * *

* * * [In] *Arizona v. Gant*, 556 U.S. 332 (2009), [the Court] analyzed searches of an arrestee's vehicle. *Gant*, like *Robinson*, recognized that the *Chimel* concerns for officer safety and evidence preservation underlie the search incident to arrest exception. As a result, the Court concluded that *Chimel* could authorize police to search a vehicle "only when the arrestee is unsecured and within reaching distance of the passenger compartment at the time of the search." *Gant* added, however, an independent exception for a warrantless search of a vehicle's passenger compartment "when it is 'reasonable to believe evidence relevant to the crime of arrest might be found in the vehicle.'" That exception stems not from *Chimel*, the Court explained, but from "circumstances unique to the vehicle context."

III

These cases require us to decide how the search incident to arrest doctrine applies to modern cell phones * * *. A smart phone of the sort taken from Riley was unheard of ten years ago; a significant majority of American adults now own such phones. Even less sophisticated phones like Wurie's, which have already faded in popularity since Wurie was arrested in 2007, have been around for less than 15 years. Both phones are based on technology nearly inconceivable just a few decades ago, when *Chimel* and *Robinson* were decided.

Absent more precise guidance from the founding era, we generally determine whether to exempt a given type of search from the warrant requirement "by assessing, on the one hand, the degree to which it intrudes upon an individual's privacy and, on the other, the degree to which it is needed for the promotion of legitimate governmental interests." Such a balancing of interests supported the search incident to arrest exception in *Robinson*, and a mechanical application of *Robinson* might well support the warrantless searches at issue here.

But * * * neither of [*Robinson's*] rationales has much force with respect to digital content on cell phones. On the government interest side, *Robinson* concluded that the two risks identified in *Chimel*—harm to officers and destruction of evidence—are present in all custodial arrests. There are no comparable risks when the search is of digital data. In addition, *Robinson* regarded any privacy interests retained by an individual after arrest as significantly diminished by the fact of the arrest itself. Cell phones, however, place vast quantities of personal information literally in the hands of individuals. A search of the information on a cell phone bears little resemblance to the type of brief physical search considered in *Robinson*.

We therefore decline to extend *Robinson* to searches of data on cell phones, and hold instead that officers must generally secure a warrant before conducting such a search.

A

We first consider each *Chimel* concern in turn. * * *

1

Digital data stored on a cell phone cannot itself be used as a weapon to harm an arresting officer or to effectuate the arrestee's escape. Law enforcement officers remain free to examine the physical aspects of a phone to ensure that it will not be used as a weapon—say, to determine whether there is a razor blade hidden between the phone and its case. Once an officer has secured a phone and eliminated any potential physical threats, however, data on the phone can endanger no one.

Perhaps the same might have been said of the cigarette pack seized from Robinson's pocket. * * * But unknown physical objects may always pose risks, no matter how slight, during the tense atmosphere of a custodial arrest. * * *

The United States and California both suggest that a search of cell phone data might help ensure officer safety in more indirect ways, for example by alerting officers that confederates of the arrestee are headed to the scene. * * * [But] such threats from outside the arrest scene do not "lurk[ ] in all custodial arrests." * * * To the extent dangers to arresting officers may be implicated in a particular way in a particular case, they are better addressed through consideration of case-specific exceptions to the warrant requirement, such as the one for exigent circumstances.

2

The United States and California focus primarily on the second *Chimel* rationale: preventing the destruction of evidence.

Both Riley and Wurie concede that officers could have seized and secured their cell phones to prevent destruction of evidence while seeking a warrant. And once law enforcement officers have secured a cell phone, there is no longer any risk that the arrestee himself will be able to delete incriminating data from the phone.

The United States and California argue that information on a cell phone may nevertheless be vulnerable to two types of evidence destruction unique to digital data—remote wiping and data encryption. Remote wiping occurs when a phone, connected to a wireless network, receives a signal that erases stored data. This can happen when a third party sends a remote signal or when a phone is preprogrammed to delete data upon entering or leaving certain geographic areas (so-called "geofencing"). Encryption is a security feature that some modern cell phones use in addition to password protection. When such phones lock, data becomes protected by sophisticated encryption that renders a phone all but "unbreakable" unless police know the password.

As an initial matter, these broader concerns about the loss of evidence are distinct from *Chimel's* focus on a defendant who responds to arrest by trying to conceal or destroy evidence within his reach. With respect to remote wiping, the Government's primary concern turns on the actions of third parties who are not present at the scene of arrest. And data encryption is even further afield. There, the Government focuses on the ordinary operation of a phone's security features, apart from any active attempt by a defendant or his associates to conceal or destroy evidence upon arrest.

We have also been given little reason to believe that either problem is prevalent. The briefing reveals only a couple of anecdotal examples of remote wiping triggered by an arrest. Similarly, the opportunities for officers to search a password-protected phone before data becomes encrypted are quite limited. Law enforcement officers are very unlikely to come upon such a phone in an unlocked state because most phones lock at the touch of a button or, as a default, after some very short period of inactivity. * * *

Moreover, in situations in which an arrest might trigger a remote-wipe attempt or an officer discovers an unlocked phone, it is not clear that the ability to conduct a warrantless search would make much of a difference. The need to effect the arrest, secure the scene, and tend to other pressing matters means that law enforcement officers may well not be able to turn their attention to a cell phone right away. Cell phone data would be vulnerable to remote wiping from the time an individual anticipates arrest to the time any eventual search of the phone is completed, which might be at the station house hours later. Likewise, an officer who seizes a phone in an unlocked state might not be able to begin his search in the short time remaining before the phone locks and data becomes encrypted.

In any event, as to remote wiping, law enforcement is not without specific means to address the threat. Remote wiping can be fully prevented by disconnecting a phone from the network. There are at least two simple ways to do this: First, law enforcement officers can turn the phone off or remove its battery. Second, if they are concerned about encryption or other potential problems, they can leave a phone powered on and place it in an enclosure that isolates the phone from radio waves. Such devices are commonly called "Faraday bags," after the English scientist Michael Faraday. They are essentially sandwich bags made of aluminum foil: cheap, lightweight, and easy to use. They may not be a complete answer to the problem, but at least for now they provide a reasonable response. In fact, a number of law enforcement agencies around the country already encourage the use of Faraday bags.

To the extent that law enforcement still has specific concerns about the potential loss of evidence in a particular case, there remain more targeted ways to address those concerns. If "the police are truly confronted with a 'now or never' situation,"—for example, circumstances suggesting that a defendant's phone will be the target of an imminent remote-wipe attempt—they may be able to rely on exigent circumstances to search the phone immediately. Or, if officers happen to seize a phone in an unlocked state, they may be able to disable a phone's automatic-lock feature in order to prevent the phone from locking and encrypting data. * * *

B

The search incident to arrest exception rests not only on the heightened government interests at stake in a volatile arrest situation, but also on an arrestee's reduced privacy interests upon being taken into police custody. * * *

The fact that an arrestee has diminished privacy interests does not mean that the Fourth Amendment falls out of the picture entirely. Not every search "is acceptable solely because a person is in custody." To the contrary, when "privacy-related concerns are weighty enough" a "search may require a warrant, notwithstanding the diminished expectations of privacy of the arrestee." One such example, of course, is *Chimel*. *Chimel* refused to "characteriz[e] the invasion of privacy that results from a top-to-bottom search of a man's house as 'minor.'" Because a search of the arrestee's entire house was a substantial invasion beyond the arrest itself, the Court concluded that a warrant was required.

* * *

The United States asserts that a search of all data stored on a cell phone is "materially indistinguishable" from searches of these sorts of physical items. That is like saying a ride on horseback is materially indistinguishable from a flight to the moon. Both are ways of getting from point A to point B, but little else justifies lumping them together. Modern cell phones, as a category, implicate privacy concerns far beyond those implicated by the search of a cigarette pack, a wallet, or a purse. A conclusion that inspecting the contents of an arrestee's pockets works no substantial additional intrusion on privacy beyond the arrest itself may make sense as applied to physical items, but any extension of that reasoning to digital data has to rest on its own bottom.

1

Cell phones differ in both a quantitative and a qualitative sense from other objects that might be kept on an arrestee's person. The term "cell phone" is itself misleading shorthand; many of these devices are in fact minicomputers that also happen to have the capacity to be used as a telephone. They could just as easily be called cameras, video players, rolodexes, calendars, tape recorders, libraries, diaries, albums, televisions, maps, or newspapers.

One of the most notable distinguishing features of modern cell phones is their immense storage capacity. Before cell phones, a search of a person was limited by physical realities and tended as a general matter to constitute only a narrow intrusion on privacy. Most people cannot lug around every piece of mail they have received for the past several months, every picture they have taken, or every book or article they have read—nor would they have any reason to attempt to do so. * * *

But the possible intrusion on privacy is not physically limited in the same way when it comes to cell phones. The current top-selling smart phone has a standard capacity of 16 gigabytes (and is available with up to 64 gigabytes). Sixteen gigabytes translates to millions of pages of text, thousands of pictures, or hundreds of videos. Cell phones couple that capacity with the ability to store many different types of information: Even the most basic phones * * * might hold photographs, picture messages, text messages, internet browsing history, a calendar, a thousand-entry phone book, and so on. We expect that the gulf between physical practicability and digital capacity will only continue to widen in the future.

The storage capacity of cell phones has several interrelated consequences for privacy. First, a cell phone collects in one place many distinct types of information—an address, a note, a prescription, a bank statement, a video—that reveal much more in combination than any isolated record. Second, a cell phone's capacity allows even just one type of information to convey far more than previously possible. The sum of an individual's private life can be reconstructed through a thousand photographs labeled with dates, locations, and descriptions; the same cannot be said of a photograph or two of loved ones tucked into a wallet. Third, the data on a phone can date back to the purchase of the phone, or even earlier. A person might carry in his pocket a slip of paper reminding him to call Mr. Jones; he would not carry a record of all his communications with Mr. Jones for the past several months, as would routinely be kept on a phone.

Finally, there is an element of pervasiveness that characterizes cell phones but not physical records. Prior to the digital age, people did not typically carry a cache of sensitive personal information with them as they went about their day. Now it is the person who is not carrying a cell phone, with all that it contains, who is the exception. According to one poll, nearly three-quarters of smart phone users report being within five feet of their phones most of the time, with 12% admitting that they even use their phones in the shower. A decade ago police officers searching an arrestee might have occasionally stumbled across a highly personal item such as a diary. But those discoveries were likely to be few and far between. Today, by contrast, it is no exaggeration to say that many of the more than 90% of American adults who own a cell phone keep on their person a digital record of nearly every aspect of their lives—from the mundane to the intimate. Allowing the police to scrutinize such records on a routine basis is quite different from allowing them to search a personal item or two in the occasional case.

Although the data stored on a cell phone is distinguished from physical records by quantity alone, certain types of data are also qualitatively different. An internet search and browsing history, for example, can be found on an internet-enabled phone and could reveal an individual's private interests or concerns—perhaps a search for certain symptoms of disease, coupled with frequent visits to WebMD. Data on a cell phone can also reveal where a person has been. Historic location information is a standard feature on many smart phones and can reconstruct someone's specific movements down to the minute, not only around town but also within a particular building.

Mobile application software on a cell phone, or "apps," offer a range of tools for managing detailed information about all aspects of a person's life. There are apps for Democratic Party news and Republican Party news; apps for alcohol, drug, and gambling addictions; apps for sharing prayer requests; apps for tracking pregnancy symptoms; apps for planning your budget; apps for every conceivable hobby or pastime; apps for improving your romantic life. There are popular apps for buying or selling just about anything, and the records of such transactions may be accessible on the phone indefinitely. There are over a million apps available in each of the two major app stores; the phrase "there's an app for that" is now part of the popular lexicon. The average smart phone user has installed 33 apps, which together can form a revealing montage of the user's life.

* * * [A] cell phone search would typically expose to the government far more than the most exhaustive search of a house: A phone not only contains in digital form many sensitive records previously found in the home; it also contains a broad array of private information never found in a home in any form—unless the phone is.

2

To further complicate the scope of the privacy interests at stake, the data a user views on many modern cell phones may not in fact be stored on the device itself. Treating a cell phone as a container whose contents may be searched incident to an arrest is a bit strained as an initial matter. *See New York v. Belton*, 453 U.S. 454 (1981) (describing a "container" as "any object capable of holding another object"). But the analogy crumbles entirely when a cell phone is used to access data located elsewhere, at the tap of a screen. That is what cell phones, with increasing frequency, are designed to do by taking advantage of "cloud computing." Cloud computing is the capacity of internet-connected devices to display data stored on remote servers rather than on the device itself. Cell phone users often may not know whether particular information is stored on the device or in the cloud, and it generally makes little difference. Moreover, the same type of data may be stored locally on the device for one user and in the cloud for another.

The United States concedes that the search incident to arrest exception may not be stretched to cover a search of files accessed remotely—that is, a search of files stored in the cloud. * * *

Although the Government recognizes the problem, its proposed solutions are unclear. It suggests that officers could disconnect a phone from the network before searching the device—the very solution whose feasibility it contested with respect to the threat of remote wiping. Alternatively, the Government proposes that law enforcement agencies "develop protocols to address" concerns raised by cloud computing. Probably a good idea, but the Founders did not fight a revolution to gain the right to government agency protocols. The possibility that a search might extend well beyond papers and effects in the physical proximity of an arrestee is yet another reason that the privacy interests here dwarf those in *Robinson*.

C

Apart from their arguments for a direct extension of *Robinson*, the United States and California offer various fallback options for permitting warrantless cell phone searches under certain circumstances. Each of the proposals is flawed * * *.

The United States first proposes that the *Gant* standard be imported from the vehicle context, allowing a warrantless search of an arrestee's cell phone whenever it is reasonable to believe that the phone contains evidence of the crime of arrest. But *Gant* relied on "circumstances unique to the vehicle context" to endorse a search solely for the purpose of gathering evidence. * * *

At any rate, a *Gant* standard would prove no practical limit at all when it comes to cell phone searches. In the vehicle context, *Gant* generally protects against searches for evidence of past crimes. In the cell phone context, however, it is reasonable to expect that incriminating information will be found on a phone regardless of when the crime occurred. Similarly, in the vehicle context *Gant* restricts broad searches resulting from minor crimes such as traffic violations. That would not necessarily be true for cell phones. It would be a particularly inexperienced or unimaginative law enforcement officer who could not come up with several reasons to suppose evidence of just about any crime could be found on a cell phone. Even an individual pulled over for something as basic as speeding might well have locational data dispositive of guilt on his phone. An individual pulled over for reckless driving might have evidence on the phone that shows whether he was texting while driving. The sources of potential pertinent information are virtually unlimited, so applying the *Gant* standard to cell phones would in effect give "police officers unbridled discretion to rummage at will among a person's private effects."

The United States also proposes a rule that would restrict the scope of a cell phone search to those areas of the phone where an officer reasonably believes that information relevant to the crime, the arrestee's identity, or officer safety will be discovered. This approach would again impose few meaningful constraints on officers. The proposed categories would sweep in a great deal of information, and officers would not always be able to discern in advance what information would be found where.

We also reject the United States' final suggestion that officers should always be able to search a phone's call log * * *. [C]all logs typically contain more than just phone numbers; they include any identifying information that an individual might add, such as the label "my house" in Wurie's case.

Finally, at oral argument California suggested a different limiting principle, under which officers could search cell phone data if they could have obtained the same information from a pre-digital counterpart. But the fact that a search in the pre-digital era could have turned up a photograph or two in a wallet does not justify a search of thousands of photos in a digital gallery. The fact that someone could have tucked a paper bank statement in a pocket does not justify a search of every bank statement from the last five years. And to make matters worse, such an analogue test would allow law enforcement to search a range of items contained on a phone, even though people would be unlikely to carry such a variety of information in physical form. In Riley's case, for example, it is implausible that he would have strolled around with videotapes, photo albums, and an address book all crammed into his pockets. But because each of those items has a pre-digital analogue, police under California's proposal would be able to search a phone for all of those items—a significant diminution of privacy.

In addition, an analogue test would launch courts on a difficult line-drawing expedition to determine which digital files are comparable to physical records. Is an e-mail equivalent to a letter? Is a voicemail equivalent to a phone message slip? It is not clear how officers could make these kinds of decisions before conducting a search, or how courts would apply the proposed rule after the fact. An analogue test would "keep defendants and judges guessing for years to come."

IV

We cannot deny that our decision today will have an impact on the ability of law enforcement to combat crime. Cell phones have become important tools in facilitating coordination and communication among members of criminal enterprises, and can provide valuable incriminating information about dangerous criminals. Privacy comes at a cost.

Our holding, of course, is not that the information on a cell phone is immune from search; it is instead that a warrant is generally required before such a search, even when a cell phone is seized incident to arrest. * * *

* * * [E]ven though the search incident to arrest exception does not apply to cell phones, other case-specific exceptions may still justify a warrantless search of a particular phone. "One well-recognized exception applies when 'the exigencies of the situation' make the needs of law enforcement so compelling that [a] warrantless search is objectively reasonable under the Fourth Amendment." Such exigencies could include the need to prevent the imminent destruction of evidence in individual cases, to pursue a fleeing suspect, and to assist persons who are seriously injured or are threatened with imminent injury. * * *

In light of the availability of the exigent circumstances exception, there is no reason to believe that law enforcement officers will not be able to address some of the more extreme hypotheticals that have been suggested: a suspect texting an accomplice who, it is feared, is preparing to detonate a bomb, or a child abductor who may have information about the child's location on his cell phone. * * * [U]nlike the search incident to arrest exception, [however,] the exigent circumstances exception requires a court to examine whether an emergency justified a warrantless search in each particular case.

* * * [T]he Fourth Amendment was the founding generation's response to the reviled "general warrants" and "writs of assistance" of the colonial era, which allowed British officers to rummage through homes in an unrestrained search for evidence of criminal activity. Opposition to such searches was in fact one of the driving forces behind the Revolution itself. * * *

Modern cell phones are not just another technological convenience. With all they contain and all they may reveal, they hold for many Americans "the privacies of life." The fact that technology now allows an individual to carry such information in his hand does not make the information any less worthy of the protection for which the Founders fought. Our answer to the question of what police must do before searching a cell phone seized incident to an arrest is accordingly simple—get a warrant.

We reverse the judgment of the California Court of Appeal * * *. We affirm the judgment of the First Circuit.

JUSTICE ALITO, concurring in part and concurring in the judgment.

I agree with the Court that law enforcement officers, in conducting a lawful search incident to arrest, must generally obtain a warrant before searching information stored or accessible on a cell phone. I write separately to address two points.

I

A

First, I am not convinced * * * that the ancient rule on searches incident to arrest is based exclusively (or even primarily) on the need to protect the safety of arresting officers and the need to prevent the destruction of evidence. * * *

* * *

* * * [Those] rationales fail to explain the rule's well-recognized scope. It has long been accepted that written items found on the person of an arrestee may be examined and used at trial. But once these items are taken away from an arrestee (something that obviously must be done before the items are read), there is no risk that the arrestee will destroy them. Nor is there any risk that leaving these items unread will endanger the arresting officers.

* * *

B

Despite my view on the point discussed above, I agree that we should not mechanically apply the rule used in the pre-digital era to the search of a cell phone. Many cell phones now in use are capable of storing and accessing a quantity of information, some highly personal, that no person would ever have had on his person in hard-copy form. This calls for a new balancing of law enforcement and privacy interests.

The Court strikes this balance in favor of privacy interests with respect to all cell phones and all information found in them, and this approach leads to anomalies. For example, the Court's broad holding favors information in digital form over information in hard-copy form. Suppose that two suspects are arrested. Suspect number one has in his pocket a monthly bill for his land-line phone, and the bill lists an incriminating call to a long-distance number. He also has in his a wallet a few snapshots, and one of these is incriminating. Suspect number two has in his pocket a cell phone, the call log of which shows a call to the same incriminating number. In addition, a number of photos are stored in the memory of the cell phone, and one of these is incriminating. Under established law, the police may seize and examine the phone bill and the snapshots in the wallet without obtaining a warrant, but under the Court's holding today, the information stored in the cell phone is out.

While the Court's approach leads to anomalies, I do not see a workable alternative. Law enforcement officers need clear rules regarding searches incident to arrest, and it would take many cases and many years for the courts to develop more nuanced rules. * * *

II

This brings me to my second point. While I agree with the holding of the Court, I would reconsider the question presented here if either Congress or state legislatures, after assessing the legitimate needs of law enforcement and the privacy interests of cell phone owners, enact legislation that draws reasonable distinctions based on categories of information or perhaps other variables.

* * *

* * * [I]t would be very unfortunate if privacy protection in the 21st century were left primarily to the federal courts using the blunt instrument of the Fourth Amendment. Legislatures, elected by the people, are in a better position than we are to assess and respond to the changes that have already occurred and those that almost certainly will take place in the future.

NOTES AND QUESTIONS

1.   In *Riley*, the United States and the State of California raised arguments about the potential destruction of evidence that can arise during an arrest. Did the Court devote sufficient attention to those concerns? Does the government's ability to seek a warrant (or to rely on exceptions to the warrant requirement) fully address those concerns?

2.   What is the Court's reasoning in reaching its decision? What is the reasoning in Justice Alito's concurrence? Is it surprising that no Justice—even in the conservative wing of the Court—agreed with the positions of the United States and the State of California?

3.   Does the Court pay sufficient attention to the devices at issue? The first defendant, Riley, was arrested with a "smart phone" in his possession. As the Court states, these devices serve an extensive and broad array of functions. The second defendant, Wurie, was arrested with a simple "flip phone," a device that has much less expansive functions than a "smart phone." The Court lumped both of those devices together in its holding. Should it have? Should the extent of the cell phone's function play a role in how much leeway police are given to search the device?

4.   As discussed in *Riley*, three landmark cases are critical to the Court's Fourth Amendment jurisprudence: *Chimel, Robinson*, and *Gant*. As described in *Riley*, what important principles are established in each of those cases?

5.   Two years prior to *Riley*, in *United States v. Jones*, 565 U.S. ___, 132 S. Ct. 945 (2012), the Supreme Court held that that the warrantless installation of a Global Positioning System (GPS) tracking device on a vehicle to monitor the vehicle's movements constituted an impermissible search under the Fourth Amendment. As the Court reasoned, while simply examining the movements of a vehicle in the public eye does not constitute a search, "[b]y attaching the device to the Jeep, officers encroached on a protected area." *Id.* at 952. In a similar case involving a satellite-based tracking device, the Supreme Court held in *Grady v. North Carolina*, 575 U.S. ___, 135 S. Ct. 1368 (2015), that monitoring a sex-offender's movements with a satellite tracking system constituted a search under the Fourth Amendment. The Court remanded the case to the lower court to determine whether the satellite tracking was a "reasonable" search. *Riley, Jones*, and *Grady* reflect the Court's ongoing effort to grapple with privacy issues presented by modern technology.

6.   One related issue that has generated controversy is the use of unmanned aerial drones for law enforcement purposes. For scholarly discussions of the issue, *see, e.g.*, Melanie Reid, *Grounding Drones: Big Brother's Tool Box Needs Regulation Not Elimination*, 20 Rich. J.L. & Tech. 9 (2014) (arguing that due to the public's increasing acceptance of cameras in public places and a diminished expectation of privacy, the use of drones by law enforcement in public should not trigger Fourth Amendment protections); Robert Molko, *The Drones Are Coming!: Will the Fourth Amendment Stop Their Threat to Our Privacy?*, 78 Brook. L. Rev. 1279 (2013) (arguing that courts should embrace the "reasonable expectation of privacy" test and thus should prohibit drone surveillance of the interior of the home, limit monitoring of the curtilage of the home to short intervals, and only allow longer surveillance operations in public places).

7.   In *Kevin Fearon v. Her Majesty the Queen*, [2014] 3 S.C.R. 621 (Can.), the Supreme Court of Canada took a different approach from that of the U.S. Supreme Court in *Riley*. Canada's high court held that police may search cell

phones immediately incident to a lawful arrest if the search is directly related to the arrest and the police take detailed notes of what they find on the device and how they examined it. As the Court explained: "[P]rompt cell phone searches incident to arrest may serve important law enforcement objectives: they can assist police to identify and mitigate risks to public safety; locate firearms or stolen goods; identify accomplices; locate and preserve evidence; prevent suspects from evading or resisting law enforcement; locate the other perpetrators; warn officers of possible impending danger; and follow leads promptly." *Id.* at 623. The Court held that these interests justified allowing officers to search cell phones incident to arrest. Which approach is more persuasive—that of the U.S. Supreme Court or that of the Supreme Court of Canada?

B. RIGHT TO COUNSEL (SIXTH AMENDMENT)

The Sixth Amendment to the U.S. Constitution also provides: "In all criminal prosecutions, the accused shall enjoy the right * * * to have the Assistance of Counsel for his defence." The following case discusses the contours of the right to counsel in criminal cases.

GIDEON V. WAINWRIGHT
Supreme Court of the United States, 1963
372 U.S. 335

JUSTICE BLACK delivered the opinion of the Court.

Petitioner was charged in a Florida state court with having broken and entered a poolroom with intent to commit a misdemeanor. This offense is a felony under Florida law. Appearing in court without funds and without a lawyer, petitioner asked the court to appoint counsel for him, whereupon the following colloquy took place:

> The COURT: Mr. Gideon, I am sorry, but I cannot appoint Counsel to represent you in this case. Under the laws of the State of Florida, the only time the Court can appoint Counsel to represent a Defendant is when that person is charged with a capital offense. I am sorry, but I will have to deny your request to appoint Counsel to defend you in this case.

> The DEFENDANT: The United States Supreme Court says I am entitled to be represented by Counsel.

Put to trial before a jury, Gideon conducted his defense about as well as could be expected from a layman. He made an opening statement to the jury, cross-examined the State's witnesses, presented witnesses in his own defense, declined to testify himself, and made a short argument "emphasizing his innocence to the charge contained in the Information filed in this case." The jury returned a verdict of guilty, and petitioner was sentenced to serve five years in the state prison. Later, petitioner filed in the Florida Supreme Court this habeas corpus petition attacking his conviction and sentence on the ground that the trial court's refusal to appoint counsel for him denied him rights "guaranteed by the Constitution and the Bill of Rights by the United States Government." * * * [T]he State Supreme Court * * * denied all relief. Since 1942, when *Betts v. Brady*, 316 U.S. 455 (1942), was decided by a divided Court, the problem of a defendant's federal constitutional right to counsel in a state court has been a continuing source of controversy and litigation in both state and federal courts. To give this problem another review here, we granted certiorari. * * * [W]e appointed counsel to represent [Gideon] and requested both sides to [address] the following: "Should this Court's holding in *Betts v. Brady* be reconsidered?"

I.

* * *

II.

* * * We have construed [the Sixth Amendment] to mean that in federal courts counsel must be provided for defendants unable to employ counsel unless the right is competently and intelligently waived. [In] *Betts* * * * the Court concluded that "appointment of counsel is not a fundamental right, essential to a fair trial." It was for this reason the *Betts* Court refused to accept the contention that the Sixth Amendment's guarantee of counsel for indigent federal defendants was * * * "made obligatory upon the states by the Fourteenth Amendment." * * *

* * *

We accept *Betts v. Brady*'s assumption, based as it was on our prior cases, that a provision of the Bill of Rights which is "fundamental and essential to a fair trial" is made obligatory upon the States by the Fourteenth Amendment. We think the Court in *Betts* was wrong, however, in concluding that the Sixth Amendment's guarantee of counsel is not one of these fundamental rights. Ten years before *Betts v. Brady*, this Court, after full consideration of all the historical data examined in *Betts*, had unequivocally declared that "the right to the aid of counsel is of this fundamental character." *Powell v. Alabama*, 287 U.S. 45, 68 (1932). While the Court at the close of its *Powell* opinion * * * limit[ed] its holding to the particular facts and circumstances of that case, its conclusions about the fundamental nature of the right to counsel are unmistakable. Several years later, in 1936 [and 1938], the Court reemphasized what it had said about the fundamental nature of the right to counsel * * *.

* * *

In light of these and many other prior decisions of this Court, it is not surprising that the *Betts* Court, when faced with the contention that "one charged with crime, who is unable to obtain counsel, must be furnished counsel by the state," conceded that "[e]xpressions in the opinions of this court lend color to the argument * * *." The fact is that in deciding as it did—that "appointment of counsel is not a fundamental right, essential to a fair trial"—the Court in *Betts v. Brady* made an abrupt break with its own well-considered precedents. In returning to these old precedents, sounder we believe than the new, we * * * restore constitutional principles established to achieve a fair system of justice. Not only these precedents but also reason and reflection require us to recognize that in our adversary system of criminal justice, any person haled into court, who is too poor to hire a lawyer, cannot be assured a fair trial unless counsel is provided for him. This seems to us to be an obvious truth. Governments, both state and federal, quite properly spend vast sums of money to establish machinery to try defendants accused of crime. Lawyers to prosecute are everywhere deemed essential to protect the public's interest in an orderly society. * * * That government hires lawyers to prosecute and defendants who have the money hire lawyers to defend are the strongest indications of the widespread belief that lawyers in criminal courts are necessities, not luxuries. The right of one charged with crime to counsel may not be deemed fundamental and essential to fair trials in some countries, but it is in ours. From the very beginning, our state and national constitutions and laws have laid great emphasis on procedural and substantive safeguards designed to assure fair trials before impartial tribunals in which every defendant stands equal before the law. This noble ideal cannot be realized if the poor man charged with crime has to face his accusers without a lawyer to assist him. A defendant's need for a lawyer is nowhere better stated than in the moving words of Mr. Justice Sutherland in *Powell v. Alabama*:

> The right to be heard would be, in many cases, of little avail if it did not comprehend the right to be heard by counsel. Even the intelligent and educated layman has small and sometimes no skill in the science of law. If charged with crime, he is incapable, generally, of determining for himself whether the indictment is good or bad. He is unfamiliar with the rules of evidence. Left without the aid of counsel he may be put on trial without a proper charge, and convicted upon incompetent evidence, or evidence irrelevant to the issue or otherwise inadmissible. He lacks both the skill and knowledge adequately to prepare his defense, even though he have a perfect one. He requires the guiding hand of counsel at every step in the proceedings against him. Without it, though he be not guilty, he faces the danger of conviction because he does not know how to establish his innocence.

The Court in *Betts v. Brady* departed from the sound wisdom upon which the Court's holding in *Powell v. Alabama* rested. Florida, supported by two other States, has asked that *Betts v. Brady* be left intact. Twenty-two States, as friends of the Court, argue that *Betts* was "an anachronism when handed down" and that it should now be overruled. We agree.

The judgment is reversed * * *.

* * *

[The separate opinion by JUSTICE DOUGLAS and the concurring opinions by JUSTICE CLARK and JUSTICE HARLAN are omitted.]

NOTES AND QUESTIONS

1.   Why did the *Gideon* Court overrule *Betts v. Brady*? Is the approach in *Gideon* preferable? Why or why not?

2.   The Supreme Court held that, under *Gideon*, the right to counsel is not limited to felonies but also applies to any case in which jail time is actually imposed. *See, e.g., Scott v. Illinois*, 440 U.S. 367 (1979); *Argersinger v. Hamlin*, 407 U.S. 25 (1972). Some scholars have contended that this rule (requiring appointed counsel only if actual incarceration is imposed) does not adequately protect defendants' rights in a modern justice system, where a criminal conviction has vast implications beyond mere incarceration. As Professor John Gross contends in his article, *What Matters More: A Day in Jail or a Criminal Conviction?*, 22 Wm. & Mary Bill Rts. J. 55, 56 (2013), " * * * [T]here are severe and lasting penalties which occur automatically as a result of a criminal conviction, even those convictions which never result in the defendant being incarcerated." Professor Gross cites numerous penalties, including driver's license sanctions, immigration consequences, and monetary penalties. He concludes that the Sixth Amendment right to counsel should apply whenever "the conviction itself will subject a defendant to a web of enmeshed penalties." *Id.* at 89. Is Professor Gross persuasive in criticizing the *Scott v. Illinois* approach?

3.   In *Douglas v. California*, 372 U.S. 353 (1963), the Supreme Court held that the right to counsel does not end after the initial trial. Instead, a defendant is entitled to court-appointed counsel during the first level of appellate review. The Court later made clear that the defendant is entitled to such appointment even if the first level of appellate review is discretionary (as was the case in Michigan). *See Halbert v. Michigan*, 545 U.S. 605 (2005). The right to appointed counsel does not apply, however, beyond the first level of appellate review (*e.g.*, to the highest court of the state from the intermediate appellate court). *See Ross v. Moffit*, 417 U.S. 600 (1974). Should the right to counsel apply beyond the first tier of appellate review?

4.   The Sixth Amendment entitles a defendant not just to actual representation, but to minimal competence. In *Strickland v. Washington*, 466 U.S. 668 (1984), the Supreme Court put forth a two-part test to determine whether a defendant is entitled to a new trial based on the performance of counsel: (1) the lawyer's performance must be deficient; and (2) the deficient performance must have prejudiced the defense in a manner that deprived the defendant of a fair trial. In explaining this test, the Court stated that the

defendant must demonstrate that counsel's representation fell below an "objective standard of reasonableness" and that there is a "reasonable probability" that, but for the deficient representation, the result of the proceeding would have been different. *Id.* at 687–88, 694. In *Strickland*, the Court applied its test and held that the defendant was not entitled to relief even though counsel failed to call a potentially helpful character witness during the sentencing hearing. For other applications of the test by the Supreme Court, *see, e.g., Rompilla v. Beard*, 545 U.S. 374 (2005) (defendant satisfied two-part test when his counsel failed to investigate the file on the defendant's prior conviction, which would have shown mitigating evidence that would have affected the severity of the defendant's sentence); *Roe v. Flores-Ortega*, 528 U.S. 470 (2000) (holding that a lawyer's failure to advise the defendant of his right to appeal is prejudicial ineffective assistance of counsel when the defendant would have actually sought out an appeal had he been advised of the right); *Cuyler v. Sullivan*, 446 U.S. 335 (1980) (holding that a conflict of interest, in which multiple defendants were being represented by the same attorney in the same matter, did not constitute ineffective assistance because that conflict did not "adversely affect" the lawyer's performance).

5. Effective assistance of counsel applies not only at trial but also during plea bargaining. *See, e.g., Missouri v. Frye*, 566 U.S. ___, 132 S. Ct. 1399 (2012) (holding that counsel must inform clients about plea bargains that they have been offered); *Lafler v. Cooper*, 566 U.S. ___, 132 S. Ct. 1376 (2012) (holding that counsel must inform the client about the risk of a longer sentence that may result from rejecting a plea offer and going to trial); *Padilla v. Kentucky*, 559 U.S. 356 (2010) (holding that counsel must provide competent advice regarding the immigration consequences that a guilty plea may have on a client's immigration status). Plea bargaining is discussed further at the end of this chapter.

6. Although the Supreme Court has protected a defendant's right to effective assistance of counsel during the plea bargaining, federal and state prosecutors sometimes require defendants to waive claims of ineffective assistance of counsel as a condition of a plea agreement. Some scholars have criticized this practice. *See, e.g.,* Peter Joy & Keven McMunigal, *Waivers of Ineffective Assistance of Counsel as Condition of Negotiated Pleas*, 29 Crim. Just. 32 (2014) (arguing that when the government seeks a waiver of ineffective assistance of counsel claims as part of the negotiated plea, the defendant should be afforded independent counsel to ensure that the defendant is fully advised of the implications of such a waiver). Should a defendant ever be permitted to waive a claim of ineffective assistance of counsel? If so, should courts at least require advice from independent counsel?

7. Although a defendant has a Sixth Amendment right to counsel, he can waive that right and proceed without a lawyer (known as appearing "pro se"). In *Faretta v. California*, 422 U.S. 806 (1975), the defendant asked for permission to appear pro se and was denied the opportunity. After being forced to accept a public defender, Faretta was convicted and sentenced to prison. The Supreme Court reversed the conviction, reasoning: "[I]t is one thing to hold

that every defendant, rich or poor, has the right to the assistance of counsel, and quite another to say that a State may compel a defendant to accept a lawyer he does not want." *Id.* at 833. Subsequently, however, in *Martinez v. Court of Appeals of California*, 528 U.S. 152 (2000), the Court held that a defendant does not have a constitutional right to proceed pro se during the appellate stage. The Court reasoned: "The Sixth Amendment identifies the basic rights that the accused shall enjoy in 'all criminal prosecutions.' They are presented strictly as rights that are available in preparation for trial and at the trial itself. The Sixth Amendment does not include any right to appeal." *Id.* at 159–60. Should a defendant have a right to represent himself on appeal? Why or why not?

C. POLICE INTERROGATIONS (FIFTH AMENDMENT)

The Fifth Amendment to the U.S. Constitution sets forth a number of rights, including the following: "[N]o person * * * shall be compelled in any criminal case to be a witness against himself * * *." This right is commonly known as the "right to remain silent." The following case discusses that right.

MIRANDA V. ARIZONA
Supreme Court of the United States, 1966
384 U.S. 436

CHIEF JUSTICE WARREN delivered the opinion of the Court.

* * *

I.

The constitutional issue we decide * * * is the admissibility of statements obtained from a defendant questioned while in custody or otherwise deprived of his freedom of action in any significant way. In each, the defendant was questioned by police officers, detectives, or a prosecuting attorney in a room in which he was cut off from the outside world. In none of these cases was the defendant given a full and effective warning of his rights at the outset of the interrogation process. In all the cases, the questioning elicited oral admissions, and in three of them, signed statements as well which were admitted at their trials. They all thus share salient features—incommunicado interrogation of individuals in a police-dominated atmosphere, resulting in self-incriminating statements without full warnings of constitutional rights.

An understanding of the nature and setting of this in-custody interrogation is essential to our decisions today. * * *

* * *

* * *   [T]he modern practice of in-custody interrogation is psychologically rather than physically oriented. * * * "[C]oercion can be mental as well as physical, and * * * the blood of the accused is not the only hallmark of an unconstitutional inquisition." Interrogation still takes place in privacy. Privacy results in secrecy and this in turn results in a gap in our knowledge as to what in fact goes on in the interrogation rooms. A valuable source of information about present police practices, however, may be found in various police manuals and texts which document procedures employed with success in the past, and which recommend various other effective tactics. These texts are used by law enforcement agencies themselves as guides. * * *

The officers are told by the manuals that the "principal psychological factor contributing to a successful interrogation is privacy—being alone with the person under interrogation." * * *

* * *

To highlight the isolation and unfamiliar surroundings, the manuals instruct the police to display an air of confidence in the suspect's guilt and from outward appearance to maintain only an interest in confirming certain details. The guilt of the subject is to be posited as a fact. The interrogator should direct his comments toward the reasons why the subject committed the act, rather than court failure by asking the subject whether he did it. Like other men, perhaps the subject has had a bad family life, had an unhappy childhood, had too much to drink, had an unrequited desire for women. The officers are instructed to minimize the moral seriousness of the offense, to cast blame on the victim or on society. These tactics are designed to put the subject in a psychological state where his story is but an elaboration of what the police purport to know already— that he is guilty. Explanations to the contrary are dismissed and discouraged.

* * *

The manuals suggest that the suspect be offered legal excuses for his actions in order to obtain an initial admission of guilt. Where there is a suspected revenge-killing, for example, the interrogator may say:

> * * * My guess is, * * * that you expected something from him and that's why you carried a gun—for your own protection. * * * Then when you met him he probably * * * gave some indication that he was about to pull a gun on you, and that's when you had to act to save your own life. That's about it, isn't it, Joe?

Having then obtained the admission of shooting, the interrogator is advised to refer to circumstantial evidence which negates the self-defense explanation. This should enable him to secure the entire story. * * *

When the techniques described above prove unavailing, the texts recommend they be alternated with a show of some hostility. One ploy often used has been termed the "friendly-unfriendly" or the "Mutt and Jeff" act:

* * * In this technique, two agents are employed. Mutt [is] the relentless investigator, who knows the subject is guilty and is not going to waste any time. * * * Jeff, on the other hand, is obviously a kindhearted man. * * * He disapproves of Mutt and his tactics and will arrange to get him off the case if the subject will cooperate. * * *

The interrogators sometimes are instructed to induce a confession out of trickery. The technique here is quite effective in crimes which require identification * * *. [T]he interrogator may take a break in his questioning to place the subject among a group of men in a line-up. "The witness or complainant (previously coached, if necessary) studies the line-up and confidently points out the subject as the guilty party." Then the questioning resumes "as though there were now no doubt about the guilt of the subject." * * *

* * *

The manuals also contain instructions for police on how to handle the individual who refuses to discuss the matter entirely, or who asks for an attorney or relatives. The examiner is to concede him the right to remain silent. * * * "[A] concession of this right to remain silent impresses the subject with the apparent fairness of his interrogator." After this psychological conditioning, however, the officer is told to point out the incriminating significance of the suspect's refusal to talk[.]

* * *

In the event that the subject wishes to speak to a relative or an attorney, the following advice is tendered:

[T]he interrogator should respond by suggesting that the subject first tell the truth to the interrogator himself rather than get anyone else involved in the matter. * * *

From these representative samples of interrogation techniques, the setting * * * becomes clear * * *: To be alone with the subject is essential to prevent distraction and to deprive him of any outside support. The aura of confidence in his guilt undermines his will to resist. He merely confirms the preconceived story the police seek to have him describe. Patience and persistence, at times relentless questioning, are employed. To obtain a confession, the interrogator must "patiently maneuver himself or his quarry into a position from which the desired objective may be attained." When normal procedures fail to produce the needed result, the police may resort to deceptive stratagems such as giving false legal advice. It is important to keep the subject off balance, for example, by trading on his insecurity about himself or his surroundings. The police then persuade, trick, or cajole him out of exercising his constitutional rights.

Even without * * * the specific stratagems described above, the very fact of custodial interrogation exacts a heavy toll on individual liberty and trades on the weakness of individuals. * * *

In the cases before us today * * * we concern ourselves primarily with this interrogation atmosphere and the evils it can bring. In *Miranda v. Arizona*, the police arrested the defendant and took him to a special interrogation room where they secured a confession. In *Vignera v. New York*, the defendant made oral admissions to the police after interrogation in the afternoon, and then signed an inculpatory statement upon being questioned by an assistant district attorney later the same evening. In *Westover v. United States*, the defendant was handed over to the Federal Bureau of Investigation by local authorities after they had detained and interrogated him for a lengthy period, both at night and the following morning. After some two hours of questioning, the federal officers had obtained signed statements from the defendant. Lastly, in *California v. Stewart*, the local police held the defendant five days in the station and interrogated him on nine separate occasions before they secured his inculpatory statement.

In these cases, we might not find the defendants' statements to have been involuntary in traditional terms. Our concern for adequate safeguards to protect precious Fifth Amendment rights is, of course, not lessened in the slightest. In each of the cases, the defendant was thrust into an unfamiliar atmosphere and run through menacing police interrogation procedures. * * * To be sure, the records do not evince overt physical coercion or patent psychological ploys. The fact remains that in none of these cases did the officers undertake to afford appropriate safeguards at the outset of the interrogation to insure that the statements were truly the product of free choice.

It is obvious that such an interrogation environment is created for no purpose other than to subjugate the individual to the will of his examiner. * * * The current practice of incommunicado interrogation is at odds with one of our Nation's most cherished principles—that the individual may not be compelled to incriminate himself. * * *

* * *

II.

* * * [The] roots [of the privilege against self-incrimination] go back into ancient times. Perhaps the critical historical event shedding light on its origins and evolution was the trial of one John Lilburn, a vocal anti-Stuart Leveller, who was made to take the Star Chamber Oath in 1637. The oath would have bound him to answer to all questions posed to him on any subject. He resisted the oath and declaimed the proceedings. * * *

* * *

On account of the Lilburn Trial, Parliament abolished the inquisitorial Court of Star Chamber and went further in giving him generous reparation. The lofty principles to which Lilburn had appealed during his trial gained popular acceptance in England. These sentiments worked their way over to the Colonies and were implanted after great struggle into the Bill of Rights. * * * The privilege [against self-incrimination] was elevated to constitutional status * * *. We cannot depart from this noble heritage.

* * *

III.

Today, * * * there can be no doubt that the Fifth Amendment privilege is available outside of criminal court proceedings and serves to protect persons in all settings in which their freedom of action is curtailed in any significant way from being compelled to incriminate themselves. * * * [W]ithout proper safeguards the process of in-custody interrogation of persons suspected or accused of crime contains inherently compelling pressures * * *. In order to combat these pressures * * *, the accused must be adequately and effectively apprised of his rights and the exercise of those rights must be fully honored.

It is impossible for us to foresee the potential alternatives for protecting the privilege which might be devised by Congress or the States in the exercise of their creative rule-making capacities. Therefore we cannot say that the Constitution necessarily requires adherence to any particular solution * * *. However, unless we are shown other procedures which are [equally protective of defendants' rights], the following safeguards must be observed.

At the outset, if a person in custody is to be subjected to interrogation, he must first be informed in clear and unequivocal terms that he has the right to remain silent. For those unaware of the privilege, the warning is needed simply to make them aware of it—the threshold requirement for an intelligent decision as to its exercise. More important, such a warning is an absolute prerequisite in overcoming the inherent pressures of the interrogation atmosphere. * * *

* * *

The warning of the right to remain silent must be accompanied by the explanation that anything said can and will be used against the individual in court. This warning is needed in order to make him aware not only of the privilege, but also of the consequences of forgoing it. It is only through an awareness of these consequences that there can be any assurance of real understanding and intelligent exercise of the privilege. * * *

The circumstances surrounding in-custody interrogation can operate very quickly to overbear the will of one merely made aware of his privilege by his interrogators. Therefore, the right to have counsel present at the interrogation is indispensable to the protection of the Fifth Amendment privilege * * *.

The presence of counsel at the interrogation may serve several significant subsidiary functions as well. If the accused decides to talk to his interrogators, the assistance of counsel can mitigate the dangers of untrustworthiness. With a lawyer present the likelihood that the police will practice coercion is reduced, and if coercion is nevertheless exercised the lawyer can testify to it in court. The presence of a lawyer can also help to guarantee that the accused gives a fully accurate statement to the police and that the statement is rightly reported by the prosecution at trial.

An individual need not make a pre-interrogation request for a lawyer. While such request affirmatively secures his right to have one, his failure to ask for a lawyer does not constitute a waiver. No effective waiver of the right to counsel during interrogation can be recognized unless specifically made after the warnings we here delineate have been given. The accused who does not know his rights and therefore does not make a request may be the person who most needs counsel. * * *

* * *

Accordingly we hold that an individual held for interrogation must be clearly informed that he has the right to consult with a lawyer and to have the lawyer with him during interrogation under the system for protecting the privilege we delineate today. As with the warnings of the right to remain silent and that anything stated can be used in evidence against him, this warning is an absolute prerequisite to interrogation. No amount of circumstantial evidence that the person may have been aware of this right will suffice to stand in its stead. * * *

If an individual indicates that he wishes the assistance of counsel before any interrogation occurs, the authorities cannot rationally ignore or deny his request on the basis that the individual does not have or cannot afford a retained attorney. The financial ability of the individual has no relationship to the scope of the rights involved here. * * *

* * * [Thus], it is necessary to warn him not only that he has the right to consult with an attorney, but also that if he is indigent a lawyer will be appointed to represent him. * * *

Once warnings have been given, the subsequent procedure is clear. If the individual indicates in any manner, at any time prior to or during questioning, that he wishes to remain silent, the interrogation must cease. * * * [A]ny statement taken after the person invokes his privilege cannot be other than the product of compulsion, subtle or otherwise. * * * If the individual states that he wants an attorney, the interrogation must cease until an attorney is present. At that time, the individual must have an opportunity to confer with the attorney and to have him present during any subsequent questioning. If the individual cannot obtain an attorney and he indicates that he wants one before speaking to police, they must respect his decision to remain silent.

* * *

If the interrogation continues without the presence of an attorney and a statement is taken, a heavy burden rests on the government to demonstrate that the defendant knowingly and intelligently waived his privilege against self-incrimination and his right to retained or appointed counsel. * * *

An express statement that the individual is willing to make a statement and does not want an attorney followed closely by a statement could constitute a waiver. But a valid waiver will not be presumed simply from the silence of the accused after warnings are given or simply from the fact that a confession was in fact eventually obtained. * * *

Moreover, where in-custody interrogation is involved, there is no room for the contention that the privilege is waived if the individual answers some questions or gives some information on his own prior to invoking his right to remain silent when interrogated.

Whatever the testimony of the authorities as to waiver of rights by an accused, the fact of lengthy interrogation or incommunicado incarceration before a statement is made is strong evidence that the accused did not validly waive his rights. In these circumstances the fact that the individual eventually made a statement is consistent with the conclusion that the compelling influence of the interrogation finally forced him to do so. * * *

The warnings required and the waiver necessary in accordance with our opinion today are, in the absence of a fully effective equivalent, prerequisites to the admissibility of any statement made by a defendant. * * *

The principles announced today deal with the protection which must be given to the privilege against self-incrimination when the individual is first subjected to police interrogation while in custody at the station or otherwise deprived of his freedom of action in any significant way. It is at this point that our adversary system of criminal proceedings commences, distinguishing itself at the outset from the inquisitorial system recognized in some countries. * * *

Our decision is not intended to hamper the traditional function of police officers in investigating crime. When an individual is in custody on probable cause, the police may, of course, seek out evidence in the field to be used at trial against him. Such investigation may include inquiry of persons not under restraint. General on-the-scene questioning as to facts surrounding a crime or other general questioning of citizens in the fact-finding process is not affected by our holding. It is an act of responsible citizenship for individuals to give whatever information they may have to aid in law enforcement. In such situations the compelling atmosphere inherent in the process of in-custody interrogation is not necessarily present.

In dealing with statements obtained through interrogation, we do not purport to find all confessions inadmissible. Confessions remain a proper element in law enforcement. Any statement given freely and voluntarily without any compelling influences is, of course, admissible in evidence. * * * Volunteered statements of any kind are not barred by the Fifth Amendment and their admissibility is not affected by our holding today.

* * *

IV.

A recurrent argument made in these cases is that society's need for interrogation outweighs the privilege. * * * [The response is that] * * * the Constitution has prescribed the rights of the individual when confronted with the power of government when it provided in the Fifth Amendment that an individual cannot be compelled to be a witness against himself. * * *

If the individual desires to exercise his privilege, he has the right to do so. This is not for the authorities to decide. An attorney may advise his client not to talk to police until he has had an opportunity to investigate the case, or he may wish to be present with his client during any police questioning. In doing so an attorney is merely exercising * * * good professional judgment * * *. This is not cause for considering the attorney a menace to law enforcement. * * *

In announcing these principles, we are not unmindful of the burdens which law enforcement officials must bear, often under trying circumstances. * * * Although confessions may play an important role in some convictions, the cases before us present graphic examples of the overstatement of the "need" for confessions. In each case authorities conducted interrogations ranging up to five days in duration despite the presence, through standard investigating practices, of considerable evidence against each defendant. * * *

It is also urged that an unfettered right to detention for interrogation should be allowed because it will often redound to the benefit of the person questioned. When police inquiry determines that there is no reason to believe that the person has committed any crime, it is said, he will be released without need for further formal procedures. The person who has committed no offense, however, will be better able to clear himself after warnings with counsel present than without. It can be assumed that in such circumstances a lawyer would advise his client to talk freely to police in order to clear himself.

Custodial interrogation, by contrast, does not necessarily afford the innocent an opportunity to clear themselves. A serious consequence of the present practice of the interrogation * * * is that many arrests "for investigation" subject large numbers of innocent persons to detention and interrogation. * * *

Over the years the Federal Bureau of Investigation has compiled an exemplary record of effective law enforcement while advising any suspect or arrested person, at the outset of an interview, that he is not required to make a statement, that any statement may be used against him in court, that the individual may obtain the services of an attorney of his own choice and, more recently, that he has a right to free counsel if he is unable to pay. A letter received from the Solicitor General in response to a question from the Bench makes it clear that the [FBI's] present pattern of warnings and respect for the rights of the individual * * * is consistent with the procedure which we delineate today. * * *

* * *

The practice of the FBI can readily be emulated by state and local enforcement agencies. * * *

* * *

It is also urged upon us that we withhold decision on this issue until state legislative bodies and advisory groups have had an opportunity to deal with these problems by rule making. * * * [T]he issues presented are of constitutional dimensions and must be determined by the courts. * * *

V.

* * * [The Court concludes that in all four cases, the] statements were obtained from the defendant under circumstances that did not meet constitutional standards for protection of the privilege.

* * *

[Opinion by JUSTICE CLARK, dissenting, and concurring in one of the four cases, is omitted.]

JUSTICE HARLAN, whom JUSTICE STEWART and JUSTICE WHITE join, dissenting.

I believe the decision of the Court represents poor constitutional law and entails harmful consequences for the country at large. * * *

I.   INTRODUCTION

* * *

* * * The new rules are not designed to guard against police brutality or other unmistakably banned forms of coercion. Those who use third-degree tactics and deny them in court are equally able and destined to lie

as skillfully about warnings and waivers. Rather, the thrust of the new rules is to negate all pressures, to reinforce the nervous or ignorant suspect, and ultimately to discourage any confession at all. * * *

* * *

II. CONSTITUTIONAL PREMISES

It is most fitting to begin an inquiry into the constitutional precedents by surveying the limits on confessions the Court has evolved under the Due Process Clause of the Fourteenth Amendment. [Justice Harlan reviewed the Court's prior case law.] * * *

* * *

There are several relevant lessons to be drawn from this constitutional history. The first is that with over 25 years of precedent the Court has developed an elaborate, sophisticated, and sensitive approach to admissibility of confessions. It is "judicial" in its treatment of one case at a time, flexible in its ability to respond to the endless mutations of fact presented, and ever more familiar to the lower courts. * * *

[Moreover,] * * * the Court has given ample recognition to society's interest in suspect questioning as an instrument of law enforcement. Cases countenancing quite significant pressures can be cited without difficulty * * *.

* * *

* * * The Court's opinion * * * reveals no adequate basis for extending the Fifth Amendment's privilege against self-incrimination to the police station. Far more important, it fails to show that the Court's new rules are well supported, let alone compelled, by Fifth Amendment precedents. Instead, the new rules actually derive from quotation and analogy drawn from precedents under the Sixth Amendment, which should properly have no bearing on police interrogation.

* * *

III. POLICY CONSIDERATIONS

Examined as an expression of public policy, the Court's new regime proves so dubious that there can be no due compensation for its weakness in constitutional law. * * *

Without at all subscribing to the generally black picture of police conduct painted by the Court, I think it must be frankly recognized at the outset that police questioning allowable under due process precedents may inherently entail some pressure on the suspect and may seek advantage in his ignorance or weaknesses. * * * Until today, the role of the Constitution has been only to sift out undue pressure, not to assure spontaneous confessions.

The Court's new rules aim to offset these minor pressures and disadvantages intrinsic to any kind of police interrogation. The rules do not serve due process interests in preventing blatant coercion since * * * they do nothing to contain the policeman who is prepared to lie from the start. The rules work for reliability in confessions almost only in the Pickwickian sense that they can prevent some from being given at all. * * *

What the Court largely ignores is that its rules impair, if they will not eventually serve wholly to frustrate, an instrument of law enforcement that has long and quite reasonably been thought worth the price paid for it. There can be little doubt that the Court's new code would markedly decrease the number of confessions. To warn the suspect that he may remain silent and remind him that his confession may be used in court are minor obstructions. To require also an express waiver by the suspect and an end to questioning whenever he demurs must heavily handicap questioning. And to suggest or provide counsel for the suspect simply invites the end of the interrogation.

How much harm this decision will inflict on law enforcement cannot fairly be predicted with accuracy. Evidence on the role of confessions is notoriously incomplete * * *. We do know that some crimes cannot be solved without confessions, that ample expert testimony attests to their importance in crime control, and that the Court is taking a real risk with society's welfare in imposing its new regime on the country. * * *

While passing over the costs and risks of its experiment, the Court portrays the evils of normal police questioning in terms which I think are exaggerated. * * * [I]nterrogation is no doubt often inconvenient and unpleasant for the suspect. However, it is no less so for a man to be arrested and jailed, to have his house searched, or to stand trial in court, yet all this may properly happen to the most innocent given probable cause, a warrant, or an indictment. Society has always paid a stiff price for law and order, and peaceful interrogation is not one of the dark moments of the law.

* * *

IV. CONCLUSIONS

All four of the cases involved here present express claims that confessions were inadmissible, not because of coercion in the traditional due process sense, but solely because of lack of counsel or lack of warnings concerning counsel and silence. For the reasons stated in this opinion, I would adhere to the due process test and reject the new requirements inaugurated by the Court. * * *

* * *

[Dissenting opinion by JUSTICE WHITE, joined by JUSTICE HARLAN and JUSTICE STEWART, is omitted.]

* * *

NOTES AND QUESTIONS

1. What is the issue that the Court addressed in *Miranda*? What Constitutional provision is involved?

2. How did the Court resolve the case? Was the Court's approach obvious from the text of the Fifth Amendment? If not, how did the Court reach its decision?

3. What concerns did Justice Harlan raise in his dissent in *Miranda*? Are his concerns justified?

4. As a result of the Court's decision, what must an officer tell a suspect before the suspect is subjected to interrogation? What are the consequences if the officer fails to provide the required warnings?

5. The Supreme Court has had the opportunity to overrule *Miranda*, but it has explicitly refused to do so. *See Dickerson v. United States*, 530 US 428, 443 (2000) (noting that "*Miranda* has become embedded in routine police practice to the point where the warnings have become part of our national culture"). Nonetheless, the Court has limited *Miranda* in several ways. For example:

 a. ***Miranda* warnings only need to be read when the suspect is "in custody."** In *Berkemer v. McCarty*, 468 U.S. 420 (1984), the Supreme Court clarified that the holding in *Miranda* only applies when an individual is arrested or otherwise in police custody. In *Berkemer*, an officer stopped McCarty after observing him weaving in and out of a highway lane. The officer suspected that McCarty was driving while impaired and asked him whether he had consumed alcohol. McCarty responded that he had consumed beer and had smoked a sizeable quantity of marijuana. McCarty repeated those admissions after his arrest. At neither time was McCarty advised of his *Miranda* rights. McCarty moved to suppress his statements under *Miranda*. The Court held that the admission of McCarty's statements at the jail violated *Miranda* but that his similar statements during the traffic stop did not. With respect to the traffic stop statements, the Court held that *Miranda* is only triggered in connection with a "custodial interrogation." Because traffic stops are presumptively a temporary and minor intrusion on an individual's affairs, questioning during a traffic stop does not constitute custodial interrogation.

 b. ***Miranda* warnings only need to be read prior to an "interrogation."** In *Rhode Island v. Innis*, 446 U.S. 291 (1980), the Supreme Court concluded that for the protections of *Miranda* to apply, the in-custody questioning must be an "interrogation." In *Innis*, the defendant was suspected of robbing a taxi driver with a shotgun (which was not found at the scene) and was later arrested. The defendant was advised of his *Miranda* rights on multiple occasions and chose to exercise his rights. The police honored the defendant's wishes and ceased their direct questioning. While transporting the defendant to the police station, two officers engaged in a conversation between themselves, stating that there were " 'a lot of handicapped children running around in this area' " because a school for such children was located nearby, and " 'God forbid one of them might find a weapon with shells and they might hurt themselves.' " *Id.* at 294–95. The defendant overheard this conversation and interrupted the officers, telling them that he "wanted to get the gun out of the way because of the kids in the area in the school." *Id.* at 295. The defendant led the police to the shotgun and was later convicted. The defendant moved to suppress the statements and the shotgun evidence, arguing that the police had violated his *Miranda* rights because they had interrogated him after he had invoked his rights. The Supreme Court disagreed, stating: "[T]he conversation between [the officers] included no express questioning of the [defendant]. Rather, that conversation was, at least in form, nothing more than a dialogue between the two officers to which no response from the [defendant] was invited." *Id.* at 302. *See also, e.g., Illinois v. Perkins*, 496 U.S. 292 (1990) (holding that a conversation in a jail cell between an in-custody suspect and an undercover officer posing as a cellmate was not interrogation of the suspect for purposes of *Miranda*).

c.   **The *Miranda* warnings do not need to be read when there is an imminent threat to public safety.** In *New York v. Quarles*, 467 U.S. 649 (1984), the Supreme Court created a "public safety" exception to *Miranda* and held that *Miranda* warnings do not need to be read if the police are questioning a suspect to investigate an immediate threat to public safety. In *Quarles*, officers were responding to a victim who told police that her attacker had just entered a supermarket and was carrying a gun. Police chased the attacker to the rear of the supermarket with guns drawn. Upon arrest, police observed that the defendant's gun holster was empty, indicating that the defendant had abandoned his weapon in the supermarket. The officers placed the defendant under arrest, and without administering *Miranda* warnings, they asked the defendant where had had discarded the gun. The defendant nodded toward an empty shelf in the supermarket and stated: "The gun is over there." *Id.* at 652. The Court found that, although this was a custodial interrogation, the missing gun posed a threat to public safety and thus M*iranda* warnings were not required.

d.   **A defendant must affirmatively invoke his right to silence.** In *Berghuis v. Thompkins*, 560 U.S. 370 (2010), the Supreme Court held that to invoke his right to remain silent, a suspect must affirmatively state that he is choosing not to speak. In *Berghuis*, the defendant remained largely silent during a three-hour interrogation. Police continued to question him, however, and near the end of the interrogation the defendant gave an incriminating answer. The defendant moved to suppress his statement, arguing that by remaining silent, he had invoked his *Miranda* rights. The Supreme Court disagreed, holding that silence, in and of itself, is insufficient to infer that the suspect has invoked his right to remain silent. Justice Sotomayor criticized the majority's approach, stating: "[A] suspect who wishes to guard his right to remain silent * * * must, counterintuitively, speak." *Id.* at 391 (Sotomayor, J., dissenting). Justice Sotomayor also expressed concern that the majority's approach undermined the traditional "heavy burden" that is placed on the government to show that a suspect has waived his *Miranda* rights. *Id.* at 400. Is Justice Sotomayor's concern valid?

**e.	A defendant who invokes his right to silence may be interrogated later regarding other crimes.** In *Michigan v. Mosley*, 423 U.S. 96 (1975), the Supreme Court held that even if a defendant unambiguously exercises his right to remain silent, he may later be interrogated regarding an unrelated crime as long as reasonable time has passed and a new warning is given.

**f.	A defendant who invokes his right to counsel can be re-interrogated after 14 days with proper warnings.** In *Edwards v. Arizona*, 451 U.S. 477 (1981), the Court held that when a defendant requests an attorney, the police may not attempt any further questioning until an attorney is present or until the defendant re-initiates the questioning on his own accord. This principle holds true even if the defendant had previously consulted with an attorney prior to the second round of questioning. *Edwards* appeared to place a bright-line restriction on questioning a defendant without counsel. In *Maryland v. Shatzer*, 559 U.S. 98 (2010), however, the Supreme Court held that the *Edwards* prohibition on re-questioning a defendant did not apply when a defendant was released from custodial interrogation and two-and-a-half years had elapsed between the initial questioning and the second interrogation. In its ruling, the Court created a bright-line rule that even if a defendant invokes his right to counsel during an initial interrogation, police may seek to re-interrogate him (even without counsel present) if 14 days have passed since his release from custodial interrogation and the *Miranda* warnings are re-administered.

6.	What are the implications of a defendant's silence—either at trial or prior to trial—on his case at trial? In *Griffin v. California*, 380 U.S. 609 (1965), the Supreme Court held that a prosecutor's comments on the defendant's failure to testify at trial violated the "Self-Incrimination Clause" of the Fifth Amendment. Similarly, if a defendant chooses to remain silent during a pre-trial interrogation after being advised of his *Miranda* rights, that silence may not be used against him at trial. *Brecht v. Abrahamson*, 507 U.S. 619 (1993). As the Court stated in *Brecht*: "This rule rests on the fundamental unfairness of implicitly assuring a suspect that his silence will not be used against him and then using his silence to impeach an explanation subsequently offered at trial." *Id.* at 628. *But see Jenkins v. Anderson*, 447 U.S. 231 (1980) (allowing prosecutor to use pre-arrest silence in some instances to impeach a defendant's testimony if the defendant later testifies at trial).

7. For thoughtful perspectives on *Miranda, see, e.g.,* Charles Weisselberg, *Mourning* Miranda, 96 Cal. L. Rev. 1519 (2008) (arguing that the Supreme Court should overrule *Miranda* because it has been rendered ineffective by police, who have found creative strategies to undermine the original protections); Charles Ogletree, *Are Confessions Really Good for the Soul?: A Proposal to Mirandize* Miranda, 100 Harv. L. Rev. 1826 (1987) (urging an expansion of *Miranda* and advocating a *per se* rule prohibiting police from interrogating a suspect in custody who has not consulted with an attorney).

D. TRIAL BY JURY (SIXTH AMENDMENT)

The Sixth Amendment to the U.S. Constitution provides: "In all criminal prosecutions, the accused shall enjoy the right to a speedy and public trial, by an impartial jury of the state and district wherein the crime shall have been committed * * *." The following case discusses the contours of the right to a jury trial in a criminal case.

DUNCAN V. LOUISIANA
Supreme Court of the United States, 1968
391 U.S. 145

JUSTICE WHITE delivered the opinion of the Court.

Appellant, Gary Duncan, was convicted of simple battery in * * * [Louisiana state court]. Under Louisiana law simple battery is a misdemeanor, punishable by a maximum of two years' imprisonment and a $300 fine. Appellant sought trial by jury, but because the Louisiana Constitution grants jury trials only in cases in which capital punishment or imprisonment at hard labor may be imposed, the trial judge denied the request. Appellant was convicted and sentenced to serve 60 days in the parish prison and pay a fine of $150. [The Supreme Court of Louisiana denied review.] * * * [We reverse.]

Appellant was 19 years of age when tried. While driving on Highway 23 in Plaquemines Parish on October 18, 1966, he saw two younger cousins engaged in a conversation by the side of the road with four white boys. Knowing his cousins, Negroes who had recently transferred to a formerly all-white high school, had reported the occurrence of racial incidents at the school, Duncan stopped the car, got out, and approached the six boys. At trial the white boys and a white onlooker testified, as did appellant and his cousins. The testimony was in dispute on many points, but the witnesses agreed that appellant and the white boys spoke to each other, that appellant encouraged his cousins to break off the encounter and enter his car, and that appellant was about to enter the car himself for the purpose of driving away with his cousins. The whites testified that just before getting in the car appellant slapped Herman Landry, one of the white boys, on the elbow. The Negroes testified that appellant had not slapped Landry, but had merely touched him. The trial judge concluded that the State had proved beyond a reasonable doubt that Duncan had committed simple battery, and found him guilty.

I.

The Fourteenth Amendment denies the States the power to "deprive any person of life, liberty, or property, without due process of law." In resolving conflicting claims concerning the meaning of this spacious language, the Court has looked increasingly to the Bill of Rights for guidance; many of the rights guaranteed by the first eight Amendments to the Constitution have been held to be protected against state action by the Due Process Clause of the Fourteenth Amendment. * * *

* * * [W]e hold that the Fourteenth Amendment guarantees a right of jury trial in all criminal cases which—were they to be tried in a federal court—would come within the Sixth Amendment's guarantee. Since we consider the appeal before us to be such a case, we hold that the Constitution was violated when appellant's demand for jury trial was refused.

The history of trial by jury in criminal cases has been frequently told. It is sufficient for present purposes to say that by the time our Constitution was written, jury trial in criminal cases had been in existence in England for several centuries and carried impressive credentials traced by many to Magna Carta. Its preservation and proper operation as a protection against arbitrary rule were among the major objectives of the revolutionary settlement which was expressed in the Declaration and Bill of Rights of 1689. * * *

* * *

Jury trial came to America with English colonists, and received strong support from them. Royal interference with the jury trial was deeply resented. Among the resolutions adopted by the First Congress of the American Colonies * * * on October 19, 1765 * * * was the declaration:

That trial by jury is the inherent and invaluable right of every British subject in these colonies.

The First Continental Congress, in the resolve of October 14, 1774, objected to trials before judges dependent upon the Crown alone for their salaries and to trials in England for alleged crimes committed in the colonies; the Congress therefore declared:

That the respective colonies are entitled to the common law of England, and more especially to the great and inestimable privilege of being tried by their peers of the vicinage, according to the course of that law.

The Declaration of Independence stated solemn objections to the King's making "judges dependent on his will alone, for the tenure of their offices, and the amount and payment of their salaries," to his "depriving us in many cases, of the benefits of Trial by Jury," and to his "transporting us beyond Seas to be tried for pretended offenses." The Constitution itself [includes the right to jury trial in criminal cases (in Art. III, Section 2 and the Sixth Amendment)].

The constitutions adopted by the original States guaranteed jury trial. Also, the constitution of every State entering the Union thereafter in one form or another protected the right to jury trial in criminal cases.

Even such skeletal history is impressive support for considering the right to jury trial in criminal cases to be fundamental to our system of justice * * *.

* * *

The guarantees of jury trial in the Federal and State Constitutions reflect a profound judgment about the way in which law should be enforced and justice administered. A right to jury trial is granted to criminal defendants in order to prevent oppression by the Government. Those who wrote our constitutions knew from history and experience that it was necessary to protect against unfounded criminal charges brought to eliminate enemies and against judges too responsive to the voice of higher authority. The framers of the constitutions strove to create an independent judiciary but insisted upon further protection against arbitrary action. Providing an accused with the right to be tried by a jury of his peers gave him an inestimable safeguard against the corrupt or overzealous prosecutor and against the compliant, biased, or eccentric judge. If the defendant preferred the common-sense judgment of a jury to the more tutored but perhaps less sympathetic reaction of the single judge, he was to have it. Beyond this, the jury trial provisions in the Federal and State Constitutions reflect a fundamental decision about the exercise of official power—a reluctance to entrust plenary powers over the life and liberty of the citizen to one judge or to a group of judges. * * * The deep commitment of the Nation to the right of jury trial in serious criminal cases as a defense against arbitrary law enforcement qualifies for protection under the Due Process Clause of the Fourteenth Amendment, and must therefore be respected by the States.

Of course jury trial has "its weaknesses and the potential for misuse." We are aware of the long debate * * * as to the wisdom of permitting untrained laymen to determine the facts in civil and criminal proceedings. Although the debate has been intense, * * * most of the controversy has centered on the jury in civil cases. Indeed, some of the severest critics of civil juries acknowledge that the arguments for criminal juries are much stronger. In addition, at the heart of the dispute have been express or implicit assertions that juries are incapable of adequately understanding evidence or determining issues of fact, and that they are unpredictable, quixotic, and little better than a roll of dice. Yet, the most recent and exhaustive study of the jury in criminal cases concluded that juries do understand the evidence and come to sound conclusions in most of the cases presented to them and that when juries differ with the result at which the judge would have arrived, it is usually because they are serving some of the very purposes for which they were created and for which they are now employed.

The State of Louisiana urges that holding that the Fourteenth Amendment assures a right to jury trial will cast doubt on the integrity of every trial conducted without a jury. Plainly, this is not the import of our holding. Our conclusion is that * * * a general grant of jury trial for serious offenses is a fundamental right * * *. We would not assert * * * that every criminal trial—or any particular trial—held before a judge alone is unfair or that a defendant may never be as fairly treated by a judge as he would be by a jury. Thus we hold no constitutional doubts about the practices, common in both federal and state courts, of accepting waivers of jury trial and prosecuting petty crimes without extending a right to jury trial. * * *

II.

Louisiana's final contention is that even if it must grant jury trials in serious criminal cases, the conviction before us is valid and constitutional because here the petitioner was tried for simple battery and was sentenced to only 60 days in the parish prison. We are not persuaded. * * * Crimes carrying possible penalties up to six months do not require a jury trial if they otherwise qualify as petty offenses. But the penalty authorized for a particular crime is of major relevance in determining whether it is serious or not and may in itself, if severe enough, subject the trial to the mandates of the Sixth Amendment. * * * In the case before us the Legislature of Louisiana has made simple battery a criminal offense punishable by imprisonment for up to two years and a fine. The question, then, is whether a crime carrying such a penalty is an offense which Louisiana may insist on trying without a jury.

* * *

In determining whether the length of the authorized prison term or the seriousness of other punishment is enough in itself to require a jury trial, we * * * refer to objective criteria, chiefly the existing laws and practices in the Nation. In the federal system, petty offenses are defined as those punishable by no more than six months in prison and a $500 fine. In 49 of the 50 States crimes subject to trial without a jury, which occasionally include simple battery, are punishable by no more than one year in jail. Moreover, in the late 18th century in America crimes triable without a jury were for the most part punishable by no more than a six-month prison term, although there appear to have been exceptions to this rule. We need not * * * settle in this case the exact location of the line between petty offenses and serious crimes. It is sufficient for our purposes to hold that a crime punishable by two years in prison is, based on past and contemporary standards in this country, a serious crime and not a petty offense. Consequently, appellant was entitled to a jury trial and it was error to deny it.

* * *

Reversed and remanded.

[Concurring opinions by JUSTICE BLACK and JUSTICE FORTAS are omitted.]

* * *

JUSTICE HARLAN, whom JUSTICE STEWART joins, dissenting.

* * * The question in this case is whether the State of Louisiana, which provides trial by jury for all felonies, is prohibited by the Constitution from trying charges of simple battery to the court alone. In my view, the answer to that question * * * is clearly "no."

* * * The Due Process Clause of the Fourteenth Amendment requires that [a state's criminal justice] procedures be fundamentally fair in all respects. It does not, in my view, impose or encourage nationwide uniformity for its own sake * * * and it does not impose on the States the rules that may be in force in the federal courts except where such rules are * * * found to be essential to basic fairness.

* * *

I.

[Justice Harlan explained that, in his view, the Sixth Amendment right to jury trial should not be applied to the states via the Fourteenth Amendment.]

II.

* * * When a criminal defendant contends that his state conviction lacked "due process of law," the question before this Court, in my view, is whether he was denied any element of fundamental procedural fairness. Believing, as I do, that due process is an evolving concept * * *, I think it appropriate to deal on its merits with the question whether Louisiana denied appellant due process of law when it tried him for simple assault without a jury.

* * *

The argument that [a] jury trial is not a requisite of due process is quite simple. * * * "[D]ue process of law" requires only that criminal trials be fundamentally fair. * * * [T]he inquiry in each case must be whether a state trial process was a fair one. The Court has held, properly I think, that in an adversary process it is a requisite of fairness, for which there is no adequate substitute, that a criminal defendant be afforded a right to counsel and to cross-examine opposing witnesses. But it simply has not been demonstrated, nor, I think, can it be demonstrated, that trial by jury is the only fair means of resolving issues of fact.

The jury is of course not without virtues. It affords ordinary citizens a valuable opportunity to participate in a process of government, an experience fostering, one hopes, a respect for law. It eases the burden on judges by enabling them to share a part of their sometimes awesome responsibility. A jury may, at times, afford a higher justice by refusing to enforce harsh laws (although it necessarily does so haphazardly, raising the questions whether arbitrary enforcement of harsh laws is better than total enforcement, and whether the jury system is to be defended on the ground that jurors sometimes disobey their oaths). And the jury may, or may not, contribute desirably to the willingness of the general public to accept criminal judgments as just.

It can hardly be gainsaid, however, that the principal original virtue of the jury trial—the limitations a jury imposes on a tyrannous judiciary—has largely disappeared. We no longer live in a medieval or colonial society. Judges enforce laws enacted by democratic decision, not by regal fiat. They are elected by the people or appointed by the people's elected officials, and are responsible not to a distant monarch alone but to reviewing courts, including this one.

The jury system can also be said to have some inherent defects, which are multiplied by the emergence of the criminal law from the relative simplicity that existed when the jury system was devised. It is a cumbersome process, not only imposing great cost in time and money on both the State and the jurors themselves, but also contributing to delay in the machinery of justice. Untrained jurors are presumably less adept at reaching accurate conclusions of fact than judges, particularly if the issues are many or complex. And it is argued by some that trial by jury, far from increasing public respect for law, impairs it: the average man, it is said, reacts favorably neither to the notion that matters he knows to be complex are being decided by other average men, nor to the way the jury system distorts the process of adjudication.

* * *

* * * I * * * see no reason why this Court should reverse the conviction of appellant, absent any suggestion that his particular trial was in fact unfair * * *.

* * * [E]ven if I were persuaded that trial by jury is a fundamental right in some criminal cases, I could see nothing fundamental in the rule,

not yet formulated by the Court, that places the prosecution of appellant for simple battery within the category of "jury crimes" rather than "petty crimes." * * *

* * *

* * * [M]any offenses that English-speaking communities have, at one time or another, regarded as triable without a jury are more serious, and carry more serious penalties, than the one involved here. * * * [U]ntil today few people would have thought the exact location of the line mattered very much. There is no obvious reason why a jury trial is a requisite of fundamental fairness when the charge is robbery, and not a requisite of fairness when the same defendant, for the same actions, is charged with assault and petty theft. The reason for the historic exception for relatively minor crimes is the obvious one: the burden of jury trial was thought to outweigh its marginal advantages. Exactly why the States should not be allowed to make continuing adjustments, based on the state of their criminal dockets and the difficulty of summoning jurors, simply escapes me.

In sum, there is a wide range of views on the desirability of trial by jury, and on the ways to make it most effective when it is used; there is also considerable variation from State to State in local conditions such as the size of the criminal caseload, the ease or difficulty of summoning jurors, and other trial conditions bearing on fairness. * * *

* * * [This] Court has chosen to impose upon every State one means of trying criminal cases; it is a good means, but it is not the only fair means, and it is not demonstrably better than the alternatives States might devise.

I would affirm the judgment of the Supreme Court of Louisiana.

NOTES AND QUESTIONS

1.   In what way did Duncan claim that his rights were violated? How did the Court decide the case? What limits, if any, did the Court place on the rule it adopted?

2.   Why did Justice Harlan disagree with the majority? Whose analysis is more persuasive—the majority's or Justice Harlan's?

3.   Although the right to a jury trial exists in both criminal and civil matters, different constitutional provisions are involved. The right in criminal cases stems from the Sixth Amendment (quoted above), whereas the right in civil cases stems from the Seventh Amendment ("In Suits at common law, where the value in controversy shall exceed twenty dollars, the right of trial by jury shall be preserved * * *."). The contours of the Seventh Amendment right to jury trial, however, are narrower than those of its Sixth Amendment counterpart. The Seventh Amendment right to a jury trial in civil cases is discussed in more detail in Chapter 3.

4. What benefits does a jury offer to a criminal defendant? Why might a defendant choose to waive his right to a jury and have his case decided by a judge? Was Duncan wise, given the charge against him, to seek a jury? For an in-depth statistical comparison of when a defendant may benefit from waiving the right to a jury trial, *see* Andrew Leipold, *Why Are Judges So Acquittal Prone?*, 83 Wash. U. L.Q. 151 (2005) (finding that federal judges acquit defendants more frequently than juries across all categories of cases). Are there certain kinds of crimes for which a defendant should be especially inclined to opt for a bench trial as opposed to a jury trial? If so, what types of crimes and why? Are there certain kinds of crimes in which a defendant should generally opt for a jury trial? If so, what kinds and why?

5. The Constitution requires not just the right to a jury, but also the right to a *fair jury selection*. To ensure a fair trial, each party in a jury trial has a right to use what are known as "for cause" and "peremptory" challenges to strike jurors from the jury pool during jury selection. "For cause" challenges are claims that a juror may harbor prejudice against (or favoritism towards) one side and thus could not fairly decide the case. If the trial judge concludes that the juror will have difficulty fairly assessing the merits of the case, the juror will be struck "for cause." Each party is entitled to an unlimited number of for cause challenges, although in most cases, only a small number of jurors will be struck for cause. Peremptory challenges, on the other hand, allow counsel to strike a specified number of jurors for virtually any reason. *See Ross v. Oklahoma*, 487 U.S. 81 (1988) (discussing the differences between "peremptory" and "for cause" challenges and their practical uses at trial). Generally, a party does not have to explain why he used a peremptory challenge, and parties are afforded broad discretion in exercising such challenges. In *Batson v. Kentucky*, 476 U.S. 79 (1986), however, the Supreme Court held that a prosecutor violates the Equal Protection Clause by striking jurors based on their race. Subsequently, in *J.E.B. v. Alabama ex rel. T.B.*, 511 U.S. 127 (1994), the Court expanded *Batson* to apply to gender as well. *Batson* remains good law, but a *Batson* challenge is rarely successful. As the Court in *Batson* acknowledged, once racially motivated strikes have been suspected, the attorney must then provide "racially neutral" justifications for the strike. 476 U.S. at 94. As demonstrated by *Purkett v. Elem*, 514 U.S. 765 (1995), that test is relatively easy to satisfy. In *Purkett*, the prosecutor was accused of striking a black juror based on race. When asked about his motivations for the strikes, the prosecutor explained:

> I struck [juror] number twenty-two because of his long hair. He had long curly hair. He had the longest hair of anybody on the panel by far. * * * Also he had a moustache and goatee type beard. And juror number twenty-four also has a moustache and goatee type beard. Those are the only two people on the jury . . . with facial hair . . . And I didn't like the way they looked, with the way the hair is cut, both of them. And the moustaches and the beards look suspicious to me.

Id. at 766.

The Court held that the prosecutor had satisfied the showing of a racially neutral explanation. It held that explanations need not be "persuasive, or even plausible." *Id.* at 768. Justice Stevens, joined by Justice Breyer, dissented in *Purkett*, stating: "The Court's unnecessary tolerance of silly, fantastic, and implausible explanations" promotes an extreme risk of pretextual challenges and "demeans the importance of the values vindicated by our decision in *Batson*." *Id.* at 777–88 (Stevens, J., dissenting). Is Justice Stevens correct? Do his concerns demonstrate that *Batson* is a constitutional doctrine with limited practical significance? For a discussion of the limitations of the *Batson* rule, *see* Gilad Edelman, *Why Is It So Easy for Prosecutors to Strike Black Jurors?*, THE NEW YORKER (June 5, 2015), http://www.newyorker.com/news/news-desk/why-is-it-so-easy-for-prosecutors-to-strike-black-jurors. (concluding that "[r]ace-based peremptory strikes are almost always invisible, or at least, as *Batson* has shown, hard to prove").

In May of 2015, the Supreme Court granted review in a case involving claims of race discrimination in jury selection under *Batson*. *Foster v. Chatman*, 135 S. Ct. 2349 (U.S. May 26, 2015) (No. 14–8349). In *Foster*, a Georgia prosecutor struck all four black prospective jurors in a capital murder case in which the defendant was black. In addition to arguing that the reasons offered by the prosecutor for striking those four jurors were pretextual, the defendant relied on notes taken by the prosecutor on a list of prospective jurors (obtained through the Georgia Open Records Act). Those notes showed, among other things, that the prosecutor had marked the four black prospective jurors with a "B" and had underlined those names with a green highlighter. As of the date that this text went to press, the Court had not yet rendered an opinion.

6.   Under the Sixth Amendment, the defendant is entitled to a jury trial from a "fair cross section" of the community. In other words, the jury pool must be selected from a fairly representative group from the community where the crime was committed. For example, in *Duren v. Missouri*, 439 U.S. 357 (1979), the Supreme Court held that Missouri's systematic exclusion of women from the jury pool—which resulted in jury venires that were on average less than 15 percent female—violated the Sixth Amendment's fair cross-section requirement. The jury pool does not need an exact representation of the community, but as *Duren* demonstrates, gross disparities in the jury pool may violate a defendant's rights. In *Berghuis v. Smith*, 559 U.S. 314 (2010), the Supreme Court held that, to demonstrate a fair cross-section violation, the defendant must show: "(1) a group qualifying as 'distinctive' (2) is not fairly and reasonably represented in jury venires, and (3) 'systematic exclusion' in the jury-selection process accounts for the underrepresentation." *Id.* at 327. The Court in *Berghuis* ultimately held that, while the defendant did demonstrate some limited disparity of African-Americans in his jury pool, he could not show that the trial court's policies had any significant effect on the underrepresentation of African-American jurors (the "systematic exclusion" prong of the test).

E. DEFENDANT'S RIGHT TO EXCULPATORY EVIDENCE (FIFTH AND FOURTEENTH AMENDMENTS)

There is no constitutional provision that explicitly guarantees a defendant a right to exculpatory evidence (*i.e.*, evidence in a criminal trial that tends to negate guilt), but courts have analyzed the question under the Due Process Clauses of the Fifth and Fourteenth Amendments. The Fifth Amendment Due Process Clause applies in federal cases and provides: "No person shall be * * * deprived of life, liberty, or property, without due process of law * * *." The Fourteenth Amendment applies in state cases and provides the same right, stating: "No state shall * * * deprive any person of life, liberty, or property, without due process of law * * *." The following case discusses the Fourteenth Amendment's Due Process Clause in the context of the prosecution's duty to disclose exculpatory evidence to the defendant prior to trial.

BRADY V. MARYLAND
Supreme Court of the United States, 1963
373 U.S. 83

Opinion of the Court by JUSTICE DOUGLAS, announced by JUSTICE BRENNAN.

Petitioner and a companion, Boblit, were found guilty of murder in the first degree and were sentenced to death, their convictions being affirmed by the Court of Appeals of Maryland. Their trials were separate, petitioner being tried first. At his trial Brady took the stand and admitted his participation in the crime, but he claimed that Boblit did the actual killing. And, in his summation to the jury, Brady's counsel conceded that Brady was guilty of murder in the first degree, asking only that the jury return that verdict "without capital punishment." Prior to the trial petitioner's counsel had requested the prosecution to allow him to examine Boblit's extrajudicial statements. Several of those statements were shown to him; but one dated July 9, 1958, in which Boblit admitted the actual homicide, was withheld by the prosecution and did not come to petitioner's notice until after he had been tried, convicted, and sentenced, and after his conviction had been affirmed.

Petitioner moved the trial court for a new trial based on the newly discovered evidence that had been suppressed by the prosecution. Petitioner's appeal from a denial of that motion was dismissed by the Court of Appeals without prejudice to relief under the Maryland Post Conviction Procedure Act. The petition for post-conviction relief was dismissed by the trial court; and on appeal the Court of Appeals held that suppression of the evidence by the prosecution denied petitioner due process of law and remanded the case for a retrial of the question of punishment, not the question of guilt. The case is here on certiorari.

The crime in question was murder committed in the perpetration of a robbery. Punishment for that crime in Maryland is life imprisonment or death, the jury being empowered to restrict the punishment to life by addition of the words "without capital punishment." In Maryland, by reason of the state constitution, the jury in a criminal case are "the Judges of Law, as well as of fact." The question presented is whether petitioner was denied a federal right when the Court of Appeals restricted the new trial to the question of punishment.

* * *

We * * * hold that the suppression by the prosecution of evidence favorable to an accused upon request violates due process where the evidence is material either to guilt or to punishment, irrespective of the good faith or bad faith of the prosecution.

The * * * [due process principle we invoke] is not punishment of society for misdeeds of a prosecutor but avoidance of an unfair trial to the accused. Society wins not only when the guilty are convicted but when criminal trials are fair; our system * * * suffers when any accused is treated unfairly. An inscription on the walls of the Department of Justice states the proposition candidly for the federal domain: "The United States wins its point whenever justice is done its citizens in the courts." A prosecution that withholds evidence on demand of an accused which, if made available, would tend to exculpate him or reduce the penalty helps shape a trial that bears heavily on the defendant. That casts the prosecutor in the role of an architect of a proceeding that does not comport with standards of justice * * *.

The question remains whether petitioner was denied a constitutional right when the Court of Appeals restricted his new trial to the question of punishment. * * *

* * *

* * * [Under Maryland law,] it is the court, not the jury, that passes on the "admissibility of evidence" pertinent to "the issue of the innocence or guilt of the accused." In the present case a unanimous Court of Appeals has said that nothing in the suppressed confession "could have reduced the appellant Brady's offense below murder in the first degree." We read that statement as a ruling on the admissibility of the confession on the issue of innocence or guilt. A sporting theory of justice might assume that if the suppressed confession had been used at the first trial, the judge's ruling that it was not admissible on the issue of innocence or guilt might have been flouted by the jury * * *. But we cannot raise that trial strategy to the dignity of a constitutional right and say that the deprival of this defendant of that sporting chance through the use of a bifurcated trial denies him due

process or violates the Equal Protection Clause of the Fourteenth Amendment.

Affirmed.

[Separate opinion by JUSTICE WHITE and dissenting opinion by JUSTICE HARLAN are omitted.]

NOTES AND QUESTIONS

1.   What was the issue in *Brady*? What constitutional principle was established? Why did Brady himself not benefit from that principle?

2.   *Brady* is a seminal case: The term "*Brady* material" is often used to refer to exculpatory evidence that must be produced, and the term "*Brady* violation" is often used to refer to the breach of the prosecutor's obligation to produce exculpatory evidence. *See, e.g., Strickler v. Greene*, 527 U.S. 263, 280–81 (1999) (using both terms). Numerous defendants have obtained reversals of their convictions because of the prosecutor's failure to disclose exculpatory evidence. *See, e.g., Smith v. Cain*, 565 U.S. ___, 132 S. Ct. 627 (2012) (new trial required because of prosecutor's failure to disclose that the sole eyewitness against the defendant had previously told police he could not identify any of the perpetrators); *Kyles v. Whitley*, 514 U.S. 419, 434 (1995) (new trial required where prosecutor failed to disclose that a key witness against the defendant had changed his story numerous times during police interviews; Court held that a defendant need only show a " 'reasonable probability' of a different result" with the undisclosed evidence); *Giglio v. United States*, 405 U.S. 150 (1972) (new trial required because of prosecutor's failure to disclose that a key witness had been promised he would not be prosecuted in exchange for his testimony). Courts are especially vigilant in enforcing *Brady* when the prosecution knowingly or intentionally presents perjured evidence at trial. As the Supreme Court stated in *United States v. Agurs*, 427 U.S. 97, 120 (1976): "In cases in which 'the undisclosed evidence demonstrates that the prosecution's case includes perjured testimony and that the prosecution knew, or should have known, of the perjury,' the judgment of conviction must be set aside 'if there is *any reasonable likelihood* that the false testimony could have affected the judgment of the jury.' " (Emphasis added).

3.   *Brady* involved the withholding of exculpatory evidence by the prosecution. The Court did not hold that the government must *preserve* evidence that may be exculpatory or pay for testing to determine whether a particular piece of evidence is in fact exculpatory. For example, in *Arizona v. Youngblood*, 488 U.S. 51 (1988), clothing was gathered at the scene of a sexual assault but the clothes (containing samples of the assailant's semen) were not properly preserved in a refrigeration unit, resulting in an inability to conduct DNA (genetic) testing on the semen. The defendant was ultimately convicted at trial and appealed, claiming that the police had violated his *Brady* rights by not preserving the evidence. Despite the improper preservation of the potentially useful evidence, the Supreme Court declined to grant the defendant relief from his conviction. As the Court stated: "[U]nless a criminal defendant

can show bad faith on the part of the police, failure to preserve potentially useful evidence does not constitute a denial of due process of law." *Id.* at 58. Subsequently, in *District Attorney's Office for the Third Judicial District v. Osborne*, 557 U.S. 52 (2009), the Supreme Court held that a defendant had no federal due process right under *Brady* to obtain potentially exculpatory DNA evidence after a conviction. Many state statutes, however, have adopted criteria for defendants to seek DNA evidence post-conviction. *See, e.g., id.* at 70 (examining Alaska's law that provided a limited right of a defendant to obtain DNA evidence).

4.   Despite the Supreme Court's refusal to find a constitutional right to DNA evidence, there is no doubt that such evidence can be very powerful. For instance, the defendant in *Arizona v. Youngblood* was ultimately convicted at trial and sentenced to a lengthy prison term. More than a decade after the Supreme Court's ruling, however, attorneys from an organization called the Innocence Project convinced law enforcement to test the poorly preserved evidence using DNA testing methods that were unavailable at the time of Youngblood's conviction. The new results exonerated Youngblood, and he was released from prison. For a detailed discussion of the case, *see* Barbara Whitaker, *DNA Frees Inmate Years After Justices Rejected Plea*, N.Y. TIMES, Aug. 11, 2000, http://www.nytimes.com/2000/08/11/us/dna-frees-inmate-years-after-justices-rejected-plea.html. Youngblood's case is just one of more than 300 instances in which the Innocence Project has demonstrated, through DNA evidence, that a defendant was wrongfully convicted. For information about the Innocence Project, *see* http://www.innocenceproject.org.

5.   Many scholars have argued that the Supreme Court has not done enough to protect defendants' rights to utilize DNA evidence. *See, e.g.,* Jason Kreag, *Letting Innocence Suffer: The Need for Defense Access to the Law Enforcement DNA Database*, 36 Cardozo L. Rev. 805, 811 (2015) (arguing that due process "requires a limited procedural right for post-conviction defendants to access the law enforcement DNA database to prove their innocence"). Some scholars have criticized *Osborne* and have advocated for an extension of *Brady* to the post-conviction context. *See, e.g.,* Jeff Spahr, *Fundamental Injustice*: Osborne*'s Rejection of a Post-Conviction Application of the* Brady *Doctrine*, 21 Sum Kan. J.L. & Pub. Pol'y 450 (2012) (arguing that, given the documented cases of wrongful convictions, the *Brady* doctrine should be extended to the post-conviction context). Should a defendant have a constitutional right after his conviction to obtain DNA evidence? What arguments can be made against establishing such a right?

F. DEATH PENALTY (EIGHTH AMENDMENT)

The Eighth Amendment to the U.S. Constitution provides: "Excessive bail shall not be required, nor excessive fines imposed, nor cruel and unusual punishments inflicted." This section focuses on the prohibition against "cruel and unusual punishment" in the context of the death penalty.

ROPER V. SIMMONS

Supreme Court of the United States, 2005
543 U.S. 551

JUSTICE KENNEDY delivered the opinion of the Court.

This case requires us to address, for the second time * * * whether it is permissible under the Eighth and Fourteenth Amendments * * * to execute a juvenile offender who was older than 15 but younger than 18 when he committed a capital crime. In *Stanford v. Kentucky*, 492 U.S. 361 (1989), a divided Court rejected the proposition that the Constitution bars capital punishment for juvenile offenders in this age group. We reconsider the question.

I

At the age of 17, when he was still a junior in high school, Christopher Simmons, the respondent here, committed murder. About nine months later, after he had turned 18, he was tried and sentenced to death. There is little doubt that Simmons was the instigator of the crime. Before its commission Simmons said he wanted to murder someone. In chilling, callous terms he talked about his plan, discussing it for the most part with two friends, Charles Benjamin and John Tessmer, then aged 15 and 16 respectively. Simmons proposed to commit burglary and murder by breaking and entering, tying up a victim, and throwing the victim off a bridge. Simmons assured his friends they could "get away with it" because they were minors.

The three met at about 2 a.m. on the night of the murder, but Tessmer left before the other two set out. (The State later charged Tessmer with conspiracy, but dropped the charge in exchange for his testimony against Simmons.) Simmons and Benjamin entered the home of the victim, Shirley Crook, after reaching through an open window and unlocking the back door. Simmons turned on a hallway light. Awakened, Mrs. Crook called out, "Who's there?" In response Simmons entered Mrs. Crook's bedroom, where he recognized her from a previous car accident involving them both. Simmons later admitted this confirmed his resolve to murder her.

Using duct tape to cover her eyes and mouth and bind her hands, the two perpetrators put Mrs. Crook in her minivan and drove to a state park. They reinforced the bindings, covered her head with a towel, and walked her to a railroad trestle spanning the Meramec River. There they tied her hands and feet together with electrical wire, wrapped her whole face in duct tape and threw her from the bridge, drowning her in the waters below.

[The following afternoon], Steven Crook * * * returned home from an overnight trip, found his bedroom in disarray, and reported his wife missing. On the same afternoon fishermen recovered the victim's body from the river. Simmons, meanwhile, was bragging about the killing, telling friends he had killed a woman "because the bitch seen my face."

The next day, after receiving information of Simmons's involvement, police arrested him at his high school and took him to the police station in Fenton, Missouri. They read him his *Miranda* rights. Simmons waived his right to an attorney and agreed to answer questions. After less than two hours of interrogation, Simmons confessed to the murder and agreed to perform a videotaped reenactment at the crime scene.

The State charged Simmons with burglary, kidnaping, stealing, and murder in the first degree. As Simmons was 17 at the time of the crime, he was outside the criminal jurisdiction of Missouri's juvenile court system. He was tried as an adult. At trial the State introduced Simmons's confession and the videotaped reenactment of the crime, along with testimony that Simmons discussed the crime in advance and bragged about it later. The defense called no witnesses in the guilt phase. The jury having returned a verdict of murder, the trial proceeded to the penalty phase.

The State sought the death penalty. As aggravating factors, the State submitted that the murder was committed for the purpose of receiving money; was committed for the purpose of avoiding, interfering with, or preventing lawful arrest of the defendant; and involved depravity of mind and was outrageously and wantonly vile, horrible, and inhuman. The State called Shirley Crook's husband, daughter, and two sisters, who presented moving evidence of the devastation her death had brought to their lives.

In mitigation Simmons's attorneys first called an officer of the Missouri juvenile justice system, who testified that Simmons had no prior convictions and that no previous charges had been filed against him. Simmons's mother, father, two younger half brothers, a neighbor, and a friend took the stand to tell the jurors of the close relationships they had formed with Simmons and to plead for mercy on his behalf. Simmons's mother, in particular, testified to the responsibility Simmons demonstrated in taking care of his two younger half brothers and of his grandmother and to his capacity to show love for them.

During closing arguments, both the prosecutor and defense counsel addressed Simmons's age, which the trial judge had instructed the jurors they could consider as a mitigating factor. Defense counsel reminded the jurors that juveniles of Simmons's age cannot drink, serve on juries, or even see certain movies, because "the legislatures have wisely decided that individuals of a certain age aren't responsible enough." Defense counsel argued that Simmons's age should make "a huge difference to [the jurors] in deciding just exactly what sort of punishment to make." In rebuttal, the prosecutor gave the following response: "Age, he says. Think about age. Seventeen years old. Isn't that scary? Doesn't that scare you? Mitigating? Quite the contrary I submit. Quite the contrary."

The jury recommended the death penalty after finding the State had proved each of the three aggravating factors submitted to it. Accepting the jury's recommendation, the trial judge imposed the death penalty.

Simmons obtained new counsel, who moved in the trial court to set aside the conviction and sentence. One argument was that Simmons had received ineffective assistance at trial. * * *

* * *

The trial court found no constitutional violation by reason of ineffective assistance of counsel and denied the motion for postconviction relief. * * * [T]he Missouri Supreme Court affirmed. The federal courts denied Simmons's petition for a writ of habeas corpus.

After these proceedings * * * this Court held that the Eighth and Fourteenth Amendments prohibit the execution of a mentally retarded person. *Atkins v. Virginia*, 536 U.S. 304 (2002). Simmons filed a new petition for state postconviction relief, arguing that the reasoning of *Atkins* established that the Constitution prohibits the execution of a juvenile who was under 18 when the crime was committed.

The Missouri Supreme Court agreed. It * * * set aside Simmons's death sentence and resentenced him to "life imprisonment without eligibility for probation, parole, or release except by act of the Governor."

We granted certiorari and now affirm.

II

The Eighth Amendment * * * is applicable to the States through the Fourteenth Amendment. As the Court explained in *Atkins*, the Eighth Amendment guarantees individuals the right not to be subjected to excessive sanctions. The right flows from the basic " 'precept of justice that punishment for crime should be graduated and proportioned to [the] offense.' " * * *

The prohibition against "cruel and unusual punishments," like other expansive language in the Constitution, must be interpreted according to its text, by considering history, tradition, and precedent, and with due regard for its purpose and function in the constitutional design. To implement this framework we have established the propriety and affirmed the necessity of referring to "the evolving standards of decency that mark the progress of a maturing society" to determine which punishments are so disproportionate as to be cruel and unusual.

In *Thompson v. Oklahoma*, 487 U.S. 815 (1988), a plurality of the Court determined that our standards of decency do not permit the execution of any offender under the age of 16 at the time of the crime. * * *

* * * [T]he *Thompson* plurality stressed that "[t]he reasons why juveniles are not trusted with the privileges and responsibilities of an adult also explain why their irresponsible conduct is not as morally reprehensible as that of an adult." * * * With Justice O'CONNOR concurring in the

judgment on narrower grounds, the Court set aside the death sentence that had been imposed on the 15-year-old offender.

The next year, in *Stanford*, the Court * * * referred to contemporary standards of decency in this country and concluded the Eighth and Fourteenth Amendments did not proscribe the execution of juvenile offenders over 15 but under 18. The Court noted that 22 of the 37 death penalty States permitted the death penalty for 16-year-old offenders, and, among these 37 States, 25 permitted it for 17-year-old offenders. These numbers, in the Court's view, indicated there was no national consensus "sufficient to label a particular punishment cruel and unusual." * * *

* * *

* * * [W]e now reconsider the issue decided in *Stanford*. The beginning point is a review of objective indicia of consensus, as expressed in particular by the enactments of legislatures that have addressed the question. * * * We then must determine, in the exercise of our own independent judgment, whether the death penalty is a disproportionate punishment for juveniles.

III

A

The evidence of national consensus against the death penalty for juveniles is similar, and in some respects parallel, to the evidence *Atkins* held sufficient to demonstrate a national consensus against the death penalty for the mentally retarded. * * * In the present case, * * * even in the 20 States without a formal prohibition on executing juveniles, the practice is infrequent. Since *Stanford*, six States have executed prisoners for crimes committed as juveniles. In the past 10 years, only three have done so: Oklahoma, Texas, and Virginia. In December 2003 the Governor of Kentucky decided to spare the life of Kevin Stanford, and commuted his sentence to one of life imprisonment without parole, with the declaration that " '[w]e ought not be executing people who, legally, were children.' " By this act the Governor ensured Kentucky would not add itself to the list of States that have executed juveniles within the last 10 years even by the execution of the very defendant whose death sentence the Court had upheld in *Stanford*.

There is, to be sure, at least one difference between the evidence of consensus in *Atkins* and in this case. Impressive in *Atkins* was the rate of abolition of the death penalty for the mentally retarded. Sixteen States that permitted the execution of the mentally retarded * * * had prohibited the practice by the time we heard *Atkins*. By contrast, the rate of change in reducing the incidence of the juvenile death penalty, or in taking specific steps to abolish it, has been slower. Five States that allowed the juvenile death penalty at the time of *Stanford* have abandoned it in the intervening 15 years—four through legislative enactments and one through judicial decision.

* * * [W]e still consider the change from *Stanford* to this case to be significant. As noted in *Atkins*, with respect to the States that had abandoned the death penalty for the mentally retarded * * *, "[i]t is not so much the number of these States that is significant, but the consistency of the direction of change." * * * Since *Stanford*, no State that previously prohibited capital punishment for juveniles has reinstated it. This fact, coupled with the trend toward abolition of the juvenile death penalty, carries special force in light of the general popularity of anticrime legislation and in light of the particular trend in recent years toward cracking down on juvenile crime in other respects. Any difference between this case and *Atkins* with respect to the pace of abolition is thus counterbalanced by the consistent direction of the change.

The slower pace of abolition of the juvenile death penalty over the past 15 years, moreover, may have a simple explanation. * * * When we heard *Stanford*, * * * 12 death penalty States had already prohibited the execution of any juvenile under 18, and 15 had prohibited the execution of any juvenile under 17. If anything, this shows that the impropriety of executing juveniles between 16 and 18 years of age gained wide recognition earlier than the impropriety of executing the mentally retarded. * * *

* * *

As in *Atkins*, the objective indicia of consensus in this case * * * provide sufficient evidence that today our society views juveniles, in the words *Atkins* used respecting the mentally retarded, as "categorically less culpable than the average criminal."

B

A majority of States have rejected the imposition of the death penalty on juvenile offenders under 18, and we now hold this is required by the Eighth Amendment.

Because the death penalty is the most severe punishment, the Eighth Amendment applies to it with special force. Capital punishment must be limited to those offenders who commit "a narrow category of the most serious crimes" and whose extreme culpability makes them "the most deserving of execution." * * *

Three general differences between juveniles under 18 and adults demonstrate that juvenile offenders cannot with reliability be classified among the worst offenders. First, as any parent knows and as the scientific and sociological studies respondent and his *amici* cite tend to confirm, "[a] lack of maturity and an underdeveloped sense of responsibility are found in youth more often than in adults and are more understandable among the young. These qualities often result in impetuous and ill-considered actions and decisions." * * * In recognition of the comparative immaturity and irresponsibility of juveniles, almost every State prohibits those under

18 years of age from voting, serving on juries, or marrying without parental consent.

The second area of difference is that juveniles are more vulnerable or susceptible to negative influences and outside pressures, including peer pressure. This is explained in part by the prevailing circumstance that juveniles have less control, or less experience with control, over their own environment.

The third broad difference is that the character of a juvenile is not as well formed as that of an adult. The personality traits of juveniles are more transitory, less fixed.

These differences render suspect any conclusion that a juvenile falls among the worst offenders. The susceptibility of juveniles to immature and irresponsible behavior means "their irresponsible conduct is not as morally reprehensible as that of an adult." * * *

* * *

Once the diminished culpability of juveniles is recognized, it is evident that the penological justifications for the death penalty apply to them with lesser force than to adults. We have held there are two distinct social purposes served by the death penalty: " 'retribution and deterrence of capital crimes by prospective offenders.' " As for retribution, * * * the case * * * is not as strong with a minor as with an adult. Retribution is not proportional if the law's most severe penalty is imposed on one whose culpability or blameworthiness is diminished, to a substantial degree, by reason of youth and immaturity.

As for deterrence, it is unclear whether the death penalty has a significant or even measurable deterrent effect on juveniles * * *. Here, * * * the absence of evidence of deterrent effect is of special concern because the same characteristics that render juveniles less culpable than adults suggest as well that juveniles will be less susceptible to deterrence. In particular, * * * "[t]he likelihood that the teenage offender has made the kind of cost-benefit analysis that attaches any weight to the possibility of execution is so remote as to be virtually nonexistent." To the extent the juvenile death penalty might have residual deterrent effect, * * * the punishment of life imprisonment without the possibility of parole is itself a severe sanction, in particular for a young person.

* * * [P]etitioner and his *amici* * * * assert that * * * jurors * * * should be allowed to consider mitigating arguments related to youth on a case-by-case basis, and in some cases to impose the death penalty if justified. * * *

We disagree. The differences between juvenile and adult offenders are too marked and well understood to risk allowing a youthful person to receive the death penalty despite insufficient culpability. An unacceptable likelihood exists that the brutality or cold-blooded nature of any particular crime would overpower mitigating arguments based on youth as a matter of course, even where the juvenile offender's objective immaturity, vulnerability, and lack of true depravity should require a sentence less severe than death. * * *

It is difficult even for expert psychologists to differentiate between the juvenile offender whose crime reflects unfortunate yet transient immaturity, and the rare juvenile offender whose crime reflects irreparable corruption. * * * If trained psychiatrists * * * refrain, despite diagnostic expertise, from assessing any juvenile under 18 as having antisocial personality disorder, we conclude that States should refrain from asking jurors to issue a far graver condemnation—that a juvenile offender merits the death penalty. * * *

Drawing the line at 18 years of age is subject, of course, to the objections always raised against categorical rules. The qualities that distinguish juveniles from adults do not disappear when an individual turns 18. By the same token, some under 18 have already attained a level of maturity some adults will never reach. For the reasons we have discussed, however, a line must be drawn. * * * The age of 18 is the point where society draws the line for many purposes between childhood and adulthood. It is, we conclude, the age at which the line for death eligibility ought to rest.

* * *

IV

Our determination that the death penalty is disproportionate punishment for offenders under 18 finds confirmation in the stark reality that the United States is the only country in the world that continues to give official sanction to the juvenile death penalty. * * *

* * *

It is proper that we acknowledge the overwhelming weight of international opinion against the juvenile death penalty * * *. The opinion of the world community, while not controlling our outcome, does provide respected and significant confirmation for our own conclusions.

* * *

The Eighth and Fourteenth Amendments forbid imposition of the death penalty on offenders who were under the age of 18 when their crimes were committed. The judgment of the Missouri Supreme Court setting aside the sentence of death imposed upon Christopher Simmons is affirmed.

It is so ordered.

[Concurring opinion by JUSTICE STEVENS is omitted.]

[Dissenting opinion by JUSTICE O'CONNER is omitted.]

JUSTICE SCALIA, with whom THE CHIEF JUSTICE and JUSTICE THOMAS join, dissenting.

* * * [T]oday's opinion announc[es] the Court's conclusion that the meaning of our Constitution has changed over the past 15 years—not, mind you, that this Court's decision 15 years ago was *wrong*, but that the Constitution *has changed.* * * * Because I do not believe that the meaning of our Eighth Amendment, any more than the meaning of other provisions of our Constitution, should be determined by the subjective views of five Members of this Court and like-minded foreigners, I dissent.

I

In determining that capital punishment of offenders who committed murder before age 18 is "cruel and unusual" under the Eighth Amendment, the Court first considers * * * whether there is a "national consensus" that laws allowing such executions contravene our modern "standards of decency." We have held that this determination should be based on "objective indicia that reflect the public attitude toward a given sanction"— namely, "statutes passed by society's elected representatives." * * *

Words have no meaning if the views of less than 50% of death penalty States can constitute a national consensus. Our previous cases have required overwhelming opposition to a challenged practice, generally over a long period of time. * * *

In an attempt to keep afloat its implausible assertion of national consensus, the Court throws overboard a proposition well established in our Eighth Amendment jurisprudence. "It should be observed," the Court says, "that * * * a State's decision to bar the death penalty altogether of necessity demonstrates a judgment that the death penalty is inappropriate for all offenders, including juveniles." * * * [This] is misleading. *None* of our cases dealing with an alleged constitutional limitation upon the death penalty has counted, as States supporting a consensus in favor of that limitation, States that have eliminated the death penalty entirely. And with good reason. * * * That 12 States favor *no* executions says something about consensus against the death penalty, but nothing—absolutely nothing—about consensus that offenders under 18 deserve special immunity from such a penalty. * * *

[In addition,] * * * the Court says a legislative change in four States is "significant" enough to trigger a constitutional prohibition. It is amazing to think that this subtle shift in numbers can take the issue entirely off the table for legislative debate.

I also doubt whether many of the legislators who voted to change the laws in those four States would have done so if they had known their decision would (by the pronouncement of this Court) be rendered irreversible. * * *

Relying on such narrow margins is especially inappropriate in light of the fact that a number of legislatures and voters have expressly affirmed their support for capital punishment of 16- and 17-year-old offenders since *Stanford* [*v. Kentucky*, 492 U.S. 361 (1989)]. Though the Court is correct that no State has lowered its death penalty age, both the Missouri and Virginia Legislatures—which, at the time of *Stanford*, had no minimum age requirement—expressly established 16 as the minimum. The people of Arizona and Florida have done the same by ballot initiative. Thus, even States that have not executed an under-18 offender in recent years unquestionably favor the possibility of capital punishment in some circumstances.

The Court's reliance on the infrequency of executions for under-18 murderers credits an argument that this Court considered and explicitly rejected in *Stanford*. That infrequency is explained, we accurately said, both by "the undisputed fact that a far smaller percentage of capital crimes are committed by persons under 18 than over 18," and by the fact that juries are required at sentencing to consider the offender's youth as a mitigating factor. * * *

It is, furthermore, unclear that executions of the relevant age group have decreased since we decided *Stanford*. * * * [T]he numbers of under-18 offenders subjected to the death penalty, though low compared with adults, have either held steady or slightly increased since *Stanford*. [The] statistics in no way support the action the Court takes today.

II

Of course, the real force driving today's decision is not the actions of four state legislatures, but the Court's "own judgment" that murderers younger than 18 can never be as morally culpable as older counterparts. * * * But the Court having pronounced that the Eighth Amendment is an ever-changing reflection of "the evolving standards of decency" of our society, it makes no sense for the Justices then to *prescribe* those standards rather than discern them from the practices of our people. * * * By what conceivable warrant can nine lawyers presume to be the authoritative conscience of the Nation?

The reason for insistence on legislative primacy is obvious and fundamental: " '[I]n a democratic society legislatures, not courts, are constituted to respond to the will and consequently the moral values of the people.' " * * *

Today's opinion provides a perfect example of why judges are ill equipped to make the type of legislative judgments the Court insists on making here. To support its opinion that States should be prohibited from imposing the death penalty on anyone who committed murder before age

18, the Court looks to scientific and sociological studies, picking and choosing those that support its position. It never explains why those particular studies are methodologically sound; none was ever entered into evidence or tested in an adversarial proceeding. * * *

* * *

We need not look far to find studies contradicting the Court's conclusions. * * * [T]he American Psychological Association (APA), which claims in this case that scientific evidence shows persons under 18 lack the ability to take moral responsibility for their decisions, has previously taken precisely the opposite position before this very Court. * * * Given the nuances of scientific methodology and conflicting views, courts * * * are ill equipped to determine which view of science is the right one. Legislatures "are better qualified to weigh and 'evaluate the results of statistical studies in terms of their own local conditions and with a flexibility of approach that is not available to the courts.' "

Even putting aside questions of methodology, the studies cited by the Court offer scant support for a categorical prohibition of the death penalty for murderers under 18. At most, these studies conclude that, *on average*, or *in most cases*, persons under 18 are unable to take moral responsibility for their actions. Not one of the cited studies opines that all individuals under 18 are unable to appreciate the nature of their crimes.

* * *

That "almost every State prohibits those under 18 years of age from voting, serving on juries, or marrying without parental consent" is patently irrelevant * * *. [I]t is "absurd to think that one must be mature enough to drive carefully, to drink responsibly, or to vote intelligently, in order to be mature enough to understand that murdering another human being is profoundly wrong, and to conform one's conduct to that most minimal of all civilized standards." * * *

Moreover, the age statutes the Court lists "set the appropriate ages for the operation of a system that makes its determinations in gross, and that does not conduct individualized maturity tests." The criminal justice system, by contrast, provides for individualized consideration of each defendant. In capital cases, this Court requires the sentencer to make an individualized determination, which includes weighing aggravating factors and mitigating factors, such as youth. * * *

The Court concludes, however, that juries cannot be trusted with the delicate task of weighing a defendant's youth along with the other mitigating and aggravating factors of his crime. This startling conclusion undermines the very foundations of our capital sentencing system, which entrusts juries with "mak[ing] the difficult and uniquely human judgments that defy codification and that 'buil[d] discretion, equity, and flexibility into a legal system.' " * * *

Nor does the Court suggest a stopping point for its reasoning. If juries cannot make appropriate determinations in cases involving murderers under 18, in what other kinds of cases will the Court find jurors deficient? * * *

The Court's contention that the goals of retribution and deterrence are not served by executing murderers under 18 is also transparently false[, as the] facts of this very case show * * *. Before committing the crime, Simmons encouraged his friends to join him by assuring them that they could "get away with it" because they were minors. This fact may have influenced the jury's decision to impose capital punishment despite Simmons's age. * * *

III

Though the views of our own citizens are essentially irrelevant to the Court's decision today, the views of other countries and the so-called international community take center stage.

* * *

* * * [T]he basic premise of the Court's argument—that American law should conform to the laws of the rest of the world—ought to be rejected out of hand. In fact the Court itself does not believe it. In many significant respects the laws of most other countries differ from our law—including not only such explicit provisions of our Constitution as the right to jury trial and grand jury indictment, but even many interpretations of the Constitution prescribed by this Court itself. * * * England, for example, rarely excludes [illegally seized] evidence found during an illegal search or seizure and has only recently begun excluding evidence from illegally obtained confessions. Canada rarely excludes evidence and will only do so if admission will "bring the administration of justice into disrepute." The European Court of Human Rights has held that introduction of illegally seized evidence does not violate the "fair trial" requirement * * * of the European Convention on Human Rights.

* * * [Moreover], [m]ost other countries—including those committed to religious neutrality—do not insist on the degree of separation between church and state that this Court requires [under the First Amendment]. * * *

And let us not forget the Court's abortion jurisprudence, which makes us one of only six countries that allow abortion on demand until the point of viability. * * *

* * *

The Court should either profess its willingness to reconsider all these matters in light of the views of foreigners, or else it should cease putting forth foreigners' views as part of the *reasoned basis* of its decisions. * * *

* * *

NOTES AND QUESTIONS

1.   What was the majority's rationale in concluding that the execution of juveniles violates the Eighth Amendment's prohibition on cruel and unusual punishment?

2.   In his dissent, Justice Scalia expressed concerns over the majority's use of international law in its analysis of U.S. law. Are his concerns justified? Do Justice Scalia's other criticisms of the majority opinion have merit?

3.   Is the Court's bright-line rule prohibiting the execution of individuals who were under the age of 18 at the time of their capital crime a sensible one? Is a 17-year-old individual any less culpable in terms of capital punishment than an individual who is merely a matter of months, or even days, older at the time he committed their crime?

4.   Is the *Roper* Court's bright-line rule preferable to a rule that considers the maturity of the defendant on an individual basis? If a case-by-case inquiry regarding maturity is preferable, how would the courts ensure consistency from case to case?

5.   In *Atkins v. Virginia*, 536 U.S. 304 (2002), a case discussed in *Roper*, the Supreme Court held that the execution of mentally disabled individuals violated the Eighth Amendment's ban on cruel and unusual punishment. As the Court reasoned: "[T]here is a serious question as to whether either justification that we have recognized as a basis for the death penalty[— retribution and deterrence of capital crimes—]applies to mentally retarded offenders." *Id.* at 318–19. The Court continued: "If the culpability of the average murderer is insufficient to justify the [death penalty], the lesser culpability of the mentally retarded offender surely does not merit that form of retribution." *Id.* at 319. As in *Roper*, the Supreme Court analyzed the current law among the states and concluded: "Construing and applying the Eighth Amendment in the light of our 'evolving standards of decency,' we therefore conclude that such punishment is excessive and that the Constitution 'places a substantive restriction on the State's power to take the life' of a mentally retarded offender." *Id.* at 321. Is the Court correct in holding that execution of a mentally disabled defendant is *per se* cruel and unusual punishment?

In *Brumfield v. Cain*, 576 U.S. ___, 135 S. Ct. 2269 (2015), the Supreme Court reinforced its decision in *Atkins*. It held that if there is any reasonable doubt regarding the defendant's intellectual competency, the defendant is entitled to an evidentiary hearing for the court to determine whether the defendant can satisfy an *Atkins* claim to preclude the death penalty. In *Brumfield*, the defendant submitted an IQ score of 75 to the trial court and asked the court to hold a hearing to determine whether he was mentally disabled (and thus not a candidate for the death penalty). Brumfield's IQ score was on the margin of mental disability, but the trial court denied the claim without holding an evidentiary hearing on the issue of his mental disability. In defendant's post-conviction attack, the Supreme Court held that because

Brumfield's IQ score was on the margin of disability, Brumfield had satisfied the "reasonable doubt" standard and was entitled to an evidentiary hearing to assess the merits of his *Atkins* claim.

6. In *McCleskey v. Kemp*, 481 U.S. 279 (1987), a black defendant was convicted of murdering a white police officer and was sentenced to death. In attempting to overturn his death sentence, McCleskey provided extensive statistical research indicating that black defendants who kill white victims are most likely to receive the death penalty. McCleskey contended that this disparity violated his Fourteenth Amendment right to equal protection as well as the Eighth Amendment's ban on cruel and unusual punishment. The Supreme Court disagreed, holding that McCleskey did not present a valid equal protection issue because he failed to establish that any of the decision-makers in his particular case acted with a discriminatory purpose. Moreover, McCleskey could not demonstrate an Eighth Amendment violation because the studies he produced merely showed a correlation with race, and thus did not rise to the level of unconstitutional racial bias in the death penalty process. There were three dissenting opinions in *McCleskey*, all of which expressed concerns that statistical research demonstrated a clear pattern of differential treatment in imposing the death penalty on the basis of race and that there was a significant risk that McCleskey's death sentence was imposed as a result of racial prejudice.

7. The Supreme Court has not only faced constitutional issues regarding *when* the death penalty may be imposed, but also *how* the death penalty can be carried out. For example, in *Glossip v. Gross*, 576 U.S. ___, 135 S. Ct. 2726 (2015), several death-row inmates who were facing the death penalty filed a lawsuit alleging that Oklahoma's lethal injection protocol created an unacceptable risk of severe pain that constituted cruel and unusual punishment in violation of Eighth Amendment. The Supreme Court upheld the lethal injection protocol, and reasoned that there was insufficient evidence to show that Oklahoma's injection protocol entailed a higher risk of severe pain than any known and available alternatives. Quoting prior precedent, the Court reasoned: "[P]risoners 'cannot successfully challenge a State's method of execution merely by showing a slightly or marginally safer alternative.' Instead, prisoners must identify an alternative that is 'feasible, readily implemented, and in fact significantly reduce[s] a substantial risk of severe pain.'" *Id.* at 2737. Accordingly, the Court held that the specific injection protocol did not constitute cruel and unusual punishment.

8. Some scholars believe it possible—or even likely—that the Supreme Court will ultimately abolish the death penalty. *See, e.g.*, Jordan Steiker, *The American Death Penalty: Constitutional Regulation as the Distinctive Feature of American Exceptionalism*, 67 U. Miami L. Rev. 329 (2013) (noting that a decision invalidating the death penalty is quite possible now that the death penalty has been so heavily eroded by both judicial and legislative restrictions). In that regard, even some states that have traditionally been categorized as "conservative" with respect to the death penalty have recently shown movement. For example, the State of Nebraska passed legislation in 2015

abolishing the death penalty within the state. *See, e.g.*, Mark Berman, *Nebraska Lawmakers Abolish the Death Penalty, Narrowly Overriding Governor's Veto*, WASH. POST, May 27, 2015, http://www.washingtonpost.com/ news/post-nation/wp/2015/05/27/nebraska-lawmakers-officially-abolish-the-death-penalty/.

Indeed, at least two sitting Justices seem prepared to declare the death penalty unconstitutional in all circumstances. As Justice Breyer, joined by Justice Ginsburg, stated in a dissenting opinion in *Glossip v. Gross, supra*:

> The [problems associated with the death penalty], such as lack of reliability, the arbitrary application of a serious and irreversible punishment, individual suffering caused by long delays, and lack of penological purpose, are quintessentially judicial matters. They concern the infliction—indeed the unfair, cruel, and unusual infliction—of a serious punishment upon an individual. I recognize that in 1972 this Court, in a sense, turned to Congress and the state legislatures in its search for standards that would increase the fairness and reliability of imposing a death penalty. The legislatures responded. But, in the last four decades, considerable evidence has accumulated that those responses have not worked.

> * * * The Eighth Amendment sets forth the relevant law, and we must interpret that law. * * *

> * * * I believe it highly likely that the death penalty violates the Eighth Amendment. At the very least, the Court should call for full briefing on the basic question.

135 S. Ct. at 2776–77 (Breyer, J., dissenting).

9.   It is important to note that the Eighth Amendment applies to *any* form of punishment the government imposes. Accordingly, some forms of punishment other than the death penalty have been called into question as "cruel and unusual." For example, the Supreme Court has held that the Eighth Amendment prohibits sentencing a juvenile offender to life in prison without the possibility of parole. *Miller v. Alabama*, 567 U.S. ___, 132 S. Ct. 2455 (2012). The *Miller* Court reasoned that, because juveniles have diminished culpability and greater prospects for reform, they are less suitable candidates for the most severe punishments.

In *Davis v. Ayala*, 576 U.S. ___, 135 S. Ct. 2187 (2015), some members of the Supreme Court debated the constitutionality of a form of punishment involving prolonged periods of solitary confinement. The issue before the Court was unrelated to the topic of solitary confinement, but in a concurring opinion Justice Kennedy raised constitutional concerns over the practice, stating: "[I]t is likely respondent has been held for all or most of the past 20 years or more in a windowless cell no larger than a typical parking spot for 23 hours a day; and in the one hour when he leaves it, he likely is allowed little or no opportunity for conversation or interaction with anyone." *Id.* at 2208 (Kennedy, J., concurring). Justice Kennedy remarked: "Years on end of near-total isolation exact a terrible price." *Id.* at 2210. As Justice Kennedy concluded: "In a case that presented the issue, the judiciary may be required, within its proper jurisdiction and authority, to determine whether workable alternative systems for long-term confinement exist * * *." *Id.* Justice Thomas responded to Justice Kennedy's statements, noting that "the accommodations in which Ayala is housed are a far sight more spacious than those in which his victims * * * now rest." *Id.* (Thomas, J., concurring). The Court has not yet ruled directly on the practice of solitary confinement in the context of the Eighth Amendment.

G. ADDITIONAL TOPICS OF INTEREST

In addition to the topics covered in detail in this chapter, the following topics are frequently addressed in an introductory criminal procedure course.

a. Right to Speedy Trial (Sixth Amendment): The Sixth Amendment guarantees that in all criminal prosecutions, the accused shall enjoy the right to a "speedy trial." For example, in *Doggett v. United States*, 505 U.S. 647 (1992), the Supreme Court held that a delay of 8 ½ years between a defendant's indictment and arrest violated his Sixth Amendment right to a speedy trial when the government could not justify the delay. Although there is no bright-line rule for when a defendant's case must be tried, the Supreme Court has articulated four factors that courts should weigh in evaluating a speedy trial claim: "[W]hether delay before trial was uncommonly long, whether the government or the criminal defendant is more to blame for that delay, whether, in due course, the defendant asserted his right to a speedy trial, and whether he suffered prejudice as the delay's result." *Id.* at 651. If a defendant's right to a speedy trial has been violated, the case is dismissed with prejudice (*i.e.*, the case can never be brought again).

In addition to the speedy trial protections granted by the Sixth Amendment, in 1974 Congress enacted the Speedy Trial Act (18 U.S.C. §§ 3161–3174), which provides that a defendant charged with a federal crime must be brought to trial within 70 days after his initial appearance in court or within 70 days from the date the government files an indictment (whichever occurs later). Although the statute appears to provide a simple rule, many specified periods are excluded from the 70-day period, such as time spent litigating pre-trial motions or an interlocutory appeal (an appeal that occurs prior to trial). *See* 18 U.S.C. § 3161(h). Consequently, establishing a violation can be difficult and complicated. Moreover, unlike the Sixth Amendment right to a speedy trial, the Speedy Trial Act states that upon a violation, a court may (in its discretion) dismiss with *or without* prejudice (meaning the case may be filed again). In addition to the federal right, state criminal courts may also have their own statutory rules regarding speedy trial rights.

b. Confrontation Clause (Sixth Amendment): The Sixth Amendment guarantees that in all criminal prosecutions, the accused shall enjoy the right to be "confronted with the witnesses against him." In *Crawford v. Washington*, 541 U.S. 36 (2004), the Supreme Court articulated the general Confrontation Clause rule that testimony by witnesses against the defendant must be normally made on the witness stand at trial. Unless the witness is unavailable and the defendant had a prior opportunity for cross-examination, the prosecution may not introduce recorded or written statements from a witness that were made outside of the courtroom. Instead, the prosecution must produce that witness to testify and be subject to cross-examination at trial. It is important to note, however, that this confrontation right only applies to *testimonial statements*. Perhaps the easiest way to define a "testimonial statement" is the formulation in *Crawford* that such a statement is one made " 'under circumstances which would lead an objective witness reasonably to believe that the statement would be available for use at a later trial.' " *Id.* at 52. *Crawford* held that the admission of a tape-recorded statement that the defendant's wife made to police—that a stabbing committed by the defendant was not done in self-defense—violated the Confrontation Clause. The defendant's wife did not testify at trial because of the State of Washington's marital privilege, and the defendant did not have a prior opportunity to cross-examine her. The Court held that the statement was testimonial because the defendant's wife would have reasonably believed that the statement would be used against the defendant at his trial. *See also, e.g., Bullcoming v. New Mexico*, 564 U.S. ___, 131 S. Ct. 2705 (2011) (holding that a blood-alcohol test that was admitted to demonstrate the defendant's level of intoxication in a drunk driving case was a testimonial report against the defendant that required confrontation of the analyst who conducted the testing); *Melendez-Diaz v. Massachusetts*, 557 U.S. 305 (2009) (holding that a state forensic analyst's lab report finding that a substance was cocaine was a testimonial report prepared specifically for use in a criminal prosecution for drug charges and, therefore, confrontation of the lab analyst was required).

In a number of circumstances, however, the Supreme Court has rejected Confrontation Clause arguments, finding that the statements at issue were not testimonial statements. *See, e.g., Ohio v. Clark*, 576 U.S. ___, 135 S. Ct. 2173 (2015) (holding that a three-year-old victim's statements to his preschool teachers regarding alleged abuse that the defendant had committed against him were non-testimonial (and thus not subject to confrontation) because they were made with the primary purpose of addressing an ongoing emergency of child abuse, not to prove the guilt of the defendant during a later prosecution); *Michigan v. Bryant*, 562 U.S. 344 (2011) (holding that a witness' identification and description of a shooter on the loose and the location of the shooting were non-testimonial (and thus not subject to confrontation) because their primary purpose was to enable the police to investigate an ongoing emergency, not to prove the guilt of the defendant during a later prosecution); *Davis v. Washington*, 547

U.S. 813 (2006) (holding that a witness' statements made during a 911 call to report domestic violence were non-testimonial (and thus not subject to confrontation) because the statements were intended to help the police resolve an ongoing emergency).

    c.   **Plea Bargaining:** Plea bargaining (mentioned at various points in this chapter) is a critical part of the criminal process. In the United States, the vast majority of criminal cases never go to trial; rather, the prosecution and the defense "bargain" on specific terms of the crime (and sometimes on the recommended sentence). For instance, if a defendant is charged with 10 separate felonies, he might agree to plead guilty to one felony in exchange for dismissal of the other nine. As noted by the Supreme Court in *Lafler v. Cooper*, 566 U.S. ___, 132 S. Ct. 1376, 1388 (2012): "Ninety-seven percent of federal convictions and ninety-four percent of state convictions are the result of guilty pleas." In a seminal plea bargaining case, *Brady v. United States*, 397 U.S. 742, 758 (1970), the Supreme Court held that a guilty plea that is "voluntarily and intelligently made" is an acceptable means of resolving a criminal case. In *Brady*, the Court held that even though Brady's guilty plea may have been motivated in part by a desire to avoid the death penalty, that fact did not render the plea involuntary. Prosecutors and defendants have broad discretion in what pleas they may agree to, but the court must always evaluate the totality of the circumstances to determine whether the defendant voluntarily and intelligently agreed to the plea.

    As *Brady* indicated, the prosecution is entitled to use negotiation tactics and bargaining leverage in an effort to entice the defendant to plead guilty. The Supreme Court later reaffirmed that principle in *Bordenkircher v. Hayes*, 434 U.S. 357 (1978). In the case, the defendant was charged with a felony offense that could have resulted in his incarceration for life (because of the defendant's prior criminal record). The prosecutor offered to recommend a five-year prison sentence to the court if the defendant agreed to plead guilty to the crime. If the defendant declined the offer to plead guilty, however, the prosecutor informed him that he would seek a life sentence upon conviction. The defendant declined to accept the offer and was ultimately convicted of the crime and sentenced to life in prison. The defendant challenged the conviction, and argued that the prosecutor's negotiating tactics violated the Due Process Clause of the Fourteenth Amendment. The Supreme Court held that, although the prosecutor engaged in a tough negotiating strategy, the strategy did not violate the defendant's due process rights.

    d.   **Eyewitness Identifications:** Eyewitness identifications of a suspect, both before and during trial, often play a significant role in the outcome of a case. Eyewitness testimony identifying the defendant as the perpetrator of a crime can often be powerful evidence to the jury. The reliability of this type of evidence, however, has been called into question.

See, e.g., The Innocence Project, *The Causes of Wrongful Conviction,* http://www.innocenceproject.org/causes-wrongful-conviction (noting that eyewitness misidentification was a contributing cause of wrongful conviction in more than 70 percent of cases where the defendant was later exonerated). Because of the potential for misidentification, the Supreme Court has addressed the issue of when a witness's identification should not be admitted at trial. In *Manson v. Brathwaite,* 432 U.S. 98, 114 (1977), the Court held:

> * * * [R]eliability is the linchpin in determining the admissibility of identification testimony * * *. [The factors for reliability] include the opportunity of the witness to view the criminal at the time of the crime, the witness' degree of attention, the accuracy of his prior description of the criminal, the level of certainty demonstrated at the confrontation, and the time between the crime and the confrontation. Against these factors is to be weighed the corrupting effect of the suggestive identification itself.

As the Supreme Court later stated in *Perry v. New Hampshire,* 576 U.S. ___, 132 S. Ct. 716, 720 (2012):

> [T]he trial judge must screen the evidence for reliability pretrial. If there is "a very substantial likelihood of irreparable misidentification," the judge must disallow presentation of the evidence at trial. But if the indicia of reliability are strong enough to outweigh the corrupting effect of the police-arranged suggestive circumstances, the identification evidence ordinarily will be admitted, and the jury will ultimately determine its worth.

CHAPTER 8

CRIMINAL LAW

■ ■ ■

Criminal law concerns governmental actions against defendants who are alleged to have committed crimes. A host of issues arise in a criminal law course, including the burden of proof, the requisite criminal intent, and elements of specific criminal offenses. The following sections discuss several of these issues.

A. REASONABLE DOUBT STANDARD

To convict an individual of a crime, the factfinder must find the person guilty "beyond a reasonable doubt." This is a high standard of proof that recognizes the serious consequences of a criminal conviction. The following case discusses that standard and whether it should apply to prosecutions of juvenile defendants.

IN RE WINSHIP
Supreme Court of the United States, 1970
397 U.S. 358

JUSTICE BRENNAN delivered the opinion of the Court.

Constitutional questions decided by this Court concerning the juvenile process have centered on the adjudicatory stage at "which a determination is made as to whether a juvenile is a 'delinquent' as a result of alleged misconduct on his part, with the consequence that he may be committed to a state institution." *In re Gault*, 387 U.S. 1, 13 (1967). *Gault* decided that, although the Fourteenth Amendment does not require that the hearing at this stage conform with all the requirements of a criminal trial or even of the usual administrative proceeding, the Due Process Clause does require application during the adjudicatory hearing of "the essentials of due process and fair treatment." This case presents the single, narrow question whether proof beyond a reasonable doubt is among the "essentials of due process and fair treatment" required during the adjudicatory stage when a juvenile is charged with an act which would constitute a crime if committed by an adult.

Section 712 of the New York Family Court Act defines a juvenile delinquent as "a person over seven and less than sixteen years of age who does any act which, if done by an adult, would constitute a crime." During a 1967 adjudicatory hearing, conducted pursuant to § 742 of the Act, a judge in New York Family Court found that appellant, then a 12-year-old boy, had entered a locker and stolen $112 from a woman's pocketbook. The petition which charged appellant with delinquency alleged that his act, "if done by an adult, would constitute the crime or crimes of Larceny." The judge acknowledged that the proof might not establish guilt beyond a reasonable doubt, but rejected appellant's contention that such proof was required by the Fourteenth Amendment. The judge relied instead on § 744(b) of the New York Family Court Act which provides that "[a]ny determination at the conclusion of [an adjudicatory] hearing that a [juvenile] did an act or acts must be based on a preponderance of the evidence." During a subsequent dispositional hearing, appellant was ordered placed in a training school for an initial period of 18 months, subject to annual extensions of his commitment until his 18th birthday— six years in appellant's case. [Both the intermediate appellate court and New York's highest court affirmed.] * * * We reverse.

I

The requirement that guilt of a criminal charge be established by proof beyond a reasonable doubt dates at least from our early years as a Nation. The "demand for a higher degree of persuasion in criminal cases was recurrently expressed from ancient times, [though] its crystallization into the formula 'beyond a reasonable doubt' seems to have occurred as late as 1798. It is now accepted in common law jurisdictions as the measure of persuasion by which the prosecution must convince the trier of all the essential elements of guilt." Although virtually unanimous adherence to the reasonable-doubt standard in common-law jurisdictions may not conclusively establish it as a requirement of due process, such adherence does "reflect a profound judgment about the way in which law should be enforced and justice administered."

Expressions in many opinions of this Court indicate that it has long been assumed that proof of a criminal charge beyond a reasonable doubt is constitutionally required. * * *

The reasonable-doubt standard plays a vital role in the American scheme of criminal procedure. It is a prime instrument for reducing the risk of convictions resting on factual error. The standard provides concrete substance for the presumption of innocence—that bedrock "axiomatic and elementary" principle whose "enforcement lies at the foundation of the administration of our criminal law." * * *

The requirement of proof beyond a reasonable doubt has this vital role in our criminal procedure for cogent reasons. The accused during a criminal prosecution has at stake interest of immense importance, both because of the possibility that he may lose his liberty upon conviction and because of the certainty that he would be stigmatized by the conviction. Accordingly, a society that values the good name and freedom of every individual should not condemn a man for commission of a crime when there is reasonable doubt about his guilt. * * * [T]he reasonable-doubt standard is indispensable, for it "impresses on the trier of fact the necessity of reaching a subjective state of certitude of the facts in issue."

Moreover, use of the reasonable-doubt standard is indispensable to command the respect and confidence of the community in applications of the criminal law. It is critical that the moral force of the criminal law not be diluted by a standard of proof that leaves people in doubt whether innocent men are being condemned. It is also important in our free society that every individual going about his ordinary affairs have confidence that his government cannot adjudge him guilty of a criminal offense without convincing a proper factfinder of his guilt with utmost certainty.

Lest there remain any doubt about the constitutional stature of the reasonable-doubt standard, we explicitly hold that the Due Process Clause protects the accused against conviction except upon proof beyond a reasonable doubt of every fact necessary to constitute the crime with which he is charged.

II

We turn to the question whether juveniles, like adults, are constitutionally entitled to proof beyond a reasonable doubt when they are charged with violation of a criminal law. The same considerations that demand extreme caution in factfinding to protect the innocent adult apply as well to the innocent child. * * * We made clear in * * * [*Gault*] that civil labels and good intentions do not themselves obviate the need for criminal due process safeguards in juvenile courts, for "[a] proceeding where the issue is whether the child will be found to be 'delinquent' and subjected to the loss of his liberty for years is comparable in seriousness to a felony prosecution."

Nor do we perceive any merit in the argument that to afford juveniles the protection of proof beyond a reasonable doubt would risk destruction of beneficial aspects of the juvenile process. Use of the reasonable-doubt standard during the adjudicatory hearing will not disturb New York's policies that a finding that a child has violated a criminal law does not constitute a criminal conviction, that such a finding does not deprive the child of his civil rights, and that juvenile proceedings are confidential. Nor will there be any effect on the informality, flexibility, or speed of the hearing at which the factfinding takes place. And the opportunity during the post-adjudicatory or dispositional hearing for a wide-ranging review of the child's social history and for his individualized treatment will remain unimpaired. Similarly, there will be no effect on the procedures distinctive to juvenile proceedings that are employed prior to the adjudicatory hearing.

The Court of Appeals observed that "a child's best interest is not necessarily, or even probably, promoted if he wins in the particular inquiry which may bring him to the juvenile court." It is true, of course, that the juvenile may be engaging in a general course of conduct inimical to his welfare that calls for judicial intervention. But that intervention cannot take the form of subjecting the child to the stigma of a finding that he violated a criminal law and to the possibility of institutional confinement on proof insufficient to convict him were he an adult.

* * * [T]he observance of the standard of proof beyond a reasonable doubt "will not compel the States to abandon or displace any of the substantive benefits of the juvenile process."

Finally, we reject the Court of Appeals' suggestion that there is, in any event, only a "tenuous difference" between the reasonable-doubt and preponderance standards. The suggestion is singularly unpersuasive. In this very case, the trial judge's ability to distinguish between the two standards enabled him to make a finding of guilt that he conceded he might not have made under the standard of proof beyond a reasonable doubt. Indeed, the trial judge's action evidences the accuracy of the observation of commentators that "the preponderance test is susceptible to the misinterpretation that it calls on the trier of fact merely to perform an abstract weighing of the evidence in order to determine which side has produced the greater quantum, without regard to its effect in convincing his mind of the truth of the proposition asserted."

III

In sum, the constitutional safeguard of proof beyond a reasonable doubt is as much required during the adjudicatory stage of a delinquency proceeding as are those constitutional safeguards applied in *Gault*—notice of charges, right to counsel, the rights of confrontation and examination, and the privilege against self-incrimination. We therefore hold * * * "that, where a 12-year-old child is charged with an act of stealing which renders him liable to confinement for as long as six years, then, as a matter of due process * * * the case against him must be proved beyond a reasonable doubt."

Reversed.

JUSTICE HARLAN, concurring.

No one * * * would contend that state juvenile court trials are subject to no federal constitutional limitations. Differences have existed, however, among the members of this Court as to what constitutional protections do apply.

The present case draws in question the validity of a New York statute that permits a determination of juvenile delinquency, founded on a charge of criminal conduct, to be made on a standard of proof that is less rigorous than that which would obtain had the accused been tried for the same conduct in an ordinary criminal case. While I am in full agreement that this statutory provision offends the requirement of fundamental fairness embodied in the Due Process Clause of the Fourteenth Amendment, I am constrained to [write separately], lest the true nature of the constitutional problem presented become obscured or the impact on state juvenile court systems of what the Court holds today be exaggerated.

I

* * *

* * * [W]e have before us a case where the choice of the standard of proof has made a difference: the juvenile court judge below forthrightly acknowledged that he believed by a preponderance of the evidence, but was not convinced beyond a reasonable doubt, that appellant stole $112 from the complainant's pocketbook. Moreover, even though the labels used for alternative standards of proof are vague and not a very sure guide to decision-making, the choice of the standard for a particular variety of adjudication does, I think, reflect a very fundamental assessment of the comparative social costs of erroneous factual determinations.

To explain why I think this so, I begin by stating two propositions, neither of which I believe can be fairly disputed. First, in a judicial proceeding in which there is a dispute about the facts of some earlier event, the factfinder cannot acquire unassailably accurate knowledge of what happened. Instead, all the fact-finder can acquire is a belief of what probably happened. * * *

A second proposition, which is really nothing more than a corollary of the first, is that the trier of fact will sometimes, despite his best efforts, be wrong in his factual conclusions. * * *

The standard of proof influences the relative frequency of these two types of erroneous outcomes. * * *

When one makes such an assessment, the reason for different standards of proof in civil as opposed to criminal litigation becomes apparent. In a civil suit between two private parties for money damages, for example, we view it as no more serious in general for there to be an erroneous verdict in the defendant's favor than for there to be an erroneous verdict in the plaintiff's favor. A preponderance of the evidence standard therefore seems peculiarly appropriate for, as explained most sensibly, it simply requires the trier of fact "to believe that the existence of a fact is more probable than its nonexistence before (he) may find in favor of the party who has the burden to persuade the (judge) of the fact's existence."

In a criminal case, on the other hand, we do not view the social disutility of convicting an innocent man as equivalent to the disutility of acquitting someone who is guilty. * * *

In this context, I view the requirement of proof beyond a reasonable doubt in a criminal case as bottomed on a fundamental value determination of our society that it is far worse to convict an innocent man than to let a guilty man go free. It is only because of the nearly complete and long-standing acceptance of the reasonable-doubt standard by the States in criminal trials that the Court has not before today had to hold explicitly that due process, as an expression of fundamental procedural fairness, requires a more stringent standard for criminal trials than for ordinary civil litigation.

II

When one assesses the consequences of an erroneous factual determination in a juvenile delinquency proceeding in which a youth is accused of a crime, I think it must be concluded that, while the consequences are not identical to those in a criminal case, the differences will not support a distinction in the standard of proof. First, and of paramount importance, a factual error here, as in a criminal case, exposes the accused to a complete loss of his personal liberty through a state-imposed confinement away from his home, family, and friends. And, second, a delinquency determination, to some extent at least, stigmatizes a youth in that it is by definition bottomed on a finding that the accused committed a crime. Although there are no doubt costs to society (and possibly even to the youth himself) in letting a guilty youth go free, I think here, as in a criminal case, it is far worse to declare an innocent youth a delinquent. I therefore agree that a juvenile court judge should be no less convinced of the factual conclusion that the accused committed the criminal act with which he is charged than would be required in a criminal trial.

* * *

With these observations, I join the Court's opinion * * *.

CHIEF JUSTICE BURGER, with whom JUSTICE STEWART joins, dissenting.

The Court's opinion today rests entirely on the assumption that all juvenile proceedings are "criminal prosecutions," hence subject to constitutional limitations. This derives from earlier holdings, which, like today's holding, were steps eroding the differences between juvenile courts and traditional criminal courts. The original concept of the juvenile court system was to provide a benevolent and less formal means than criminal courts could provide for dealing with the special and often sensitive problems of youthful offenders. Since I see no constitutional requirement of due process sufficient to overcome the legislative judgment of the States in this area, I dissent from further straitjacketing of an already overly restricted system. What the juvenile court system needs is not more but less of the trappings of legal procedure and judicial formalism; the juvenile court system requires breathing room and flexibility in order to survive, if it can survive the repeated assaults from this Court.

Much of the judicial attitude manifested by the Court's opinion today and earlier holdings in this field is really a protest against inadequate juvenile court staffs and facilities * * *. The lack of support and the distressing growth of juvenile crime have combined to make for a literal breakdown in many if not most juvenile courts. Constitutional problems were not seen while those courts functioned in an atmosphere where juvenile judges were not crushed with an avalanche of cases.

My hope is that today's decision will not spell the end of a generously conceived program of compassionate treatment intended to mitigate the rigors and trauma of exposing youthful offenders to a traditional criminal court; each step we take turns the clock back to the pre-juvenile-court era. I cannot regard it as a manifestation of progress to transform juvenile courts into criminal courts, which is what we are well on the way to accomplishing. We can only hope the legislative response will not reflect our own by having these courts abolished.

* * *

[Dissenting opinion by JUSTICE BLACK is omitted.]

NOTES AND QUESTIONS

1.   Why is the "beyond a reasonable doubt" standard the applicable one for criminal cases? What was the majority's basis for holding that that standard should apply even in juvenile cases? What was Justice Harlan's rationale? Why did the dissent disagree with the majority? Which opinion is more persuasive?

2.   In civil cases, courts generally use a "preponderance of the evidence" standard rather than the more rigorous "beyond a reasonable doubt" standard. Under the preponderance standard, the factfinder must determine whether it is more likely than not that the defendant is liable. In *Winship*, both the majority and Justice Harlan explained why a higher burden is required in criminal cases. Are their explanations persuasive? Are there situations in which the burden in a civil case should be as great as (if not greater than) the burden in a criminal case? Does the answer depend on the seriousness of the charges?

3.   There are certain narrow categories of civil cases in which courts apply a "clear and convincing" standard, which requires a level of proof greater than the preponderance standard but less than the reasonable doubt standard. For example, the Supreme Court has used that intermediate standard in denaturalization proceedings (proceedings to take away a person's U.S. citizenship):

> In its consequences[, denaturalization] is more serious than a taking of one's property, or the imposition of a fine or other penalty. For it is safe to assert that nowhere in the world today is the right of citizenship of greater worth to an individual than it is in this country. It would be difficult to exaggerate its value and importance. By many it is regarded as the highest hope of civilized men. * * * [S]uch a right once conferred should not be taken away without the clearest sort of

justification and proof. * * * [The] burden [on the government] must be met with evidence of a clear and convincing character that when citizenship was conferred upon petitioner * * * it was not done in accordance with strict legal requirements.

Schneiderman v. United States, 320 U.S. 118, 122–23 (1943). Does it make sense in denaturalization cases to have a standard that is more rigorous than the civil standard but less rigorous than the criminal standard? The "clear and convincing evidence" standard is applied in other types of civil proceedings as well. *See, e.g., Santosky v. Kramer*, 455 U.S. 745 (1982) (holding that that the Due Process Clause of the Fourteenth Amendment requires the state to produce clear and convincing evidence of neglect or abuse before it may take a child away from his or her parents); *Addington v. Texas*, 441 U.S. 418 (1979) (holding that that the Due Process Clause of the Fourteenth Amendment requires the state to produce clear and convincing evidence of a dangerous mental illness before it may commit an individual involuntarily (and for an indefinite period) to a state mental hospital).

4. In several post-*Winship* cases, the Supreme Court has addressed the reasonable doubt standard. For example, in 1979, the Supreme Court emphasized that the application of that standard must be rigorously scrutinized for error:

> The *Winship* doctrine requires more than simply a trial ritual. A doctrine establishing so fundamental a substantive constitutional standard must also require that the factfinder will rationally apply that standard to the facts in evidence. * * * Yet a properly instructed jury may occasionally convict even when it can be said that no rational trier of fact could find guilt beyond a reasonable doubt, and the same may be said of a trial judge sitting as a jury. * * * [I]t follows that when such a conviction occurs in a state trial, it cannot constitutionally stand.

Jackson v. Virginia, 443 U.S. 307, 316–18 (1979).

5. For additional discussion of burdens of proof, *see, e.g.*, Ronald Allen & Alex Stein, *Evidence, Probability, and the Burden of Proof*, 55 Ariz. L. Rev. 557 (2013) (arguing that the current system works well, and criticizing proposals for a statistical or numerical based proof system); Edward Cheng, *Reconceptualizing the Burden of Proof*, 122 Yale L.J. 1254 (2013) (advocating for the reconceptualization of burdens of proof that compares the statistical likelihood of the competing narratives advanced by the parties, rather than simply requiring one party to meet a specific probability threshold); Louis Kaplow, *Burden of Proof*, 121 Yale L.J. 738 (2012) (analyzing burdens of proof from the perspective of maximizing social welfare).

6. *Winship* involved a prosecution within the juvenile justice system. Typically, juveniles are prosecuted in separate juvenile courts, and their cases are assessed by a judge rather than a jury. *See, e.g., McKeiver v. Pennsylvania*, 403 U.S. 528, 545 (1971) ("[W]e conclude that trial by jury in the juvenile court's adjudicative stage is not a constitutional requirement."). Other

jurisdictions allow most juvenile criminal cases to be determined by juries. *See, e.g., I.J. v. State*, 182 P.3d 643, 644 (Alaska Ct. App. 2008) ("The Alaska Constitution guarantees minors the right to trial by jury in delinquency proceedings if the delinquency petition is based on allegations of criminal conduct that, if committed by an adult, could result in incarceration."); *In re L.M.*, 286 Kan. 460, 473, 186 P.3d 164, 172 (2008) ("[J]uveniles have a right to a jury trial[.]"). All jurisdictions also permit trial of some juveniles outside of the juvenile court system when the crimes are particularly serious or are otherwise deemed unfit for juvenile court. *See, e.g., R.W.G. v. State*, 2014 Ark. App. 545, 444 S.W.3d 376 (2014) (affirming that 17-year-old could be prosecuted as an adult when he willingly participated in the abduction, robbery, and murder of a man and had previously demonstrated an inability to rehabilitate in community programs for juvenile criminals); *In re Welfare of R.D.M., III*, 825 N.W.2d 394 (Minn. Ct. App. 2013) (affirming that the public interest would be better served by transferring a case to the adult criminal court when the defendant broke into a pharmacy and stole thousands of pills, had two previous convictions for felony assault, admitted to four other felonies, and was nearly 19-years-old at the time of the court proceedings).

B. SUFFICIENCY BASED ON CIRCUMSTANTIAL EVIDENCE

In a criminal case, there are two types of evidence: direct and circumstantial. Direct evidence provides direct support for the allegation that the defendant committed a crime, such as a witness's testimony that he saw the defendant kill the victim. By contrast, circumstantial evidence supports the allegation through inference, such as a statement by a witness that he saw the defendant enter the victim's house the night that the victim was killed. Often, the prosecutor will present both types of evidence, but sometimes the prosecutor will bring a case based solely on circumstantial evidence. The following case provides an example of a court's reliance entirely on circumstantial evidence.

OWENS V. STATE

Court of Special Appeals of Maryland, 1992
93 Md. App. 162, 611 A.2d 1043

MOYLAN, JUDGE.

This appeal presents us with a small gem of a problem from the borderland of legal sufficiency. It is one of those few occasions when some frequently invoked but rarely appropriate language is actually pertinent. Ironically, in this case it was not invoked. The language is, "[A] conviction upon circumstantial evidence *alone* is not to be sustained unless the circumstances are inconsistent with any reasonable hypothesis of innocence."

We have here a conviction based upon circumstantial evidence alone. The circumstance is that a suspect was found behind the wheel of an automobile parked on a private driveway at night with the lights on and with the motor running. Although there are many far-fetched and speculative hypotheses that might be conjured up * * *, there are only two * * * likely inferences that could reasonably arise. One is that the vehicle and its driver had arrived at the driveway from somewhere else. The other is that the driver had gotten into and started up the vehicle and was about to depart for somewhere else.

The first hypothesis, combined with the added factor that the likely driver was intoxicated, is consistent with guilt. The second hypothesis, because the law intervened before the forbidden deed could be done, is consistent with innocence. With either inference equally likely, a fact finder could not fairly draw the guilty inference and reject the innocent with the requisite certainty beyond a reasonable doubt. We are called upon, therefore, to examine the circumstantial predicate more closely and to ascertain whether there were any attendant and ancillary circumstances to render less likely, and therefore less reasonable, the hypothesis of innocence. Thereon hangs the decision.

The appellant, Christopher Columbus Owens, Jr., was convicted in the Circuit Court [in a bench trial] of driving while intoxicated. Upon this appeal, he raises the single contention that [the trial court] was clearly erroneous in finding him guilty because the evidence was not legally sufficient to support such finding.

The evidence, to be sure, was meager. The State's only witness was Trooper Samuel Cottman, who testified that at approximately 11 P.M. on March 17, 1991, he drove to the area of Sackertown Road in Crisfield in response to a complaint that had been called in about a suspicious vehicle. He spotted a truck matching the description of the "suspicious vehicle." It was parked in the driveway of a private residence.

The truck's engine was running and its lights were on. The appellant was asleep in the driver's seat, with an open can of Budweiser clasped between his legs. Two more empty beer cans were inside the vehicle. As Trooper Cottman awakened him, the appellant appeared confused and did not know where he was. He stumbled out of the vehicle. There was a strong odor of alcohol on his breath. His face was flushed and his eyes were red. When asked to recite the alphabet, the appellant "mumbled through the letters, didn't state any of the letters clearly and failed to say them in the correct order." His speech generally was "slurred and very unclear." When taken into custody, the appellant was "very argumentative . . . and uncooperative." A check with the Motor Vehicles Administration revealed, moreover, that the appellant had an alcohol restriction on his license. The appellant declined to submit to a blood test for alcohol.

After the brief direct examination of Trooper Cottman * * *, defense counsel asked only two questions, establishing that the driveway was private property and that the vehicle was sitting on that private driveway. The appellant did not take the stand and no defense witnesses were called. The appellant's argument as to legal insufficiency is clever. He chooses to fight not over the fact of drunkenness but over the place of drunkenness. He points out that his conviction was under the Transportation Article, which is limited in its coverage to the driving of vehicles on "highways" and does not extend to driving on a "private road or driveway."

We agree with the appellant that he could not properly have been convicted for driving, no matter how intoxicated, back and forth along the short span of a private driveway. The theory of the State's case, however, rests upon the almost Newtonian principle that present stasis on the driveway implies earlier motion on the highway. The appellant was not convicted of drunken driving on the private driveway, but of drunken driving on the public highway before coming to rest on the private driveway.

It is a classic case of circumstantial evidence. From his presence behind the wheel of a vehicle on a private driveway with the lights on and the motor running, it can reasonably be inferred that such individual either (1) had just arrived by way of the public highway or (2) was just about to set forth upon the public highway. The binary nature of the probabilities— that a vehicular odyssey had just concluded or was just about to begin—is strengthened by the lack of evidence of any third reasonable explanation * * *. Either he was coming or he was going.

The first inference would render the appellant guilty; the second would not. Mere presence behind the wheel with the lights on and the motor running could give rise to either inference, the guilty one and the innocent one. For the State to prevail, there has to be some other factor to enhance the likelihood of the first inference and to diminish the likelihood of the second. We must look for a tiebreaker.

The State had several opportunities to break the game wide open but failed to capitalize on either of them. As Trooper Cottman woke the appellant, he asked him what he was doing there. The appellant responded that *he had just driven* the occupant of the residence home. Without explanation, the appellant's objection to the answer was sustained. For purposes of the present analysis, therefore, it is not in the case. We must look for a tiebreaker elsewhere.

In trying to resolve whether the appellant (1) had just been driving or (2) was just about to drive, it would have been helpful to know whether the driveway in which he was found was that of his own residence or that of some other residence. If he were parked in someone else's driveway with the motor still running, it would be more likely that he had just driven there a short time before. If parked in his own driveway at home, on the other hand, the relative strength of the inbound inference over the outbound inference would diminish.

The driveway where the arrest took place was on Sackertown Road. The charging document (which, of course, is not evidence) listed the appellant's address as 112 Cove Second Street. When the appellant was arrested, presumably his driver's license was taken from him. Since one of the charges against the appellant was that of driving in violation of an alcohol restriction on his license, it would have been routine procedure to have offered the license, showing the restriction, into evidence. In terms of our present legal sufficiency exercise, the license would fortuitously have shown the appellant's residence as well. Because of the summary nature of the trial, however, the license was never offered in evidence. For purposes of the present analysis, therefore, the appellant's home address is not in the case. We must continue to look for a tiebreaker elsewhere.

Three beer cans were in evidence. The presence of a partially consumed can of beer between the appellant's legs and two other empty cans in the back seat would give rise to a reasonable inference that the appellant's drinking spree was on the downslope rather than at an early stage. At least a partial venue of the spree, moreover, would reasonably appear to have been the automobile. One does not typically drink in the house and then carry the empties out to the car. Some significant drinking, it may be inferred, had taken place while the appellant was in the car. The appellant's state of unconsciousness, moreover, enforces that inference. One passes out on the steering wheel after one has been drinking for some time, not as one only begins to drink. It is not a reasonable hypothesis that one would leave the house, get in the car, turn on the lights, turn on the motor, and then, before putting the car in gear and driving off, consume enough alcohol to pass out on the steering wheel. Whatever had been going on (driving and drinking) would seem more likely to have been at a terminal stage than at an incipient one.

Yet another factor would have sufficed, we conclude, to break the tie * * *. [T]he thing that had brought Trooper Cottman to the scene was a complaint about a suspicious vehicle. The inference is reasonable that the vehicle had been observed driving in some sort of erratic fashion. Had the appellant simply been sitting, with his motor idling, on the driveway of his own residence, it is not likely that someone from the immediate vicinity would have found suspicious the presence of a familiar neighbor in a familiar car sitting in his own driveway. The call to the police, even without more being shown, inferentially augurs more than that. It does not prove guilt in and of itself. It simply makes one of two alternative inferences less reasonable and its alternative inference thereby more reasonable.

The totality of the circumstances are, in the last analysis, inconsistent with a *reasonable* hypothesis of innocence. They do not, of course, foreclose the hypothesis but such has never been required. They do make the hypothesis more strained and less likely. By an inverse proportion, the diminishing force of one inference enhances the force of its alternative. It makes the drawing of the inference of guilt more than a mere flip of a coin between guilt and innocence. It makes it rational and therefore within the proper purview of the factfinder. We affirm.

* * *

NOTES AND QUESTIONS

1.   The Court of Special Appeals in *Owens* noted that the evidence for conviction was "meager." Yet, the court found the evidence to be sufficient. In the court's view, what evidence satisfied the beyond a reasonable doubt standard? Did the court correctly apply that standard? Can "meager" evidence ever satisfy that standard?

2.   What "circumstantial evidence" was presented in the *Owens* case? Was any "direct" evidence presented?

3.   What arguments can be made that the evidence in *Owens* did not establish proof beyond a reasonable doubt? Was there additional evidence that the prosecutor could have used to bolster the government's case?

4.   In cases involving circumstantial evidence, the court will typically give the jury an instruction on when it is permissible to rely on such evidence. For instance, in California the instruction is as follows:

> Before you may rely on circumstantial evidence to conclude that a fact necessary to find the defendant guilty has been proved, you must be convinced that the [prosecution has] proved each fact essential to that conclusion beyond a reasonable doubt. Also, before you may rely on circumstantial evidence to find the defendant guilty, you must be convinced that the only reasonable conclusion supported by the circumstantial evidence is that the defendant is guilty. If you can draw two or more reasonable conclusions from the circumstantial evidence, and one of those reasonable conclusions points to innocence and another to guilt, you must accept the one that points to innocence. However, when considering circumstantial evidence, you must accept only reasonable conclusions and reject any that are unreasonable.

Judicial Council of California Criminal Jury Instructions, *Instruction 224— Circumstantial Evidence: Sufficiency of Evidence* (2015). The court must give that instruction if the prosecution "substantially relies on circumstantial evidence to establish any element of the case." *Id.* at Bench Notes— Instructional Duty. In some jurisdictions, however, the instruction is only required when a case is based *solely* on circumstantial evidence. For instance, in *Osby v. State*, 139 So.3d 98 (Miss. App. 2013), the defendant was convicted of theft. On appeal, he alleged that his counsel was constitutionally ineffective (a concept that was discussed in Chapter 7) for not requesting a circumstantial evidence instruction at trial. The government, however, had produced three eyewitnesses who (1) had seen the defendant leaving the house where the burglary had occurred, and (2) had seen objects similar to the stolen property in the defendant's car. In addition, the defendant had made inculpatory statements. As a result, the court noted that "the eyewitness testimony, in addition to Osby's statements, which amounted to an admission, obviated the need for a circumstantial-evidence jury instruction." *Id.* at 100. Should a circumstantial evidence instruction be required even in cases in which some direct evidence has been offered in addition to the circumstantial evidence? Alternatively, should courts dispense with a circumstantial evidence instruction in all cases?

5. For additional analysis of circumstantial evidence (and the circumstantial-direct evidence distinction), *see, e.g.,* Eugenée Heeter, *Chance of Rain: Rethinking Circumstantial Evidence Jury Instructions*, 64 Hastings L.J. 527 (2013) (arguing that direct and circumstantial evidence are equally probative, because circumstantial evidence is no more unreliable than eyewitness testimony and confessions); Richard Greenstein, *Determining Facts: The Myth of Direct Evidence*, 45 Hous. L. Rev. 1801 (2009) (criticizing the distinction between direct and circumstantial evidence and arguing that even direct evidence is inherently subjective); Kevin Jon Heller, *The Cognitive Psychology of Circumstantial Evidence*, 105 Mich. L. Rev. 241 (2006) (explaining that jurors often undervalue circumstantial evidence and proposing a jury instruction that would encourage jurors to discredit circumstantial evidence only when it is likely, and not just conceivable, that the evidence is not inculpatory).

C. MENS REA

Many crimes require the prosecution to prove that the defendant had a certain mental state when committing a crime. For example, the required mental state may be intent, recklessness, or negligence in committing the crime. Courts sometimes use the term "mens rea," meaning mental state, to express this idea. Another concept, scienter, is related to mens rea. Some courts use the terms scienter and mens rea interchangeably, while others treat scienter as having a more specific definition, such as knowingly or intentionally. In the following case, the defendant claims on appeal that she did not have the requisite state of mind to be convicted of the crime.

CAROSI V. COMMONWEALTH
Supreme Court of Virginia, 2010
280 Va. 545, 701 S.E.2d 441

KOONTZ, JR., JUSTICE.

In this appeal, we consider whether the Court of Appeals erred in finding that three convictions for child endangerment * * * were supported by sufficient evidence that the defendant endangered the lives of her three children by permitting illegal drugs to be kept in her home in a place accessible to the children.

BACKGROUND

* * * [T]he evidence adduced at trial showed that shortly after 10 P.M. on February 28, 2008, Virginia State Police Special Agent Richard Boyd, Jr. executed a search warrant * * * where Angela Marie Carosi lived with her three children, ages 10, 5 and 3[;] all * * * were present in the home at the time of the search. Cavell Thomas, the father of two of the children, also frequently stayed in the residence. However, Thomas was not present at the time of the search, as he was being held in custody on drug charges in another jurisdiction.

In the master bedroom of the home, which Carosi shared with Thomas, Boyd found a glass jar containing marijuana, two "bongs" or smoking devices, a digital scale with a powdery residue, and plastic bags in an upper cabinet of an unlocked wardrobe. In an unlocked safe inside the wardrobe, Boyd also found prescription bottles containing oxycodone and methylenedioxymethamphetamine, commonly known as MDMA or ecstasy. On top of the safe was a plate with two razor blades and powdered cocaine. Boyd further observed that there was no lock on the master bedroom door and that all the drugs in the wardrobe would be within the reach of a small child.

Boyd subsequently testified at trial that Carosi told him the smoking devices were in the wardrobe, that she kept clothing in the drawers of the wardrobe, and that the safe belonged jointly to her and Thomas. She denied any knowledge of the drugs that Boyd had found inside the safe.

On August 4, 2008, the Stafford County Grand Jury indicted Carosi for three counts of child abuse * * * and three counts of child endangerment * * *. Carosi was also indicted for possession of marijuana with intent to distribute * * * and three counts of possession of cocaine, oxycodone, and MDMA * * *. The Commonwealth subsequently dismissed the felony child abuse charges * * *.

On March 4, 2009, a two-day jury trial on the child endangerment and drug possession charges commenced in the Circuit Court of Stafford County. Boyd testified concerning the February 28, 2008 search of Carosi's home as described above. After presenting evidence from a forensic expert, who identified the marijuana, cocaine, oxycodone, and MDMA, the Commonwealth rested its case.

Carosi moved to strike the child endangerment charges, contending that "[t]here is no evidence whatsoever that the children knew that there were drugs in the house. There is no evidence whatsoever that there was drug use going on in front of these children. There [is] no evidence whatsoever that [the children] actually had access to the bedroom and they could go in there." Thus, Carosi contended that the jury would have to speculate as to whether the children had actually been placed in a situation endangering their lives through her alleged willful or negligent conduct.

The Commonwealth responded that the children had "access to dangerous drugs" because there were no "locks or any prohibitions on the door to prohibit the [children] from coming into their mother's room." Thus, the Commonwealth asserted that the elements of * * * [child endangerment] could be satisfied "solely on the children's access to the Schedule I or Schedule II drugs and marijuana."

Carosi responded that children merely having potential access to drugs was different from a case where "there is drug dealing going on in front of the children." She contended that the possibility of access to drugs is "no different than * * * [having knives, chemicals, or prescription drugs in the house]. The circuit court denied the motion to strike the child endangerment charges.

Thereafter, Thomas was called as a witness for the defense. Thomas took full responsibility for the drugs found in the home, stating that the wardrobe was his "and I wanted to hide [the drugs] there." He denied that Carosi kept any belongings in the wardrobe and maintained that he did not use drugs in the home. On cross-examination, Thomas gave equivocal answers to a series of questions concerning whether any of Carosi's clothing was kept in the wardrobe. Nevertheless, he insisted that "all the drugs were mine" and that, other than the marijuana, he had placed the drugs in the wardrobe the day before the search was conducted.

Concerning ownership of the safe, Thomas testified that while he purchased the safe, Carosi might have told Boyd that she and Thomas owned the safe jointly because "everything [of mine], is basically hers. . . . if she wanted to claim the safe, she could." He further testified that although there were two bongs in the wardrobe, both belonged to him. Asked why he would keep two bongs in the home if Carosi did not smoke marijuana, * * * Thomas replied that the two were "total different instruments if you look at them clearly" and that they were of "[d]ifferent styles."

The Commonwealth concluded its cross-examination of Thomas by impeaching him through prior inconsistent statements he had made to a probation officer for a pre-sentence report following his conviction on drug trafficking charges. Specifically, the Commonwealth established that Thomas had denied using marijuana, cocaine, or other drugs recently. Thomas responded either that he could not recall what statements he had made or that he did not know what had been stated in the pre-sentence report.

Carosi testified on her own behalf. She maintained that Thomas brought the wardrobe to the home. Carosi denied that she kept any clothing or other property in the wardrobe, though she conceded that she sometimes would borrow a pair of Thomas's socks that were kept in the wardrobe. She further testified that while her children "[s]ometimes" would go into her bedroom, she had never seen them playing in the wardrobe.

Carosi specifically denied having any knowledge of the drugs or the bongs, and denied that she smoked marijuana or used any type of illegal drugs. She further maintained that Thomas did not use drugs in the home, though she had "seen him take pills" for pain after he had two teeth pulled.

On cross-examination, Carosi denied that she had told Boyd that she kept clothes in the wardrobe. She also denied having told Boyd that the bongs were located in the wardrobe. Asked whether she could offer a reason that Boyd would fabricate this testimony, Carosi replied that she had been "overcritical" of him during the search of her home and had "told him how to do his job better." Carosi also testified that she had purchased the safe for Thomas as a gift and did not "know why he said he purchased it."

After the Commonwealth called the probation officer who had prepared Thomas's pre-sentence report as a rebuttal witness, Carosi renewed her motion to strike the child endangerment charges * * *. The circuit court again denied the motion to strike.

The case was submitted to the jury, which returned verdicts acquitting Carosi of the four drug possession offenses, but convicted her of the three child endangerment charges. The jury fixed her punishment at a fine of $500 for each offense. * * * After receiving testimony from Carosi and her sister, the circuit court confirmed the jury's verdict and imposed $1500 in fines on Carosi.

Carosi filed a petition for appeal to the Court of Appeals. The sole issue asserted in her petition was that the evidence was insufficient to support the three convictions for felony child endangerment. * * * [T]he Court of Appeals refused Carosi's petition. * * *

DISCUSSION

In relevant part, * * * [the Penal Code] provides, "It shall be unlawful for any person . . . having the custody of any child willfully or negligently to cause or permit the life of such child to be endangered." * * *

Carosi contends that the Commonwealth's evidence was insufficient * * * because it failed to show that she actually endangered the life of her children as proscribed by [the Penal Code]. Carosi advances two separate challenges to the sufficiency of the evidence, contending that the Commonwealth failed to prove both the necessary scienter, in that the evidence did not show that she had actual knowledge of the presence and character of the illegal drugs in her home, and the requisite mens rea, in that the evidence did not show that her acts or omissions rose to a level of criminal negligence. We will address Carosi's contentions in that order.

With respect to the issue of scienter, Carosi asserts that "the only facts before the [jury] are that there were drugs and drug paraphernalia in a closed cabinet belonging to [Carosi's] boyfriend." Because the jury acquitted Carosi of all the drug possession charges, she contends that there was no evidence that she was actually aware that the drugs were present in the wardrobe. Absent that knowledge, she asserts the evidence that she permitted the children to occasionally enter and play in the master bedroom would be insufficient to prove that she knowingly permitted the children's lives to be endangered. We disagree.

When a defendant challenges the sufficiency of the evidence on appeal "[i]t is the appellate court's duty to examine the evidence that tends to support the conviction and to uphold the conviction unless it is plainly wrong or without evidentiary support." * * * Applying this standard of review, we * * * [reject Carosi's scienter challenge].

* * * Boyd's testimony that Carosi told him that the two bongs were in the wardrobe, that she kept clothing in it, and that the safe belonged jointly to her and Thomas would give rise to a reasonable inference by the trier of fact that Carosi was also aware of the presence and character of the marijuana and other drugs in the wardrobe and safe and that she jointly exercised dominion and control over them with Thomas. * * * The evidence presented by the defense, specifically Carosi's adamant denial that she used the wardrobe or was aware of what Thomas stored in it and that she had not made the statements during the search that Boyd attributed to her, as well as Thomas's assertion that all of the drugs and drug paraphernalia were his alone, thus created a question of fact to be resolved by the jury based upon its assessment of the credibility of the witnesses.

A jury is not required to accept the self-serving testimony of the defendant or of witnesses with a potential bias in favor of the defendant, but may rely on such testimony in whole, in part, or reject it completely. Thus, the jury reasonably could have accepted Thomas's assertion that the drugs were his, while rejecting Carosi's assertion that she was ignorant of the fact that the drugs were being stored in the wardrobe. Accordingly, while the jury may have found that the Commonwealth had not proven beyond a reasonable doubt that Carosi exercised dominion and control over the drugs, it could also have found the evidence was sufficient to prove that she was nonetheless aware of the presence and character of the drugs for purposes of determining whether she was guilty of the child endangerment charges.

We now turn to * * * Carosi's contention that the mens rea element of [the Penal Code] cannot be established solely upon the fact that a parent or other custodian knowingly permitted a child to be present in a home where illegal drugs were kept unsecured in an area accessible to the child. * * * Carosi asserts that keeping illegal drugs in this manner was no more likely to endanger her children than would "the possession of sharp knives in the kitchen, chemicals under the sink, prescription drugs in the medicine cabinet, and a lawfully possessed unloaded gun in the closet." * * *

* * *

* * * [W]e reject Carosi's * * * contention * * *. It is self-evident from Carosi's own characterization of the two circumstances that they differ in [an] important respect[:] the latter items, though unquestionably dangerous if left accessible to unsupervised children, are possessed by the parent or custodian for lawful purposes, whereas drugs that are illegally present in the home are not.

Finally, in order to accept Carosi's argument that the evidence was insufficient to establish the mens rea of criminal negligence in this case, we would have to conclude that reasonable minds could not differ on whether rearing children in a home where illegal drugs are readily accessible may constitute endangering the children for purposes of [the Penal Code]. The myriad factors to be considered in such cases—such as the ages of the children, the length of the exposure, the level of supervision or lack thereof, and the quantity and variety of the drugs—suggest that as with most cases where criminal negligence is at issue, this determination is necessarily fact-specific. Such determination is best left to the jury, which is in the best position to assess the weight and credibility of the evidence. In that respect, and considering the totality of the evidence, we cannot say that the jury's finding of criminal negligence in this case was plainly wrong or without support in the record.

CONCLUSION

* * * [T]he judgment of the Court of Appeals will be affirmed.

NOTES AND QUESTIONS

1.   Carosi argued that her convictions were invalid because there was insufficient proof of her state of mind. What were her arguments? How did the court rule? Is the court's decision persuasive? What arguments can be made against the court's decision?

2.   As discussed in *Carosi*, mental state requirements are essential to understanding criminal culpability. It is important to note, however, that not all crimes require a specific mental state. For example, in *United States v. Humphrey*, 608 F.3d 955 (6th Cir. 2010), the defendant was convicted of production of child pornography based on videotaping a minor engaged in sexual acts. On appeal, he argued that he did not know that the girl was a minor and that he should have been able to raise that defense at trial. The Sixth Circuit disagreed, holding that the child pornography statute did not require proof that the defendant knew the victim's age. *See also, e.g., United States v. Indelicato*, 800 F.2d 1482 (9th Cir. 1986) (holding that there is no scienter requirement for the crime of possessing a firearm while under indictment); *Case v. Commonwealth*, 63 Va. App. 14, 27, 753 S.E.2d 860, 866

(Va. Ct. App. 2014) (holding that there is no mens rea requirement in Virginia's statute criminalizing the act of driving under the influence of alcohol); *State v. Eaton*, 143 Wash. App. 155, 177 P.3d 157 (Wash. Ct. App. 2008) (noting that there is no mens rea requirement for possession of a controlled substance), *aff'd*, 168 Wash. 2d 476, 229 P.3d 704 (2010).

3.   Even when a mental state is required in a particular case, it may not be required as to all of the elements of the crime. For example, in *United States v. Andino*, 627 F.3d 41 (2d Cir. 2010), custom officials found a package, addressed to the defendant, that contained cocaine. The government set up a controlled delivery of the package to the defendant's address. Subsequently, the defendant took the package to another residence and left it there without opening it. At trial, the defendant argued that he did not know what specific controlled substance the package contained and thus could not be convicted of conspiracy to violate the narcotics laws. The Second Circuit disagreed, stating: "In cases like the present one, where the defendant personally and directly participated in the drug transaction underlying the conspiracy charge, the government need not prove that the defendant had knowledge of either drug type or quantity." *Id.* at 47.

4.   Traditionally, courts have presumed that criminal statutes require some degree of intent. The Supreme Court has held that this presumption does not apply to so-called public welfare offenses, *i.e.*, safety laws that are designed to protect the public from harm. *Staples v. United States*, 511 U.S. 600, 607 n.3 (1994) (characterizing public welfare offenses as " 'dispensing with' or 'eliminating' a mens rea requirement or 'mental element' "). But such crimes are the exception. Some scholars have criticized the usual presumption that a specific mental state is required. *See, e.g.*, Eric Johnson, *Rethinking the Presumption of Mens Rea*, 47 Wake Forest L. Rev. 769 (2012) (proposing a presumption that requires only proof of general criminal intent (*i.e.*, that the defendant intended to do the basic criminal act in and of itself), and not specific intent (*i.e.*, that the defendant intended to accomplish a specific result by committing the criminal act)). Strict liability offenses are discussed further in the following section.

5.   Although it may be difficult to determine exactly what an individual was thinking when he committed a crime, courts can sometimes infer intent from the behavior and circumstances involved. For example, in *People v. Conley*, 187 Ill. App. 3d 234, 543 N.E.2d 138 (1989), the defendant was convicted of aggravated battery causing permanent disability after he hit an individual in the face with a wine bottle, breaking bones in the victim's face and causing permanent damage to his mouth and lip. On appeal, the defendant argued that the government had failed to prove that he intended to cause permanent injuries to the victim. The court noted that the crime was a specific intent crime, but that such intent could be based on "the ordinary presumption that one intends the natural and probable consequences of his actions." *Id.* at 242, 543 N.E.2d at 143. The court thus held that the government presented sufficient evidence of intent through "the surrounding circumstances, the use

of a bottle, the absence of warning and the force of the blow." *Id.* at 242–43, 543 N.E.2d at 143–44.

6.   For additional discussion of mens rea, *see, e.g.*, Stephen Smith, *Proportional Mens Rea*, 46 Am. Crim. L. Rev. 127 (2009) (arguing that mens rea requirements should incorporate a proportionality analysis by considering not only whether an individual is culpable, but also whether his level of blameworthiness fits the punishment for the crime); Note, *Mens Rea in Federal Criminal Law*, 111 Harv. L. Rev. 2402 (1998) (arguing that a high mens rea requirement should be used in federal court to limit federal prosecutions and thereby allow states to control prosecution of most local criminal activity); Ira Robbins, *The Ostrich Instruction: Deliberate Ignorance as a Criminal Mens Rea*, 81 J. Crim. L. & Criminology 191 (1990) (noting that some people remain willfully ignorant to avoid the knowledge required for mens rea and proposing to address the problem through the adoption of a willful ignorance or recklessness alternative to mens rea).

D. NOTICE AND STRICT LIABILITY

As noted in the prior section, some crimes (known as "strict liability" crimes) do not have an intent requirement, meaning that individuals can be criminally culpable even when they had no criminal intent. Such crimes raise potential issues of notice and due process because an individual may not subjectively know that his conduct will subject him to criminal liability. The following case concerns a strict liability offense.

GARNETT V. STATE

Court of Appeals of Maryland, 1993
332 Md. 571, 632 A.2d 797

MURPHY, CHIEF JUDGE.

Maryland's "statutory rape" law prohibiting sexual intercourse with an underage person is codified in Maryland Code Art. 27, § 463, which reads in [relevant part]:

Second degree rape.

(a) *What constitutes.*—A person is guilty of rape in the second degree if the person engages in vaginal intercourse with another person:

(1) By force or threat of force against the will and without the consent of the other person; or

(2) Who is mentally defective, mentally incapacitated, or physically helpless, and the person performing the act knows or should reasonably know the other person is mentally defective, mentally incapacitated, or physically helpless; or

(3) Who is under 14 years of age and the person performing the act is at least four years older than the victim.

(b) *Penalty.*—Any person violating the provisions of this section is guilty of a felony and upon conviction is subject to imprisonment for a period of not more than 20 years.

* * * [W]e consider whether under the present statute, the State must prove that a defendant knew the complaining witness was younger than 14 and, in a related question, whether it was error at trial to exclude evidence that he had been told, and believed, that she was 16 years old.

I

Raymond Lennard Garnett is a young retarded man. At the time of the incident in question he was 20 years old. He has an I.Q. of 52. His guidance counselor from the Montgomery County public school system, Cynthia Parker, described him as a mildly retarded person who read on the third-grade level, did arithmetic on the 5th-grade level, and interacted with others socially at school at the level of someone 11 or 12 years of age. Ms. Parker added that Raymond attended special education classes and for at least one period of time was educated at home when he was afraid to return to school due to his classmates' taunting. Because he could not understand the duties of the jobs given him, he failed to complete vocational assignments; he sometimes lost his way to work. As Raymond was unable to pass any of the State's functional tests required for graduation, he received only a certificate of attendance rather than a high-school diploma.

In November or December 1990, a friend introduced Raymond to Erica Frazier, then aged 13; the two subsequently talked occasionally by telephone. On February 28, 1991, Raymond, apparently wishing to call for a ride home, approached the girl's house at about nine o'clock in the evening. Erica opened her bedroom window, through which Raymond entered; he testified that "she just told me to get a ladder and climb up her window." The two talked, and later engaged in sexual intercourse. Raymond left at about 4:30 a.m. the following morning. On November 19, 1991, Erica gave birth to a baby, of which Raymond is the biological father.

Raymond was tried * * * on one count of second degree rape under § 463(a)(3) proscribing sexual intercourse between a person under 14 and another at least four years older than the complainant. At trial, the defense * * * proffered evidence to the effect that Erica herself and her friends had previously told Raymond that she was 16 years old, and that he had acted with that belief. The trial court excluded such evidence as immaterial, explaining [that a good faith belief that the victim was not underage is not a defense].

* * *

The court found Raymond guilty. It sentenced him to a term of five years in prison, suspended the sentence and imposed five years of probation, and ordered that he pay restitution to Erica and the Frazier family. [Raymond appealed the judgment.] * * *

II

* * *

[The statute under which Raymond was convicted] does not expressly set forth a requirement that the accused have acted with a criminal state of mind, or mens rea. The State insists that the statute, by design, defines a strict liability offense, and that its essential elements were met in the instant case when Raymond, age 20, engaged in vaginal intercourse with Erica, a girl under 14 and more than 4 years his junior. Raymond replies that the criminal law exists to assess and punish morally culpable behavior. He says such culpability was absent here. He asks us either to engraft onto subsection (a)(3) an implicit mens rea requirement, or to recognize an affirmative defense of reasonable mistake as to the complainant's age. Raymond argues that it is unjust, under the circumstances of this case * * * to brand him a felon and rapist.

III

* * *

The precise legal issue here rests on Raymond's unsuccessful efforts to introduce into evidence testimony that Erica and her friends had told him she was 16 years old, the age of consent to sexual relations, and that he believed them. Thus the trial court did not permit him to raise a defense of reasonable mistake of Erica's age, by which defense Raymond would have asserted that he acted innocently without a criminal design. At common law, a crime occurred only upon the concurrence of an individual's act and his guilty state of mind. In this regard, it is well understood that generally there are two components of every crime, the actus reus or guilty act and the mens rea or the guilty mind or mental state accompanying a forbidden act. The requirement that an accused have acted with a culpable mental state is an axiom of criminal jurisprudence. * * *

* * *

To be sure, legislative bodies since the mid-19th century have created strict liability criminal offenses requiring no mens rea. Almost all such statutes responded to the demands of public health and welfare arising from the complexities of society after the Industrial Revolution. Typically misdemeanors involving only fines or other light penalties, these strict liability laws regulated food, milk, liquor, medicines and drugs, securities, motor vehicles and traffic, the labeling of goods for sale, and the like. Statutory rape, carrying the stigma of felony as well as a potential sentence of 20 years in prison, contrasts markedly with the other strict liability regulatory offenses and their light penalties.

Modern scholars generally reject the concept of strict criminal liability. * * * [T]he consensus [is] that punishing conduct without reference to the actor's state of mind fails to reach the desired end and is unjust * * *.

* * *

Conscious of the disfavor in which strict criminal liability resides, the [American Law Institute's] Model Penal Code states generally as a minimum requirement of culpability that a person is not guilty of a criminal offense unless he acts purposely, knowingly, recklessly, or negligently, *i.e.*, with some degree of mens rea. The Code allows generally for a defense of ignorance or mistake of fact negating mens rea. The Model Penal Code generally recognizes strict liability for offenses deemed "violations," defined as wrongs subject only to a fine, forfeiture, or other civil penalty upon conviction, and not giving rise to any legal disability.

The commentators similarly disapprove of statutory rape as a strict liability crime. In addition to the arguments discussed above, they observe that statutory rape prosecutions often proceed even when the defendant's judgment as to the age of the complainant is warranted by her appearance, her sexual sophistication, her verbal misrepresentations, and the defendant's careful attempts to ascertain her true age. Voluntary intercourse with a sexually mature teen-ager lacks the features of psychic abnormality, exploitation, or physical danger that accompanies such conduct with children.

Two sub-parts of the rationale underlying strict criminal liability require further analysis at this point. Statutory rape laws are often justified on the "lesser legal wrong" theory or the "moral wrong" theory; by such reasoning, the defendant acting without mens rea nonetheless deserves punishment for having committed a lesser crime, fornication, or for having violated moral teachings that prohibit sex outside of marriage. Maryland has no law against fornication. It is not a crime in this state. Moreover, the criminalization of an act, performed without a guilty mind, deemed immoral by some members of the community rests uneasily on subjective and shifting norms. * * * We acknowledge here that it is uncertain to what extent Raymond's intellectual and social retardation may have impaired his ability to comprehend imperatives of sexual morality in any case.

IV

The legislatures of 17 states have enacted laws permitting a mistake of age defense in some form in cases of sexual offenses with underage persons. In Kentucky, the accused may prove in exculpation that he did not know the facts or conditions relevant to the complainant's age. In Washington, the defendant may assert that he reasonably believed the complainant to be of a certain age based on the alleged victim's own declarations. In some states, the defense is available in instances where the complainant's age rises above a statutorily prescribed level, but is not available when the complainant falls below the defining age. In other states, the availability of the defense depends on the severity of the sex offense charged to the accused.

In addition, the highest appellate courts of four states [California, Alaska, Utah, and New Mexico] have determined that statutory rape laws by implication required an element of mens rea as to the complainant's age. * * *

* * * Two-fifths of the states, therefore, now recognize the defense [of reasonable mistake of age] in cases of statutory sexual offenses.

V

We think it sufficiently clear, however, that Maryland's second degree rape statute defines a strict liability offense that does not require the State to prove mens rea; it makes no allowance for a mistake-of-age defense. The plain language of § 463, viewed in its entirety, and the legislative history of its creation lead to this conclusion.

It is well settled that in interpreting a statute to ascertain and effectuate its goal, our first recourse is to the words of the statute, giving them their ordinary and natural import. While penal statutes are to be strictly construed in favor of the defendant, the construction must ultimately depend upon discerning the intention of the Legislature when it drafted and enacted the law in question. * * *

Section 463(a)(3) prohibiting sexual intercourse with underage persons makes no reference to the actor's knowledge, belief, or other state of mind. As we see it, this silence as to mens rea results from legislative design. First, subsection (a)(3) stands in stark contrast to the provision immediately before it, subsection (a)(2) prohibiting vaginal intercourse with incapacitated or helpless persons. In subsection (a)(2), the Legislature expressly provided as an element of the offense that "the person performing the act *knows or should reasonably know* the other person is mentally defective, mentally incapacitated, or physically helpless." In drafting this subsection, the Legislature showed itself perfectly capable of recognizing and allowing for a defense that obviates criminal intent; if the defendant objectively did not understand that the sex partner was impaired, there is no crime. That it chose not to include similar language in subsection (a)(3) indicates that the Legislature aimed to make statutory rape with underage persons a more severe prohibition based on strict criminal liability.

Second, an examination of the drafting history of § 463 during the 1976 revision of Maryland's sexual offense laws reveals that the statute was viewed as one of strict liability from its inception and throughout the amendment process. * * *

* * *

This interpretation is consistent with the traditional view of statutory rape as a strict liability crime designed to protect young persons from the dangers of sexual exploitation by adults, loss of chastity, physical injury, and, in the case of girls, pregnancy. The majority of states retain statutes which impose strict liability for sexual acts with underage complainants. * * *

VI

Maryland's second degree rape statute is by nature a creature of legislation. Any new provision introducing an element of mens rea, or permitting a defense of reasonable mistake of age, with respect to the offense of sexual intercourse with a person less than 14, should properly result from an act of the Legislature itself, rather than judicial fiat. Until then, defendants in extraordinary cases, like Raymond, will rely upon the tempering discretion of the trial court at sentencing.

* * *

[Dissenting opinion by JUDGE ELDRIDGE is omitted.]

JUDGE BELL, dissenting.

* * *

I do not dispute that the legislative history of Maryland Code may be read to support the majority's interpretation that [Section 463](a)(3) was intended to be a strict liability statute. Nor do I disagree that it is in the public interest to protect the sexually naive child from the adverse physical, emotional, or psychological effects of sexual relations. I do not believe, however, that the General Assembly, in every case, whatever the nature of the crime and no matter how harsh the potential penalty, can subject a defendant to strict criminal liability. To hold, *as a matter of law*, that section 463(a)(3) does not require the State to prove that a defendant possessed the necessary mental state to commit the crime, *i.e.* knowingly engaged in sexual relations with a female under 14, or that the defendant may not litigate that issue in defense, "offends a principle of justice so rooted in the traditions of conscience of our people as to be ranked as fundamental" and is, therefore, inconsistent with due process.

In the case *sub judice*, according to the defendant, he intended to have sex with a 16, not a 13, year old girl. This mistake of fact was prompted, he said, by the prosecutrix herself; she and her friends told him that she was 16 years old. Because he was mistaken as to the prosecutrix's age, he submits, he is certainly less culpable than the person who knows that the minor is 13 years old, but nonetheless engages in sexual relations with her. Notwithstanding, the majority has construed section 463(a)(3) to exclude any proof of knowledge or intent. But for that construction, the proffered defense would be viable. I would hold that the State is not relieved of its burden to prove the defendant's intent or knowledge in a statutory rape case and, therefore, that the defendant may defend on the basis that he was mistaken as to the age of the prosecutrix.

* * *

To recognize that a State legislature may, in defining criminal offenses, exclude mens rea, is not to suggest that it may do so with absolute impunity * * *. It is ordinarily the Due Process Clause, either of the federal constitution, or the * * * state constitution, which will determine its validity.

* * *

* * * The failure of section 463(a)(3) to require proof of a culpable mental state conflicts both with the substantive due process ideal requiring that defendants possess some level of fault for a criminal conviction of statutory rape and the procedural due process ideal requiring that the prosecution overcome the presumption of innocence by proof of the defendant's guilt beyond a reasonable doubt. * * * [As interpreted by the majority], section 463(a)(3) not only destroys absolutely the concept of fault, but it renders meaningless, in the statutory rape context, the presumption of innocence and the right to due process.

I respectfully dissent.

NOTES AND QUESTIONS

1.   In *Garnett*, what arguments did Garnett make to overturn his conviction? What did the court of appeals hold? What did the dissent argue? Which opinion is more persuasive? As a matter of "fairness," should Garnett have been convicted based on the circumstances of the case?

2.   Due process requires that criminal defendants have notice that their conduct is criminal, and thus defendants sometimes argue that the crimes at issue are unconstitutionally vague. In *Johnson v. United States*, 576 U.S. ___, 135 S. Ct. 2551 (2015), the Supreme Court discussed vagueness in the criminal law context, stating: "[T]he Government violates th[e] guarantee [of due process] by taking away someone's life, liberty, or property under a criminal law so vague that it fails to give ordinary people fair notice of the conduct it punishes, or so standardless that it invites arbitrary enforcement." *Id.* at 2556. The Court addressed whether a clause of the Armed Career Criminal Act was unconstitutionally vague. The Act increases an individual's prison term for certain firearm offenses to a minimum of 15 years if the individual has three prior convictions that fall into certain categories. One such category is: "any crime [that] * * * is burglary, arson, or extortion, involves use of explosives, *or otherwise involves conduct that presents a serious potential risk of physical injury to another*." 18 U.S.C § 924(e)(2)(B) (emphasis added). The Supreme Court held that the language was unconstitutionally vague, stating: "We are convinced that the indeterminacy of the wide-ranging inquiry required by [that

language] both denies fair notice to defendants and invites arbitrary enforcement by judges. Increasing a defendant's sentence under the clause denies due process of law." *Id.* at 2557.

3.   In *McNeely v. United States*, 874 A.2d 371 (D.C. Cir. 2005), a man was prosecuted for violating the District of Columbia "Pit Bull and Rottweiler Dangerous Dog Designation Emergency Amendment Act" after his two pit bulls attacked a neighbor. The defendant [McNeely] argued that he did not have "fair warning" that his conduct, *i.e.*, owning the dogs that engaged in the attack, was criminal under the Act. The court interpreted defendant's arguments to be that the law was vague and ruled that the Act was not vague because it clearly set forth the elements of the crime. Accordingly, the court upheld the defendant's conviction. In terms of moral culpability, who is the greater offender: McNeely or Garnett?

4.   For additional reading on strict liability, *see, e.g.*, Paul Larkin, Jr., *Strict Liability Offenses, Incarceration, and the Cruel and Unusual Punishments Clause*, 37 Harv. J.L. & Pub. Pol'y 1065 (2014) (arguing that incarceration of individuals based on convictions for strict liability crimes is unconstitutional); Darryl Brown, *Criminal Law Reform and the Persistence of Strict Liability*, 62 Duke L.J. 285 (2012) (noting that the Model Penal Code does not favor strict liability but that the states have not followed the Code's lead); Kenneth Simons, *When Is Strict Criminal Liability Just?*, 87 J. Crim. L. & Criminology 1075 (1997) (arguing that strict liability is incompatible with culpability-based punishment).

E.   INFERENCES

In some cases, often those involving circumstantial evidence, the only way to conclude that a defendant committed a crime is based on inference. Inferences, however, may only be made based on facts proven at trial. The following case discusses the inappropriateness of inferences that are made without a factual basis.

DLUGASH V. NEW YORK

United States District Court, Eastern District of New York, 1979
476 F. Supp. 921

NICKERSON, DISTRICT JUDGE.

Petitioner Melvin Dlugash [asserts] that his conviction in the New York State Courts for attempted murder violated his right to due process under the Fourteenth Amendment.

Dlugash was indicted on January 9, 1974 in Kings County for the murder of Michael Geller. Although charged with acting in concert with one Joseph Bush, Dlugash was tried alone.

At the trial the only evidence describing Geller's death was Dlugash's statement to the police. According to that statement he and Bush were at

Geller's home on the night of December 21, 1973, all three having been out drinking. During the course of the evening Bush had carried on a heated argument with Geller concerning money and had made frequent threats to shoot him. Finally in the early morning of December 22, 1973, Bush pulled out a pistol and fired three shots into Geller's chest.

Geller fell to the floor mortally wounded. Within a few minutes, perhaps as many as five, Dlugash went over and fired his own pistol five times into Geller's face. Dlugash told the police that he fired his gun believing Geller already dead and fearing for his own life at Bush's hands.

Medical experts for both the prosecution and the defense testified that the shots by either Bush or Dlugash would have been fatal. But none of the experts could say whether Geller was still alive when Dlugash fired.

The trial judge * * * presented the case to the jury on two theories, intentional murder and attempted murder.

Before defining the crime of murder the judge told the jury that "the big contention evidently is whether the deceased was alive at the time that Mr. Dlugash shot him." He then instructed that "a person is guilty of murder when with intent to cause the death of another person he causes such death." "Intent" he defined as "a doing of an act deliberately, willfully, knowingly, feloniously as distinguished from doing an act by mistake or by accident or by negligence or by carelessness." After stating that criminal intent could be "inferred from all the facts and circumstances in the case connected with the individual upon whom you are inquiring," the judge charged that "under our law every person is presumed to intend the natural and probable consequences of his acts but this presumption, like all presumptions, may be accepted or rejected by you."

After completing the instructions as to murder, the judge turned to the charge of attempted murder. He told the jurors they should not consider this crime if they found petitioner guilty of murder. The critical portion of the instructions on attempted murder [was] as follows: "Now, ladies and gentlemen, * * * even though it was factually or legally impossible to kill the deceased because of his prior death, you would be warranted in convicting this defendant of an attempt to murder if you found beyond a reasonable doubt that at the time the defendant discharged the bullet into the body of the deceased he, the defendant, actually intended to kill the deceased, believing in his own mind that the deceased was living, even though he was dead."

The jury returned a verdict of guilty of murder and Dlugash was sentenced to fifteen years to life. * * * [T]he Appellate Division, Second Department, reversed, holding that in the light of the experts' testimony the prosecution had not proven beyond a reasonable doubt that Geller had been alive when Dlugash shot him. The District Attorney, apparently conceding the lack of evidence to convict of murder, asked the court to modify the judgment and enter a judgment of conviction of attempted murder. The Appellate Division declined to do so, finding that there was no proof that Dlugash believed Geller alive. The court accordingly dismissed the indictment.

On the District Attorney's appeal the New York Court of Appeals affirmed the dismissal of the murder charge. But the court ruled that there was sufficient evidence for the jury to find that Dlugash believed Geller alive and held that the Appellate Division should have modified the judgment to reflect a conviction for attempted murder. The court's opinion reasoned that by rendering a guilty verdict as to murder the jury necessarily found intent to kill a live person and that subsumed within this finding was a finding that Dlugash believed Geller alive. Concluding that there was no need for further findings of fact by a jury, the court reversed and remanded.

* * * On August 2, 1978, Dlugash was sentenced to up to three years. * * *

Dlugash contends that the modification of the judgment to convict him of attempted murder denied him due process. He argues, among other things, that, while a belief that the victim is alive is an element of both * * * murder and attempted murder, the jury instructions permitted, indeed invited, the jurors while considering the crime of murder to "presume" the necessary belief once they found Geller alive. Dlugash therefore says the verdict of murder cannot consistently with due process be the foundation for a conviction of attempted murder which requires a finding that he "actually" believed Geller alive.

The pertinent part of the New York Penal Law provides that a person is guilty of murder when "[w]ith intent to cause the death of another person, he causes the death of such person." Under [the Penal Law,] one who "with intent to commit a crime" engages "in conduct which tends to effect the commission of such crime" is guilty of an attempt. * * * [I]f a person's conduct otherwise constitutes an attempt, it is no defense to a prosecution for attempt "that the crime charged to have been attempted was, under the attendant circumstances, factually or legally impossible of commission, if such crime could have been committed had the attendant circumstances been as such person believed them to be." As the New York Court of Appeals stated and as the trial judge charged, Dlugash could be found guilty of an attempt under these sections only if he actually believed Geller alive.

Although the jury rendered a verdict of murder, Dlugash stands convicted of attempted murder. Due process entitled him to a jury trial of that crime, and required that the prosecution prove and the jury find beyond a reasonable doubt every element of the crime. Therefore, in order to sustain the conviction of attempted murder it must be shown that the prosecution proved and the jury properly found that when he fired his gun

Dlugash believed that Geller was alive. Due process further requires that any such findings have been based on instructions which appropriately described under the proof in the case the intellectual process whereby the jurors might make the finding.

The question is not whether the trial court's charge properly instructed the jurors as to murder. We may assume that and accept the reasoning of the New York Court of Appeals that Dlugash's belief that Geller was alive was subsumed in the finding of intent to kill necessary to a murder conviction. The question before this court is whether a conviction for attempted murder can consistently with due process be based on the instructions as to murder. In deciding that question we must consider what the jurors fairly could have understood they must find in order to conclude that Dlugash had an "intent to kill." * * *

In his instructions as to murder, the judge focused the jury's attention on whether Geller was alive when Dlugash fired. That was the "big contention." Although the judge made it clear that there must be an "intent to kill," he defined "intent" not in terms of Dlugash's belief as to Geller's condition but as the doing of an act deliberately and knowingly as distinguished from mistakenly or negligently. Finally he charged that "under our law every person is presumed to intend the natural and probable consequences of his acts but this presumption, like all presumptions, may be accepted or rejected by you."

The instructions as to the element of intent in attempted murder were in striking contrast to those on intent as applied to the murder charge. To convict of attempted murder, the jurors were told, they must find that Dlugash "actually" intended to kill Geller, "believing in his own mind that the deceased was living."

By concentrating the jury's attention in the murder instructions on the "big contention" of whether Geller was alive when Dlugash fired, and by reciting in the murder instructions that "our law" "presumed" an intent to attain the natural and probable "consequences" of one's acts while requiring "actual" intent in the attempt instructions, the judge led the jurors to understand that in considering the crime of murder they could "presume" Dlugash had an intent to kill once they made a finding that Geller was alive.

The District Attorney suggested on oral argument that the presumption language should be read as meaning no more than that the jury might infer from the fact that Dlugash pulled the trigger of his loaded gun that he intended the "natural consequences" that bullets would be discharged and hit the object at which he aimed. There is no warrant for this argument. The "intent" to which the jury's attention was directed was "intent to kill", not a more generalized intent to hit an object. Clearly the instructions invited the jurors to "presume" intent to kill from the "natural consequences" of shooting a live person.

As the jurors considered the crime of murder the logical sequence of their deliberations could well have been as follows. First they would have focused on the "big contention," whether Geller was alive. Having decided that Geller was alive they would have concluded that the "natural and probable consequence" of shooting five times into a live man's face would have been to kill him. From that they would have understood they could "presume" the requisite intent.

Since the jurors found that Geller was alive when Dlugash fired, it certainly does not appear that their conclusion that Dlugash had the requisite intent was reached by considering only sources independent of their determination that Geller was alive. It follows that whether the jurors understood the word "presume" as having its common dictionary meaning of "to suppose to be true without proof," Webster's New Collegiate Dictionary 911 (1974), or merely as permitting an inference, the conviction cannot stand under the Due Process Clause.

If the instruction is read merely to permit an inference, the conviction of attempted murder is based on a finding of intent to kill which may well, and probably does, rest on an inference drawn from an unproven supposition. Since no expert could say whether Geller was alive or dead, there was no evidence on which to base a finding * * * that he was living. To comport with due process inferences may only be made from proven facts.

If the instruction is construed to allow a presumption shifting the evidentiary burden as to intent and to permit a finding of intent to kill on the false hypothesis that the prosecution had proven Geller alive, the conviction plainly denies due process.

Whichever of the two interpretations is adopted there is no assurance that the jury properly found beyond a reasonable doubt the essential element, namely, Dlugash's belief that Geller was alive. * * *

Although no objection was made to the trial judge's instructions as to murder, Dlugash did not thereby waive the due process contention he makes here and made in the state appellate courts. Nor does the District Attorney urge that there was a waiver. This is not a case where an objection in the trial court would have avoided error. The violation of due process claimed did not occur at the trial but as a result of the action of the New York Court of Appeals in directing the entry of judgment of conviction of attempted murder. * * *

* * *

The conviction having been obtained in violation of Dlugash's right to due process * * * he shall be released unless the State grants him a new trial within sixty days. So ordered.

NOTES AND QUESTIONS

1.   Although Dlugash's trial initially took place in state court, the court decision set out here is by a federal court. The reason is that incarcerated individuals may attack their convictions by seeking a writ of habeas corpus in federal court (meaning literally "produce the body"), regardless of whether they were initially convicted in state or federal court. State court convictions may be attacked under 28 U.S.C. § 2254 on the grounds that the conviction violated the Constitution, laws, or treaties of the United States. *See Wainwright v. Sykes*, 433 U.S. 72, 87 (1977) ("The federal habeas petitioner who claims he is detained pursuant to a final judgment of a state court in violation of the United States Constitution is entitled to have the federal habeas court make its own independent determination of his claim, without being bound by the determination on the merits of that claim reached in the state proceedings."); *Harrington v. Richter*, 562 U.S. 86, 102–03 (2011) ("[H]abeas corpus is a 'guard against extreme malfunctions in the state criminal justice systems,' not a substitute for ordinary error correction through appeal."). *See generally* U.S. CONST. art. I, § 9 ("The privilege of the Writ of Habeas Corpus shall not be suspended, unless when in Cases of Rebellion or Invasion the public Safety may require it."). The writ of habeas corpus is also discussed in Chapter 2.

2.   The *Dlugash* case generated a variety of approaches. What did the jury find? How did the Appellate Division rule? Why did the New York Court of Appeals (the state's highest court) disagree with the Appellate Division? Why did the federal district court disagree with the New York Court of Appeals?

3.   The issue of intent—and how intent should be determined—is at the forefront in *Dlugash*. What did Dlugash likely intend when he shot Geller? What tools should courts use to analyze an individual's intent? For an analysis of the case, *see* Gideon Yaffe, *Trying to Kill the Dead: De Re and De Dicto Intention in Attempted Crimes, in* PHILOSOPHICAL FOUNDATIONS OF LAW & LANGUAGE 184 (Andrei Marmor & Scott Soames eds., 2011) (concluding that Dlugash could not properly be found guilty of attempted murder).

F. PROVOCATION

In some cases, an individual may not be fully culpable for his actions because he was provoked. The analysis is fact-specific and depends on whether the provocation was sufficiently serious to cause a reasonable person to commit the crime. The following case addresses verbal provocation in the marital context.

GIROUARD V. STATE

Court of Appeals of Maryland, 1991
321 Md. 532, 583 A.2d 718

COLE, JUDGE.

* * * [W]e must determine whether words [of provocation] alone are provocation adequate to justify a conviction of manslaughter rather than one of second degree murder.

The Petitioner, Steven S. Girouard, and the deceased, Joyce M. Girouard, had been married for about two months on October 28, 1987, the night of Joyce's death. Both parties, who met while working in the same building, were in the army. They married after having known each other for approximately three months. The evidence at trial indicated that the marriage was often tense and strained, and there was some evidence that after marrying Steven, Joyce had resumed a relationship with her old boyfriend, Wayne.

On the night of Joyce's death, Steven overheard her talking on the telephone to her friend, whereupon she told the friend that she had asked her first sergeant for a hardship discharge because her husband did not love her anymore. Steven went into the living room where Joyce was on the phone and asked her what she meant by her comments; she responded, "nothing." Angered by her lack of response, Steven kicked away the plate of food Joyce had in front of her. He then went to lie down in the bedroom.

Joyce followed him into the bedroom, stepped up onto the bed and onto Steven's back, pulled his hair and said, "What are you going to do, hit me?" She continued to taunt him by saying, "I never did want to marry you and you are a lousy fuck and you remind me of my dad." The barrage of insults continued with her telling Steven that she wanted a divorce, that the marriage had been a mistake and that she had never wanted to marry him. She also told him she had seen his commanding officer and filed charges against him for abuse. She then asked Steven, "What are you going to do?" Receiving no response, she continued her verbal attack. She added that she had filed charges against him in the Judge Advocate General's Office (JAG) and that he would probably be court martialed.

When she was through, Steven asked her if she had really done all those things, and she responded in the affirmative. He left the bedroom with his pillow in his arms and proceeded to the kitchen where he procured a long handled kitchen knife. He returned to Joyce in the bedroom with the knife behind the pillow. He testified that he was enraged and that he kept waiting for Joyce to say she was kidding, but Joyce continued talking. She said she had learned a lot from the marriage and that it had been a mistake. She also told him she would remain in their apartment after he moved out. When he questioned how she would afford it, she told him she would claim her brain-damaged sister as a dependent and have the sister move in. Joyce reiterated that the marriage was a big mistake, that she did not love him and that the divorce would be better for her.

After pausing for a moment, Joyce asked what Steven was going to do. What he did was lunge at her with the kitchen knife he had hidden behind the pillow and stab her 19 times. Realizing what he had done, he dropped the knife and went to the bathroom to shower off Joyce's blood. Feeling like he wanted to die, Steven went back to the kitchen and found two steak knives with which he slit his own wrists. He lay down on the bed waiting to die, but when he realized that he would not die from his self-inflicted wounds, he got up and called the police, telling the dispatcher that he had just murdered his wife.

When the police arrived they found Steven wandering around outside his apartment building. Steven was despondent and tearful and seemed detached, according to police officers who had been at the scene. He was unconcerned about his own wounds, talking only about how much he loved his wife and how he could not believe what he had done. Joyce Girouard was pronounced dead at the scene.

At trial, defense witness, psychologist, Dr. William Stejskal, testified that Steven was out of touch with his own capacity to experience anger or express hostility. He stated that the events of October 28, 1987, were entirely consistent with Steven's personality, that Steven had "basically reach[ed] the limit of his ability to swallow his anger, to rationalize his wife's behavior, to tolerate, or actually to remain in a passive mode with that. He essentially went over the limit of his ability to bottle up those strong emotions. What ensued was a very extreme explosion of rage that was intermingled with a great deal of panic." Another defense witness, psychiatrist, Thomas Goldman, testified that Joyce had a "compulsive need to provoke jealousy so that she's always asking for love and at the same time destroying and undermining any chance that she really might have to establish any kind of mature love with anybody."

Steven Girouard was convicted * * * of second degree murder and was sentenced to 22 years incarceration, 10 of which were suspended. Upon his release, Petitioner is to be on probation for five years, two years supervised and three years unsupervised. The Court of Special Appeals affirmed the judgment * * *. We granted [review] * * *.

Petitioner [argues] that the provocation to mitigate murder to manslaughter should not be limited only to the traditional circumstances of: extreme assault or battery upon the defendant; mutual combat; defendant's illegal arrest; injury or serious abuse of a close relative of the defendant's; or the sudden discovery of a spouse's adultery. Petitioner argues that manslaughter is a catchall for homicides which are criminal but that lack the malice essential for a conviction of murder. Steven argues that the trial judge did find provocation (although he held it inadequate to mitigate murder) and that the categories of provocation adequate to mitigate should be broadened to include factual situations such as this one.

The State counters by stating that * * * [w]ords spoken by the victim, no matter how abusive or taunting, fall into a category society should not accept as adequate provocation. According to the State, if abusive words alone could mitigate murder to manslaughter, nearly every domestic argument ending in the death of one party could be mitigated to manslaughter. This, the State avers, is not an acceptable outcome. Thus, the State argues that the courts below were correct in holding that the taunting words by Joyce Girouard were not provocation adequate to reduce Steven's second degree murder charge to voluntary manslaughter.

Initially, we note that the difference between murder and manslaughter is the presence or absence of malice. Voluntary manslaughter has been defined as "an *intentional* homicide, done in a sudden heat of passion, caused by adequate provocation, before there has been a reasonable opportunity for the passion to cool" (emphasis in original).

There are certain facts that may mitigate what would normally be murder to manslaughter. For example, we have recognized as falling into that group: (1) discovering one's spouse in the act of sexual intercourse with another; (2) mutual combat; (3) assault and battery. There is also authority recognizing injury to one of the defendant's relatives or to a third party, and death resulting from resistance of an illegal arrest as adequate provocation for mitigation to manslaughter. Those acts mitigate homicide to manslaughter because they create passion in the defendant and are not considered the product of free will.

In order to determine whether murder should be mitigated to manslaughter we look to the circumstances surrounding the homicide and try to discover if it was provoked by the victim. Over the facts of the case we lay the template of the so-called "Rule of Provocation." The courts of this State have repeatedly set forth the requirements of the Rule of Provocation:

1. There must have been adequate provocation;

2. The killing must have been in the heat of passion;

3. It must have been a sudden heat of passion—that is, the killing must have followed the provocation before there had been a reasonable opportunity for the passion to cool;

4. There must have been a causal connection between the provocation, the passion, and the fatal act.

We shall assume without deciding that the second, third, and fourth of the criteria listed above were met in this case. We focus our attention on an examination of the ultimate issue in this case, that is, whether the provocation of Steven by Joyce was enough in the eyes of the law so that the murder charge against Steven should have been mitigated to voluntary manslaughter. For provocation to be "adequate," it must be " 'calculated to inflame the passion of a reasonable man and tend to cause him to act for the moment from passion rather than reason.' " The issue we must resolve, then, is whether the taunting words uttered by Joyce were enough to inflame the passion of a *reasonable* man so that that man would be sufficiently infuriated so as to strike out in hot-blooded blind passion to kill her. Although we [believe] that there was needless provocation by Joyce, we also [believe] that the provocation was not adequate to mitigate second degree murder to voluntary manslaughter.

* * *

* * * [W]ords can constitute adequate provocation if they are accompanied by conduct indicating a present intention and ability to cause the defendant bodily harm. Clearly, no such conduct was exhibited by Joyce in this case. While Joyce did step on Steven's back and pull his hair, he could not reasonably have feared bodily harm at her hands. This, to us, is certain based on Steven's testimony at trial that Joyce was about 5' 1" tall and weighed 115 pounds, while he was 6' 2" tall, weighing over 200 pounds. Joyce simply did not have the size or strength to cause Steven to fear for his bodily safety. Thus, since there was no ability on the part of Joyce to cause Steven harm, the words she hurled at him could not * * * constitute legally sufficient provocation.

Other jurisdictions overwhelmingly agree with our cases and hold that words alone are not adequate provocation. One jurisdiction that does allow provocation brought about by prolonged stress, anger and hostility caused by marital problems to provide grounds for a verdict of voluntary manslaughter rather than murder is Pennsylvania. * * * [Under Pennsylvania law,] the determination of the weight and credibility of the testimony regarding the marital stress and arguments [is left] to the trier of fact.

We are unpersuaded by [Pennsylvania law given] a sea of opposite holdings. * * *

Thus, with no reservation, we hold that the provocation in this case was not enough to cause a reasonable man to stab his provoker 19 times. Although a psychologist testified to Steven's mental problems * * *, "there must be not simply provocation in psychological fact, but one of certain fairly well-defined classes of provocation recognized as being adequate as a matter of law." * * * We cannot in good conscience countenance holding that a verbal domestic argument ending in the death of one spouse can result in a conviction of manslaughter. We agree with the trial judge that social necessity dictates our holding. Domestic arguments easily escalate into furious fights. We perceive no reason for a holding in favor of those who find the easiest way to end a domestic dispute is by killing the offending spouse.

We will leave to another day the possibility of expansion of the categories of adequate provocation to mitigate murder to manslaughter. The facts of this case do not warrant the broadening of the categories recognized thus far.

NOTES AND QUESTIONS

1.   Was the *Girouard* court correct in finding that mitigation from murder was not warranted? Was the situation faced by Girouard really less provocative than the kinds of situations in which mitigation has been allowed by the Maryland courts?

2.   For examples of cases in which courts have found justification for a provocation instruction, *see, e.g., State v. Ventre*, 811 A.2d 1178 (R.I. 2002) (holding that the trial court erred in refusing to give an involuntary manslaughter instruction based on provocation (in addition to a self-defense instruction) in a murder case when the defendant's car was intentionally damaged by the victim and the victim also attacked the defendant during the incident); *Rogers v. State*, 819 So. 2d 643 (Ala. Crim. App. 2001) (holding that a heat of passion provocation instruction was warranted when the defendant saw the victim on top of the defendant's brother holding a gun and the victim had previously shot the defendant's brother months earlier); *State v. Craig*, 33 S.W. 3d 597 (Mo. Ct. App. 2000) (holding that the trial court erred in failing to give a provocation instruction when the victim weighed approximately 230 pounds, was intoxicated, cursed at the defendant, and brandished a 12-inch knife during the argument).

3.   For a discussion of provocation and the rights of provocateurs, *see, e.g.,* Kimberly Kessler Ferzan, *Provocateurs*, 7 Crim. L. & Phil. 597 (2013) (contending that when words make a defendant extremely angry, such words might justify a partial excuse for the defendant's behavior). Should verbal provocation ever be egregious enough to justify the provocation defense? If so, under what circumstances?

G. ATTEMPT

Individuals who try to commit crimes are not always successful. Failure to complete a criminal act, however, does not always eliminate an individual's culpability. The following case involves an "attempt crime" by a minor.

STATE V. REEVES

Supreme Court of Tennessee, 1996
916 S.W.2d 909

DROWOTA, JUDGE.

The defendant, Tracie Reeves, appeals from the Court of Appeals' affirmance of the trial court's order designating her a delinquent child. The trial court's delinquency order, which was entered following a jury trial, was based on the jury's finding that the defendant had attempted to commit second degree murder—a violation of * * * [Tennessee law]. The specific issue for our determination is whether the defendant's actions constitute a "substantial step" * * * toward the commission of that crime. For the following reasons, we hold that they do, and therefore affirm the judgment of the Court of Appeals.

FACTS AND PROCEDURAL HISTORY

On the evening of January 5, 1993, Tracie Reeves and Molly Coffman, both twelve years of age and students at West Carroll Middle School, spoke on the telephone and decided to kill their homeroom teacher, Janice Geiger. The girls agreed that Coffman would bring rat poison to school the following day so that it could be placed in Geiger's drink. The girls also agreed that they would thereafter steal Geiger's car and drive to the Smoky Mountains. Reeves then contacted Dean Foutch, a local high school student, informed him of the plan, and asked him to drive Geiger's car. Foutch refused this request.

On the morning of January 6, Coffman placed a packet of rat poison in her purse and boarded the school bus. During the bus ride Coffman told another student, Christy Hernandez, of the plan; Coffman also showed Hernandez the packet of rat poison. Upon their arrival at school Hernandez informed her homeroom teacher, Sherry Cockrill, of the plan. Cockrill then relayed this information to the principal of the school, Claudia Argo.

When Geiger entered her classroom that morning she observed Reeves and Coffman leaning over her desk; and when the girls noticed her, they giggled and ran back to their seats. At that time Geiger saw a purse lying next to her coffee cup on top of the desk. Shortly thereafter Argo called Coffman to the principal's office. Rat poison was found in Coffman's purse and it was turned over to a Sheriff's Department investigator. Both Reeves and Coffman gave written statements to the investigator concerning their plan to poison Geiger and steal her car.

Reeves and Coffman were found to be delinquent by the Carroll County Juvenile Court, and both appealed from that ruling to the Carroll County Circuit Court. After a jury found that the girls attempted to commit second degree murder in violation of * * * the "criminal attempt" statute, the trial court affirmed the juvenile court's order and sentenced the girls to [a juvenile detention center] for an indefinite period. Reeves appealed from this judgment to the Court of Appeals, which affirmed the judgment of the trial court. Reeves then applied to this Court for permission to appeal. * * * [W]e granted that application.

PRIOR AND CURRENT LAW OF CRIMINAL ATTEMPT

Before the passage of the reform legislation in 1989, the law of criminal attempt, though sanctioned by various statutes, was judicially defined. In order to submit an issue of criminal attempt to the jury, the State was required to present legally sufficient evidence of: (1) an intent to commit a specific crime; (2) an overt act toward the commission of that crime; and (3) a failure to consummate the crime.

Of the elements of criminal attempt, the second, the "overt act" requirement, was by far the most problematic. By attempting to draw a sharp distinction between "mere preparation" to commit a criminal act, which did not constitute the required overt act, and a "direct movement toward the commission after the preparations had been made," which did, Tennessee courts construed the term "overt act" very narrowly. The best example of this extremely narrow construction occurred in *Dupuy v. State*, 204 Tenn. 624, 325 S.W.2d 238 (1959). In that case, the Memphis police sought to lay a trap for a pharmacist suspected of performing illegal abortions by sending a young woman to request these services from him. After the woman had made several attempts to secure his services, he finally agreed to perform the abortion. The pharmacist transported the young woman to a hotel room, laid out his instruments in preparation for the procedure, and asked the woman to remove her clothes. At that point the police came into the room and arrested the pharmacist, who then admitted that he had performed abortions in the past. The defendant was convicted under a statute that made it illegal to procure a miscarriage, and he appealed to this Court.

A majority of this Court reversed the conviction. After admitting that the defendant's "reprehensible" course of conduct would doubtlessly have resulted in the commission of the crime "had he not been thwarted in his efforts by the arrival of the police," the majority concluded that:

> * * * [T]he element of attempt [overt act] does not appear in this record. The proof shows that [the defendant] did not use any of the instruments and did not touch the body of the girl in question. Under such facts we do not think that the defendant is guilty under the statute.

To support its holding, the *Dupuy* court [differentiated between] actions that constituted "mere preparation," as opposed to actions that would satisfy the overt act requirement * * *.

To * * * illustrate the [point] the majority provided the following example: "the procurement by a prisoner of tools adapted to breaking jail does not render him guilty of an attempt to break jail."

* * * [T]he sharp differentiation in *Dupuy* between "mere preparation" and "overt act," or the "act itself," was characteristic of the pre-1989 attempt law. In 1989, however, the legislature enacted a general criminal attempt statute, as part of its comprehensive overhaul of Tennessee's criminal law. In that statute, the legislature did not simply codify the judicially-created elements of the crime, but utilized language that had up to then been entirely foreign to Tennessee attempt law. Section 39–12–101 provides, in pertinent part, as follows:

(a) A person commits criminal attempt who, acting with the kind of culpability otherwise required for the offense:

(1) Intentionally engages in action or causes a result that would constitute an offense if the circumstances surrounding the conduct were as the person believes them to be;

(2) Acts with intent to cause a result that is an element of the offense, and believes the conduct will cause the result without further conduct on the person's part; or

(3) Acts with intent to complete a course of action or cause a result that would constitute the offense, under the circumstances surrounding the conduct as the person believe them to be, *and the conduct constitutes a substantial step toward the commission of the offense.*

(b) Conduct does not constitute a *substantial step* under subdivision (a)(3) unless the person's entire course of action is corroborative of the intent to commit the offense.

[Emphasis added by the court.]

THE SUBSTANTIAL STEP ISSUE

As stated above, our task is to determine whether the defendant's actions in this case constitute a "substantial step" toward the commission of second degree murder under the new statute. The * * * question is made more difficult by the fact that the legislature declined to set forth any definition of the term, preferring instead to "leave the issue of what constitutes a substantial step [to the courts] for determination in each particular case."

In addressing this issue, we first note that the legislature, in enacting § 39–12–101, clearly looked to the criminal attempt section set forth in the Model Penal Code. That section provides, in pertinent part, as follows:

(1) Definition of attempt. A person is guilty of an attempt to commit a crime if, acting with the kind of culpability otherwise required for commission of the crime, he:

(a) purposely engages in conduct which would constitute the crime if the attendant circumstances were as he believes them to be; or

(b) when causing a particular result is an element of the crime, does or omits to do anything with the purpose of causing or with the belief that it will cause such result, without further conduct on his part; or

(c) purposely does or omits to do anything which, under the circumstances as he believes them to be, is a *substantial step in a course of conduct planned to culminate in his commission of the crime*

Model Penal Code, Section 5.01 (emphasis added [by the court]).

The State argues that the striking similarity of Tenn. Code Ann. § 39–12–101 and the Model Penal Code evidences the legislature's intention to abandon the old law of criminal attempt and instead adopt the Model Penal Code approach. The State then avers that the model code contains examples of conduct which, if proven, would entitle, but not require, the jury to find that the defendant had taken a "substantial step;" and that two of these examples are applicable to this case. The section of the model code relied upon by the State, § 5.01(2), provides, in pertinent part, as follows:

(2) * * * [T]he following, if strongly corroborative of the actor's criminal purpose, shall not be held insufficient as a matter of law:

. . .

(e) possession of materials to be employed in the commission of the crime, which are specially designed for such unlawful use or which can serve no lawful purpose of the actor under the circumstances;

(f) possession, collection or fabrication of materials to be employed in the commission of the crime, at or near the place contemplated for its commission, where such possession, collection or fabrication serves no lawful purpose of the actor under the circumstances;

. . .

The State concludes that because the issue of whether the defendant's conduct constitutes a substantial step may be a jury question under the model code, the jury was justified in finding her guilty of attempting to commit second degree murder.

The defendant counters by arguing that despite the similarity of Tenn. Code Ann. § 39–12–101 and the Model Penal Code's attempt provision, the legislature intended to retain the sharp distinction between "mere preparation" and the "act itself" characteristic of such decisions as *Dupuy*.

She supports this assertion by pointing out that although the legislature could have easily included the examples set forth in § 5.01(2) of the model code, the Tennessee statute does not include the examples. The defendant concludes that the new statute did not substantially change Tennessee attempt law, and that her conviction must be reversed because her actions constitute "mere preparation" under *Dupuy*.

Initially, we cannot accept the argument that the legislature intended to explicitly adopt the Model Penal Code approach, including the examples set forth in § 5.01(2). Although § 39–12–101 is obviously based on the model code, we agree with the defendant that the legislature could have, if it had so desired, simply included the specific examples in the Tennessee statute. That it did not do so prohibits us from concluding that the legislature explicitly intended to adopt the model code approach in all its particulars.

This conclusion does not mean, however, that the legislature intended to retain the distinction between "mere preparation" and the "act itself." * * * [W]hile we concede that a strong argument can be made that the conviction conflicts with *Dupuy* because the defendant did not place the poison in the cup, but simply brought it to the crime scene, we also are well aware that the *Dupuy* approach to attempt law has been consistently and effectively criticized. One persistent criticism of the endeavor to separate "mere preparation" from the "act itself" is that the question is ultimately not one of kind but of degree * * *. Therefore, distinguishing between "mere preparation" and the "act itself" in a principled manner is a difficult, if not impossible, task. The other principal ground of criticism of the *Dupuy* approach bears directly on the primary objective of the law—that of preventing inchoate crimes from becoming full-blown ones. Many courts and commentators have argued that failing to attach criminal responsibility to the actor—and therefore prohibiting law enforcement officers from taking action—until the actor is on the brink of consummating the crime endangers the public and undermines the preventative goal of attempt law.

The shortcomings of the *Dupuy* rule with respect to the goal of prevention are particularly evident in this case. As stated above, it is likely that under *Dupuy* no criminal responsibility would have attached unless the poison had actually been placed in the teacher's cup. This rigid requirement, however, severely undercuts the objective of prevention because of the surreptitious nature of the act of poisoning. Once a person secretly places a toxic substance into a container from which another person is likely to eat or drink, the damage is done. Here, if it had not been for the intervention of the teacher, she could have been rendered powerless to protect herself from harm.

After carefully weighing considerations of *stare decisis* against the persuasive criticisms of the *Dupuy* rule, we conclude that this artificial and potentially harmful rule must be abandoned. We hold that when an actor possesses materials to be used in the commission of a crime, at or near the scene of the crime, and where the possession of those materials can serve no lawful purpose of the actor under the circumstances, the jury is entitled, but not required, to find that the actor has taken a "substantial step" toward the commission of the crime if such action is strongly corroborative of the actor's overall criminal purpose. For the foregoing reasons, the judgment of the Court of Appeals is affirmed.

* * *

[Opinion by JUSTICE BIRCH concurring in part and dissenting in part is omitted.]

NOTES AND QUESTIONS

1.   As in *Winship*, the defendant in *Reeves* was tried within the juvenile justice system. Features of the juvenile justice system are described in the notes following *Winship*.

2.   What was Reeves's argument in the Tennessee Supreme Court for contesting the conviction for attempted second-degree murder? What facts were crucial to her argument? How did the court rule? Is the court's opinion persuasive?

3.   For additional discussion of inchoate (incomplete) crimes, *see* Ira Robbins, *Double Inchoate Crimes*, 26 Harv. J. on Legis. 1 (1989) (discussing the prosecution of incomplete crimes, such as attempts, and concluding that some degree of judicial discretion is necessary to allow inchoate crimes to be prosecuted when they pose a risk to society).

H. JUSTIFICATION DEFENSE

The justification defense applies when an individual must commit a crime to prevent some other bad act. For example, the defense often applies in cases of self-defense or defense of others—situations when the defendant needs to commit a crime to prevent a violent act. The following case discusses the justification defense.

PEOPLE V. GOETZ

Court of Appeals of New York, 1986
68 N.Y.2d 96, 497 N.E.2d 41

WACHTLER, CHIEF JUDGE.

A Grand Jury has indicted defendant on attempted murder, assault, and other charges for having shot and wounded four youths on a New York City subway train after one or two of the youths approached him and asked for $5. The lower courts, concluding that the prosecutor's charge to the Grand Jury on the defense of justification was erroneous, have dismissed the attempted murder, assault and weapons possession charges. We now reverse and reinstate all counts of the indictment.

I.

The precise circumstances of the incident giving rise to the charges against defendant are disputed, and ultimately it will be for a trial jury to determine what occurred. We feel it necessary, however, to provide some factual background to properly frame the legal issues before us. Accordingly, we have summarized the facts as they appear from the evidence before the Grand Jury. We stress, however, that we do not purport to reach any conclusions or holding as to exactly what transpired or whether defendant is blameworthy. The credibility of witnesses and the reasonableness of defendant's conduct are to be resolved by the trial jury.

On Saturday afternoon, December 22, 1984, Troy Canty, Darryl Cabey, James Ramseur, and Barry Allen boarded an * * * express subway train in The Bronx and headed south toward lower Manhattan. The four youths rode together in the rear portion of the seventh car of the train. Two of the four, Ramseur and Cabey, had screwdrivers inside their coats, which they said were to be used to break into the coin boxes of video machines.

Defendant Bernhard Goetz boarded this subway train at 14th Street in Manhattan and sat down on a bench towards the rear section of the same car occupied by the four youths. Goetz was carrying an unlicensed .38 caliber pistol loaded with five rounds of ammunition in a waistband holster. The train left the 14th Street station and headed towards Chambers Street.

It appears from the evidence before the Grand Jury that Canty approached Goetz, possibly with Allen beside him, and stated "give me five dollars." Neither Canty nor any of the other youths displayed a weapon. Goetz responded by standing up, pulling out his handgun and firing four shots in rapid succession. The first shot hit Canty in the chest; the second struck Allen in the back; the third went through Ramseur's arm and into his left side; the fourth was fired at Cabey, who apparently was then standing in the corner of the car, but missed, deflecting instead off of a wall of the conductor's cab. After Goetz briefly surveyed the scene around him, he fired another shot at Cabey, who then was sitting on the end bench of the car. The bullet entered the rear of Cabey's side and severed his spinal cord.

All but two of the other passengers fled the car when, or immediately after, the shots were fired. The conductor, who had been in the next car, heard the shots and instructed the motorman to radio for emergency assistance. The conductor then went into the car where the shooting occurred and saw Goetz sitting on a bench, the injured youths lying on the floor or slumped against a seat, and two women who had apparently taken cover, also lying on the floor. Goetz told the conductor that the four youths had tried to rob him.

While the conductor was aiding the youths, Goetz headed towards the front of the car. The train had stopped just before the Chambers Street station and Goetz went between two of the cars, jumped onto the tracks and fled. Police and ambulance crews arrived at the scene shortly thereafter. Ramseur and Canty, initially listed in critical condition, have fully recovered. Cabey remains paralyzed, and has suffered some degree of brain damage.

On December 31, 1984, Goetz surrendered to police in Concord, New Hampshire, identifying himself as the gunman being sought for the subway shootings in New York nine days earlier. Later that day, after receiving *Miranda* warnings, he made two lengthy statements, both of which were tape recorded with his permission. In the statements, which are substantially similar, Goetz admitted that he had been illegally carrying a handgun in New York City for three years. He stated that he had first purchased a gun in 1981 after he had been injured in a mugging. Goetz also revealed that twice between 1981 and 1984 he had successfully warded off assailants simply by displaying the pistol.

According to Goetz's statement, the first contact he had with the four youths came when Canty, sitting or lying on the bench across from him, asked "how are you," to which he replied "fine." Shortly thereafter, Canty, followed by one of the other youths, walked over to the defendant and stood to his left, while the other two youths remained to his right, in the corner of the subway car. Canty then said "give me five dollars." Goetz stated that he knew from the smile on Canty's face that they wanted to "play with me." Although he was certain that none of the youths had a gun, he had a fear, based on prior experiences, of being "maimed."

Goetz then established "a pattern of fire," deciding specifically to fire from left to right. His stated intention at that point was to "murder [the four youths], to hurt them, to make them suffer as much as possible." When Canty again requested money, Goetz stood up, drew his weapon, and began firing, aiming for the center of the body of each of the four. Goetz recalled that the first two he shot "tried to run through the crowd [but] they had nowhere to run." Goetz then turned to his right to "go after the other two." One of these two "tried to run through the wall of the train, but * * * he had nowhere to go." The other youth (Cabey) "tried pretending that he wasn't with [the others]" by standing still, holding on to one of the subway hand straps, and not looking at Goetz. Goetz nonetheless fired his fourth shot at him. He then ran back to the first two youths to make sure they had been "taken care of." Seeing that they had both been shot, he spun back to check on the latter two. Goetz noticed that the youth who had been standing still was now sitting on a bench and seemed unhurt. As Goetz told the police, "I said '[y]ou seem to be all right, here's another,' " and he then fired the shot which severed Cabey's spinal cord. Goetz added that "if I was a little more under self-control * * * I would have put the barrel against his forehead and fired." He also admitted that "if I had had more [bullets], I would have shot them again, and again, and again."

II.

* * * Goetz was * * * arraigned on a felony complaint charging him with attempted murder and criminal possession of a weapon. The matter was presented to a Grand Jury in January 1985, with the prosecutor seeking an indictment for attempted murder, assault, reckless endangerment, and criminal possession of a weapon. Neither the defendant nor any of the wounded youths testified before this Grand Jury. On January 25, 1985, the Grand Jury indicted defendant on one count of criminal possession of a weapon in the third degree, for possessing the gun used in the subway shootings, and two counts of criminal possession of a weapon in the fourth degree, for possessing two other guns in his apartment building. It dismissed, however, the attempted murder and other charges stemming from the shootings themselves.

Several weeks after the Grand Jury's action, the People, asserting that they had newly available evidence, moved for an order authorizing them to resubmit the dismissed charges to a second Grand Jury. Supreme Court, Criminal Term * * * granted the motion. Presentation of the case to the second Grand Jury began on March 14, 1985. Two of the four youths, Canty and Ramseur, testified. Among the other witnesses were four passengers from the seventh car of the subway who had seen some portions of the incident. Goetz again chose not to testify, though the tapes of his two statements were played for the grand jurors, as had been done with the first Grand Jury.

On March 27, 1985, the second Grand Jury filed a 10-count indictment, containing four charges of attempted murder, four charges of assault in the first degree, one charge of reckless endangerment in the first degree, and one charge of criminal possession of a weapon in the second degree [possession of a loaded firearm with intent to use it unlawfully against another]. Goetz was arraigned on this indictment on March 28, 1985, and it was consolidated with the earlier three-count indictment.

On October 14, 1985, Goetz moved to dismiss the charges contained in the second indictment alleging, among other things, that the evidence before the second Grand Jury was not legally sufficient to establish the offenses charged, and that the prosecutor's instructions to that Grand Jury on the defense of justification were erroneous and prejudicial to the defendant so as to render its proceedings defective.

On November 25, 1985, while the motion to dismiss was pending before Criminal Term, a column appeared in the *New York Daily News* containing an interview which the columnist had conducted with Darryl Cabey the previous day in Cabey's hospital room. The columnist claimed that Cabey had told him in this interview that the other three youths had all approached Goetz with the intention of robbing him. The day after the column was published, a New York City police officer informed the prosecutor that he had been one of the first police officers to enter the subway car after the shootings, and that Canty had said to him "we were going to rob [Goetz]." The prosecutor immediately disclosed this information to the court and to defense counsel, adding that this was the first time his office had been told of this alleged statement and that none of the police reports filed on the incident contained any such information. Goetz then orally expanded his motion to dismiss, asserting that resubmission of the charges voted by the second Grand Jury was required because it appeared, from this new information, that Ramseur and Canty had committed perjury.

In an order dated January 21, 1986, Criminal Term granted Goetz's motion to the extent that it dismissed all counts of the second indictment, other than the reckless endangerment charge, with leave to resubmit these charges to a third Grand Jury. The court * * * held, however, that the prosecutor * * * had erroneously introduced an objective element into this defense by instructing the grand jurors to consider whether Goetz's conduct was that of a "reasonable man in [Goetz's] situation." The court concluded that the statutory test for whether the use of deadly force is justified to protect a person should be wholly subjective, focusing entirely on the defendant's state of mind when he used such force. It concluded that dismissal was required for this error because the justification issue was at the heart of the case.

Criminal Term also concluded that dismissal and resubmission of the charges were required * * * because the *Daily News* column and the statement by the police officer to the prosecution strongly indicated that the testimony of Ramseur and Canty was perjured. Because the additional evidence before the second Grand Jury, as contrasted with that before the first Grand Jury, consisted largely of the testimony of these two youths, the court found that the integrity of the second Grand Jury was "severely undermined" by the apparently perjured testimony.

On appeal by the People, a divided Appellate Division affirmed Criminal Term's dismissal of the charges. * * *

* * *

* * * We [hold] * * * that neither the prosecutor's charge to the Grand Jury on justification nor the information which came to light while the motion to dismiss was pending required dismissal of any of the charges in the second indictment.

III.

[New York] Penal Law * * * recognizes the defense of justification, which "permits the use of force under certain circumstances." One such set of circumstances pertains to the use of force in defense of a person, encompassing both self-defense and defense of a third person. [New York] Penal Law * * * sets forth the general principles governing all such uses of force: "[a] person may * * * use physical force upon another person when and to the extent he *reasonably believes* such to be necessary to defend himself or a third person from what he *reasonably believes* to be the use or imminent use of unlawful physical force by such other person" (emphasis added [by the court]).

[The law] sets forth further limitations on these general principles with respect to the use of "deadly physical force": "A person may not use deadly physical force upon another person * * * unless (a) He *reasonably believes* that such other person is using or about to use deadly physical force * * * or (b) He *reasonably believes* that such other person is committing or attempting to commit a kidnapping, forcible rape, forcible sodomy or robbery" (emphasis added [by the court]).

Thus, consistent with most justification provisions, [New York] Penal Law permits the use of deadly physical force only where requirements as to triggering conditions and the necessity of a particular response are met. As to the triggering conditions, the statute requires that the actor "reasonably believes" that another person either is using or about to use deadly physical force or is committing or attempting to commit one of certain enumerated felonies, including robbery. As to the need for the use of deadly physical force as a response, the statute requires that the actor "reasonably believes" that such force is necessary to avert the perceived threat.

Because the evidence before the second Grand Jury included statements by Goetz that he acted to protect himself from being maimed or to avert a robbery, the prosecutor correctly chose to charge the justification defense in * * * the Grand Jury. The prosecutor properly instructed the grand jurors to consider whether the use of deadly physical force was justified to prevent either serious physical injury or a robbery, and, in doing so, to separately analyze the defense with respect to each of the charges. * * *

When the prosecutor had completed his charge, one of the grand jurors asked for clarification of the term "reasonably believes." The prosecutor responded by instructing the grand jurors that they were to consider the circumstances of the incident and determine "whether the defendant's conduct was that of a reasonable man in the defendant's situation." It is this response by the prosecutor—and specifically his use of "a reasonable man"—which is the basis for the dismissal of the charges by the lower courts. * * * [B]ecause [the statute] uses the term "*he* reasonably believes," the appropriate test, according to [the Appellate Division], is whether a defendant's beliefs and reactions were "reasonable *to him.*" Under that reading of the statute, a jury which believed a defendant's testimony that he felt that his own actions were warranted and were reasonable would have to acquit him, regardless of what anyone else in defendant's situation might have concluded. Such an interpretation defies the ordinary meaning and significance of the term "reasonably" in a statute, and misconstrues the clear intent of the Legislature * * * to retain an objective element as part of any provision authorizing the use of deadly physical force.

Penal statutes in New York have long codified the right recognized at common law to use deadly physical force, under appropriate circumstances, in self-defense. These provisions have never required that an actor's belief as to the intention of another person to inflict serious injury be correct in order for the use of deadly force to be justified, but they have uniformly required that the belief comport with an objective notion of reasonableness. * * *

[The court discusses the development of the justification defense between the late 1800s and the 1930s.]

* * *

In 1961 the Legislature established a Commission to undertake a complete revision of the Penal Law and the Criminal Code. The impetus for the decision to update the Penal Law came in part from the drafting of the Model Penal Code by the American Law Institute, as well as from the fact that the existing law was poorly organized and in many aspects antiquated. Following the submission by the Commission of several reports and proposals, the Legislature approved the present Penal Law in 1965, and it became effective * * * [in] 1967. The drafting of the general provisions of the new Penal Law, including the article on justification, was particularly influenced by the Model Penal Code. While using the Model Penal Code provisions on justification as general guidelines, however, the drafters of the new Penal Law did not simply adopt them verbatim.

The provisions of the Model Penal Code with respect to the use of deadly force in self-defense reflect the position of its drafters that any culpability which arises from a mistaken belief in the need to use such force should be no greater than the culpability such a mistake would give rise to if it were made with respect to an element of a crime. Accordingly, under Model Penal Code, a defendant charged with murder (or attempted murder) need only show that he *"believe[d]* that [the use of deadly force] was necessary to protect himself against death, serious bodily injury, kidnapping or [forcible] sexual intercourse" to prevail on a self-defense claim (emphasis added [by the court]). If the defendant's belief was wrong, and was recklessly, or negligently formed, however, he may be convicted of the type of homicide charge requiring only a reckless or negligent, as the case may be, criminal intent.

The drafters of the Model Penal Code recognized that the wholly subjective test * * * differed from the existing law in most States by its omission of any requirement of reasonableness. The drafters were also keenly aware that requiring that the actor have a "reasonable belief" rather than just a "belief" would alter the wholly subjective test. This basic distinction was recognized years earlier by the New York Law Revision Commission and continues to be noted by the commentators.

New York did not follow the Model Penal Code's equation of a mistake as to the need to use deadly force with a mistake negating an element of a crime, choosing instead to use a single statutory section which would provide either a complete defense or no defense at all to a defendant charged with any crime involving the use of deadly force. The drafters of the new Penal Law adopted in large part the structure and content of [the] Model Penal Code, [with respect to the use of deadly force,] but, crucially, inserted the word "reasonably" before "believes."

The * * * [Appellate Division] agreed with defendant's argument that the change in the statutory language from "reasonable ground," used prior to 1965, to "he reasonably believes" * * * evinced a legislative intent to conform to the subjective standard contained in [the] Model Penal Code. This argument, however, ignores the plain significance of the insertion of "reasonably." Had the drafters of * * * [the legislation] wanted to adopt a subjective standard, they could have simply used the language of * * * [the Model Penal Code]. "Believes" by itself requires an honest or genuine belief by a defendant as to the need to use deadly force. Interpreting the statute to require only that the defendant's belief was "reasonable to *him*," as done by the plurality below, would hardly be different from requiring only a genuine belief; in either case, the defendant's own perceptions could completely exonerate him from any criminal liability.

We cannot lightly impute to the Legislature an intent to fundamentally alter the principles of justification to allow the perpetrator of a serious crime to go free simply because that person believed his actions were reasonable and necessary to prevent some perceived harm. To completely exonerate such an individual, no matter how aberrational or bizarre his thought patterns, would allow citizens to set their own standards for the permissible use of force. It would also allow a legally competent defendant suffering from delusions to kill or perform acts of violence with impunity, contrary to fundamental principles of justice and criminal law.

We can only conclude that the Legislature retained a reasonableness requirement to avoid giving a license for such actions. The * * * [Appellate Division's] interpretation * * * excises the impact of the word "reasonably."

* * *

The conclusion that * * * [the New York law] retains an objective element to justify the use of deadly force is buttressed by the statements of its drafters. The executive director and counsel to the Commission which revised the Penal Law have stated that the provisions of the statute with respect to the use of deadly physical force largely conformed with the prior law, with the only changes they noted not being relevant here. Nowhere in the legislative history is there any indication that "reasonably believes" was designed to change the law on the use of deadly force or establish a subjective standard. To the contrary, the Commission, in the staff comment governing arrests by police officers, specifically equated "[he] reasonably believes" with having a reasonable ground for believing.

Statutes or rules of law requiring a person to act "reasonably" or to have a "reasonable belief" uniformly prescribe conduct meeting an objective standard measured with reference to how "a reasonable person" could have acted. * * *

* * *

Goetz * * * argues that the introduction of an objective element will preclude a jury from considering factors such as the prior experiences of a given actor and thus, require it to make a determination of "reasonableness" without regard to the actual circumstances of a particular incident. This argument, however, falsely presupposes that an objective standard means that the background and other relevant characteristics of a particular actor must be ignored. To the contrary, we have frequently noted that a determination of reasonableness must be based on the "circumstances" facing a defendant or his "situation." Such terms encompass more than the physical movements of the potential assailant. * * * [They] include any relevant knowledge the defendant had about that person. They also necessarily bring in the physical attributes of all persons involved, including the defendant. Furthermore, the defendant's circumstances encompass any prior experiences he had which could provide a reasonable basis for a belief that another person's intentions were to injure or rob him or that the use of deadly force was necessary under the circumstances.

Accordingly, a jury should be instructed to consider this type of evidence in weighing the defendant's actions. The jury must first determine whether the defendant had the requisite beliefs under * * * [New York law], that is, whether he believed deadly force was necessary to avert the imminent use of deadly force or the commission of one of the felonies enumerated therein. If the People do not prove beyond a reasonable doubt that he did not have such beliefs, then the jury must also consider whether these beliefs were reasonable. The jury would have to determine, in light of all the "circumstances," as explicated above, if a reasonable person could have had these beliefs.

The prosecutor's instruction to the second Grand Jury that it had to determine whether, under the circumstances, Goetz's conduct was that of a reasonable man in his situation was thus essentially an accurate charge. It is true that the prosecutor did not elaborate on the meaning of "circumstances" or "situation" and inform the grand jurors that they could consider, for example, the prior experiences Goetz related in his statement to the police. We have held, however, that a Grand Jury need not be instructed on the law with the same degree of precision as the petit jury. This lesser standard is premised upon the different functions of the Grand Jury and the petit jury: the former determines whether sufficient evidence exists to accuse a person of a crime and thereby subject him to criminal prosecution; the latter ultimately determines the guilt or innocence of the accused, and may convict only where the People have proven his guilt beyond a reasonable doubt.

* * * [W]e [have] stated that the prosecutor simply had to "provid[e] the Grand Jury with enough information to enable it intelligently to decide whether a crime has been committed and to determine whether there exists legally sufficient evidence to establish the material elements of the crime." Of course, * * * where the evidence suggests that a complete defense such as justification may be present, the prosecutor must charge the grand jurors on that defense, providing enough information to enable them to determine whether the defense, in light of the evidence, should preclude the criminal prosecution. The prosecutor more than adequately fulfilled this obligation here. His instructions were not as complete as the court's charge on justification should be, but they sufficiently apprised the Grand Jury of the existence and requirements of that defense to allow it to intelligently decide that there is sufficient evidence tending to disprove justification and necessitating a trial. The Grand Jury has indicted Goetz. It will now be for the petit jury to decide whether the prosecutor can prove beyond a reasonable doubt that Goetz's reactions were unreasonable and therefore excessive.

IV.

Criminal Term's second ground for dismissal of the charges, premised upon the *Daily News* column and the police officer's statement to the prosecutor, can be rejected more summarily. * * *

* * * Canty and Ramseur have not recanted any of their Grand Jury testimony or told the prosecutor that they misunderstood any questions. Instead, all that has come to light is hearsay evidence that conflicts with part of Canty's testimony. There is no statute or controlling case law requiring dismissal of an indictment merely because, months later, the prosecutor becomes aware of some information which may lead to the defendant's acquittal. There was no basis for the Criminal Term Justice to speculate as to whether Canty's and Ramseur's testimony was perjurious, and his conclusion that the testimony "strongly appeared" to be perjured is particularly inappropriate given the nature of the "evidence" he relied upon to reach such a conclusion and that he was not in the Grand Jury room when the two youths testified.

Moreover, * * * the testimony of Canty and Ramseur was not the only evidence before the Grand Jury establishing that the offenses submitted to that body were committed by Goetz. Goetz's own statements, together with the testimony of the passengers, clearly support the elements of the crimes charged, and provide ample basis for concluding that a trial of this matter is needed to determine whether Goetz could have reasonably believed that he was about to be robbed or seriously injured and whether it was reasonably necessary for him to shoot four youths to avert any such threat.

Accordingly, the order of the Appellate Division should be reversed, and the dismissed counts of the indictment reinstated.

* * *

NOTES AND QUESTIONS

1.   The trial court in *Goetz* dismissed the attempted murder, assault, and weapons possession charges, and the intermediate appellate court affirmed. The New York Court of Appeals (New York's highest court) reversed, holding that those counts should be reinstated. What were the concerns raised by the trial and intermediate courts? Why did the New York Court of Appeals disagree? Which approach is more persuasive?

2.   Following the ruling of the New York Court of Appeals, Goetz went to trial and was acquitted of the most serious charges (attempted murder, criminal assault) but was convicted of unlawful gun possession. He served less than a year in prison. Subsequently, Darrell Cabey filed a civil action against Goetz, and Goetz was found liable for $43 million. Goetz later declared bankruptcy. For further details, *see, e.g.,* http://www.biography.com/people/ bernhard-goetz–578520#trials-and-public-image.

3.   The Goetz shootings were widely publicized in the United States and abroad. *See, e.g.,* Michael Coakley, *Jury to Hear Goetz Testify on N.Y. Subway Shootings,* CHI. TRIB., Mar. 26, 1985; Suzanne Daley, *Man Tells Police He Shot Youths in Subway Train,* N.Y. TIMES, Jan. 1, 1985; Richard Stengel, *A Troubled and Troubling Life: Who is Bernhard Goetz, and Why Did He Do What He Did?,* TIME, Apr. 8, 1985; Margot Hornblower, *Intended to Gouge Eye of Teen, Goetz Tape Says; "My Problem Was I Ran Out of Bullets",* WASH. POST, May 14, 1987; Charles Bremner, *"Subway Vigilante" Cleared,* TIMES (Eng.), June 17, 1987; Alan Attwood, *New Trial for Goetz,* AGE (Austl.), Apr. 12, 1996. Why was the case newsworthy, given that, on average, five people were murdered every day in New York City in 1984? *See* Steve Chapman, *How New York Won the War on Crime—Against all Expectations, a Dangerous City Became Safe,* N.Y. TIMES, Nov. 13, 2011, *available at* http://articles.chicago tribune.com/2011–11–13/news/ct-oped–1113–chapman–20111113_1_national- crime-rate-number-of-violent-crimes-homicide-rate   (containing   crime statistics).

4.   In addition to the press coverage, the *Goetz* case has received substantial scholarly commentary. *See, e.g.,* Stephen Carter, *When Victims*

Happen to Be Black, 97 Yale L.J. 420 (1988) (discussing the role of race in determining who is the victim in violent encounters and arguing that Goetz's acquittal on the serious charges can be explained by the fact that the victims were black); Nadine Klansky, *Bernard Goetz, A "Reasonable Man": A Look at New York's Justification Defense* People v. Goetz, 53 Brook. L. Rev. 1149 (1988) (examining the *Goetz* court's application of the New York justification statute and suggesting that the court's approach violated precedent by using an objective element and failing to give weight to the defendant's actual intent in using force for self-defense); David Posner, *The Proper Standard for Self-Defense in New York: Should* People v. Goetz *Be Viewed As Judicial Legislation or Judicial Restraint?*, 39 Syracuse L. Rev. 845 (1988) (discussing the self-defense standard used in *Goetz* and arguing that the hybrid objective-subjective approach is more effective because it holds individuals accountable when their subjective fears are unreasonable, but suggesting that the standard should be clarified by the legislature because it is unclear how much subjective fears should be considered in limiting liability).

5.   Justification as a defense to a criminal charge can be asserted in a variety of ways. *See, e.g., LaPradd v. Commonwealth*, 334 S.W.3d 88 (Ky. 2011) (holding that the defendant, who was convicted of "possession of a handgun by a convicted felon," was improperly denied a "choice of evils" instruction when he claimed that he picked up a handgun in order to prevent teenagers from obtaining and using the gun); *Commonwealth v. Cabral*, 443 Mass. 171, 819 N.E.2d 951 (2005) (holding that a "use of force in law enforcement" justification defense was appropriate when the defendant was charged with kidnapping and assault, but claimed that he was acting at the direction of the superior court by apprehending the victim and delivering him to the court due to the victim's failure to appear in court); *Smith v. State*, 268 Ga. 196, 486 S.E.2d 819 (1997) (holding that the defendant was entitled to a "battered person" justification defense when the defendant killed her abusive husband, and reversing defendant's conviction because she was denied the instruction at trial); *Calhoun v. State*, 526 So. 2d 531 (Miss. 1988) (holding that a "protection of others" defense was justified when the victim threatened the defendant's girlfriend on numerous occasions, including on the night of the killing); *Poteete v. Commonwealth*, 701 S.W.2d 416 (Ky. Ct. App. 1985) (holding that an "execution of a public duty" defense was justified when the defendant, an inmate at a correctional facility, was prosecuted for possessing a weapon, but claimed that he purchased the weapon from another inmate in order to turn it over to guards and improve the safety of the facility).

6.   For discussions of the justification defense in the context of battered women, *see, e.g.,* John Roberts, *Between the Heat of Passion and Cold Blood: Battered Woman's Syndrome as an Excuse for Self-Defense in Non-Confrontational Homicides*, 27 Law & Psychol. Rev. 135 (2003) (discussing the phenomenon of battered women killing their abusers and proposing that defendants in those cases are entitled to a jury instruction allowing jurors to fully consider the mindset of the battered woman); Richard Rosen, *On Self-Defense, Imminence, and Women Who Kill Their Batterers,* 71 N.C. L. Rev. 371 (1993) (discussing self-defense for battered women and proposing an

adjustment to the typical requirement that the defendant be facing imminent harm by also allowing self-defense when an individual believes that it is necessary to use force to prevent harm, even if the harm is not imminent).

INDEX

References are to Pages